3

A HISTORY OF
THE JEWS

A HISTORY

OF

THE JEWS

by

ABRAM LEON SACHAR, Ph.D.

President of Brandeis University

FIFTH EDITION, REVISED AND ENLARGED

NEW YORK : ALFRED · A · KNOPF

1965

L. C. catalog card number: 64–17704

THIS IS A BORZOI BOOK,
PUBLISHED BY ALFRED A. KNOPF, INC.

PUBLISHED MARCH 1930; REPRINTED SIX TIMES.
SECOND EDITION, REVISED, AUGUST 1940; REPRINTED FOUR TIMES.
THIRD EDITION, REVISED AND ENLARGED, JULY 1948; REPRINTED ONCE.
FOURTH EDITION, REVISED AND ENLARGED, JUNE 1953; REPRINTED FIVE TIMES.
FIFTH EDITION, REVISED AND ENLARGED, JANUARY 1965.

To
MY
PARENTS

PREFACE TO THE FIFTH EDITION

NEARLY thirty-five years have passed since this volume was published. Now, some nineteen printings and four editions later, I have found it necessary once again to effect major revisions in the text, primarily in its last chapters. The events of the past few decades have been cataclysmic beyond human imagination. For the chronicler of Jewish history, the changes of our own generation have surely been more profound than those that occurred during any other period in the annals of the Jewish people since the fall of the Second Commonwealth in A.D. 70.

Which of us even twenty-five years ago would have conceived that a Europe steeped in the traditions of the Renaissance and the Enlightenment, of classical liberalism and public, secular education, was capable of methodically destroying its entire Jewish community? In one terrifying convulsion, world Jewry was deprived of a third of its population; the entire demographic structure of Jewish life was thereafter altered more traumatically and irretrievably than at any time in its long and tragic history.

Conversely, only a generation ago the dream of a Jewish National Home in Palestine was still equated with an autonomous enclave within the British imperial system, a kind of sheltered agricultural experiment station, dependent for protection upon a garrison of some one hundred thousand British troops. Today that garrison is gone. An Israeli army has taken its place. The Star of David waves from flagpoles where once the Union Jack fluttered. Two and a quarter million inhabitants, an ingathering of Jews from the far corners of the earth, are the proud citizens of a resurgent sovereign nation. Foreign ambassadors present their credentials to a Jewish president. Israeli delegates in the United Nations vote on issues affecting the fate and fortune of other nations, a dramatic change from the time, only yesterday, when the destiny of the Jews was almost totally dependent upon the good will, or lack of it, of the non-Jewish world.

These two revolutions in recent Jewish history—the destruction of Jewry's European hinterland, and the rebirth of its independent homeland—the one a tragedy of unimaginable proportions, the other an event pregnant with incalculable opportunities for creativity and enrichment, would surely of themselves require a basic revision in any volume dealing with Jewish life. But there is another factor, as well, which suggests the need for continual reassessment. Jewish historiography has grown enormously in the past thirty-five years. Thousands of articles, many hundreds of books, nearly a score of learned journals, have appeared to provide a new depth and dimension to our understanding of the Jewish scene. I cannot claim to have incorporated even a fraction of this extensive bibliography in my revision. But I believe that enough new material has been included in the section on the modern period to provide a significantly better focus and perspective.

My basic approach, however, to the writing of a history of the Jews, has not altered since those days—they seem so long ago—when I first embarked on this project as a junior member of the history department at the University of Illinois. It seemed to me then, as it does now, that the task of interpreting more than three thousand years of Jewish history was far too presumptuous for one man to take upon himself. Such an undertaking ought properly to be organized as a kind of Cambridge Jewish History, the collective effort of many historians, each providing chapters or sections in the area of his specialty. Yet such a joint enterprise did not appear to be in the offing in the late 1920's, nor unaccountably, has it in the decades that have followed. Thus, it seemed to me a vacuum continued to exist in the field of Jewish historiography. The volumes that addressed themselves to the totality of the Jewish experience were, and still are, primarily religious or social in their interpretation. The impact of secular forces upon the Jews has been largely ignored.

My aim, therefore, in undertaking a one-volume survey of Jewish history was, at least temporarily, to bridge this gap: to set down, first of all, in as lucid a fashion as possible, the salient events, ideas, and influences that have shaped the destiny of the Jews and their role on the world scene; and, secondly (because I was trained as a European historian, and was deeply influenced by the schools of Robinson and Beard), to pay what I considered proper attention to economic, political, and diplomatic factors, as well as to the purely social and religious. In the subsequent editions of the book, I have continued, as far as possible, to stress this diversified interaction between Jewish and non-Jewish life. For this approach has more validity than ever before.

In the preface to the first edition I expressed my indebtedness to many helpful friends. It was possible then to list by name those who had generously shared with me their specialized information and experience. Through subsequent revisions my obligation to others has grown manyfold, especially during my trips to Europe, Israel, Asia, and Latin America. Accordingly, it is no longer possible to express my appreciation to these countless benefactors—many of whom unhappily are no longer with us—within the limits of a few paragraphs, or even a few pages. Only to my wife, the companion of my public as well as my private life, and the partner of its sacrifices no less than its creative satisfactions, must my thanks once again be extended for her sustaining patience and devotion.

Waltham, Massachusetts

August 1, 1964

LIST OF MAPS

CONTENTS

PART ONE

xi

CONTENTS

ⴕⴖⴕⴖ

PART TWO

CONTENTS

CONTENTS

ᒍᒍᒍᒍ

PART THREE

CONTENTS

CONTENTS

PART ONE

CHAPTER ONE

THE CAST OF CHARACTERS

I. THE PROCESSION OF PEOPLES

WE usually begin the story of Western civilization in the little bow-shaped strip of territory known as the Fertile Crescent, skirting the vast Arabian desert. It is, on the whole, a grudging soil, nourished by few life-giving rivers, uninviting, surrounded by sheet rock and burning sand. Yet it has offered an irresistible temptation to countless peoples. Its history has been an unceasing struggle between the northern mountain folk and the southern desert nomads for possession of its few and scattered fertile districts. Today the great wastes and uninspiring ruins, scorched by the blasting summer sun and whipped by the dreary winter rain, cause the tourist to wonder how this, of all areas, could be the nursery of Western civilization. His guide-book, however, marshals the relentless facts. Here tradition has placed the garden of Eden. Here were built the splendid empires of the Sumerians, the Babylonians, the Assyrians, the Hittites, the Chaldeans, and the other ancient peoples who stormed and fretted for brief periods and then were gone for ever. Here, moreover, were enacted the spirit-moving scenes which made Palestine the holy shrine of three powerful religions.

The little Crescent world, however, was long in preparing itself for the actors who were to make it immortal. The Semitic races were comparative latecomers on the scene. For tens of thousands of years other forgotten races had lived there, slowly working through successive stages which have marked the progress of every historical people. Men fought with animals and with each other for possession of rude and vile-smelling cave homes. They discovered new metals which helped them to control nature and conquer their enemies. They learned to draw sustenance from the soil and to dress themselves with skins crudely sewed together with bone needles. They developed institutions with which to regulate their simple society. Undoubtedly they relied upon primitive practices, forms of magic rather than of religion, to bend the spirits to their bidding, pouring water over cliffs to induce the rain to fall, sacrificing animals, or even human beings, to propitiate the unseen supernatural powers which they dreaded. The light of history is not yet powerful enough to illuminate those long, dark periods, so that we know little about them, except that civilization moved along lazily, unconcernedly, as if unable or unwilling, in the climate of the area, to bestir itself.

The light is still very dim when it begins to play on the fourth millenium B.C., but certain forms are now vaguely to be distinguished. On the fertile soil between the Tigris and the Euphrates, the choicest spot of the ancient world, lived a sturdy race, the Sumerians, already advanced to a high degree of culture. They were a non-Semitic people, part of the great white race, capable and energetic. They probably invented cuneiform writing, cumbersome indeed and inadequate, but a vast improvement over the pictographic writing which preceded it. They were far enough advanced to fashion utensils of copper, though they had not yet learned to manufacture the sturdier bronze. They could cut gems with a fair degree of artistry; some of their personal seals, cut in stone, were unequalled by those of any ancient Oriental people.

Most of them lived in towns, in little groups of houses, built usually of the baked clay which was plentiful in the valley. They brought water into these towns and into their fields by a system of artificially constructed canals. Agriculture was, of course, a long and arduous process, but it was less primitive among them than among any people of their little world. They understood the simple movements of the stars. Already, so early, they had developed a faith and a system of religious practices regulated by a priesthood, the first known priesthood, indeed, in all history. We have remains of imposing tower-temples, later imitated by the Babylonians, and destined to become the ancestors of our church steeples.

While the Sumerians built their cities and their temples and wrote boastful memoirs into their baked tablets, other non-Semitic races were established in Palestine and Syria, less gifted, but settled, progressive, and quick to lend themselves to the influences which came from the Euphrates and the Nile.[1] In between, wherever life was possible, wherever good soil or water beckoned, there were tiny communities — men struggling with nature and with each other for food and wealth; women bearing heavy burdens and ministering to their lords and masters; children, sallow and drawn from drinking bad water, playing near tents and huts; sheep and cattle grazing on meagre grass-land. Endless tribes, sprung from obscurest corners of nowhere, living out simple, forgotten existences.

Into this area came the historic Semites, probably from the desert which lay on its outskirts. The desert has been a most potent force in the development of the life and thought of the ancient world. From its depths nomads have been pouring out, clan by clan, since the dawn of history, hunting for food and for better soil, drawn to the Fertile Crescent as by an irresistible magnet. Sometimes it has been a leisurely emergence, a few families or tribes at a time,

---

[1] Recent excavations of ancient sites in Palestine reveal the presence, among the earliest inhabitants, of a race of New Stone men who dwelt in caves and grottoes and burnt their dead in crude crematoriums, and who may have been the Horim of the Biblical narrative. How long they lived on in Palestine cannot be ascertained.

to some temporary settlement in another place. Sometimes it has been a vast migration, like the Arab sweep of Mohammed's day, set in motion by sudden pressure within, forcing out great numbers of tribes and compelling them to attempt the violent conquest of neighbouring lands.

From the desert, as early perhaps as 5000 or 6000 B.C., groups of Semitic tribes began to emerge, in waves of growing strength.[1] They took every route that was open and made new ones when the old ones offered no promise. Some moved west to the ever hospitable Nile and profoundly modified the already matured civilization of Egypt. Others moved north and east, attracted by the fertility of the lower Tigris and Euphrates valley. Dribbling in for generations, they ultimately conquered the Sumerian peoples; but apparently they were conquered by the Sumerian civilization, for they adopted many of its arts and manners and ways of life. In time they developed notable city-states — Ur, Nippur, Larsa, Erech, and others, which were later united under the leadership of powerful kings. In these golden days even a literature developed and there is an interesting record of a fortunate hero who, having built an ark, survived the flood which the gods had sent to overwhelm the earth.

Meanwhile the waves of migration spilled into the less attractive corners of the little world. Palestine and western Mesopotamia became the objective of the Amorites, who wrestled for many years with the natives and then unceremoniously dispossessed them. The new-comers were apparently a vigorous people, for they not only developed a fine agricultural and commercial civilization, but subsequently a hardy offshoot fought its way into some of the strongest Babylonian cities and conquered them. From the dynasty established by them sprang Hammurabi, the most important of ancient legislators.

Still the procession of peoples came pouring out of the desert. Those who rooted themselves in Syria and northern Mesopotamia became the ancestors of the Biblical Aramæans. They were the famous traders of antiquity. Their caravans travelled to the remotest corners of the earth, to the frontiers of India, spreading their culture, their language, their very alphabet, and bringing back to their cities luxuries that were the source of endless wonder. Later a section of them established a powerful kingdom, centring in Damascus, which became one of Israel's formidable rivals and against which the Hebrew prophets thundered anathemas.

As part of the engulfing wave which brought in the shrewd, commercial Aramæans, came the progenitors of the Ammonites, the Edomites, the Moabites, and the other tribes who have found their way into the Biblical story. These wanderers settled just east of the Dead Sea, " far from the fat places of the

---

[1] It was once thought that the earliest invaders already had the marked characteristics of the modern Semites, high cheek-bones and aquiline noses. But authoritative anthropological research throws doubt on the old theory that these characteristics were limited to the Semites, or that they were even part of the earliest Semitic features.

earth, and from the dew of the heaven above "; and in their wake, clambering over them into the reaches of Palestine, came the ancestors of the Hebrews.

These immense tribal movements continued for centuries and were not completed even by 1000 B.C. But the most important peoples had already taken their places some two centuries earlier. The stage was set for the characters who were to enact a mighty and impressive drama.

2. PALESTINE BEFORE THE HEBREWS

The little land of Palestine, no larger than the state of Vermont, thus early sought out by the desert nomads, was the result of a geological accident. At the beginning of the diluvial period the country took form after an unsuccessful attempt of nature to extend the Mediterranean farther to the east and the south-east. A providential whim, as it were, rescued from the sea the tiny province that was to become the world's most important spiritual centre.

Yet it never had outward physical beauty or grace to recommend it. By comparison with luxuriant Egypt and Babylon it was mean and humble indeed. Its few fertile areas were but oases in long reaches of barren hills and mountain ridges. Only a deep cleft, forming the miserably hot, well-nigh uninhabitable Dead Sea valley, separated the country from the trackless desert on the east. Perhaps its peoples have produced so little in the field of art because of the drabness of the environment. Art usually requires beauty for its inspiration and there was little in Palestine to stir an æsthetic nature.

Even a few spots of green, however, were not to be despised by way-worn nomads. For them the land always had a lure; it promised shelter and ease. In contrast with the wastes that gave them birth, it seemed a veritable land of milk and honey. So they came in hordes, throwing themselves against the country; repelled, they tried again or sent forth others. Some were doubtless mere vandals who killed and burnt and pillaged as they raided. Others were genuine home-seekers who settled down and became staunch defenders of their hard-earned plots of soil against the new waves of adventurers who followed fast on their heels.

Yet Palestine was not merely the dumping-ground for homeless peoples. It drew the most enterprising types. For nature had placed it at the cross-roads of the ancient world, and it was always close to the heart of civilized life. The great highways ran through it, and the caravans, moving from the busy marts of Babylon, filed through its little villages on the way to Egypt or the unknown world of the West. Its strategic situation gave the country no rest from the ambitions of conquerors, but it raised its people above the level of gaping peasants.

By the third millenium B.C. the country, as far north as the Lebanon district, had been conquered by the Amorites or tribes closely related to them, who poured in from the desert or from Mesopotamia. The earliest records tell of close relations between their Palestine and the great empires that towered on both sides of it. The country oscillated between Egyptian and Babylonian control, influenced meantime by both, the north more profoundly by Babylon, the south by Egypt. The Palermo Stone tells of an expedition of forty ships to bring cedarwood from the Lebanon in the reign of Snefru, a king of the fourth dynasty (2840–2680 B.C.) Throughout the third millenium there were Egyptian expeditions into Palestine. Often they worked havoc among the fig-trees and the vines and the little farmsteads, patiently built; more often they were peaceful and of enduring benefit to the country. There are records of Amorite merchants who visited Egypt and exchanged their humble wares for the fine creations of the artisans of the Nile.

Babylonian influence, however, was of deeper significance in this early period. Lugalzaggisi, perhaps the first Babylonian imperialist, claimed to rule all of the western lands in 2600. Sargon of Agade, whose early story suggests a parallel with the fables woven about the career of Moses, boasts of his con-quests in the Mediterranean a century later. The control in these instances may have been slight, but at the end of the third millenium Palestine was certainly a part of the empire which acknowledged the authority of the gifted king Hammurabi, who not only collected booty and tribute, but gave his subject provinces the benefits of a wise administration and a well-matured culture. The language of Babylon, its writing, its customs, its laws, even its myths, took firm root in Palestine.

From the account of an Egyptian exile, Sinuhe, who wrote about 2000 B.C., we get a glimpse of Palestinian life at the height of Babylonian influence. The more fertile parts of the country are well cultivated and fairly prosperous. " It is an excellent land," Sinuhe says. " Figs are there and grapes; wine is more plentiful than water; honey abounds in it; numerous are its olives and all the products of its trees; there are barley and wheat without end, and cattle of all kinds. . . ." From other sources we learn that the high places are dotted with little towns, each with its laboriously constructed walls, bulwarks against the invaders from the desert. The inhabitants live in frail huts or houses built of unburnt clay or baked brick. Much ingenuity is shown in making oil- and winepresses, pottery, and amulets, and particularly in constructing wells. The tunnel discovered in Gezer, leading outside of the town to a precious spring, is astonishingly long and deep, considering that it was worked only with stone tools. Its excavator remarks that it so greatly impressed the later inhabitants of Gezer that they were wont to say that the Great Flood began from the hill of Gezer and returned to it at the close.

But the country was hopelessly backward politically; there was no union, or even semblance of union. It was composed of a hodge-podge of petty clannish entities, each jealous of the other, an easy prey for every foreign conqueror.

Somewhere in the beginning of the second millenium the Canaanites, another Semitic offshoot, must have come into the country. The Biblical accounts clearly distinguish between them and the Amorites. Since there is no sharp break in the development of the country, however, the supersession was probably gradual, almost imperceptible. The turning-point in this period was not the Canaanite infiltration, but rather the substitution of Egyptian for Babylonian supremacy. Egyptian influence became most pronounced after the eighteenth century B.C., when the Kassites, invaders from the east, destroyed the powerful Babylonian state and established a new dynasty, destined to last for nearly six hundred years. Early in the fifteenth century B.C. the Egyptian imperialist Thutmose III (1501–1447 B.C.) completely reduced the country, appointed its rulers, built garrisons, and enriched his already overflowing coffers with spoil and heavy tribute. His soldiers lived on the fat of the land and "were drunk every day and anointed with oil, as at festival times in Egypt." Thutmose did his best to ground Egyptian influence thoroughly by carrying off the children of the princes for education in the Egyptian court. Fortunately we are not left in the dark about the life of Palestine in this period and that of the immediate successors of the new conqueror. The Annals of Thutmose give surprisingly full accounts of the products of the country. And the Tel el Amarna letters, discovered in 1887 by a peasant woman, open up a mine of other contemporary material.[1]

It appears that the rather large population lived largely by agriculture. The Annals make frequent reference to harvests cut down by the king's forces in the Canaanite fields and include grain among the captured plunder. There was, besides, oil, wine, fruits of all kinds, honey, and other numerous products of a well-cultivated land. Evidently some of the people were clever artisans, weavers, woodworkers, gold- and silversmiths, and pottery-makers.

But with all of its economic advantages the country was still divided by the jealousies and animosities of its princelings. In the Amarna letters they protest their loyalty in phrases oozing humility and submission. They are dust under the Pharaoh's feet, his dog, his stable-boy, his groom. They prostrate themselves before him " seven times seven," some even " both on their breasts and on their backs." But they accuse one another of treachery and urge the great master of the Nile to put the upstarts in their place. Many of them are in distress because of the attacks of invaders from the north and the east, and they beg for assistance from the Egyptian overlords. Typical is the plea of Abd Khiba, prince of Jerusalem, who appeals for help against the ruthless Chabiru, desert tribes who are attacking from the east, and over whom historians have been

[1] They are a series of about three hundred and fifty tablets of baked clay, written between 1411 and 1358, the correspondence sent to the Egyptian kings from the petty princes of Palestine and the ancient world. They deal with every aspect of life, diplomatic, religious, social, and economic. It is significant that though Egypt was now in complete political control, the language and script of the letters are Babylonian.

debating for years in a vain attempt to establish definitely whether or not they were the vanguard of the Hebrew invading hordes. " Let the king attend to his country," Abd Khiba pleads, " and let the king secure troops for the country, for if troops are not here this year, all the lands of my lord the king will be lost."

It was becoming a very troubled world and urgently required the strong arm of Egypt to keep it peaceful and secure. But just at this time the deformed, dilettante King of Egypt, Amenhotep IV, or Ikhnaton, was too much concerned with his new religious and artistic conceptions to care very much about his Asiatic provinces, and they cried in vain for succour. The Hittites, a strong and aggressive people from the north, kept pushing down, penetrating as far as southern Palestine, and threatening even the nominal Egyptian supremacy. Rameses II, in a revival of Egyptian imperialism, was later able to stem their advances for a moment, and in 1271 B.C. he even concluded a treaty with them. But the tide was irresistible. Other peoples kept pressing in on the country, tribes from the sea and from the desert, eager, rapacious, unscrupulous. The natives found themselves hemmed in on all sides, fighting half a dozen enemies at once. A new and fearful crisis in their lives was impending.

But a veil now falls over the story. We are left without definite evidence of what occurred during these long centuries of race movements and conflicts. From the twelfth century to the ninth Egypt was in decline; the Hittite power was broken; Babylon and Assyria were too busy watching and fighting each other to concern themselves with Palestine, and their records throw no light on what occurred. Perhaps it was their lack of interest which gave the smaller peoples an opportunity to insinuate themselves into the country and to carve out places for themselves. The Philistines came in from the west, the Aramæans spread down, ever south, penetrating farther into Syria. The Hebrews, anxious for a cranny in the Fertile Crescent, probably now also entered. The details of the shifting and changing are unknown. Very few contemporary memorials have been left to tell the story of the settlements.

When the veil is at last lifted, five centuries later, and zealous historians begin to tell, in the Biblical narrative, the story of their ancestors, the Hebrews are already long settled in Palestine, holding the strategic places, loosely united in a monarchy, worshipping a strange god, known as Yahweh. Where they came from, who moulded them into a people, how they entered Palestine, their oldest traditions cannot answer with certainty. The most influential history in the world is lost in the grey morning of folk-memory and fable. It is the central problem of early Hebrew history to discover just what happened in these critical centuries, to explain how a group of scattered tribes, pressing into the country from many directions, became a nation, and how their varied religious experiences evolved into the national religion which the prophets built upon and expanded.

CHAPTER TWO

THE ORIGINS OF THE HEBREWS

I. THE BIBLE AS HISTORY

A CENTURY ago the Biblical account of Hebrew origins was too sacred to question. The stories had been sanctified by the devotion of the ages; they had been the moral pabulum of generations of children who were reared with piety. Men and women had reverently woven them into their religious faith. This reverence, often bolstered up with unreasoning dogmatism, made the orthodox unwilling to submit the Bible to ordinary scientific tests. It was difficult even to suggest that the delightful folk-lore of the Holy Writ could not serve as history, that it was, indeed, not meant to be an exact account of the development of Hebrew life.

Today, while there are still, in every faith, earnest conservatives who protest, men are more willing to submit the old traditions to reasonable analysis. Even the most pious are recognizing that it does not detract one jot or tittle from the richness and usefulness of the age-hallowed volume to admit that it is the record of an amazing people's spiritual progress rather than an infallible document of divine origin. Stanley Cook suggests that it deepens the value of the Bible and brings out its central truths to regard it as " man's account of the divine rather than a divine account of man." It is a great human document, with all the loves and hates, the feelings sublime and sordid, that animate human beings. In its pages are naïve cosmogonies written when the nation was young, and magnificent prophecies written when suffering had curbed the worldliness of national life. The boulevardier is there, and the fashionable roué, mocking the virtues, and glorifying the philosophy of Me and Mine. The elegant agnostic is there, squeezing the lemon of life to its last drop and then bewailing the emptiness of the lemon. The priest is there too, chronicling his pious hopes, distributing blessings and curses to the heroes and villains of the past. They are all brought together, under one cover, a tribute to the versatility and candour of Hebrew genius.

Patient puzzling over the earlier historical books of the Bible has made it plain they were the compilation of a number of hands, written in different periods for different purposes. Some chroniclers told their story simply as they heard it; others adorned their tales to point significant morals. Many, humiliated by the contemporary experiences of their people, turned for comfort to the past, changing it, glorifying it, pouring all of their thwarted hopes, their vain longings for peace and ease, into the ancient characters, the patriarchs, the legendary figures who lived sublime lives. The tired prophetic historians, turning to the ancient fathers for solace, remind one of poor Faust, wearied and disillusioned, turning for rest to the beautiful types of motherhood.

This process of history-writing, so closely akin to history-making, was not unique in Israel. The time-honoured traditions of Greece and the earliest Saxon experiences were similarly compiled. The monks of the Middle Ages also built on each other's work, incorporating old manuscripts into their accounts after revising them for their own purposes. Such documents usually throw more light on the mind of the period in which they were written than on the period which they describe.

The earliest Hebrew historians wrote probably in the ninth and eighth centuries, when some measure of stability came to the country. Their chronicles form the basis of what modern Biblical critics call the J and E documents. Later, after the eighth century, when the prophetic influence became more pronounced, a moral and religious tone crept into the stories. Under these Deuteronomistic writers the old traditions were retouched and expanded to teach lessons. Hortatory paragraphs were inserted. Historians became preachers, their histories became sermons. The idea of retribution was introduced and good and bad fortune were attributed to piety or sinfulness. Still later, in the fifth and fourth centuries B.C., the priestly leaders of the people, the P historians, added their interpretations to the story of the Hebrew origins. The previous accounts were again rewritten to stress the importance of such institutions as sacrifice and purification. Long sections of systematized Levitical laws were incorporated. By the end of the fourth century the Hebrew story resembled geological strata, layer resting upon layer, in some places clearly cut and clearly defined, in other places twisted, confused, corroded.

Largely from such heterogeneous material — for the extra-Biblical sources are few — we must construct the occurrences of the eventful years when the scattered tribes amalgamated to become a nation. Even the oldest documents are several hundred years removed from the events that are described. The fragments that come from the northern chroniclers have survived through the channel of Judæan recensions. What, then, is history and what legend? What is deprecation and what idealization? Who was Moses and what was his law? Was the conquest of Canaan accomplished by a united people or by scattered tribes? Was the monarchy forced on the country or was it a peacefully developed institution? Was Saul a great king or a great failure? Was David a genius or a rascal? The answers seem to depend upon the mood and purpose of the chronicler. Biblical criticism has been struggling with its fascinating problems for generations, stretching the meagre evidence on conjectures and beliefs. It has striven to resolve the literature into its component documents, to weigh what has been modified and to reconstruct what has been eliminated.

There must be many mistakes and misinterpretations. Yet more and more is being unravelled. Every year adds its mite to the knowledge of the past.

It will be most useful to tell the story of Hebrew origins in terms of the old traditions preserved in the Biblical literature. But one must steer between the Scylla of credulity and the Charybdis of scepticism. The Bible can serve as a very useful historical document if it is kept in mind that its editors have recast tribal traditions and reinterpreted them from a national standpoint, that the story is the idealized product of prophetic and priestly imagination, written down many centuries after the events supposedly occurred.

2. THE AGE OF FABLE

All primitive peoples begin their history with an account of the foundation of the world and the origins of man. The Hebrews developed several theories and blended them in the Biblical narrative. In the beginning there was a divinely created pair, Adam and Eve, and they were the original ancestors of everybody. There was a single pure stock to begin from, a single language, a definite home. But as men multiplied, life became debased and cruel and the pleasant simplicity of Eden went for ever.[1] Then came the raging flood, as a punishment for the past and a lesson for the future. All of mankind was destroyed, except Noah and his three sons, from whom have come the known races of the earth. The descendants of Shem, the Semites, settled themselves in western Asia; they included not only the Hebrews, but the Aramæans, the Assyrians, and other mighty peoples. The descendants of Ham centred themselves in Africa and were father to the Egyptians, the Turanians, the Cushites, and their kinsmen. And the European peoples, far off to the unknown west, sprang from the loins of the kindly Japhet. So the generations passed and multiplied until from the city of Ur, in Mesopotamia, came a descendant of Shem whose name was Abraham. To him was vouchsafed the discovery of the one true God, Yahweh, and with him the Hebrew chroniclers definitely begin the history of their people.

It is a naïve account and of historical usefulness principally to give us an insight into the mind of the generations that conceived it. Some of it was borrowed from Babylonian traditions; but the moral genius of the Biblical writers expurgated it, refinished it, and charged it with ethical meaning. God made everything and it was good, the Hebrew writers say again and again, with simple eloquence. Even labour, the bane of nomadic life, can be good; the sweat of a man's brow can be the most dignified baptism.

It is significant that in the Babylonian stories the creation is the result of a conflict between the gods, and ultimately rival kingdoms are established in the heavens and on the earth. Even where one god, Marduk, is able to conquer

[1] Like the Greeks and the Romans, the early Hebrews placed the golden age at the beginning of their history.

chaos and establish himself over an orderly world, his victory comes only after a fearful battle with the rebellious forces of nature. The Hebrew writers, however, stress a peaceful, unchallenged creation. God wills it, and it comes to pass. He rules over all things, heaven and earth, light and darkness.

The Flood story was a rather inconsequential tale in the Babylonian traditions, with capricious gods who were jealous of each other, who swore and plotted and erred. Utnapishtim, the Babylonian Noah, was a favourite of Ea, who gleefully frustrated the plans of the other gods by counselling his protégé to build his ark. When the flood came, the gods who turned on the destructive forces were unable to turn them off, and mankind was thus wiped out, almost inadvertently. If, as is now generally believed, the Hebrew writers took over the story, they completely changed its meaning and purpose. To them God was not made in the image of man; man was made in the image of God. Since God was good and just, only the good and the just were held up as models. Noah was singled out from all mankind to be saved because he lived well and walked humbly with his God.

Here are fine examples of the moral ardour of the prophetic and priestly historians. They miss no opportunity to preach. The story of the Hebrew beginnings is excellent material to impress a love of one God and an ideal of righteousness on their people. They pour into the account all of their own idealism. This moral tradition has never been discontinued. To this day the ancient words are pondered over, analysed, interpreted, weighed, read in context and out of context, to teach mankind how to live. The zealous old preachers of the past wrought more than they knew.

The Biblical narrative passes from general accounts of human beginnings to the origins of the Hebrews. The historical difficulties involved in reconstructing the dim days of tribal beginnings do not seem to daunt the sturdy chroniclers. They see the ancient scenes clearly. With minutest detail they spin tales of the patriarchs who first organized the Hebrew people, of fearful experiences in Egypt, of a miraculous deliverance, of further wanderings in the barren Sinaitic peninsula, of new religious revelations, and finally of the conquest of Canaan. Many of the stories were doubtless told to establish a common ancestor, as Greek writers developed a single founder in the character of Hellen, and Roman writers strained their imagination to create a Romulus. Other tales probably had their origin in the sanctuary myths current in Canaan when the Hebrews first entered the land. But some of the legends must be rooted in authentic soil, and much critical ingenuity has been applied to the discovery of these roots.

The patriarchs, who seemed to wander all over the ancient world, with no one to molest them, present the most difficult problem. Some scholars believe that they were originally merely tribal deities who were later brought down from their heavens, in the familiar ways of folk-lore, to become the progenitors of

Israel. Others believe that they were semi-divine Canaanite heroes who were adopted by the Hebrews after the conquest of Canaan. Still others believe that their lives reflect the early history of some wandering tribes, that the experiences of the desert nomads were all thrown together into a composite account of the patriarchs. Perhaps tradition is dimly reaching out to the distant days of the Aramæan migrations, which brought a great number of Semitic tribes, at least temporarily, into Palestine. At some stage in the wanderings of these tribes a few unusual characters may have impressed themselves on the memory of the people, through kindness or wisdom, through strength or courage, or through all of them together, so that later historians clustered about their names the legends and stories which have endeared themselves to every lover of the Bible.

Every old tradition points to a long sojourn in Egypt as an important part of the earliest Hebrew experiences. It may be that the first arrivals in Palestine, unable to get a permanent foothold there and impelled by famine or restlessness, kept moving southward until they found their way into the hospitable delta of the Nile. Or perhaps while most of the early Hebrews took root in Palestine, assimilating rapidly with the natives, a part of them, unable or unwilling to remain and attracted by the flesh-pots of Egypt, wandered southwards and established themselves in Goshen in the eastern Nile delta. Such an interpretation would mean that there were Hebrews in Palestine at the same time that there were Hebrews in Egypt, and that both groups united their blood and their traditions many centuries later. This view has the authority of most modern historians. Actual evidence for a Hebrew settlement in Egypt is, in either case, of the scantiest and most doubtful kind. Biblical critics who maintain that folk-lore is preserving a historical fact must rest their beliefs almost entirely on faith. Many of them do so frankly. They hope that some day evidence will be unearthed to tell the story of the penetration of the Hebrews into Egypt, of their friendly relations with the Egyptian rulers, and of their prosperous life in the Nile delta, with a definite tribal organization, a separate language, and distinct religious beliefs.[1]

Following the Biblical account, we must assume that a little group of Hebrews settled in Egypt during the middle of the second millenium. They lived their quiet, pastoral life, multiplying, growing wealthy, some filtering back into the desert, others coming in to take their places. Then suddenly conditions changed. " A Pharaoh arose who knew not Joseph." For some unexplained reason a sharp, anti-Asiatic reaction began, rising steadily and affecting the alien Hebrew tribes who dwelt in the country. Egyptian animosity reached out against all strangers in the land; they were heckled and disturbed and preyed upon. At last,

---

[1] One interesting theory, held by a few scholars who do not believe in an Egyptian sojourn, suggests that the southernmost tribes of Palestine, close to Egyptian influence and for some time under Egyptian control, developed the whole Exodus saga on the basis of local experiences of their own.

actual oppression came, and reduction to serfdom. Folk-lore tells in sharp, concise sentences how galling was the making of bricks and other forced manual labour to a free, nomad people.

Controversy is not yet exhausted on the identity of the Pharaoh of the oppression. There are as many theories as there are Egyptian dynasties. The difficulties in the way of a satisfactory solution can be readily understood when it is remembered that the very fact of the oppression is open to serious question. For long it was believed that the doubtful distinction of being the Hebrew taskmaster belonged to Rameses II, who reigned long and prosperously in the thirteenth century B.C. He had an extraordinary mania for erecting memorials and he built continuously, almost throughout his reign, using the princely booty from his conquests to write himself into stones and sites. Countless serfs were needed, of course, to take care of so much building in a day when machinery was unknown. Perhaps the Hebrews were among the serfs who " toiled in mortar and in brick and in all manner of service in the field." Exodus tells how they built Rameses and Pithom, and in 1883 the sites of both places were discovered, with bricks bearing the name of Rameses. Today, at the rock temple of Abu Simbel, facing the Nile with solemn grandeur, are four giant statues of Rameses; at the base of each throne there are captives with the ropes in the hands of the Pharaoh. These facts and others are marshalled as evidence that the oppression occurred in the time of Rameses.

But there are serious chronological difficulties that have to be faced if this view is accepted. Much of the evidence, too, does not necessarily point to Rameses. A number of critics wish to push back the beginning of the oppression about two centuries, to the reign of Thutmose III. Until there is more satisfactory evidence, one theory is as likely as the other.

The oppression probably lasted until the powerful nineteenth dynasty began to founder, in the thirteenth century. The last kings were not very able statesmen. Internal dissensions began to gnaw at the heart of the State. Libyan invaders came in upon the country from the west, and hordes of Cretans swept in from the sea; pirates from Cyprus and Asia Minor followed in the wake of these troubles, and all together probably gave a basis for the plague stories, which the Hebrew writers dwelt upon with relish. It is not unlikely that during the distress and confusion the Hebrew serfs broke their bondage and left, to go back into the wilderness that bore them.

The influence of the long, Egyptian oppression remained. Even if the whole episode was a myth, the later generations implicitly believed that it was a fact, and it left an eternal mark on them. They hated oppression and tyranny with all the intensity of their Semitic natures. They wrote their hate into every one of their laws; many of them are prefaced, significantly, with " Remember your bondage in Egypt." Sometimes as a people they forgot and became taskmasters themselves. But their prophets were quick to remind them that they had once eaten of the bread of affliction, and pleaded fervently for tenderness and sympathy for the slave, the alien, the widow, and the orphan. This is why a tiny revolution, which may never have occurred, looms so large in history. The tradition of it burnt into the soul of a people, destined to teach the world the meaning and responsibilities of freedom.

3. MOSES

The central hero of the Exodus and what follows is Moses, who, Heine says, makes Sinai seem puny by his grandeur, and who is to Napoleon the one man of mark in all Biblical history, not excluding Jesus! Tradition portrays him in the dual role of leader and priest-prophet, the maker of the nation and the organizer of the Hebrew religion. In fact, the two roles were inseparably connected and arose out of each other. Moses created the Hebrew people when he united them by the bonds of religion. His immense influence easily marks him as the outstanding character in Hebrew history, one of the moral giants of all time. Yet of his life, of his very existence, we have no conclusive proof. Not a contemporaneous document, not a stele, not a shred of evidence, has been found to authenticate his historicity. Perhaps some day his existence, too, will be scientifically demonstrated, as Hammurabi's was, when, in 1902, the tablets of his laws were discovered. Until then the paradox must remain that the most influential personality in Jewish history may be merely the product of Jewish imagination.

Moses was born, by the Biblical accounts, in the bitterest years of the Egyptian oppression, when the venom of the Pharaoh had gone so far that all male children of Hebrew parents were ordered slain. The child was hidden by his mother in the rushes of the Nile and rescued from a watery grave only by the providential intervention of Pharaoh's own daughter, who adopted him and brought him into the king's household. He was reared in the midst of the astonishing luxury common in the decadent period of the nineteenth dynasty, but he never forgot the bondage of his people. It cut deep into his soul when he thought of their degradation and helplessness. And one day as he beheld an ignorant taskmaster beating a terrified Hebrew serf, his indignation ran away with his discretion and he slew the tormentor. He thereby sacrificed his protected position and his privileges and was compelled to flee from the wrath of the Pharaoh.

The young rebel took refuge in the desert with some wandering Midianite tribes, and there married the daughter of the priest-chief. In the solitude of the desert he came to know Yahweh, who, according to some of the Biblical documents, had not revealed himself until he appeared to Moses. Inspired by the vision, Moses now felt that he had the strength to save his people. He returned to Egypt to break the fetters which they had borne too long and too patiently.

His fiery zeal and the troubles which just then engulfed Egypt combined to make his mission successful, and the little people went forth into the desert to begin life anew.

One of the first acts of Moses after the departure from Egypt was to consecrate the new freedom of his people by bringing them into a covenant with Yahweh. He led them to Mount Sinai, at the foot of which they were to learn of their sacred religious and social responsibilities. The imagination of the Hebrew writers glows with the dramatic possibilities of the scene. Here was a people just emancipated, the marks of slavery still in their souls, if not on their bodies, trembling at the foot of Sinai, dense clouds obscuring the peak, where Moses stood face to face with Yahweh, lightning and thunder, smoke and flame adding to the awfulness of Yahweh's proximity. It was a worthy setting for the promulgation and acceptance of the deathless Decalogue.

The Biblical accounts are confused as to the nature of the religious and ethical messages of Moses. Hence the most diverse principles are attributed to him, laws simple and complex, hardened with desert cruelty, tempered with sublimest gentleness. Even the rules of conduct for a great state are there and the elaborate details of priestly procedure. What were probably the results of generations of trial and experiment were fathered upon the versatile nomad chieftain.

But tradition adds a few more cubits to his stature. He was a masterful leader as well as a lawgiver, a giant personality who could bend a rabble to his bidding. Through all the weary years of wandering he guided his people and taught them, schooled them, watched them develop from a bondage-born and bent race into a strong, virile, fearless, bedouin nation, capable of winning a home and settling in it. There were battles, of course, and distressing trials, which made the craven yearn for the flesh-pots which they had left behind in Egypt. The Amalekites were inveterate enemies, and there were other hostile tribes who made life a trial. There were dissensions and rebellions, some reaching formidable proportions. But Moses was a rod of iron in the face of every danger. He showed his people that the staff of leadership in the wrong hands turned invariably into a serpent; that only tried, responsible guides and patient followers could make the staff blossom and bear choice fruit.

So leading and teaching, Moses brought the Hebrews to Canaan, which they were destined to make their own. It was left for other leaders to accomplish the conquest. Moses died seeing the land from afar, never entering it himself. Tradition says that God kissed him as he went to his rest; "and no man knoweth of his sepulchre."

It has been suggested that even if this whole picturesque account were purely mythical, even if there were no Moses, it would be necessary to create one to account for the developments which transformed the early history of the Hebrews. From the point of view of actual influence it matters little; for the towering

Moses of tradition has conquered the possible Moses of fact. Authentic or not, created by God or created by the literary genius of men, his personality has become one of the enduring influences of mankind. " A pillar of light," the Hebrew philosopher Ahad Ha'am calls him, " on the threshold of history." Even as a myth he represents the idealism of the prophetic writers who fashioned him, and he becomes thus more truly than ever the great Hebrew type; for his life is just what the best in Hebrew genius has wished him to be. He becomes the greatest Hebrew who never lived.

But from the more strictly historical point of view we cannot dimiss Moses so lightly. Upon his existence depends an understanding of the major problems of early Hebrew history. The development of the tribes into a nation, the evolution of the religion to the prophetic times — these and other matters cannot be accurately analysed if the problem of Moses and the nature of his work are not taken into account.

Most modern critics are inclined to accept Moses as a definite historical character. Though there have clustered about him innumerable legends, the work of historians who revelled in the art of literary decoration, the core of the stories is authentic. Moses, they suggest, was a magnificent nomad leader, associated with the Levi-Simon-Judah tribes who entered Palestine, probably from the south, and who, in the course of Israel's evolution, made the largest contribution to the religion of the Hebrews. Moses profoundly influenced his own tribes, and these in turn influenced the tribes in Palestine with whom they were later united. Moses, then, was not a national leader as portrayed by the later chroniclers who aimed to reinterpret local history in national terms; but he was a tribal chieftain who guided his people in critical days and permanently united them by impressing upon them a new religious outlook.

Just what this new religion was cannot be understood without first taking into account the general Semitic background. For the early Hebrews were part of the old desert world. They emerged from it, and doubtless their earliest religious experiences were moulded by it.

4. THE MOSAIC FAITH

The desert and its peoples have changed slowly. The forces of nature, strange, contradictory, full of perplexities, awakened practically the same response in the nomad breast when the desert was young, when Moses was overcome by the presence of Yahweh, when Mohammed fled from Mecca to save his life.

The desert was extremely stingy with its gifts, and its native tribes could never stay long in one place. Their homes were rude tents; their industry was usually limited to cattle-breeding. They ate and drank simple food — milk, cheese, and wild fruits, and, when they came into contact with civilized centres, corn and bread. Since there was little rainfall, fertile spots were rare. Hence every shady

tree, every cool spring, every alluring oasis, was regarded with grateful veneration.[1] Behind them all were spirits that watched over them and over the dusty
travellers who came to them for relief from the rigours of the desert. The world
was filled with spirits, many life-bringing, many malignant. Jinn, demons,
lurked in dark places. They brought plagues and pestilence; they carried sickness and death. Exorcism had to be resorted to frequently to drive out or placate
the demons who " possessed " men. Every clan had its soothsayer or magician,
with special charms, which were calculated to destroy the influence of these
malignant spirits.

It was natural in a world which stood in awe of spirits, good and evil, to
practise sacrifice. The spirits needed food. They were more inclined to grant
favours when hunger had been appeased; they were more kindly disposed when,
by sacrifice, a bond had been established with the petitioner. Rude stone
altars, or circles of stones, were set up, connected with favoured places that had
become shrines.[2] Here were offered the animals of sacrifice, perhaps even human
beings. Since the blood was very life, it was spilled out or smeared upon the
altar. Later the whole sacrifice was burnt.

How many of the desert beliefs and customs the early Hebrews lived by it
is impossible to know, but they formed the background out of which the
Hebrews emerged. All through the Biblical narrative we have references to
similar ways of life, and it is not improbable that many of them were survivals
from these primitive forms. The early Hebrew must have been polydemonistic,
fearful of every phenomenon, grateful for every blessing. The world was filled
with supernatural mysteries, and it was necessary for man to be careful of his
actions. The spirits were harsh and jealous, demanding cruelty to enemies, exulting in the complete destruction of those who sought to harm the tribes that
they had chosen to protect. Perhaps there was a degree of ancestor worship connected with the veneration of the spirits. Oracles from the dead occur frequently
in the Bible, and the teraphim, which often resembled human form, may have
been meant for ancestral images.

From this period, too, date many of the customs which were carried over
into later Hebrew life. The law of retaliation, the grim response of the desert
to actual or fancied injury, was part of Hebrew tradition until late in the
prophetic age. Kinsmen avenged each other's wrongs with relentlessness. *Lex*

[1] " To one who has wandered in the Arabian wilderness, traversing day after day stony plateaus,
black volcanic fields, or arid sands walled in by hot mountains of bare rock, and relieved by
no other vegetation than a few grey and thorny acacias or scanty tufts of parched herbage; till
suddenly at a turn of the road he emerges on a Wady where the ground-water rises to the surface, and
passes as if by magic into a new world, where the ground is carpeted with verdure and a grove of
stately palm-trees spreads forth its canopy of shade against the hot and angry heaven, it is not
difficult to realize that to early man such a spot was verily a garden and habitation of the gods."
Robertson: *The Religion of the Semites* (1889), pp. 97–8.

[2] It is commonly believed that the pillars and asherahs which stood at many of the shrines
were sexual symbols, venerated and worshipped to ensure fertility.

talionis was the only justice conceivable. The Song of Lamech is an echo of the desert days of Israel:

> A young man I slew for wounding me;
> A young man, too, for bruising me.
> Avenged may Cain be sevenfold,
> But Lamech seven-and-seventy fold!

The taboos on certain animals come from the desert days also. And the practice of circumcision was shared by many Semitic peoples and goes back beyond the Hebrews. There are records of the operation in Egyptian reliefs before 2500 B.C. The later Hebrews read into the practice a special ethical meaning; they believed that it was a symbol of their separation from other peoples, a separation to enable them to fulfil a special mission. Modern physicians have praised the practice as hygienic; but in its origin it was probably meant as a sacrifice, either of a part in lieu of the whole person, or as a means of ensuring fertility, or both.

Social organization, whatever its earlier form, became definitely patriarchal.[1] The father was the absolute ruler of the family. Women were reduced to practical serfdom; wives were frequently bought or captured and were little better than slaves. Polygamy was a common practice among those who could afford to support a large establishment.

This reconstruction of the desert life of the Hebrews may be justly challenged. The way is tangled, the facts that throw light upon it are few and dim. Yet, whether the details are accurate or not, it cannot be easily denied that the earliest Hebrew religious and social conceptions were neither greatly in advance of nor greatly behind the conceptions of kindred desert tribes.

The development from these primitive notions to the idea of Yahweh and its ethical content may have taken place on Palestinian soil, under Egyptian or Babylonian influence. But every tradition points to a remarkable religious revolution wrought by the genius of the desert chieftain Moses, who imbued his people with a sense of their unity and sanctified the bond by a common devotion to the god Yahweh. As suggested above, most critics accept his historical existence, as a member of the Levi-Simon-Judah tribes, and, while discounting the subsequent idealization of his character and career, place him among the great religious leaders of all time. For his God and his law are immortal.

There is much dispute whether Yahweh was an original conception of Moses or the adopted god of some local tribe. In the reaction against the idealization of Moses many scholars have attempted to trace every religious innovation to surrounding influence, regarding Moses simply as a clever

[1] There is a tendency among the more radical Biblical critics to support the theory that Hebrew society retained matriarchal forms until well into David's day.

popularizer. Others, more generous, credit him with some originality, but point out that his borrowings were liberal. Some years ago Budde perfected the theory that Yahweh had been the god of the Kenites, the tribe of Moses' father-in-law, and was adopted by Moses when the Kenites threw in their destinies with the Hebrews. There is evidence for and against every theory. But whether or not Yahweh was a borrowed god, the content which Moses gave to his conception, and the spiritual values which he drew from it, were essentially different from any that had been previously developed.

To Moses Yahweh was indissolubly bound up with the lives of men and the moral order of the universe. He was the sanction for all the laws which governed society. They were not made simply for the convenience of men; they were Yahweh's will and part of an inscrutable divine scheme. To break the law, then, was more than a crime against society; it was a sin against Yahweh, a flouting of His wishes.

There followed from this a unique relation between Yahweh and his people. Yahweh, indeed, sought to help Israel. He was the Lord of hosts, fighting for His people, shielding them, exulting in the destruction of their enemies. But never at the expense of the moral order. This was absolute and unchangeable. The moral nature of other gods was perhaps not inferior to Yahweh's; but other gods were not so bound up with the moral law. They could stretch it, change it, forget it, when their own favourites were involved. Yahweh could not unbend even for His chosen people. He was limited by His own law.

It is this magnificent austerity, this undeviating loyalty to a principle of law, suggested in the monumental masterpiece of Michelangelo, that raises Moses to the heights in religious history. His Yahweh was often narrow and jealous; his laws were often steeped in the primitive spirit of the desert. But he had linked his people to Yahweh and the moral law in a sublime, indissoluble trinity. The union remained the basis for the faith of the prophets, of the great teachers of mankind, when they had exalted both the concept of Yahweh and the moral code which He demanded.

Such a god, as Söderblom suggests, could touch the emotions deeply. He was not cold, hard, external, but a great consuming flame, taking complete possession of men, filling their souls. To a nature such as Moses' He came with overwhelming power, in the burning bush, in the thundering storms of Sinai. To the Hebrews who worshipped Him, as to Moses, He was a god of awe, of terrifying majesty; and yet holy, demanding holiness in His people, a high standard, faithfully kept.

The nature of the law proclaimed by Moses has been variously interpreted. There are a number of codes scattered through the Pentateuch, all attributed to Moses, many of which, however, must have been of much later composition. The simple Decalogue of Exodus xxxiv. 14–26 is probably the oldest and is incorporated in all of the other codes. Simply expressed, admirably suited for the needs of a nomad people, it has been usually accepted as approximating the norm of conduct proclaimed by Moses as the irreducible minimum of the moral life.

The code established that Yahweh was the god of the Hebrews, that none other could be worshipped; and it forbade the making of graven images. Festivals, either borrowed or commemorating early experiences in the life of the Hebrews, were to be carefully celebrated. Sacrifices and the redemption of firstlings were several times emphasized. And the sabbath was established as a day of rest.[1]

These precepts seem to be very bald and primitive, not at all suited to the moral grandeur that has been assigned to Moses. Yahweh is more like a stern uncle than an indulgent father. He is attached to His people, but He grumbles and complains and constantly reminds them of duties. Many critics feel that it would not be straining the evidence too far to attribute the essence of the Deuteronomic Code to the genius of Moses. It was a remarkable document. It established, as the other codes had, that Yahweh was the god of Israel; it forbade the making of graven images. But it went much farther. It forbade stealing, adultery, murder, coveting, and bearing false witness. It called for the suppression of passions and instincts which remain uncurbed in modern society. It went far beyond the limited vision of the ancient peoples; it became the burden of the prophetic teaching.

Perhaps Moses towered sufficiently above his time and his people to proclaim such a gospel. But even if the Deuteronomic Code is not attributed to him, his place as a nation-builder and religious leader does not suffer. The later ethical developments in Israel were made possible when he established the premise that human relations must be regulated by religious principles, and that these principles are a manifestation of Yahweh's will.

Moses, then, as a tribal and religious leader was the most important influence in the life of Israel. He used spirit to cement into a people a group of rude nomads. He brought them to worship one God, to stand in awe of Him, to adjust their acts to His will. The worship which he introduced was narrow, not completely emancipated from the heathen customs of the desert, but it was clean and wholesome and connected with none of the sexual excesses that marred the practices of many another people. In later history Israel too went a-whoring after more attractive gods and vulgarized their worship. But the degeneration was due to alien influence and was checked by the prophets, who rested on the Mosaic faith. The religion of Moses was as clean as the fires that scorched his soul when he saw and talked to his God.

1 Jastrow has suggested that the sabbath may have been borrowed from Babylon. Among the Babylonians the sabbath was originally a taboo day falling upon the seventh, fourteenth, twenty-first and twenty-eighth days of the lunar month.

CHAPTER THREE

THE HEBREWS ENTER PALESTINE

I. QUEST AND CONQUEST

THE first Hebrews who penetrated into Palestine were not, of course, rude savages descending suddenly, like a plague of locusts, upon a well-ordered country. The transition from the nomadic stage was not usually precipitate. Many of the nomadic tribes had lived for long periods in settled areas before breaking camp and moving on. Modern travellers often tell of nomad valleys sown each year and abandoned after the harvest.

Yet the new-comers were assuredly far from understanding the ways of settled communities. They were, even in the idealized Biblical accounts, a disunited, untutored folk, amazed even by the primitive civilization of the Canaanites. Fate orders its miracles capriciously. From such crude and unpretentious beginnings there were to develop sages and saints and prophets who consecrated the soil on which they preached; a religion of tremendous power, from whose body sprang two others of enduring force and vitality; and a literature of rare, spiritual quality, the autobiography of a God-intoxicated people.

There are a number of Biblical accounts which recall the memorable history of the conquest. In the Book of Joshua the whole episode is simple, a well-planned and well-executed campaign. Joshua, the high-spirited successor of Moses, led the invading hosts across the Jordan and in a series of courageous attacks and subtle stratagems took possession of Palestine. He then divided up the country by lot among the twelve tribes who helped in the conquest, and, after a stirring farewell oration to his people, went to his reward.

This account, with its miracles and its lessons, is, of course, the romantic fabrication of the Deuteronomistic and priestly historians. They were anxious to father a common history upon the tribes who afterwards made up the little Hebrew nation, and to prove through that history how munificent was Yahweh's reward to an obedient people. To them the Hebrews were already a united nation when they came to the threshold of Palestine, and the conquest was accomplished in a few brilliant and miraculous strokes. The first two chapters of the Book of Judges, representing an older version, suggest another view-point, which, undoubtedly, approximates the truth much more closely. The settlement of the country, according to them, was not accomplished in one violent effort. It was a slow, filtering-in process, wave by wave, tribe by tribe. Hordes of land-hungry nomads fought for a foothold, fell back, returned, conquered, settled down, intermarried, assimilated, and were not certain, even after the passing of several generations, that they would succeed in rooting themselves in the soil.

It is likely that long before the invasion of other Hebrew tribes Asher was already settled in the north, closely associated with Phœnicia. The Asher clans are mentioned in inscriptions which go back to the days of Rameses, the traditional Pharaoh of the Exodus. In the Biblical stories Asher is accounted the son of a handmaiden of Jacob, perhaps a hint that union with the more legitimate Hebrew tribes came after a period of separate historical development. The powerful Joseph clans, including Ephraim and Manasseh and Benjamin, probably came in from the east, conquering the territory on the farther side of the Jordan, some of the clansmen settling there, and then pushing across the river and gradually spreading, after years of fighting, from the barren highlands into the more fertile central parts of the country. Last of all, about 1200 B.C., came Judah and associated clans, such as Levi, Simon, and the Kenites, who pushed into the southern part of Palestine from the desert. These brought with them their worship of Yahweh and their devotion to the memory of their great leader, Moses.[1]

It is all a very complicated story, bristling with problems for the historians and archæologists of the future. In the present state of our knowledge one can be certain only that the conquest was not an act, but a process, and that it must have taken years for the nomads to break down the resistance of the natives.

From the Tel el Amarna letters we can understand how formidable this resistance was, what serious obstacles to the path of the invaders were presented by the many cities that dotted the country, with their walls, their fortifications, and their watch-towers, defended by natives superior in culture, greater in numbers, and possessing far better weapons. The war-chariots of the Canaanites were deadly effective and struck terror into the hearts of the Hebrews. Only the wretched political weakness of the natives undermined their natural advantages and brought them low. Their disunion was evidently as marked as it appeared to be in the Tel el Amarna days, each little community concerned only with its own safety, worrying little about the fate of its neighbour. " The whole country," writes the excavator of Gezer, was " a mass of little clans, scarcely more than a collection of independent villages, with such highly developed mutual jealousy that union for a common purpose, even for the public safety, was out of the question." [2] The desperate ardour of the invaders could win even fortified cities from a population so distraught. One recalls the con-

[1] If this interpretation is correct, Moses came later, in point of time, than Joshua, whom tradition associates with the Joseph clans.
[2] Macalister: *A History of Civilization in Palestine*, p. 48.

quest of the Celts in ancient Britain by the Saxons, dribbling in little by little, but overcoming the opposition of a whole country made feeble by internal dissension and fratricidal hostility.

2. THE PROCESS OF AMALGAMATION

Conquest was one matter; security after conquest was quite another. For generations the new-comers had no peace. They held only scattered portions of the country, and even in the days of David it was necessary to conquer Jerusalem before it could be made the country's capital. The Hebrews were often hemmed in on all sides by other alien tribes. Where there were peaceful relations, there was rapid assimilation and very often a loss of identity. Simon could not retain its corporate existence and very early was merged in the tribes of the south. Asher took to the sea and was lost among the Phœnicians. Even Judah received a large infusion of Canaanite blood if the tradition of the marriage with the Canaanite is the record of tribal experiences (Genesis xxxviii. 2).

More often, however, relations between the new-comers and the older inhabitants were not peaceful. Warfare was constant. And no mercy was shown by either side. Captured communities were given over to massacre; men, women, and children were all exterminated " with the edge of the sword." A man's life was unsafe outside of his own village. " In the days of Jael the highways were in disuse, and the travellers walked in bypaths." [1] Egypt had completely withdrawn, and, with none to keep the peace, intertribal hostility was given every opportunity for free play. In the Book of Judges, which describes with gusto the long and desperate wars of the local Hebrew chieftains against the enemy tribes of Palestine, we have an idealized but fundamentally sound record of the early Hebrew struggle to maintain life and independence in the newly won communities.

On the east the little tribe of Benjamin found a constant menace in the Moabites, who were able to reconquer many of the old towns which the Hebrews had taken. Benjamin withstood their fierce onslaughts for years, but at length was reduced to degrading tribute. Tradition preserves the exploit of a left-handed hero, Ehud, who assassinated the Moabite king and brought temporary peace to his tribe.

In central Palestine the Canaanite tribes were relentless enemies, and they made life miserable for the scattered Hebrews. They raided their fields, burnt their homes, and killed off their young men. Only when the oppression became unbearable was there a concerted thrust for freedom by a few of the Hebrew tribes. The crisis is responsible for one of the oldest pieces of literature in the Bible, the Song of Deborah, perhaps a contemporary document. It tells of the

[1] Judges v. 6.

desperation of the Hebrews, the martial inspiration of the prophetess, her pleas with the tribes to unite in self-defence, the leadership of Barak, the long-fought battle on the banks of the Kishon, the final, overwhelming victory of the Hebrews against the chariots of the mighty Sisera. So vivid is the account that in the Hebrew verse one catches the sound of the grinding of the horses' hoofs. There is genuine art in the conclusion of the poem, which describes the anxiety of Sisera's mother as she sits waiting at the palace window for his triumphal return, while he lies dead, with a tent-pin in his temple, slain by the cunning of a woman.

The Midianites were yet other foes, who specialized in raids at harvest time. Here it was a young farmer of Manasseh, Gideon, who fought the enemy with guile and strategem, and conquered. And from the Ammonites, who disturbed the peace of the Hebrews well on into Roman days, it was the outlaw chief Jephthah who brought temporary relief to his tribe.

The whole turbulent period is filled with such struggles, the circumstances calling forth local heroes from all ranks and all walks of life. But the common danger did not for long bring the scattered Hebrew tribes together. Sometimes a few tribes co-operated, as in the battle against Sisera, but the union was only temporary, and after a spurt of enthusiasm each little clan relapsed into its own petty concerns. At the most critical moments there were jealousies and animosities, and in the Bible there is a graphic account of a civil war among the Hebrew tribes on the west. This internal strife, when there were so many dangers to be resisted, was the most serious barrier to stability and normal development. For long the ever watchful enemies took advantage of tribal separateness to perpetrate raids and outrages. It was not until the advent of the terrifying Philistines, whose hammer-blows endangered the existence of all the tribes of Palestine, that union among the Hebrews was at last achieved.

But before discussing the pressing danger and the reaction to it, which opened a new era in Hebrew history, it may be profitable to analyse the influence of the conquest of the country upon the social and religious life of the Hebrews.

3. THE MEETING OF BAAL AND YAHWEH

The entrance of the Hebrew tribes into Canaan completely changed their destiny. Their outlook had been nomadic, their habits and customs largely bedouin. They now became settlers on a fixed soil, acquired homes, took pride in personal possession. Everything in the civilization of the land astonished their half-open minds; the little towns and hamlets, walled and protected with fortresses, the fields and their abundant products, the weapons of war, especially the devastating, swiftly moving chariots, the implements and utensils of peace. They watched and imitated. For the Canaanites were not all exterminated, nor was their civilization effaced. Most of the conquered lived on in the land among their despoilers, often side by side. From them the Hebrews learned how to till the soil, to make garments, and to manufacture tools. They began to produce corn, wine, oil, and figs and to exchange their surplus for the products of Tyre and Sidon. With new means of sustenance their population increased materially. They began to think of the future and to wonder about the past. They learned the alphabet, and though at first, perhaps, it served merely for a charm on a weapon or a name on a stone, it was soon employed to record the lusty songs and the extraordinary deeds of legendary heroes. By the time of David we read of scribes attached to the court who, like the Saxon Widsith, were eager " their word-horde to unlock."

Hebrew religion was naturally also vitally affected by the contact with Canaanite life. From the evidence of Biblical and extra-Biblical sources it is possible to glimpse the more important religious ideas of the Canaanites. They were the result of many influences. In the Tel el Amarna period they had crystallized into a mixture of old Semitic polydemonism and Babylonian and Egyptian polytheism. Reverence was paid to active natural phenomena, to wind, storm, lightning, rain, to springs and trees, to solitary stones of peculiar shape, to the spirits of ancestors. Worship, as Jeremiah afterwards exclaimed, was conducted " on every high hill and under every green tree." Life, health, happiness, all depended on the favour of the gods, the Baals or Baalim, who inhabited these objects of nature or manifested themselves through them. The land was so much dependent upon rain and sun that its inhabitants were completely at the mercy of the powers of nature and nature worship was almost inevitable. Baal was a nature god, the patron of the husbandman. He sent the rain, he made the ground productive, he induced fertility in the domestic animals.

The Baals were often represented by symbols — cows, doves, bulls, and other animals and birds of prey. It has been customary to compare the worship with that of Catholic communities in the Middle Ages, each of which had individual madonnas. The Mary of one Italian town was not the Mary of another, yet it was the same Holy Virgin which was being adored. Such a comparison, however, stretches the idea of the Baal into a one-god concept. Perhaps among the more thoughtful natives there was a general god idea, but it could not have been highly developed.

There were female counterparts of Baal as well, the Baalith, usually associated with the miracle of fertility. The worship of the Baalith, usually Astarte, was carried on with sensual practices, meant originally to consecrate the mysteries of the renewal and creation of life, but in practice degenerating into crude, barbarous lasciviousness.[1]

---

[1] " The emotional side of Semitic heathenism was always very much connected with the worship of female deities, partly through the associations of maternity, which appealed to the purest and

The first contact of Yahwism and Baalism was doubtless a dramatic clash; each people clung desperately to its gods, appealing for assistance in the hour of direst need and ruthlessly uprooting all institutions which seemed alien. But after the Hebrews had settled down to a stable life, antagonisms diminished and a process of assimilation began. By degrees, loyalty to Yahweh wavered as Baal beckoned alluringly. Baal was definitely associated with agriculture. The husbandman depended upon his goodwill during all the slow, tedious processes of raising crops; he needed him for sunshine, for rain, for an abundant crop. Perhaps the simple Hebrew, wielding his crude flail, thought of his desert god as he prayed, but Baal was closer and seemingly more useful. A curious but natural transposition occurred. Yahweh himself became a Baal. Sacrifices were made to him on the high places, but with all the rites and ceremonies connected with the Baal worship. Even images crept in, though they were expressly forbidden by the Mosaic tradition. Teraphim became common household objects; we read that King David himself possessed one, in human form, large enough to pass for himself.

Soon the shrines of the Canaanites were taken over by the Hebrews. The high place at Shechem, devoted for ages past to the worship of the Baal Berith, became a Hebrew shrine too, sanctified by the tradition that there Yahweh had promised Canaan to the seed of Abraham. The ancient Canaanite sanctuary at Bethel was associated with Jacob's dream and became a popular Hebrew shrine in the days of the monarchy. Hebron was thought to be the burial place of the patriarchs, and its Cave of Machpelah is to this day holy ground for Hebrews, Christians, and Mohammedans. In a sense the Canaanites were revenged upon their conquerors, for the illustrious Hebrew dead of antiquity were made to sleep in Canaanite sepulchres!

It was natural for the Hebrews to absorb the festivals of the country, for they were nearest to the life of the masses. To the simple, nomadic Passover, with its lamb offering, there was now attached an agricultural festival of unleavened cakes, marking the beginning of the corn harvest, " when thou puttest the sickle into the corn." Seven weeks later, with the close of the corn harvest, came the Feast of Weeks. The most important festival of Canaanite life came in the autumn, commemorating the end of agricultural operations for the year, and was known as the Feast of Booths, or simply " the Feast." This was celebrated with much festivity, often with excessive exuberance. As with the shrines, traditions developed around the festivals to explain them in terms of early national experiences.

Gods, shrines, festivals, customs, habits, all found their way into Hebrew life. The assimilation has been often compared to the astonishing process by

---

tenderest feelings, and partly through other associations connected with woman, which too often appealed to the sensuality so strongly developed in the Semitic race." W. R. Smith: *Religion of the Semites*, pp. 58–9.

which a great body of pagan practices was built into the structure of early Christianity. Doctrines and dogmas were taken from pagan philosophies; rites and ceremonies were borrowed from pagan temples. The Church Fathers gave them new meanings and glibly associated them with events in the history of Jesus and Christianity. This religious synthesis is not uncommon wherever two civilizations come into close contact. In the case of the Hebrews the inter-mingling was fraught with much good, opening their minds and developing their spiritual potentialities. But it also proved a grave danger. Shrines and festivals, even superstitions, beliefs in witchcraft and necromancy, might be assimilated without serious hurt. But there also crept into the religion of the Hebrews pernicious sex practices and a devastating polytheism. These threat-ened to debilitate Hebrew life. For long the Hebrews lived on a plane no higher than any contemporary people, profaning their altars with the sorriest rites and desecrating their shrines with the vulgarest practices. The agricultural festivals became orgies of eating and drinking, with music and dancing and such sexual indulgence as would please the Baalith as a patroness of fertility. It was little wonder that when the early prophets appeared, aflame with anger at the degradation of the old desert faith, they demanded a root and branch reformation, the complete destruction of the alien influences, good and bad alike.

But these were developments which came much later. We must turn now to the events that moulded the Hebrew tribes into a nation.

CHAPTER FOUR

THE GROWTH OF NATIONAL
CONSCIOUSNESS

I. ON THE PHILISTINE ANVIL

AMONG the many invaders who kept throwing themselves into the Mediterranean coastland during these momentous migration periods were the powerful and aggressive Philistines, destined for centuries to be the *bête noire* of Hebrew life. They were probably a non-Semitic people, hailing from Crete and the Greek islands, where their splendid Mycenæan civilization had been suddenly overthrown by other adventurers. All through the early twelfth century B.C. they had been drifting by various routes into the coastland and had even penetrated as far as the Egyptian frontier. The riches and splendour of the Nile were not for them; in 1180 they were effectively checked in their southern expansion by Rameses III. However, they crept farther and farther north and east, meeting there only the feeble opposition of petty tribes. Carrying with them the remnants of their Mediterranean culture, they developed opulent cities, such as Gaza, " the outpost of Africa, the door of Asia," quite superior to any in Palestine. They created busy markets fed by the bedouin caravans of Edom and southern Arabia and by the merchants of Mesopotamia and Babylon. They built splendid temples to Dagon and other gods whom they may have borrowed from the Canaanites. They conquered and built and prospered, and when, at last, they had ground out the remnants of the sorry coastland tribes, they stood face to face with the Hebrews, ready to contest with them the supremacy of Palestine.

The little tribe of Dan, closest to the Philistine scourge, was the first to feel the pressure. Around the conflicts, which went on for years, a whole cycle of Samson legends was woven, the thrilling adventures of a genial Hebrew giant among the people who were afflicting his kinsmen. Samson slew his enemies by the thousands; he carried the gates of their cities for miles on his back; he was as marvellous in his subtle stratagems as in his superhuman strength. Tradition revels in the victories which he should have won. But the Philistines did most of the winning. Even a gigantic Samson was no match for the problem which his little tribe had to solve. Ultimately the Danites were squeezed out of their corner and were compelled to migrate to the north, where they settled close to Phœnicia, to become the outpost of Hebrew influence in Palestine.

30

The trip-hammer blows of the Philistines at last aroused the other Hebrew tribes to their own danger. Ephraim and Manasseh hastily united to keep the invaders out of the hill country. All in vain. The Philistines were irresistible. They won a crushing victory at Aphek, on the outskirts of Benjamin, and took a terrifying toll of lives. The Hebrews tried a last desperate resort to turn the tide. They brought from its sanctuary at Shiloh the Ark of Yahweh, their sacred palladium, and carried it into battle with them, praying as they fought. But even the visible presence of their god was unavailing. An undisciplined infantry was useless against the terrible power of the scythed chariots, which cut the Hebrew forces into shreds. The miserable remnants fled as before the Furies. The Philistines carried off the Ark to their own temples and crowned their triumph by burning the town of Shiloh. They surged exultantly into the country, occupied other cities, established their garrisons, pressed their captives into their army, stamped out uprisings, and drew a heavy tribute.

The Ark of the Lord of hosts in a pagan sanctuary, under the bloody, lustful eye of Dagon; Shiloh a heap of embers and debris; the country overrun by the hated enemy! It seemed as if the Hebrews were to share the fate of the other unhappy tribes that had obstructed the path of the Philistines. But the disasters had their sobering effect. The blows that sent the disunited tribes reeling were ultimately to prove a national blessing. All the hammering did not break the Hebrews. It made them. The Philistines smote them on an anvil and forged them into a people.

First, however, they forged them into a sword, and an obscure son of Benjamin rose to wield it. The occasion came on the eastern borders, across the Jordan, where desert and highland merge. The Ammonites, taking advantage of the Hebrew troubles, had delivered some telling blows and had made humiliating demands on the towns of Gilead. Now the tide turned. A powerful young farmer, Saul, gathered about him some of the stricken clans of his own tribe and turned with desperate fury on the foe. He crushed them so effectively that a thrill of courage ran through his people. They turned to Saul as to a saviour, confident that through him their woes were to be ended. One tradition has it that after his spectacular victories over the Ammonites he was at once crowned king at Gilgal.

Saul now struck out against the invincible Philistines. The issue was long in doubt. Saul played Alfred against the Danes; he required as much patience as skill and courage in the face of early disasters. After one defeat his army of three thousand melted away to barely three hundred, and these " followed him trembling." But destiny could no longer be forestalled, and the sword which the Philistines had forged conquered at last. Saul became the king of the Benjamin clans whom he had led in discomfiting the enemy.

2. THE CREATION OF THE MONARCHY

The origins of the Hebrew monarchy are lost in a maze of conflicting Biblical accounts. We know definitely only that wars were fought and that a little kingdom was created after them, perhaps out of them. Around these two series of developments the Book of Samuel has been built. The framework is probably sound, and many of the details are undoubtedly authentic, though they are not necessarily ascribed to the right persons.

One tradition presents Saul as the choice of Samuel, the famed sage of Ramah. A simple farmer lad, seeking his father's lost asses, Saul is told of his historic destiny by the seer and is anointed as Yahweh's instrument of salvation. By another account, probably written in the early post-exilic period, when the chroniclers were anxious to discredit the monarchy, a classic denunciation of kingship is placed in the mouth of the prophet Samuel, who anoints Saul very unwillingly. This interpretation is distinctly hostile to Saul and seeks to minimize him at the expense of his brilliant successor, David. Both of these accounts were later merged, but only fragments survived and were included in the Books of Samuel. It is from such fragments that we must interpret the history of the period. It is possible that we thereby unjustly libel worthy characters or unwarrantably praise knavish ones, but so long as the past preserves its inexorable silence, we must build our estimates on the flimsy material that is alone available.

The resounding victories of Saul made him the hero of the Hebrew tribes and elevated him to a kind of glorified judgeship. Even prejudiced accounts cannot deprecate his exploits or take from his prowess. But the kingship was not conceived in the heat of battle alone. There is a persistent tradition of prophetic influence in the establishment of the monarchy. It may be that Samuel, who hoped for the union of all the tribes, welcomed Saul as the chosen of Yahweh when he emerged triumphantly from his Ammonite battles. Thus, singled out by war and consecrated by the prophet's blessing, Saul launched his people in the monarchic tradition.[1]

All through his reign, however, he could not sheathe his sword. Despite his victories over the Philistines, they always returned, bringing with them greater numbers and greater doggedness. There were jackals too, lean, hungry, familiar figures that scented spoils while the lions fought. Moab, Edom, Ammon, slunk in again and again, snarling, barking, and occasionally biting. The fierce Amalekite showed poisonous fangs. Saul was for ever brandishing the sword. His ministers were rough frontiersmen like himself; his court was the camp. He won victories, he held his own, but the cries of battle continued, to the end of his life, to waken echoes in the Palestinian hills.

Saul lived simply and democratically, as befitted a Cincinnatus, and did little

[1] Kittel and others accept the Biblical account literally, that Saul was first chosen by Samuel and then began a momentous career of victory against the Ammonites.

to outrage the feelings of a people not yet accustomed to royal despotism. We read of meetings with his councillors under a sacred tree at Gibeah, of meals with only four places laid on the royal table, for the King, Jonathan, his son, David, his minstrel, and Abner, his cousin, the "captain of the host." No crown, no court ceremonial, none of the gorgeous trappings of Solomon's day.

So simple and courageous a warrior deserved to found a strong, stable dynasty. But it was not to be. It is clear from every source that the struggles waged against foreign enemies were matched by struggles in his own little domain. There was a sharp break with the prophets, who had been his most enthusiastic champions. Where and why the conflict began, it is impossible to say with assurance. In one story the King was not thorough enough in destroying the heathen Amalekites and their possessions, "man and woman, infant and suckling, ox and sheep, camel and ass." Samuel was so angry with Saul for his lack of zeal that he hewed the Amalekite king in pieces with his own hand! According to another account Saul evidently wounded the prophet's dignity, paying little attention to his importance in the new State. Probably the man of war was without the tact needed for difficult statesmanship.

There soon developed a considerable spirit of antagonism to the unhappy warrior king. This antagonism is presented as commendable by the Judæan chroniclers, who, throughout their narrative, seem to be bitterly hostile to Saul. They dwell at length on the genial personality of David, on his chivalry and his splendid, buoyant strength, and they contrast his virtues with the growing meanness and pettiness of the king. Saul became so jealous of David's popularity that he drove him from his presence, even seeking his life. When the priests apparently came to David's assistance during his exile, the old king went insane with fury. The story is told with pious horror how an entire company of priests were massacred at the sanctuary of Nob by the orders of Saul.

The end was near. Harassed by internal difficulties and Samuel's animosity, and worn down by the enemies on every frontier, Saul turned moody and violent. He is presented in decline as a half-crazed, jealous despot, governed by whim, impelled by rage, no match for the Philistines, who were just now on the crest of a new martial enthusiasm. Before the decisive battle of Mount Gilboa Saul was a beaten man.

But his end was in a major key. He died as he had lived, with the din of battle in his ears, by the side of three stalwart sons. The next day the exultant Philistines, stripping the fallen enemy, stumbled upon the royal body. They cut off the head and nailed the corpse on the walls of Bethshean. There it hung, proclaiming the degradation of Israel, until the men of Jabesh-Gilead, who had been rescued from the Ammonite incursions by the valour of the youthful Saul, risked their lives to recover the body and give it a reverent burial.

Saul is a pathetic character, undeserving of the harsh verdict of the Judæan writers. He was a failure only in the sense that he probably did not retain his early hold on his people. He lacked tact and geniality, qualities essential for the builder of a state. And perhaps there slumbered in his nature the beginnings of a dangerous melancholy which, under the pressure of hostility, wakened into a fatal madness, sapping his strength and paralysing his judgment. But his achievements cannot be buried beneath his shortcomings. As a soldier he was a living flame who kept his enemies at bay for a generation. As an organizer he left his people with a cluster of glorious victories, the memory of which was the best cement to build a united nation.

3. DAVID: FAVOURITE SON OF YAHWEH

David of Bethlehem, as drawn by the Biblical historians, was an extraordinary type, combining every happy talent and every winning quality. Never was mortal more fortunate. His very reverses struggled to bring him success. Of no Biblical character are there so many attractive legends of magnanimity, of cleverness, of brave dealings with enemies, of wisdom in statesmanship. Robbing the rich for the poor, he was Robin Hood; whipping the mighty against odds, he was Bruce; winning the friendship of Jonathan, he was Damon. He played exquisitely, he fought heroically, he loved titanically. Withal he was a profoundly simple being, cheerful, despondent, selfish, generous, sinning one moment, repenting the next, the most human character of the Bible.

As a youth he was attached to the king's retinue and easily won unparalleled fame by his gallant conduct on the field and his amiable manners in the camp. When his too fulsome popularity earned for him the animosity of Saul, he became an outlaw in the recesses of the stern Judæan hills, gathering about him a loyal band of kindred spirits. " And everyone that was in distress, and everyone that was in debt, and everyone that was discontented gathered themselves unto him; and he became captain over them."[1] They lived on plunder and throve on warfare. Now they sallied out against the unwary Geshurite; now they despoiled the camp of the sleeping Gezrite; now they laid tribute on the terrified Amalekite. All the while the vengeance of the king pursued the little band, until at length they went over to the Philistines, carrying on the same raids and the same freebooting from the other side of the frontier. Such was the early training of David. To such a tempestuous character even the Hebrew kingship seemed not remote.

When the tidings of the death of Saul reached David, he was already in control of Judah and its outlying districts, and on very friendly terms with the neighbouring sheikhs of the south. Soon after, it seems, he was actually crowned king in Hebron. In the north Abner, the faithful general of Saul, at once seized control in the name of Ishbaal, the son of the dead King. The ghost of old tribal animosities again stalked Israel in a tragic hour. The general of the north,

[1] I Samuel xxii. 2.

towering over his pygmy ruler, prepared to destroy the bandit of the south, and the Philistines rejoiced as the two rivals faced each other. It seemed as if the toy kingdom which had been built with such travail was to be finally destroyed.

There was still David, however, to be reckoned with, stolid, resourceful, supremely patient. For eight or ten years he steered a tortuous course with masterful diplomacy. He flattered his friends, he bribed his enemies, and dexterously used them all to further his ambitions. There were accidental murders and timely assassinations. Abner fell in a blood feud, Ishbaal lost his head by treachery. David buried them both with tears. At the end of the decade he emerged from the mire of bloodshed and sordidness, smiling, triumphant, and, what is most astonishing, with the goodwill of all parties behind him!

David was now recognized as ruler in a much wider area than Saul had ever controlled. He proceeded to consolidate his position further by establishing himself in a capital city. Saul had done nothing to focus the loyalty of the people; he had lived on in Gibeah, the little hamlet that had bred him. David made no such tactical mistake. The scattered tribes, he saw clearly, needed a centre of unity, a religious and national rallying-point, the tangible symbol of the common bond that united them. He chose from no tribal territory for fear of arousing jealousies. Instead he conquered a new, centrally located town, held by a Jebusite clan which had resisted the Hebrews since the conquest. Jerusalem, high up among the Judæan hills, was well-nigh impregnable; so strong, it was said, that the lame and the blind alone could effectively defend it. David captured it by a ruse, the exploit adding greatly to his prestige.

When founded, it was a miserable little town, vile-smelling, crooked, and ugly. David began at once to make it a worthy capital. He enlarged it by uniting to it the fortress of Zion, on a neighbouring hill, taking in the valley which separated the two, and surrounding the whole with a good stout wall. Then with dramatic pageantry he brought into Jerusalem the Holy Ark of Yahweh, which had gone through a troubled history since its capture by the Philistines. With this act of consecration began the romantic history of Jerusalem, now the religious and civil centre of the State, the physical symbol of Hebrew unity. Pilgrims in holiday garb, bearing presents, later flocked to its sacred shrines; merchants filled its bazaars and market places. Sentiment glorified the ancient scenes until they furnished inspiration to countless generations of patriots and singers. And the brigand David, who founded the city, became, in the eyes of the future, a pious religious leader, a favourite son of Yahweh.

Meantime the restless warrior was striking steadily and effectively at the ring of foes that hemmed in his new-born kingdom. His exuberance seemed to have no bounds. Soon he had carved out an empire that extended from Lebanon to the Red Sea. He became a leading power in the Syrian world. The Philistines were beaten back, losing even their capital, Gath, and the humiliation of Mount Gilboa was avenged by Saul's own rival. The Moabites were assailed hip and thigh, and if the Biblical narrative is authentic, nearly two out of three were killed off. The Ammonites, the Edomites, the Aramæans, the Amalekites, all felt the resounding blows of the new monarch, who conducted his wars with the ruthlessness and brutality of the time. He gave as he received. These were no milk-and-water days. Men fought desperately for hearth and home.

The victories changed the complexion of Hebrew life. Government became more complicated, and though David served as king and judge and general, there were subordinates who helped to knit the country closer politically. David's victories opened up the commercial highways, and new products as well as new fashions and ideas began to come in from Phœnicia, Damascus, Arabia, and farther points. The Hebrews were no longer an inconsequential group of adventurers. They had fused and become, at least superficially, an important Eastern people.

If David had died now, at the height of his fame, he might have a more honourable place in the history of his people. But he lived on to dissipate the glories that he had wrought with brain and sword. He lived on to become a typical despot, with all the vices that sadden the history of a mediæval Oriental court. The chroniclers detail, with remarkable objectivity, the story of his moral decay.

The harem, we are told, grew until it swarmed with women, some of them the pompous daughters of neighbouring kings. David found himself under the obligation of maintaining a court in keeping with their dignity. His own unruly passions, stimulated by the enervating life of the harem, eventually conquered his earlier military austerity. He stole Bath-sheba, the attractive wife of one of his faithful soldiers, and sent the poor man off to die for the glory of the king. He compounded adultery with murder, and soon his children began to profit by his example. Many concubines meant many royal princes, with palace plots and intrigues. The contrast is spectacular between the simplicity of Saul's little court and the court of David, in which princes already had ranks and privileges far above those of the common citizen. When rebellions broke out, David was not his old self. He showed only maudlin weakness in the crises and drew further and further into the luxurious repose of the harem. His prestige sank so low that when his handsome, temperamental son Absalom led a hare-brained revolt to drive his father from the throne, David was compelled to flee the capital amidst the curses and insults of all who bore him ill will. Only the iron arm of his loyal general, Joab, retrieved the situation, and Absalom's head was brought to the weeping father.

The last few years of David's reign were filled with plots and counterplots, engineered by the rivals for the throne. The eldest son, Adonijah, seemed to have the support of the army, while the king's favourite, Solomon, was thrust forward by his ambitious mother, the notorious Bath-sheba. The kingdom had been only just born, and already its life was threatened by the ugly struggles of adventurers for personal advancement. Solomon was ultimately proclaimed king in the last days of his father's lifetime, but only after some very slippery diplomacy.

Despite his beclouded end David was by no means a failure. Measured by results, he was the greatest statesman in the history of the Hebrew monarchy. He came to a country rent with strife, bewildered by the blows of enemies. Constant warfare imperilled every man's life and threatened every man's home. Yahweh was discredited, his Holy Ark was in the hands of the enemy. David cleared the frontiers and then pushed them back until they touched the mountains in the north, and the desert in the south. He created Jerusalem and made it not only a capital, but also a shrine.

Future generations, however, remembered his personality even better than his achievements. Every quality of leadership was his — bravery, Oriental cunning, affability. He had a genius for friendship; the love of Jonathan and David has become a byword. His smile was as potent as his sword. Even his outrageous actions had a winning quality about them. Who could be angry with his ingenuous, boyish impulsiveness? It is easy to understand how a people, embittered by misfortune and hounded by persecution, would look back upon the days of David with loving yearning, and how the shining figure of the poet-warrior would grow to epic proportions, the dross transformed, the good exaggerated, until even the Messiah Himself was to spring from the house of the peerless king.

4. SOLOMON AND CLASS DIVISIONS

Solomon inherited much of his father's winning personality and added to it a wit of his own, keen, worldly, searching, admirably adapted to endear him to an Eastern people. He was a shrewd judge of character and had no misgivings about human virtue. He had been brought up amidst political intrigues and harem jealousies and he realized how much perfidy and duplicity could be concealed beneath an obsequious demeanour. He gauged accurately men who kissed his hand in public and reviled his name in private.

These qualities won for him a reputation for remarkable wisdom, and, as usual, time and circumstance conspired to magnify his accomplishments. Solomon was counted by tradition the wisest of men. Yahweh had blessed him with a discerning heart, and nothing was hidden from him. He knew the speech of birds and trees, he could read the very hearts of men. Much of the Wisdom literature in the Bible, the pithy Proverbs, the cynical Ecclesiastes, and parts of the Apocrypha, were fathered upon him to enhance their prestige and authority. Hebrew and Arabic sources are filled with stories of his rare sharpness.

All this enthusiastic homage in the face of his undoubted extravagance and its disastrous consequences has called forth an angry reaction. It has become fashionable to side with the stern old northern historians, who betray little love for Solomon. Many modern critics describe him as the king of pomp and glitter, the despoiler of his people, his life one long extravagance, without a constructive feature.

This judgment too is grossly unfair. Solomon deserves neither romantic adulation nor sweeping abuse. He made grievous mistakes. He was often a petty Oriental despot. His genius was never of a moral or spiritual quality. But seen on the canvas of his day, he was no worse than the other figures who thronged it; rather, a great deal better. He opened the Hebrew world to new and far-reaching influences. He expanded the cultural boundaries of Israel. The price was perhaps too high; too many backs were bent and too many purses drained to pay for the royal projects. But they helped to enrich the narrow life of Israel as much as they helped to satisfy the vanity of the king.

The new reign was inaugurated with a series of executions motivated as much by revenge as by policy. Solomon was particularly relentless towards the opponents of his succession. Adonijah, who had almost captured the throne by a skilful coup, was quickly dispatched. The valiant Joab, victor in a score of glorious combats, who had served David with unstinting loyalty in every crisis, was hunted down like a dog and denied the immunity even of sanctuary in the house of Yahweh. His assassin was made the new commander of the king's forces. A number of military leaders who had supported Adonijah's candidacy were slain without the formality of a pretext. Abiathar, who had shared David's adventures since the lean, hungry days of his outlaw period, was deposed as high priest and banished. The sternness of the new monarch was a clear sign, soon made unmistakable, that the clever master of phrases was also a harsh master of men.

His father's impressive victories having secured him from external danger, and his unsentimental execution of rivals and opponents having established his throne, Solomon turned from problems of war to problems of peace. Edom and Moab broke away at the very beginning of the reign, but Solomon seemed to mind more the loss of revenue involved than the loss of dominion.[1] There followed the successful rebellion of the Aramæans, under the gifted leadership of the adventurer Rezon, who laid at Damascus the foundations of a state which sorely troubled the Hebrew kingdom in the future. Solomon may have made more determined efforts to re-establish himself than the Biblical writers cared to reveal. It was easy to suppress accounts which reflected little credit on Hebrew arms. But it is likely, from what we know of Solomon's inclinations, that he did not trouble himself greatly about the defections. The line of least

[1] Edom, or part of it, was probably recovered later, for the approach to the Red Sea at Eziongeber was used by Solomon in his commercial expeditions.

resistance was perhaps the line of wisdom. Surely it was statesmanlike not to attempt to retain an uncertain hold over a group of restless, alien peoples.

Instead Solomon strove to strengthen and consolidate his own territory. He divided up the country into twelve districts, deliberately disregarding tribal boundaries. He was anxious to superimpose national loyalty upon tribal loyalty. He was not entirely successful, as events after his death showed. Yet it was a great step towards national amalgamation. It was also an effective means of meeting his financial requirements, although many of the old tribes bitterly resented his tactics.

Solomon was already engaged in a vast building-program, which occupied most of his reign. His ambitions were dazzling. He yearned for large cities, beautiful, well constructed, well protected; for great markets and busy bazaars, alive with the trade that crossed his country from the ends of the world. He yearned for a palace equal to those which his neighbours boasted, splendidly built, sumptuously appointed; for a temple more elaborate than the temporary dwelling built by David, a temple that would be a worthy symbol of the majesty of Yahweh and the dignity of His priests. These were loftly ambitions for the king of a simple people, who were still too loosely bound together to make easy sacrifices, who were naïve enough to expect as much from the State as they gave. It was too early for them to take pride in common property built from the meagre earnings of the plough and the pruning-hook. Solomon gave them the gorgeous trappings of a respected state, but they remembered only its cost. There lay Solomon's mistake. He created institutions before he created loyalty. He erected a temple before he made his people understand its importance. He was quick-sighted rather than far-sighted.

All through the early years of Solomon's reign the work of construction proceeded. The country throbbed with effort; the building of a state from its foundations was, in Israel, a physical reality. For invaluable assistance in all his building-efforts Solomon was indebted to Hiram of Tyre, the capable king of the flourishing little Phœnician state, which specialized in the industrial and commercial arts. Friendly relations between Israel and Tyre had already been established by David; Solomon made the relationship almost an alliance. Hiram supplied Solomon with the materials of construction, the precious cedars and pines of the Lebanons; with skilful architects, who alone could satisfactorily execute Solomon's ambitious plans; with seamen for the first commercial fleets of Israel sent to venture on the seas. In return Solomon agreed to pay huge consignments of corn and oil and other provisions for Hiram's household.

All elements of the population contributed in the work, especially the non-Hebrew peoples, Gibeonites, Jebusites, and other wretched, Canaanite groups, who were pressed into a serfdom as odious as the Israelites had borne in Egypt. The trees of the Lebanons had to be cut down and carried hundreds of miles to the capital; the quarries around Jerusalem demanded patient labour before they yielded the giant blocks of stone which went into Solomon's buildings.

Work alone was not enough. Payments fell due for materials, plans, and architects, as well as for the upkeep of the State. The tax-gatherer went abroad and collected more thoroughly and systematically than the Hebrews had ever known. Every direct tax is odious and occasions grumbling. Solomon's taxes fell heavily on a part of the nation, the poorest part, and there was more than the usual grumbling, especially in the north, which took no pride in the knowledge that Judah and Jerusalem alone seemed to benefit from the king's exactions. The northern chroniclers, incensed for religious reasons also, later revenged themselves by blackening Solomon's reputation, describing with much asperity how every expenditure went to gratify a selfish despot's whim.

Slowly the new buildings grew until at length the Temple and the palaces were completed. There was nothing original in them; they followed the orthodox Phœnician patterns, but as they stood in the glare of the Jerusalem sun, they seemed to rival the best creations of the surrounding states. Every step, every stone, every furnishing, humble, almost tawdry in comparison with the most mediocre of the great buildings of today, caused astonishment to the Hebrews. The palace buildings alone took thirteen years of continuous labour to complete. There were halls for waiting, for receiving, for judging, for entertaining; pillars with the labour of thousands of serfs in them; floors and walls from all over the world, all beautiful enough to spin fairy-tales about! To the humble folk of Jerusalem the magnificent throne of ivory and gold must have seemed worthy to stand in the judgment halls of heaven. The drinking-cups were surely too magnificent to be used. " None were of silver," the chronicler remarks, with a suspicion of bitterness; " it was nothing accounted of in the days of Solomon." Then there were the private apartments of the king and those for his many queens. There were elaborately equipped rooms for a numerous retinue and for the luxurious harem of the king. There were endless other marvels. Even the detractors of Solomon breathe wonder at the creations wrought by his magic wand.

Such an elaborate palace required an elaborate table. The Book of Kings (I Kings iv. 22–3) preserves an inventory, probably much exaggerated, of the daily necessities of Solomon's court. There were needed thirty thousand kor of fine flour (a kor is about eighty gallons!), sixty thousand kor of ordinary flour, ten stalled oxen, twenty oxen out of the pasture, a hundred sheep, and endless game and fowl, to say nothing of wine and other liquors. Even when this catalogue of riotous luxury is much discounted, one may sympathize with the resentment of prophets and people.

The Temple took half as long to build as the palace, but it was as elaborate in its material and workmanship, and a far more momentous undertaking. When first built, it was almost a royal chapel, part of the palace buildings, closed in and cut off from the city. But the custom grew for the nation to assemble in the capital on the great religious festivals. They flocked in from all parts of the country and brought their little gifts to the shrine. Gradually the Temple became part of the nation's heritage, the centre of its religious life. The sacrifices that went into its construction, the extravagances that were paid for by peasant sweat, were forgotten. To generations whose pride rested only on their memories, the Temple grew until it overshadowed Jerusalem. It became more than an object of worldly greatness. It was a symbol of peace, of social justice. Ethical meanings were read into its blocks and stones; allegories were found hidden in its measurements! No iron, it was said, went into the construction of the Temple, for iron is a weapon of war. The Temple site, the rabbis taught, was chosen because on it two brothers had shown for each other a divine, self-sacrificing love. These and other legends clustered about Solomon's work of pride until the Temple rivalled Sinai in its religious significance.

In immediate fact, however, the Temple had a very different meaning. For good or ill it became the centre of a sacerdotal faith, with priests and sacrifices, prayers, and elaborate ceremonial. Perhaps it was an unavoidable development. The example of surrounding peoples was irresistible, the political value of religious unity was too important to overlook. But many of the later prophets, who hated the development and the religious defections which came in subsequent reigns, placed the blame upon the pleasure-loving king, whose ambition, they insisted, was largely responsible for destroying the clean simplicity of early days.

All the while that the splendour of Jerusalem was being developed, Solomon was busy with the more prosaic task of consolidating the rest of his kingdom. He built fortresses in key centres and strengthened the border cities of the north and south. We read of arsenals and cities of store, of chariots, long used by other peoples, but new in little Israel. We read of roads cut through the wildness of the country to serve for commercial as well as military purposes. Forts were established on the Red Sea, and several places of calling for caravans were developed. The products and arts of the Semitic world began to penetrate into the country. Israel was becoming a respected member in the circle of ancient peoples.

The mental horizon of Israel was further widened by relationships which Solomon now found it necessary to establish. He made a series of political and commercial treaties with every people whose friendship could bring him trade or security. In keeping with the custom of the time, he sealed his treaties by marriages. His harem was a register of the multiplicity of his friendships. There were princesses from Moab and Edom, from the farthest north and the extreme south. Even powerful Egypt was not too haughty to value cordial relations with the little State crossed by so many roads. The king was perhaps not so much married as some chroniclers would have us believe, but the Song of Songs mentions " sixty queens and eighty concubines and virgins without number." Many of these brought with them their gods and their priests, and soon the worship of Yahweh went on side by side with the worship of Baal and other alien deities. It rankled in the hearts of those to whom the old worship was dear to find the King so lightly sacrificing his very God to promote the interests of his dynasty.

Buildings, fortresses, roads, an expensive household, a luxurious harem — the problem of making ends meet was one to test the ingenuity even of the wisest king. The people were poor, their loyalty was strained. The taxes were already too high; the tolls on passing caravans could not be raised without risk of altogether killing a lucrative trade. Solomon went into business. He bought horses and sold them at a handsome profit. He entered into a partnership with Hiram of Tyre, equipping vessels and sending them out on the seas as far as India, to trade, perhaps to pirate, to steal. They brought back wealth — gold, silver, sandalwood, peacocks, apes, ivory. But there were always larger bills to pay. Solomon borrowed from Hiram and gave him twenty worthless cities in the north to meet his debt. He twisted and turned, he drained every legitimate and illegitimate source. Still the deficit grew. It was a grisly skeleton at every feast. But Solomon refused to diminish his expenses. He lived with prodigality to the end, leaving to his successor a tradition of splendour and a bankrupt treasury to maintain it.

He had reigned forty years, momentous years that changed the life of the nation. Palestine had become an important country, Jerusalem a great capital, with palaces, and buildings, and a Temple worthy of its new dignity. But there was much sorrow beneath the grandeur. Probably about this period a class of wealthy men began to develop, accumulating capital at the expense of the whole community. The poorer folk were compelled to mortgage their belongings to pay their taxes and save enough to subsist. It did not appease them to know, as the prophets afterwards exclaimed, that the aristocrats ate of the finest and drank of the best; that they reclined on soft cushions in imported couches, inlaid with ivory. The class divisions, appearing so early in the history of the monarchy, were to have sorry fruit in a later day.

Despite the evil tendencies in his reign, Solomon was not a mere wastrel. His desire for the pomp and vanity of power had a utilitarian side. With all of his shortcomings, he was statesman enough to sense the importance of placing his people in contact with the civilization of the world about him. His policy did not affect the life of the masses, who lived and died in the traditional groove. But the sublime prophets, who deplored the social and religious decay that grew with Solomon's reign, were indebted more than they knew to the very innovations which they denounced. The provincialism of the country had to be broken down before Yahweh could develop into a conception broader than Israel and the little Hebrew world.

CHAPTER FIVE

A HOUSE DIVIDED AGAINST ITSELF

I. THE REVOLT OF THE NORTH

EVEN before the death of Solomon a solid phalanx of resentment, based on financial and religious grievances and on tribal jealousies, had been built up against the royal house. The Grand Monarch had too quickly turned a simple state into a rigid despotism. Only the legend of his crushing strength and the memory of his inexorable vengeance held the opposition of his detractors to whispers and gestures. When an attempt at revolution, led by Jeroboam, a former royal employe, was smashed without difficulty, other rebels learned to restrain their hostility. But the iron-handed ruler's death created a new situation. To continue with impunity the methods of the old regime his successor had to be, not a chip of the old block, but the old block himself, fortified by the courage of a Saul and the tact and geniality of a David. As it happened, young Rehoboam seemed to inherit only the tastes and temper of his father and none of his wisdom, and his councillors were as indiscreet and arrogant as himself.

Events moved rapidly to teach the young monarch the penalties of irresponsibility. He had journeyed to Shechem to receive the formal allegiance of the northern tribes. Their leaders utilized the occasion to appeal for a reduction of taxes and the abolition of forced labour. Rehoboam answered bluntly in words which set the haughty northern leaders aflame, and a revolt broke out at once. When the cocky fledgling returned, in all haste, to Jerusalem, he found that only Judah and Benjamin remained loyal. The other northern tribes rallied about the rebel chief, Jeroboam, who now became in fact the successor of Solomon; for the little province that remained to Rehoboam was too tiny to be other than a mere political appendix.

The historic rupture, never healed, destroyed a united kingdom which had endured rather precariously for seventy-odd years. It proved the turning-point in the political history of the Hebrews. Powerful states were growing up in the east and the west. The days of militant empire were recommencing, bespeaking woe to the smaller peoples of the ancient world. Even firmly united, made vigorous by an active sense of religious and national loyalty, the Hebrews could not long have withstood the onslaughts of their ambitious neighbours. Divided into two toy kingdoms, constantly fighting against each other and torn by rabid dynastic struggles, the Hebrews destroyed any possible hope for survival. Judah, indeed, was not so great an offender. Despite internal feuds, the monarchy remained in the line of the house of David for several centuries, until its extinction. But Israel wallowed in revolution and assassination. Nine dynasties were established in little more than two hundred years; nineteen kings followed each other, usually compelled to hack a bloody way to the throne. The political history of the Hebrews in these two dizzy centuries, disgraced by selfish and undisciplined turbulence, is little different from the history of any petty Oriental people. To recount even the outstanding events of such a story would be serving no useful purpose were it not that these events were the sombre background in which the sublime Hebrew prophets ministered.

Jeroboam, whom fortune suddenly brought to the kingship of Israel, was evidently a strong and forceful personality. Risen from humble origins, at one time the royal supervisor of the labour gangs of Ephraim, rebel, exile, conspirator, he had run the gamut of human experience. He was recalled to Israel from his refuge in Egypt, hardened, toughened, and necessarily more interested in the wedge which divided north and south than in the ties that bound them. He turned at once to rendering his kingdom completely independent of Judah. The task required ingenuity, for the seat of the Yahweh worship was in Jerusalem, and the growing prestige of the Temple was difficult to overcome. Jeroboam, a thorough opportunist, fertile in resource and untroubled by religious qualms, was just the man for the task.

He proceeded to establish rival sanctuaries, one in the extreme north, at Dan, and the other in the south, at Bethel, on the road to Jerusalem. Both places were already shrines, long held in reverence by the people of the north, and they needed only to be re-established under royal patronage to become popular centres of pilgrimage. Jeroboam probably had no intention of abandoning the Yahweh worship. He went annually to Bethel to sacrifice upon its altar and to offer his respects to the old desert god. He posed as a preserver of old traditions. But he carefully clipped the worship of all Judaean reminders, changing the rites and the festival dates, and completely transforming the spiritual meaning of Yahweh. He set up two golden calves in Bethel and Dan and urged his supporters to worship them as tangible representations of their god. Since the masses were too close to Canaanite practices to be shocked, they readily lapsed into pure idolatry. The prophetic historians never forgave Jeroboam for his daring religious manipulations. He goes down in their chronicles as a wicked king, who ruined a noble faith by a wayward heart and who, by causing his people to sin, was responsible for all of their later misfortunes. Jeroboam, however, worried little about the verdict of posterity. He accomplished his immediate purpose. Without a struggle he broke down the spirit of dependence on Jerusalem, the feeling that there was an indispensable, mystic holiness in the kingship of the house of David.

Politically the wily rebel was less successful, but this was due less to his incapacity than to the international situation. He was able, of course, to hold his own against Rehoboam, who made only feeble and ineffectual attempts to recover his patrimony. But soon both kingdoms were overrun by Shishak (Sheshonk) of Egypt and placed under a heavy tribute. In the inscriptions on the walls of the Temple of Karnak the invader triumphantly lists more than sixty captured cities of Israel and ninety of Judah. The southern country suffered most. Shishak entered Jerusalem as a conqueror. The palace and the Temple, only recently completed, were ravished; the treasury was plundered; and the rich ornaments, which had been the pride of Solomon, were carried off. Whatever sovereignty Judah still exercised over the bordering provinces now altogether disappeared.

But Israel too was stripped and given a bitter foretaste of experiences to be repeated often in the future. Pious persons who saw a divine plan in every event must have regarded the Egyptian invasion as the righteous judgment of Yahweh for Jeroboam's iniquitous desecration of His altars.

Both peoples, thoroughly cowed, went about their humble labour, tilling their soil, building their homes, weaving their garments, little concerned with problems of prestige. Rehoboam lived out a stupid reign, execrating Israel, occasionally reopening the feud, but consoled by a harem of eighteen wives and a numerous offspring. Jeroboam fought a few battles with the successor of Rehoboam, but otherwise ruled quietly, rebuilding some of his cities, instilling loyalty into his dynasty. He was able to pass his kingdom intact to his son Nadab, after a reign that had lasted more than twenty years.

The crash came soon after, and for half a century Israel struggled in the throes of anarchy. The revolutionary precedent which Jeroboam began was followed by his successors. In thirty-seven years there were six kings, half of whom died violent deaths, and only twice did son succeed father. Israel was an agricultural people, but military despots were the rule and prophets and professional fighters were the king-makers. There were no real reigns, only wars of succession.

Jeroboam's son attempted to carry on his father's policies, but at the end of two years was cut down by one of his generals, Baasha, who, with true Oriental thoroughness in such matters, proceeded to massacre every living scion of the first dynasty. Baasha's son Elah was killed in a drunken debauch by a military comrade, Zimri, the commander of the war-chariots, and again a whole royal family was wiped out. When the news of the new revolution reached the army, which was just then besieging a Philistine city, another general, Omri, was elevated to the kingship. He marched at once to the capital and laid siege to the palace. The hapless Zimri, realizing that resistance was useless, set fire to his place of refuge and was burnt alive amidst the ruins. Still there was no peace. A portion of the population put forward another pretender for the throne, who plunged the country into a disastrous civil war. Only after four years of further strife was the pretender slain and Omri able to claim an undisputed kingship.

In Judah meantime there was comparative stability. Evidently the influence of the prophetic school was becoming paramount, for there was feverish activity to intensify the popular devotion to Yahweh. The easy-going, tolerant policy of Solomon, who permitted the worship of many gods, in many forms, was changed. During the long reigns of Asa and Jehosaphat, lasting forty and twenty-five years respectively, none but Yahweh could be worshipped. Asa went so far in his zeal that he punished the aged queen-mother for having teraphim in her possession and had the infamous emblem solemnly burnt in the valley of Kidron.

Perhaps the reformers were unable to do more than graze the surface, but they began a policy of strict religious exclusion destined later to have far-reaching consequences. The Temple, gradually recovering from the vandalism of Egypt, became more and more a national shrine, and even the prophets became reconciled to its existence. As the territory of the kingdom shrank, the Temple grew in importance and influence, overshadowing the State. And as the dynasty rooted itself, the legend of David, its founder, grew, adding strength and prestige to the reigning kings.

During Asa's reign warfare went on intermittently between Judah and Israel; at one time Asa went so far as to bribe Damascus to attack his northern rival. But under Jehosaphat even these quarrels petered out. With laudable foresight both he and the King of Israel were eager to re-establish friendly relations, to permit the two peoples, related by language and tradition, to build up a firm alliance.

The history of the first few decades after Solomon's death had not been distinguished in either kingdom. It is a wearisome tale and it is not relieved by the pious platitudes of the chroniclers, who portion out praise or blame to the succession of sovereigns in accordance with their zeal or lack of zeal for the Yahweh worship. With the rise of the house of Omri the situation changes. Israel and Judah are drawn into world affairs. Their destinies depend upon the movements of Egypt and the Hittites, Babylon and Assyria. Freedom of action is no longer possible. The orbit of the little world is definitely fixed by the larger luminaries. The change proves the undoing of Israel and Judah as states, but it has immense consequences for their religious and cultural life.

2. THE HOUSE OF OMRI

Omri was one of the outstanding kings in the history of Israel, the founder of its only important dynasty. Little is told of him in the Biblical narrative — he was not a pious king — but from the Moabite Stone of the ninth century, one judges that he was an able statesman and a fairly successful soldier. In Assyrian records the northern kingdom is called by his name, and years later, when his whole house was destroyed by Jehu, the regicide is called " son of Omri," a rare tribute to Omri's reputation.[1]

He has often been called the " David of the North." The lives of both state-builders have many interesting parallel experiences. When Omri fought his way to the throne, he found the State disrupted internally and in danger from foreign enemies. The anarchy of several generations had to be righted and pretenders had to be suppressed. Omri turned at once to setting his house in order. The country, he saw, required a better capital than the little ham-let Tirzah, where former kings had made their quarters. With a soldier's insight he picked Samaria, on a hill site, about three hundred feet above the plain. It must have been physically as attractive as Tirzah and was immensely stronger. Isaiah calls it "the proud crown of Ephraim on the head of a rich valley." Here Omri built his palace with great limestone blocks quarried from the conical hill. Here his soldiers settled, watching their opportuni-ties if the new sovereign could not prove his mettle. Omri fortified his new capital with such success that later even the well-trained hosts of Assyria, masters in the technique of the siege, took three years to break down its resistance.

Throughout Omri's reign there were cordial relations with Judah, now ruled by the peaceful Asa. Their successors, Ahab and Jehosaphat, were often associated in war, and their co-operation bespeaks almost a united Palestine. Omri further allied himself with the revived state of Tyre, marrying his son Ahab to the daughter of the priest-king. The alliance encouraged Phœnicians to settle in Israelite territory and helped materially to extend commerce and develop trade.

Secure on his throne and strengthened by his alliances, Omri was able to deal with the Moabites, who had broken from Hebrew control when the historic schism took place. We learn from Mesha's Moabite Stone that Chemosh, the god of the Moabites, was angry with his people and permitted Omri to conquer many cities. Soon herds of lambs and rams and other precious offerings were pouring into Israel as tribute. Later the Moabites called in Damascus, and Omri was compelled to relinquish most of his holdings and to give the Aramæan merchants commercial privileges in Samaria. But in the mean time

---

[1] It may, of course, also mean that the kingdom of Israel made only a slight impression on Assyria and that its rulers were very little known.

Omri was the suzerain, and Moab endured in silence, waiting for a favourable opportunity to strike back.

So far the western Asiatic world had been left comparatively free to live, to prosper, and to quarrel to its heart's content. With the exception of the brief conquests of Tiglath-Pileser I of Assyria before Solomon's day, and of Shishak of Egypt in Jeroboam's time, the great empires of the East and the West did not attempt to extend their control into Syria and Palestine. Now all was changed. The rise of the new Assyrian empire revolutionized the history of the ancient world. Thence on, it was one of the dominating factors in Hebrew history, playing an ever greater role and compelling the divided kingdoms to take a part in international affairs. Its full significance was not yet realized. For a great part of the ninth century B.C. it remained a distant menace. Nevertheless there was already a rush of princes to protest loyalty, and Omri, together with the other petty rulers of the Fertile Crescent, laid tribute at the feet of the new power.[1]

After a reign of twelve years Omri was succeeded by his son Ahab. The new ruler inherited his father's ability and proved to be, on the political side, perhaps the strongest King of Israel. In the Biblical story he is counted as a double-dyed scoundrel, for his religious policy was disapproved by the later historians. But Assyrian and Moabite evidence leaves no such impression. He seemed to have his wits about him in every undertaking. He continued a conciliatory policy with surrounding nations, striving always to accomplish by peaceful negotiation what was usually settled by war. Probably an acute perception of the Assyrian menace helped him to remain at peace with most of his neighbours.

There were commercial relations, of course, with Tyre, from whose luxurious court came his ambitious wife, Jezebel. Judah, ruled by the pious Jehosaphat, was brought closer to Israel when Ahab's daughter, Athaliah, was married to the son of the king. All through the reign Moab continued to pay heavy tribute in raw wool, and Ahab doubtless sold the material at a heavy profit to the merchants and weavers of Phœnicia. At friends with the world, his kingdom growing in economic strength, his dynasty becoming solidly rooted in the affections of his people, Ahab appeared to have regained the glory of the regal days of Solomon. He even built a sumptuous palace, decorated with rare ivory, probably imported for him, from Cyprus.

Only the Aramæans were a source of irritation. Ahab had paid tribute to them as his father had done, but when their king, Ben-hadad II, made unreasonable demands, Ahab threw off his meekness. After many vicissitudes he not only freed himself, but cooped up his former oppressor at Aphek.

---

[1] With the beginning of Assyrian interest in Palestine we have a great deal of light thrown on the period. Royal inscriptions and lists, in cuneiform, fill in many gaps left by the Biblical editors.

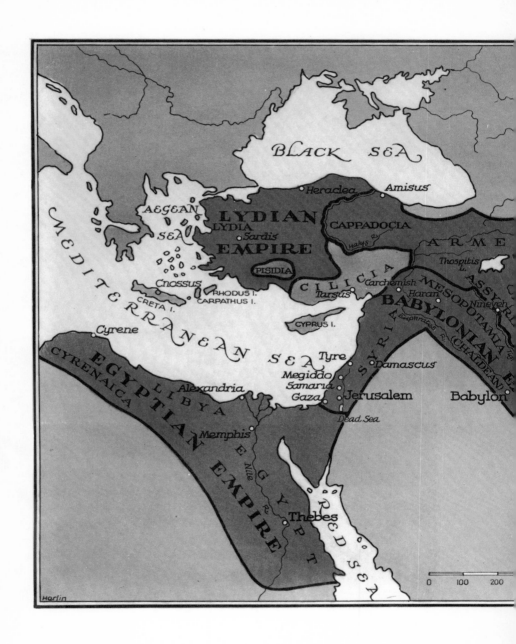

BLACK SEA

Heraclea • • Amisus

AEGEAN
SEA
LYDIAN
LYDIA
• Sardis
EMPIRE

CAPPADOCIA

ARME

Halys R.

Thospitis
L.

ASSYR

PISIDIA

CILICIA

Carchemish

Haran • • Nineveh

MESOPOTAMIA

Cnossus
CRETA I.

RHODUS I.
CARPATHUS I.

Tarsus

BABYLONIAN (CHALDEAN) E

Euphrates R.

CYPRUS I.

MEDITERRANEAN SEA

Cyrene

Tyre

SYRIA

• Damascus

EGYPTIAN
CYRENAICA

LIBYA

Alexandria

Megiddo
Samaria
Gaza

Jerusalem

Babylon

Dead Sea

EMPIRE

Memphis

E
G
Y
P
T

Nile R.

RED SEA

Thebes

Herlin

0   100   200

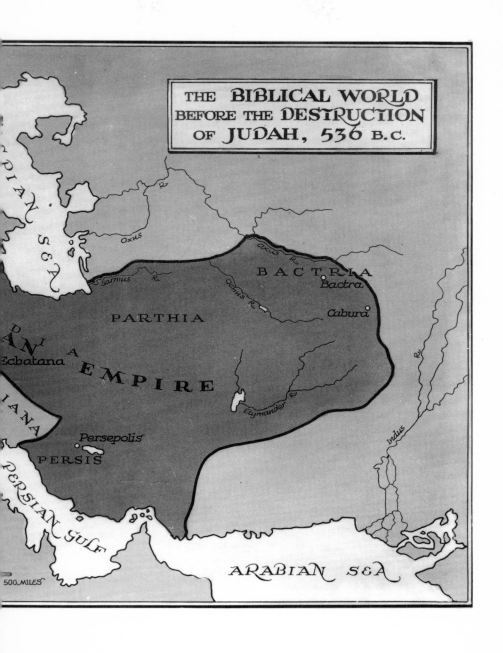

THE BIBLICAL WORLD BEFORE THE DESTRUCTION OF JUDAH, 536 B.C.

CASPIAN SEA

Oxus R.

Oxus R.

BACTRA

Bactra

Sarnius R.

Ochus R.

PARTHIA

Cabura

Ecbatana

MEDIA

EMPIRE

Elymander R.

Indus

Persepolis

PERSIS

CARMANIA

PERSIAN GULF

ARABIAN SEA

500 MILES

Ben-hadad, his boastfulness completely gone, was compelled to send ambassadors in sackcloth, with ropes about their necks, to sue for his life. The prophets bitterly upbraided Ahab when he released his prisoner after obtaining a promise from him that Israelite merchants were to have trading-privileges in Damascus. But here, too, Ahab was purposely lenient. He was watching the political situation carefully. Assyria was now moving westward and Ahab felt that he needed every ally. His prescience was quickly rewarded. In 853 B.C. a great coalition was formed to resist Assyria. At Karkar Israel fought side by side with the Aramæans, Phœnicians, and other little peoples. Shalmaneser III claimed the victory; in his inscriptions he boasted of having slain more than twenty-nine thousand enemies, their corpses choking the Orontes and filling the fields. But it was evidently a Pyrrhic victory, gained at such a heavy cost that the Assyrian king did not repeat the invasion for another twelve years.

The truce with Aram lasted only as long as the danger. Ben-hadad soon broke his promises, and the desolating wars recommenced. Judah had now become definitely a vassal of Israel; at least Ahab, calling upon Jehosaphat for assistance against Aram, received the meek reply: " I am as thou art, my people as thy people, my horses as thy horses." But even with Judæan assistance Ahab could no longer prevail. The tide had turned again. During a decisive battle against Ben-hadad, Ahab was suddenly smitten by a chance arrow. He continued fighting throughout the day, propped up in his chariot. But the wound was fatal, and as the Aramæans pressed forward, the Israelite army disbanded in dismay, " every man to his city, every man to his country."

Ahab had reigned for twenty-two years and in this period had played no unworthy part. He had built up the commerce of his country, had ended ancient rivalries, and until the last tragic war had held his own fairly successfully against every enemy. If it were not for his religious policy, his name would not have been execrated by the prophetic historians.

3. THE MANTLE OF ELIJAH

Nearly a century had passed since Jeroboam had created the kingdom of Israel and had set up separate sanctuaries. To the later historians the few military victories, the conquests over surrounding peoples, the booty, and the tribute brought no solace. For Yahweh had been abandoned and outraged. Native Baals and alien gods lorded it in the high places. What mattered the petty royal conquests when the kings abetted idolatry? They were all sinners, worthy of censure. And the worst of the lot was surely Ahab, who is portrayed as an insane bigot, completely under the thumb of Jezebel, hating Yahwism and persecuting its devotees.

In fact, Ahab, like Solomon, was guilty, not of religious bigotry, but of tolerance. He permitted the Baal worship to go on side by side with the

Yahweh worship. He gave Jezebel her way when she wished to raise a temple in Samaria to Baal-Melkart, the patron god of Tyre. He offered no opposition when the sacrifices, with all the gorgeous trappings of the pagan Tyrian ritual, were offered publicly.

Ahab assuredly had no intention of abandoning Yahweh. His advisers worshipped in the old faith; he followed their example. His children were given names compounded with Yahweh. But he saw no good reason for an exclusive monotheism. To pursue a tolerant policy towards other deities and forms of worship made for foreign friendship and for domestic peace.

But to the Puritans of Ahab's day, and to the chroniclers, this subordination of religion to diplomacy was unendurable. Tolerance was not a virtue. It was treason to the old faith. Perhaps in the prophetic opposition there was also an element of hatred against the whole complex civilization which the house of Omri was building up, with its foreign customs and habits, its luxuries, its artistic developments, its abandonment of the rustic simplicity of the patriarchal ideal. There were doubtless many contributing causes. But primarily the revolt of the prophets was inspired by what they considered the blasphemous apostasy of the royal house.

Fundamentally their instinct was sound. In theory, tolerance was a broadening, civilizing policy. But actually, in Israel, it dissolved the unique outlook of the people. It weakened national loyalty. It destroyed the characteristics which distinguished Israel from other peoples. Worse still, since the Tyrian Baal worship had in it alluring immoral elements, it debilitated the national character. Tolerance of Baal meant tolerance of child sacrifice and sacred prostitution. It meant licence for the foreign priests to display themselves, during their sacrifices, in their mad frenzies, dancing, leaping, gesticulating, cutting and tearing their flesh. It was a sore sight to the little band of Yahwist patriots to watch the painted priests of Baal wailing and whirling on the high places of Israel in adoration of imported gods and goddesses. It grieved them more to note the growing popularity of the cult.

A bitter war soon began which went on for many years, with growing intolerance on both sides. The court, persistently attacked, was under the necessity of harrying its critics, who, of course, raised the cry of persecution and redoubled their efforts. We have few authentic details of the religious crisis, but out of it one dramatic figure emerges. The prophet Elijah bestrides the narrow world of Ahab like a colossus.

He is the most popular personality in Hebrew history, the patron saint of Jewish life. Dean Stanley calls him the grandest and the most romantic character that Israel ever produced. Curiously enough, in the Biblical narratives he shows few of the gentle qualities calculated to endear him to a peace-loving people. He is harsh, severe, relentless, of the typical dervish type, intolerant of all the effeminate corruptions of civilized life. Yet through centuries of folk-lore the austere figure who never knew the meaning of peace, whose every word was a challenge, is mellowed and softened into the gentle comforter, the solicitous friend, the chivalrous champion of the weak and the oppressed. In the memory of his people it is Elijah who opens secret doors through which the martyred escape, who provides dowries for the unfortunate daughters of the poor, who saves the defenceless victims of powerful swindlers. There is a chair for him at every circumcision, and a cup of wine on every Passover table. He is stationed at the cross-roads of paradise to welcome every worthy person; he weaves garlands for God from the prayers of the truly pious. He will be the precursor of the Messiah, ushering in the new world in which the sufferings of Israel and of all peoples will be no more.

Elijah was doubtless a historical figure whose exploits were much magnified after the house of Omri was violently overthrown. He crystallized the growing opposition to the religious tendencies in Israel. It is significant that he put forward no new concept of Yahweh. He made no outcry against the rites which had crept in before the days of Omri. He protested solely against the Tyrian influences which had been degrading Yahweh. And here he was adamant. There could be no compromise; dualisms were repugnant to him. "How long limp ye between two opinions? If Yahweh be God, follow Him; but if Baal, then follow him."

Tradition preserves the story of a long, dramatic contest on the peaceful slopes of Mount Carmel between the solitary Elijah and all the prophets of Jezebel. In the story, Elijah wins a spectacular victory. Yahweh performs astonishing miracles, and the discomfited priests of Baal are all slaughtered by the banks of the river Kishon. Of course Elijah's views did not prevail with the spectacular suddenness of the Biblical account. The old ways were too firmly rooted to be completely cast out by a prophet's curse. Yet Elijah's work cannot be overestimated. He created a powerful opposition and was, at least indirectly, the cause of the revolution that was soon to plunge Israel into chaos and ruin.

The consequences of the subtle propaganda carried on against the house of Omri were soon made painfully clear. After the death of Ahab and his son Ahaziah, a second son, Jehoram, came to the throne, and the prophets of Elijah's school worked harder than ever. There were whole guilds of them, hotbeds of revolution, violently opposed to the alien tendencies in the religious life of the State. Perhaps they rejoiced secretly when Jehoram was disastrously defeated by Mesha of Moab, who, on the famous Moabite Stone, exultantly described his victory and the booty in territory that it brought.

The leader of the revolutionary group was Elisha, the disciple of Elijah, but a man of entirely different mould. He was evidently widely travelled, a man of the world, a skilful diplomat. Elijah had thundered and stormed and was anathema at court; Elisha was smooth and bland, familiar with court

etiquette and often consulted by the dynasty of Jehu. The miracles ascribed
to him by the Biblical narrative are a clear indication of the immense hold
that he had on popular imagination then and later. Beneath the gentleness,
however, there seems to have been a will of steel. He watched every opportunity to turn public opinion against the royal house.

At last the great chance came. In Damascus the powerful warrior Ben-hadad
had been smothered and one of the palace officials, Hazael, had usurped the
throne. Jehoram took advantage of the confusion that followed to recover
the Gilead territory which had been lost to Damascus some years before.
Wounded in battle, the Israelite king retired to Jezreel, together with his guest
and kinsman Ahaziah, King of Judah. He left his garrison in the command
of a young general, Jehu.[1]

Jehu had already been selected by Elisha as the instrument to carry out
the long-planned revolution. He had every quality to ensure success. He was
alert and ambitious, and his immense energy was indicated by the watchman's
cry, which became proverbial: "He drives like Jehu." An emissary from
Elisha anointed him king, and the officers of the army at once proclaimed him.
Jehu acted quickly. He started in hot haste for Jezreel, thirty miles away. The
two kings came forward to meet him. In the field of Naboth the carefully laid
plans of Elisha were consummated. Jehu denounced the King as a tool of
Jezebel, and when he turned to flee, Jehu shot an arrow through his heart.
The body was left in the field, to be disposed of by the dogs. The bewildered
King of Judah was also overtaken and mortally wounded before he could reach
his own kingdom. Jezebel, now a venerable grandmother, courageous to the
end, determined to die like a queen. Attired in all her finery she taunted Jehu
when he approached the palace. She was flung down into the court by her
eunuchs at the command of Jehu, who drove his chariot and horses over her
body. After dinner, when his men went out to bury her, they found that the
prophecy of Elijah had been fulfilled; the dogs had done their work. So ended
the house of Omri in Israel.

But the bloody revolution had only just begun. Every one of Ahab's
descendants in Samaria was hunted down. The elders, terrorized, sent seventy
heads to Jehu, as he demanded. All who were connected with the royal house,
all who were friendly to the Tyrian religion, the priests, the worshippers, all
were destroyed in the root-and-branch revolution. Even princes of Judah,
captured in northern territory, were slain, and the friendly relations between
the two kingdoms were for ever severed.

The effects of the revolution were felt in Judah also. When Ahaziah's body
was brought back, his mother, Athaliah, a true daughter of Jezebel, at once
seized the throne, massacring all who stood in the way, even her descendants

---

[1] The name "Jehu" is probably part of a longer name, compounded with Yahweh. Only
the deity form has survived.

and relatives. Baal Melkart was again established in Jerusalem. For six years she held on grimly, defying the infuriated prophets and the sullen populace. Then the high priest, who had saved one little son, Joash, and had secretly reared him, brought on a revolution and wiped out the last remnants of the house of Omri in Judah. The little king received the acclamations of the prophets and people, who tore down the altars of Baal and destroyed his priests. Elijah and Elisha had triumphed everywhere. Yahweh reigned supreme.

Politically the price was high. The cordial relations of Tyre, Judah and Israel, sealed by marriage, came to an abrupt end. Each little kingdom struggled on by itself and soon fell a prey to the powerful enemies who surrounded them. Assyria, warring on the peoples of the west, passed through Israel and was meekly submitted to, at once. Jehu paid his tribute and his homage, hoping only to be left alone. In the famous black obelisk of Shalmaneser II one sees Jehu prostrate before the great Assyrian king, with forehead to the ground, the servants bearing tribute behind him.[1]

The energetic Hazael, who had won his throne at the same time that Jehu had won that of Israel, and by similar means, now also rode rampant through unhappy Israel. He ravaged the territory on the east of the Jordan, pillaged, slew, burnt, with barbarous cruelty and terrible thoroughness. The Biblical description is short, but eloquent. " The King of Aram destroyed the Israelites and made them like the dust in the threshing." The hunger was so great in Samaria that popular tradition tells of women eating their own children. When Aram departed, the kingdom of Israel had been reduced to about four miles around its capital.

Even if Israel had been strong and stable, the powerful Assyrian could not have been staved off, nor perhaps the Aramæan. But the bloody revolution helped materially to weaken the resistance of the kingdom. In the Biblical narrative, however, Jehu is not reproached. He was suffering defeats on every side only because he had not been thorough enough in his massacres of Yahweh's enemies! Only Hosea, the prophet of love, later condemned the whole orgy of brutality.

4. THE DOWNFALL OF ISRAEL

The close of the ninth century B.C. marked the nadir of the northern kingdom. Dynastic quarrels drained it of vitality; military reverses completed its collapse. Oppression by Damascus continued during the reigns of Jehu's son and grandson; in fact, the shadow of Damascus hung heavy over Israel until

---

[1] The story of Jehu's revolution is told entirely from the point of view of the prophets, with no reference to Assyria. It may be that Jehu was enabled to establish himself on the throne through Assyrian assistance or connivance. The whole episode is not yet fully clear and forms a fundamental problem in Biblical criticism.

the kingdom was destroyed. Heavy tribute was paid to Assyria as well. Israel counted as nothing among the peoples of the eastern Mediterranean.

Suddenly the tide turned. The warriors of Damascus who were besieging Samaria, unexpectedly rose and abandoned their tents. The chroniclers describe the miracle of the deliverance with awe. "Yahweh raised up a saviour for Israel." Recent Biblical research has made clear the allusion. The hitherto obscure kingdom of Hazrak, in northern Syria, pounced upon Damascus, and the ancient enemy of Israel ceased, for a while, to be a scourge. Assyria was also compelled to guard other interests for a number of years. When she did turn, in 797, to sweep most of the little nations of Asia Minor into her tribute net, she struck hard at stubborn Damascus and permanently crippled her. The King of Israel, Jehoash, seized his opportunity. He took the offensive against the unfortunate kingdom and won back all that had been lost by his predecessors. When Amaziah of Judah challenged his growing authority, he was sharply chid for his impudence — the thistle would be trodden underfoot for presuming to meddle with the cedar of Lebanon. Jehoash was as good as his word. He met Amaziah in a Judæan battlefield, captured him, tore open part of the wall of Jerusalem, and looted the palace and the Temple. From then on to the end of the history of Israel, Judah was definitely a vassal state.

Jehoash's successor, Jeroboam II, enjoyed a remarkably long reign, of more than forty years, during which the material development of his kingdom continued. His territorial holdings were now almost as impressive as David's had been. He lived at peace with his neighbours; Damascus was stunned, Assyria was inactive, Moab was subdued, and the other little nations no longer gave any trouble. Only a generation before, Israel had prayed for mere life. Now it had become a real power in the Syrian world.

It was only a temporary respite, however. On Jeroboam II's death there was anarchy again. Within fourteen years six kings had succeeded each other, four of whom died by an assassin's hand. "Each eats the flesh of his own arm," Isaiah said, referring to the effects of the dynastic struggles. It was a particularly unfortunate time for internal strife. Assyria was girding herself for world supremacy. The powerful Tiglath-Pileser IV, by revolution, had laid the foundation of the famous dynasty which spread its conquests to the remotest parts of the Asiatic world. Soon he was marching westward, and almost before the dire prophecies of Hosea had ceased, he came down upon the little kingdom. Menahem, the new king, himself a pretender, quickly yielded and purchased immunity with an enormous bribe, perhaps a thousand talents of silver, obtained by desperate taxation. The heavy tribute placated Assyria and assured Menahem a very shaky throne. But the populace was outraged. The burden of the tribute lay heavily on the wealthier classes, and though Menahem died in peace after a reign of ten years, his son was quickly murdered, in 736 B.C.

The new regicide, Pekah, who came from the east of Jordan, changed the

policy of the State. He became pro-Damascan and joined in a league of kings
to defy Assyria. Tiglath-Pileser could not allow his authority in Syria to be
questioned. He swept down like a hungry vulture upon the rebellious little
world. Rezon of Damascus was killed, along with his whole house, and his
kingdom was finally annexed to Assyria. The other conspirators were sent
shivering into their hiding-places. Then the monarch turned upon the Hebrews.
In 734 B.C. he conquered nearly all the Israelite territory, uprooted thousands
of its most important inhabitants, and scattered them through his empire. He
annexed all of Israel with the exception of the little district about Samaria.
Pekah was deposed, and a puppet, Hoshea, was set up in his place.

Although the kingdom survived the awful desolation, Tiglath-Pileser's attack
was really the death-blow. Hoshea, the last king, bowed to every Assyrian
whim, until the death of the great conqueror. Then, untaught by experience,
and relying upon the promises of wily Egypt, he again challenged Assyria's
might. The new king, Shalmaneser, now gave the *coup de grâce*. Samaria
gallantly defended itself for three years, but it was the final stand of despair.
Nearly thirty thousand inhabitants were deported and the country was re-
settled with captives from other lands. No strong sense of nationalism had
developed in Israel, and it was therefore not strange that the deported tribes
quickly assimilated.

After a life story of two centuries the northern kingdom came to an inglorious end. Dynastic strife, incompetent statesmanship, and an unfortunate geographical situation, all contributed to bring about her debacle. The identity
of the desolated kingdom did not, of course, disappear. Despite its newly-
assimilated population, it retained some hold on its past, some remnants of the
old Yahwism. The country had so far become stabilized in the time of Ezekiel
that it was termed by him " the elder sister." Despite a superficial continuity,
however, the life of Israel as a separate kingdom was ended in 721 B.C., when
the Assyrians burst through the walls of Samaria. The country fell out of the
ken of history and was mentioned only when it came into contact with communities more virile and creative.

What had the little kingdom to show after two centuries of independent
existence? Little apparently but the melancholy bickering of petty tyrants and
the characteristic civil wars of any Oriental people. There was more, however.
Almost lost in the confusions of political life were the gentle messages of a few
prophets and the beginnings of a religious literature. This humble contribution
loomed large in history. It was destined to outlast the more resounding clatter
of the conquerors of Israel.

5 · THE DECLINE AND FALL OF JUDAH

Until the crash of the Israelite state Judah had been completely overshadowed. Politically and intellectually she was the vassal of the northern kingdom.

Now Judah took up the guardianship of the Hebrew tradition. She was doubtless enriched by the genius of many of the exiles who came from the north, just as Renaissance Italy was enriched when she welcomed the Greek scholars who fled from Constantinople after its capture by the Turks.

At first Judah continued her tradition of non-intervention in the complicated and dangerous politics of the little Asiatic world. She had maintained a precarious existence by a policy of submission. While Israel defied Assyria and lost both independence and national existence, Judah felt that discretion was the better part of valour, and yielded meekly to whichever nation became the dominant power. Her king, Hezekiah, exchanged political freedom for the freedom to live and prosper, to instruct his people in the true faith of Yahweh, to build cities and aqueducts and extend commerce. Who could challenge the wisdom of his policy as tales dribbled into the country of battles and wars, of capitulations and massacres, of ruin and desolation?

But the situation soon changed completely. To the patriots it was shameful to continue indefinitely a policy of cravenness. They formed a powerful party at court and they were completely carried away by the glowing hopes held out for them by the envoys from other peoples.

Those who came from Egypt were the most importunate. They urged the creation of a strong alliance to break the humiliating hold of Assyria on the world. The time was opportune, for Assyria was in desperate difficulty with the Chaldean invaders of Babylon. If the Mediterranean nations would only unite and co-operate, the haughty Assyrian would be completely humbled; the crushing tributes would cease; the subject peoples would breathe freely again. The arguments were plausible and were presented with the glibness and smoothness of practised diplomats. The patriots began to clamour for action. Hezekiah hesitated. The temptation was great. His old adviser, Isaiah, pleaded with him to preserve the traditional policy of submission, not to be won over by any phrases. "In sitting still, and rest, shall be your salvation," he cautioned; "in quietness and confidence your strength." But ultimately the jingoes triumphed. Hezekiah joined in a league with Egypt, the Philistine cities, Moab, Edom, and other provinces, and when Azuri, King of Ashdod, withheld his tribute in 714 B.C., all who were in the league boldly followed his example.

Sargon acted quickly. He moved westward and soundly trounced the Philistine cities that had begun the rebellion. Their homes were desolated, their inhabitants transported, and settlers from other parts of the empire were brought in to build up the ruins. The example was a salutary one, and the other conspirators ran to cover at once and kept their peace for a number of years.

Secretly, however, the plotting continued. Those whose fingers had not yet been burnt continued to play with the dancing flames of intrigue. Isaiah begged

Hezekiah to profit by the experiences of the Assyrian victims. He walked about Jerusalem with bare feet, in sackcloth, prophesying that those who relied on Egypt would soon be reduced to a similar state. Desperately he appealed over the heads of the pro-Egyptian party to the good sense of the populace. He could not keep Hezekiah altogether out of the councils of the conspirators, but for a number of years he kept Hezekiah out of alliances.

Then in 705 B.C. the mighty Sargon, most powerful of all Assyrian rulers, fell in battle or was murdered, and his empire fell to pieces. The new monarch had to prove his mettle. He had to reconquer all of his provinces at the same time that Babylon was making a bid of its own for world supremacy. The Palestinian world was aglow with excitement. Egypt was again on the alert, planning, plotting, exhorting. Isaiah exercised every diplomatic talent that he possessed to keep Judah neutral. Some of the sermons that he preached, now preserved in the twenty-eighth to the thirty-first chapters of the book which bears his name, illustrate the desperation with which he battled. But all of his artistic vehemence was in vain. When the wily Babylonian king sent an embassy to console Hezekiah for his illness, the Hebrew king had so far yielded to the pressure of the jingoes that he showed his guest the arsenals and all his fortifications. Soon after, when Assyria joined in a life-and-death struggle with Babylon, he entered the Egyptian league.

In 701 B.C. came the vindication of Isaiah's foresight. Sennacherib disposed of his rivals in the Tigris and Euphrates districts and then came down like a thunderbolt on the league, which was already divided by suspicions and animosities. One by one the conspirators were scattered. The Phœnician cities were punished first, particularly Tyre and Sidon, active movers in the rebellion. Isaiah rejoiced in the fall of the cities of the hated Baal worship, but there was sadness in his happiness. The net was drawing close about Judah. After the Philistine cities fell, followed by the capitulation of Edom and Moab, Sennacherib came through Judah.

In his inscription he boastfully tells the story. He spared no one; his soldiers pillaged and slew and spread fire and destruction wherever they passed. Jerusalem itself was besieged; but here the conqueror ran into unexpected obstacles. The capital which David had built proved provokingly strong. The impatient besieger was able to boast of shutting up the Hebrew king "like a bird in his cage in the midst of his royal city"; but there was no surrender. At length a truce was made. It was not death for Judah, but it was only a footstep from it. Hezekiah lost most of his territory. He was stripped of his treasure and his palace ornaments. Even his daughters went to enrich the conqueror's harem. He was left with only his crown and the ruined city of Jerusalem.

The conqueror marched on triumphantly to meet Egypt. The subsequent incidents have long puzzled Biblical scholars. In the midst of triumph, with every expectation of further success, the Assyrian army suddenly abandoned its plans and turned back. Herodotus tells a story of field-mice who gnawed at the military equipment of the Assyrians and rendered it useless. In the Biblical story there is hint of a plague which struck down the enemy. Perhaps the fearful bubonic epidemic smote the victorious Assyrians in their most triumphant moment and caused them to abandon their plans.

The miraculous discomfiture of the Assyrian hosts did not long impede their march to world supremacy. All through the seventh century their sovereigns wrote boastful inscriptions of unending military successes. Under the brilliant leadership of Esar-haddon and Assur-bani-pal, Assyria extended its conquests into Egypt itself and reduced the proud mistress of the Nile to vassalage.

Tiny Judah was of course bound body and soul. Cuneiform dockets discovered at Gezer imply that garrisons were established in Judah to ensure allegiance. The little country supplied precious timber for use in Nineveh and even sent contingents of troops to fight in Assyrian armies against Egypt. Above all, the culture of Assyria, largely borrowed from Babylon and now fashionable everywhere, deeply influenced Judah too.

A large part of this period of Assyrian dominance was spanned by the reign of Manasseh, who ruled over Judah for fifty-five years. He has an odious name among Hebrew historians, who bitterly resented his immersion in Assyrian heathenism. They trace every misfortune which followed his death to his apostasy. It appears, however, that at least economically and politically his reign was a period of recovery. The half-century of peace healed the wounds of earlier devastations. The people, a little wearied by the gloomy puritanism foisted upon them in the nervous hysteria of Hezekiah's day, turned in relief to wear a lighter mood. They welcomed Assyrian ideas and were happy that imports again flowed in from Egypt and Phœnicia and made life comfortable, even luxurious.

So long as Assyria remained all-powerful, there was peace. Who could challenge the might of Assur-bani-pal, who harnessed four captive kings to his chariot and compelled them to drag him to the Temple of Ishtar in Nineveh? But towards the end of the seventh century the crushing grip of Assyria relaxed. New enemies appeared, from strange corners of the world, to threaten the Semitic dominance which had lasted for more than a thousand years. Powerful Median tribes emerged from the mountains on the east of Assyria; the long-menacing Chaldeans at last conquered Babylon and made ready to challenge Assyria; fierce hordes of Scythians poured out of the passes north of the Black Sea.[1] The world was filled with fears and rumours. Diviners read entrails for omens, sorcerers mumbled incantations, prophets preached

---

[1] Herodotus describes how they drank the blood of their enemies, using skulls as drinking-cups and making cloaks for themselves out of the scalps of the slain.

doom, and humble folk everywhere, wanting only peace, waited, trembling for their meagre security.

Judah was as frightened as the rest of the world. When the Scythians swept down into Syria, leaving ruin and devastation behind them, the blood of its inhabitants froze with fear. But the northern hordes skirted Judah and went rumbling on towards Egypt, where they were repulsed, and Judah in thankfulness turned again to puritanism. Yet the respite was brief. As Assyria weakened, Egypt took heart and made a new bid for empire. Her navy swept the Phœnician coast. Her army, bolstered with hordes of Libyans and Ethiopians, marched north to subjugate unhappy Judah. Josiah, a young, popular king, bravely met the invaders at Megiddo. The defence seemed hopeless, but had not Yahweh once before placed victory in the hands of the Hebrews and cut to pieces Sisera's Canaanite forces? Alas! The glorious days of Deborah were not repeated. Josiah was killed and Egypt once again ruled Syria and Palestine. An appointee of Egypt sat on the throne of David, mulcting the people of tribute for his suzerain.

Still there was no peace. The Assyrian empire crashed before the combined assaults of the Medians and the Chaldeans, and the latter turned at once to meet Egypt. At Carchemish, in 601 B.C., one of the decisive battles of the ancient world was fought. Egypt was shattered and the new Chaldean state began its sensational climb to world supremacy. It was now headed by Nebuchadrezzar, the greatest Eastern king since Hammurabi. Conquest to him meant more than tribute. In his long reign, of forty-three years, he spread the authority and the civilization of the new Babylon throughout the world. Where his armies came, cities grew up, with temples, canals, dikes, palaces, and all the arts of life.

Naturally, Judah changed hands, but so long as it submitted peacefully Nebuchadrezzar did not interfere. The king, however, refused to remain a vassal and, despite the denunciations of the prophets and the more sober statesmen, defied the Chaldean potentate. At first Nebuchadrezzar contented himself with sending Chaldean guerrilla troops into Judah and with fomenting attacks by Moabites, Ammonites, and other none too friendly tribes. Jerusalem and its outlying districts suffered intensely. Jeremiah gives vivid descriptions of the ruin brought on the country by the king's foolhardiness — beasts devouring the earth, brigands infesting it. At last, in 597 B.C., Nebuchadrezzar himself came to invest the little capital, which quickly submitted. Not only was the city sacked and plundered, but the king followed the Assyrian policy of transporting the most important elements of the population and carried away with him the warriors, the artisans, the craftsmen, and all who could give vitality to the State. The miserable remnants were left, amidst the lonely ruins, under Zedekiah, the last of the Hebrew kings.

Nebuchadrezzar thought to destroy the resistance of the stubborn Judæan state by transporting its heads. He did not realize the immense vitality which surged in the body of Jewish life. " The bad figs," as Jeremiah contemptuously termed the remnants, refused to remain passive. They seized every opportunity to stir up trouble. They listened eagerly to rebellious suggestions by envoys from the borders of the desert, from Tyre and Sidon, from Egypt. At length Zedekiah flung down the gauntlet and ceased to pay tribute. Nebuchadrezzar, angry, with patience exhausted, swept down to end the bickerings in his western dominions. Jerusalem was invested and slowly starved into submission. The sufferings of the besieged, prolonged for more than a year and a half, were dreadful. The people perished so fast that it was impossible for the survivors to bury them properly. Corpses decayed in streets and cellars. Pestilence, engendered by the poisonous stench of the city and by the unwholesome diet forced upon the people, added further horrors to the siege. At last the Chaldean troops broke through and the resistance ended abruptly. The Temple was razed, its columns broken up, its huge stones sent rolling to the bottom of the valley of Kidron. The princes, the priests, and the elders were tortured and put to death before Zedekiah, who was himself blinded and carried off to Babylon in chains of brass.

A sorry remnant remained in the country-side. Over these Nebuchadrezzar placed, as royal governor, a respected leader, Gedaliah. A seat of government was set up at the ancient sanctuary of Mizpah, five miles north-west of Jerusalem. Gedaliah was an able ruler and he evoked the loyalty, not only of the humble citizens, who wished for peace above all, but also of the wandering guerrilla bands. Fugitives began to return and settled again into the normal routine of an agricultural life. But a curse seemed to hang over the country. There were still hotheaded fanatics who refused to accept the situation. Miserable worms, hacked asunder, the parts continued to wriggle and squirm. Within a few months the governor was assassinated at a community meal, and a large body, fearful of the consequences of this new defiance of Babylon, fled to Egypt, dragging with them the aged prophet Jeremiah.

Life in Palestine continued despite all the military disasters. Modern criticism has rejected the traditional view that the country was left empty after the assassination of Gedaliah — a mass of ruins and debris — and was only restored by returning exiles. A considerable population remained and gradually recovered a little of their economic strength. Yet the desolation was serious enough to prove almost fatal.

The Jews in Palestine and in the places which received the exiles might easily have been lost for ever, their history no more important than the history of petty Damascus or Philistia. But the Jews would not die. Three centuries of prophetic teaching had given them an unwavering spirit of resignation and had created in them a will to live which no disaster could crush.

CHAPTER SIX

THE PROPHETS: THE LIVING HEBREW CONSCIENCE

I. RISE OF THE PROPHETS

Out of the mire of Hebrew political life the prophets rose like strange exotic blossoms. Their work is as surely the contribution to civilization of ancient Israel as Hellenic art is the Greek contribution, and imperial law and government the Roman. Extraordinarily complex spirits they were: supreme individualists, yet preaching restraint and conformity to law; intensely patriotic, yet upbraiding the nation and threatening it with destruction; innately religious, yet despising the forms that religion took. They smote the idea of a national god and a narrow patriotism, often making military and diplomatic action impossible by their uncompromising attitude. They laboured to substitute plain, moral requirements for elaborate ceremonial and formal creed. They were the stern guardians of individual and national conduct, the living Hebrew conscience, the poets of statesmanship. And they were completely fearless in pursuing their self-appointed mission, bearing abuse with sublime patience, defying kings and priests and populace alike, eternal rebels.

How came they to Palestine? Endless processions of peoples lived there before them, lived and worked and died, mute and uninspired. Endless processions of peoples followed them without a breath of life issuing from them. Alone of them all, the prophets spoke, somehow drawing inspiration from the barren soil, the stony mountains, the gaping ravines, awakening in men a new moral zeal.

They must not be identified with the generations of quacks who preceded them and called themselves prophets. From time immemorial, in every land, there were seers and soothsayers who were believed to possess clairvoyant powers, who could interpret dreams or speak to the dead, or tell fortunes, or divine the intentions of the gods. Samuel is linked up in the old traditions with this brand of fakir. When Saul seeks his father's lost asses, he risks a quarter shekel to consult the sage of Ramah; he interviews his spirit, through the witch of Endor, on the eve of his last battle. Such seers had little in common with the moral giants of the eighth century B.C. They came, of course, in response to the natural human craving for supernatural guidance in a fearsome crisis. But they answered the craving in a very primitive way, with signs and with

61

wonders. They were little in advance of the Assyrian baru who interpreted the wishes of the gods by inspecting the entrails of specially slaughtered animals.[1]

Nor was there any relationship with the half-distraught epileptic individuals who seemed to primitive minds to be "possessed" by a divine afflatus. In the ancient world such prophets were common. The report of an Egyptian envoy, Wen-amon, describes a case of frenzied prophesying at Gebal in Phœnicia as early as 1100 B.C. In the seventh and sixth centuries B.C. there were itinerant Orphic prophets who travelled over Greece in the service of the ecstatic cult of Dionysus. Early Hebrew history is filled with the antics of these men, who later travelled together in guilds. In their crude way they helped Israel to survive in the dual struggle against external enemies and alien beliefs. Fierce as modern dervishes when preaching religious wars, the prophets travelled up and down the country whipping the masses into loyalty to the old desert faith. During the long wars with the Philistines and with Damascus they worked with hysterical fervour to make courage a sacred duty. Elisha was evidently closely associated with such prophetic groups, though he himself seems to have been unable to bring on an ecstatic mood except by artificial means.

Genuine prophecy was not primarily concerned with prediction or with working charms. It was related to the reformation of the moral order. The true progenitors of the prophets were the few isolated spirits who fought to raise the standard of social righteousness. They were not daunted by great names or great titles; they reached into the sacred precincts of royalty itself to thunder out their message. Such a type was Nathan, who boldly took David to task for his iniquitous conduct in the affair with Bath-sheba.[2] Such was Ahijah, who denounced the tyrannous practices of Solomon and even fomented rebellion against him. And such was Elijah, who upbraided Ahab for robbing Naboth of his humble patrimony.

It is probably to such men that we are indebted for the beginnings of Hebrew history. From the ninth and eighth centuries, when the social conscience was wakening, come the first anonymous fragments that form the basis of the later Biblical redactions. Their authors found inspiration in the tribal traditions, orally preserved. They gathered them reverently, pieced them together with material already written as early as David's day, and steeped them all in their own moral fervour. Some wrote in Judah; some wrote in Ephraim; each had different notions about the twilight days of the past, and different ethical standards by which to judge. But a common

[1] If prophecy arose out of soothsaying, and many modern scholars believe that it did, it is to the credit of Israel that it could purify divination and make it a powerful religious force.
[2] There is grave suspicion that the story of Nathan and David is a product of later prophetic emendation.

impulse lay beneath all differences — the eternal presence of Yahweh in life. Everything had significance only as it had relation to Him. Nothing was ever done but that He dictated it. Good and evil came to men only because Yahweh judged their acts.

There is an element of pathos in the simple fervidness of the early prophetic chroniclers. One thinks of the three sisters whom Jason consulted for guidance to the Golden Fleece, three sisters with only one eye among them, which was passed about from one to the other. It made all things clear to them; without it they stood blind and helpless, at the mercy of every adventurer who crossed their path. Thus the Hebrew historians saw life and all of its manifestations through Yahweh. Without Him they were lost — their people were stray sheep groping in abysmal darkness.

But there was sublimity in such tender narrowness. It was fanaticism controlled and reasoned, a combination which, Lecky has well said, is one of the most powerful agents in moving the passions of men. It moved the moral passions of the choicest spirits in Israel. Ultimately it leavened the worldliness of nations other than those for whom the prophets wrote.

Men who could thus refashion the potter's clay were not unworthy spiritual progenitors of the great prophets of the eighth century B.C. whose names we know and a precious residue of whose writings has survived.

2. AMOS AND HOSEA

As was noted in discussing the political history of Israel, the middle of the eighth century B.C. ushered in a period of magnificent ease such as had never before been enjoyed by the kingdom. Unexpectedly, after two centuries of turmoil and civil strife there came a quick recovery, followed by more than a generation of surgent prosperity. Assyria was quiet; the Aramæans were turned back; the petty tribes that bordered on Israel were reconquered. Commercial relations were re-established with friendly nations. As wealth poured into the country, and fortunes were quickly made, cities began to grow in number and in size. The wealthier classes imported new comforts and undreamed-of luxuries.

But beneath the glamour there were terrible social evils which rankled in those who cared nothing for the flesh-pots of a metropolitan civilization. Of course one should not take too literally the blasting indictments of the prophets who drew damning pictures of the country's inner life. To judge from the catalogue of crimes which they listed, ancient Israel was a sink of iniquity, sufficiently immersed in vice and crime to merit the sufferings and misfortunes which soon came upon the country. It must be remembered that every reformer must exaggerate; his messages must be filled with brimstone and fire if he is to make any impression. And if his standard is high, his keen eye will ferret out abuses everywhere. The prophets were maximum men, demanding more than a moral minimum, and in consequence their analysis of the social scene was a mounting crescendo of denunciation.

Yet there were enough actual evils present to lend reality to their messages. Israel in this period has been aptly compared with fourteenth-century England, whose economic abuses evoked Langland's *Vision of Piers Plowman*. The Aramæan wars had wrought enduring social changes in the life of the people. Thousands of the middle and lower classes, always on a bare margin of subsistence, had been impoverished and had mortgaged and lost their little holdings to the powerful wealthy caste. As was said of nineteenth-century Ireland, dispossession was nine points of the law. Many unfortunates had even become slaves because of their default. The new commercial relations with foreign countries brought profit only to those who had capital to invest; those who had none only sank deeper in the bogs of ruin. Justice as usual was on the side of the wealthy; bribery was a common practice, conducted with finesse, but "leaving a taste in the mouth like wormwood." The luxurious habits of the wealthy brought out all the more glaringly the poverty of the disinherited. It was whispered in the streets that behind the closed doors of newly erected mansions the wealthy mocked the poor by their heartless waste; that lewdness and depravity were the daily routine of those who enjoyed silken cushions in their beds.

Yet who could bring the wastrels to account? They were models of technical goodness. They held their heads high in righteousness. They did nothing that was not within the limits of the law. They were fervid patriots, quick to uphold national honour, ever ready to defend the sanctity of property rights and social stability. They adhered strictly to all the ritualistic demands of religion. Theirs were the fattest sacrifices, theirs the most generous tributes of thanksgiving and free-will offering; theirs the sweetest words to the bowing priests. Who could challenge these pillars of respectability, except social radicals, rebels who demanded more than legality, who refused to weigh actions in the conventional scales, who sought to introduce a gentle spirit of equity into the rigid legalism of the period?

The first of these lofty figures was Amos, a simple herdsman from Tekoah, a tiny hamlet between Jerusalem and Bethlehem. Living on the edge of the Dead Sea wilderness, often in solitude, wrestling with nature for barest subsistence, Amos was particularly unfitted to condone the vices of organized life. Yet he was no ignorant rustic, decrying a civilization that he could not understand. St. Jerome was grossly unfair when he described the prophet as crude and unlettered, an *imperitus sermone*. His humble origin did not predicate ignorance, nor did it hinder his speech. Amos had a power of imaginative imagery and an unerring instinct for realities, which lent unique virility to his eloquence. He knew life and the world. Selling his wool at the frequently held fairs, he met and studied all types of people, and his writings reveal an understanding of international affairs.

It was probably during the most prosperous period of Jeroboam's reign that Amos came to the religious festival at Bethel. Careless crowds of merry-makers swarmed the streets and the courts of the shrine. Prosperous merchants vied with well-fed nobles in the lavishness of their sacrifices. Suddenly Amos began to speak, in the manner of the modern dervish. He mocked the self-righteous who came with prayers and with offerings to satisfy the ritualist demands of Yahweh. Yahweh needed none of them. He abominated their sacrifices. What good were fatlings when the hearts of the givers were sodden with filth, when men lay before the altar in the clothes torn from debtors, when they drank sacramental wine purchased with the sweat money of the oppressed?

> I hate, I despise, your feasts,
> And I will not smell the savour of your festivals,
> And the peace-offerings of your fatlings I will not regard with favour.
> Banish from me the noise of your songs,
> For to the melody of your lyres I will not listen.
> But let justice roll on as a flood of waters,
> And righteousness like an unfailing stream.

Yahweh had indeed chosen Israel from among other peoples, but the choice did not release Israel from the moral law. Justice was demanded from all peoples, and Israel was doomed if it did not meet its responsibilities.

> Do horses run upon crags,
> Does one plough the sea with oxen,
> That you turn justice into poison,
> And the fruit of righteousness into wormwood?

Amos, in his prophetic wrath, spared no one, neither the unctuously righteous nobles, nor the feather-headed masses, nor the sleek daughters of Samaria who urged their lords into more and more rapacity to satisfy every selfish whim. "Kine of Bashan" they were, trampling down everything that was sacred or beautiful. Nor were the priests and the prophets exempted, nor even royalty itself. So must Savonarola have denounced the iniquities that he found in Rome; so must Knox have thundered before Mary Stuart.

Amaziah, the high priest, was furious and sneeringly implored Amos to save his prophecies for his own Judæan people, who needed them and who would better compensate him. Amos, not at all abashed, retorted that he was no professional prophet, that he spoke from an earnest conviction of the iniquity of Israel's life. The country would assuredly suffer. All might seem well for the moment, but no people could long survive where the leaders were corrupt and self-seeking, where the middle class was impoverished, and where there was no faith except in material things. Israel was like a basket of Oriental fruit, ripe, juicy, luscious, but soon to rot, already, indeed, in the process of rotting.

Amos was no more immediately successful than any radical reformer. He was expelled from Bethel and went back to his hut to pen his words. But he turned a sharp corner in the history of religious thought. His denunciations of social evils were not new. Right-minded men must have been sickened by the abuses that existed. Keen-visioned statesmen had long realized that no state could survive when its leaders sapped its strength for personal uses. But Amos linked up his social ideals with a concept of Yahweh far in advance of his age. He rose above the idea of Yahweh as merely a national god. Yahweh had created and brought Israel forth from Egypt, but He had also brought the Philistines from Caphtor and the Aramæans from Kir. He was the god of all peoples, pleased when they were honourable, and angered when they erred. Foreign nations would be punished, not because they harmed Israel, but because they violated their social responsibilities. And Israel would be treated no more indulgently than any other people. Yahweh drew no distinction between them and the dusky Cushites, who lived farthest from Jerusalem. Israel perhaps stood in a special relation to Yahweh. It had known Him before the others—it had enjoyed the privilege of His guidance longer. But this closer relationship meant greater responsibilities. " You only have I known of all the families of the earth; therefore I will visit upon you all your iniquities." More was expected of a maturer people. Here Amos was harking back to the stern faith of Moses, who placed Yahweh in a special relation with Israel, but never privileged Israel therefore to violate His moral law.

Amos thought in terms of justice and said little of more fundamental ideals. These were to be stressed by other prophets. But his message challenged the complacency of those who identified goodness with ritualist piety. Yahweh's justice could not be satisfied with empty forms. Those who brought in sacrifices did not wash away their guilt—they heightened it, for they compounded evil with hypocrisy. Such a message is elementary, but Amos thundered it in the bazaars of Samaria twenty-seven hundred years ago. Perhaps it can still be read with profit.

Scarcely had Amos ceased preaching when the evils which he had predicted were fulfilled with startling precision. Jeroboam II died in 743 B.C., and when his strong grip was relaxed, anarchy came. The house of Jehu came to an end when Zechariah was assassinated six months after he ascended the throne. His murderer was killed within a month. Menahem, who followed, maintained himself only by mulcting the country to pay a huge tribute to Tiglath-Pileser of Assyria, whose vassal he became. His priests were rascals who cloaked themselves in religious sanctities for the better success of their corruption. After

Manahem there was another fever of assassination. Finally "the Assyrian came down like the wolf on the fold" and ended the independent life of the little kingdom. The catastrophe could not perhaps have been avoided even if the social life of the kingdom had been healthy. But Israel might have died honourably; it might have been spared the degradation of a putrifying decay.

Before the end a second prophet had risen in Israel to continue the work of Amos. Hosea was as bitter as his predecessor had been in his denunciation of the evils of the time. Renan compares his passionate vigour with that of the Puritan pamphleteers in the time of Cromwell. His tongue swept every class which was contributing to the ruin of the kingdom, false prophets and rapacious profiteers, priests, rulers, and nobles. His keen eye saw to the roots of the social disease, society unbalanced, justice outraged, discontent undermining patriotism. Israel was "a cake unturned, burnt on one side, the heart raw and sour." What could follow but destruction?

Yet, with all the severity, there was a new note. Perhaps Hosea's own tragic experiences taught him a profound tenderness. His wife, Gomer, who had been his pride and happiness, proved unfaithful and turned to sin. Hosea's sensitive nature was shaken to its roots; dirt and dishonesty appalled him. He pleaded with her to abandon her adultery at least for the sake of their children. She was obdurate and went openly to her lover. When he wearied of her love and abandoned her, she sank to the lowest degradation. Hosea could not give her up to her punishment. He loved her the more for her sufferings and took her back to live with him. His domestic tragedy taught him that he could not cease to love that which was dear to him. It taught him that he who loves truly can only be pained, never exultant or callous, at the sinner's hurt.

Perhaps the whole episode was a beautiful allegory, developed by Hosea to draw a moral. It matters little. Upon its lesson he built his teachings. Israel had sinned. She had betrayed Yahweh. By all the laws of justice she deserved all the evils that came upon her. But Yahweh was not merely a god of justice. He was a god of love. He loved Israel. He had nourished her, cared for her, watched her develop; and it pained Him to see her go astray.

> How can I give thee up, Ephraim,
> Abandon thee, Israel?
> How can I make thee like Admah,
> Treat thee like Zeboim?
> My heart is turned within Me,
> My compassions are kindled together.
> I cannot work out the heat of My wrath,
> I cannot again make havoc of Ephraim;
> For I am God, and not man —
> The Holy One is in the midst of thee;
> I come no more to consume.

Hosea preached the doctrine of a God who cared, with all the solicitude of a loving father, for the welfare of His children. Doom was not irrevocable. It need not come if Israel would only see the light. And Hosea was convinced that Israel would. The nation was not perverse. Ignorance was its undoing. The people were being "destroyed for lack of knowledge." They needed a heart of wisdom.

With Hosea mankind climbed another step in its struggle upward. His God was far removed from the Yahweh of the wilderness, the relentless, warlike Yahweh who revealed himself in flame and whose voice was the voice of thunder. He was far removed, too, from the Yahweh of justice that Amos took as his sanction, a sublimely austere, rational god who predicated a moral law. Hosea felt God in a warm personal relation. His religion was more than a religion of the mind; it grew from a heart overflowing with sympathy. As Robertson suggests, Amos based religion on morality, whereas Hosea deduced morality from religion. His god was a god of love, love not merely as a thin sentiment, but as a principle of life.

Jeremiah and nearly all of the other prophets based their teachings upon a god of love. The heart of the message of Jesus was the gospel of love. But before Jeremiah and more than seven centuries before Jesus, Hosea stood forth on the threshold of the ruin of Israel, heart-broken by its plight, a lonely, solitary figure, gently striving to bring his people to a god of love.

3. ISAIAH AND MICAH

Amos and Hosea ministered in Israel, and their memorable words remained as an epitaph for the kingdom. Very soon after Hosea's voice fell silent, the Assyrians conquered and uprooted the house of Israel. Thence on, the prophetic genius manifested itself in the southern kingdom and helped to leaven the tasteless lump of its life.

Judah had fallen out of sight since the disruption of the Solomonic monarchy. It had been completely overshadowed by Israel; for nearly a century it remained in the position of vassal to the kings of Samaria. It was rarely mentioned in foreign inscriptions. Quietly, sluggishly, almost stupidly, generation followed generation into the reign of Uzziah, the contemporary of Jeroboam II.

This middle-eighth-century period, a golden age for Israel, was also a bright interlude in the history of Judah. There was a sudden release of prosperity following peace with Damascus and Assyria. There were victories over ancient enemies—Philistines, Arabs, Edomites. There were considerable accessions of territory. But material prosperity was accompanied, as in Israel, by the usual social evils, the craze for foreign fashions, the oppression of the poor, the subversion of justice, the subordination of morality to comfort. Society was not so decadent as in Israel, but to sensitive souls with high ethical standards life was unbearable.

The outstanding figure in the period was Isaiah, the most eloquent and one of the profoundest of all the prophets. In training and temperament he was vastly different from Amos or Hosea. He was no recluse, suddenly appearing to deliver his message and then disappearing into the simplicity of a shepherd existence. He was an aristocrat of an old noble family, a constant attendant at court, the friend of kings. For forty years or more he helped to guide Judah's foreign policy. He was the one strong force amid a host of weaklings who pulled Judah now in one direction, now in another. It was largely due to his acumen that the kingdom survived the first flushed victories of an awakened Assyria.

But it was as a prophet more than as a statesman that Isaiah achieved immortality. His diction was magnificent — beautiful, lilting poetry that preserves its charm and vigour even in translation. Like his predecessors, he was affected by social abuses and religious hypocrisy as by physical pain — "moral ipecacuana," Carlyle once called it. Isaiah denounced the priests and the professional prophets, whose example awakened only contempt. "They reel during their visions, they totter while giving judgment." He was a son of the aristocracy, yet he turned upon his own class to upbraid them for the cruelty of their ambition, for the heartlessness with which they added "field to field and house to house." He assailed the vanity of the pampered daughters of Jerusalem, who would soon exchange their finery for the garb of slaves. "Instead of artificial curls there will be baldness, instead of a girdle a rope, instead of a mantle a girdling of sackcloth, branding instead of beauty." He insisted that the fundamental weakness of the State lay in its blind reliance on material forces. In every crisis men thought at once of chariots and horses, of fortresses and arsenals. Faith was needed too, simple, reverent faith. "If ye will not have faith, ye shall not endure."

So far there was little that was startlingly original in Isaiah's message except the eloquence in which he dressed it and the vigour with which he applied it to Judæa. But there was another aspect to his teachings, a unique concept of Yahweh and of the mission which He had ordained for His people.

Yahweh was a holy god, with a splendour so awesome as to be well-nigh incomprehensible to men. He demanded holiness in His people. Holiness meant a spirit of consecration for the highest purposes, a sense of separation from what was common. Israel was a chosen people only in the sense that it was chosen to live above the average. *Noblesse oblige!* Such a standard of conduct could not appeal to all, nor even to the greater number. It did not matter. Those who went on desecrating their own lives and enervating the life of the State were dry, rotten branches. They would wither and die. But a remnant would remain, a spiritual aristocracy, to continue serving a holy god, to preserve a holy Israel, to rebuild a holy Zion.

The doctrine of holiness and the "saving remnant" profoundly influenced subsequent Jewish life. It explained the inexplicable sufferings of the nation. It was balm of Gilead in the midst of the most fiery judgments. The Assyrians sacked and plundered Jerusalem, the Babylonians visited the ancient city with sword and death, the Greeks trampled upon the chosen people, the Romans crucified them, endless other conquerors harried them without mercy. What did it matter? Israel was immortal. The State might perish, its inhabitants might be scattered to the winds, but a saving remnant, or, rather, a saved remnant, chosen by Yahweh and hallowed by Him, must survive.

Inspired by the eloquence of Isaiah, another great prophet appeared during the reign of Hezekiah. The simple democrat Micah had none of Isaiah's profundity, none of his vision. He knew little of statesmanship and was little concerned with religion. But the social problem set his soul on fire. He despised the professional religious leaders who condoned the social evils, who pandered to the wealthy classes, and who were ever ready with venom for those who would not throw a bite into their jaws.

The predecessors of Hosea had also concerned themselves with the exploitation of the poor by the powerful. But Micah expressed his feelings with a vivid terseness all his own. He came from the afflicted class and spoke from out of their heart. His bitterness for the oppressors of the poor sent him to cannibalism for his imagery: "Ye who hate the good and love the evil; who pluck off their skin from off them, and their flesh from off their bones; who also eat the flesh of my people and flay their skins from off them and break their bones, and chop them in pieces as for the pot, and as flesh for the cauldron" (Micah iii. 1–3).

From Micah, too, we have perhaps the finest summary of religious duty in any language:

> What doth the Lord require of thee
> But to do justly, to love mercy,
> And to walk humbly with thy God? [1]

Here was a simple, beautiful recapitulation of all that Amos, Hosea, and Isaiah had taught. The future centuries could improve it little. Huxley, the agnostic, found in it the perfect ideal of religion; "a conception of religion which appears to me as wonderful an inspiration of genius as the art of Phidias or the science of Aristotle!"

4. DEUTERONOMY

The pleas for social righteousness of Isaiah and Micah would have made little impression in Judah but for new political exigencies. Suddenly the

---

[1] Many scholars believe that chapter vi, in which the verse appears, is a post-exilic addition to the text of Micah.

Assyrians, under Sennacherib, swept down upon the country. King Hezekiah, certain that the country was being punished for its waywardness, was driven into puritanism. He destroyed the more important high places, centres of a revived heathenism, and hewed down the brazen serpent, long since become a fetish, now deemed unworthy to remain in the Temple. He restored Jerusalem as the only legitimate place for sacrifice. But Hezekiah's reformation did not long survive the crisis that created it. Soon after his death came a reaction which swept out every vestige of prophetic puritanism. Judah was now vassal to Assyria, the easy-going Manasseh was king, and both circumstances contributed to loosening the strictness of Yahwism. Old gods, long flung into limbo, almost forgotten, emerged again for another brief period of power. The Assyrian Ishtar invaded the Temple itself. Witchcraft, divination, and wizardry became common and even child sacrifice was again practised in the valley of Hinnom.

If we are to take the chronicles literally, Manasseh mercilessly persecuted the old reformers. The sword of reaction " devoured the prophets like a destroying lion," and Jerusalem was filled with innocent blood. According to a Talmudic tradition, even the aged Isaiah was not spared; despite his grey hairs and his long years of unselfish service he was sawed asunder. But persecution could not destroy the prophets. Secretly they contniued to spread their propaganda. It is likely that they now rewrote the history of the kingdom, combining the Judæan traditions with those which came from Israel, revising the whole to drive home the moral that Yahweh never failed to reward loyalty and punish apostasy.

Ultimately the prophetic patience was well rewarded. After Manasseh's death and the assassination of his son, the impressionable Josiah came to the throne. The prophets emerged from retirement. They began to lift their voices as they had in Hezekiah's day. And when, in 630 B.C., the dreaded Scythians poured down from the north and threatened the life of Judah, their prophecies echoed in every corner of the city. Jeremiah began his ministry in these critical days; Zephaniah's terrifying voice rang out all through the period.

Zephaniah reminds one of Isaiah. He came from the house of Hezekiah and had the blood of reformers in him. He was a brilliant, forceful orator and he had Isaiah's high standard of the holiness of Israel. But there was no gentleness, no kindliness, in his prophecies. In the events about him he saw only doom for Israel, the well-merited destruction of the Jewish State. In mediæval art Zephaniah is appropriately portrayed as a dread denouncer, seeking sinners with the lantern of the Lord. His picture of the desolation of the day of Judgment inspired the hymn *Dies iræ, dies illa,* the most magnificent hymn of the mediæval church. Only once did he hold out the slightest hope for his people: " Seek righteousness, seek meekness; it may be that ye will be hid in the day of Yahweh's anger! "

Evidently there was a personal conversion of the terror-stricken Josiah. He put himself entirely in the hands of the Puritans, and the pendulum swung back to the other extreme. The worship of strange gods was sternly repressed. The altars of Manasseh were torn down; the horses and chariots dedicated to the sun were removed. Above all, the Temple was thoroughly cleansed of every abomination. Those who had been ridiculed through the long reign of Manasseh now had their innings and trod the host of mockers underfoot.

The impetus for the reformation was a newly " discovered " code of laws, said to have been devised by Moses, which very opportunely helped to crystallize the reforms desired by the prophets. The code, which is now contained in parts of the Book of Deuteronomy, was no doubt written by the prophets during the period of reaction and smuggled into the Temple. It was partly history and partly law and was ascribed to Moses to win prestige and authority for it. The work was based upon the old Mosaic tradition, recast and amplified and steeped thoroughly in the prophetic spirit. The social, political, and religious ordinances so much abused and violated were plainly recited. The Hebrews were constantly reminded that they were a holy people, separate, unique, with a high standard of conduct. The *Shma,* the credo of Israel through the ages, was prefixed as an introduction to the whole code.

The code made a tremendous impression on the people then and after. Josiah proclaimed it as the law, and for twelve years Judah abided by it. To the later chroniclers this brief era of Josiah was looked back upon as a golden age. The people had peace; the laws of the Mosaic faith were carefully practised. The king was a model of piety and set a worthy example for his people.

Then came the unfortunate war with Egypt, and the premature death of the reforming king, and Judah was swallowed up again in the great international convulsions which shook the world. Assyria, Egypt, Babylon, in turn smote the little State. The most brilliant diplomacy would have been utterly futile in such a day and ultimately the Holy City, long regarded as inviolate, was destroyed. Throughout this last period the personality of Jeremiah, perhaps the greatest of the prophets, stands out in solemn grandeur to lend a tragic dignity to the final act.

5. THE SOLITARY JEREMIAH

The sixth century B.C. produced several supreme religious geniuses whose lives profoundly influenced the progress of civilization. In the Far East Lao-Tse wrought a moral revolution when he laid the foundations of Taoism; Confucius impressed himself even more indelibly on Chinese life by his incomparable moral precepts; Guatama taught the gentle philosophy of the Eightfold Path, which became the heart of Buddhism. And Israel produced Jeremiah, whose career is one of the epics of history. His life was as impressive as his work. He was a gentle, sensitive, melancholy type, yearning for affection, for love, for the comforts of home and the normal life, and yet he was impelled by the prophetic fire within him to preach doom, to antagonize the people whom he loved, to undermine their national existence. Throughout his life he was fearfully alone, now a pacifist, now a traitor, kings imprisoning him, associates reviling him, the mob crying for his blood. Often he cursed the fate that condemned him to a living hell. "Woe is me, my mother," he cried, "that thou hast borne me a man of strife and contention to the whole earth!" Some of his poems, born of the struggle between his natural impulses and his consciousness of a divine destiny, are among the most poignant in Hebrew literature.

But he stood his ground with magnificent courage. He never lost faith in the goodness of God and the justice of His decrees. He found excuses in his own unworthiness for the stern discipline to which he was compelled to submit. Out of his suffering came a new understanding of God. His intense emotionalism, his tortuous introspection, often interpreted as a sign of weakness, was his greatest strength. It brought him into a personal relationship with God. He felt close to Him, he found relief in Him, and he came to the realization that an individual fellowship was possible. God had not chosen nations, He had chosen individuals. He was in every man's heart. He was not a stern master of the world, off somewhere in space. He was in every form of nature, the divine in man. His presence in each individual linked all men in kinship and made them all brothers.[1] This doctrine Jeremiah preached in season and out until death stilled his voice.

Jeremiah was born, of an old priestly family, in Anatoth, an hour's walk from Jerusalem. His call came early, about 626 B.C., but his first messages, in which he expressed disapproval of the degeneration of religion and the cruelty of social life, had nothing original in them. They were largely modelled on what he had learned from the older prophets, especially Hosea. But they were sufficiently vigorous to obtain his expulsion from Anatoth. He probably came to Jerusalem soon after, to find the inhabitants in a panic because of the threat from the pitiless, desolating Scythians. He joined with Zephaniah and the other prophets in filling the city with Cassandra forebodings of a great world-convulsion.

> Behold, like clouds he comes up,
> His chariots a storm-wind;
> Swifter than vultures his horses!
> Woe to us; we're undone.
> O Jerusalem, wash thee from sin
> If thou wouldst be saved.
> How long shall lodge in thy heart
> Thy dissolute thoughts?[2]

[1] It may be, however, that these portions of Jeremiah are post-exilic.   [2] Jeremiah iv. 13–14.

The Scythians skirted Judah without harming the country, but the young king, Josiah, converted either by fear or by persuasion, proceeded to work some drastic reforms in the religious life of the State. The Deuteronomic reformation, previously discussed, attempted to undo the evils which had grown up during the long Assyrian hegemony and the kingship of Manasseh.

For some years Judah was untroubled. We have little information about the activities of Jeremiah during this Indian summer. Perhaps the Deuterono-mistic reforms satisfied him; perhaps he found defects to quarrel about. He must have hated those who submitted only to the letter of the code — who gave lip-service to its principles and slipped back to the old hypocritical piety which every prophet vigorously attacked.

His real mission began when international difficulties again overwhelmed the little kingdom. Egypt, sweeping towards the Euphrates for a new empire, attacked Judah, killed Josiah, and took possession of the country. It, in turn, was soon overwhelmed by Babylon, which succeeded as the lord of Judah. So long as the puppet king, Jehoiakim, remained loyal, the country was not harmed. But the patriotic party was soon nibbling at alliances with surrounding nations, aiming to break loose from Babylon.

Jeremiah awoke. From then on, the full blaze of publicity was upon him. He pleaded for loyalty to the suzerain power, insisting that Judah, wedged between mighty nations, could find salvation only by remaining outside of alliances and coalitions. He did not share the popular belief that the Holy City could not be destroyed. There was too much faith in the inviolability of Jerusalem. It had hardened into a dogma of popular religion, further strength-ened by a vulgar interpretation of Deuteronomy. God would assuredly destroy Jerusalem and the people who had desecrated it; it would be as Shiloh. For the Temple had become a house of sin, a mockery —

> What has my darling to do in my house?
> Vile are her doings!
> Can scraps of fat and sacred flesh
> Turn calamity from there? Then mightest thou rejoice! [1]

Jeremiah was the most unpopular man in Jerusalem. The priests derided him, the patriots denounced him, the mobs reviled him. He was publicly struck by a Temple priest and placed in the stocks to be taunted by the passing crowds. He would have been executed, but one feared to kill a prophet. Yet he did not flinch. When the king renounced the authority of Babylon and prepared for war, he continued with his pacifist propaganda. As soon as he had been released, he wrote out the sermons which he had preached and sent them to the king. When Jehoiakim destroyed them in anger, Jeremiah rewrote them, elaborated upon them, and continued to preach his treasonable doctrines.

[1] Jeremiah xi. 15.

He prophesied that Judah would fall; it was unworthy to continue. Yahweh would have to refashion His work, for Judah had failed Him. The potter was often obliged to do his work over when the clay proved to be not good.

Even as Jeremiah spoke, Nebuchadrezzar swept down upon the little western world and overwhelmed Judah. The king and the leading citizens were transported, leaving only a hapless remnant under the rule of Josiah's youngest son, Zedekiah. Jeremiah now turned to give advice to the exiles, offering them solace and comfort, assuring them that a remnant would spring from them in God's own time that would bring about a resurrection of Jewish life. Meantime they must needs make themselves worthy of the rehabilitation.

It was more difficult to speak to Jerusalem. There Zedekiah was soon in the hands of fire-brands who still hoped to be freed from Babylonian control. Again Jeremiah took up the unpopular cause of pacifism. Again he ran counter to the popular prophets. But his previous experiences did not leave him frightened. He was still undaunted. He walked through Jerusalem with a yoke on his shoulders to illustrate what must soon happen to Judah if it adopted the suicidal policy of resistance. The yoke was torn off and Jeremiah spat upon. Still he persisted.

Nebuchadrezzar again descended upon the city, determined to end the resistance of the stiff-necked people. Jerusalem held out with astonishing courage. For more than two years the city was invested and the inhabitants were reduced to every desperation. Jeremiah continued to preach doom, to denounce the gallant defenders. Hundreds daily deserted to the Babylonians. The prophet was surely undermining loyalty. He became a serious menace. He was starved, beaten, cast into a vile cistern to die. But he would not surrender, he would not keep his peace. He would not be loyal to a state that was not worthy of loyalty. When Zedekiah brought him forth, secretly, to receive his advice, the prophet still insisted: " Surrender or perish."

The tragedy was coming to an end. After two years and a half Jerusalem was taken and utterly destroyed. Zedekiah was blinded, his sons were executed, and the survivors of the first ruin were dragged off to Babylon. Only a miserable remnant was left in Mizpah under Gedaliah. Jeremiah chose to remain with his people. But they were destined to have no peace. The high-minded governor was assassinated and many of the Hebrews, in terror, rose and fled to Egypt. Poor Jeremiah, white with age and suffering, was dragged along. There, according to a tradition which has come down from Jerome, he was stoned to death by his infuriated people for continuing to preach doom at Daphne. His last gesture was defiance.

The statesmanship of Jeremiah was not his most important contribution. Running all through his writings are confessions laying bare the conflicts of his inner life — his doubts, his fears, his hopes. They are the profoundest in all Hebrew prophecy and they add immensely to the importance of his work.

In his search for light he reveals his deepest nature. He went far beyond his predecessors in his conception of God. To them Yahweh had made a bond with Israel, and Israel had to be holy to be worthy of the bond. To Jeremiah God was more personal. His bond was with each individual, not alone with the nation. "They shall all know Me, from the least of them unto the greatest." [1] Jeremiah was the prophet of personal religion.

But his career was as inspiring as his thought and work. "The Book of Jeremiah," it has been well said, " does not so much teach religious truths as present a religious personality. Prophecy had already taught its truths, its last effort was to reveal itself in a life." [2] Jeremiah's sufferings, and the patience with which he bore them, his doubts, and the faith with which he triumphed over them, embody the finest spiritual qualities of his people. He is the symbol of eternal Israel. Surely the sublime prophet of the exile was thinking of Jeremiah when he painted his magnificent portrait of God's chosen servant: " He was despised and rejected of men; a man of sorrows and acquainted with grief; and as one from whom men hide their face he was despised and we esteemed him not. Surely he hath borne our griefs and carried our sorrows; yet we did esteem him stricken, smitten of God, and afflicted. But he was wounded for our transgressions; he was bruised for our iniquities; the chastisement of our peace was upon him, and with his stripes we were healed." (Isaiah liii. 3–5).

The great religious geniuses of the eighth, seventh, and sixth centuries B.C. — Amos, Hosea, Isaiah, Micah, Zephaniah, and Jeremiah — changed the religion of the Hebrews. They crystallized the progressive thought which had been developing for three centuries and gave it an expression which influenced the subsequent history of three religions. They became a model for all rebels who placed national and individual life on a moral basis, holding conscience higher than law. It is little wonder that the reformers of the sixteenth and seventeenth centuries came so frequently to them, that their glowing words were ever on the tongue of Calvin, Knox, and Cromwell. Thus, the prophets, the outcasts of their own generation, became the spiritual heroes of those which followed, the exemplars of true religious faith. For it is the fashion of the world to idealize dead saints and to persecute living ones.

It is sometimes suggested that the prophets repudiated all ritual and ceremonial. Superficially it would seem so. Amos hated the festivals; the psalms and songs were din in his ears. Isaiah called the entrance of sacrifice into Yahweh's courts a desecration. Jeremiah's most pointed barbs were directed at " scraps of fat and sacred flesh." Yet the prophets did not repudiate the forms of religion. They repudiated their abuse. When they lived, the dogmas had

---

[1] As was suggested above, many scholars regard these passages as of post-exilic origin.
[2] A. B. Davidson, in Hastings's *Dictionary of the Bible*, II, 576.

become charms, magical formulas, intended to induce the deity to favourable action. There was no spirit in organized religion; it had sunk to heathen levels. It was the degeneration which the prophets smote without fear and without stint. They had no quarrel with a cultus practised sincerely and with understanding hearts.

The destruction of Jewish national life did not, miraculously, destroy the Jewish people. They lived on to play out impressive roles in every age, in every land. History presents no parallel for the phenomenon. Many peoples have survived the destruction of their states — the Poles, the Irish, the Serbs, and others who have lived to see the rebirth of hopes never fully lost. But these people were never torn from their soil; however bitter the oppressions which they bore, they remained united and drew courage to go on from every site and every grave that was linked to the past. The Hebrews were almost completely dispersed. Only a ragged, dejected minority remained or, after many years, again returned. But into this remnant the Hebrew prophets breathed a spirit which could not be extinguished. It was a spirit that was not dependent for life on temples, or national sacra, or ceremonial requirements. It was a faith that was not bound up with a city or a book. Thus the unpopular, misunderstood fanatics who derided narrow nationalisms and narrow religious zeal endowed their people with a sense of nationalism and a sense of religious solidarity which no power was able to destroy. Nor was it merely the ability to endure. Immortality alone is not a blessing. The mother of Tithonus begged the gods to grant her son eternal life, but forgot to ask for eternal youth, and Tithonus grew old and gnarled and senile, his life a burden and a curse. The Hebrews grew old in experience, older in suffering, but retained a spirit youthful enough to be for ever productive.

CHAPTER SEVEN

THE RISE OF JUDAISM

I. THE EXILE AND ITS CONSEQUENCES

THE miracle of Jewish survival after the collapse of Judah seems more extraordinary when it is realized into what tiny fragments the State was shattered. A remnant of the population lived on in Palestine, another was carried off to Babylon, a third fled to Egypt. All three together probably did not number more than a hundred and twenty-five thousand, about a third of the present Jewish population of Chicago. Yet a few centuries later, just before the Christian era, the Greek geographer Strabo wrote of the Jews: "They have penetrated already into every state, so that it is difficult to find a single place in the world in which their tribe has not been received and become dominant!"

The greatest number lived in Palestine, poor, ignorant peasants who gained a precarious livelihood from the soil and who needed to be for ever on guard against the raids of marauding neighbours. The Ammonites, the Moabites, and the Philistines coveted their meagre harvests and neglected no opportunity to harass them. The Edomites, driven northward by the Nabathæans and other tribes which pressed on their own borders, were a particular scourge. Ezekiel curses them for their cruelty (xxv. 12–15), and the historians to whom the memory of Edomite encroachments was fresh wrote their bitter hatred into their accounts. The glory of Judah was gone. Its survivors ceased to hope for better days as they wrestled with the soil. They intermarried with the heathen about them and forsook the god who had evidently forsaken them.

In Egypt the situation was much more promising. Here Jews had been dribbling in for centuries, and even before the destruction of Jerusalem there were flourishing Jewish communities in many parts of Pharaoh's dominions. All through the sixth century B.C. Jews fleeing from the successive assaults of Babylon settled on the east borders of Egypt. Some returned to Palestine; others drifted into other lands and were lost; still others took over completely the Egyptian ways of life and were absorbed in the native population. But the majority who came settled permanently, remained faithful to their traditions, and helped to build up the wealth and strength of the Elephantine region. Several centuries later the Egyptian communities had become the leading commercial and cultural centres in the Jewish world.

In Babylon lived the smallest number. They represented the best elements, the wealthiest and most cultured classes who had been successively deported from Judah. They lived together in little colonies, where they enjoyed an almost autonomous life. They did not permit their homogeneity to disappear and at first made every effort to continue the life which they had led in Palestine. But despite a superficial continuity the exile completely changed their mental outlook. No people could remain uninfluenced when transplanted from the narrow, barren confines of a hinterland to the splendid kingdom in the heart of the Mesopotamian garden lands. How vast was this world — "this land of traffic," as Ezekiel termed it, "with its cities of merchants, its fruitful soil, beside many waters"! It was rich, powerful, teeming with life. Where were there such luxurious buildings, such towers and temples and palaces, such gigantic walls? Was there anywhere so remarkable a creation as the hanging gardens of Babylon, built merely to satisfy a whim of the king's lonesome Median wife? Everything astonished the provincial Hebrews, as a metropolis astonishes rustics during a first visit.

Many of the exiles, carried away by the splendours of the new civilization, snapped all associations with their past and entered completely into Babylonian life. Every opportunity was theirs. The king placed no difficulties in their way so long as they held their peace and paid their taxes, and apparently there was little prejudice against them among the natives. They became merchants, traders, artisans; and, rising on the wings of their shrewdness, developed into an influential group in the land that had transported them.

Many who did not completely lose their identity were vitally affected by the cultural influences that were brought to bear upon them. They remained Jews, outwardly loyal to their people, but they probably dropped most of the practices and ideas which made them unique. Gradually they drifted out of Jewish life, and their children remembered the country of their fathers' origin with the chagrin of parvenus who dislike to be reminded of their humble beginnings.

But there was a strange unhappy minority in the midst of all the Babylonian splendour — fervid nationalists who refused to forget. They sat by the waters of Babylon and wept. They yearned for the little blue hills of Judah. They regarded the civilization and religious forms of the Babylonians as abominations. They kept, almost desperately, every custom which bound them to their past, and they worshipped Yahweh with more fervour now that they were set down in an alien environment. Their religious concepts became clearer, more mature. They began to understand the deeper significance of the prophetic messages. Yahweh was not dependent on temples and sacrifices. He was a god of the heart, as near in Babylon as in Palestine, present wherever men sought Him.

One of the most potent forces in stimulating the tiny minority and nourishing their hope was the vigorous young nationalist Ezekiel. He had been trained in the priesthood and was among the ten thousand and more better families

who were first transported when the Babylonians sacked Jerusalem in 597 B.C.
He became a trusted leader of the exiles and for more than twenty years ministered to them. The priest and the prophet were admirably blended in him.
He never tired of explaining the destruction of national life as the deserved
castigation of an erring people. But he always held high the hope for a
speedy restoration. Soon, very soon, the exile would be ended, a theocracy
would be established, the Temple would be restored, and a chastened people
would again bring sacrifices to the ever gracious Yahweh. "I will give you a new
heart, and will put a new spirit within you . . . and ye shall keep statutes, to do
them" (xxxvi. 26–7).

Today the prophecies of Ezekiel are scarcely read. They have neither the
warmth nor the strength that immortalize the words of Amos or Hosea or
Jeremiah. Ezekiel's messages are involved, confusingly florid, filled with difficult symbolisms, rightly called by a modern critic "architectonic." The prophet
was thoroughly saturated with priestly ideas, and the commonwealth which
he envisioned was one carefully regulated by ritual laws. Whole chapters of his
prophecies are taken up with plans for the new Temple and its restored sacrifices.

But the constant emphasis on the liturgical forms of the new life in Zion
was based on good psychology. Ezekiel was speaking to heart-sick exiles who
yearned to be reminded of days gone by, whose nostalgia could not be fed
with empty hopes. Abstractions, however vivid, however beautiful, could not
long keep up their confidence in an ultimate restoration. They might serve
for a few months, for a few years even, but not for decades. Ezekiel talked
of a Temple rebuilt, of ritual and ceremony, of bronze ornaments and cubic
inches. He spoke of future undertakings with the precision of an architect
or a surveyor. He encouraged people to plan with him as if the return were
to begin tomorrow. And they ceased to be depressed exiles; they became
hopeful builders.

Yet Ezekiel was no mere syrup-feeder. When occasion demanded, he could
carry his people away with visions as thoughtful as they were vivid. He saw
the Hebrews as dry bones in a barren valley, until the breath of God was
breathed into them; then they stirred and moved, became men, prepared for
God's service. He saw them as poor scattered sheep, betrayed by faithless
shepherds, led again, after a spiritual awakening, to fragrant pastures and clear
water, guided by God Himself.

For years Ezekiel preached such messages and enabled the homesick exiles
to resist every assimilatory influence. They waited eagerly for the moment when
they would return to fulfil the prophecies of their leaders.

It was probably during this period that the history of the Jewish kingdoms,
and the words of the great prophets, were rewritten in what has been called the
Deuteronomistic tradition. The main parts of Joshua, Judges, Samuel, and

Kings underwent new redactions, and, wherever possible, morals were tacked on to demonstrate the deplorable consequences of religious infidelity. An important part of this literary activity was the new collection of laws, called the Holiness Code, which was projected into the Book of Leviticus and which re-emphasized the distinction between a holy Israel and other peoples.

It was during this period too that the institution of the synagogue developed, destined to survive until the present time. Bereft of Temple and of religious centres, each little community created its own meeting-place. The exiles would congregate, usually on the sabbath, to hear their elders read to them the prayers which had been handed down by tradition. Alms would be distributed, and perhaps there would be instruction in the ritual that was practicable in a strange land. When the exile was over, the synagogue was brought back to Palestine. And when national life was again snuffed out, the synagogue went with the wandering Jews into every corner of the globe. All through the ages there was never a place where Jews could not meet to keep alive the faith of their ancestors.

2. THE REBUILDING OF THE TEMPLE

During the forty-three years that Nebuchadrezzar sat upon the throne of Babylon, his kingdom remained the firmest and mightiest of the ancient world. But when the illustrious monarch died, in 561 B.C., there was no successor with the strength to continue the tradition. Four ineffectual monarchs followed each other, two of whom died by the hands of assassins. While Babylon was besieged on every side by eager enemies, its last king, Nabonidus, turned to pious archæological enterprises — digging in ruins, restoring old temples, interested above all in centralizing the worship of the provincial gods in the capital.

Already far off to the east a new star was rising, the star of Cyrus of Anshan, which, in a little more than a decade, was to dazzle the whole world. Cyrus was a vassal of the King of Media and controlled a little principality on the east of the Zagros Mountains. Military genius and unique organizing capacity enabled him within three years to send a handful of peasant soldiers forward to become the conquerors of the whole Median kingdom. Then began a triumphant march westward which filled the East with terror and wonder. Cyrus became a legend in his own lifetime; Herodotus brings together extraordinary traditions from the remotest corners of the earth, a tribute to the awe which his name inspired. Soon his empire comprised the territory from the Indus River to the shores of the Ægean. Only Babylon stood in the way of world supremacy, and in 539 B.C., Cyrus prepared to overcome the sole obstacle.

For three years the proud city withstood his siege, confident that no enemy was mighty enough to crash through its powerful walls. Treason eased the task of Cyrus. One night the priests of Babylon, embittered by the religious

practices of Nabonidus, opened the gates of Babylon, and the Persians poured
in. Belshazzar, who had taken his father's place as head of the State, was slain
at a midnight feast as he drank to the glory of his throne.

The colossus of the ancient world had fallen at last. " Thou art cast out from
thy sepulchre like an abhorred abortion, like those who are pierced with the
sword; thou goest down to the lowest pit like the corpse that is trodden under
foot " (Isaiah xiv. 19). The control of Asia passed from the Semites to the hands
of the hardy Aryan peoples of the north and east—a control to be retained until
the days of Mohammed and his fierce, inspired Arabs.

It was probably during this period of political cataclysm that a new prophet
arose to interpret the bewildering events and to turn them to spiritual significance. We do not even know his name, this genius whose prophecies follow
the fortieth chapter of the Book of Isaiah. We call him Deutero-Isaiah, the
Great Unknown. He explained the reason for the glaring disparity between the
prosperity of the heathen Babylonians and the desolation of Yahweh's people.
Yahweh had not forsaken the Hebrews. They were a chosen people—chosen,
however, to be disciplined by suffering, to be a martyr for the world's redemption. " I will also give thee for a light to the gentiles, that thou mayest be My
salvation unto the end of the earth " (Isaiah xlix. 6).

No other ideal was worth pursuing. Material success soon turned to emptiness. Power and pomp were tinsel. Armies and fortresses and empires brought
no inner satisfaction.

> All flesh is grass,
> And all its glory as the flower of the field.
> Grass withers, flowers fade,
> But the word of God shall stand for ever. (Isaiah xl. 6–7.)

Babylon today stood high in the world. Its magnificent cities were the envy
of the earth. Its legions carried fear wherever they went. No matter; its power
was mere emptiness; it would pass as the driven stubble. Already a rival was
rising in the east, and tomorrow Babylon would sit in ruins. She would be
stripped of her purple and torn from her gorgeous throne. She would sit on
the ground and toil with the grindstone like any peasant.

The words of the anonymous prophet, teaching the futility of material
strength, the mission of Israel to be purified by sorrow, to serve at the cost of
pain, transformed the spirit of Israel. No burden was now too heavy to bear
—Israel was the suffering servant whose stripes healed others. " Thou art My
servant, Israel, in whom I will be glorified." The message brought solace to the
weary and the heavy-laden. It taught them resignation in every national sorrow
and strengthened them for other fiery ordeals. Every cloud, as St. Jerome put it,
was an angel's face.

The century following the Persian conquest of Babylon is an obscure period in Jewish history. Virtually all that we know is based on the accounts in the Books of Ezra and Nehemiah. But recent criticism has cast considerable doubt upon their reliability. They were written certainly not before 300 B.C. and probably long after then. Their authors were removed by nearly two hundred and fifty years from the events that they described. Perhaps they had access to well-established facts, but it appears now that their own emendations and revisions helped only to obscure them.

According to the traditional account, which most scholars now discredit, as soon as Cyrus conquered Babylon, he issued a sensational edict of emancipation. He explained that since Yahweh had given the kingdoms of the earth into his hands, the Jews who lived in Babylon could, if they wished, return to their Holy Land. They would receive every assistance from him and he would co-operate in the rebuilding of the Temple. The Jews hailed the edict with unrestrained joy. Cyrus was indeed the saviour proclaimed by the prophets. An impressive exodus to Palestine began, led by Zerubbabel, a scion of the house of David. Those who remained behind blessed the expedition and sent gifts for the new house of God.

When the little band arrived in Jerusalem, their rosy dreams evaporated. The city was an ugly heap of ruins, the whole country was terrifyingly bare and uninspiring. The pioneers had expected no luxuries; they were prepared for hardships. But this! They were compelled to scrape aside debris even to clear a stone for an altar to God. The men of the older generation who still remembered the Temple of their childhood broke down and wept.

With frozen hearts the disillusioned colonists began to erect temporary shelters for themselves. Even this work could not proceed in peace. Enemies swooped down from all sides to harass the builders. In the fierce struggle for bare existence, complicated by droughts and failing crops, many wished they had never left the banks of the Khaibar. Hundreds deserted and went back to decry the whole enterprise. Those who remained turned sour and callous, every spark of their early idealism extinguished.

It was not until fifteen years or more had passed that the construction of the Temple began. The impetus came from two eloquent prophets, the aged Haggai and the youthful Zechariah, who flayed the people for neglecting the Temple while they built panelled houses for themselves. Even when a sense of shame had been revived, the work proceeded slowly. The apathy of the people was matched by the animosity of neighbouring tribes, and it was not until 516 B.C., twenty years after the edict of Cyrus, that the house of God was finally completed.

Such is the account of the return from exile detailed by the authors of Ezra and Nehemiah. It premises an almost deserted Palestine and ascribes the re-creation of Jewish life entirely to Cyrus and the immigration from the east.

But this interpretation raises more problems than it solves. It is difficult to believe that Cyrus issued the edict quoted in Ezra, exalting the name of Yahweh. It is more difficult to understand how the return to Palestine could have included so many families. The list in the Book of Ezra is, as a matter of fact, simply an enumeration of the families who, in the days of Nehemiah, a century after Cyrus, claimed to belong to the district of Jerusalem. The prophets Haggai and Zechariah, whose words are contemporary, show no knowledge either of the edict of Cyrus — surely an event miraculous enough to excite at least a reference — or of a return from Babylon.

Because of these and other difficulties modern critics have been guided by the words of the prophets rather than by the words of the chroniclers in their reconstruction of the period. It is likely that there was no grandiloquent edict issued by Cyrus nor a tremendous exodus to Palestine. Perhaps when Cyrus conquered Babylon, a number of Jews actually came to live in Palestine. But there cannot have been very many, certainly not more than a few thousand. The rank and file had been weaned too long from Palestine to make genuine sacrifices for it. Their homes, their business, their friends, their interests, were all in Babylon. In the leading cities — Ecbatana, Susa, the capital itself — they had attained commanding positions. Only zealous nationalists would uproot themselves from such an environment to travel for months across scorching deserts back to a land overrun by enemies, uncultivated, ugly, primitive, all for an abstract love of a fatherland removed by three generations from them. The restoration of Palestine, then, depended not upon an element returned from Babylon, but upon the Palestinian Jews themselves, upon the poor folk who had survived the successive deportations. For long they had lived in dumb apathy, striving to heal the scars of many conflicts. They heard with wonder how their brethren were prospering by the banks of the Nile and the Khaibar. Occasionally travellers came through bringing news of growing Jewish settlements and enterprises in the busiest markets of the world. But they were little moved. Nothing mattered to them, cut off from the world, except the harvest and security from marauding neighbours.

It was impossible, however, to remain completely unstirred by the political convulsions that shook the world. The advent of Cyrus brought new settlers into the country, with new ideas, new zeal, new hopes. Men began to speak again of the national destiny, of a mission; they began to plan a Temple. Then enthusiasm cooled. Cyrus died. Years of chaos followed before the reins of power were firmly seized by the able and genial Darius. While rebellions were flaring up everywhere in the empire, the poor peasant Jews of Palestine, bowed with their own troubles, remained loyal. But among the leaders hopes fluttered anew. Perhaps from out of all the strife would come the salvation predicted by the old prophets. Perhaps by some miracle complete independence would be restored. Taking advantage of the excitement, new prophets arose to urge the rebuilding of the Temple. Haggai and Zechariah, both whole-souled patriots, upbraided the people for allowing the house of God to remain an empty hope while they built houses for themselves. Surely all the tribulations that had come upon Israel since the Babylonian disaster were due to the neglect of the Temple. If the Temple were rebuilt, the fortunes of the country would change. Judah would again be an established kingdom. A son of the house of David would again rule in Jerusalem.

The messages of Haggai and Zechariah seem almost a retrogression. The prophets speak little of social justice; they revert to an emphasis on the institutional side of religion. To them the Temple service is the centre of religious life. But the problems of the age perhaps required just such an emphasis. The trappings of religious ceremonial were needed to awaken faith. The prophets felt that until Judah again had its Temple to symbolize the restoration of Zion, there could be no genuine loyalty.

The task of rebuilding the Temple now proceeded. It was slow and difficult work. Every communal enterprise is consummated only after strenuous effort. But the usual difficulties were here accentuated because life itself was not yet comfortable and every family had needs which seemed more immediately essential than a Temple. Suddenly the Persian satraps became suspicious of the Jewish motives and almost put an end to the enterprise. It required earnest pleading to gain permission to continue the building. But all hope for national independence disappeared when Zerubbabel, the last of the royal house, was put aside. The Davidic dynasty thus came to a quiet, inglorious end.

But in 516 B.C. the Temple was completed and dedicated with great joy. Humble, plain, undecorated it was, but it is difficult to overestimate its importance in Jewish history. It stood for five hundred years, a century longer than its predecessor. It was the centre of a restored worship, and every pious Jew contributed to its maintenance. All the sentimental yearning of the Jews scattered through the world was now focused in the Temple, which thus effectively bound together the whole Jewish people.

3. THE CREATION OF THE TORAH

For the seventy years following the rebuilding of the Temple we again have only scanty and unreliable records. It is clear, however, that life in little Judah was hard and bitter. The Persian yoke was ordinarily not difficult to bear; the kings were tolerant and were little concerned about the internal affairs of subject peoples. But in this period the Persian and the Greek were engaged in a titanic struggle for the supremacy of the West. Marathon, Salamis, Thermopylæ, and Platæa were bloody examples of the desperation with which the Greeks defended their liberties. Then came the Egyptian uprisings, and the distraught Persian kings turned to lead expeditions to chastise the rebels on the Nile. Judah, along with other subject lands, paid for these expensive enterprises. Persian armies marched and countermarched through Syria and Palestine. There were increased taxes, compulsory contributions and provisions, perhaps impressment into the Persian forces. And the country was pathetically poor. Even in times of peace it was difficult to eke out a livelihood; war burdens made the inhabitants reflect bitterly on the beautiful visions which the prophets had painted for them. To fill the cup of sorrow there were rascals in Judah who took advantage of the helpless. Even the Temple did not help to raise the tone of life. A corrupt priesthood had established itself, preying on all who could be cajoled or terrified.

A few lone voices cried out from the darkness against the degradation of Jewish life. Attached to the Book of Isaiah are the eloquent protests of an anonymous prophet whose heart was torn by the corruption of the so-called religious leaders. " Blind they are, without knowledge; dumb dogs that cannot bark, dreaming, lying down, loving to slumber; yea, greedy dogs that can never have enough." Of what use were all the pious fasts and the mortifications of the flesh?

> Is not this the fast I have chosen —
> To loosen the bonds of wickedness
> And undo the cords of violence;
> To let the oppressed go free,
> And every yoke to snap?
> To break for the hungry thy bread,
> And the homeless to bring to thy house;
> When thou seest the naked, to cover him,
> And to hide not thyself from thy flesh? (Isaiah lviii. 6–7.)

Another prophet, whom we call Malachi, spoke with equal fervour and firmness. While pleading with the people not to lose faith, he denounced those who, by their cruelty and selfishness, forced men into darkness. The obsequious priests and the pious hypocrites were honouring the Persian satrap more than they honoured God. Better to close the Temple than to continue with a travesty of worship. The heathen, who venerated bits of stone or tusks of ivory, were truer sons of God, for they at least worshipped from the heart, according to their light. Far better ignorant idolatry than the word-mumbling of the Hebrew hypocrites!

The early fifth century resounded with these vigorous denunciations. The prophets were still the living Hebrew conscience, still true to their thankless task. Then suddenly came a series of epoch-making events, told at length in the memoirs of Nehemiah. Nehemiah was a Jew of Susa, who had risen to the position of cup-bearer to the Persian king, Artaxerxes. He was profoundly stirred by the mournful tales which reached him of the plight of " the remnant who were left of the captivity." He determined to use his influence to bring about a change. Apparently he stood very high in the favour of the king, for he received not only a limited leave of absence to rebuild the ruins of Jerusalem, but permission also to make levies of wood in the king's forests for his purpose. He departed with a military escort and plunged at once into the many problems which troubled the Jewish community.

His first object was to protect Jerusalem and its environs from the incursions of hostile neighbours. The Ammonites, the Edomites, and prowling Arab tribes had long been a menace to the Jews. Nehemiah determined to rebuild the walls of Jerusalem, exhibiting immense vigour and statesmanship in carrying out the difficult project. Every neighbourhood was to take care of its own section of the wall; rich individuals were to build opposite their own homes. None were exempted from either financial or actual service. Soon a whole community was at work. Some built; some stood guard, for treacherous neighbours required watching. Nehemiah pushed the work forward feverishly, fearful lest sinister influences should poison the mind of the Persian king and destroy his plans. There were, indeed, foundations for his fears. Old enemies spread lies in the courts of Susa about Nehemiah's ambitions, and many of the priestly leaders, who were unwilling to lose their authority in Jerusalem, wished Nehemiah no good. All obstacles were overcome, however, by the persistence of Nehemiah, and after fifty-two days the walls were complete. They were larger than those which had been replaced, and they enclosed not only Jerusalem but the near-by villages as well. After one hundred and fifty years of desolation the famous old capital was again habitable and secure.

Temple and walls rebuilt, the Jews at last tasted peace and comfort. The Persian wars had ceased and life under Persian control was not now onerous. The Jews enjoyed a large measure of freedom and were not disturbed so long as they contributed taxes and tribute. Material conditions began to improve and numbers of Jews from Babylon, Egypt, and other far-away places came to settle. The country, now much smaller than the pre-exilic kingdom, never grew large enough to attract widespread attention. Herodotus, who is delightfully loquacious about the Near East in this period, does not appear to know of the Jews. He speaks only of " the Syrians of Palestine." Yet the community grew and the twenty square miles which comprised the State became a complex little organism.

It was inevitable that easy contact with the heathen world should encourage a latitudinarian spirit in Jewish life. As intermarriages became common and the orthodox religious practices were not observed, Jewish leaders became alarmed that the growing laxity would destroy the nation and its faith. A new puritanism came to life, impressing a rigid conformity to the law. The leadership in the reaction against laxity has been credited to a zealous Babylonian scribe, Ezra. The book which bears his name relates how he led an expedition of colonists from Babylon to strengthen Jewish life in Palestine. He was armed with a pious proclamation of the Persian king, which ordered inhabitants of Jerusalem to obey the laws of Yahweh on pain of death, banishment, fine, or imprisonment. Arrived in Jerusalem, Ezra, assisted by Nehemiah, at once began his reformation. He insisted upon a strict observance of every law — the sacrifices, the sabbath, the prayers, the ceremonies. Above all he waged relentless war upon the practice of intermarriage. Those who had taken non-Jewish wives were to put them aside at once under peril of ostracism. Homes were broken up, families were wrecked. The cost was fearful, but the end, Ezra insisted, justified the means.

Parts of the account in Ezra are probably the imaginative interpretation of events by the pious chroniclers who wrote many generations later. The grandiloquent proclamation of Artaxerxes, and the account of a second general migration to Palestine, seem, at best, dubious. Many modern critics even question whether Ezra is a historical character; they lean to the view that he is the impersonation of the Puritan tendency which dominated the middle fifth century.

Despite difficulties in detail, the essential fact is clear. All through the fifth century there was a steady reaction against religious laxness, a reaction sponsored by the scribes, who were becoming ever more influential. The scribes, forerunners of the Pharisees, were the interpreters of the law, the leaders in the synagogues. They were closer to the heart of the people than the priests. Zealous in their belief that the law of God must be strictly observed and that Israel must remain a separate people, they fought every attempt at compromise. It was due to them that, after the fifth century, Israel threw itself into complete dependence on the Torah (the Mosaic law) as the guide of life.

The law, which had been orally preserved for generations, was now carefully brought together and consecrated as the foundation of Jewish civil and religious life. "Turn it and turn it again," the scribes admonished their people, "for everything is in it." And the Jews responded with unparalleled devotion. All existence was centred in the law. The Jews became the people of the book. The early Hebrews had created the Bible out of their lives; their descendants created their lives out of the Bible.

But the Torah in itself contained only general principles. These required application and elaboration. New laws were therefore deduced from the old ones, new meanings were ferreted out of every sentence and every clause. Soon a school of expounders developed, whose work continued for centuries and became the foundation of the Talmud.

The process was not devised by petty spirits to chain men to the letter of the law. On the contrary, it was hoped to make the ancient law practical in the life of later generations. In the field of civil law the new principles were decidedly useful. Those which were afterwards embodied in the Mishnah were sound and humane and were a distinct improvement on many of the Biblical injunctions.

In the field of religious practice, too, many of the new interpretations helped to enrich the spiritual life. The sabbath became a useful day of rest, with many of its onerous prohibitions modified.

It was inevitable, however, that the endless spinning of meanings from the old texts should go to extremes and become burdensome. The Biblical law which prohibited the eating of meat torn in the field was based upon the sensible hygienic principle that carrion was dangerous as food.[1] In the hands of the dialecticians the law was elaborated into a complex dietary machinery. If meat torn in the field was prohibited, why not also meat torn in the city? But what was torn meat? If it were not properly slaughtered, it was surely torn. What was proper slaughter? A whole code, the basis for the practice of *Shehita* (ritual slaughter), grew up to meet these problems — rules governing the knife to be used and the manner of using it, rules governing the competency of the ritual slaughterer and his training, the prayers to be recited when the throat was cut and when the blood was covered with ashes. A simple Biblical precept grew into a labyrinth of petty observances.

There was a similar expansion of the Biblical law which forbade seething the kid in its mother's milk. It was amplified until meat and milk could not be eaten at the same table; separate dishes were required for each kind of food, separate bowls in which to wash them, separate towels to dry them; and there grew a long list of subsidiary practices and prohibitions. Orthodox housewives observe the rules to the present day.

The scribes could not, of course, conquer without a struggle. Then, as yesterday, and today, there were men who would not be bound by what they considered narrow and choking loyalties. These unconstrained spirits fought the scribes in school and synagogue, in the court and the market place. Some of them embodied their protests in literature and two anonymous specimens have been preserved and are among the choicest parts of the Bible.

The Book of Jonah is an impressive allegory written in this period to combat the narrow chauvinism of the scribes. Jonah typefies the Jew who thinks in terms of strict Judaism and who regards God as in a special relation with his own people. He is commanded to preach to the people of Nineveh and to win them from their evil ways. He is angry at such a request, for he sees no usefulness in saving the heathen from their just deserts. He flees to escape from his task, but God's hand reaches farther than Palestine. Jonah is swallowed by a whale and released only when he humbly agrees to preach God's message. To his indignation, his message is impressive enough to bring about the repentance and the salvation of his audience. He chides God for making a fool of him, and the little book concludes with the benign words which teach Jonah that all peoples are the children of God.

[1] There was a primitive taboo against eating meat torn in the field, and the law, originally, was related to this taboo.

The Book of Ruth is another product of protest. The beautiful idyll points out that even King David descended from a daughter of Moab. Though Ruth was a heathen, sprung from a tribe which, by the laws of Deuteronomy, could never acquire full citizenship in Israel, she proved a model of piety, filial devotion, and feminine sweetness. If she had been excluded there would have been no David, no monarchy, no Temple, and no priesthood and there would be no Messiah. Surely it was wrong to make the law of exclusion so severe.

The two tendencies, one calling for adherence to a revealed way of life, the other resenting the imposition of dogmatic authority, produced a fundamental antinomy, never to be reconciled. They continue to struggle for expression in Judaism and in all organized religions. It is easy to stigmatize the first as a harsh legalism which breeds intolerance and exclusiveness and impoverishes spiritual life by robbing it of spontaneity and freedom. A clever Frenchman once suggested that Pharisaic Judaism was not a *re*ligion (binding men together), but an *ab*ligion (keeping them apart). Yet each type of faith is immortal and draws adherents from men of opposite temperaments. The scribes built their ideals upon what they accepted as a divine revelation. They insisted that men could live best only by following the precepts of this divine law as interpreted by its great teachers.[1]

In the fifth and fourth centuries B.C. the scribes triumphed and the Torah became the guide of life. Unfortunately its interpretation did not always give release to the noblest religious enthusiasm. The scribes were not all lofty spirits, and their attempts to draw hidden meanings from the law often degenerated into meaningless formulas and stupid restrictions. These hardened into custom, which soon became an unrelenting tyrant. " The divinative chains of habit," says Johnson shrewdly, " are seldom heavy enough to be felt till they are too strong to be broken."

Yet, as a whole, the work of the scribes was not stultifying, nor was it built upon sand. It gave solidity to the religious idealism of some of the noblest Jewish teachers of all time. To pious souls it gave a practical outlet for high earnestness and moral zeal. In creating a clear set of principles by which to live, it helped to link up Jews scattered in all parts of the known world. Above all, it preserved Jewish solidarity in the crisis soon to follow, when nations and religions were all beset by the seductive power of the Greco-Roman civilization.

[1] " The mechanism of religion, while not necessarily an end in itself, was thought to be the indispensable vehicle by which men might hope to rise higher and higher in God's esteem. This was an attitude not unlike that of a later Christian ecclesiastic who affirmed that one who will not have the church for a mother cannot have God for a father. Such is the distinctive trend of institutional piety in all ages." Case: *Jesus*, p. 314.

CHAPTER EIGHT

LIFE AND LABOUR IN BIBLICAL PALESTINE

1. "IN THE SWEAT OF THY BROW . . ."

THUS far we have been discussing political and religious developments, grouping them about the careers of the outstanding characters — princes and prophets, war lords and seers. We have noted how a group of scattered tribes, of diverse origin, stamped by different traditions, were fashioned by strong fingers into a virile nation, conscious of a unique destiny. But this is not the whole of the early Hebrew story, nor perhaps even the most important part. What of the masses of average men, who toiled in the fields or plied their humble trades in the congested little villages and towns? How did they live and work? What of their family life and their social customs and institutions? What did they think about?

It is not easy to resurrect their story. The chronicles of the period are meagre and the fragments that survive deal with the most numerous class hardly at all. The chroniclers naturally sought out the uncommon, the spectacular; a description of huts and peasants, of trades and clothes, was beneath their notice. Yet the story is fortunately not blank. From indirect statements in the Biblical literature, from the heart of folk-lore, we may reconstruct at least the main features of life and labour in Biblical Palestine.

Life was largely conditioned by the character of the land. Good soil was rare and the water-supply was never plentiful. Since most of the Hebrew peasants lived by agriculture and cattle-breeding, they were thrown in complete dependence upon the forces of nature. They dreaded the drought, which meant famine and death. They dreaded the hot desert wind, the sirocco, which burnt up vegetation and was as great a menace to security as the drought. They dreaded the terrible locusts, which came often thick as clouds, seeming to darken the very sun, devouring the hardly-raised crops.

The methods of agriculture were pathetically crude. Men used scythes and sickles for mowing; their ploughs were of wood, rarely shod with iron; and threshing was done laboriously with the clumsy flail. Small, undersized oxen, hardly as large as modern calves, dragged the ploughs back and forth, barely scratching the surface of the earth. Nothing, of course, was known of fertilizing or of rotating crops, and the yield was never very large even when nature was kind.

All Orientals regarded labour as a curse and the early Hebrews were no exception to the general rule. It is significant that in the Hebrew traditions about Eden an ideal scene was built about the time when Adam and Eve frolicked in a lovely garden with little to do; God's punishment for their disobedience was the awful curse which compelled them and their descendants to toil for their food by the sweat of their brow.

Women did most of the menial labour; they pounded the hand-mill, ground the corn, prepared the meals, spun the clothing, took care of the many children, bore the burdens, and often toiled with the men in the fields under the blazing sun. Chivalry did not require that women be relieved of hard labour.

In the nomadic days families lived in tents and changed their dwellings frequently. But as a settled life developed, little villages grew up and, in a few places, towns and cities. Modern excavations have revealed the narrowness and dinginess of the living-quarters, even in the larger places. The houses were built of baked clay and consisted usually of but one large room, in which whole families lived; at night the animals were brought in as well. There were few windows and these were constructed only to let out the smoke from the hearth. Beds were known only by the wealthiest, and pillows were a luxury, the objects of prophetic sarcasm. Thatch on the floor was good enough for the common run of men. Even in the larger towns the streets were narrow and crooked and filled with dirt; the dogs were the only scavengers. The stench of a town was proverbial and was made tolerable only by habit. Wagons could make their way only through the larger streets, and pedestrians were often compelled to wade through mud and filth, pushing aside squalling children, sad-eyed cows and dogs, dead and alive. Wells were dirty and disease-breeding, and whole communities were often carried off once the plague began its dread invasion.

Yet men were tolerably happy. They knew no better life. When times were good and there was enough to feed all the hungry mouths, they could sing at their toil. Often there was wine to gladden the table. Until well into the days of the monarchy only the chronic grumblers envied the privileged few who could buy the luxuries from the travel-worn pedlars who brought strange and wondrous goods from far-off lands.

In Jerusalem and Bethel and the larger centres living conditions were not so primitive. Here trade and commerce quickened the domestic pulse, and educated men's tastes and desires. An important part of the population were clever artisans, bronze-workers, pottery-makers, smiths who produced tools, workers in precious metals, all of whom developed considerable skill in their crafts. For the construction of public buildings, reservoirs, ships, and the better homes a constant supply of labour was required, and though the workers were sometimes imported, natives were most frequently used. But the wealthiest and most important elements in the cities were the merchants who financed the caravans which went to other lands or traded with those that passed through Palestine. Jerusalem, which Ezekiel rightly called "the door of the nations," was admirably situated to profit from a thriving carrying-trade. Intercourse with other peoples, which increased after Solomon's day, brought comforts and luxuries into the country and profoundly altered economic and social life.

The climate and the general poverty compelled most men and women to dress very simply. But a natural liking for finery impelled those who could afford more elaborate outfits to deck themselves out. Bright colours — reds, purples, and scarlets, trimmed with gold and silver — were very fashionable. The girdle was especially important and was often adorned with the finest handiwork in gold and precious stones. Jewels and ornaments of all kinds were the heart's desire of every maiden, despite the protests of the Puritans. Armlets, bracelets, and tinkling anklets, ear-rings and finger-rings, and gorgeous crowns for the head were often all worn together by the Biblical coquette.

Men and women both wore their hair long and they prided themselves on anointing it with costly oils and cosmetics. Scent was also used by both sexes, and even the rustic beauty carried her bundle of myrrh in her bosom. The ladies were vain even in Biblical days and constantly consulted their mirrors of polished bronze. The fashionable beauties sometimes carried such small mirrors about their persons.

2. SOCIAL LIFE AND CUSTOMS

All of the ancient writers refer to the Hebrews as divided into clearly defined tribes. In the Priestly Code, which includes a brief history of Israel, twelve tribes are enumerated, with divisions and subdivisions into clans and families. All such accounts of systematic divisions are of course idealized; there was no well-arranged political organization. Tribes grew up out of a union of families and developed some common traditions, but during migrations or after wars they were often as quickly dissolved or were divided and separated, new ones growing up in their place. Jacob and Joseph early disappeared and Ephraim and Manasseh were formed out of them. Reuben was lost among the southern desert tribes soon after the conquest of Canaan, and Asher was swallowed up among the hardly Phœnicians.

Throughout early Hebrew history, however, the tribe, loosely united as it was, served as the centre of gravity. Families rallied about its standard; they cherished their common traditions, lived together, and fought together. In the days of the judges tribal pride was particularly strong and there were devastating civil wars among them to avenge affronts.

As the Hebrews became adjusted to their life in Palestine and developed towns and cities and forms of political organization, the tribes began to diminish in importance. New religious associations and traditions held in common, the growth of the monarchy, and the expansion of the country, all helped to create a national consciousness in which tribal loyalties were absorbed. The destruction of the State by the Babylonians and the subsequent exile completely obliterated the importance of the tribes and they now had value only for the historian or for families who wished to awe their neighbours with impressive genealogical tables.

Social life revolved about the father, who was the head of the family and the master of the house. As in Roman law, he had absolute power over his kin, even to the point of inflicting death, though this power was sharply limited by custom. Children could do nothing without his consent, and daughters who rebelled against marriage arrangements made for them could be forced to comply. Marriage in all Oriental countries was not an affair of personal affection, but of family convenience. The wife was merely the chattel of the husband. " Her desire is towards the husband, but he rules over her." The man could divorce his wife at will. His power over her was so sweeping that in the Deuteronomic Code, published in the seventh century b.c., it was necessary to place some limitations upon it. There were few legal restrictions on a man's sexual life. He could live with whom he wished so long as he violated no other man's property rights. Women, on the other hand, were strictly guarded and made to answer to another law. A wife whose infidelity was proved was stripped naked and publicly stoned to death.

The only class of women whom the law did not bind were the hetæras or the harlots, who in the earliest period were an important part of the social order, recruited mostly from foreigners. They could appear in public unveiled, could converse freely with men, without any restraint, and could conduct themselves otherwise as they wished. But they were a dishonourable class and their lives were filled with wretchedness. Though occasionally a Jephthah could spring from among them and make his mark in the world, usually they and their offspring were regarded as the dust in the street.

As in all Oriental countries, polygamy was a well-established institution, and though it died out among Jews some centuries before the Christian era, it was not legally forbidden until the edict of Rabbi Gershom was issued, well along in the Middle Ages. A man could have any number of wives so long as he supported them. But since it required wealth to maintain them, only kings and princes usually permitted themselves the luxury of a large harem. We are told that Gideon had seventy wives and we know the names of at least seven of David's wives. Solomon probably maintained the largest harem in Jewish history. These were exceptional cases, however, dictated largely by political exigencies. In practice few men had more than two women in the house, a wife and a concubine.

The purpose of marriage was procreation, and a woman's greatest sorrow was to be left childless. " Give me children or I die," Rachel cried, echoing the deepest desire of all of her people. Motherhood was the Jewish patent of nobility and crowned a wife with glory. The blessing of a bride was the wish for her to become "the mother of thousands of millions" (Genesis xxiv. 60). "Like arrows in a hero's hand, so are sons of youth," exclaimed the Psalmist. "Happy the man who has filled his quiver with them!" (Psalm cxxvii. 4-5.) So great was the horror of a barren stalk that the Deuteronomic Code established the principle of the levirate marriage, which compelled a man to marry his deceased brother's widow if she was left childless. Release from this obligation could be secured only if the brother went through the humiliating ceremony of Chalitza, during which the rejected woman spat upon him and cursed him for his callousness.[1] The story of Tamar and Judah in Biblical literature is another indication of the lengths to which a childless woman could go in her desire to perpetuate the name of her deceased husband (Genesis xxxviii).

Children, thus eagerly sought, were usually in the hands of their mothers until they were able to bear the burden of work. There were no schools, and all that the young people learned they assimilated at home or gleaned from their limited contact with life. Early in their teens they were already at work in the fields or at the anvil, helping to meet the many needs of the household. Sons were consequently more desired than daughters and they were favoured in every relationship, particularly in the matter of inheritance. Until the children passed out of the house and set up homes of their own, they were completely subordinate, and death could be meted out to those who crossed or dishonoured their parents.

Slavery was also an integral part of the social system. There is no way to estimate accurately the number of slaves in Biblical Palestine, but they could not have totalled less than twenty per cent of the population. They were recruited from among conquered peoples and those who had fallen into debt or crime. Hebrew masters were obliged to emancipate their Hebrew slaves at the end of six years unless the slaves themselves wished to remain. The ears of voluntary slaves were bored with an awl and they remained the property of their masters until the jubilee year.

The status of the ancient slave differed vastly from the status of the modern slave. He became a part of the family and often rose high in the household. There were brutal and despotic masters, of course, who treated their slaves with less indulgence than they treated their beasts of burden; but the ancient teachings urged kindness upon them, and public opinion brought pressure into the same direction. Even when their consciences were silent, the desire to save their property from injury restrained them from undue acts of cruelty. Biblical literature

---

[1] "Then shall his brother's wife come unto him in the presence of the elders and loose his sandal from off his foot and spit in his face, and shall answer and say: 'So shall it be done unto that man that will not build up his brother's house.' And his name shall be called in Israel: the house of him that hath his sandal loosed." Deuteronomy xxv. 9-10.

contains a number of charming stories of slaves who were counted as a master's own kin in the household. Eleazar was given the important commission of seeking a wife for Isaac, his master's son, and there are numerous instances of slaves who became the heirs to their master's fortunes. A childless wife often gave her handmaiden to the husband so that the children of the union could be counted as her own. After Bilhah had given birth to a son by Jacob, Rachel, her mistress, exclaimed: "God has given me my rights, and has also heard my voice and has given me a son." "Therefore she called his name Dan" (Genesis xxx. 6).

In the earlier desert days justice was based upon the simple principle of *lex talionis,* common to all primitive peoples. When a man was killed or injured, the act was avenged by his own people on the kin of the criminal. When damages were to be extorted, they were taken from property belonging to any who were allied to the guilty. "If any mischief follow, then thou shalt give life for life, eye for eye, tooth for tooth, hand for hand, foot for foot, burning for burning, wound for wound, stripe for stripe" (Exodus xxi. 23–5).

As the Hebrews progressed in civilization, they submitted to the saner and more reasonable laws ascribed to Moses. A fine spirit of humanitarianism pervaded the venerable code. It aimed to protect the weak and the defenceless, the widow and the orphan, the stranger and the slave. It established principles to govern social relationships which very perceptibly raised the tone of Hebrew life. A wide latitude was given to the judges in their application and administration, and this permitted them to interpret and elaborate the laws until they developed into a mighty code of common law, influential through all Jewish history.

Much that was primitive of course remained. Thus, in cases where there were witnesses, their testimony was decisive, but if there were no witnesses, Providence was often called in. When a woman was accused of adultery, the priest compelled her to submit to divine tests to prove her innocence. Holy water was placed in a vessel, and after incantations had been pronounced, she drank. If there were no ill effects, she was declared innocent; but if her body swelled and her thigh rotted, she was adjudged guilty and punished. Perhaps the test was based upon good psychology; often the fear of the consequences drove the guilty woman to confession. But the test was one of many survivals of a primitive inheritance.

It was to be expected that the life of the early Hebrews should be largely influenced by their environment. The hot desert blood in their veins often called to them, and they learned from their neighbours not only that which was admirable, but also that which was despicable. In times of peace the sober traditional teachings and the prophetic words helped to restrain them. In times of war they were the helpless slaves of their passions, as relentless as those who went against them.

All peoples were cruel, and enemies expected no quarter. Perhaps the famous boast of the Assyrian king Assur-nazir-pal was extreme: "Many prisoners I burnt to death; many I buried alive; I cut off the hands and arms of some, the noses and ears of others, and I gouged out the eyes of many." But scattered through the books of the Bible are horrible tales, exultantly recited by the chroniclers, which demonstrate all too clearly that cruelty was not an Assyrian monopoly. The Hebrews also destroyed cities and sowed them with salt; they choked up wells and cut down trees and put men, women, and children to the sword.

Despite the reforms introduced by the prophets and the lawgivers, life was harsh in Biblical days. Nature and men conspired to endanger the humble worker's security. Civilization was, after all, only a thin veneer, and the animal in man constantly escaped. There was still a long road to travel before other inspired teachers and seers arose and by precept and example helped to educate the hearts of men and to emancipate their minds.

CHAPTER NINE

THE MEETING OF HELLENISM AND HEBRAISM

FOR more than a century after the rebuilding of the Temple the Jews lived quietly by the principles of the Mosaic law. Persian dominance was not oppressive and each people within the empire pursued its ends without let or hindrance. Imperial tolerance enabled priests and scribes to regulate the minutest acts by religious rites and to make the Temple the centre of existence. Gradually the Jewish state became a theocracy, with priests and law supreme.

The whole development seemed providential, for at the close of the long period of discipline the integrity of Jewish life was suddenly menaced by the most serious danger which it had ever faced. With the conquest of Europe and Asia by Alexander the Great and Hellenism a new, alluring way of life was placed before the ancient world. Every people, great and small, sooner or later succumbed, except the stubborn little folk of Palestine, who were also sorely tempted to follow the popular gods of the forum and the market place. For four centuries, until the destruction of the State, the nationalists waged a life-and-death struggle, first against the Greeks themselves and then against the Romans, who assimilated Greek culture. In the end, though Jewish thought was unmistakably influenced by the long contact with Hellenism and by the struggle against it, Judaism survived distinct and more militant than ever.

I. THE RISE OF HELLENISM

Alexander was one of history's spoiled favourites. He had everything that a mighty king could desire, high physical courage, a fervid imagination, limitless power, unparalleled opportunity, loyal followers. He inherited from his father an invincible army and a burning desire to use it for the subjugation of the world. No obstacle long blocked him. Wherever he led his legions, they were victorious. He conquered the teeming Greek world and invaded the wild country beyond the Danube. In 334 B.C. he burst into Asia, ready to contest with the Persians the supremacy of the East. Within a year he had put the mighty Darius to flight at Issus and had taken over Asia Minor. Next year he was in Egypt inquiring from the god Ammon Ra whether a common mortal like Philip could indeed have been his father. Thence he marched on through Mesopotamia, through Assyria, to the very borders of India, where mothers still frighten their babes with the threat that the dread Iskander will take them if they do not behave! When he died, in his thirty-third year, worn out by toil and dissipation, he was master of the most impressive empire which the ancient world had known.

Wherever Alexander went, he founded cities, peopling them with Greek colonists and beautifying them with Greek works of art. Through them he conquered civilizations as well as peoples. It is difficult to tell, of course, whether this policy was dictated by the desire to disseminate Greek culture or whether it was the product of his military plans. Certainly the frivolities and eccentricities which marked his career, his almost childish sacrifice of principle to indulgence, make one wonder whether his primary interest was to bring the blessings of Hellenism to the barbarian world; whether, indeed, the genius of " Macedonia's madman" has not been much overrated. It has been often suggested that he was not a cause, but merely a part, of the spread of Hellenism. Historians will probably never be unanimous in their judgment of Alexander's motives, but they cannot quarrel over the enormous consequences of his actions. The seeds of Hellenism which he planted took root everywhere and even the chaos which followed his death did not stultify their development.

Alexander had trained no successors to follow him, nor had he made any plans for the future, and when he succumbed to the effects of a night of carousal, in 323, his vast empire fell apart. The struggle of his generals to possess themselves of the fragments continued for decades and brought desolation to every province over which their armies marched and countermarched. " His servants bare rule, every one in his place . . ." writes the author of Maccabees, " and evils were multiplied on the earth" (1 Maccabees xiv. 5). Ultimately a few empires emerged from the chaos of the wars of succession. The debonair Ptolemy, Alexander's most trusted lieutenant, succeeded in making himself master of Egypt and established a dynasty which continued unbroken until the days of Cæsar. The wily Seleucus after more than fifty years of constant combat became the founder of an empire in Asia Minor extending north to Armenia and east to Mesopotamia.

Judah and the petty tribes of Palestine and Syria stood between the two rivals, and, as the caravan routes to India and Arabia ran through their territory, it was bitterly contested. Josephus compares Judah in this period with a ship in a storm, smitten by waves on either side. The political history of the country, as so often before and after, depended almost exclusively upon the policies of its powerful neighbours. The territory passed from one to another; no one knew to whom tribute would be due on the morrow. Judah itself suffered little, for Jerusalem was on the heights, and most of the military marches were confined to the Philistine coast or the plains of Galilee. It was a relief, however, when the Seleucid dynasty, in 198 B.C., finally established its supremacy in Palestine, and Egyptian legions no longer troubled its peace.

The details of the diplomacy of the period are of little importance. The

Jews were accustomed to the frequent change of suzerains, and so long as they were permitted to live in peace, they were little troubled whether the house of Ptolemy or the house of Seleucus controlled the country. But Hellenism, throughout the long wars and after, made mighty inroads in Palestine. The country was completely circled by Greek cities and exposed to their influence everywhere. Sacrifices to the Greek gods were held daily in the Philistine cities on the west coast and in the temples on the Nile, where once the Egyptian gods had ruled. Greek fashions, Greek speech, Greek buildings, and Greek sports were as common in the hamlets east of the Jordan as in the great centres of population in Syria. Judah could not long remain unaffected, and the more daring of the younger generation early began to adapt themselves to the new influences. The long conflict began. Could Judaism survive if Hellenism became dominant in the civilization of the country? Or were the two spirits mutually exclusive and a menace to each other?

The Hebraic and the Hellenic views of life have been often contrasted. The Hebrew stressed reliance upon an omnipotent God and conformity to a divinely sanctioned moral law; he was essentially serious, restrained, willing to recognize his finite limitations. To seek God was the ultimate wisdom, to follow His precepts the ultimate virtue. The Greek accepted no revelation as ultimate; he strove to penetrate to the core of his conceptions, analysing the very bases of his knowledge. He was blessed with a delicate, subtle reason and with a keen desire to use it, to probe with it, to open the very heart of reality. The Hebrew was inclined to mysticism; he accepted the moral law and would not go beyond it. The Greek bowed to no law but that of complete self-expression. He loved beauty and art, the outdoor life, and every aspect of nature which appealed to his æsthetic sensibilities. Where the Hebrew asked: " What must I do? " the Greek asked: " Why must I do it? " Matthew Arnold has put the difference between the two spirits in a series of famous epigrams. The uppermost idea with the Greek was to see things as they really are; the uppermost idea with the Hebrew was conduct and obedience. The Hebrew believed in the beauty of holiness, the Greek believed in the holiness of beauty.

The two points of view could not very well be reconciled in an individual. One could not accept a revealed law as ultimate, and yet honestly question the very foundations of life; or submit to a moral law and yet exploit one's capacities without restraint. But was it not possible for both spirits to be present in a whole people, residing in individuals who were splendid examples of each? National life would indeed be ideally rounded out if it developed at once the burning zeal for social righteousness of an Amos or an Isaiah, and the serene wisdom of a Socrates or a Plato, the moral fervour of a Jeremiah and the artistic genius of a Praxiteles.

Unfortunately, the best in the Greek spirit did not meet the best in the Hebrew spirit. The splendid achievements of the philosophers and the artists, their search for truth and beauty, their mellowed humanistic approach, did not come to the East in the wagons of the Greek conquerors. There came instead a degraded imitation of Hellenism, externals with the glowing heart burnt out, a crude paganism, a callousness for the common weal, a cheap sophistry, a cynicism easily undermining old conceptions and older loyalties, but substituting nothing constructive in their place. Too often the gymnasium and the amphitheatre meant lewdness and licentiousness; the search for intellectual clarity meant dishonest banter and trickiness; the pursuit of the beautiful meant moral irresponsibility. And these empty trappings of a wondrous culture enslaved the East. For who could withstand the splendid examples of the new spirit, men of exuberant energy and physical strength, with quick, biting tongues, thrilling with their irreverence and their intellectual daring?

In Judah, coming after a long period of priestly sternness and puritanic piety, the Greek ideals wrought havoc. At first only a few more daring souls stepped out of the established conventions. But as their numbers grew, the older generations stook back aghast. The youth of the land were aping names and manners; they were shamelessly displaying their nudeness in the Greek palæstra. More too. They were assimilating the whole Greek *Weltanschauung*. They were even attacking the laws and customs in which they were reared This was no mere passing fad, to be treated indulgently.

The masses were, as usual, not the decisive elements in the conflict. They were fuddled, bewildered, and inarticulate. They travelled in the beaten path, perhaps vaguely wondering where the quarrel lay. But the two extreme factions, the *Hasidim* and the *Letzim,* Puritans and Hellenists, filled the synagogues and the market places with their din as they sought to discredit each other.

Soon Judah was rent by the quarrels of two factions who could not understand each other. Almost every family found itself divided. What was earnest to one group was jest to the other; what was pleasure to one was torment to the other; and neither side gave quarter. Those who loved the Greek ways found Judaism crude and soul-repressing. They looked upon the sacerdotalists as fools if sincere, and as hypocrites if not ready with answers. The stern nationalists, on the other hand, alarmed by the assaults on their mode of life, drew no distinctions in judging the alien culture. Hating lasciviousness, they decried all that was beautiful in Greek art; hating sophistry and irreverence, they decried all that the philosophers taught. There could be no compromise.

Victory, quite naturally, as usual seemed to go at first to the Hellenizers. They gathered to them the youth of all classes, the aristocracy, and even some of the priests. Ambitious men discovered that the way to advancement, at least socially, lay in living like Greek gentlemen. By the beginning of the second century the old Judaism was in serious danger of dissolution, threatened with death, not by the mellowed wisdom of ancient Hellas, but by the bastard culture which called itself an offspring. Perhaps Judaism would have been quietly swallowed up as so many other civilizations had been; but at the dramatic moment history worked one of its miracles. Suddenly the Hellenizers were thoroughly discredited in a reaction which shifted the whole balance of the Near East, a reaction brought about by the harshness and stupidity of a new Syrian monarch who usurped the throne in 175 B.C.

2. THE MACCABEAN REVOLT

Antiochus IV, who surnamed himself Epiphanes (the God made manifest) was the unconscious saviour of the Jewish faith. He was a despot of immense ability and energy, a sincere lover of Hellenism, vitally interested in its dissemination. Partly to indulge his vanity, but partly also to satisfy his tastes, he encouraged art and building-enterprises, and by his patronage Antioch became one of the most brilliant centres of the ancient world. All of the king's abilities, however, could not repress the vein of irresponsibility and restlessness which made him a slave to his whims. At times his foolish excesses verged on madness; the wits of the time, punning on his name, called him Epimanes (the mad). The Jewish apocryphal writers, embittered by his persecution of their own kin, found no good in him at all and portrayed him as an insane bigot, hard of heart, fashioned by pride and fraud.

On his accession the little Jewish state was in a turmoil because of rivalries for the lucrative priestly offices. One clever blackguard, Jason, leading Antiochus to believe that a Hellenizing program would be strenuously urged by him, was awarded the high priesthood, only to have it snatched from him by a greater blackguard, Menelaus, who made more lavish promises and paid a larger bribe. While these rascals ruled the country, the pietists had no peace. Their sanctuary became a Greek temple; Yahweh was identified with Zeus, and in every community sacrifices were offered to the hated Greek deities. For a few years the outraged populace submitted in despair, hating the blasphemers, but offering no active resistance. Then word came to Jerusalem that Antiochus, while battling against the Egyptians, had been killed. A furious reaction at once swept the city. The apostate priests and the sychophants who hung on them were massacred and all the filth which they had brought into the Temple was cast out. For a moment the old regime was in control. Only for a moment. The rumour which precipitated the riot was false. Antiochus was very much alive, and on his return from Egypt, disgruntled by his defeats and maddened by the stiff-neckedness of the Jews, he turned upon those who had dared to flout his authority. Led by the vile Menelaus, he looted the Temple and took away whatever of value remained in it. The survivors of the mob's anger were restored to their places. Then Antiochus began a systematic persecution of those who would not be Hellenized.

He issued an edict prohibiting, on pain of death, further observance of Jewish practices and then added insult to injury by compelling loyalty to the pagan abominations which he substituted. To enforce the edict twenty-two thousand soldiers were sent into the country, most of whom were quartered in the citadel of Akra, overlooking the Temple. These faithfully carried out their master's instructions. They dismantled the Temple, tore down homes, burnt, pillaged, looted, and wherever they met with opposition, killed without mercy. Hundreds of women and children were sold into slavery.

It was in this period of darkness that the Book of Daniel was written. It sought to show how Israel had been successively plagued by powerful enemies — Babylonians, Medes, Persians — but had neither yielded nor lost hope. This new persecution by the Syrians was the last trial which God had in store for His people. In God's own time this trial too would end and all would be well again. Even as Daniel had passed through the fires of the furnace unscathed, so too would those who had retained their faith. The enemy would soon be discomfited.

Persecution bred a new spirit and reunited the quarrelling factions among the Jews. Even those who had dabbled in the Hellenistic ways were frightened by the extremes to which the Syrians had gone. The incidents of worship were no longer the issue; Judaism itself was at stake. Only for a while longer did the nation submit, dumbly mourning its heroic martyrs. At last " horns grew upon the lambs," the Book of Enoch suggests. As Antiochus' hirelings came blustering through the village of Modin, north of Jerusalem, an aged priest, Mattathias, rose to defy them. He slew a craven Jew who came forward to sacrifice upon a pagan altar, and also the officer who stood by to superintend the ceremony. Then, with five stalwart sons, the Maccabees, he escaped to the mountains, there to raise the standard of revolt. Judah was at war with the invincible Syrian empire.

A motley crew, drawn from every walk of life, joined the rebels, all determined to resist to the end the excesses of the pagans. Jerusalem was as amazed as Antioch. Resistance seemed suicidal. Judas, who became captain of the little band on the death of his father, Mattathias, led men untrained, unequipped, unsupported — men who had learned only to obey. Opposed to him were the best soldiers of the East, well clad, well armed, led by generals who had won fame on fields of international importance. Judah was not even united in its resistance. Renegade Jews led on the oppressors and pointed out the hidden nooks and corners which guerrilla bands could use.

Fortunately the international situation favoured the Maccabean insurgents. Antiochus was harassed by uprisings far to the east and could not concentrate his attacks. "He endeavoured to root out the Jewish superstition, but was hindered by a Parthian war from reforming the vilest of people," writes the unfriendly Tacitus (*Hist.* V. 8). Meantime the troops of Judas fought like supermen. So Cromwell's Ironsides must have fought as they faced the Stuart legions, and the inflamed soldiers of Mohammed as they swept across three continents for Allah and his Prophet. Judas won four important battles in rapid succession and Antiochus himself could not bring victory to his forces.

Near the Maccabean home in Modin was the narrow pass of Emmaus guarding the ascent from the coastal plains into the hills. Here, a thousand years before, according to the well-loved tradition, Joshua had put the Amorites to flight. Here, thirteen hundred years later, Richard the Lion Hearted cut his way through the Moslem forces. Here in our own day General Allenby advanced on his way to the Holy City. And here, as the Greeks came up the famous pass, Judas fell upon them and sent their whole camp flying for life towards the coast.

Before the next battle, at Mizpah, the Syrian general was so confident of victory that he brought merchants with him to buy the captured Jewish slaves, whose prices were already posted in neighbouring cities! Judas triumphed decisively enough to take control of the Temple. He destroyed its pagan altars and ornaments, cleansed it thoroughly, and then rededicated it to the God of Israel amid the joyous acclaims of his people. The anniversary of the miraculous restoration is still celebrated in every Jewish home as the Festival of Rededication (Hanukah).

Flushed by his astonishing victories, Judas now cleared the circle of his lesser enemies. He pushed back the Idumæans and the Ammonites and controlled a kingdom almost as large as David's. But neither these victories nor those which he had gained over the Syrians brought liberation. The warfare against Antiochus continued for years. Even after the king's death, in 163 B.C., the Syrian citadel of Akra still towered menacingly in the very heart of Jerusalem. Lysias came down with a great host of infantry and cavalry and, reinforced with a terrifying cavalcade of elephants, determined to end the stubborn resistance of the Jews. One of the Maccabean brothers sacrificed himself to kill the Syrian general, but Judas was badly beaten and compelled to retreat. All would have been ended now if foreign complications had not again providentially recalled the Syrians. When hostilities were resumed, Judas was killed at Beth-horan, and his brother Jonathan was assassinated. But always some new enemy prevented the Syrians from stamping out the revolt completely. At length, in 142 B.C., Simon, the last of the five Maccabean brothers, was granted complete remission from tribute and recognized as the high priest and leader of Judah. The little Jewish state after centuries of servitude was again independent.

It was a far cry from the days of the unhappy Zedekiah and the prophet Jeremiah. Many tears had since been shed, much blood had been spilled. But the faith of Israel had been deepened by suffering and enriched by contact with new civilizations. There was an opportunity now to profit by the experiences of the past, to live on a different plane, to follow in paths different from those which inevitably brought other Oriental states to quick decay and ruin. By an astonishing combination of courage and luck Judah had won another chance to play a national role. Would she live up to her opportunity? Would she justify the sacrifices of those who had died that the nation and its faith might live?

3. THE DECLINE OF THE MACCABEAN STATE

The first years of independent life were characterized by a creditable political and spiritual virility. Simon, the ablest of the Hasmonæans, proved an admirable ruler for a reconstruction period. Although he combined civil and military leadership with the high priestly office and possessed all of the substance of power, he refrained from calling himself king. He was too much interested in strengthening the foundations of the resuscitated State to be concerned about the trappings of power. After several fruitless attempts he captured the citadel of Akra and freed his people from the menace of a foreign garrison in their midst. He took control of Gazara and Joppa on the coast and through these ports established a thriving commerce between Judah and foreign lands. He negotiated a treaty with Rome which guaranteed him the friendship of the expanding Mediterranean state. He even struck Jewish coins for the first time in Jewish history. Men became proud of their Judaism and, exulting in their strength, sought to spread the principles of the Holy Writ. This was one of the rare proselytizing periods in Jewish history. It is small wonder that during Simon's reign some of the most exuberant psalms were written, throbbing with the joy of life; that the author of the Book of Maccabees bubbles over with enthusiasm. " The Jews," he writes, " tilled the land in peace, and the land gave her increase, and the trees of the plains their fruit. The old men sat in the streets, they talked together of the common good, and the young men put on glorious and fine apparel. . . . Simon strengthened all the distressed of his people."

Material prosperity continued under John Hyrcanus, who succeeded to the headship of the State when Simon, his father, was treacherously assassinated. Perhaps there was now too much prosperity; Hyrcanus' head was turned by ambitions to play a role in the eastern Mediterranean world. He created a mercenary army, with which he proceeded to carve out an empire. He subjugated the Samaritans and destroyed their temple. He gave Israel's ancient enemies, the Edomites, the alternative of exile or conversion to Judaism. It was a sorry commentary upon the perverseness of human nature that Hyrcanus was already spreading his faith by the point of the sword, although he was only one generation removed from those who had poured out life and fortune for religious freedom. His son Aristobulus continued and improved upon his example. He pushed his conquests up through Galilee and ultimately crowned himself king. He reintroduced the dreadful Oriental custom of destroying the members of his family who could become a threat to the security of his throne.

Meantime a formidable party had developed that vigorously opposed the policy of the rulers and their abandonment of Hasmonæan idealism. In recent years a whole literature has grown up about this influential group, the Pharisees, written primarily to correct the traditional view that they were rigid obscurantists who opposed all change, who adhered to the letter of the law while they violated its spirit, and who hampered the progress of Jewish life. In the new exposition they are shown to be genuine liberals, aiming to reinterpret the law to fit new conditions, tolerant, sunny spirits, who, far from stultifying Judaism, helped each generation to give it renewed vitality.

But one must not press this view too far. The Pharisees were indeed interpreters of the law and helped to make it more flexible. But they changed and elaborated it precisely because they wished to retain it as the fundamental law of life. The basic principles remained unchallenged despite the most ingenious modifications. In truth, Pharisaic liberalism arose out of their conservatism.

This fact makes clearer the uncompromising political attitude of the Pharisees. While their opponents, the Sadducees, supported the royal policy of imperialism, they stood sternly opposed to it. They felt instinctively that it must mean the break-down of their faith, the introduction of the paganism against which the Hasmonæans had fought so long and so bitterly.

Their opposition reached the point of civil war in the reign of Alexander Jannæus, who succeeded his brother Aristobulus. Jannæus had a genius for alienating his people. He drove every honest citizen into opposition and before he drank himself to death, in 78 B.C., he succeeded in thoroughly exhausting the country. During the Feast of Tabernacles early in his reign he boldly departed from the usual ritual, and the people pelted him with citrons. He retaliated by inaugurating a persecution in which nearly six thousand Pharisees lost their lives. Though his own house was not in order, he continued his wars of aggression on surrounding peoples. There was a limit to endurance, however. When he returned from a futile war against some of the Arab desert tribes, he found that nearly the whole nation had risen behind him.

For six years the civil strife continued. Jannæus was merciless when opposed. At one time eight hundred rebels who had held a fortress against him were crucified and the throats of their wives and children were cut before their dying eyes. Eight thousand others were driven into Egyptian exile. Even in the worst days of the Israelite monarchy there had been no such bloody bickering.

After the death of Jannæus his wife, Alexandra, who succeeded to the throne, reversed his policy and favoured the Pharisees. For a moment there was peace in Judah. The exiles returned, foreign wars ceased, and the old faith was practised without hindrance. But the Pharisees had been too sorely outraged to allow their enemies to escape without punishment. Firm in their belief that their rancour was virtue, they instituted a series of persecutions and judicial murders which opened every old wound.

The sides now grouped themselves about the two sons of Alexandra, Hyrcanus II and Aristobulus, who disputed the succession when their mother died, in 69 B.C. The next few years were again filled with intrigue and fighting, treachery and assassination. In one period Jerusalem was beleaguered for weeks, and as the Passover approached, the inhabitants begged the besiegers to allow cattle for the sacrificial offerings to be brought into the city. They passed money through an opening in the wall only to discover that their brethren were taunting them. There were no Passover sacrifices that year in the Holy City. War was war even between Jews. Antiochus would have rested easier in his grave could he have seen the two hostile camps thus struggling for power and revenge under the leadership of scions of the Maccabean house in the shadow of the Temple.

In this extremity one of the ambitious captains of Rome swooped down upon Judæa. The redoubtable Pompey was creating an empire in the East for the new mistress of the Mediterranean and looked greedily upon the fortresses of south-western Asia. Both warring factions in Judæa appealed to him in 64 B.C. to judge between them, and after a show of deliberation he supported Aristobulus and bade his rival begone. He sent to Rome the magnificent golden vine which the grateful Aristobulus sent him as a present.

Next year the Pharisees begged Pompey to abolish the kingship altogether, take control of the country, and remove the curse of dynastic war. Pompey acted with alacrity and sent his legions to take over the Holy City. It was not a simple task, even for the conqueror of Marius and Cinna. The infuriated followers of Aristobulus struggled heroically against his might. For three months they held the Temple site and their desperate defence would have kept them longer unbeaten were it not that Pompey pushed the fighting on the sabbath, when the Jews refused to defend themselves. When the Romans carried the last barrier on a sabbath-day, they found the defenders standing calmly by, praying, the priests at the altars pouring out libations. Few resisted in the carnage that followed. Nearly twelve thousand Jews perished as the independence of Judah came abruptly to an end.

Freedom was again crushed out because the Jews had not learned how to use it. The selfishness of the ruling houses and the strife of political and religious factions exhausted the strength of the State. A curse seemed to lie on the Jews which prevented them from reaching the highest levels of moral power except when they were hammered and beaten by oppression.

4. JEWISH COMMUNITIES OUTSIDE OF PALESTINE

Jewish life in these eventful centuries of Greek and Roman supremacy was not confined to Palestine. In every thriving centre of the ancient world, to the furthermost corners of Africa and Asia, Jewish communities had evolved, fed by enterprising merchants and wandering adventurers, by exiles and emancipated slaves. Though they formed a tiny minority in the heart of a vigorous pagan world, they quickly adapted themselves to their new environment and rose to wealth and influence. In Mesopotamia the Jews became powerful enough to contribute materially to the defeat of the Roman emperor Trajan when he sought conquests in the valley. The strength of the Jewish population of northern Syria may be gauged from the fact that in the later Roman wars eighteen thousand Jews are said to have perished in Damascus alone.

The most important Jewish communities of the pre-Diaspora were centred in Egypt. Philo estimates that nearly a quarter of a million were scattered up and down the Nile valley in his own day. In Alexandria, which had become the leading city of the world and boasted a population of more than a million, two of its five sections were almost exclusively Jewish. Although they were heartily detested by their Greek fellow-citizens, who often assailed them, the Jews held leading positions in the community and were well treated by their imperial masters.

The far-flung Jewish communities, despite the alien influences which surrounded them, retained their affection and reverence for the Holy Land. The sense of unity, built up by centuries of religious enthusiasm, could not be easily effaced. Jews in every corner of the earth looked upon the Temple as their religious centre in much the same way as Catholics everywhere regard the Vatican. They paid the Temple tax, respected the decisions and edicts of the Sanhedrin, and whenever possible made pilgrimages to Palestine, bearing with them very generous gifts.

This extraordinary compactness, preserved decade by decade in a day of easy assimilation, often drew down upon the Jews the reproach of exclusiveness. The Greek grammarian and commentator on Homer, Apion, was never tired of reiterating this charge against the Jews, and, in A.D. 38, he headed a delegation of Alexandrians to complain to the Roman emperor, Caligula, that the Jews were haters of mankind. An earlier emperor knew Apion for a *cymbalum mundi* — a world drum — filling the air with empty sound. But there were others more willing to listen to calumnies, and Apion's charges were widely believed. "Whereas today," shrewdly remarks a modern expositor of Hellenism, "the charge is made that the Jews are cosmopolitan in a national society, then the current complaint was that they were national in a cosmopolitan society." [1]

Yet it was impossible for the Jews of the Diaspora to escape being profoundly affected by the civilization of their adopted lands. Greek became their common speech. Greek ideas and customs penetrated into their lives. Even Hebrew thoughts and religious conceptions came to the younger generation through the medium of Greek translations.

Many Jews, unable or unwilling to preserve a continuous nonconformity,

[1] Bentwich: *Hellenism*, p. 133.

succumbed and were lost to Judaism. But the majority, though Greek in speech and manners, retained the essentials of their heritage. They were proud of their faith and conscious of its superiority to the decaying religions of the pagan world. Their attitude was made articulate in a vigorous Hebraic-Hellenistic literature, which became increasingly important through the second and first centuries B.C. Most of what was written was intended to expound the essentials of the Hebrew faith to the Jews themselves, but some of the new literature had a distinct missionary object. It sought to establish the superiority of the Jewish beliefs, to show how much that was apparently original in the pagan classics was taken from Hebrew sources.

Many writers, anxious to gain acceptance for their views, adopted the old expedient of attributing them to venerable names of the past. Moses, Solomon, and the prophets again became authors of a variety of concepts, ranging from the uniqueness of God to the exact time of the end of the world. Nor were the classic Greek writers left in peace. Oracles were suddenly discovered purporting to come from them. Homer and Sophocles, Plato and Aristotle, and innumerable other divine pagans were found extolling the virtues of a moral code suspiciously Hebraic in spirit. There is extant a fragment of a religious epic called *Exodus* which illustrates how the methods of the Greek drama were utilized to explain the essentials of Judaism to the pagan world. The hands were the hands of Esau, but the voice was the voice of Jacob.

One of the most vital literary and religious influences on Jew and pagan alike was the translation into Greek of the Pentateuch — a work known as the Septuagint. It was probably compiled late in the third century B.C., and the other books of the Testament were gradually added. By the first century B.C. legends had grown up about the translation, calculated to increase pagan respect for Hebrew learning. A letter was discovered from one Aristeas which described in great detail how Ptolemy II, the Egyptian king, anxious to secure a copy of the Torah for his unexcelled Alexandrian library, imported seventy-two scholars from Palestine to make a translation. The sages were isolated on the island of Pharos and laboured in separate rooms for seventy-two days, and when their manuscripts were compared, it was found that their seventy-two versions were miraculously identical. It was quite plain that the divine spirit rested on the enterprise.[1]

The legends were but another proof of the far-reaching influence of the Septuagint. The translation made the Scriptures accessible to the vast numbers of Jews living outside of Palestine. It introduced Hebrew learning to the Hellenistic world. It was consequently a mighty agent in the fusion of the Hebraic and the Hellenic strains which modified the creative spirit of subsequent generations. " Like the opening of the Suez Canal it let the waters of the

---

[1] The spuriousness of the letter was established in 1684 by Humphrey Hody, Regius Professor of Greek in Oxford.

East mingle with those of the West, bearing with them many a freight of precious merchandise."

There was another result of the famous translation, however, which compelled the rabbis to frown upon the whole work. The authors often altered the original to fit in with their advanced ideas. They consciously substituted expressions for the frequent anthropomorphisms of the Bible and they excluded altogether stories which were likely to discredit Judaism in the Greek world. God spoke to Moses not face to face, but in a vision; the rather indecorous tale of Tamar and Judah was omitted. Such methods alienated the conservative groups who insisted that every part of the Bible was holy and was not to be tampered with. The rift became extremely important in the early Christian centuries, when the conservatives were assailed on every side.

The most important representative of Hellenistic Judaism was Philo Judæus, who was born in Alexandria about the first or second decade B.C. Little is definitely known of his life, but his voluminous writings give a fairly full account of his views. Philo loved the old Greek classics, particularly Plato, who was to him "most holy." In style, in feeling, in outlook, he was completely Greek. Yet he was bound by blood and temperament to Jewish tradition and he devoted his life to the task of squaring it with his beloved Hellenism.

As Maimonides later built upon Aristotle, so Philo built upon Plato. The Scriptures were for him the final authority, but by skilful exegesis and dialectic he found in the Scriptures all that his Greek masters had taught. Philo did not begin the school which drew allegorical meanings from antiquated Biblical phrases, but he was its most influential representative. Through his interpretations he was able, without scrapping anything, to eliminate the crudeness and primitiveness of concepts developed centuries before, enriching them with new meaning.

In still another way Philo's work was of enduring importance. His concept of God, combining in curious fashion Platonic idealism and Hebrew monotheism, baffled as much as it edified many succeeding generations. To Philo God was without limitation either in time or in space and therefore was bare of qualities which could limit Him. None could say *what* He is, only *that* He is. It was necessary, however, to relate the ineffable Being with the corporeal world, and Philo built up a theory of intermediaries. The chief instrument of God's activity was the Word, the Logos. Through the Word the world was created and all living forms. Exactly what the Word was is lost in a maze of words. Sometimes it was associated with the sum of the Platonic ideas — sometimes it was mystically termed the first-born son of God. In one passage Philo suggested that the Logos was begotten by God of the truly virgin Wisdom. Perhaps Philo himself was groping. But the idea of intermediary potencies profoundly influenced the theology of early Christianity.

As in the matter of the Septuagint, many of the rabbis decried the work of

Philo. His rationalizations and his allegories were dangerous, for often, in stressing the inner spirit of the laws, the actual practice was overlooked. And his Logos could easily undermine the cardinal principle of Judaism, a pure, unadulterated monotheism. The rabbis consequently turned from Philo, and in the centuries following his death he was much better known among Greek and Christian philosophers than among Jews. But in the Middle Ages he again became a vital Jewish influence, the patron saint of the more understanding Cabalist.

Enough has been said of Jewish literary activity to demonstrate the immense vitality of Judaism in the centuries preceding the triumph of Christianity. Its sages and interpreters were no longer on the defensive. They sought to proselytize, to carry the message of their faith to the jaded world in which they lived.

The conditions were highly favourable. The old paganism, especially in the Near East, was decaying, and sensitive minds were repelled by it. The clear-cut monotheism and the rational practices of the Hebrews, expounded with charm by the Hellenized Jewish writers, made a deep impression. There were great numbers of converts, if not officially to Judaism, at least to Jewish practices and ideals. Sabbath lights gleamed through the darkness from many cultured Roman homes. The converts, referred to in the Acts as " God-fearing Greeks," were welcomed by the scattered Jewish communities and freely admitted to the services of the synagogue.

Seneca remarked that Jewish customs were everywhere predominant and bitterly lamented that the virile Roman conquerors were being vanquished by the humble conquered! In 59 B.C., when Cicero defended the proconsul Flaccus, who had, among other things, embezzled money intended for the Temple in Jerusalem, the great orator pretended that he feared to speak above a whisper lest he arouse the enmity of the numerous Jews who were present. It was among those whose spirits were leavened by Jewish concepts that the early Christians made their first converts.

CHAPTER TEN

THE END OF THE JEWISH STATE

I. THE HOUSE OF HEROD

For a quarter of a century after Rome assumed control of Judæa, the little State was in a turmoil. It is difficult and of little profit to follow its complicated and distressing politics. The people suffered not only from the insensate feuds of the Hasmonæan princes, but also from the civil strife of their Roman masters, during which Palestine changed hands four times. For twenty years the Roman civil war raged, from the time that Cæsar crossed the Rubicon until the suicide of Antony, in 30 B.C. There were successive wars between Pompey and Cæsar, Antony and Cassius, Octavian and Antony; and though the Jews abstained from becoming partisans, it was inevitable that the strife should affect them disastrously. When Crassus, of the second triumvirate, became proconsul of Syria, he plundered the Temple, and in the revolt which followed, he sold thirty thousand Jews into slavery. Not the least tragic element in the situation was the fact that Jewish pretenders had golden opportunities to win temporary support for their most vulgar ambitions by appealing to one or another of the rival Roman war lords.

It was during these disturbances that the house of Herod supplanted the decaying Hasmonæan dynasty. The founder was Antipater, an astute Idumæan, one of the cleverest statesmen of the age. The ruler of a petty province bordering on Palestine, he took a keen interest in the rivalries of the Hasmonæan princes and began a policy of supporting one candidate against another. When the sluggish Hyrcanus II won the kingship, it was Antipater who became the power behind the puppet throne. Thence on, Antipater managed with extraordinary finesse to retain the goodwill of the changing Roman dictators, whose quarrels filled the world. While Pompey was all-powerful, Antipater ate honey out of his hand. On Pompey's death, in 48 B.C., Antipater turned quickly to Cæsar, earning the gratitude of the great consul by lending him valuable military assistance against Egypt. In consequence Hyrcanus was made ethnarch in Judah, and the Jews were granted protection and valuable commercial privileges. Antipater became a Roman citizen and virtually ruled the country. Two of his sons became prefects in the districts of Jerusalem and Galilee. Antipater's spectacular career was suddenly cut short by a cup of poison as he feasted at a banquet with Hyrcanus. But he could die in peace; the foundations of his family's fortune had already been firmly laid.

Herod continued to build upon the work of his father, and Hyrcanus remained a puppet in his hands too. For a moment, indeed, it appeared as if his career would be wrecked at its beginning. Rome's most dangerous and persistent enemy, the Parthians, taking advantage of the inactivity of Antony, who was enslaved by the charms of Cleopatra, swept into Syria and Palestine, carrying all before them. Hyrcanus was captured, his ears were shamefully mutilated, and he was sent into exile beyond the Euphrates. Herod, after desperate fighting, barely escaped from Jerusalem, where, as Josephus relates, "the Jews, more even than the Parthians, harassed him in his flight and fought against him for a distance of sixty-nine stadia from the city" (*War*, I, xiii, 8). The Parthians set up as king one Antigonus, an old rival of Hyrcanus and Antipater. The last of the Roman legions in Palestine were driven out and it appeared as if all that Rome had built in Palestine would be demolished.

But Herod did not easily give up. He made his way to Rome to lay his grievances before the Roman rulers. Antony had now returned to Rome and had arranged a truce with Octavian, whose sister he married to seal the bargain. Both the triumvirs were fully conscious of the services of Antipater and they realized that Herod was just the man to hold Palestine for Rome against the troublesome Parthians. Consequently, by senatorial decree, Herod was made King of Judæa, a position which he had not dreamed of soliciting. History presents few sights stranger than the spectacle which followed the senatorial decree. Herod, half Jew and half Idumæan, accompanied by Antony and Octavian, proceeded to the Temple of Jupiter on the Capitoline hill and there offered sacrifices in thankfulness for having been named King of the Jews!

In 39 B.C. Herod arrived in Palestine to take over the kingdom which Rome had assigned. The Roman legions cleared the country of Parthians, but Jewish opposition to Herod proved more serious and thousands of patriots who supported the cause of Antigonus paid with death for their desperate loyalty. Opposition was especially fierce in Galilee, the stronghold of guerrilla bands who never yielded easily to tyrants. They were no match for the Roman troops, however, and gradually they were hunted out of their hills and caves. Their resistance was not entirely crushed, but it was confined to petty skirmishes and raids.

Meantime Jerusalem itself was besieged and, after much slaughter, was taken, exactly twenty-seven years to the day after Pompey's ominous victory. The hapless Antigonus, the last of the Maccabean dynasty, was scourged as a common criminal and then ignobly beheaded. The Roman fury was so great that Herod himself protested. "Would the Romans deprive the city of all its inhabitants and possessions and leave me a king of the wilderness?"[1] Satiety, not mercy, ended the terror, and Herod became king in fact as well as in name.[2]

---

[1] Josephus: *War*, I, xviii, 2.

[2] It is estimated that in the thirty years since Alexandra's two sons began the fearful civil war, more than a hundred thousand Jews had fallen.

The new king proved to be one of the strongest and ablest rulers in Jewish history. Endowed with immense energy and resourcefulness, a consummate diplomat, possessed of the high esteem of the Roman emperor, he had unparalleled opportunities to bring peace to peaceless Judah. His reign was a genuine Augustan age for Palestine. The bandits who had thriven on the disorders of the civil strife were ruthlessly suppressed and men could again plough their fields or ply their trades in security. Herod strengthened the defences of the country and encouraged commerce and peaceful foreign intercourse. He developed a splendid harbour at Cæsarea, which became important enough ultimately to supplant Jerusalem as capital. He reduced the taxes when the times pinched; and when the spectre of famine stalked the land, he sold the plate and furnishings of the palace to help relieve the needy. Personally he cared little for Judaism, but he respected the scruples of the Pharisees as far as he was able, introducing no offensive statues into Jerusalem and omitting his likeness from his coins. He built a magnificent Temple, which was far larger and more beautiful than the already legendary Temple of Solomon. Neither labour nor expense was spared. Josephus writes that "when the morning sun burst upon the white marble of the Temple, Mount Moriah glittered like a hill of snow; and when its rays struck the golden roof of the sacred edifice, the whole mount gleamed and sparkled as if it were in flames" (*Antiquities,* XV, xi, 1ff.).

By all the laws of compensation Herod should have been one of the best-loved rulers in history. It was his fate to be the most despised. He was popular among the Gentiles of Galilee and Samaria and among the Jews of the Dispersion, whom he invariably befriended. But his subjects in Judæa hated him. They hated his despotism, though it was no more severe than that of any Hasmonæan predecessor and much more necessary after decades of dynastic bickering. They hated his Hellenism — the heathen temples which he endowed, the games and races which he sponsored, the baths and the stoæ which he built, although his predecessors had also found comfort in foreign fashions. They hated his generosity and his acts of kindness, for the fountain was poisoned at its source.

Perhaps some of the hatred sprang from the knowledge of his ignoble origin. He came from the stock of Idumæa; the cursed blood of Edom flowed in his veins. This the Pharisees never forgot. They despised all aliens, but for the sons of Esau hate was compounded with venom. An understanding of the spirit existing between the two peoples may be glimpsed in the Book of Jubilees, written probably in the first Christian century. Esau says of Israel: " When I can change the skin and bristles of a pig into wool, and when horns grow out of its head like the horns of a ram, then shall I regard thee with brotherly love, and when wolves make peace with the lambs, then shall there be peace with thee in my heart." [1] Herod tried to obliterate the stain of Edomite descent. He manufactured a genealogy which traced his ancestry back to Babylonian Jews.

---

1 Chapter xxvii. Cited by Morrison: *Jews under the Romans,* p. 85.

But the ruse was not successful. Until the bitter end he was referred to contemptuously as " the Idumæan slave."

But even more important in awakening the antipathies of the Jews towards him was Herod's unfortunate temperament. Few men in history have stained their hands with so much blood of dearest kin. Towards the end of his life Herod executed mercilessly, almost wantonly, wife, children, relatives, friends, all who opposed him, until Augustus exclaimed: " Better to be Herod's swine than his son! "

Perhaps the mania which possessed the king did not rise entirely out of his own nature. He was brought to it by the hatred and bigotry of the people. He craved affection and the goodwill of his subjects, but they seethed with sedition regardless of what he did. His own household were implicated in the plots which threatened his throne and his life. Living in an atmosphere so charged, seeing only frozen, sullen faces wherever he turned, imagining curses and sneers wherever he listened, Herod was driven to virtual insanity. Skilful intriguers worked upon the weaknesses in his nature until they brought him to paroxysms of rage impossible to check. He drowned his brother-in-law. He put to death the aged Hyrcanus II, now eighty-two years old and completely harmless. In a dreadful moment he ordered the execution of his wife, Mariamne, a beautiful Hasmonæan princess whom he dearly loved. He had two of his sons strangled, another drowned; and the memory of the horrible deeds never gave him peace thereafter. He wandered about the palace dishevelled, inconsolable, crying aloud for those who could no longer answer. Every murder increased the hatred of his subjects and drove him into deeper despair.

At last he lay dying, racked by the pain of an incurable intestinal cancer, and daring Pharisees tore the royal eagle from the Temple. He had strength enough to crush the premature uprising, and the rebels paid for their daring by being burnt alive. It was destined that he should go down to the grave with the cry of new victims still ringing in his ears.

After his death all the glories of his reign were forgotten. The rabbis who built legends about the reconstructed Temple execrated its builder. Christian writers remembered him only as a jealous, suspicious sovereign who earned the infamous reputation which he left. Jewish writers pictured him as an insolent and godless king, with an unrestrained hand and a heart bent on bloodshed. His epitaph is contained in the words of the historian who writes of him that " he stole along to the throne like a fox, he ruled like a tiger, and he died like a dog."

2. THE DESTRUCTION OF THE STATE

The Jewish state now rushed rapidly to its ruin. As if the persecutions of Herod were not a sufficient ordeal, an earthquake shook Judæa in 31 B.C., killing thousands of its inhabitants and destroying incalculable property. Seven years later came crop failures bringing famine, plague, and pestilence. It was not astonishing that the distracted Jews listened with awe to the words of self-appointed prophets who proclaimed that these trials were but the " pangs of the Messiah," introducing the end of the world.

Meanwhile political hardships continued. Herod had divided his kingdom among three sons, and the eldest, Archelaus, who was blessed with none of his father's talents, was assigned Judæa, Samaria, and the outlying Idumæan territory. While he waited for the Roman emperor to give formal approval to his succession, the Jews broke out in revolt, infuriated by the last executions of Herod. Archelaus inaugurated his reign by massacring three thousand people in the Temple court, crowded with Passover pilgrims. " The people were slaughtered like sheep, side by side with their Temple offerings," Josephus writes, " and the Temple was filled with the dead " (*War*, II, ii, 5).

No sooner was one rebellion crushed than another began and the ten years of Archelaus' reign were a long, bloody feud. In a common opposition to Archelaus the Samaritans and Jews forgot their hatred of each other and united to appeal to the emperor for relief. At last, in A.D. 6, the petition was granted and the king was banished to Gaul, where he lived out the remainder of an unhappy life.

Rome determined now to end the policy of native rulers for Palestine. Strategically the country was too important and its people were too turbulent to do without direct Roman surveillance. A procurator was therefore placed in control, responsible directly to the emperor.

Most of the procurators tried honestly to respect the sensibilities of their high-mettled subjects. The Sanhedrin, the supreme Jewish judicial body, was permitted to retain control of religious affairs and of all local concerns. Roman troops entering Jerusalem invariably left behind them the offensive imperial images. But several of the procurators were rascals from whom anything could be obtained for money. Of Felix, risen from slavery, Tacitus writes: " He exercised the prerogative of a king in the spirit of a slave, with superlative cruelty and licentiousness." He and several of his successors were merciless in the levying of taxes, and those who collected them were hated more than thieves. " The officials of the Roman provinces are like flies on a sore; but those already sated with blood do not suck so hard as the new-comers," Josephus remarked on the tax situation (*Antiquities*, XVIII, vi, 5).

There were also governors who were earnestly intent upon Romanizing their charges, little realizing to what pitch of desperation the Jews could be roused when their religious susceptibilities were involved. Pontius Pilate, the procurator who sentenced Jesus to death, was such a governor. He ruled for ten years, until his recall, A.D. 36, quarrelling almost continuously. Characteristic of his tactics was the famous order to smuggle soldiers into the Holy City by night, bearing silver images of the emperor on their ensign. He was besieged for five days by the outraged pietists and yielded only when the whole nation seemed ready to rise. He insisted upon using some of the Temple treasure to build an aqueduct for Jerusalem and he dispersed with clubs the mobs who cried out against the diversion of sacred funds for secular purposes. Ultimately a magnificent aqueduct, several miles in extent, was built, but the rabbis always regarded it as accursed of God.

Under all the procurators, good and bad alike, there were clashes and the land seethed with rebellion. The most serious opposition came from Galilee, where the Zealots became the leaders. They were extremists who shrank from nothing to bring down their heathen masters. Their watchword was: "No God but Yahweh, no tax but to the Temple, no friend but the Zealot." The crucifixions which followed every unsuccessful flouting of imperial power only had the effect of arousing avengers, who fought on until they too hung in agony on a public gibbet.

Ultimately Roman patience was thoroughly exhausted and the procurators introduced measures of barbarous severity. Soldiers slew on the slightest provocation. Eminent Jewish leaders were crucified, whole villages were razed. All in vain. A fever of martyrdom seemed to seize upon the harassed people. Fanatics went up and down the country, wild-eyed and frantic, prophesying the end of the world, and the advent of the Messiah. Multitudes were ready to follow every impossible visionary who claimed inspiration from heaven. Zealots rushed to their deaths crying out in hysterical exaltation. What was one to do with such a nation? The Romans were frankly bewildered. They had dealt with many turbulent peoples, but with none so contrary—so insanely intractable.

The last few procurators, by their rapacity, helped to turn even moderate people into revolutionaries. One of them, Florus, apparently to recover arrears of tribute, more probably to provide for his own needs, seized seventeen talents of the Temple treasure. Some of the bolder revolutionaries determined to pay their master in kind. They went about among the masses with baskets begging coppers for the impoverished procurator. Florus, stung to fury by the insult, sacked the upper city and killed more than six hundred Jews. Almost immediately the great national rebellion broke, destined to bring the unfortunate State to a bloody and inglorious end.

The war began when the fortress at Masada was captured by a rebel band, and the Romans were put to the sword. Immediately after, the daily sacrifice, which had been offered since the days of Augustus, was discontinued. Three thousand cavalry were rushed to Jerusalem to protect the Roman fortress, but the people had now risen *en masse;* all counsels of peace were drowned out by the ferocity of the Zealots. After some bloody street-fighting the Romans were disarmed and driven out. The soldiers of the fortress offered to surrender, asking only to be permitted to leave the country. The terms were accepted, but the rebellion had become a holy war; every pagan was hell-born and not to be left alive. Consequently as soon as the Romans had laid aside their arms, they were savagely slaughtered. The fever spread through every part of the country, and the reprisals against the Romans proceeded with all the fury of a desperate people suddenly released.

Cestius Gallus, the Syrian proconsul at Antioch, realizing that this was no insignificant rising, made elaborate preparations to crush it before it passed out of hand. With twenty thousand soldiers and as many auxiliaries he marched upon Jerusalem. For six months he besieged the city, but the Jews resolutely held their own and ultimately routed the invaders. Cestius retreated in confusion, leaving six thousand dead behind him and immense quantities of war material, which the Jews quickly appropriated. After the victory the peace party in Jerusalem disappeared; those who were still frightened by the alarming boldness of the Zealots' acts either preserved silence or smuggled themselves out of the country. Palestine was quickly cleared of Romans, its militia was reorganized, its fortresses were strengthened, and the war-maddened populace waited confidently to see what the emperor himself would do.

Nero now dispatched Vespasian, a trusted and capable officer, who had covered himself with glory on the battlefields of Germany and Britain. He was given fifty thousand men and unlimited powers to crush the rising of the stubborn folk in Palestine. Vespasian did his work systematically and coolly. In his first campaign he circled Galilee, where Josephus, the future historian, was in command. Vespasian won the open fields easily enough, but the fortresses for long defied the skill and experience of the besiegers. Many thousands of Jews were killed in the bitter conflicts during the long months which the siege required. Before the end Josephus went over to the enemy and sought to bring about the surrender of his unyielding co-religionists. Failing in this, he retired to write the history of the Jewish defence, and it is from his eloquent pages that we have the detailed story of the tragic end of the Jewish state.

After Galilee fell, the Romans moved south and east. In the winter of 68 the trans-Jordanic country was subdued; in the spring the southern territory and Idumæa. By the middle of 68 resistance had nearly everywhere been crushed out. Only Jerusalem itself remained and Vespasian made ready for what was destined to be one of the most desperate sieges in all history.

Before Jerusalem had been long invested, Nero died and a civil war shook the Roman world, while ambitious generals struggled for the purple. Vespasian was proclaimed by the Eastern legions and after a year was brought victoriously to the throne. The change in his fortunes did not alter Vespasian's determination to reduce the Holy City. He sent his son Titus to complete the work, placing at his disposal the choicest of his legions.

Titus needed as much patience as powerful resources. The city was magnificently fortified, protected externally by a triple circle of walls and internally by numerous towers and defences. And the Jews, fired by a holy zeal, were determined not to give in to the Romans while the breath of life remained in them. Courage and defiance went for naught, however, in the face of the cursed factional strife, which cropped up again even in this most critical moment of Jewish national life. Crammed within the few square miles of Jerusalem were nearly a million people, natives, soldiers, refugees, pilgrims, brave to the point of death, but distracted by quarrels which would not be stilled.

Three factions fought each other, divided by temperament, by personal animosities, by disputes over war methods. One held the upper town, one the lower, and one the Temple area in between. None co-operated with another; riots and assassinations were frequent, while the most powerful legions in the world pounded at the gates.

It was a miracle how a city so torn and disorganized could withstand the siege even a month. Yet even in its most hopeless days none dared speak of submission, and Jerusalem held out so long that the prestige of the new imperial house was at stake.

After the overtures of the Romans had been rejected, Titus began his assaults on the north wall. He used the *ballista,* a gigantic sling-shot, which threw stones weighing a hundred and twenty-five pounds more than a quarter of a mile into the city. He crashed his huge battering-rams against the walls, and the two outer ones soon gave way. The last wall was the hardest obstacle, and though the battering-rams and the *ballista* continued their deadly work, Titus waited for starvation to bring the city to submission.

The Jews died by thousands, more from famine and plague than from the wounds of war. Bodies could hardly be buried. Children and parents fought each other for refuse. The wife of the high priest, accustomed to walk on carpets and to eat the choicest morsels, skulked through alleys in search of scraps. Wretches who stole out at night to pick up roots were captured by the vigilant Romans and crucified, five hundred and more in a night. Those who returned were robbed of their precious cargo or murdered for it. Soon it was necessary to discontinue the sacrifices which had been offered every morning and evening.

Titus implored the city to surrender, but the Zealots steadily turned back every deputation. At night they repaired the breaches in the wall made during the day. They rested only when death came for them or when they collapsed from sheer exhaustion. Those who could rushed out to fight with bare hands, biting, tearing, struggling like wild animals. Steadily the imperial legions moved forward. The outer wall fell. Then the second. But when the last wall fell and the Romans burst into the city, the survivors withdrew into the Temple and continued their resistance. For six days the battering-rams pounded at the holy citadel, and then it, too, was taken. Titus perhaps tried to save the Temple, but his infuriated soldiers burnt it to the ground and butchered all whom they found alive. Still the district about Herod's beautiful palace remained and another month of fighting passed before its defenders had also been cut to pieces. Then at last, after four years, all of Jerusalem lay at the feet of the conquerors.

Of those who survived, thousands were transported to fight wild beasts in the amphitheatres of Cæsarea and Antioch, or to slave to death in the mines of Sinai. The hardiest and the handsomest were reserved to grace the triumphal procession of the victorious general in Rome. There was an old Roman custom that on this occasion the enemy leader should be hurled from the Tarpeian rock, as a sacrifice to the Roman gods. Simon bar Giora, one of the most valiant and uncompromising of the Jewish rebels, was thus executed to complete the Roman holiday. Further to commemorate the occasion Titus struck coins on which Judah was represented by a woman sitting desolate under a palm-tree, while around the coin was the melancholy inscription: *"Judæa devicta,"* or *" Judæa capta."* The sacred symbols which were borne away from the Temple were placed in the Roman Temple of Peace. The Torah was deposited in the palace of the emperor. These tokens have long since disappeared, but the beautiful arch which Titus erected, with reliefs of the candlesticks and holy vessels of the Temple, still stands. Today it is a monument, not to the Romans, but to the heroic little people who outlived their conquerors.

3. THE AFTERMATH

Quiet was not completely restored to Judah even after the Temple had gone up in flames. Some outlying districts of Jerusalem continued to resist. One fortress, Masada, where the rebellion actually began, defied Rome for three years; before it was taken its defenders slew each other so as not to come alive into the hands of the pagan despoilers. Even after this, fanatical Zealots arose sporadically to throw themselves to death against the spears of the Romans. Even Jewish stubbornness gave out, however. The quick suppression and summary punishment of every rebellion at length taught the lesson that resistance against the power and might of Rome was useless.

The Jews gradually adjusted themselves to the tragedy that had come upon them. The fall of the Temple and the dissolution of the State destroyed all of the outward symbols by which the religious and national life of the people had been regulated. Fortunately Judaism was not dependent for existence on a sanctuary and sacrifices. The life-blood of the nation was the law and the traditions which had grown up about it. The truest defenders of the faith were now, not the desperate Zealots who sacrificed themselves with sublime stupidity, but the scribes and sages who devoted their lives to teaching the masses the meaning of the ancient heritage. Such was Johanan ben Zakkai, who established an academy at Jabneh at the very moment that the physical State was being destroyed. The light which smouldered out in Jerusalem was again rekindled.

Study throve and teachers were developed who went forth with enthusiasm into broken Palestine and the Diaspora to preserve the integrity of Israel.

For a generation and more there was peace, and the Jews lived quietly, enjoying equal political rights with the non-Jewish subjects of Rome. Domitian harried them a little, but usually only when they sought to evade the poll-tax, which went to the imperial treasury. Under Nerva even this source of trouble was mitigated, for the emperor was anxious to have the tax levied kindly and discreetly. Coins were struck commemorating his tolerance, bearing his image on one side and on the other the inevitable palm-tree and the inscription: "*Fisci Judaici calumnia sublata* (Accusations on account of the Jew's tax are at an end)."

But after Nerva's all too brief reign the old animosities flared up again. The new emperor, Trajan, was one of the most attractive characters in ancient history: a brilliant soldier, an able and economical administrator, a genial and modest person. He placed no onerous burdens upon his Jewish subjects, and apparently they shared the general prosperity which characterized his reign. But an irreconcilable minority kept alive an opposition which no prosperity could quench. They remained quiet so long as revolt seemed useless, but at the first sign of imperial weakness their hopes drove them into sedition.

In 115 Trajan, then sixty years old, was compelled to take the field to combat the Parthians, who, despite all the warfare of the Romans, had not yet been subdued. Trajan had fought his way into the heart of the Parthian kingdom and had captured its famous capital when news came to him that a series of formidable revolutions had broken out behind him. The Jews rose with the other rebel peoples, not only in Mesopotamia, but all over the western Mediterranean world. In Mesopotamia thousands of Jews were killed before quiet was restored and the desolation was so great that brides were requested by the rabbis not to adorn themselves with wreaths. The Jews of Egypt, taking advantage of Roman difficulties, began to riot against their Roman and Greek enemies, and their disturbances grew into a formidable rebellion. This had hardly been suppressed when even more serious disturbances occurred in Cyrene and in Cyprus. The Roman historian Dio Cassius paints a sensational picture of the uprisings. The Jews wiped out nearly half a million people in both places, eating their flesh, besmearing themselves with their blood, sawing them asunder, feeding them to wild beasts! The account is the distorted version of a prejudiced historian, but evidently the Jews were in the grip of a wild and irresponsible fanaticism, which drenched Cyprus and Cyrene with blood. Trajan was compelled to send one of his ablest generals to cope with the fury of the Jews. The devastation was complete; when the last embers of the rebellion had been extinguished, it was necessary to rebuild Cyprus from its foundations. No Jew was thereafter permitted to set foot on the island, and even shipwrecked

Jewish merchants who sought temporary refuge were done to death when found.

Trajan died in 117, before he could carry out his ambitious schemes for strengthening his vast empire. His successor, Hadrian, at once concluded peace with the Parthians and adopted a pacific policy towards all subject peoples. The Jews, sick unto death of warfare, hailed him as a second Cyrus. Hadrian, however, had little understanding of the peculiarities of the Jews and their fanatical reverence for what seemed to him pure sentimentality. Towards the end of his reign he issued two edicts which again plunged his Judæan province into rebellion. His first was a plan for the rebuilding of Jerusalem. Since its destruction it had lain destitute and barren, a haunt for the beasts of the field. But the new city was not to be a centre for Judaism. It was to be purely Roman, a seat of Roman culture, known as Ælia Capitolina, in honour of the patron god of Rome. At the same time, and again with the best intentions, Hadrian issued another ominous edict. He was determined to rid the Roman dominion of the heinous practice of mutilation, and, mistakenly placing circumcision in such a category, he forbade the practice. Both edicts set the Jews afire, and they rose in their final rebellion against Rome, one of the most serious and protracted in Roman history.

The centre of the revolt was Judæa. The soul of the revolt was the venerable rabbi Akiba, one of the ablest of Israel's spiritual leaders. His genius lay far from war and rebellion. He was the first teacher to bring together the vast mass of oral traditions and to classify them according to subject-matter, a forerunner, therefore, of the makers of the Mishnah. His learning was held in high esteem; the saying was current that the power of Moses was weak until his teachings were interpreted by Akiba. His wisdom sat lightly upon him, however; all his life he laboured for the masses, travelling through the eastern Jewish world to interpret and awaken a love for Judaism. The Roman oppression roused the peaceful rabbi to active conflict. He centred all his hopes on a brilliant young warrior, Bar Kokba, who became the brain and sword of the revolt. Little is known of the antecedents or personality of the young captain. He appeared suddenly, to symbolize the yearnings of his people and to give them meaning. Apparently he claimed to be divinely inspired, and to his loyal followers he seemed the long-awaited Messiah. His personality must have been indeed irresistible, for the singularly rational Akiba fervidly believed in him and considered it an honour to become his armour-bearer.

Led by the intrepid pair, a new revolution began. Everywhere throughout the country the word was heard that the end of suffering was at hand; the tyrant who had dared to desecrate the house of God would be swept away like chaff; the country would again belong to the people that had made it sacred. Every village, every hamlet, was stirred. Only the newly-formed sect of Christians rejected the authority of the Jewish leaders. The might of Rome was forgotten—its endless resources, its terrible efficiency, its summary execution of unsuccessful rebels. The Jews believed that this last stand against the Roman eagle was like no other. It was the prelude to the establishment of God's kingdom on earth.

The amazing zeal of the aroused nation brought them unexpected successes in the early months of the rebellion. They completely routed the Roman legions and cleared the country of the enemy. The aged high priest Eleazar rededicated the altar, and Judah glowed with pride at this apparent revival of Maccabean days. Hadrian was obliged to recall from Britain Severus, the most distinguished soldier of the age. Severus adopted the tactics of Vespasian and reduced the country gradually, town by town, district by district. Soon every Jewish stronghold had fallen except Bethar, south-west of Jerusalem, where the heart of the resistance lay. Here Bar Kokba with a dwindling handful of followers defied the Roman legions until the usual blockade starved the fortress into submission. Bar Kokba and Akiba were both executed, along with all their followers. A virtual campaign of extermination concluded the tragedy. For Rome had suffered too, and the emperor in making his report to the Senate omitted the usual formula: "Both I and my army are well."

The Jews paid for the omission. Their casualties were much greater than attended the destruction of the State in 70. It is not improbable that a half-million lives were sacrificed in the hopeless cause. Those who escaped death were rushed to the slave markets of the East or to the gladiatorial arenas in the chief cities of the West. On the site of the sanctuary a Temple was built in honour of Jupiter Capitolinus. On the south gate of the city was placed the head of a boar, the emblem of the tenth legion. The very name of Judah was discarded and the province which had given the Roman legions so much trouble was renamed Syria Palestina. Jews were forbidden on pain of death ever again to set foot in Jerusalem. Only on the ninth of Ab—the traditional anniversary of the destruction of the Temple—could Jews pay for the right to weep on the site of the old sanctuary. For centuries thereafter they "bought their tears," weeping over the lost glories of the past, yet never abandoning the hope that some day, in God's own way, a restoration would come and the Holy Land would once again rise from the ruins, tenderly built up by Jewish hands.

CHAPTER ELEVEN

THE RISE OF CHRISTIANITY

THE four generations of Roman rule which followed Pompey's capture of Jerusalem were filled with vain sedition. No year passed without its toll of lives, and gibbets and crosses at every cross-road proclaimed the foolhardiness of the Zealots who continued to defy the Roman legions. At length the masses ceased to hope for relief by martial means and submitted sullenly and bitterly to the inevitable.

A small group turned for solace to the promises of the prophets, promises of a Messianic day when bloodshed would cease and justice would again prevail. With pathetic earnestness they searched the prophetic words, striving by computation and interpretation to deduce the exact date for the advent of the kingdom of God. A whole apocalyptic literature grew up dealing with the Messiah and his coming. Little sects appeared, some living simple, quiet lives, aloof from the harshness of the world, others practising mystical rites in preparation for the inauguration of the new era. Every few years a new prophet arose, claiming to be the long-expected Messiah and carrying with him to ruin hundreds of desperate followers.

It was in these years of political despair and Messianic hope that the ministry of Jesus of Nazareth fell. His career was destined to change the history of the world more profoundly than that of any other single individual who ever lived.

I. THE SOURCES FOR THE STORY OF JESUS

It is difficult to write of the man Jesus. About his name innumerable legends have clustered, about his teachings endless theological quibbles. His birth has been made divine, his life a long series of miraculous achievements, his death the prelude to a triumphant resurrection. Millions in every generation have venerated him as the son of God; other millions have worshipped him as an integral part of the Godhead. The labours of twenty centuries of pious churchmen have so completely obscured his genius and his humanity that it is wellnigh impossible to extricate the historical Jesus.

Jews have known little of him and have wished to know less. Throughout their long history he was not, to them, the Prince of Peace, the harbinger of goodwill. In his name every conceivable outrage was perpetrated on the despised and cursed race that gave him life. When the crusaders set fire to Jewish villages, plundered Jewish homes, and outraged Jewish daughters, it was in the shadow of the cross they bore. When Torquemada burnt thousands of wretched *marranos* at public *autos-da-fé* in every Spanish city and capped his career by driving two hundred thousand peaceful Jews out of the country, it was in the name of the gentle Saviour who preached the message of brotherly love. When Pobedonostsev, the procurator of the Holy Synod, counselled his tsar, the Little Father of his people, to solve the Jewish problem of Russia by baptizing, expelling, and destroying the stiff-necked race, he did so in the name of the Master who called to all the weary and the heavy-laden. Hounded from one land to another, burnt, hanged, spat upon, compelled to live in filthy ghettos and to wear degrading badges, denied the right to exist as human beings, to work as others worked, to play as others played, in no country, in no age, at peace, all because of Christian bigotry, it was impossible for Jews to regard the Prophet of Nazareth as other than the scourge of God, a fiend unmentionable. It was natural for legends to grow up about him, libelling his name and perverting his messages. In the *Toldos Yeshu,* a collection of hideous tales purporting to be his life story, read eagerly during the Middle Ages by an embittered people, one finds the response to centuries of persecution in the name of Jesus.

Now, in a brighter day, Jews are turning open-mindedly to learn the truth about the prophet who sprang from their midst and was converted to Christianity long after his death. Jewish scholars are joining with the more liberal Christian scholars to analyse the problems of the Gospels and the Acts, to understand better the essence of the prophet's message and the meaning of his career. It is now possible to speak with less doctrinal heat about the sources for the life of Jesus and their historical value, the influences which shaped his career, the reasons for his success, the causes for his failure, and the forces which separated him from his people.

The sources for the life of Jesus, other than the canonical Gospels, are few and ambiguous. In the first years after his death he was practically forgotten except by a devoted band of disciples, and the world knew nothing of him until he had become a legendary figure. In Hebrew literature there are only scattered references, none of which do more than authenticate his existence. Early Roman historians, too, say little: Tacitus and Suetonius alone mention "Christos" in connexion with Roman persecutions. Jesus himself did not write, relying entirely upon his disciples to perpetuate his teachings. They, too, probably committed nothing to writing. It was not until long after the death of Jesus, when it became urgent to spread the gospel to newly-converted Christians, to teach the lessons of the Master's life to communities in all corners of the earth, that the first accounts were compiled. These were circulated, expanded, and elaborated, and from them the Gospels of Mark, Matthew, Luke, and John were subsequently developed.

New Testament scholars have virtually established that the common basis for the first three, the synoptic, gospels, is a document or a group of documents, conveniently labeled Q, from the German *Quelle* (source). Relying upon this account, upon an "Ur-Mark" version, and doubtless upon considerable oral material, the gospel of Mark was written, about A.D. 65, a simple narrative of the life and death of Jesus, with little embellishment. Somewhat later, in response to the growing demand for new versions of the Master's career, the Gospels of Matthew and Luke appeared, both based upon Q and upon some Aramaic collections of the sayings of Jesus, but also drawing materially upon the work of Mark. Matthew, originally a Jew, emphasized the teachings of Jesus and reorganized them as connected discourses. Bitterly antagonistic to his former co-religionists, he assailed the Jews at every point for rejecting the Messianic claims of Jesus. Luke, apparently a Gentile physician, summarized what had been previously told, in the most beautiful and most polished of all the Gospel accounts. Many years later, perhaps not until the beginning of the second century, the Gospel of John was written, definitely Christological,[1] concerned primarily with the theological implications of the life and death of Jesus.[2]

All the sources together conceal more than they reveal and even the splendid scholarship of the last few generations has not solved the most important synoptic problems. It is because the sources are as untrustworthy as they are fragmentary that there have been so many varying interpretations of Jesus, ranging from the conceptions of fundamentalist Catholics, to the ultra-rationalist accounts of many modern writers. Until more information is available, every treatment of Jesus must remain essentially subjective, no more authoritative than any others that are based upon reasonable deductions from the meagre facts on hand.

2. THE CAREER OF JESUS

Jesus was born about 4 B.C., of humble Galilean parents, the oldest of five brothers and at least two sisters. The doctrine of the virgin birth[3] was developed long after his death; the gospel accounts name Mary as his mother, and Joseph, a carpenter, as his father, and they trace his lineage through Joseph from the royal stock of David.

Jesus shared the simple living of his family, wielding hammer and trowel as one of the great army of toilers. He probably had not the intensive Jewish

[1] Many modern scholars, notably Burney, are tending to the view that the Gospel of John may prove to be more valuable as source material for the life of Jesus than any of the so-called synoptic gospels.

[2] The epistles of Paul were written before any of the gospels, but since Paul, too, was concerned with a resurrected saviour, his work is more valuable for the history of the Christian Church than it is for the life of Jesus.

[3] The doctrine of the Immaculate Conception is a Roman Catholic concept and refers to the preservation of the mother of Jesus from original sin. It was defined by the Pope in 1854.

training characteristic of the Pharisees, but he knew and loved the stories of the Biblical heroes, the exalted messages of the prophets, and the moving poetry of the Psalms. At the age of twelve he was taken by his parents to Jerusalem, and to the Temple, and thenceforth there may have been many similar trips. Perhaps he listened to the utterances of the benignant Hillel, whose teachings were very much like those which Jesus preached many years later. Luke relates how he grew in wisdom as he grew in stature, all unaware until he was nearly thirty that he was preparing for a historic task.

Nothing influenced Jesus more in these formative years than the natural beauty of his Galilean environment. He loved its brilliant skies and its gentle green fields, its fresh streams, its vines and fig-trees, and the lovely gardens, breathing fragrance and bearing fruit. In most of his later messages he drew inspiration from the beloved scenes in the midst of which he had been reared. Here, as rumours of Roman brutality and Jewish hardships reached him, he dreamed over the allegorical meanings hidden in the prophets, over the Messianic promises of the contemporary apocalyptic literature. The belief in the advent of a deliverer was common in Judæa, and Jesus doubtless shared it, though his dream was not of a military conqueror nor of an ordinary emancipated Jewish state.

Then came an eventful day when a zealous Hebrew prophet called and stirred Jesus out of his dreams. John the Baptist was another in the unique succession of spiritual geniuses who appeared in nearly every critical period of Hebrew history. His manner of living and preaching recalled that of Elijah; indeed, it was believed by some that he was Elijah, restored to earth to carry through a new dispensation of the divine will. Like the thunderbolt of Ahab's day, John lived in the desert wastes, sternly ascetic, intolerant of all moral lapses. His sharp tongue reached into the highest places, and though he paid for his boldness with his life, he fearlessly denounced Herod Antipas, the tetrarch of the Galilee district, for an illegal and incestuous marriage.

But John was not primarily an ethical teacher. He identified himself with the messenger proclaimed by Isaiah, destined to clear the way of the Lord in the wilderness.[1] His mission was to usher in the kingdom of heaven and to prepare his people for its advent. The ax was already laid at the foot of the tree, and the tree would soon be cast into the fire.[2] He pleaded for preparation by repentance, for only those who were worthy would survive. The simple masses were attracted by the magnetism of his personality and the appeal of his message. They flocked in hundreds from all walks of life, to the river Jordan, where they were baptized by him, in a rite which was intended to symbolize moral purification.

The centre of the Baptist's influence was Judæa, but his fame spread to Galilee, and Jesus was irresistibly drawn to him. With a small group of followers

[1] Isaiah xl. 3.   [2] Matthew iii. 10.

he came to John, and his baptism began a new epoch in his life. Perhaps even so early the thought may have flashed into his mind that he himself had been divinely ordained to be the Messiah. But if the thought did not come till later, or perhaps at all, the decision was now made to devote his life to evangelism. The succeeding days were a time of earnest introspection. Jesus recalled the dangers and hardships of the way he had chosen, the fate of other men who had bared their souls to the sceptical world, the thorns and thistles that tangled the path of the prophet. But he rose superior to all doubts and fears and launched forth on a ministry which was to change the history of civilization.

The entire public activity of Jesus extended over little more than a year, or, by the tradition of the fourth gospel and the early Church Fathers, parts of three years. Yet the fruits of this short period were of enduring influence. What Jesus taught was perhaps not new. He pieced together, from the noblest portions of the Bible, beautiful prayers which brought solace to the masses who followed him. The God whom he worshipped and whose measureless mercy he offered to the weary was the God of love whom the gentle Hosea and the lonely Jeremiah had sought in their spiritual travail. Like these prophets too he urged his people to keep the law and follow the moral precepts which the genius of Israel had developed, though never to rely upon a mechanical loyalty to words and rites. When the sick and the downtrodden, the wounded in body and spirit, came to him, he sought to heal them with faith, as did many of the rabbis in his day. His words and his acts were like those of the moral giants whom he took as models. His ministry was not unique.

But the manner in which Jesus ministered was unique. Few had ever prayed and taught with such charm and power. His radiant personality, his tenderness and humility, captivated the masses wherever he went, and inspired confidence. As a teacher he was superb. He had the divine gift of a lucid tongue and a colourful imagination. His parables, pregnant with thought and rich with spiritual meaning, were yet simple enough for a child to follow. When he spoke, men listened enthralled, and begged for his blessing. Faith in his power to heal may have relieved many who were afflicted, and the word spread through the country-side that a new prophet had risen the magic of whose touch restored the blind and animated the halt. As the account of his activity spread from mouth to mouth in a hysterical age, it was magnified and exaggerated until the most astonishing marvels were attributed to him.

In all that Jesus said and did, there seemed to be little in conflict with Jewish tradition as interpreted even by the rigid Pharisees. He preached in the synagogues; he praised the law; he fulfilled the commandments. " For verily I say unto you, till heaven and earth pass away, one jot or one tittle shall in no wise pass away from the law, till all things be accomplished."

His ethical ideals, to be sure, were more ascetic, more unworldly, than Jewish tradition had sponsored. But Jesus was speaking to people on the threshold of the kingdom of heaven; a "new creation" was soon to supplant the trivialities and vanities of life. Hence, as Klausner suggests, he taught an "end-of-the-world morality," an "Interim-Ethic," calling upon men to distribute their possessions among the poor, to forsake their families, to follow those who proclaimed the kingdom. "Whosoever smiteth thee on thy right cheek," he taught, "turn to him the other also." "If any would take away thy coat, let him have thy cloak also." "It is easier for a camel to go through the eye of a needle than for a rich man to enter the kingdom of heaven." Even such teachings, however, so extremist as to become impossible of fulfilment, were not heretical. To love one's enemy, to return good for evil, to follow reasonable ideals of social justice, were essentially Jewish doctrines and had been preached by the prophets and teachers of Israel since their memorable succession began.[1]

Unfortunately the time was out of joint for the liberalism of Jesus. Many of the men whom he encountered were Pharisees who mistook the inner meaning of Pharisaism. For them the ideal of a life consecrated by religious rites, a life in which every step, from the eating of a meal to the wearing of a new cloak, was a sacred act, had degenerated into a blind, fanatical adherence to forms. The type had been often denounced, far back in the eighth century B.C. in the bazaars of Bethel, and in Jesus' own day. The Talmud contains many bitter protests which date from before the time of Jesus, protests against "making the law a burden," against "laws that hang on hairs," against wicked priests and Pharisees "who do evil deeds like Zimri and require a goodly reward like Phinehas." In an evil hour Jesus was brought into conflict with such men, as he spread his gospel of an ethical life. He hinted that clean living was more important than the keeping of every religious rite; that food, however prepared, could not defile a man; only bad qualities could. He healed the sick on the sabbath-day, though they may have been in no immediate danger. He associated with sinners and publicans and forgave them their sins when they repented. Undoubtedly no pious Jew could look with approval on the methods of Jesus, especially in a time when every rite and custom was doubly endeared by persecution. But active opposition came only from the narrowest, from

[1] Abba Hillel Silver, in his recent volume *Messianic Speculations in Israel,* throws an entirely different stress upon the ministry of Jesus. By his interpretation Jesus was not a Jewish prophet, nor was he primarily concerned with a gospel of social amelioration. He was essentially a child of the Messianic speculation of his day, when men were led to believe on the basis of their chronology that the sixth millennium — *the* millennium — was near at hand and that therefore the Messiah would soon appear. The essential preachment of Jesus was that "the time is fulfilled and the kingdom of God is at hand," and that men must swiftly repent if they wished to escape "the wrath that is to come" — the birth-throes of the Messianic times. These apocalyptic thoughts dominated all his teachings, and he was put to death by the Roman masters of the country as a political agitator. The words "King of the Jews," which were written over his head when he was crucified, are the key to the whole situation. Dr. Silver's brilliant thesis adds another to the many conflicting interpretations which baffle the modern student of Jesus.

the least worthy. These vehemently denounced Jesus as a betrayer and a seducer.

It was another of the tragic misunderstandings which have so often darkened the pages of history. Jesus assuredly had no quarrel with Judaism. His diatribes were directed at the fanatics who perverted its essence. In later years, however, as the chasm widened between Christians and Jews, many Christian writers and missionaries read back into Jesus' teachings all the venom and hatred which they felt towards the Jews of their own day. And " scribes and Pharisees " were taken as synonyms for hypocrisy. The class whose self-righteousness Jesus denounced became, in the eyes of purblind Christians, the symbols of a narrow Jewish faith which Christianity came providentially to supplant.

There was another note in the teachings of Jesus which no Jew could receive with favour and which therefore complicated the Jewish attitude towards the new prophet. Jesus taught, not in the name of God, but in his own name. No prophet, not even the greatest of them, had spoken with such assurance. No one of them had brought a message to Israel without proclaiming that it was spoken in the name of the Lord. Jesus, however, seemed to be an authority in himself. " But I say unto you . . ." he insisted with every message. " And they were all amazed at his teachings," writes Mark, " for he taught them as one that had authority and not as their scribes " (Mark i. 22).

Very likely by now Jesus had reached the conviction that he was the long-awaited Messiah. And at Cæsarea, after several months of adventurous preaching, the disciples who had thrown away all and had followed him elicited an affirmation from him. At the foot of the magnificent Mount Hermon he asked them who they thought he was. And Simon, the fisherman, who was later to become the head of the Church, answered: " Thou art the Messiah." Then Jesus answered and said unto him: " Blessed art thou, Simon bar Jonah, for flesh and blood hath not revealed this to thee, but my Father in heaven." [1] Jesus had at last been revealed as the Messiah, but he forbade his followers to tell what had happened. The time was not yet ripe, nor was Galilee the place for the public announcement. This must be made in Jerusalem. Jesus now planned to enter the capital to prepare it for the kingdom of heaven. His disciples, fearing the consequences of a public appearance in the centre of Pharisaic and Roman strength, remonstrated with him, but Jesus could not be dissuaded. He sensed the dangers which his mission involved, but he was confident that after " the pangs of the Messiah " he must triumph.

Jesus chose the Passover time for his journey to Jerusalem, for then the capital was thronged with pilgrims from every community where Jews lived. He made his way almost alone to Judæa, where he was met by disciples and followers who led him to the wall of Jerusalem. There he procured the colt of an ass on which to ride through the gate, in keeping with the tradition that

[1] Matthew xvi. 17.

the Messiah would thus enter the Holy City. The holiday crowds who jostled each other in the narrow, dingy streets gazed in astonishment at the strange caravan of enthusiasts, waving palms, shouting " Hosannah," and blessing the name of Jesus as they preceded him.

In the days which followed, Jesus spent much of his time in the Temple courts, observing, preaching, and praying. He criticized the priests for their complacency, the scribes for their apparent legalism. He refused to be impressed by the beauty of the Temple, and, to the horror of bystanders, he scoffed at its apparent inviolability even as Jeremiah had done in another unhappy day: " Seest thou these great buildings? There shall not be left here one stone upon another which shall not be thrown down." There were many bitter arguments with the leaders of orthodoxy, now over questions of law, now over questions of policy. Jesus spared no words. He denounced his opponents as hypocrites, blind leaders of the blind, whited sepulchres, outwardly beautiful, but inwardly full of uncleanness. " Woe unto ye, scribes and Pharisees," he exclaimed, " hypocrites, for ye tithe mint and anise and cumin and leave undone the weightier matters of the law, judgment and mercy and faith; but those ye ought to have done and not to have left the other undone. Ye blind guides, which strain out the gnat and swallow the camel, woe unto you."

Soon after his entrance into Jerusalem, Jesus brought the heated disputes to a climax by an act of sensational boldness. In the outer court of the Temple were booths in which venders sold doves and pigeons for the sacrifices, and where money-changers converted into negotiable coins the currency of those who came from afar. It was a long-established custom, as little offensive as the modern practice of selling candles for holy purposes in churches and cathedrals. But the shouts of the venders and purchasers, their bickering and bargaining, the whole commercial atmosphere in the court of the house of God, grated on Jesus as they must have grated on other sensitive pilgrims who came to the Temple in a reverent spirit. At length the evil irked Jesus beyond endurance. With the aid of his faithful disciples he drove the traders out of the court, overthrew the tables of the money-changers, and " suffered no man to carry any vessel through the Temple." The priests and Levites were outraged by the act of violence, but nothing could be done at once and the rebel withdrew unharmed to his dwelling on the outskirts of Jerusalem.

Jesus had now thoroughly aroused the leading citizens of Jerusalem. The Sadducee high priests, who were responsible to the Romans for the peace of the community, were especially alarmed. Jerusalem, crowded with pilgrims, had never been so restless; the procurator, Pontius Pilate, as a precaution, had taken up residence there, and, according to Luke, Herod Antipas had also come in with additional troops. Already one Barabbas had begun a rebellion, and it seemed not unlikely that this newly-proclaimed Messiah from Galilee would begin another, more serious and more dangerous. The Jewish leaders had bitter memories of former revolts, the sudden descent of the Roman legions, the indiscriminate slaughter of the innocent and the guilty, ruined homes, broken families. Jesus must be removed or restrained. It did not make the position of the young Galilean more secure that he had aroused the hatred of the uncompromising Pharisees by his straightforward, guileless attacks upon their religious observances.

The hours before the arrest of Jesus are described with simple, poignant eloquence in each of the gospels. Here the drama is unspoiled by any vulgar pettiness. In the evening the Master sat for the last time at supper with his disciples. He was moody and worried, sensing the doom which hung over him. The melancholy did not leave him after all of his followers had fallen asleep. He walked wearily in the Garden of Gethsemane, in agony, wrestling with himself whether to flee or to stay and face the consequences of his boldness. He had already suffered more than a sensitive nature could bear — the scorn of the Pharisees, the hatred of the Sadducees, the derision of the mob. Surely it was enough. Half the night he searched his soul and prayed for guidance. Then his faith returned stronger than ever and he determined to shrink from nothing to fulfil the vision that called him.

By every tradition Jesus was arrested that very night, betrayed by Judas of Kerioth, one of his own disciples. What followed has been the subject of more controversy than any other aspect of Jesus' career. Was Jesus tried at once and condemned by the Sanhedrin in the dead of night, contrary to all legal procedure? Was he turned over to the Romans as a rebel and not tried at all by the Sanhedrin? Or was there a preliminary investigation conducted by the Sanhedrin to determine the guilt of the accused and was he then turned over to the Romans to be legally dealt with? No theory can be definitely proved, though the last has the authority of most modern scholars. Regardless, however, of when the trial was held and under whose auspices, it is well-nigh incontrovertible that the burden of the Sadducee indictment was that Jesus falsely claimed the Messiahship and therefore merited the most extreme punishment. Every account relates that, to the direct question of the high priest Caiaphas: " Art thou the Messiah? " Jesus answered: " Thou sayest " or: " I am he " and added: " And ye shall see the Son of man sitting at the right hand of power and coming with the clouds of heaven." This was positive proof that Jesus was too dangerous a rebel to remain uncontrolled in restless Jerusalem.

The Sanhedrin had no authority to act in capital cases and Jesus was therefore probably turned over to the Roman procurator, accused of blasphemy and of Messianic pretensions. In all the Gospel accounts except that of John, Pontius Pilate is made out to be a merciful and tender judge, eager to save poor Jesus from his fate, but rendered powerless when a Jewish mob howled for the blood of the prisoner. Ultimately he yielded, throwing the responsibility upon the Jewish people, who, according to Matthew, accepted it, crying out: " His blood be on us and on our children" (Matthew xxvii. 24-5). It is highly improbable that Pilate, with a long record of cruelty and rapacity, was much concerned about the fate of a Jewish prisoner, accused of being a dangerous rebel. The story of Pilate's anxiety to save a "just man perishing through his righteousness" was evidently a creation of the late first century, when it had become clear to the Christian brotherhood that the future of their faith depended not on Jews, but on Gentiles; it was impolitic to implicate the powerful Roman empire in the execution of the Saviour.[1] Pilate took no account of the charge of blasphemy, but when Jesus admitted his Messianic claims, he was condemned to die as a Roman rebel.

The tragedy was drawing to a close. The Romans, experienced in suppressing disorders, had devised the agonizing torture of crucifixion as a punishment for criminals and political offenders. Jesus was first scourged until his poor broken body was reduced to a mass of bleeding wounds. He was then fastened to the cross at Golgotha, outside of Jerusalem, with the derisive words over his head: "The King of the Jews." He drank his cup of sorrow to the dregs. Flies and gnats settled in his wounds, but, nailed hand and foot to the beams, he could not drive them out. All day he hung in agony. Perhaps he recalled now the pleasant hills of Galilee which he had deserted, the gardens in which he had played, the lake by which he had preached and where simple, loving crowds had hung on his words. All his high hopes, his plans to help his people, crucified on a gibbet! The thought must have pierced him more sharply than the nails. And in his agony he cried out in the words of the Psalms which he had so loved: "My God, my God, why hast Thou forsaken me?" One sorrow, however, was spared him. "He had not to suffer the pain of mocking his own visions by any disloyalty or weakness in himself."[2]

He expired late in the afternoon. The sabbath was coming on and the body was therefore taken down as soon as death had claimed it. It was hastily deposited in a near-by tomb, and a stone was placed at the entrance. Only a few women, faithful to the Master even unto death, stood by, weeping silently.

3. JEWISH CHRISTIANITY

The martyred prophet lived and died a Jew. At no time during his ministry, even in his most iconoclastic moments, had he any intention of separating himself from his people. Throughout his ministry he toiled to enrich their spirit by bringing to them, and to them alone, the inner meaning of the prophetic

[1] The dominating concern of the Christian preachers in the gospel-making age was to cast the blame upon the Jews and to relieve the Gentiles of responsibility. The guilt of the Jews was magnified when Pilate was made to order the execution against his will. In the original situation certainly the procurator acted freely and probably with full satisfaction to himself. He saw in Jesus a potential revolutionist whose removal would be a warning to all future agitators. Case: *Jesus*, p. 325.

[2] Leonard: *The Poet of Galilee*, p. 77.

messages. The Gentile world was out of his ken. "I was not sent," he said when asked to heal the daughter of a Canaanite woman, "except to the lost sheep of the house of Israel." His disciples were Jews too, loyal to Jewish traditions and abiding by the commandments.

The death of Jesus, however, made a vast difference. As the years passed and the numbers of those who believed in his Messiahship grew, the Jewish elements in his teachings were subordinated. The simple faith of the earliest disciples, brought into contact with the Greco-Roman world, was overlaid with new ideas and new doctrines. At length the whole of the Mosaic law was subordinated. And Jesus, shorn of his simple humanity and transformed into a divine figure, every act of whose life was a miracle, became the sanction for an elaborate religion which disowned its mother and set out to conquer the world.

The sources for this period in which the new religion developed and triumphed are few and conflicting. Historians have relied almost exclusively upon the closing chapters of the four gospels and the opening chapters of the Acts. The apocryphal Acts of Peter, John, Thomas, and Andrew, written in the second century and massed with legendary material, have not been seriously considered as historical sources. Because of the meagreness of evidence the origins of Christianity and its separation from Judaism still remain obscured. But modern scholarship, toiling patiently on the most ancient texts available, has established the more important general facts.

The death of Jesus left his few, frightened disciples despondent and bewildered. Their whole world had suddenly collapsed about them. The Messianic claims of their Master seemed to die with him on the cross at Golgotha. Then came a miraculous restoration of faith, inspired, according to all gospel accounts, by the resurrection and reappearance of Jesus. It seems that on the Sunday following the Crucifixion, some of the women who had been the most ardent followers of Jesus came to his tomb to pay their last respects. They found the stone rolled away and the tomb empty. Then followed visions in which first the women and then the disciples saw their beloved leader again. The resurrection of Jesus and his reappearance to the little body of faithful believers became the corner-stone of the new Christian religion.

It is not likely that the women and the disciples who told of their Master's reappearance after his crucifixion were deliberately deceitful. Their amazing devotion to his memory, their unshaken conviction that he was the Messiah, their exaltation and enthusiasm, were not artificial. Doubtless their imagination was set on fire when the body disappeared, and they sought no rational explanation.[1] They actually saw their crucified Master as vividly and as truly as Isaiah saw his heavenly visions, and as other sensitive spirits, in exalted religious moods, were certain of transcendental experiences.

[2] Klausner believes that Joseph of Arimathæa, the owner of the tomb, secretly removed the body of the crucified teacher and buried it elsewhere.

The reappearance of Jesus fortified the conviction of his disciples that he would return to establish the kingdom of heaven for the righteous. Nothing could daunt them now. Death itself had no fear for them. Had not the Master conquered it?

Such were the humble beginnings of the triumphant Christian Church: a little brotherhood, united by love of a divine Master, determined to live together by the principles which had guided his life. None of them, with the possible exception of Peter, were men of outstanding ability, but they made up in devotion what they lacked in intellect. They remained observant Jews, abiding by the Jewish law, and worshipping in the Temple. They differed from other Jews only in their belief that the Messiah had already come and in their manner of life, which approached an ideal communism. Only two rites were part of their new cult, baptism and the Lord's supper, the two earliest rites of the Christian Church. Since Judah was filled with strange sects, the followers of Jesus were not molested so long as they kept their peace.

Soon new followers were added to the tiny body, deeply impressed by its enthusiasm and its way of life. Peter, its moving spirit, endlessly expounded the new faith and promised salvation to all who repented. These conditions involved no abrogation of Judaism and on the Day of Pentecost the little band had grown to more than three thousand. Even now the society was animated by Jewish principles.

There was bitterness, of course, towards the authorities for the part which they had played in the crucifixion of Jesus but this bitterness brought no breach with Judaism. At the meetings, which were probably held daily, the apostles gave instruction not only in the life and teachings of Jesus, but in the meaning of the Old Testament. No one thought yet of proselytizing the Gentiles. The Master had ministered only to the lost sheep of Israel, and his disciples were inclined to follow his example and await his return.

The schism between the new sect and Judaism began when many Hellenistic Jews, already weaned from strict adherence to Jewish practices, and a number of converted Gentiles, were added to the growing band of Nazarenes. One of the neophytes, Stephen, now boldly insinuated that Jesus the Messiah had freed those who followed him from their obligation to the Mosaic law. The Pharisees were highly incensed, and during a riot he was stoned to death for his heresy. There followed an active persecution, sanctioned and assisted by the king, Herod Agrippa, of all who shared the belief of the slain radical. The brotherhood was disrupted, and many of the refugees sought shelter outside of Jerusalem, where they began to spread their faith among non-Jews. Samaritans were baptized in large numbers, and, in Galilee, the zeal of the disciples brought many Gentiles into the fold. In Antioch a Church was organized and the name Christian was first applied there to the new sect.

In recent years new insights for an understanding of early Christianity have been provided by the dramatic discovery of what are now called the Dead Sea

Scrolls. These were manuscripts of approximately the first century B.C., in Aramaic and in Hebrew, that were stumbled upon in 1947 by wandering Bedouin in the Qumran caves near the northwest corner of the Dead Sea. When the documents were deciphered by the gifted Jewish archæologist, Eliezer Sukenik, and by reliable Christian scholars, they cast light on one of the religious sects, probably the Essenes, that flourished during the immediate pre-Christian era.

The Scrolls d scribed the ascetic practices of the sect, the group's emphasis upon "uprightness and humility," its idea of shared possessions, and a form of social organization which resembled the way of life of the early Christians. Some scholars assume that there may have been a relationship between John the Baptist and this sect, for the manuscripts refer to a revered Teacher of Righteousness who was persecuted by a Wicked Priest and who predicted the impending fall of the Sons of Darkness, the Kittim (very likely the Romans). Others assume that Jesus himself may have emerged from this sect and that his teachings and his practice were substantially influenced by its rites and beliefs. The intensity of the disputes over the Scrolls in the scholarly world during the past decade may be explained by the impact that the validation of any of these assumptions would have on Christian theology. They would open the possibility that the sources of the New Testament were Jewish, rather than Greek— as had formerly been assumed. But though scores of manuscripts have now been recovered and deciphered, the evidence is still too scanty and fragmentary for any of these theories to be asserted with conclusive assurance.

Yet the Scrolls have already deeply influenced Biblical scholarship. They have helped further to establish the authentic text of the Old Testament, since they are a thousand years older than any of the traditional—i.e. Masoretic—texts that have been preserved. Indeed, one of the Scrolls was an original version of the Book of Isaiah, the only one in existence. And they corroborate the diversity of religious experience in the days of Jesus, the apocalyptic climate of the period, when so many troubled souls hoped for the alleviation of their sorrows and insecurities through the coming of a Messiah.

Meantime the rapid influx of proselytes brought new problems. What was to be the relation of the Jewish to the Gentile Christians? Were all converts obliged to keep the Jewish law or was faith in the mission of Jesus enough? Was there to be one way of life for Jews and another for Gentiles? The problems called for an early solution. A decisive answer was supplied by one of the mightiest forces in history, the real founder of Christianity, Saul of Tarsus, the Paul of the New Testament.

4 · PAUL AND THE TRIUMPH OF THE NEW FAITH

Of Paul we know more than of any other influential religious character of antiquity. The main facts of his career have been recorded, probably by a companion of his travels, and the mainsprings of his character as clearly revealed in his own letters, addressed to the religious communities which he founded. Every generation reinterprets him anew, and he has been as roundly denounced as he has been idealized. Renan was violently repelled by "the ugly little Jew." Nietzsche found in him "one of the most ambitious of men, whose superstition was equalled only by his cunning." But to Luther he was a rock of strength and to many earnest churchmen in all denominations he has been considered as the second founder of Christianity, inferior only to the Master himself.

He was born, about the same time as Jesus, in Tarsus, the commercial centre of Cilicia. Evidently he came of a well-to-do family, for he was both a citizen of Tarsus and a free-born Roman. His birthplace was one of the great cities of the Mediterranean world, with half a million population, and a noted university, the centre of Stoic and Cynic philosophy, the meeting-place for Greco-Roman culture. Paul was vitally influenced by his cosmopolitan environment, and, unlike Jesus, he became a man of the world, with a broad and sensitive culture. He learned from every experience. "I am debtor," he wrote later, "both to Greeks and to barbarians, to the educated and the uneducated classes." He was equally at ease before the crowds whom he harangued in Jerusalem "in the Hebrew dialect" (Aramaic), and the intellectually select to whom he spoke in Greek on the Areopagus at Athens.

Yet he remained a strict Pharisee until he was well in his prime. "A Hebrew of Hebrews; as touching the law, a Pharisee; as touching the righteousness which is in the law, found blameless." He travelled several times to the Holy City, and there sat at the feet of the sage Gamaliel, a grandson of Hillel, one of the most broad-hearted and liberal of the Pharisee leaders. He probably took part in the early disputes with the Nazarene sect and joined in persecuting those who assailed Jewish practices.

All the time, however, he was sorely troubled by a sense of sin which no rationalizing and no amount of learning would still. Something was lacking for him in the faith of his fathers. Then came a sudden vision to him, a tremendous psychological experience, which changed his whole balance. The prophet whose disciples were being persecuted suddenly appeared and opened a new way of life to Paul. For several days the bewildered Pharisee searched himself and prayed for guidance; then he asked for baptism and the gift of the Master's spirit. This famous experience, the outstanding event in the history of the early Church, is as bewildering today as to the chroniclers who first recorded it, in four variant accounts. Perhaps Paul was won by his very failure to shake the persecuted sect, which displayed an astonishing serenity in the face of all trials. Perhaps his restless spirit could find no peace in Judaism and sought for it in the brotherhood which had consecrated itself to live by the teachings of Jesus. Jesus had conquered sin; surely other men could conquer it too through spiritual union with him. So Paul thought when he said: "We all with unveiled face, reflecting as a mirror the glory of the Lord, are transformed into the same likeness as Himself from glory to glory." Once converted, Paul gave himself body and soul to his new Master, Jesus, who became for him the living Christ and dominated his whole life. He was now as eager to spread the doctrines which had brought him peace as formerly he had been to condemn them.

So began a life of missionary activity which transformed a despised and hunted creed into a world-wide religion. Armed with faith, Paul was daunted by nothing. His success was phenomenal when it is recalled what a fragile vessel he was. Small in size, bandy-legged, unattractive, with a great hook nose, meeting eyebrows, and a bald head, intensely nervous, afflicted with sick-headaches, it seemed impossible for him to carry, almost single-handed, the immense burden which he undertook. But the weak little body was thoroughly controlled by an immense will and inexhaustible energy. "I have often been at the point of death," he writes in describing the difficulties which he conquered in spreading the gospel to the Gentiles. "Five times I have received lashes from the Jews, three times have I been beaten; once I was stoned, three times shipwrecked; I have been adrift on the sea a night and a day, in many journeys, in perils from rivers, from robbers, in town and desert, on the sea, in perils among false brothers, through labour and hardships, through many a sleepless night, through hunger and thirst, often starving, cold, and ill clad" (2 Corinthians xi. 24–7). All of this supernormal energy he attributed to the divine power "energizing mightily" in him when he felt weakest in himself (2 Corinthians xii. 9).

Wherever the ubiquitous apostle travelled, he denounced the evils of pagan society, "hateful and hating one another," and pointed to the blessed communities of Christians, who accepted Jesus and lived by his light. "Walk by the spirit, and desire of the flesh ye shall not fulfil." He called to the persecuted, to the slaves, to the despised and the downtrodden, to the sick in body and spirit, to refresh themselves in a brotherhood where all were equal, where life was clean and pure and peaceful. The world was shackled by forms and rites and there was too little genuine faith. Men must therefore free themselves from external laws and throw themselves on their conscience. "Only," he added significantly, "turn not freedom into an opportunity for the flesh, but through love serve one another. For the whole law stands fulfilled in this: 'Thou shalt love thy neighbour as thyself.'" The moral crusade which Paul fought through every misery and privation is the most beautiful part of his career.

It was during his long missionary activity, which carried him throughout the Roman empire and which ultimately brought him martyrdom at the hands of Nero, that Paul developed and crystallized the beliefs which made him the intellectual founder of Christianity. Judaism, he now saw clearly, had been a long preparation for the work of Jesus. It embodied a fine moral code, but it was not sufficient to bring men to a knowledge of their Heavenly Father. It lacked the power, the vitality, to induce men to realize this knowledge. Jesus alone had fulfilled the inner essence of the law and had understood the meaning of God. Faith in Jesus could help others to do as he had done. Paul felt the nearness of God so overwhelmingly through his faith in Jesus that it seemed inconceivable to him that others would not similarly feel it. The Jew had come to God through the law. To Paul, Christ now took the place of the law; he now served as the form and the medium of relation between God and man. This is what he meant when he spoke of " Christ in man and man in Christ."

But Jesus, who brought men so near to God, could not then be other than a superhuman, heavenly being, God's own representative, the very Son of God, who had humbled himself and suffered to emancipate mankind from the burden of the law. This principle became the corner-stone of his faith, and upon it the Church Fathers built up the elaborate theology which became Christianity.

It was Paul who solved the difficult problem of the Christian relationship to the Jewish law. As his faith became clearer to him, the claims of Judaism hung more and more loosely on him, until at length he determined that it must not hinder his mission to the Gentiles.

Paul came to Jerusalem several times to discuss with the leaders of the Christians there the problems created by Gentile converts. Peter was at first quite conservative, and a compromise was reached whereby Jewish Christians would continue to observe Jewish practices while Gentiles would be under no obligation to do so. It was impossible, however, to maintain for long such a relationship. Jewish and Gentile Christians met together, ate together, prayed together, and the compromise was found onerous on both sides. Paul, now at the close of a long and arduous life of missionary activity, refused to be any longer shackled, and he broke completely from the Jewish law, denouncing it as a burden to Jew and Gentile alike. Opposition angered him and the Epistle to the Galatians, in which he let forth a torrent of abuse on the Judaizers, is an eloquent indication of the distance which he had travelled since his own conversion. Gradually the Jewish Christians were won over to his views, until only a little community remained in Jerusalem, and this too virtually died out after the Temple was destroyed. The breach was complete, and, as time passed, Christianity, in contact with the great Roman world, grew more and more unlike its parent. The faith which Paul founded developed amazing doctrines, which flowered into the *Summa Theologiæ* of St. Thomas Aquinas.

It was a tragedy for Jesus that historic circumstances conspired to make some of the leaders of his people intolerant of his ethical teachings. A revival of the militant prophetic liberalism was sorely needed to revitalize the Judaism of his day. Perhaps if Messianic claims had not been intertwined with his teachings, his own and later generations would have taken him to heart and given him a deserved place among the noblest of the Jewish prophets.

But a greater tragedy was his acceptance by the Greek Fathers who took his name and made it the sanction for a new theology. The Roman world was indeed made better for the conquering faith which it adopted, but Jesus was not honoured by the adulteration of his teachings. Through the thick cloud of religious incense, offered by the piety of countless generations, it is difficult to recognize the magnetic teacher of Galilee, who preached a gospel of love in an era filled with hate, whose simple humanity was a solace to those who lived in darkness.

PART TWO

CHAPTER TWELVE

THE DEVELOPMENT OF THE TALMUD

MODERN liberals who have been reared in a secularist environment and are impatient of religious legalism look upon the historic Talmud in no friendly spirit. They regard its growth and its complete domination during the Middle Ages as deterrents to the creation of a virile Judaism. They explain the phenomenon as a combination of stubborn conservatism and superstition. Once men lived by the plain Mosaic law. As parts grew antiquated, new interpretations and traditions grew up about it. But the old was not discarded; every jot and tittle was precious. It was carried along through the years, and the Mosaic law developed into the Mishnah, the Mishnah into the Gemara, the Gemara into innumerable commentaries and codes. Ultimately the observant Jew was compelled to carry a staggering load, and Judaism was mummified by the very forces which were meant to give it freedom and resilience.

The verdict is harsh and unjust. The Talmudic development, which spun out a simple law into an enormous body of tradition, was the natural result of nearly ten centuries of virile Jewish life. The huge tomes which frighten the novice and perplex the liberal contain not only the laws and customs which were to be observed by the pious, but the discussions which created them; ideas and concepts embracing every aspect of life—science and art, labour and literature, wisdom and superstition. They are the record of the intellectual and religious activity of the Jews during their most trying centuries, centuries which spanned the Maccabean struggles, the rise and fall of the house of Herod, the destruction of the State, and the adventures which followed in Palestine and Babylon. Some of the vast stores later proved worthless and a burden. But much more was lofty and edifying, as stimulating as anything in contemporary thought, a river of life in a barren desert of despair.

I. THE MISHNAH

There were well-beloved traditions intertwined with the Mosaic law even before it was arranged and canonized. This was natural, for the many experiences of Israel during the first monarchy, the Babylonian exile, and the rebuilding of the State had all left their mark. Men's outlooks had broadened, life had

143

become more complex, and new customs had developed spontaneously out of the old. Yet it was not until the Mosaic law had been officially defined, either by Ezra or by his successors, that an appreciable expansion of the law began. Once the Scriptures had been set down, the scribes and Pharisees joyously took up the duty of teaching and explaining the sacred work. In their hands the body of tradition grew enormously, and when the Jewish state passed under Roman hegemony, there were regulations for almost every act and relationship of life.

Nothing was yet written, except the Scriptures themselves, which were read on the sabbath from long, hand-made scrolls and conned over during what little leisure there was on week-days. There was a natural fear that the supremacy of the Holy Writ would be endangered if any of the oral traditions were committed to writing. Consequently the teachers and their disciples preserved their wealth of learning by memory and transmitted it by word of mouth. The practice developed men of extraordinary erudition. To this day, many of the old-fashioned rabbis carry whole tomes in their minds, without missing so much as an accent.

It was during the height of the Roman tyranny, some twenty or thirty years before the birth of Jesus, that Shammai and Hillel, two of the most influential teachers of antiquity, flourished. Folk-lore is enriched by many charming stories which illustrate their varied temperaments, Shammai the stern, rigorous stickler for the letter of the law, Hillel the liberal, benignant humanitarian. Shammai could not have been a repellent personality, for in his own day he carried more weight than Hillel; until after the destruction of the Temple it appears that his disciples outnumbered the Hillelites.

The genius of Hillel, who was probably a native of Babylon, became clearer in the generations which followed his death. The great *Tannaim* (teachers) recalled affectionately the serene beauty of his life, his generosity, his devotion to learning, his modesty, his extraordinary patience. When Jesus taught his followers to love their fellow men as they loved God, to do unto others as they would have others do unto them, to value humility as the highest virtue, he was repeating the teachings of the master who had preceded him by a generation. Hillel loved the traditions which he had inherited, and he toiled all his life to link them up with the Scriptures, to demonstrate exactly how they had been developed. In the course of this work he laid down the Seven Rules for deduction and analogy, which became the established principles of interpreting the Scriptures. He was thus one of the creators of rabbinical hermeneutics.

Some time after the death of Shammai and Hillel the rebellion against Rome began which ended with the destruction of the State. As the Roman legions closed in on the doomed capital, the more moderate Pharisees strove desperately to restrain the war-mad Zealots, anxious at all costs to save the

Temple. Most of the Jewish practices depended upon a temple and a home-land; sacrifices, priestly rites, purifications, Temple prayers, agricultural laws — the entire ritual and cultus. How could Judaism survive the annihilation of its framework?

When the catastrophe came and the light seemed to depart for ever from Judah, the teachers alone were calm and clear-headed. They began at once to adapt the orphaned religion to the new conditions. It is related that, even before the destruction of the State, one of Hillel's most distinguished successors, Johanan ben Zakkai, escaped from Jerusalem and established himself at Jabneh, near the coast, where he began to train a body of disciples to continue the traditions of Jewish learning. The fall of the Temple, the end of its picturesque and symbolic ritual, were deplorable incidents, Johanan felt, but the Jewish faith was still strong in spiritual power and rich in traditions which could be observed. Johanan substituted a new patriotism for the old. The most gallant soldier, he declared, was he who studied longest, who taught best, who raised up a host of disciples.

Johanan, however, did more than build an academy. To preserve the organic body of Judaism it was essential to have an authoritative body to take over the duties of the defunct Sanhedrin. Johanan therefore organized a council of teachers, the *Bet Din,* which served as senate, as court, as parliament — in short, as the articulate voice of scattered Israel.

For sixty years after the destruction of the Temple the teachers of Jabneh toiled heroically to rebuild the broken foundations of Jewish life. They went carefully through all of the written and unwritten law, and, a few years after Johanan's death, the long-standing controversy between the Shammaites and the Hillelites was settled by the decision that, though the teachings of both schools were inspired by the living God, the decisions of Hillel were to be followed in practice. In this period, too, came the final delimitation of the Scriptures; after long debate Ecclesiastes and the Song of Songs were admitted, but the Book of Ben Sira was kept out, and it was decreed that nothing which came after his day should be added.

As the study of the law proceeded, it continually yielded new meanings; learning was intimately linked with dialectic ingenuity. In the period before the final revolt against Hadrian the palm for such erudition went to the rabbi Akiba. Akiba was by no means a pious pedant. In the Talmudic stories he plays roles fit for the heroes of romance. He began life as an illiterate shepherd who had the boldness to fall in love with the daughter of one of the wealthiest men in the land. After winning her hand, both were set adrift and the courageous wife toiled to subsidize his study until he became the leading light of his generation.

Akiba perfected the practice of deducing laws and principles not only from the clear text of the Bible, but from its arrangement, its superfluous words, its very dots and dashes. He discovered new meanings in the most hidden nooks and crannies. Later in life he began to systematize the developing body of tradition, bringing it together in six divisions, with numerous subdivisions, thus materially facilitating its study and transmission.

His work was interrupted by the uprising of the Jews against Hadrian. The revolt was led by the restless, irreconcilable Zealot Bar Kokba, and Akiba backed the fiery soldier by every means within his power, leading most of his colleagues into the war. Pious scholar, uncompromising rebel, Akiba was also a mystic. He was so far carried away by the Messianic speculation of his day that he hailed Bar Kokba as the promised "Star out of Jacob" of Balaam's prophecy. It required more than three years for Rome to lay the country prostrate; when it was finally triumphant, it went beyond the limits of brutality to wreak vengeance on the whole people. Akiba, in his last and noblest role, exulted in the opportunity to die for the God whom he had until then served without genuine sacrifice. According to a popular legend, the Romans tore his flesh to bits with pincers and burnt him alive, but he retained his serenity to the end, perishing with the name of God on his lips. The painful, laborious exegesis of Akiba has roused wonder, but the heroic teacher answered his critics through his devotion. "He interpreted the Law," says Israel Abrahams, "by his utter self-surrender to it." [1]

Through the remainder of Hadrian's reign a ruthless war of extermination was carried on against the religion of the Jews, which, the emperor shrewdly realized, was the head and front of the resistance. It was forbidden to circumcise children, to keep the sabbath and the festivals, to observe any of the Jewish rites. The study and the teaching of the law was made a capital offence; those who were found in possession of a copy of the Torah were speedily executed. Jabneh was, of course, destroyed, and those who were able to escape martyrdom were hunted through the caves and the hills, like wild beasts. Usha, near Haifa, and the larger towns in Galilee, whose ignorance and illiteracy had long been a subject for jest among the scholars of the south, now became the rallying-points of those who loved the law. Here the remnants of Jabneh and the other centres of learning gathered, broken in body and spirit, but guarding their few precious scrolls. The pursuers managed to ferret out their retreats, but the fugitives were able, with their dying breath, to ordain new disciples, young, resourceful, courageous, and passed on to them the pious labours of the generations.

The simple, kindly Antoninus Pius, who succeeded to the Roman emperorship in 138, relaxed the severe restrictions of his predecessor, and the persecuted scholars were able, at last, to emerge from their hiding-places. Judah was too completely devastated to continue as the centre of learning, and new academies took root in the northern part of Palestine, especially in Galilee, where

[1] Peake: *The People and the Book*, p. 431.

they remained until they were later eclipsed by those of Babylon. As soon as some stability had been attained, each school went carefully over the traditional lore to make sure that nothing had been lost during the chaos of the rebellion. Then, as if nothing had happened, the work of systematization which Akiba had begun was continued.

The most eminent scholar in this new period of reconstruction was Rabbi Meir, a man of wide culture and tolerance, whose outlook had not been soured by continuous Jewish adversity. He was admirably fitted to assume the mantle of Akiba. He enjoyed the friendship of the pagan cynic Oinomaos of Gadara, "a condemner of all things divine and human," whose keen criticism poured ridicule on the old heathen gods and their oracles. He continued to reverence the sober wisdom of Elisha ben Abuyah even after this noted teacher had denounced Judaism and turned atheist. He was equally at home in the midst of needle-witted scholars and among the masses, to whom he preached on Friday evenings in the little synagogue of Tiberius. His shrewd and homely parables and his clever fables are among the most delightful parts of the Talmudic literature.

Meir virtually completed Akiba's work of codification; his prestige stood so high that, in the latter part of the third century, an outstanding scholar announced: "When no authority is specifically cited in the Mishnah, it is understood to be Rabbi Meir."

Now at last the time was ripe for a final redaction of the teachings of the sages. To be sure, the country was peaceful, and the labours of Akiba and Meir had made it easier to study and transmit the law, but the Jews were living on a volcano, and another unexpected political catastrophe might well destroy the precious heritage of the past. It fell to Judah, the head of the *Bet Din,* to consummate the work of his zealous predecessors. Judah was himself the most erudite teacher of his age. Sprung from a family of scholars, he was trained in the tradition of Meir, enjoying the friendship of some of the most distinguished of his contemporaries, among them the emperor-philosopher Marcus Aurelius. Judah was ideally fitted for his historic task. In his home the pure Hebrew of the Bible was spoken, and many of his disciples who were familiar only with the vernacular Aramaic were able to clear up disputed passages in the Scriptures by listening to the conversation of his domestics.

For half a century Judah and his disciples toiled on the mountain of tradition, using the redaction of Meir as a basis. At length, about A.D. 220, the decisions and opinions of a hundred and forty-eight *Tannaim,* from the time of Hillel to his own day, were neatly grouped in six categories. In the tractate on "Seeds" were contained all the agricultural laws, many now rendered obsolete by the destruction of the State, and the laws dealing with prayers, blessings, and the rights of the poor. "Feasts" dealt with the sabbath and the Jewish holidays and fast-days, their customs, their ritual, and the methods of determining their exact dates. The tractate on "Women" discussed the laws of betrothal, marriage, divorce, the levirate, and the regulations which governed vows. Civil and criminal laws, the most practical parts of the Mishnah, were included in a long division on "Damages." "Sacred Things" dealt principally with the now discontinued sacrifices and ritual of the Temple. "Purifications," which codified the Levitical rites, also contained much that was no longer useful, but there were important sections dealing with hygienic regulations for men and women.

Even yet the Mishnah was not committed to writing; the fear of setting up a rival authority to the Torah was still too strong. But with the code now whipped into order, conflicts settled, decisions clearly made, the rabbis were no longer perturbed by the thought that an unexpected calamity could destroy even a single decision of the sainted *Tannaim*.

Nearly six hundred years were spanned by the Mishnah, and it faithfully mirrored the varied life of the changing centuries. Some of its traditions came from the days when the cultures of the Greek and the Hebrew were locked in mortal combat, some when the Romans sought to break down Jewish persistence, and some when all was quiet and peaceful and study could proceed without hindrance. Those who contributed to the code came from all walks of life, for neither the teachers nor their disciples devoted themselves exclusively to study. They earned a livelihood as merchants, artisans, farmers, doctors, or even menial labourers. One of the heads of the academies of Palestine was a humble charcoal-burner. Men worked during the day and studied in their hours of leisure. Even the most distinguished teachers scorned "to use the Torah as a spade." The dignity of labour was unquestioned. "A tradesman at his task," the rabbis said, "need not rise before the most learned teacher."

The compilation of the Mishnah marked a turning-point in Jewish history. It was never intended to be authoritative legal code, but in effect it became just that. Even the obsolete laws which it preserved — laws of sacrifice, of Temple ritual, of agrarian procedure — became sacred and were discussed and expounded as if they still had vitality. No attempt was made to distinguish between fundamental laws and petty regulations. All were alike important. The Mishnah itself set up the rule: "Be equally conscientious in small as in great precepts, for ye know not their individual rewards." Future generations regulated their lives by the Mishnah, and what some of the rabbis had feared came true. The great compilation tended to overshadow the Scriptures which it was created to expound.

2. THE GEMARA

It was inevitable that the exegetical genius of the Jewish teachers should continue to spin new interpretations and concepts even after the Mishnah had been codified. For the next three centuries the Mishnah became the text about which another and vastly greater body of tradition developed. It must be remembered that the practice of dialectic interpretation was not limited to the rabbis. All over the civilized world men were sharpening their wits in legal and philosophical casuistry; the academies of Palestine and Babylon had their counterparts in the famous schools of Rome and Alexandria. The Church Fathers developed the elaborate theology of Christianity, which stood supreme until the Protestant Reformation, while the *Amoraim* (the disciples of the great teachers) elaborated the teachings of their forbears and created the Talmudic Judaism which remained dominant, despite all challenge, until the eighteenth century.

The Palestinian academies continued for two centuries after the completion of the Mishnah. Their discussions were carefully transmitted from generation to generation until they were codified in the Palestinian Talmud in 390. But the centre of intellectual activity had already shifted to Babylon. Despite its academies, Palestinian life decayed; there was no enthusiasm, no confidence in the future. The country was economically debilitated and the Eastern schools called too temptingly to the best teachers and scholars for them to resist. Early in the fourth century the Palestinian schools, after a distinguished history, were closed, and in 425 the Emperor Theodosius II abolished the patriarchal office, which had been held by the head of the academy.

Babylon had not ceased to be an important centre of Jewish life since the days when Nebuchadrezzar had dragged the leading Jewish families of Palestine into captivity. Augmented by exiles and colonists, the population increased enormously until, when the Mishnah was closed, it ran well beyond a million. The opulent cities of Nehardea, Nisibis, and Mahoza, on the grand canal, and Pumbedita and Sura, in the interior, contained influential Jewish communities, numbering among them the wealthiest caravan merchants and the most skilful artisans. On the country-side the Jews were prominent as farmers, cattle-breeders and landowners. The Jews formed a practically autonomous unit, and their head, known as the *Resh Galuta* (the prince of the Captivity or exilarch), was accorded almost royal honours. Usually he was a man who combined outstanding ability with a courtly bearing, and, because of the lavish gifts which poured in upon him from his co-religionists everywhere, he was able to maintain a regal establishment.

But the glory of Babylonian Jewish life lay, not in its princely exilarch nor in its wealthy landowners, but in its academies and scholars. In the middle of the third century two exceptional teachers, Samuel and Rab, were able, by their erudition and their organizing ability, to wrest the intellectual supremacy from Palestine. Both accepted the Mishnah of Judah as the basis for their scholarship, but they utilized it much more ingeniously than the scholars in the land which gave it birth.

Samuel was a man of remarkable versatility for the third century. He had been trained in the field of medicine, and, though he became head of the academy at Nehardea, he was as much sought after for his prescriptions as for his Talmudic judgments. He studied astronomy until the ways of the heavens seemed as clear to him as the ways of Nehardea, but he did not fall victim, as so many other astronomers did, to the wiles of astrology. Despite his scientific turn of mind Samuel wrote some excellent poetry, and a number of his prayers went to enrich the Jewish liturgy. His thorough knowledge of civil law made his decisions authoritative in all disputes. He was an excellent statesman, recognizing that Jews must share fully, as far as they were able, in the life of their community. One of his dicta, accepted ever after, made the law of the State binding on all Jews in matters not affecting religious life.

Abba Arika, affectionately known as Rab, surpassed his younger contemporary in depth and original ability. He was a striking personality, towering in height, affable, and able to win the friendship of Gentiles as well as Jews. It is not improbable that he numbered among his correspondents Jerome and Origen, the latter perhaps the most distinguished theologian of the early Church. Early in his career Rab served as inspector of markets, and his travels gave him exceptional opportunities to come into contact with all types of men. After having refused the presidency of the academy in Nehardea, he established at Sura, in 219, a new academy, which was destined to last for eight centuries and to outshine all of the other Babylonian schools. Here Rab taught early in the morning and late at night, the only times when his students were free to devote themselves to learning. At festivals he spoke in the synagogues to vast audiences, and during the two Kalla months, when there was freedom from labour, more than twelve thousand young and old gathered in Sura to follow his keen and original mind through the highways and by-ways of the Mishnah.

Even as the two brilliant scholars illuminated the intellectual life of Babylon, deplorable changes were robbing the Jewish population of their hard-earned security. In 226 the old dynasty of the Arsacids, which had been favourable to the Jews, came to an end and was succeeded by the Sassanian dynasty, a succession of fanatical fire-worshippers. Ardashir I began the tradition of intolerance with an edict which called for the sacrifice, on the Magian altars, of a part of all meat intended for food. He prohibited the burial of the dead, since burial polluted the soil, and great numbers of bodies were flung out of their graves to satisfy his religious scruples. The synagogues were a standing eye sore to him, and many of them were burnt down at his orders. Samuel was able for a while to conciliate the ruler, but persecution continued intermittently all through the century. During the wars which were waged against the Romans and surrounding peoples, the Jews were frequently assaulted, and in 259 the academy of Nehardea was razed.

Even the fiercest persecutions, however, were unable to put an end to

Jewish study. Business decayed, homes were darkened, worshippers were driven underground, but learning withstood all trials. As the lights went out in one academy, the disciples rescued brands here and there to start the blaze anew elsewhere. When Nehardea was destroyed, a new academy rose to take its place in Pumbedita, which soon rivalled Sura and continued to flourish side by side with its sister academy until the tenth century. During the fourth century another school was founded at Mahoza by the erudite Raba, the most gifted teacher of his age. The prestige of the heads of the various academies rose so high during the fourth century that they, rather than the exilarch, became the spokesmen for the Jewish population.

Meantime the commentaries on the Mishnah, which were being steadily augmented by more than two centuries of discussion, were getting out of hand. Very little had been committed to writing; at most only rough notes had been preserved, and the vast literature which had developed since the days of Rab and Samuel was still being transmitted by memory from school to school and from generation to generation. The task of transmission was very much more difficult than it had been in the third century, before the Mishnah was compiled. Then it was primarily the laws that were studied; but the commentaries now included all the countless disputes which had grown out of the laws — theories, concepts, parables, stories, everything that the teachers and their disciples had said. Often there were thousands of lines of commentary on one clause of the Mishnah.

Late in the fourth century the head of the Sura academy, Ashi, began a labour of nearly fifty years to bring together the vast body of learning that had come down to him. Tractate by tractate he and his colleagues explored the whole field, rescuing the obscurest bits, striving to omit nothing. Soon after his death the impetus towards codification was strengthened by new disasters which threatened to submerge Jewish life completely. Under Yazdegerd II (438-57) it became a capital offence even to recite the *Shma*. His successor was an undisguised persecutor and many of the scholars, including the exilarch himself, fell victim to his bigotry. Hence the new head of Sura, Rabina II (474-99), took the unprecedented step of committing to writing all that Ashi had brought together. Scribes worked for years with him and his disciples, the faithful *Saboraim,* until, at the opening of the sixth century, another turning-point in Jewish history had been reached. The Gemara was at last completed. Together with its text, the Mishnah, it comprised the monumental Babylonian Talmud.

3 · THE TALMUD IN JEWISH HISTORY

A clever Hebrew satirist has described how God, infuriated by the unworthiness of Israel, demanded that His law be returned and was astonished at the never-ending number of folios that came rolling in. The quip is justified, for the process of elaborating the law continued even after the Talmud had been completed. Commentaries grew up around every one of its volumes, and then there were commentaries upon these commentaries. But the Talmud was never displaced. It became the citadel of Jewish life all through the bitter Middle Ages and, in eastern Europe, down into modern times. Almost as soon as the Jewish youngster was able to lisp his alphabet he was set to pore over the pages of the bulky tomes; most often his mind was steeped in Talmudic discussions long before he had clearly grasped the Bible itself. And the study of the Talmud continued until the very day of death. No other literature was worthy of serious consideration. The works of Christians and pagans were not only dangerous, but a stupid waste of time which could better be devoted to the sacred lore. Pages of the Talmud, like pages of the prayer-books which had been torn and tattered in use, were reverently placed aside and buried with the dead.

It was natural that enemies should look for the soul of Jewish persistence in the mysterious pages of the Talmud. Surely there was some elixir there which nourished an indomitable spirit. In every generation the Talmud was treated as if it were endowed with life, excommunicated and burnt, torn and banned. Emperors and their subordinates vied with popes and churchmen in condemning the cursed volumes, the contents of which few of them knew.[1] As late as the middle of the nineteenth century Emperor Nicholas I of Russia declared ceaseless war on the Talmud in the attempt to disintegrate the unassimilable Jewish masses.

The instinct was sound. For preserved in those musty old pages was an unquenchable flame of life. The words of the Jewish sages were there, wise and reverent words explaining the Holy Writ. The injunction was there, oft repeated, that the words must be carefully guarded, patiently fulfilled, at any cost. Had not the sages themselves suffered for them to the extent of sacrificing life and honour and security? Their example could only stir similar devotion and heroism.

Within the Talmud all was tangled and confused, curious jumbles of regulation and information without apparent connexion. It seemed as if there had been embodied in one magnificent anthology not only the decisions of the leading scholars and the discussions germane to such decisions, but also all the conversations which pertained to their external life, their views of the morning news, the occurrences in the home last night, excerpts from a fine sermon, legends which had traversed the ages — helter-skelter, like a dream, images fleeting by quickly, disconnectedly, but therefore a true summary of the life of the epochal centuries during which the Talmud grew. For life itself was unsys-

---

[1] One Capuchin friar, Henricus Seynensis, gave as the authority for a dictum which he was discussing: "*Ut narrat Rabbinus Talmud* (Thus said Rabbi Talmud)"! Cited in Deutsch: *The Talmud*, p. 6.

tematic, throbbing with many impulses, here narrow and dingy and lack-lustre, there warm and virile and glowing with richest colour.

The Talmud faithfully reflected the beliefs and notions of its people. In close proximity were the crassest superstitions and the most commendable ethical ideals. The rabbis believed with Pliny and the ancient world that the lion is frightened by the crowing of the cock, that the salamander can extinguish fire. They had faith in the Shamir, a tiny worm as large as a barley grain, which had been created during the twilight of the sixth day and whose look could cleave rocks. Many of them burdened their disciples with petty, burdensome rites and regulations that enslaved their spirit and warped their outlook.

But the rabbis also knew how to regulate their lives by a touching piety, by charity and self-sacrifice. " He who gives charity in secret," they said, " is greater than Moses himself." They taught an exalted concept of God and the true meaning of tolerance. "Into a well from which you have drunk, cast no stone." Lovers of learning, they cherished kindness more than wisdom, a clean spirit above a world of knowledge. " He who has more learning than good works is like a tree with many branches, but few roots, which the first wind throws on its face; whilst he whose works are greater than his knowledge is like a tree with many roots and fewer branches, but which all the winds of heaven cannot uproot." Their ideals were often limited by the world in which they lived, but more often they soared high above its passions and hatreds. When they taught, the Roman empire was fast decaying and the barbarian hordes, not yet tinctured by Christianity, dissipated their energies in wars.

Two types of learning were embodied in the Talmudic literature, the law, known as the Halakah, and the narrative, known as the Haggada. The first, already discussed, dealt with the structure of Jewish life, civil as well as religious, personal as well as social. The other, the *obiter dicta,* was the genuine literature, less important, but more engrossing. It appeared in the most unexpected places. A group of teachers would be discussing a clause in the Mishnah and then, to illustrate their points, would suddenly dart off into parable or proverb and, twisting and turning for four or five pages, would slowly return by another path. Heine was repelled by much in the Talmudic literature, but he loved the Haggada.

> He would turn to seek refreshment
> In the blossoming Haggada,
>
> Where the beautiful old sagas,
> Legends dim, and angel-fables,
> Pious stories of the martyrs,
> Festal hymns and proverbs wise,

And hyperboles the drollest,
But withal so strong and burning
With belief — where all, resplendent,
Welled and sprouted with luxuriance!

The Haggada has been the source and inspiration of many of the beautiful legends which have enriched mediæval Christian and Mohammedan literature. Some of the choicest tales embedded in the classics of Dante and Boccaccio, Cervantes and Milton came, consciously or unconsciously, from this forgotten source.

Many Talmud enthusiasts are lavish in their praise of its virtues. They find therein not only the finest expressions of the religious spirit, but hints for every advance which the modern world has made, from evolution to airships. Others, sceptical of Jewish genius in the benighted Middle Ages, have taken the gargoyles "that mount their thousand years' guard over our cathedrals, for the gleaming statues of the Saints within." [1] No view is worth while which fails to consider that the Talmud is a complex document, a cross section of the heart and mind of the Jewish nation during the rise and fall of the Roman empire. Its inadequacies are all too patent, but no nation may be judged solely by the moments in which it drags wearily along with the rest of an unemancipated humanity. Its contribution to progress is to be found in the frequent times in which it rises out of its environment to lift the human spirit to worthier ideals and better hopes.

[1] Deutsch: *The Talmud*, p. 7.

CHAPTER THIRTEEN

THE NEW MOSLEM WORLD

FOR a large part of the sixth and seventh centuries the Persian and the Eastern Roman empires were locked in deadly combat. At several stages of the long struggle it appeared as if the Christian empire would be shattered. The illustrious Justinian was driven insane when the Persian forces penetrated to the very shores of the Mediterranean, taking over the chief cities and capturing more than three hundred thousand men. Early in the seventh century the Persians won more stupendous victories, even carrying off the holy cross from Jerusalem. But the victors were not without wounds either. The battles of nearly two centuries, which rocked the Eastern empire, also exhausted the Persian kingdom, and when the peace of 628 was signed, both rivals were in a state of prostration.

The ground was thus well laid for the triumph of a new force, the inspired army of Islam, which was soon to emerge from the Arabian desert to destroy both the Persian and the Byzantine empires. The rise and development of the new Arabian faith, which transformed the political and religious history of Europe and the East, affected Jewish life more profoundly than any development since the triumph of Christianity.

I. MOHAMMED AND ISLAM

Long before the rise of Islam there were flourishing Jewish communities in the Arabian peninsula. They were usually centred in the more habitable parts, especially in the oases of the south and the north-west. Yathrib, or Medina, where Mohammed rose to power and where his tomb lies, may have been founded by Jews; when it first emerges into history, it was held by the Jews. The town of Khaibar, farther north, and one of the most prosperous settlements in all Arabia, was another Jewish centre. In Yemen in the fifth century one of the pagan princes, Dhu Nuwas, became enamoured of Judaism and carried his whole province with him into the Jewish fold. There is evidence that it became a proselytizing state and even persecuted non-believers. But it was not destined to endure. It came to an end later in the century, when it was successively overrun by the Christian Abyssinians and the heathen Persians.

The Jews were evidently thoroughly at home in Arabia. Like the pure Arabs, they were organized into tribes, and often engaged in the internecine feuds which were the bane of desert life. Their names were Arabic, their speech was Arabic, and some of the finest work in early Arabic literature was the product of Jewish poets and singers. In most respects, however, they lived on a higher level than the Arabs. They were much better equipped for agriculture and were proficient in industries which were virtually unknown to the natives. They probably introduced the culture of the date-palm into the peninsula. They formed the artisan class, and many of them rose to wealth and power as gold- and silversmiths and as manufacturers of arms. Their religion, to which they clung with great devotion through every trial, was another factor which raised them above the natives, who worshipped the heavenly hosts and were a prey to every desert superstition. The Arabs wondered at the facility with which the Jews could read and write, and their respect for the queer people of the Book was almost a fear. "Novelists," writes the biographer of Mohammed, " sometimes depict the awe which book-learning evokes in those who are abso- lutely without it; and this, which for a time was Mohammed's attitude, was, if not normal, at any rate common among the pagans of Arabia who had come into contact with Jews and Christians." [1]

The founder of Mohammedanism was born in Mecca in 570, when Arabia was suffering most from its ignorance and disunity. His family boasted of a noble lineage, but materially it had evidently seen its best days. On the early death of Mohammed's father and mother the young orphan was cast upon the world with nothing but the sturdy constitution which enabled him to bear his many privations. All his life he was a prey to melancholy and given to strange fits. He often alarmed his intimates when his trances rendered him virtually unconscious and left him thoroughly exhausted.

He had very little education and could never read or write. But he has seldom been surpassed as a man of practical affairs. Quickness substituted for learning, and organizing genius for genuine spiritual fervour. As a camel-driver, he travelled considerably and was able to assimilate scraps of information which intrigued him. He was at the mercy of circumstances, however, and he learned nothing well. The Biblical phraseology which he gleaned from Jews and Christians was fragmentary and inaccurate; almost to the end of his life he did not distinguish between the sister of Moses and the mother of Jesus. Naturally he imbibed many of the superstitions of his day and trusted in charms and incantations to drive away evil. Later when he discovered that a serpent's bite had been healed by the recitation of some verses of the Koran, he claimed a part of the fee!

Until well into the prime of life he lived from hand to mouth. His enemies never forgot his humble birth and his early vagabondage, and they often mocked him as a " palm sprung from a dung-hill." Then suddenly his privations ended. The gentle widow Kadijah, one of the wealthiest women in the land, whose

[1] Margoliouth: *Mohammed*, p. 41.

caravans Mohammed had safely conducted to Syria, offered her hand to the young and handsome eccentric whose blazing black eyes and tense face strangely fascinated. Mohammed never regretted the union, though Kadijah was many years older than he was. She not only restored him to the station of his ancestors and released him from further cares about a livelihood, but made him an excellent wife.

During the years of his maturity Mohammed became strangely concerned with religious problems and brooded over them continually. The religion of his fathers seemed hollow and empty. He hated the idolatry that disgraced Arabia, the blood feuds, the degraded, wasted lives. Was it not possible to unite all Arabs and perhaps all godly men by a simple faith in the one God who ruled all creation and whose spirit could regenerate the life of the desert? The more Mohammed thought, the more the conviction grew upon him that he was divinely ordained to bring a new message to his people. He was broad enough to recognize the genius of the religious leaders of the past who had helped to elevate the human spirit — Abraham, Moses, Jesus, and other Biblical characters. But, naturally enough, he felt that he, the last of the prophets, transcended them all.

Westerners find little that stirs the soul in the record of Mohammed's revelations, collected reverently after his death and incorporated in the hundred and fourteen suras of the Koran. It seems to be an incoherent rhapsody of fable, precept, and declamation, " which sometimes crawls in the dust and is sometimes lost in the clouds." But behind the confused messages was a powerful personality, an ardent, passionate soul capable of carrying his followers through every impossible sacrifice. Mohammed was his own greatest contribution to his faith.

At first the new religion made little headway, for Mohammed dared not proclaim himself openly. There were too many vested interests in the three hundred and sixty-five idols of Mecca; too much loyalty was bound up with the sacred stone of the Caaba. It seemed wiser to work secretly until the little band of proselytes had grown to respectable proportions. In ten years there were less than a hundred converts, mostly slaves and lowly persons. But there was also the faithful Abu Bekr, a tower of strength to Mohammed in every crisis; and the gallant Omar, a masterful soldier and the fiercest rider in all Arabia. These men later became the apostles of a militant Mohammedanism; they carried it out of Arabia and spread it throughout the Eastern world.

The little group lived by the teachings of Mohammed, practising the ceremonies, reciting the prayers, and pinning their faith to the Prophet's revelations, which now came frequently through the angel Gabriel. Mohammed made few demands — sincere prayer, fasting, alms-giving, and complete submission to the will of Allah. His precepts could be understood by the simplest. They embodied, in Gibbon's summary, the hope "that prayer will carry the true believer half way to God, fasting will bring him to the door of his palace, and alms will gain him admittance."

At last, when Mohammed was in his fortieth year, the angel Gabriel came to him in a vision and commanded him to proclaim his faith.

> "Cry, in the name of Allah!
> In the name of Allah, who hath created man!
> Oh, arise and preach
> And magnify Allah."

The Meccans at first ridiculed the new sect; obviously its adherents were unbalanced or under the influence of malignant jinn. Then they bitterly denounced Mohammed as an enemy of the ancient gods and would have killed him but for the influence of his relatives. Evil days were now ahead of the prophet. Kadijah died and her property passed into other hands. The pinch of poverty was added to the persecutions of the authorities. The number of converts had grown to over a hundred, but most of them required assistance, and their miserable condition tore Mohammed's heart. The situation was intolerable, and in 622, when Mohammed discovered that his enemies were plotting his death, he fled with his followers to Medina, where a small group of Arabs who had been impressed with his teachings welcomed him. The year of the flight, the Hegira, became the year one of the Mohammedan calendar.

In Medina Mohammed made more encouraging progress; among his converts were some of the leading members of the Khazraj tribe. But above all he was anxious to win over the Jews. They were the wealthiest inhabitants of Medina and their adhesion to his cause would bring not only prestige, but material strength. He felt that of all groups they should feel closest to him. He had accepted the revelations of the Biblical seers and prophets. He was proud of his descent, through Ishmael, from Abraham. He ordered his followers to fast on the Day of Atonement and to turn in prayer towards Jerusalem. He rose reverently when Jewish funerals passed by him. He even arranged his hair as the Jews wore theirs!

All in vain. Only a few Jews would be won over. The leaders pointed out his colossal ignorance of the Bible and scoffed at his pompous and blasphemous pretensions. The more he yielded, the more they jeered. Mohammed was obliged to content himself with sullen words, for his power was by no means firmly established in Medina. But he bided his time.

Meantime he seemed to be at the end of his resources in Medina also. His followers were starving and went about in rags. Neither the Jews nor the Christians would lend him money without heavy security. He himself knew the pangs of hunger. At last he determined to turn robber. He sent out his followers to waylay some of the better-laden caravans. Were not their owners idolaters? It was surely just to punish unbelievers. The first few raids brought little success; then Mohammed gave orders to attack in the sacred month during which no fighting was permitted. His ruthlessness and his dishonourable tactics horrified the pagans, but a special revelation came to Mohammed just in time to justify the procedure, and the booty helped the believers through their most precarious period.

Mohammed was now, in 624, strong enough to risk battle against the powerful Meccans. At Badr he led three hundred followers against over a thousand of his infuriated former townsmen and utterly crushed them. The victory was hailed as the Day of Deliverance and it proved to be the turning-point in Mohammed's fortunes. The booty and the ransom relieved his followers from all material difficulties and strengthened their faith in the prophet's destiny. He returned to Medina a hero.

Mohammed had now broken completely with the hated Jews. He turned again in prayer to Mecca; he set aside the whole month of Ramadan as a season of fasting; and he changed every rite and custom which suggested Jewish practices. The revelation which is contained in the long Sura of the Cow is filled with invective against the stiff-necked race.

In keeping with his feelings, Mohammed turned to avenge himself upon the Jewish tribe, the Kainuka, who were strongly entrenched about the market places of Medina. The Kainuka, in a panic, appealed to the other Jewish tribes near by. Had there been an immediate response, Mohammed's career might have ended abruptly, for his forces did not yet number more than a few hundred. But the Jewish tribes, lulled by a false sense of security, would not co-operate, and after a brief siege the resistance of the Kainuka collapsed. Mohammed would have put the whole population to the sword but for the intervention of Abdallah, a converted Jew, who stood high in the favour of the Prophet. Mohammed satisfied himself by packing off the Jews out of the land and confiscating their possessions. The goods of the seven hundred wealthiest inhabitants of Medina, distributed among the faithful, raised many of them to fortune and power. The rewards of Islam were of this world also.

Next year there was a momentary set-back when the Meccans, strongly reinforced, roundly defeated Mohammed at Uhud. The defeat was a heavy blow, but there were still Jewish tribes within reach to retrieve the situation. Mohammed marched upon the wealthy Banu Nadir, who were concentrated in a village three miles from Medina. Those who were assailed appealed to the other Jewish tribes to help protect themselves from future disaster by sending immediate assistance. But again there was no response, and the Banu Nadir were left to their fate. They resisted manfully for weeks, and Mohammed, to hasten their capitulation, again broke a sacred practice of the desert and cut down the date-palms outside of the village. This act of vandalism was even more shocking than the destruction of unarmed caravans during the sacred month, but again there was a special revelation which justified the outrage.

The Jews were compelled to submit and were soon flying towards Syria, while their possessions were divided among the followers of Mohammed.

Within the next few years, through one pretext or another, Mohammed destroyed the strength and influence of the Jewish settlements which remained. More than six hundred families had been living comfortably in a suburb of Medina. They entered into negotiations with the Meccans to destroy Mohammed and drive his followers from the city. The alliance was shattered even before the warfare began and Mohammed, seeking vengeance, refused to be restrained by any consideration. The whole population were put to the sword, their bodies were flung into a rude ditch, and their wealth and arms were confiscated. Then came the turn of the most prosperous of all Jewish communities, Khaibar, which had steadily refused to assist the other Jewish tribes in their distress. Instead of slaughtering the unfortunate inhabitants, Mohammed took half of their possessions and permitted them to remain on the soil, when they submitted to the condition that one half of what they produced belonged to the conqueror.

The fall of Khaibar ended the vigorous Jewish life of the peninsula. Jews remained, but they were a subject class, living always with the fear of the sword over them. Another religion had sprung from Judaism, but again the parent became an outcast and a pariah.

After the death of Mohammed all of Arabia was won to Islam. The discredited palm of the dung-hill became the unifying force about which the whole peninsula rallied. The grosser things of his life were forgotten — his sensuality, his duplicity, his cruelty to enemies. Only his faith was remembered, his perseverance, his fervent, moving messages. Stories of his miraculous powers grew up, of course. He had healed the sick and raised the dead. He was lord of trees and plants and animals. Water had gushed from his fingers, a shoulder of mutton had warned him that it was poisoned. A word from him had split the orb of the moon. But through all the legend that inevitably attached itself to him his genuine contribution shone out bright and clear. He had united a feud-ridden peninsula into a religious nation; he had abolished idolatry; he had ended intoxication; he had placed polygamy on a responsible basis; and he had introduced a splendid moral code among the primitive Arabs.

The subject of Jewish influence on Islam has not yet been thoroughly explored and it is too intangible to satisfy scientific minds. Yet it is clear that though Mohammed's work bore the stamp of original genius, he was signally indebted to Judaism for its content. The Arab prophet borrowed from Judaism his God, the foundations of his theology, the heroes of the Old Testament, many of his prayers, the laws of cleanliness and uncleanliness, and much of his moral code. Mohammedan jurisprudence has been vitally influenced by Jewish practice, and even a superficial examination reveals how much of Islamic legend and literature has been inspired by Jewish sources. Whatever Mohammed borrowed he changed and adapted to the needs of his desert people. But his religious principles and his early reliance upon Judaism demonstrate his instinctive realization of the debt due to the mother faith.

Islam now emerged from the wastes of Arabia to conquer the world. It seemed to be invested with irresistible power. Religious zeal, added to hunger and unparalleled opportunities for plunder, were a most efficient combination. Within five years of the Prophet's death all of Syria had fallen, except Jerusalem and Cæsarea. Babylon was conquered in 637 and its splendid capital at Ctesiphon, the residence of the Sassanids, was entered without a struggle. By 641 all of the once magnificent Persian empire had been reduced to vassalage. Forward, ever forward, the Mohammedan armies surged, and at the end of the century the haunting muezzin, calling the faithful to prayer, was heard from minarets throughout northern Africa and nearly all of western Asia.

After the first impetuous sweep the conquerors did not compel their subjects to adopt Islam. They were content to accept homage and a heavy tribute. Theoretically the restrictions which were established reduced the vanquished Christians and Jews to slavery. By the Code of Omar they were not permitted to bear arms or to raise their dwellings above those of the Mohammedans. They could not worship in a loud voice, nor build new houses of prayer, nor rebuild their old ones. They could hold no judicial or administrative office, nor employ Moslem slaves. They were compelled to wear marks by which they might be easily distinguished from faithful sons of Islam.[1] But fortunately most of these restrictions were dead letters. A schism had occurred in the Moslem world, and the caliphs of Bagdad, in contact with Western civilization, refused to be bound by the strict letter of the code. They overlooked many of its intolerant commands, and so long as subjects kept their peace and paid their poll-tax and their ground-rent, they were content. They interfered little in their affairs and allowed them to live an almost autonomous life. From the eighth century onward, therefore, the Jews of the East enjoyed a period of unprecedented peace and freedom, rivalled only in France during the tolerant and distinguished reign of Louis the Pious.

2. THE REVOLT AGAINST THE TALMUD

Jewish religious life in these tranquil, unmolested centuries was governed by the Geonim, the heads of the famous academies. They were the spiritual descendants of the sages who had created the Talmud. They drew students from all over the world and trained them to carry unbroken the traditions which they had inherited. Their position gave them prestige which challenged

[1] It is interesting to note that practically all of the disabilities in the Code of Omar were taken over by the Moslems from the Christians.

the supremacy of the exilarchs and the masses unquestionably accepted their regulations. By the eighth century the authority of the Talmud was supreme in all matters—from the prayers for a new garment to the amount of dough which the pious housewife was obliged to burn at each baking.

Yet there was always a current of opposition which challenged the supremacy of the Talmud and, all through the eighth century, attempts were made to burst through its restraint. Some of these attempts arose from other causes, political and personal, but even these gained their strength when they were associated with the opposition to the Talmudic interpretation of Judaism.

One formidable protest came early in the eighth century when a certain Serene proclaimed himself, in Syria, as the long-awaited Messiah, divinely ordained to expel the Moslems from the Holy Land. He released his followers from dependence upon the Talmud, abolishing the dietary laws, the regulations that governed the holidays, and the other practices which, he thought, pressed heavily on the people. Serene gained thousands of adherents, and his fame spread as far as Spain. He was soon captured, however, by the caliph, Yazed II, who turned him over to the Jews for punishment and thus effectively ended his Messianic pretensions.

Thirty years later there was another uprising, led by Obaiah Abu Isa, centring in Ispahan, the capital of Persia. The time seemed opportune, for revolts were everywhere shaking the foundations of the Omayyad dynasty, and no man could trust his neighbour. One pretender, Abdullah, trapped ninety Omayyads at a banquet, had them clubbed to death, and then, throwing leather covers over the corpses, ordered the banquet to be served on them. Pious souls saw in the bloodshed and brutality the end of the world and listened eagerly to every gifted personality who seemed to have a divine message. Abu Isa was an illiterate tailor, but he was endowed with great courage and was honestly convinced that he was the last of the five forerunners of the Messiah. He, too, denied the authority of the Talmud and returned to the clear principles of the Bible. More than ten thousand Persian Jews joined his standard. He led a spectacular career as a soldier and religious reformer until 755, when he fell at the head of his troops. The movement at once collapsed, though a small sect of Isavites remained to cherish his memory and to follow his principles, until late in the tenth century.

The most serious and important revolt against the authority of the Talmud, however, originated in Bagdad, in the very heart of Gaonite strength, and was led by Anan ben David, the founder of the Karaite sect. Little is known of Anan except that he sprang from a distinguished family and was undoubtedly a man of great force and iron will. The disciples who knew him idolized him and acclaimed him as a model of piety and holiness, who, "if he had lived at the time when the Temple was still standing, would have been vouchsafed the gift of prophecy."

According to the traditional story, which may or may not be true, Anan stood in line for the exilarchate, but, because his orthodoxy was suspected, he was passed over in favour of a younger brother. Anan had powerful friends, many of whom shared his distaste for the Talmudic despotism, and, in 767, they proclaimed him as counter-exilarch and urged him to defy the Geonim. A conflict began at once and the caliph was appealed to. He construed Anan's defiance as treason. The rebel was cast into prison and narrowly escaped being executed. By a ruse he succeeded in gaining his release and migrated to Palestine, where he became the head of a new sect, which quickly spread through Syria and Egypt and even into south-eastern Europe.

Just what Anan believed, it is impossible to say, for most of his writings have been lost and his views have survived only through the refutations of bitter opponents. It is clear, however, that Anan accepted the Bible as the supreme authority in Jewish life and vigorously denied the pretensions of the Talmudic traditions. His followers believed that the battle had been fought often before; most of them regarded Jesus as a magnificent teacher and prophet who had come not to found a new religion, but to re-establish the supremacy of the Torah against the restrictions imposed by the rabbis. Because of their strict adherence to the clear, written word of the law, unobscured by casuistical interpretation, the new sect later became known as the Bnai Mikra (the children of the text) or the Karaites.

The new doctrines released the Karaites from many heavy burdens. The dietary laws were made less stringent, the phylacteries were abolished, and many other restrictive practices were dropped. Yet much new severity was also introduced when the Talmudic modifications of the Biblical word were denied authority. No lights shone in Karaite homes on the sabbath; fast-days were multiplied; the only meat that could be eaten was deer meat; the only fowl, pigeon. Physicians were barred, for did not the Scriptures say clearly: "I am the Lord that healeth thee."

Characteristically there was no orthodox Karaism; Anan himself had insisted that his followers " search the Scriptures diligently and lean not upon my opinion." Each little Karaite community interpreted the Scriptures by its own light and made its own regulations. The differences which naturally developed were often fundamental, for little was known of pure Hebrew and scientific exegesis was still in its infancy.

The movement might have degenerated into a variety of petty sects, each clinging to its own innovation. It was momentarily saved from such a fate half a century after Anan's death by a deeply learned rationalist, Benjamin Nahavendi, who was honoured by the Karaites almost as greatly an Anan. Benjamin was not averse to independent thinking. "Inquiry," he taught, "is a duty, and errors occasioned by inquiry do not constitute a sin." Yet he thought it necessary to crystallize the Karaite ideas to prevent the disintergration of the movement. In constructing the system he modified much of the harshness which strict adherence to the letter of the law had made necessary.

The Karaite heresy spread, and for a time it threatened to become supreme in Jewish life. But with the rise of Saadiah, a powerful champion of Talmudic Judaism who flourished in the middle of the tenth century, Karaism began to lose its vitality. It depended for its strength upon the very principles that weakened it. Its individualism, the ideal that called it into being, prevented its organization. Hence despite Benjamin's work the Karaites split into quarrelling sects, each holding different views. After the eleventh century their numbers steadily declined and they ceased to play an influential part in Jewish life. They gained a temporary importance during the Reformation when Catholics hurled the epithet "Karaei" at Protestants, in contempt for their slavery to the Biblical text, a term which the Protestants gladly accepted. Today Karaites number no more than twelve thousand, most of whom live in Russia, where they have often been released from the restrictions placed upon the Jews.

The Karaite rebellion, though it failed, was a useful development in Jewish life. To be sure, the view is no longer tenable that the Karaites, building their fortress solely upon the Bible, were the first to study Hebrew scientifically and were the pioneers in the field of Hebrew philology. There were many rabbinical scholars who long preceded them in such research. Yet it cannot be denied that their reliance upon the Bible gave an immense impetus to the study of Hebrew, for they compelled their followers to equip themselves and their opponents to defend themselves. " Their very existence as a schismatic sect, their negative attitude toward traditional Judaism, and their active propaganda, in speech and in writing, for the new cause, could not have failed to incite a counter-activity among the Rabbinites." [1]

There was another useful consequence of the revolt. Talmudic Judaism required periodic protests against its supremacy to prevent it from ossifying. It was helpful to remind the rabbis that, while interpretation of the Bible was highly commendable, when the process was carried too far it could easily become pernicious.

3. SAADIAH AND THE LAST GEONIM

One of the most important figures in the political and religious history of mediæval Judaism was Saadiah ben Joseph, who came like a bright star to light up the darkness of his age. In western Europe learning had almost completely decayed, and in the east intellectual life stood at a level only a little higher. Among Jews nothing of value, with the exception of certain Midrashim, had been produced since the days when the Talmud was closed. Saadiah was

[1] Malter: *Life and Works of Saadiah Gaon*, p. 46.

the first religious philosopher since the time of Philo who attempted to elaborate the doctrines of Judaism into a philosophy and to harmonize this system with the thought of the day. His work released a tradition of religious learning and speculation which vitally influenced his own and later generations.

Saadiah was born in the Fayum in upper Egypt towards the close of the ninth century. Little is known of his early life, but from his subsequent activity it is clear that his education was wide and thorough. He absorbed Mohammedan as well as Talmudic learning and he familiarized himself with the Karaite literature and point of view. His was a robust and alert mind, supported by courage which did not flinch in any struggle. While still a very young man, he published his first work, a vigorous attack on the principles of Anan and the Karaites, and an able defence of the authority of tradition. For three years he continued his onslaught on the Karaite heresies, not contenting himself, as other rabbinical champions had, with mere abuse. He was thoroughly at home in the issues involved and met his opponents thought for thought.

Taking a leaf from the Karaite book, Saadiah began to translate the Bible into Arabic, with commentaries, to enable the masses to understand the sources of Talmudic inspiration and to counteract the Karaite propaganda. Though little was known of the principles upon which the Hebrew language and grammar were based, he also developed a lexicon (*Iggaron*), an important pioneering effort, despite all of its limitations.

Soon after, he began a series of migrations through Palestine, Syria, and the East, which ultimately brought him to Babylon. He was at once engaged in other literary and religious controversies and again demonstrated the soundness of his learning and the perfection of his dialectic skill. When Ben Meir, a well-respected scholar of Palestine, and the head of one of its academies, sought to make innovations in the calendar, Saadiah routed him in a brilliant work which established beyond cavil the case for the traditional methods.

Saadiah's vigorous championing of the Talmudic cause made him its inevitable leader; when a vacancy occurred in the headship of the Sura academy, a few years after his controversy with Ben Meir, he was offered the position. He showed himself to be no closet philosopher, but gave himself unstintingly to teachers and students, who flocked in from everywhere to come under the wing of his versatile genius. He soon re-established Sura as the Mecca of Jewish culture.

Unfortunately a bitter quarrel broke out between Saadiah and the exilarch, which threatened to undermine all of his achievements. The ill feeling had existed since Saadiah's installation; in fact, the Geonim and the exilarchs, rival authorities in Jewish life, were not usually in harmony. In this instance Saadiah disapproved of the methods by which the exilarch was raising funds for the maintenance of his regal establishment. The issue came to a head when the conscientious gaon refused to approve a case in which it seemed that the exilarch was rendering judgment unjustly to bring profit to himself. In the venomous quarrel which followed, both sides appealed to the caliph, the drunken Al Kahir, who ordered the deposition of Saadiah. This act split the Babylonian community and threatened to nullify all leadership. The gaon's health was seriously undermined by the aggravation.

Yet the whole affair had its advantage. Saadiah was now able to devote himself exclusively to his literary labours, and the four years of retirement in Bagdad were the most productive period in his career. Freedom from responsibility was urgently needed if he was to round out his work. For though a reconciliation finally came and Saadiah was reinstated with every mark of honour, he did not long survive. Before he had lived out his prime, he was tired unto death and soon after went to his rest.

Until recently the true importance of Saadiah's influence on mediæval life was not realized. His works were written mainly in Arabic, and with the closing of the Babylonian schools, soon after his death, they could be easily studied only in Spain. When the Moors and the Jews were expelled in the fifteenth century, Arabic became an unknown tongue there too, and much of Saadiah's work was forgotten and lost. Though it was recognized that he, more than any one else, had destroyed the effectiveness of the Karaite movement and that he had given a genuine impetus to scriptural study through his exegetical enterprise, he remained an obscure figure. His name was reverenced and he was termed a classic, but, like all classics, he was neither read nor known.

Since the discovery of fragments of Saadiah's work in the Genizah at Cairo, there has been a reawakening of interest in the old intellectual warrior, and a renewed appreciation of his influence. It is now clear that his chief contribution was neither in controversy with the Karaites nor in exegesis. He was the creator of mediæval Jewish philosophy, the forerunner of a school that sought to systematize Jewish thought and to harmonize it with the most advanced conceptions of the time. He was conservative enough to insist that pure speculation was futile and that the basis of any Jewish system must be the divine revelation vouchsafed to Moses and the prophets. But within these limits genuine and sincere speculation was useful and, indeed, necessary. It was narrow to argue that it was dangerous because it led to scepticism. Then astronomy was dangerous too, since there were many stupid people who believed that the moon went into eclipse because a dragon swallowed it.

After all, revelation and reason were complementary, two means of reaching the truth. Reason was the patient, practical way. Revelation was the way of intuition; " without it men would have to go a long way round to reach clearness through their own thought." Saadiah's suggestion that revelation and reason were complementary was taken over by Maimonides and became the foundation of his own philosophical system, from whom it passed on into the epochal theology of St. Thomas Aquinas, the most important of mediæval Catholic philosophers.

After Saadiah's day conditions were no longer favourable in the East for the perpetuation of learning. Babylon was engulfed in serious political troubles brought on by the inroads of the Turks. The exilarchate began to founder and, after a glorious tradition of seven centuries, lost its influence in Jewish life. The decay of the great schools soon followed. Six years after Saadiah's death the academy in Sura was closed and all attempts to revive it failed. Pumbedita still lingered, and under the popular Geonim Sherira and Hai it preserved its leadership in the Jewish world. But when the caliph imprisoned the unfortunate Hai, tortured him to discover his treasures, and then executed him, in 1040, the Gaonate, too, ceased to be an effective force. It continued to exist for several centuries, but the universal prestige which it had once enjoyed was gone for ever.

Meantime a new centre of learning had grown up. At the other end of the sea, in sunny Spain, the light which went out in Babylon was rekindled. The Babylonian scholars migrated to the west, carrying with them the precious scrolls which had been so long housed in the academies of the East. In the new world, under the tolerant rule of the Spanish Moslems, the Jewish spirit created new works of genius, and the few centuries of Jewish life in Moslem Spain are among the happiest and most fruitful in all Jewish history.

CHAPTER FOURTEEN

THE GOLDEN AGE IN MOSLEM SPAIN

I. THE RISE OF THE OMAYYADS

JEWS had been settled in Spain at least as early as the Carthaginian days. Traders, merchants, artisans, exiles, and adventurers found their way to the Pillars of Hercules in the wake of the Romans, the Suevi, the Alans, the Vandals, the Visigoths, and the other Gothic tribes who successively flooded the country and helped to form its racial character. They lived as quietly as the troubled times allowed, suffering few hardships for their faith among either pagans or Arians. In 589 the tide turned sharply when the politic Visigothic king, Reccared I, hoping to strengthen his throne, accepted the Catholic faith. Thereafter for more than a century, until the Moslem conquest (711), the Jews, along with other heretics, were constantly in the shadow of persecution. Reccared's restrictions undermined their economic life; the farmers were particularly affected by the edict which forbade the ownership of slaves. The Jews were further harried by the Twelfth Council of Toledo in 681, when the Archbishop Julian, himself the son of converts, again proved the dictum that men hate most those whom they have injured most. The culmination of a century of vicious persecution came under Egica, who confiscated the possessions of the Jews, reduced them to the status of slaves, and prohibited the practice of their faith.

It was natural for the unhappy folk to watch with hope the rise of the Saracens, who were sweeping triumphantly through the East and were now turning to the countries of the West and North. By 670 the conquering Okba had pushed to the outskirts of Algeria, and twelve years later he rode his horse into the waves of the Atlantic. The fierce Berber tribes were not easily subdued, but in 705 they, too, recognized, at least nominally, the suzerainty of the caliph. Then the Arab hosts crossed the straits into Spain, and in 711, aided by the decadent condition of the Visigothic kingdom, and, doubtless, by the sympathetic attitude of the oppressed Jews, they made themselves masters of the land.

The Moslem conquest of Spain, destined to endure for nearly seven centuries, marked a new epoch in the history of western Europe. Already with the first Omayyad, the romantic Abd Ar Rahman, who fled from the East when his family was ruined, and established himself in Córdoba in 755, a tradition of culture was begun. Under the enlightened rule of Abd Ar Rahman and his successors Spain helped dissipate some of the darkness that enveloped the

rest of Europe. Beautiful palaces and mosques, busy streets and markets, flourishing fields and orchards were the outward marks of a glorious era. The
sovereigns were patrons of learning, and authors and singers laid at their feet
the fruits of a rich genius. Abd Ar Rahman III, who assumed the title of caliph
to symbolize the passing of the Moslem headship to his brilliant Córdoba,
prized a good poem above a brave deed in battle.

For the Jewish population in Spain the coming of the invaders was a godsend. The Moslem was more concerned about poll-taxes than about converts
and therefore most of the old restrictions disappeared. Jews entered fully into
the life of the country and soon rose to wealth and power. Many of them became
leading landowners and financiers; others, prominent physicians and statesmen.
They took advantage of the exceptional cultural opportunities and added to
the glories of the age. They made a definite contribution to mediæval civilization by serving as the intermediaries between the Arabs and the Christians;
their translations and adaptations of Arabic and Greek writings bridged the
Dark Ages. The admirable work of the Arabs in mathematics and astronomy,
and their enlightened interpretation of the old Greek philosophers, came to
Europe through the Jews.[1]

The happy union of Hebrew and Moslem culture produced a renaissance
in literature and philosophy, in science and religion. Even architecture flourished and some of the most beautiful churches in Spain speak to the modern
pilgrim of their glory in a day when they served as synagogues and received
the prayers of a proud and wealthy Jewish community.

2. TWO JEWISH STATESMEN: PATRONS OF LEARNING

The long succession of distinguished Jews in Spain was begun with Hasdai
ibn Shaprut (915-70), who held the most honourable posts in the court of
Abd Ar Rahman III. Hasdai was one of Fortune's favourite sons. He inherited
wealth and a noble name from his father and was well trained in Jewish lore
and in the sciences. As a physician he had few superiors in his time. Amiable,
witty, generous, he won enduring friendships in every quarter. He was soon
attached to the court of Abd Ar Rahman, serving variously as physician, interpreter, and inspector of the customs. His tactfulness and subtlety won him
ever higher commissions, and at length his master called upon him to treat
with the diplomats from foreign lands. Though he did not enjoy the title,
Hasdai became in fact the vizier of the famous caliph. When the envoys of the
Emperor Otto the Great returned to Germany, they declared that the Jew
Hasdai surpassed any diplomat with whom they had negotiated. When Sancho,

[1] Of course even the Jewish scholars in Spain knew no Greek, but they had access to the
Arabic translations of the Greek writings, which, in turn, had come to the Arabs most frequently
through the Syriac.

the ruler of Leon, sought a cure for the excessive fatness which made him a jest to his subjects, he came to Hasdai, who incidentally engineered an alliance which the Moslem king had been anxious to have. Even the bigoted Byzantine emperor, the scourge of the Eastern Jews, found that he could not gain the ear of Abd Ar Rahman without treating through Hasdai.

Hasdai's good fortune at the court did not drive out the remembrance of his people. He was the model patron of learning, not only assisting men of talent with unstinted generosity, but himself joining in their activity. He wrote relig- ious and liturgical poetry and, though he was not a literary genius, he had exquisite taste and could hold his own with the best satirists and epigramma- tists. "In Hasdai's time," writes Ibn Daud in the twelfth century, "the poets first began to chirp."

> His goodness made the dumb to speak his name,
> Yea, stubborn hearts were not unyielding long;
> And bards the starry splendour of his fame
> Mirrored in lucent current of their song.

Perhaps Hasdai's most enduring achievement was the founding and financ- ing of a Spanish academy for Talmudic study, which soon became the most important in the world. According to the familiar legend, Fate co-operated most dramatically with his desires. Several distinguished scholars had started from the East to gather contributions for the support of the declining academy in Sura. Misfortunes overtook them and scattered them to all parts of the world. One came to Alexandria, another to Kairuwan; in each place as a result of their activity new academies were established. A third, Moses ben Enoch, was captured by Abd Ar Rahm's admiral and, after many disastrous experiences, was brought to Córdoba to be sold as a slave.[1] The Jewish community at once ransomed him, and when his astonishing knowledge of the Talmud became known, he was made the head of the new academy which Hasdai helped to establish. The generous patron brought copies of the Talmud from the East and encouraged scholars from everywhere to pursue their studies in the con- genial environment of Córdoba. Almost at the moment that the light of learn- ing went out in Sura and Pumbedita, new lights were thus kindled in the most populous centres of the Mediterranean world, the brightest of which shone in the capital of Moslem Spain.

All through the tenth century the Jews shared in the phenomenal prosperity of the country. Many of them amassed wealth in the slave trade, supplying troops for the armies, eunuchs for the harems, and servants for the home. The leading families, with long, impressive names, proud of their lineage, rode in beautiful carriages, dressed in the handsome, ornamented garments of the day,

---

[1] A fourth exile is supposed to have landed in Narbonne and begun a literary tradition there. This is solely the creation of Graetz.

in all respects like the contemporary princes and nobles. Downtrodden Jews who lived in the East and heard rumours of the splendours among which their Western brethren moved could not help discounting them as the idle fairy-tales of imaginative travellers.

Early in the eleventh century the illustrious Omayyad dynasty, after more than two hundred and fifty years, began to decline, and a long civil war at once followed. In 1031 the last of the Omayyads was deposed in a bloody palace revolution. Córdoba itself was sacked and plundered by the Berbers, who took advantage of the internal anarchy to risk a number of raids. The country split up into conflicting principalities or Taifa states, each ready to co-operate with the Christian princes to destroy the others. The unity of Moslem Spain disappeared, and the centre of Moslem power shifted to northern Africa.

It was in Granada, one of the few Spanish provinces that retained its prestige, that another versatile Jew, Samuel ibn Nagdela, rose to the highest position in the State. Like Hasdai, Samuel was a gifted statesman, a discerning critic and writer, and a generous patron of learning. But, unlike Hasdai, he rose from the humblest ranks to his exalted station. He was twenty when the disastrous civil wars began which brought the wild Suleiman and his Berber cohorts into his native Córdoba and well-nigh ruined the city. Samuel, nearly penniless, now established himself in a little shop in Málaga, selling spices and writing and interpreting letters for those who needed such service. His beautiful script brought him to the attention of the vizier, and in 1025 the fortunate young merchant was made his private secretary. Thereafter his advancement was rapid. His master consulted him in the most difficult diplomatic negotiations and soon relied upon him completely. Before the vizier died, he counselled the king, Habus, to give the Jewish interpreter his place. Habus was a Berber with few prejudices, and Samuel, the former spice-dealer, was placed in charge of the diplomatic affairs of one of the leading states in Spain.

The new position was no sinecure. Samuel had many powerful enemies in court and out. They worked on the weaknesses of the king and dinned him with tales of his vizier's favouritism and incompetence. But Samuel was adroit as well as capable. He could be hard when hardness was necessary, but his tongue dripped honey when flattery seemed to be the most effective weapon. He humoured the king better than any Moslem and at one time wrote a poem of praise which extolled his master in seven languages. For about three decades he steered his way through the problems and difficulties of his office, foiling every plot and rarely committing a blunder. When Habus died and the succession was in dispute, Samuel ranged himself with the side that was eventually victorious. The new ruler, Badis, was more interested in drinking wines and making love than in statesmanship, and Samuel, who could manage him easily, virtually became the master of the country.

The vizier gave considerable thought to the problems of the Jewish community and was its official leader. He earned the title "*Nagid*" (prince), which was bestowed upon him in gratitude. He presided over the rabbinical school in person and lectured on the intricacies of the Talmud. His works included a collection of Halakic decisions and grammatical commentaries which unfortunately have been lost. He was in constant communication with the Geonim of Babylon and the scholars of North Africa, and some of his *responsa* which are extant furnish important information about his period. His *Introduction to the Talmud* is still useful to students of rabbinical literature. As a poet he won no fame and it was said in jest that few things could be so cold as the snow of Hermon or as the songs of the Levite Samuel. Yet he was never cold to the needs of the poor scholars and teachers who thronged Granada and he contributed generously to their support. Yearly he sent olive-oil from his own estates for the synagogues of the Holy Land. Well beloved, as much at home in the Moslem world as in the Jewish, his fame spread everywhere. He was indeed worthy to introduce the brilliant succession of Jewish poets and savants who made the eleventh and twelfth centuries a golden age.

3. THE LITERARY APOGEE

The two outstanding poets in the history of mediæval Jewish literature are Solomon ibn Gabirol and Judah Halevi, and both were developed in the same environment and the same era. In depth and lyrical quality Gabirol has been rarely excelled. The noblest philosophic concepts were expressed by him in rich, vibrant tones as if blown through golden trumpets. Heine, a sensitive critic, called Gabirol "a nightingale singing in the darkness of the Gothic mediæval night." Enthusiastic admirers rank him, for the texture of his verse and his breadth of vision, with Dante and Milton.

He was born in Málaga about 1021, when Samuel was still dispensing spices in his little shop near the vizier's palace. His youth was clouded by bereavements and personal misfortunes, and he was early thrown upon the goodwill of friendly patrons. "Grieved, without mother or father, inexperienced, lonely, and poor, I am alone, without a brother and without friends, save my own thoughts." Doubtless the wistful note characteristic of many of his early poems is to be traced to the circumstances in which they were written. Fortunately, before he was entirely soured, the generous Samuel, now a powerful prince, took him under his wing. Though Gabirol's restless nature often induced quarrels with his patron, the friendship was maintained until the poet's death.

Already at sixteen Gabirol was deftly turning verses on the Arabic model, inaugurating a tradition which stimulated later Jewish poets. His fancy and his energy led him into every field. In one long poem, still chanted on the *Shabuot* in the Sephardic synagogues, he brought together the six hundred and thirteen precepts of the rabbinical code. Again, he put to rhyme and metre, with acrostical complications, the grammatical laws of the Hebrew language! And then, in another mood, he ranted gaily against wineless banquets:

> Good Moses of old caused the waters to flee
> And led all his people dry-shod o'er the sea;
> But Moses our host at the precedent frowns,
> And us, his poor guests, he unflinchingly drowns
> In water, cold water.[1]

These were diversions, however. Gabirol's genius lay in his delicate lyrics and in his ethical and religious works. The former have been compared to the products of the romantic school in nineteenth-century France and England; the latter have earned him the title " the Jewish Plato "; both have enhanced the richness and beauty of the Jewish liturgy. All of Gabirol's work was written in pure, limpid Hebrew, with Biblical phrases, like garlands, adroitly woven into the pattern. His most famous hymn is *The Royal Crown,* a series of beautiful poems extolling the magnificence of God.[2] Its science has become antiquated, but its grasp of monotheism, the basic concept of the Jewish faith, has rarely been so powerfully presented. To Gabirol, it is the recognition of the mystery and infinity of God which makes man divine and gives him hope in the midst of hopelessness.

> From Thee to Thee I fly to win
> A place of refuge, and within
> Thy shadow from Thy anger hide,
> Until Thy wrath be turned aside.
>
> Unto Thy mercy I will cling
> Until thou hearken pitying;
> Nor will I quit my hold of Thee,
> Until Thy blessing lighten me.

Towards the close of his life Gabirol capped his reputation as a philosopher by writing *Fons Vitæ (The Fountain of Life)*, a little volume in which he developed more completely his conceptions of God and the universe. It is a lively discussion, cast in dialogue form, and it had an immense vogue when it was later translated into Latin. Its authorship was forgotten, however, and until the middle of the nineteenth century, when Solomon Munk demonstrated that it came from the pen of Gabirol, it was thought to be the work of a brilliant Church Father, called Avicebron. *Fons Vitæ* was the first genuine philosophical speculation in Europe since Rome, many centuries earlier, had shut down the daring schools of Athens. It was widely used by Duns Scotus and other mediæval

---

[1] Translation by J. Chotzner.

[2] The translation of *The Royal Crown* into Spanish several years ago by José Faroché is the first Jewish work published by a Jew in Spain since the Expulsion of 1492.

thinkers, through whom its ideas were woven into the philosophical systems of the schoolmen.

Gabirol was cut off in the midst of his greatest promise, perhaps as early as his thirtieth year. In only a few fugitive years he revealed a sensitiveness to reality combined with a mystic aloofness from reality which stamped his poetry as unique. What altitudes he might have reached if he had been blessed with a full measure of years!

Shortly after Gabirol died, Judah Halevi, an even more illustrious successor, was born, a "wondrous fiery pillar of song, guiding the mournful caravan of Israel through the wilderness of exile." Halevi represented the perfect union of Hebrew and Spanish culture. He was brought up in Old Castile in the midst of the strife between the Moslems and the Christian kingdoms in the north, but the disorders did not affect the thoroughness of his education. He steeped himself in Jewish and Arabic literature, and though he mastered both, he did not allow them to take his whole heart. Science fascinated him also, and like many of his predecessors he followed medicine as a profession.

In his youth he turned, with every other Spanish gallant, to themes of wine and beauty. He sang of beautiful eyes and raven hair, of the jealous pangs of love, of the blessings of friendship. No wedding passed without an ode from him, no gathering without one of his witty sallies. To one love, real or imaginary, he wrote:

> How canst thou plead that thou art innocent
> Of mine heart's blood? Behold!
> > Against thee speak
> Two witnesses in silence eloquent —
> > The ruby of the lips,
> The ruby and the rose — thy lips, thy cheek!

His delightful ode "To the First Grey Hair" has been frequently quoted:

> I spied a white hair lurking in my beard,
> > And straightway plucked it thence,
> > "Thou'rt brave," it sneered,
> > "'Gainst a lone scout — quite brave.
> > But wilt thou be
> As plucky when my troop comes, seeking me?"[1]

Halevi never lost the merry twinkle of his eye, but his lighter efforts became less frequent as he grew older. He turned more and more to capture life's deeper emotions, and the most beautiful and moving poetry since the Psalter flowed from his pen.

[1] Translations by Solis Cohen.

> Spirit and flesh are Thine,
> O Heavenly Shepherd mine;
> My hopes, my thoughts, my fears, Thou seest all;
> Thou measurest my path, my steps dost know.
> When Thou upholdest, who can make me fall?
> When Thou restrainest, who can bid me go?
> O would that I might be
> A servant unto Thee,
> Thou God by all adored.
> Then, though by friends outcast,
> Thy hand would hold me fast,
> And draw me near to Thee, my King and Lord.[1]

Hundreds of such poems have been taken into the liturgy, and their lustre has not been dimmed by the ages. Alharisi, who wrote a century later, says of them:

> With master craftsman's skill, his verse is wrought
> Of luminous phrase and piercing thought.

Heine, fascinated by them, called their author "the crowned king of souls."

In his maturity Halevi also wrote *The Cuzari*, a famous defence of Judaism. He took as his framework the spectacular story of the Tartar kingdom of the Khazars, which had been converted to Judaism in the eighth century. His work, in five parts, written in the favourite dialogue form of the day, traced imaginatively the steps by which the convert king reached Judaism after analysing the elements of the other dominant faiths. *The Cuzari* not only added prestige to its author, but inspired an unusual number of commentators, whose activity helped to clarify the principles of Judaism.

Halevi's noblest genius, however, was not revealed in his philosophy or even in his religious hymns. It found its perfect expression in his deathless love for Zion. All Jewish poets wrote more or less eloquently of Zion and wept for her widowhood, but to Halevi Zion was a genuine passion.

> Oh city of the world, with sacred splendour blest,
> My spirit yearns to thee from out the far-off West,
> A stream of love wells forth when I recall thy day,
> Now is thy temple waste, thy glory passed away.
> Had I an eagle's wings, straight would I fly to thee,
> Moisten thy holy dust with wet cheeks streaming free.
> Oh, how I long for thee! albeit thy King has gone,
> Albeit where balm once flowed, the serpent dwells alone.
> Could I but kiss thy dust, so would I fain expire,
> As sweet as honey then, my passion, my desire.[2]

[1] Translation by Zangwill.   [2] Translation by Emma Lazarus.

Not content with the conventional passion of words, Halevi determined to seek out the sacred spots that had set his imagination on fire. His friends sought to dissuade him, for a trip to the Holy Land was an ordeal. But the poet rejected all advice and set out, in his fiftieth year, after a lifetime of luxurious ease in sunny Spain, to follow his dream. The sea was rough, the miserable cabin gave no comfort, illness wracked the body. But Halevi's soul exulted in the thought that he was bound for Jerusalem.

> The billows rage — exult, oh soul of mine,
> Soon shalt thou enter the Lord's sacred shrine!

Arrived in the Holy City, Halevi is lost in legend. Doubtless he wept over the desolation which he found and probably his " Zionide," recited in the synagogues to this day on the ninth of Ab, was composed in his spiritual agony. He may have left Palestine and died soon after. But it is possible, as legend says, that he was run down by an Arab horseman as he stood praying under the ruined wall of Jerusalem. Thus he fulfilled his own words:

> Could I but kiss thy dust,
> So would I fain expire.

Meantime the ceaseless quarrels of the petty Moslem states gave the Christian kings in the Peninsula a long-awaited opportunity to fight their way to the Tagus. Zealots from all over Europe joined in the crusade. French, German, Norman, and Italian warriors stood under the Castilian banners, and in 1085 their concerted efforts drove the Moslems out of Toledo, the ancient Visigothic capital. For a moment it seemed as if the cross would regain the supremacy of the whole country. For a moment only. The hard-pressed Moslems called in from Morocco the fanatical Berber Almoravides, who, scenting spoils, responded with enthusiasm. They inflicted a signal defeat upon the combined Christian forces at Zalaka, near Badajoz, and then proceeded to make themselves masters of the south.

Though there were occasional outbursts of fanaticism, the Jews did not suffer hardships under the new regime. During nearly half of the twelfth century their economic position was stable and their intellectual life continued undisturbed. Talmudic studies were greatly advanced under the enlightened leadership of Alfasi whose famous academy at Lucena drew the most distinguished students from all over the world. Secular learning went forward too and Jews and Arabs toiled together to build the bridge which linked up old and new cultures. In Toledo " were to be found a wealth of Arabic books and a number of masters of the two tongues, and with the help of these Mozarabs and resident Jews there arose a regular school for the translation of Arabic-Latin books and science, which drew from all lands those who thirsted for knowledge . . . and left the signature of Toledo on many of the most famous versions of Arabic learning." [1]

The Almoravide empire crumbled soon after the death of its masterful creator. Almost immediately it was succeeded by another, which spread from the mountains of Morocco, aiming to restore the pure faith of Mohammed to the Moslem world. Its adherents were known as Almohades, Unitarians, for they fought against the degrading anthropomorphisms which had crept into the Moslem practices. Their organizing genius was Mohammed ibn Tumart, the mis-shapen son of a lamplighter, who was assisted by Abd al Mumin, a soldier of astonishing zeal and power, one of the outstanding leaders produced by Moslem civilization. By 1149 all of northern Africa had been conquered and Abd al Mumin pushed into Córdoba. Next year the richest provinces of Andalusia fell into his hands.

The conquerors made a clean sweep of all who did not share their beliefs and practices. The flourishing Jewish schools in Córdoba, Seville and Lucena were closed, the impressive synagogues, which had added beauty to every Spanish city, were torn down, and the Jews themselves were offered the alternative of conversion or exile. Fortunately, in this crisis the Christian states in the north were ruled by tolerant sovereigns. The King of Castile welcomed the refugees who fled from the wrath of the Almohades, and the Castilian Jewish communities became their solicitous hosts.

It was in Toledo, which rapidly became the centre of Jewish life in Spain, that the restless, witty Abraham ibn Ezra developed his many-sided talents. He was one of the most attractive characters of the Middle Ages. With never a penny in his pockets, he laughed at his misfortunes.

> If I sold shrouds, no one would die;
> If I sold lamps, then in the sky
> The sun, for spite,
> Would shine all night.

He travelled everywhere, he knew everyone, he wrote about everything. 1140 found him in Rome, toiling over Hebrew grammatical works and commentaries on the Scriptures. A few years later he was concerned with Biblical exegesis somewhere in the heart of France. In London he wrestled with the problems of Jewish theology. Again in France, he translated important astronomical treatises from Arabic into Hebrew. Nor were his labours superficial. His expositions of the Scriptures were keen and searching and of immense interest for future commentators. To this day they are used with profit. He never openly doubted the verbal inspiration of the Holy Writ, but his innuendoes, his sudden,

---

[1] V. Rose: "Ptolemæus und die Schule von Toledo" in *Hermes*, VIII, 327 (1874). Cited in Haskins: *Renaissance of the Twelfth Century*, p. 52.

sharp, biting questions, suggested a new approach to the Bible. In a sense Ibn Ezra was the father of higher criticism.

Another interesting character developed in the same period, even more significant in European than in Jewish history, was Benjamin of Tudela, who travelled for thirteen years in Europe and Asia and whose memoirs have been edited in an *Itinerary*.[1] Though he was credulous and accepted impossible tales as historical truth, many of his observations have become valuable for a knowledge of twelfth-century institutions. He was particularly interested in the Jewish communities which he visited, and he described their habits and ways of life fully. His information about the Karaite sects and the Samaritans is source material. From him comes corroboration of the knowledge that the Jews of Palestine and the East excelled in the arts of dyeing and glass-making.

There were hosts of other notable personalities, scholars and administrators, dreamers and men of affairs, whose keenness of mind and breadth of spirit helped to create the golden age. By far the most important was Moses Maimonides, who best represented and summed up the era at the culmination of which he stood.

4. MOSES MAIMONIDES

"From Moses till Moses there arose none like unto Moses," was the verdict of posterity upon Maimonides, the most influential Jewish thinker in the Middle Ages. As an expounder of Judaism, as a philosopher, as a lover of learning, as a gentle, human character, few have surpassed him in Jewish history.

He was born in Córdoba in 1135, probably near the little street or alley which today bears his name, Calle Maimónides. The Almoravide rulers, still firmly rooted in the country, patronized all branches of learning, and the precocious youngster was soon deeply immersed in the arts and sciences and in all branches of Jewish scholarship. His father dreamed of a brilliant career for him in the congenial atmosphere of Córdoba. Soon after Maimonides had reached his thirteenth year, however, the onrushing Almohades stormed the city, and the little family joined thousands of other exiles who fled to Africa and to all parts of the Peninsula. Maimonides spent the most formative years of his life wandering about in various Spanish centres. Perhaps the adventures were a very useful part of his education, for he learned to know life and men and was saved from the narrow pedantry of a scholarly recluse. Moreover, his wanderings did not seem to affect his industry. Before he was twenty-three he had prepared a treatise on the calendar and was at work on a critical commentary, in Arabic, on the Mishnah. Already so early he displayed his clear, orderly mind, which cut through confusion and obscurity like a keen drill.

After innumerable hardships the little family arrived in Fez. Here the

---

[1] The editor evidently retained the language of Benjamin's notes.

Almohade scourge had driven thousands of Jews into a nominal submission to Islam. Many of them, shaken by a decade of bigotry, had cut themselves altogether adrift from Judaism. Maimonides and his father, as secret Jews, strove to steady those who wavered and wished to assimilate completely. The authorities, justly suspicious of their activities, tormented them until they took up the staff again. More wandering, more trials, more adventure, until at last in Egypt the family found rest and security and ample facilities for scholarship.

Misfortune could not be shaken off. The old father, an inseparable comrade and an inspiring influence, died soon after settling in Egypt. An older brother, David, who traded in precious stones, perished in the Indian Ocean, and with him was lost the meagre family fortune. Maimonides turned to his practice of medicine, and, though he was later highly successful, the early years were filled with struggle. Ill health stretched him on a bed of sickness and quarrels with the Karaites disturbed his peace of mind. Fortunately Maimonides was blessed with an indomitable will which conquered all difficulties. He was able to work under the most adverse conditions. "I wrote notes on many an *halakah*," he said later, "on journeys by land, or while tossed on the stormy waves at sea." In the very year in which he completed the *Siraj,* upon which he had been engaged through all his travels, old Cairo was destroyed by fire.

The *Siraj,* a masterly commentary on the Mishnah, the first of a magnificent trilogy, showed no effects of its troubled authorship. It is a model of clarity and keen thinking. Maimonides had the rare gift of bringing the most abstruse conceptions close to the mind of the common man. In the *Siraj* he summed up the essence of the Mishnah, illustrating his points from a wide and varied learning, often filling old themes with original meanings. Modern authorities hold that it is still indispensable for the study of the Mishnah. At the close of his work Maimonides entered upon a discussion of the principles of Judaism and formulated them in the Thirteen Articles, which became, to most Jews, the authoritative creed of the Jewish faith.

Fortune began to show Maimonides favours. Soon after the *Siraj* was completed, Saladin, the most genial character in Moslem history, became master of Egypt and inaugurated an enlightened reign, which lasted nearly twenty-five years. His vizier, Alfadhel, to whom he left the administration of the country, was also a chivalrous spirit and a patron of learning, "sovereign of the pen, who threaded discourse with pearls of style." He sought out the friendship of Maimonides, and the intimacy ripened until, in 1185, the Jewish philosopher was added to the royal staff as a court physician. Here he was so cordially welcomed that when an attractive offer reached him from Richard Cœur de Lion to accept a similar post in the English court, he refused.

Meantime Maimonides had completed his second great work, the *Mishneh-Torah*,[1] a codification, in fourteen books, of all Biblical and rabbinical law.

---

[1] Or *Yad Ha-Hazakah* (*The Strong Hand*). (The numerical value of *Yad* is 14.)

It had required more than ten years of steady labour; but it was a stupendous achievement to bring together the vast material even in ten years. "The Talmud," says Graetz, "resembles a Dædalian maze, in which one can scarcely find his way even with Ariadne's thread, but Maimuni designed a well-contrived ground-plan, with wings, halls, apartments, chambers, and closets, through which a stranger might easily pass without a guide, and thereby obtain a survey of all that is contained in the Talmud. Only a mind accustomed to think clearly and systematically, and filled with the genius of order, could have planned and built a structure like this." [1] Maimonides covered the whole range of Jewish learning and impregnated it with the Aristotelian spirit. He virtually created a new Talmud, eliminating, however, its confusion and its non-essentials.

The *Mishneh-Torah* gained immediate recognition and was discussed and commented upon by students everywhere. The Jewish world, impressed by Maimonides's immense learning, turned to him in every difficulty. Communities appealed to him for advice on policy, individuals wrote to him to solve legal problems, and all alike heaped praises and honours upon him. Maimonides became the intellectual arbiter of the Jewish world, an Erasmus of the twelfth century.

In each of his treatises Maimonides had been deeply interested in philosophical problems, but their analyses had been merely incidental. Now, in the full vigour of his early fifties, he determined to construct a philosophical interpretation of Judaism. *The Guide for the Perplexed,* which was completed in 1187 or 1190, became the most important of his works. It was written for men who wished to place their faith upon a rational basis, for those who sought to reconcile revelation with the truths of science. Maimonides worked upon the premise which Saadiah had developed, that the law was perfect and complete and would be found rational in all its parts if one only searched long enough. He proceeded to prove the assumption by rationally interpreting every Biblical precept.

The courageous philosopher had none of the modern scientific equipment with which to approach the inner problems of the Bible; his thoughts on God and the universe were later antiquated. But the intellectual honesty which he applied to his problems remained an influence long after his content was superseded. In his own generation he led men open-eyed and questioning into every avenue of faith. He rescued many of his people from degrading superstitions by interpreting away all of the anthropomorphisms of the Bible, often giving them exquisitely beautiful ethical meanings. He explained rationally the miracles, the practice of sacrifice, and the nature of prophecy. The theme ran through all his work, like a golden thread, that faith and reason lead equally to the truth, that God must be worshipped with understanding, that religion is

---

[1] Graetz: *History of the Jews.* III, 466

not only an emotional phenomenon, but an answer as well to the deepest searchings of the mind.

The remaining years of Maimonides's life were filled with ceaseless activity. He continued to write, to dispute, to advise, to perform his duties as court physician. But though he was spared for another fourteen or seventeen years, his task was completed when the *Guide* was published. He died in 1204, the idol of his people; the whole world mourned as his remains were borne to Tiberius for burial. There is a legend that a host of bedouins attacked the funeral train; when they were unable to move the coffin, they joined reverently in the procession!

After his death and even during his lifetime Maimonides was fiercely attacked by conservative forces that distrusted his philosophical views and regarded his interpretations of the law as heretical. They were also fearful that his *Mishneh-Torah,* as a concise code of Jewish law, would supersede the Talmud itself. His disciples defended him vigorously and a controversy raged about his writings for more than a century. The *Guide* was even excommunicated and burnt. But as time passed, Maimonides rose to a foremost place in the estimation of all his people, and his influence became enduring. Spinoza quoted portions of his work with undisguised admiration and Mendelssohn found in the *Guide* an endless source of inspiration. Solomon Maimon, the restless vagabond-philosopher of the eighteenth century, took the very name of the sage who had most influenced his intellectual life.

European thought too was indebted to the Jewish philosopher. His *Guide* contained trenchant and independent criticism of Aristotle's principles. His masterly analysis of the dual role of revelation and reason was taken over by Albertus Magnus (d. 1280), Thomas Aquinas, and other scholastics. It was from the works of Maimonides that the mediæval Church received its authoritative knowledge of the synagogue.

A mind of such fine texture placed Maimonides far beyond the men of the Golden Age. But he was perhaps no less conspicuous as a personality than as a philosopher. He taught men how to think, but also how to live. He was a fervently pious Jew, yet a model of tolerance, never attacking except when falsehoods were uttered; ever seeking the light, serene in the face of all trials, the personification of the true humanist, a fitting climax to a glorious era.

5 · THE ANTI-MAIMUNISTS

The writings of Maimonides were constantly under fire because he applied reason not only to ethics and metaphysics, but to the very sanctities of religion. Already as early as Judah Halevi's day the protest had been voiced against such rationalization of religious concepts. Halevi's mystical poetry played constantly upon the theme of complete submission, and poets and thinkers in

Maimonides's own day stressed the same approach to the fundamental problems of existence.

After the death of Maimonides the quarrel became rancorous. His opponents and his supporters both, in the heat of their disputes, too often allowed personal abuse to take the place of cogent thought. Bans and counter bans were flung about which rejoiced the enemies of Israel and perplexed the pious. Fortunately the two outstanding intellectual opponents of Maimonides, Nahmanides and Crescas, were men of tolerance and discretion, and, while they took issue with the Maimunist position, they gallantly defended the sage of Fostat against those who sought to calumniate his memory. Intellectual disagreements, Nahmanides said, were the life of Judaism, and its sages were all to be venerated.

Nahmanides, who was born in Gerona, Spain, about 1194, came of a distinguished family of scholars. He combined the clearness and lucidity of the scientific mind with the warm emotionalism of the mystic. "If he was not a profound thinker, like the author of the *Guide of the Perplexed*," writes Schechter, "he had that which is next best — 'he felt profoundly.'"[1] His commentaries on the Bible and the Talmud display considerable originality and acumen. He followed the French school of Talmudists in his studies, but he was careful to avoid their dialectic methods and their over-subtlety. "They wish to force the elephant through the eye of a needle," he was frank to admit.

Nahmanides's most important achievement was to build a strong defence against the views and methods of the Maimunist school. He was the outstanding mystic of the middle of the thirteenth century. To him life was a mysterious process; God's will was ever performing acts which man's poor finite mind could never understand. Religious truths could therefore not be tested by reason. The miracles of the Bible were not to be explained rationally, nor was prophecy to be reduced to ordinary psychological phenomena. Faith in God's law, as revealed on Sinai, could alone serve as the way of life.

> Thou gavest me a light my path to guide,
> To prove my heart's recesses still untried;
> And as I went, Thy voice in warning cried,
> "Child, fear thou Him who is thy God and King!"[2]

Disagreeing with Maimonides upon fundamentals, Nahmanides necessarily opposed the corollaries of his system. In his *Sacred Letter* he attacked not only Maimonides's disparagement of the flesh "as an obstacle to spiritual perfection," but similar attacks which came from the more ascetic Christian sects. The body, Nahmanides insisted, with all of its functions, came from God and was, there-

---

[1] Schechter: *Studies in Judaism*, first series, p. 130.
[2] From Nahmanides's hymn for the New Year, "The King." Translated by Alice Lucas.

fore, as perfect as the soul. "It is only sin and neglect that disfigure God's creations."

It is easy to understand Nahmanides's influence upon the Cabalist movement, and the other forms of mysticism which were just beginning to stir themselves. He never identified himself with the Cabalists, but he supported their doctrines and he gave them a firm basis upon which to build an attractive interpretation of Judaism.

Another immensely able opponent of Maimonides was Hasdai Crescas, who laboured amidst the darkness which clouded fourteenth-century Spanish life. Crescas also came from a family of scholars and inherited much of their ripe powers of mind. He stood high in the social world and was friendly with the King of Aragon who often consulted him upon State questions. Because of his wealth he was able to assist his unfortunate people in other states during the disasters which now quickly overtook them.

Like Nahmanides, Crescas refused to base Judaism upon speculative philosophy and resented the dominating position which Aristotle had assumed in Jewish thought. In his *magnum opus, The Light of the Lord,* he took up in detail the problems of the existence and nature of God, His omniscience, His providence, His power, and built the conclusion from his analysis that man could reach God only through love, not through reason. Man's fundamental duty was to attain perfection, and this could be achieved, not through speculation, but through love of God as expressed in obedience to His divine will.

Crescas checked the adulation of Maimonides and stopped the tendency which had induced enthusiastic disciples to swallow Aristotle whole. He was the first Jewish thinker who succeeded in penetrating the weak spots of Aristotle's armour and he helped to dethrone him as the intellectual autocrat. Crescas was also a stimulating influence in the life of Spinoza, who derived from the philosopher of Barcelona his views on creation and free-will and his magnificent conception of the intellectual love of God.

With Crescas the golden age in Spain came to an end. A glorious succession of statesmen and thinkers had begun in the tenth century under the tolerant regime of Abd Ar Rahman and his dynasty. It had produced the benevolent statesmanship of Ibn Shaprut and Samuel ibn Nagdela, the sublime poetry of Judah Halevi and Ibn Gabirol, the sunny irony of Ibn Ezra, the philosophy of Maimonides, and the vigorous commentaries of those who supported and opposed his ideas. But by the fourteenth century the sun no longer shone for the Jews of Spain. Thereafter men struggled merely to keep alive and thought little of the creative arts. Though rabbinic studies continued well into the fourteenth century, the blossoms of genius dried up and died and the golden age became a memory.

CHAPTER FIFTEEN

FOUR BLOODY CENTURIES IN
CHRISTIAN EUROPE

Surely a limit boundeth every woe,
But mine enduring anguish hath no end;
My grievous years are spent in ceaseless flow,
My wound hath no amend. . . .

Ibn Gabirol

WHILE the Jews of Moslem Spain basked in an Andalusian sunshine,
Christian Europe seethed with hatred. After the eleventh century the story of
Jewish life in France, England, and the several hundred states of the Holy
Roman Empire was one long succession of indignities and brutalities, culminating in wholesale massacres and expulsions. To be sure, the Jews were
not alone in their misery. These were barbaric centuries, in which civilization
moved slowly and very painfully. Though there were magnificent creations
to light the darkness, particularly during the twelfth-century Renaissance, the
common man's lot was not enviable — exploited by the Church, oppressed by
the nobles, harassed by economic restrictions. Yet the fate of the Jews was
infinitely more wretched and not to be compared. Living in an alien faith,
they were outside the pale of civilization, completely at the mercy of their rulers'
whim. Even their homes were not secure, and none could say what new visitations the morrow would bring. The very hardships which the peasants endured induced them to seek scapegoats and they usually found them in the
unhappy Jewish communities. *Cherchez le juif!* With the exception of a brief
Talmudic renaissance in the Rhine districts, in the eleventh century, when
Gershom and Rashi flourished, one seeks in vain for a respite. The crusaders
spread destruction while they blessed the name of their Saviour, popes vied with
princes in creating new methods of terrorizing and harassing their subject
Jews, the Talmud was ever on trial and inevitably condemned and mutilated
or burnt. So the centuries passed, a succession of hideous memories, until
every country began to expel its Jews wholesale, first robbing them and then
driving them into nowhere. "If there be an ascending scale of suffering," Zunz
writes in an oft-quoted passage, which discusses the horrors of mediæval
Jewish existence, "Israel has reached its highest degree. If the duration of
afflictions, and the patience with which they are borne ennoble, the Jews may
vie with the aristocracy of any land. If a literature which owns a few classical

tragedies is deemed rich, what place should be assigned to a tragedy which extends over fifteen centuries in which the poets and actors were also the heroes? "

I. GERSHOM AND RASHI

Until the eleventh century the Jews lived in moderate comfort in French and German cities. While the feudal system made it extremely difficult for them to own land and excluded them from the social organization, there was always an outlet in commerce, and many of them earned an honourable livelihood as artisans. They lived amicably with their neighbours, often enjoying Christian friendships and serving in professional capacities in Christian homes.

In this peaceful environment it was possible to develop a virile intellectual life, and Talmudic studies were prosecuted with zeal in a number of cities on both sides of the Rhine. The founder of the schools was Gershom of Mayence, whose solid learning and benignant personality earned for him the title " Light of the Exile." He dedicated himself to the task of expounding the intricacies of the Talmud and he succeeded well enough to end the dependence of the Western countries upon the interpretations of the Eastern academies.

Gershom's prestige made him an unwitting rival of the last Geonim; indeed, he was recognized as the leading religious authority in Europe. Questions came to him from every land, and his pronouncements had the force of law in France, Italy, and Germany. About 1000, among other edicts, he forbade the practice of polygamy,[1] insisted upon the consent of both parties to a divorce, and modified the severity of the law in relation to those who had been forcibly baptized. He manifested a degree of tolerance unique in his troubled era. When, towards the close of his life, many forced converts returned to Judaism, he threatened to excommunicate any who dared to reproach them or who refused to admit them to every social activity.

In the very year in which Gershom died, 1040, the outstanding Jewish scholar in Christian Europe was born. Rabbi Solomon ben Isaac, familiarly known, from the Hebrew initials of his name, as Rashi, did more to popularize Biblical and Talmudic learning than any other commentator in Jewish history. The legends which have clustered about his name, praising his miraculous intellectual achievements and his well-nigh supernatural physical feats, are a significant tribute to his lovable personality and to the deep impression which his work made alike upon contemporaries and posterity.

After a wretched youth of privation, spent in study and travel, Rashi settled, at the age of twenty-five, in Troyes, " in want of food, in ragged clothes, and bearing the yoke of matrimony." He was appointed rabbi of the community, though, as usual in the Middle Ages, the post was merely an honorary one and he earned a livelihood by tending his vineyard. Like Gershom, Rashi devoted

[1] Actually the practice of polygamy had ceased many centuries before.

the better part of his life to the elucidation of the Bible and the Talmud. His genius was not in original research or in critical interpretation. He was a born teacher and his concise, graphic commentaries on the thousands of obscure passages in Jewish literature have been a joy to endless generations of students. He never slurred over difficulties or enveloped them in a maze of words. The first task of an editor, he realized, is honesty, and when he was stumped, he said frankly: " I cannot understand — I do not know." Many of his explanations were written in French, with Hebrew characters, and the two thousand and more such expressions are valuable examples of the earliest French. Without Rashi's commentaries the Talmud would doubtless have become an obscure and inaccessible document. To the present day his work is part of the Biblical and Talmudic text, and his interpretations are used in all academies of Jewish learning.

Mediæval Christian scholars turned to the delightful popularizer for the representative synagogue interpretation of Jewish thought. Thus in the fourteenth century Nicholas de Lyre consulted Rashi for his own commentaries on the Bible, and since Nicholas vastly influenced Luther's translations, Rashi became an indirect contributor to the Reformation.

After Rashi's death his work was continued by a number of very able sons-in-law, who, in turn, developed a school of commentators, the Tossafists. These French and German scholars, with their dialectic subtlety, were not always as clear as their masters, and often they obscured more than they elucidated. But at least they continued an intellectual tradition in an era of intense ignorance. " The Jewish schools in the Rhineland," remarks Abrahams, " flourished not, as in Moorish Spain, in imitation of neighbouring illumination, but in contrast to surrounding obscurantism." [1] In the bitter persecutions which now swallowed the Jews, they were pillars of strength and comfort.

2. THE CRUSADES

As the influence of the clergy widened and the Church orders gained in power, local persecutions became common. An envenomed sermon by an ignorant fanatic often impelled the simple folks of a community to burn down synagogues and homes and to lay violent hands on the Jews. It became an annual custom in Béziers, in the week between Palm Sunday and Easter Monday, when the priests described the sufferings of Jesus, to pelt the Jews with mud and stones whenever they appeared. In Toulouse the count in the city had the right to slap the face of the Jewish leader on Good Friday, and it was only at the beginning of the twelfth century that the shameful practice was commuted for a heavy money-payment.

All through the eleventh century the tide of hatred rose and the leaders in

1 Abrahams: *Jewish Life in the Middle Ages*, xxii.

Church and State helped rather than thwarted its ravages. When the autocratic Hildebrand became Pope Gregory VII, nearly all of Europe knelt at his feet and followed his commands, which included severe restrictions against the Jews. In 1078 he issued a law forbidding Christian kingdoms to employ Jews in any public capacity.[1] When Alphonso X opened Castile to Jews fleeing from the Almohade terror and gave them every opportunity to advance, Gregory protested vigorously. "We admonish Your Highness that you must cease to suffer the Jews to rule over the Christians and exercise authority over them. For to allow the Christians to be subordinated to the Jews, and to subject them to their judgment, is the same as oppressing God's Church and exalting Satan's synagogue. To wish to please Christ's enemies means to treat Christ himself with contumely." Fortunately Alphonso disregarded the admonitions and the wretched exiles found a temporary haven in Castile.

So far the Jews suffered only from local disturbances. More terrifying visitations were now in store for them as the eleventh century ended. For then began the crusades, a long series of religious wars which kept Europe and western Asia in a ferment for nearly two hundred years. The wars, unique in European history, were actuated by the purest motives, the desire to wrest Palestine and the Holy Sepulchre from the hands of the Moslems. Its appeal, in a devoutly-minded age, was irresistible. It aroused a clean, holy zeal in men of all countries, of all classes, and impelled them to sacrifice comfort, worldly goods, and life itself, for the honour and glory of the cross.

But mixed with these nobler motives were more questionable ones. Side by side with the devout pilgrims who prayed as they fought and asked only that they might serve their Saviour were adventurers, younger sons of nobles seeking fortune and a career, shrewd traders anxious for the emporiums of the East, disappointed men, outcasts, criminals, all the scum that so often poisons the heart of the holiest cause. It is significant that the Pope appealed especially to those who had been "contending against their brethren and relatives" and urged "those who have hitherto been robbers now to become soldiers of Christ." Just before the first crusade, in 1096, a pestilence raged through Europe from Flanders to Bohemia, followed by a famine in Lorraine. These new afflictions drove into the ranks of the crusaders thousands of men who used the name of religion to fill their bellies and their purses. "A stream of emigration set towards the East," writes Barker, "such as would in modern times flow towards a newly discovered gold field, a stream carrying in its waters such refuse, tramps, and bankrupts, camp followers and hucksters, fugitive monks and escaped villains, and marked by the same motley grouping, the same fever of life, the same alternations of affluence and beggary, which mark the rush for a gold field today."

[1] These laws, like so many others in the Middle Ages, came from the Theodosian and Justinian Codes of the fifth and sixth centuries.

The first crusade was preached for months by fiery evangelists who stormed up and down the Rhine valley calling upon the faithful, declaring that service in this most sacred cause was equivalent to the best kind of penance, promising the remission of all sins to those who followed the cross. Knights and nobles began to gather in one great group, peasants and paupers in another. The masses were the first to begin their pilgrimage, and a boisterous, impatient division under William the Carpenter crossed the Rhine in April.

The Jews, who lived in large numbers in the Rhenish valley, very soon felt the presence of the crusading hordes. Those on the French side of the Rhine happily escaped without harm, but there was no security for those who dwelt in the German cities. The mobs, passions inflamed, thirsting for blood and plunder, were uncontrolled; their mentality may be gauged by the fact that they insisted upon a van with a goose and a herd of goats who were to show the way to Jerusalem. The word spread that there were enemies of Christ much nearer home whose destruction would bring salvation to those who accomplished the blessed work. Some of the more maggoty-headed leaders took an oath not to pass out of Germany without first killing at least one Jew with their own hands.

The pious orgies began in Lorraine, where the rich fields and the flourishing cities were irresistible bait. In Metz twenty-two Jews were killed, and though the toll of lives was smaller in other communities, innumerable homes were pillaged and destroyed. Early in May the crusaders straggled into Spires, where the Jews had been recently granted new privileges by the authorities. The synagogue was surrounded by a howling mob and but for the sturdy resistance of the worshippers and the quick precautionary measures of the kindly bishop the Jews would have fared badly. Failure, however, served only to increase the fury of the pilgrims. On May 18, greatly reinforced, they fell upon the Jews of Worms. About eight hundred had fortunately sought safety in the episcopal palace, but those who remained in their homes were butchered without mercy. The corpses were stripped and lay naked until the refugees in the palace could smuggle out clothing for the poor mutilated bodies. The following Sunday, despite the protestations of the bishop, the rabble attacked the episcopal palace itself. For two days the besieged resisted, and then those who had not taken their own lives were cut to pieces, for the glory of God. Only a few saved themselves by submitting to baptism. From Worms " the wolves of the forest," as they were called by one Jewish chronicler, moved on to Mayence, whose citizens at once opened the gates and pointed out the Jewish hiding-places. Again the greater number committed suicide, and the rest were massacred.

> The pious wives dispatch the work
> And offer up their guileless babes.
> The fathers quickly slay their sons,

And wish not to survive their dead.
To render homage to Thy unity,
The young, the fair, prepare for death,
With " Hear, O Israel! " on their lips.
The bride and bridegroom now breathe forth
The dying words: " The Lord is one! "
They who in life were wedded,
Through hallowed death are reunited.

Kalonymos Ben Judah

The dead, numbering about thirteen hundred, were flung, stripped, into ditches, and their property was plundered. One Jew fired the synagogue before killing himself, and the blaze destroyed nearly all of the city. A small number who escaped the notice of the rabble by hiding in the treasury of the cathedral attempted to steal away at midnight, but were soon overtaken and also butchered.

In this spirit the crusaders crossed Germany, leaving behind them a trail of plundered homes and broken lives. Perhaps as many as twelve thousand Jews perished in the Rhenish valley in the wild *Judenhetze,* which lasted for three months.

The persecuting zeal of the crusaders was not yet exhausted when they entered Bohemia. Here the Jews had lived in peace, untouched by the currents which affected the lives of their people in other lands. Taking advantage of the absence of the powerful duke, who was fighting a foreign war, the motley horde brought the Prague community into Jewish history by virtually destroying it.

At last, in August, the plague was stayed. The crusaders swept into Hungary, where most of them were scattered to the winds by the natives, who rose in rebellion against their rapacity and vandalism.

Meantime a second group, composed of knights, nobles, and their numerous retainers, had been making their way, in small bands and by diverse routes, to Constantinople. From this rendezvous an immense host, totalling more than a hundred and fifty thousand, began to cut a path southward through Asia Minor into Syria and Palestine. For more than three years they fought furiously, gradually overcoming the desperate opposition of the Moslems. In May of 1099 twenty thousand survivors stood under the walls of Jerusalem, which held out for more than a month before it succumbed. The slaughter was fearful. The conquerors waded through streets which were ankle-deep with the blood of the vanquished. At nightfall they knelt in prayer before the Holy Sepulchre, sobbing with joy at their victory over the non-believers. And then they drove all the Jews of the city into a synagogue and burnt them alive within it.

The outrages which marked the march and the triumph of the crusaders were not condoned by the better elements of the population. The archbishops and bishops in every diocese pleaded against serving Christ with hatred and bloodshed, and the responsible burghers, horrified by the brutality and the greed which were masked by religious zeal, sought to help the afflicted Jews wherever they could. After the Harpagons had passed through Germany, those who had been forcibly baptized were permitted to return to Judaism, and property was restored to many of those who had been robbed. In other localities, however, the fever was not burnt out so quickly. Many Jews in Bohemia, severely shaken by their experiences, attempted to leave the country. The ruler, Wratislaw, at once confiscated their property and expelled them. They had come into the country naked and penniless, he said, and they could leave in the same condition.

Life was not the same in Europe after the holocausts of the first crusade. The Jews in the oldest and best-established communities lost their buoyance and their sense of security. Learning decayed and the Arts which ornamented civilized life — who would think of poetry and song with ten thousand martyrs perished along the Rhine? Who could write of Talmudic principles when every community still bore scars from the murderous frenzy of the crusaders? The Jews lived in mortal fear of other outbursts, knowing only too well that the ignorant masses believed every stupid and malicious tale that was circulated. Their whole mode of life changed. They drew within their shells and had little to do with Christians. Only gradually, as the horrors of the crusades and their aftermath faded into memory, did the Jews begin to forget their fears. And then the second crusade burst upon them.

The little Latin kingdoms established by the crusaders in Palestine and Syria were expanded by war until they reached from Beirut to Egypt. For half a century they remained strong and firm, attracting pilgrims from all parts of the world. But they could not endure permanently. They were rooted in lust and greed, and their founders conducted themselves like brigands. The Moslems, led by two gifted chieftains, Zengi and Nureddin, united to drive the interlopers from the land. In 1144 they succeeded in capturing Edessa, a powerful outpost, and the entire fabric that the crusaders had built was threatened with disaster. In this crisis an appeal went out over Europe for a new crusade to save Jerusalem from the enemies of Christ.

The time was propitious. Europe was profoundly stirred by the danger to the Holy Sepulchre, and the eloquence of St. Bernard set whole communities in motion. The appeal was heeded by kings as well as princes. Louis VII of France and Conrad III, Holy Roman Emperor, both took the vow. Yet, with all the pomp and pageantry that gave prestige to the new crusade, it failed miserably. The crusaders of northern Germany did not even leave the country, and those who finally reached Syria, tried vainly to capture Damascus and also turned back.

Nevertheless, success or failure, the Jews suffered. A contagion seemed to sweep the world. Just when the Jews of Morocco and Spain were being hounded by the Almohades, the communities along the Seine, the Rhine, and the Danube were made to feel the fury of the restless crusaders. St. Bernard was a kindly, pious soul who several times endangered his life when he sought to restrain the masses from assaulting the Jews; but few of his brethren were as broad-spirited. The abbot Peter of Cluny virtually called for the destruction of the hated race. It was of little use, he proclaimed, to smite the Saracens in far-off lands when there were so many blasphemers of the Saviour living in comfort among Christians. "You ought not to kill them," he advised Louis VII, "but to afflict them in a manner befitting their baseness." Another scourge was Rudolph, a devout ignoramus, who lit up the Rhine with his denunciations and who was responsible for the riots which followed nearly every one of his sermons.

The Jews were assailed not only by the bigots. The trade with the East had created a strong class of merchants who were anxious to destroy all rivals, and, since the Jews were among the most successful, they turned the fury of the mobs against them. Fortunately, in France the influence of St. Bernard and the intervention of the king prevented wholesale massacres. Yet at Ham a hundred and fifty Jews were murdered, and at Carenton, though the Jews resisted heroically, the whole community was destroyed.

In Germany as the danger of a crusade against the Jews became imminent, the emperor appealed to the princes to keep order, and set aside Nuremberg and other imperial cities as havens of refuge for the Jews. The imperial edict prevented the carnage which disgraced the first crusade, but it could not restrain rioters in a number of cities, and when the emperor left the country, hundreds of Jews fell victim to their fury.

Then came the third crusade, and the fourth, and the fifth. It seemed as if the end would never come. Every defeat of the crusaders brought the wrath of failure; every victory brought the assaults of pride.

In France, Philip Augustus, who had elevated hatred of Jews into an art, stepped into the third crusade fresh from the massacre of Bray in the province of Champagne. He had already expelled all Jews from his own dominions about Paris. In England just before Richard the Lion-Hearted joined Philip Augustus in the crusade, ominous riots spread through the country which even the gallant king could not check. No sooner had he crossed the Channel than five hundred Jews of York were besieged in a castle where they had taken refuge. The siege lasted six days, and while the Jews within prayed for courage to remain steadfast, a monk, in white robes, celebrated mass daily under the walls of the castle, spurring on the rabble who howled for blood. When rations at last gave out, nearly all of the besieged took their own lives. Those who were left were at once torn to pieces by the mob, which then proceeded to the cathedral repository where the records of indebtedness lay, and exultantly destroyed them.

The crusades are a turning-point in Jewish history. They mark the end of settled Jewish communal life in Europe, the beginning of intense race-aversions. They usher in the Jewish caricature who stalked through Europe until the eighteenth century, the pariah, with bent back and hunted look and obsequious manner, bitter over his yesterdays and fearful of his tomorrows.

For the Jews of Germany there was another important consequence of the crusades. The emperor extended protection to them and they paid a goodly sum for his generosity. They repeated their gifts when a new emperor ascended the throne or when new dangers threatened them. The practice developed into a tradition, and the Jews became the special vassals of the emperor. At first the change in status saved their lives; later it robbed them of their freedom. They became "*servi cameræ*," servants of the chamber, wards of the emperor. Formerly, though they had been hunted and plundered, they had remained freemen. Now they were bondsmen, chattels, to be bought and sold at the whim of their patron. Emperors often consigned the revenues from "their" Jews to barons and nobles in return for lump sums. The Jews did not rise out of this humiliating status for more than six hundred years!

3. INNOCENT III AND THE JEWISH BADGE

The thirteenth century was the culmination of an inspiring era in European history. It saw the rise of towns and cities, the expansion of trade and industry, the growth of municipal institutions and liberties. It was the age of Magna Charta and the enlightened Frederick II, of the gentle St. Francis and the vigorous St. Dominic. It was distinguished by Dante's immortal work, by Aquinas's immense philosophical efforts, by the development of natural science. It marked the highest excellence in cathedral-building, with beautiful façades and stained-glass windows and astonishing flying buttresses.

For the Jews the glorious epoch meant only an intensification of the torments which they had endured in the eleventh and twelfth centuries. Never did the hand of the Church militant and triumphant rest so heavily upon them; never were they so degraded in body and spirit. They were compelled to wear a badge of shame, to witness the destruction of their sacred books in public celebrations, to learn the awful meaning of wholesale expulsions from countries where they had lived longer than their persecutors. They lost self-respect and degenerated in mind and in spirit. Byron's words never had truer application:

> The wild-dove hath her nest, the fox his cave,
> Mankind their country — Israel but the grave!

When the century opened, the Church was in the keeping of one of the ablest statesmen in history, Innocent III. Of an ancient and honourable family, eloquent, well versed in legal and theological learning, he distinguished himself early, and though the youngest of the cardinals, he was elected Pope at the age of thirty-seven. He proved himself a man of affairs as well as a man of learning. In the very first year of his pontificate he wrested control of Italy from imperial hands and began a successful drive to make the papacy the supreme power in the Christian world. A Byzantine visitor remarked, as he witnessed the phenomenon of a pope bending kings to his will, that " Innocent was the successor, not of Peter, but of Constantine."

Innocent's primary concern was Christian unity and he used his own resourcefulness and the vast powers of the Church to combat those who opposed his ideal. He fiercely uprooted the heresies that threatened the Church, not shrinking from a bloody crusade to exterminate the evil. He empowered the Inquisition to ferret out the secrets of men's souls, and the world trembled as he thundered his excommunications and penalties. " I have no leisure to meditate on supermundane things," he once sighed; " scarce I can breathe. So much must I live for others that almost I am a stranger to myself."

It was natural for such a strong, imperious fanatic to be an enemy of the Jews. No one ever did them more harm; upon him rests the responsibility for most of the woes of the bitter thirteenth century. Yet his attitude was not the result of cruelty or hatred. Innocent was one of the many good men of history who, convinced that they have a monopoly of truth, are determined to bend others to their views, and not even conscience restrains them in their pious war for souls. Macaulay has admirably summarized the creed of all bigots: " I am in the right, and you are in the wrong. When you are the stronger, you ought to tolerate me, for it is your duty to tolerate truth. But when I am the stronger, I shall persecute you, for it is my duty to persecute error." Innocent honestly believed that the Jews were an accursed people, suffering for rejecting Christ and never to be given rest and peace. At the beginning of his pontificate, when a new crusade was being preached and Jews were everywhere being assaulted and plundered, he issued his *Constitutio Judæcorum,* prohibiting good Christians from attacking Jews or converting them by force. Yet when Philip Augustus recalled the Jews whom he had driven out of France, and allowed some of them to hold public office, Innocent protested vigorously and denounced the king for preferring the descendants of crucifiers to the heirs of the crucified. In May of 1205 he threatened to excommunicate Alphonso, the King of Castile, if he continued to employ Jews in his court. To Count Nevers he wrote several years later, summing up his policy: " The Jews, like the fratricide Cain, are doomed to wander about the earth as fugitives and vagabonds, and their faces must be covered in shame. They are under no circumstances to be protected by Christian princes, but, on the contrary, to be condemned to serfdom."

It was Innocent who destroyed the flourishing communities of southern France, almost the only spot in Europe where the breath of free thought remained. Religious dogmas and doctrines sat lightly upon the inhabitants, and Christian, Jew, and Moslem lived together in peace, developing the brilliant Provençal culture. Here lived Raymond VI, Count of Toulouse, the wealthiest feudal lord of the region, friendly to heretics and Jews and suspected of being lax in his own religious loyalties. For years Innocent tried persuasion to bring the district to its senses; when he failed, he turned to coercion. In 1207 an example was made of Count Raymond, who was dragged naked to church, scourged, and compelled to promise, at the point of the sword, that he would become a faithful son of the Church. Raymond's humiliation did not end the Provençal defiance, and the Pope's patience was soon exhausted. He ordered the Cistercians to preach a crusade against the heretics, and an army of eager adventurers, led by the redoubtable Simon de Montfort, was let loose into the fertile district. The terror raged through the whole country-side. No mercy was shown. "We spared neither dignity, nor sex, nor age," wrote Arnold of Citaux, one of the monkish leaders; "nearly twenty thousand human beings perished by the sword. After the massacre the town [Béziers] was plundered and burnt and the revenge of God seemed to rage upon it in a wonderful manner." Hundreds of Jews were cut down in the general massacre.

For eighteen years Innocent ruled Europe with a grip of iron. Men who opposed the papacy were executed as criminals and blasphemers, and their works were publicly burnt with them. Then in 1215, at the culmination of his career, Innocent called the Fourth Lateran Council. The assembly was an impressive tribute to his universal power; more than fifteen hundred dignitaries came to Rome from all over the world, to consider the problem of disciplining heretics and Jews, and the proclamation of a new crusade. The questions affected every dominion, but so strong was Innocent that there was little debate at the sessions; the Pope simply read his suggestions and received formal approval.

By the orders of the Lateran Council, Jews could neither hold public office nor employ Christian domestics. They could not charge high rates of interest for loaning money and the crusaders were released from all payments. Severe punishments were hinted at for converts who were lax in their new faith. These restrictions Jews had known for many centuries. The ingenuity of the over-righteous, however, is the eighth wonder of the world. Innocent rose to the occasion and imported into Christian Europe an institution which had been sometimes used by Moslems, but had been almost entirely discontinued. It was decreed that all Jews were to wear a distinctive garment or a special badge, to set them apart from other men.

In some places the edict was fought and evaded, but nearly everywhere it was enforced; often it was elaborated to work greater hardship. The Vienna Church synod in 1267 adopted a hideously disfiguring pointed cap — the *pileum cornutum* — which frequently excited the masses to bloodshed. St. Louis of

France, before departing for a new crusade against the Turks, insisted upon a badge of red or saffron-yellow in the form of a wheel, to be worn on back and breast both, " so that those who were thus marked might be recognized from all sides."

Nothing could have more quickly and more completely broken the proud spirit of Israel. The distinguishing mark called for ridicule and insult, and the ignorant populace was not slow to respond. The Jew was stoned and pelted, spat upon and cursed, compelled to slink through by-ways and side streets, in darkness and in shame. He ceased to dress with care, to walk with head erect. He lost the power to speak with ease, and, as he bowed and scraped his way through his tormentors, his self-respect disappeared. He was at last just what the Church had hoped he would become, a fugitive and a vagabond.

4 · THE TALMUD ON TRIAL

Innocent III died in the year after the creation of his masterpieces at the Lateran Council. His mantle fell upon two men, Louis IX of France, and Pope Gregory IX, who found it no difficulty to continue his Jewish policies.

Louis has been represented as the ideal mediæval king. He was reared by a strong-willed, imperious mother, who would rather have seen him dead than fall into laxity or the least sinfulness. He required no artificial stimulus, for he loved his faith unswervingly and kept every detail with the most exacting devotion. He rose at midnight for matins like a monk, read religious literature, confessed on Fridays, and had himself whipped with small chains. He hated beer, but he drank it all through Lent in the place of forbidden wine. He seemed more suited for the monastery than for the throne. His piety earned him the title of saint, and not long after his death he was officially canonized.

Sincere as was Louis's piety, however, it ran to formality. To him masses and mortification were the essence of religion. They did not prevent a stern political policy, which sat heavily upon all who challenged his authority. Recent researches have revealed that the sainted king was not the ideal friend of the communes, as portrayed by tradition, but, rather, a hard master who mulcted and extorted all he could. He nearly ruined the clergy by his exactions, and at the end of his reign most of the sees and monasteries in the kingdom were in debt to Lombard bankers. He introduced the pontifical Inquisition into his dominions and made it his personal concern to keep it busy.

From the beginning of his long reign, in 1226, the Jews fared miserably in Louis's dominions. For his strongest prejudice had to do with Jews. His hatred was almost an illness; he could not look at them. He fought Jewish usury, but opened no other means of livelihood to the helpless people. He released his subjects from one third of their indebtedness to them. The only road to his favour lay through apostasy. All his life he strove for converts. It was a personal satisfaction to him when Jews came to the baptismal font and he frequently served as godfather to the most distinguished.

In his zeal for conversion he was reinforced by Pope Gregory IX, whose paramount aim in life was to render the papacy supreme. Gregory's rules against heretics remained in force until the time of Sixtus V. He perfected the Inquisition and entrusted its management to the Dominicans, who strove to fulfil the narrow papal ideals. His activities in Provence completed Innocent's policy and ruined the Albigenses. Between Louis and Gregory the Jews of the middle of the thirteenth century ate to surfeit the bread of affliction.

Not content with impoverishing and degrading the Jew physically, the two potentates now turned to rob the Jewish spirit of its sustenance. They were helped by a vicious apostate, who had taken the name of Nicholas Donin, and who hated his people with all the fury that a traitor feels for those whom he has betrayed. Nicholas was probably the instigator of the bloody persecution of Poitou and of riots in other districts. A clever student of the Talmud, he brought together, in 1239, a number of passages and denounced them before Pope Gregory as libelling Christianity. He explained that the Talmud distorted the Bible, represented God blasphemously, and vilified the personality of Jesus. Culling extracts from the obscurest of the *Amoraim* and twisting their meanings, he deduced that it was permissible for Jews to deceive Christians and that oaths to them had no sanctity.

Gregory at once dispatched letters to the Church heads of Christian Europe calling upon them to seize all copies of the Talmud on the first sabbath in Lent. In most countries the order was neglected, for Gregory was by no means the king of kings that Innocent had been. But he found a ready ally in Louis, who hastened to comply. All copies of the Talmud were ordered surrendered on pain of death. The king went further. He arranged for a disputation between Nicholas and four representative rabbis, to decide the merits of the Talmud. Six centuries of Jewish literature were placed on trial for maligning Christianity, before a king who had vilified the Jews until they were thought to be fiends.

The strange trial was held at the royal court before the king, his mother, Blanche, and a host of Church and lay dignitaries, who came from far and wide to witness the spectacle. The rabbis were not called upon to argue the relative truths of Judaism and Christianity. They were only to answer the charges of Talmudic blasphemy against God and Jesus. It was not difficult to reply to the first indictment, but the second gave the rabbis considerable trouble. The Talmud contained not only the important laws of Judaism, but also volumes of discussion; the irrelevant words of the most mediocre *Amoraim* had been included. Instead of making this plain, however, and pointing out that the Haggadic portions of the Talmud carried no weight, the defending rabbis chose to insist that the offensive passages pointed out by Nicholas did not refer to Jesus. For three days the debate continued; in the intervals, to bolster up the courage of the rabbis, converts were continuously paraded before them. Finally it was decreed that all copies of the Talmud should be burnt, and in June of 1242 twenty-four cart-loads of Talmudic literature were destroyed in the public squares of Paris. The elegy written by Meir of Rothenburg in commemoration of the melancholy affair is still recited as part of the liturgy on the ninth day of Ab.

A second public burning was held two years later, when Louis destroyed the volumes that had escaped the first general destruction. The passing years made the king harsher and more relentless. He confiscated considerable Jewish property to pay for a new crusade, and when the venture failed, he expelled all the Jews living in his dominions. Sixteen years later, in 1270, the pious king died of a plague, and at the end of the century he was canonized for his righteousness.

5 · EXPLOITATION AND EXPULSION

As decade followed decade in the thirteenth century, the world began to take for granted that Jews were not men, but tools to be used and thrown away or targets to be fired upon in any contingency — when crops were bad or the wine mounted to the head, when an Easter sermon struck home too literally or a noble's purse was pinched. In the German provinces and in Austria the least provocation set off riots and massacres. In Frankfurt am Main a hundred and eighty Jews were slaughtered when parents attempted to prevent the baptism of a youthful convert. In 1241, when the Mongol invasions reached across the borders of Germany, devastating the land and bringing misery to its inhabitants, the rumour spread that among the invaders were descendants of the lost ten tribes of Israel, who had been locked by Alexander the Great in the Caspian Mountains. These were in a league with the German Jews and were responsible for the pitiless ravages of the Mongols.

Even the enlightened emperor, Frederick II, the most attractive figure of the century, followed the fashion. He was assuredly no religious bigot; he laughed at the pious and declared publicly that the world had been deluded by three great impostors, Moses, Jesus, and Mohammed. From his Sicilian court, up to the middle of the century, he took pleasure in defying the popes and befriending persecuted scholars and intellectuals. Yet he enforced the restrictions against the Jews and compelled them to wear the hideous badge. He excluded them from all public offices, and in his capital at Palermo he shut them up in a ghetto.

For more than twenty years after the death of Frederick a disastrous civil war rent the country, until, in 1273, the powerful Rudolph of Habsburg became emperor and restored order. In the general loosening of discipline Jewish martyrs fell in their hundreds. Many of the synagogue laments which are still preserved in the old service commemorate the mournful story of the period. In Sinzig the whole Jewish community was burnt alive by the mob as it stood in prayer in the synagogue. It is said that some of the ringleaders, proud of their exploits against the helpless Jews, took the name of *Judenbreter* (roasters of Jews).

Rudolph was powerful enough to put an end to the persecutions. But when hundreds of Jewish families took advantage of restored order to attempt to leave the country, he sternly forbade the exodus. Jews were still *" servi camaræ ";* they were much too desirable as a steady and lucrative source of income and too valuable to lose. When the renowned Jewish leader, Meir of Rothenburg, was apprehended leading a group of exiles towards Palestine, he was imprisoned in an Alsatian fortress, from 1286 to 1293. The Jews offered immense sums to ransom the aged scholar, but he preferred to end his years in captivity rather than create a precedent which could bring further vexations to his people. When death finally claimed him, Rudolph refused to surrender the body for fourteen years, until a goodly sum of money had been paid for its redemption. The emperor was setting a noble example of Christian benevolence to a hated race of " money-grubbers."

How Jews were regarded even by the cultured may be gauged from the satiric verses of a thirteenth-century poet, Siegfried Helbling. He complained that there were too many Jews in the land, that thirty Jews, indeed, were enough to fill the largest city with " stench and belief." He suggested that all the Jews be burnt or sold at thirty for a penny.

The virus of hate brought on a veritable epidemic to close the century fittingly. In 1298 the Jews of Rottingen in Franconia were charged with the desecration of a sacramental wafer; they had pounded it in a mortar, the report said, and blood had flowed from it. An uprising began at once, led by a dissolute nobleman, Rindfleisch, who declared that he was divinely authorized to destroy the accursed race of blaspheming unbelievers. Under his direction the whole Jewish community was burnt alive at the stake. Then the conflagration spread from town to town, from province to province, through Franconia, Bavaria, and Austria. Only those who accepted baptism could avert destruction. Those who remained steadfast either committed suicide or fell before the besotted mobs. For six months the hounds of hell hunted down their prey. Perhaps a hundred thousand Jews were massacred and a hundred and forty communities were completely destroyed. The Emperor Albert I sought to punish the imperial cities for maltreating " his property " and destroying " his revenues." But the homes had already been broken and the graves had already been dug.

In England the riots which had disgraced the reign of Richard were followed by further persecutions and exactions under succeeding kings. Richard's brother John, who plotted and murdered his way to the throne of England, proved a tyrant to all classes and above all to the Jews. Pressed for money, he was completely shameless in the methods of his exactions. In 1210, under the fiercest threats, he dragged sixty-six thousand marks out of the Jews. One Abraham of Bristol, who refused to pay his quota of ten thousand marks, had his teeth extracted one by one until he saw the error of his ways and paid the sum demanded.

Henry III's long reign, which covered a large part of the thirteenth century, virtually destroyed Jewish life in England. The regents who controlled policy early in the reign enforced every restriction of the Lateran Council and the English Church synods added further indignities. Jews were forbidden the right to emigrate; it was their fate to be slowly drained of wealth and manhood. In 1230 the king taxed away one third of all Jewish property, and, year by year, new means were devised to cut further into the Jewish possessions. In less than twenty years more than one hundred thousand pounds escheated to the Crown from Jewish legacies alone.

While the Jews paid taxes and fines, the Dominican monks continued to fan the flames of hatred against them. Their propaganda was largely responsible for the terrible tragedy of 1264, when during Easter-week fifteen hundred London Jews were murdered and the whole community reduced to beggary. By now the Jews had plainly become chattel. In 1255 all rights to them for one year were sold by the king to his brother for five thousand marks! Before the end of the year a child, Hugh of Lincoln, was found murdered and the Jewish community was charged with using his blood for ritual purposes. Confessions were forced by torture, and eighteen Jews were executed and scores imprisoned. The guilt of the Jews was firmly believed, little Hugh was canonized and his native city became a shrine.[1]

At last, with the accession of Edward I, came the end. Edward was one of the most popular figures in English history. Tall, fair, amiable, an able soldier, a good administrator, he was the idol of his people. But he was filled with prejudices, and hated foreigners and foreign ways. His Statute of Judaism, in 1275, might have been modelled on the restrictive legislation of his contemporary St. Louis of France. He forbade all usury and closed the most important means of livelihood that remained to the Jews. Farming, commerce, and handicrafts were specifically allowed, but it was exceedingly difficult to pursue those occupations. Well-nigh impoverished and no longer necessary in England, since the Lombards had begun to take over the banking interests, the Jews became mere nuisances in the eyes of the king. The inevitable doom came in 1290, when an order for a general expulsion was issued. The Jews were required to leave the country within a few months, taking with them only their movable property. Sixteen thousand Jews, completely demoralized by more than a century

[1] In the enlightened nineteenth century the gentle Charles Lamb was still repeating the story of Jewish bloodthirstiness in the case of little Hugh.

of pitiless baiting, were uprooted by the edict and sent flying to France and Flanders.

The thirteenth century had opened with Innocent's restrictions and the degrading Jew badge. It closed now with the destruction of every Jewish community in England. The world looked back with satisfaction upon the accomplishments of the century — beautiful Gothic architecture, brilliant philosophical achievements, the development of great Church orders, which carried the message of Christianity to the ends of the earth. But Jews could only sit and weep. "A people long used to hardships," says Swift, "lose by degrees the very notions of liberty: they look upon themselves as at mercy."

6. THE BLACK DEATH AND AFTER

The fourteenth century opened ominously with the expulsion of the Jews from all of France. The example of England was infectious. The French king, sorely pressed for money, listened willingly to advisers who were remarkably fluent on the subject of Jewish opulence. In 1306 the property and the holdings of the Jews were confiscated and they were ordered out of his dominions. For a thousand years they had lived on French soil; now they were sent out into the darkness with only the clothes on their backs. The king filled his exchequer from their savings and smiled at the quick and easy solution of his financial difficulties. He was in a good enough humour to present his coachmen with a synagogue.

After 1306 the Jews were several times readmitted, always on payment of liberal sums. But expulsion invariably followed soon after. The final edict, signed by the mad Charles VI in 1394, on the Day of Atonement, ended Jewish history in France until modern times.

Germany, too, in the early fourteenth century gave the Jews no respite. In 1336, scarcely two generations after the fearful holocaust of victims sacrificed by Rindfleisch and his rabble, another general massacre, again incited by noblemen, devoured the Jewish communities. Five thousand peasants followed the Armleder, two self-appointed leaders, and spread destruction from Alsace to Swabia.

All of these sufferings, however, were as nothing in comparison to the terror of the Black Death, which swept out of Asia in the middle of the century and penetrated into every nook and corner of Europe. Men were suddenly stricken with boils and black patches, vomited blood, and dropped down dead. The virulence of the plague well-nigh eradicated human society; even the plague days of Pericles and Gregory the Great had not wrought such desolation. Hecker estimates that twenty-five million people died, a fourth of Europe's population. Two thirds of the students of Oxford were carried off; the grass grew long in the once flourishing streets of Bristol; and every day more than five hundred bodies were taken from the hospital of Paris. " The sheep and the cattle strayed through the fields and corn," a contemporary writes, "and there were none left who could drive them." The cities were choked with the dead; they could not be buried quickly enough. Wagons went through the streets of death collecting the poor blackened bodies, missing scarcely a house. Men were beside themselves, desperately trusting every remedy, following every quack, and believing every grandmother's tale.

And then in an evil hour the rumour spread that the cursed Jews had done it all. They were revenging themselves for their degradation by poisoning the wells, the food, the very air. It was told in the market places that the poison had been actually found; that it was manufactured in Toledo by Jewish doctors of sorcery and spread through Europe in boxes by devilish messengers. It was compounded of spiders and lizards, of frogs and flesh, and of the hearts of Christians mixed with the dough of the sacred host. Frantic people listened wild-eyed; stupid people believed willingly; and debtors and rascals, scenting rich spoils, pretended to be convinced. The poor Jews, themselves suffering grievously from the plague, were now subjected to the worst outrages in their history. The Pope, the kings, the city councils, all pleaded for sanity and sought to curb the fury of the masses. But the terror was too great, the hysteria altogether unmanageable.

The massacres spread from one end of Europe to the other. Among the beautiful lakes of Switzerland and the fertile valleys of the Rhine, in the cultured cities of Germany and the affluent cities of Austria, flame and sword devoured Jewish homes and cut down Jewish lives. Everywhere captured Jews were put on trial and tortured and confessions were forced from lips wrung with pain. Sixty large communities were destroyed and one hundred and fifty smaller ones. Property losses were staggering, but the toll of lives made these pale. In Strassburg, despite the protests of the council, eighteen hundred Jews were dragged out to the cemetery on the sabbath and there burnt alive, after which their possessions were distributed. In Mayence six thousand Jews perished; in Erfurt three thousand. And in the shadow of every visitation the Flagellant monks stood, in flowing robes, like ghouls, crying in one voice for penance and blood.

At last pity came back to human hearts, and the orgy of bloodshed ended. The Jews crept back to their homes, weeping for the past and trembling for the future. In Germany they had reason to tremble. By the Golden Bull, of 1356, many of the electors were granted the right to keep and control the Jews in their dominions. It was significant that the dispensation appeared between clauses dealing with the exploitation of mines and the collection of taxes. The Jews were now herded in special quarters, and every restriction was placed upon their movements. Life was never safe either under the emperor or under his vassals. The least provocation kindled the rage and the lust of the mobs. On Easter Sunday in 1389 a riot was begun in Prague during which the synagogue was torn down, three thousand Jews were destroyed, and the very dead were flung out of their graves.

The new century brought little relief. The Emperor Sigismund (1410–37), while decrying the persecution of his Jewish subjects, was most resourceful in expedients for robbing them of the little wealth that they still possessed. At a time when the regular annual revenue for all the empire was thirteen thousand golden gulden, nine Jewish families in Frankfurt were compelled to contribute five thousand. Most of the others contributed little only because they had virtually nothing left.

Early in the fifteenth century the Church was confronted by a formidable heresy in Bohemia. Its leader was John Huss, a young reformer whose sincere devotion to the interests of Bohemia and the purity of its religious life made him a national hero. Huss was requested to appear at the Council of Constance to explain his views and was given a safe-conduct with the promise of freedom to return to Bohemia. The promise was not kept and Huss was burnt at the stake in 1415. The spirit of resistance could not be destroyed, however. Huss's gallant death was a living inspiration to his devoted followers and, according to the legend, the skin of another martyr, Ziska, was spread upon a drum to waken resistance in every corner of the land.

The day was not made for tolerance. The Dominicans, fighting the Hussite heresy, included the Jews in their denunciations. A wave of persecution spread over Germany and Austria which the Emperor Albert II did nothing to avert. The massacres were accompanied by the usual forced baptisms and the whole-sale suicide of Jewish communities. In 1421 in Vienna men and women were ruthlessly cut down, homes were burnt, synagogues were razed, and their stones were dragged away for the new University buildings. For a while not a single Jew remained in Austria.

By the middle of the century the fury of the Hussite wars died down, but other means of abusing the Jews were not lacking. Eugenius IV, who became Pope only after a series of shameful and unworthy political manœuvres, took a leaf from the books of Innocent and Gregory. He ordered Christians not to eat with Jews, not to employ them as physicians, not to allow them in any public office. Jews were to remain in their homes all through Passion Week, closing their windows and doors. They were obliged to live in special quarters and wear a special costume. In Italy they were forbidden to read the Talmudic literature.

Only one other account need be singled out from the martyrology of these unhappy days. This time the villain of the piece is the papal legate John of Capistrano, a Franciscan monk whose persecuting zeal earned him the unenviable title of " Scourge of the Jews." It was the mission of this gaunt, emaciated fanatic to uproot heresy in eastern Europe. Wherever he went, thousands who could not understand his Latin addresses were carried away by his immense sincerity, his ferocious energy. Riots were common in Germany and the Slavic lands after his tongue had lashed heretics and Jews. In Silesia and Franconia the Jews were expelled and their possessions were confiscated by State and Church. In Breslau a Bernadine chapel was built with Jewish money after nearly the whole community had been burnt alive for blasphemy. The town-clerk, Eschenloer, who could not lift his voice against the outrage, wrote in his diary: " Whether this is godly or not I leave to the judgment of the ministers of religion."

So went the tale of woe decade after decade, endlessly. Four hundred years had now passed since the hideous nightmare had begun. Hounded by successions of crusaders, by the restrictions of the Church councils, the torments of Rindfleisch and the Armleder, the accusations of ritual murder and blasphemy, the hatred of Dominicans and Jew-baiters, the Black Death and the libels which it engendered, the Hussite wars and Capistrano, Jewish life at the opening of the fifteenth century was a poor, hopeless, broken thing. It meant shame and horror to continue living in the land, yet no man dared to stir. Even if the death penalty did not prevent, where indeed was a Jew to go? Half the countries of Europe had expelled their Jews or were as ruthlessly persecuting them. Even sunny Spain was beginning to use the thumb-screw and the torch. Everywhere there was war in the name of peace, hate in the name of love. Jews turned to their Bibles and prayer-books, scanning the tear-stained pages in vain for the consolation which the living world denied them.

In the next century Martin Luther, early in his career, summed up the dreadful hypocrisy of the Church with characteristic sharpness: " Our fools, the popes, bishops, sophists, and monks, have hitherto conducted themselves towards the Jews in such a manner that he who was a good Christian would have preferred to be a Jew. And if I had been a Jew and had seen such blockheads and louts ruling and teaching Christianity, I would have become a swine rather than a Christian, because they have treated the Jews like dogs, and not like human beings."

One wonders how flesh and blood could survive such trials: not years, nor decades, but centuries of unremitting woe, and more to follow. The Jews, however, seemed to have remarkable powers of adjustment. When they suffered an apparently crushing calamity, they turned submissively to God to thank Him for all that they might have borne, but had mercifully escaped!

CHAPTER SIXTEEN

THE DECLINE AND FALL OF JEWISH LIFE IN SPAIN

I. TWILIGHT IN CASTILE

FOR some time it appeared as if the course of Jewish life in Spain would belie the developments in the rest of Europe. The long wars against the Moors continued and step by step the Peninsula was reclaimed for the cross. But the little kingdoms that emerged with each Christian victory showed little animosity towards their Jewish inhabitants. The kings were usually men of tolerance and were statesmanlike enough to appreciate the stupidity of driving an important commercial element into the arms of the still powerful Moorish enemies. While France and England, Germany and Austria ransacked chambers of horror to discover new torments, the two hundred and fifty Jewish communities of Spain throve in comfort and security. Jews rose to high State positions, often serving with conspicuous ability as linguists, diplomats, and financiers. In thirteenth- and early fourteenth-century Castile, under a succession of excellent rulers — patrons of learning, unhindered by prejudice — Jewish imagination was again given release and bloomed afresh. The benevolent Alfonso XI employed several Jewish financiers who became influential enough to affect the politics of the country.

Unfortunately these halcyon days were soon interrupted and then ended. Towards the close of the thirteenth century several of the Christian provinces of Spain began to turn from their policy of tolerance. Navarre fell to France in 1285 and its Jews were soon subjected to the restrictions and degradations endured by their co-religionists on the other side of the Pyrenees. The French example was sufficiently impressed upon Navarre by 1328 and there were massacres in Estella, Tudela, and other large centres, in which more than six thousand Jews lost their lives. Clerical agitators helped to bring Aragon into line with Navarre, and soon the statute-books reflected the general animosity of the masses.

Only Castile remained fairly faithful to its tradition of tolerance. When the Black Death itself evoked no outrages, the Jews congratulated themselves that there was at least one spot in Europe where freedom was not crushed out by bigotry.

Then Castile turned too, and Christian Spain could boast of a uniform Jewish policy. The downfall of the Jews began during a virulent civil war which threatened to destroy the prosperity of the province. Pedro, a lad of unrestrained passions and immense ego, ascended the throne in 1350. Though he protected merchants and their trade, the nobles and the clergy could not forgive his extortions and the murders by which he dispatched those who opposed his will, and they fastened upon him the title "Pedro the Cruel." Perhaps it was because the Jews and the Moslems were the instruments of his tyranny that the hatred against both peoples became so fierce in Castile. Pedro used none but Jews as his tax-gatherers and none but Moslems as his personal guard. He had no religious scruples and surrounded himself with Jewish advisers. Samuel Abulafia, a shrewd and rather shifty politician, became his right-hand man until the king suddenly put him to death for treason and confiscated his vast estates.[1]

The unpopularity of Pedro offered an excellent opportunity to pretenders who coveted his throne. A civil war began in 1366, when Pedro's bastard brother, Henry, invaded Castile with several legions of military adventurers, including the romantic ruffian Bertrand du Guesclin. Pedro fled without giving battle, and Henry entered Burgos in triumph. He immediately increased his popularity by punishing the Jewish community for Pedro's partiality. He fined the Jews fifty thousand doubloons and cancelled all Christian obligations to them. The silver was stripped from the scrolls of the law to help realize the assessment, and many humble Jews who could not contribute were sold as slaves. In the capital, Toledo, which Henry entered soon after, the Jews were fined one million maravedis.

Even yet the strife was not over. Pedro struggled on with the assistance of the English Black Prince, and his efforts were desperately supported by the Jewish population. Before Toledo was captured a second time by Henry, more than eight thousand Jews fell by sword and famine. At last, in 1369, came the end. Henry confronted his brother in the tent of Du Guesclin, taunting him: "Where is the Jew, the son of a harlot, who calls himself King of Castile?" Pedro was then stabbed to death, his stormy career ending before he had reached the age of thirty-six. Pope Urban sent his congratulations and wrote that "at the death of such a tyrant, a rebel against the Church, a favourer of the Jews and Saracens, the righteous exult in retribution."

Thenceforth there was little peace for the Jews of Castile. Henry, to be sure, was shrewd enough to temper his dislike of Jews with an appreciation of their economic importance. He was deeply in debt to the free lances who had helped him to win his kingdom and he needed capital and expert administration to discharge his obligations. During the ten years of his reign he even employed several able Jewish financiers.

[1] It is fair to add that Samuel was a generous benefactor. He built several synagogues in Castile; the magnificent one which he erected in Toledo, now known as El Tránsito, is the finest monument of its kind.

But the nobles and the clergy scented spoils and longed for revenge. In the first Cortes at Toro in 1371 they clamoured for restrictive legislation, and the king found it politic to submit. The wearing of the Jewish badge, which no pope could formerly enforce in Castile, was now made compulsory, and Jews were forbidden to retain Spanish names. Such regulations were unimportant in themselves, but they marked a turning-point in Spanish-Jewish history. For centuries the Castilian Jew had held his head high and had borne himself with grace and dignity. Now he, too, was a branded pariah, compelled to skulk through street and alley to escape the insults of the masses.

2. THE FURY OF 1391

During the latter half of the fourteenth century hostility towards the Jews spread through the Peninsula, but the civic authorities furnished the Jews some protection, and usually the outrages were summarily suppressed. Official protection, however, ultimately proved disastrous. On Ash Wednesday of 1391 an unreasoning Church dignitary, Ferrand Martinez, incited a riot in Seville, during which the Jewish quarter was burnt down. The governor at once arrested two of the ringleaders and, as a warning to other rioters, ordered them to be flogged. The severity of the governor infuriated the community, and when an opportunity came, in June, to assault the Jews with impunity, an orgy of bloodshed began. In Seville several thousand were butchered, other thousands were driven into baptism to escape death, and hundreds were sold as slaves to the Moors.

The riots spread like a plague, undoubtedly stimulated as much by the desire for plunder as by religious bigotry. In Córdoba, once the proudest centre of Jewish life, the whole Jewish quarter was destroyed, and the two thousand Jews who were slain were left in heaps in the streets. Toledo, with the largest Jewish population in Spain, was ravaged, probably on the ninth of Ab, the anniversary of Jerusalem's downfall, and the brutality of the mobs gave the day a doubly tragic meaning. About seventy cities of Old Castile were thus devastated and a trail of broken homes and broken hearts was left in the wake of the bloody hooligans.

From Castile the fury spread to Aragon, where the well-meaning king, John I, was too weak to make his authority felt. One town learned quickly from another how to pillage and destroy. The fertile province of Valencia, the prosperous seaport of Barcelona, even the islands off the coast of Spain, were all swept by the ferocity of the persecutors. After three months the orgy ended, with thousands of Jewish lives snuffed out and tens of thousands of forced baptisms. Germany and Austria were paradise now in comparison with ensanguined Spain.

One can perhaps forgive the animosity of the sincere, benighted pietists who believed that they were saving souls when they split skulls with crucifixes. But among the most relentless persecutors were converted Jews who, desperately striving to prove their loyalty to their adopted faith, moved heaven and earth to embitter the existence of their former co-religionists. Jews have suffered in every generation from the zeal of renegades, and not least from the outstanding convert of the period, Solomon Levi, who, as a Christian, took the name Paul de Santa Maria and became one of the leading men in the State.

Paul had been an exceptionally gifted rabbi in Burgos, well trained in Biblical and Talmudic lore and familiar with the outstanding works in Christian literature. Restless, ambitious, chafing at the restrictions which Jewish life entailed, he yearned for a wide field in which to exercise his undeniable talents. The persecutions of 1391 probably swept him into Christianity, and, anxious to make a success of his new life, he determined upon a career in the Church. He studied theology in Paris, where his knowledge of Hebrew gave him an exceptional advantage, and he was soon qualified for the priesthood. Once ordained, he rose from post to post; he won the friendship of the Pope and became the archbishop of the city in which he had formerly functioned as a despised rabbi. He was now a powerful leader in Castile, serving as keeper of the royal seal under Henry III and as a member of the regency during the minority of John II.

Paul worked diligently to bring other Jews into the Christian fellowship. He wrote treatises, he expostulated, he debated, and, when friendly methods of persuasion availed him little, he turned to the more effective weapons of force which a powerful position placed at his disposal. He was responsible for much of the new restrictive legislation which came from the court and which served further to cripple Jewish enterprise.

He was supported in his activity by a Dominican preacher, the outstanding evangelist of the age, Vicente Ferrer, who was later sainted for his activity. Vicente marched through the land with a troop of devoted followers, fasting, praying, scourging himself, and crying out for repentance. He went into every synagogue, attended by his followers and an unruly mob, to spread his gospel of love and brotherhood. With a cross in one hand and the Torah in the other he called upon the Jews to turn from their waywardness and to win salvation before it was too late.

To thousands of miserable, broken Jews there seemed to be no alternative but conversion or death. Most occupations were forbidden, the frontiers were closed, the enemy was at the gate, in the very centre of worship. Self-respect was gone. Even the proudest Jews were compelled now to dress in the coarsest garments and to live in the vilest quarters. It was more than flesh and blood could bear. A steady stream of converts made their way to baptismal fonts and Vicente exulted that he alone was responsible for more than thirty-five thousand rescued souls.

It was during these difficult days, in 1413, that a new disputation, instigated by the papal physician, the apostate Joshua ibn Vives Lorque, was ordered by Pope Benedict XIII to be held in the kingdom of Aragon. Again the Jews were called upon to answer the charge that their Talmudic literature calumniated the Saviour and Christianity and blasphemed against God. Twenty-two Jewish leaders were chosen to conduct the defence in Tortosa, before the Pope and a brilliant assembly of clericals and statesmen. It was made plain, however, that Christianity was not on trial, and that it was dangerous to be too bold. The text of the sermon which opened the proceedings was taken from Isaiah: "If ye be willing and obedient, ye shall eat the good of the land; but if ye refuse and rebel, ye shall be devoured with the sword." The Jewish disputants needed no elaborate commentary to understand.

For a year and nine months the farce continued, with quibbles and arguments, deliberate distortion of words, and threats. The morale of the rabbis was not improved by the practice of regularly leading new Jewish converts into the disputation chamber. In the end the usual decree was issued condemning the Talmud and forbidding Jews to read it. Thrice a year, moreover, they were to listen in their synagogues to a Christian conversion sermon. The edict was placed in the hands of a son of Paul for execution. It was not fully carried out because the Council of Constance soon afterwards deposed Pope Benedict, and Vicente himself turned to preach against his claims.

3. THE MARRANOS AND THE INQUISITION

The wholesale conversions which began in 1391 changed the course of Spanish and Jewish history. Until then converts had been welcomed with open arms and had been denied no opportunity to advance as far as their talents could carry them. There was genuine rejoicing when a new soul found the true Catholic way and was saved from the horrors of eternal perdition. This relationship continued so long as converts were few and humble. But after 1391, when the pressure upon the Jews became fierce, whole communities went into the Christian faith. The majority of the converts eagerly took advantage of their new position. They flocked in their hundreds and thousands to the places from which they had formerly been excluded by their faith. They entered forbidden professions and the quiet cloisters of the universities. They won important State positions and penetrated even into the sanctum sanctorum of the church. Their power increased with their wealth, and many became eligible for admission into the oldest and most aristocratic families in Spain. Intermarriages were frequent, and within half a century virtually every noble house had infiltrations of Jewish blood. It is said, although without authority, that His Most Catholic Majesty, King Ferdinand, who later signed the edict expelling the Jews from Spain, and Torquemada, the relentless master of the Inquisi-

THE WANDERING JEW IN THE MIDDLE AGES

LEGEND OF MIGRATIONS

——— from K. of Spain   ▬▮▬ from K. of France
– – – from K. of Portugal   ▬▭▬ from A. of Austria
–·–·– from K. of England   ═══ from Holy Roman Empire

The dates are those of migrations

K. OF SCOTLAND

IRELAND

K. OF ENGLAND

ATLANTIC

OCEAN

NORTH SEA

K. OF DEN

HOLY

ROMA

EMPIR

NETH.

LUX.

BURGUNDY

LORRAINE

SWISS CONFED.

AUST

1290

1298
1348

129
134

1306
1322
1394

KING. OF FRANCE

DAUPHINY

SAVOY

MILAN

PROVENCE

GENOA

D. OF SAVOY

PAPAL

STA

KING OF PORTUGAL

NAVARRE

KING. OF

ARAGON

CASTILE

SPAIN

GRANADA

1496

1492

FEZ

ALGIERS

MEDITERR

K. OF SARDINIA

K. O
SICI

TUNIS

MOSLEM STATES

KIN
O
NOR

KINGDOM OF SWEDEN

BALTIC SEA

DOMAIN OF THE TEUTONIC ORDER

MUSCOVY

DUCHY OF PRUSSIA

KING. OF POLAND

GRAND PRINCIPALITY OF LITHUANIA

OF HUNGARY

OTTOMAN

BLACK SEA

Constantinople

EMPIRE

CORFU

A N   S E A

CRETE

Herlin

0   100   200   300   400   500
MILES

tion, were themselves descendants from Jewish ancestors! An almost contemporary Italian remarked that the Jewish converts were practically ruling Spain while their covert adherence to Judaism was ruining the Christian faith.

Inevitably a wedge of hate cut through the relations of the old Christians and the new. The converts were known as *marranos,* (probably " the damned " or " the swine "). They were despised for their success, for their pride, for their cynical adherence to Catholic practices. It rankled in the hearts of old Christians to see the *marranos* in positions of trust and honour, in court, in camp, in Church, lording it over ancient families. They looked upon the converts as a mean and cunning people, amassing riches at the expense of true believers, mocking them as they exploited them.

While the masses looked with sullen bitterness on the success of the new Christians, the clergy denounced their disloyalty and insincerity. They sensed the truth that the majority of the converts were still Jews at heart, that the forced conversion had not erased the heritage of centuries. Tens of thousands of the new Christians conformed outwardly, went mechanically to church, mumbled prayers, performed rites, and observed customs. But the spirit had not been converted. There was a suspicion that the converts did not baptize their children or that they immediately wiped the stain of baptism from their heads. It was believed that they secretly observed the Jewish holidays, ate Jewish food, retained Jewish friendships, and studied the ancient Jewish lore. The reports of numerous spies tended to confirm every suspicion. What pious son of the Church could remain calm as these hypocrites — mockers of Christian practice in their hearts — accumulated wealth and honours?

How deep the hatred against the new Christians had become was demonstrated in 1449 when Toledo was called upon to contribute a million maravedis for the defence of the frontier. The community refused and tax-gatherers — most of them *marranos* — were sent into the city to enforce the collection. Not only were they assaulted, but the houses of all the new Christians were destroyed and those who attempted to defend them or their property were brutally beaten or killed. All of the king's attempts to restore order failed, and he was compelled to watch feebly as the council passed an edict forbidding new Christians to hold any public office. The envenomed wording of the edict, the *Sentencia Estatuto,* demonstrated clearly that the animosity sprang from more than a religious difference. It had become a genuine race-hatred.

Unchristian Christians fanned the smouldering hostilities. One Franciscan monk, Alonso de Spina, a Spanish edition of Capistrano, proved to be a living hurricane. He was a man of brilliant parts, well educated, honestly pious, yet so blinded by religious hatred that he believed whatever childish tittle-tattle he heard of Jews and *marranos.* In a Latin work which he issued in 1460, he repeated every libel which the enemies of the Jews had invented to create trouble. Jews poisoned wells, they murdered innocent Christian children, they spread plagues, they venerated the law, which encouraged the spoliation of Christians. They were a curse in every society, and they were destined to become terrible scourges with the advent of Antichrist. For then unbelievers and treacherous converts would join with the myriads of Jews locked up in the Caspians since the days of Alexander, to overrun and ruin Christian Europe. The monk called repeatedly for the establishment of an Inquisition to check the influence of the Jews and uproot the heresies of the *marranos*. In 1463 he lamented: "Some are heretics and Christian perverts, others are Jews, others Saracens, others devils. There is no one to investigate the errors of the heretics. The ravaging wolves, O Lord, have entered Thy flock, for the shepherds are few; many are hirelings, and as hirelings they care only for shearing and not for feeding Thy sheep."

While De Spina spouted filth by the yard, disturbances made a bedlam of every city. In Toledo, in 1465, no efforts were made to punish the perpetrators of a riot in which a hundred and thirty *marranos* were slain and sixteen hundred homes were burnt. No incident was too trivial to set off a blaze of horror. In 1473, during an important religious procession in Córdoba, a *marrano* girl, either accidentally or intentionally, splashed the image of the Virgin with water, and a hideous massacre followed. For three days the cry *Viva la fe de Dios* rang through the city as the crazed multitude burnt *marrano* dwellings and slaughtered all who came in their way. When the hysteria had worn itself out, the city authorities banished the survivors for ever, casting them out upon the roads to be robbed and murdered with impunity.

The converts began to wonder whether they had gained by deserting the Jewish fold. Conversion, it was clear, had not solved the problem of security. A deeper hate than ever had been engendered and wealth and honour were no badge of safety. Yet the *marrano* troubles had only begun. At the end of the century there was forged for their undoing an instrument so deadly, so effective, that it seemed to have been created by the very demons of hell.

For many years a continuous agitation had been carried on, supported by every monkish order, for the introduction of the Inquisition into Spain. Even Alonso de Spina's eloquence, however, was unavailing. The usefulness of a powerful instrument for the suppression of heretics was not disputed. To be effective, however, the tribunal had to be under secular control, and the fifteenth-century State was weak and unorganized, a prey to lawlessness and disorder. The sovereigns were struggling with a thousand political difficulties and were obliged to push the problem of religious conformity into the background.

In 1479 Ferdinand of Aragon and Isabella of Castile, who had been married several years before, became the joint rulers of the States and inaugurated a new era in Spanish history. They were determined to reconquer the whole Peninsula, to unify it in a Christian bond, and to centralize its institutions. Their combined resources and their energy and ability enabled them to ride roughshod over all opposition and they soon fashioned Spain into one of the most strongly organized states in Europe. As their grip on the country tightened, the advocates of the Inquisition became more importunate.

Torquemada, the confessor of the queen, was particularly persistent; he pointed out the advantages of religious conformity, and the political value of a powerful tribunal in the hands of the State. Isabella, who was intensely pious, according to her lights, had long been convinced. Ferdinand was probably more swayed by the thought that the Inquisition would curb the nobles who had been obstructing the development of the royal power. In 1478 the sovereigns applied to Rome for authority to organize the tribunal, and after several delays, occasioned because Ferdinand insisted that it must be under royal control, the permission was granted. In September 1480 two Dominicans were appointed to supervise the operation of the new institution in Seville.

It was highly effective from the very beginning. The inquisitors found heresy and apostasy wherever they turned. A declaration had been issued offering grace to those who confessed their errors; though many guilty families fled in terror, hundreds of others, the majority *marranos,* offered themselves for reconciliation. They soon discovered that they had fallen into a trap. They were called upon to betray all whom they suspected of similar relapses, and torture was applied to loosen their unwilling tongues. In February 1481 came the first executions of impenitent heretics — a public *auto-da-fé,* in which six men and one woman were burnt alive. The number of victims increased daily and the city authorities were obliged to establish a permanent execution ground, where, for more than three centuries, men and women were done to death for the glory of God. By November, in Seville alone, three hundred victims had been executed and eighty had been imprisoned for life. Tribunals were then established in the districts of Cádiz and Christian Andalusia, and the fires of the Quemadero soon lit up all of southern Spain.

No new Christian was safe. Bonuses were offered to those who betrayed secret relapses, and a premium was placed on the most hideous forms of treachery. Rules were issued to guide pious Christians in the detection of apostasy. If men wore clean linen on the Jewish sabbath, or ate specially prepared meat, or drank specially prepared wine, or observed Jewish customs in the Passover season, or did or did not do a hundred odd things related to Jewish practice, they were likely to be dragged before the tribunal to answer the charges of accusers whom they were not permitted to see or to know. Even the dead were not safe in their graves. If witnesses came forward to make accusations, the dead were tried, exhumed, and burnt, and, what was perhaps more important, their property was confiscated and turned into the royal treasury.

For three years the work of the Inquisition went forward, its technique steadily improving. The Dominicans in charge earned their title of "*Domini canes* (dogs of the Lord) " for they ferreted out errors in the most hidden places and tore their unfortunate victims to bits.

Thus far, however, the Inquisition had been confined to southern Spain. In the remaining provinces the opposition of the nobles and the influence of many wealthy *marranos* had prevented its introduction. In May 1483 the rulers decided to extend its operations all through their dominions and to centralize its activity by appointing as Inquisitor-General the queen's own confessor, Torquemada. The decision inaugurated the most searching and relentless persecutions in all history.

Torquemada was made for the new post. He was now sixty-three and had spent a lifetime in devoted service to the Dominican order and the Church. He had been well educated and was personally not unkindly. But conformity was a passion with him and he was pitiless in his attitude to those who deviated by one hair from the faith as he interpreted it.[1] His sincerity and his inflexible will gave him unbounded influence over the king and queen and he used this influence adroitly to accomplish his lifelong ambition — purging the country of all heresy and apostasy.

As soon as he was appointed Inquisitor-General, Torquemada drafted rules for his subordinates which left no loop-hole of escape for unfortunate suspects. Men were given a little more than a month to confess their relapse from the true faith. Those who took advantage of this grace escaped with a fine and a public penance, saving their skins and their goods. But those who were accused and remained impenitent suffered every penalty — torture, death, confiscation of property. The rack was freely used not only to drag confessions from the accused, but to obtain incriminating evidence to damn other suspects. Torquemada refused, under any circumstances, to mitigate the rigour of his tribunals. The Pope often censured him for undue severity, and three times Torquemada was obliged to send envoys to the papal court to defend his acts. But to the end of his life the tribunals continued with their deadly work, unrestrained by any considerations of statesmanship or common humanity. In the sixteen years of Torquemada's administration hundreds of *marranos* were burnt. Llorente, one of the secretaries who had access to the archives, placed the number of cases investigated as high as ten thousand.[2]

To Torquemada it was all a labour of love. He was saving Spain from the corruption of heresy. The Pope, the infamous Borgia, now showered him with

---

[1] " Lean, ascetic, ominous, with black fires in his hollow eyes, Torquemada reminds one of certain Spanish landscapes that look like suburbs of Hell. Nature in these landscapes never smiles; she is either sallow or livid, with a sinister glare of the end of the world, and a cheerless, cadaverous concentration, as if one were bending over the pale lips and waxen grin of death. The Spaniard who has taken into his soul the aspect of these desolate mountains, these bitter valleys, these sardonic forests, and who has felt in his bones the sweltering and solemn heat of these macabre heights and blistering voids, is all ready to believe in a God of fire and blood and sacrifice, not so far removed from the deity of ancient Mexico." Hackett: *Henry VIII*, 7.

[2] Lea: *A History of the Spanish Inquisition*, I, 220.

praise, writing to him in 1496 that "he cherishes him in the very bowels of affection for his immense labors in the exaltation of the faith." [1] Despite various attempts to dislodge the Inquisition, it continued to function, its severity unabated, for three centuries, destroying not only all heresy, but all freedom of thought. It was not finally abolished until 1834.

4. THE EXPULSION OF THE JEWS

Meantime the dominion of the cross was being steadily extended by the energy of the Catholic sovereigns. Step by step the Moslems were pushed back until Granada, the last bulwark of Moslem strength, fell. In January of 1492, Ferdinand and Isabella entered the capital in triumph and set themselves up in the wondrous citadel of Alhambra. The conquered Moors were permitted to remain in the land and to practise their faith unmolested; they were obliged to pay only such taxes as they had formerly paid to their own sovereigns. Yet they had the status of aliens, and thousands whose pride sat heavily upon them followed the tearful Boabdil, the last of the Moorish kings, and withdrew to the more friendly soil of Africa. After nearly eight centuries Spain was again Christian, as it had been in the days of the Visigoths.

With the *marranos* crushed and the Moors conquered, the Inquisitor-General now turned to the Jews. There was no longer any hope of converting them. They had too long resisted the pressure of the kings and the persecutions of priests and populace. The melancholy example of *marrano* suffering had strengthened them in their steadfastness. They were a source of annoyance to pious Christians, a hated remnant by whose connivance the *marranos* managed to continue affiliations with their abandoned faith. For it was known that Jews supplied the *marranos* with books, secretly prayed with them, instructed their children, and subtly undid all that the Church was hoping to accomplish. Torquemada was determined to expel them from the country, root and branch. Spain could never be cleansed until this maleficent, stiff-necked people had been driven out.

Already in 1480, when the Inquisition was established, Torquemada had urged upon Ferdinand to expel the Jews from the province of Andalusia, where they lived in the greatest numbers. The order had been actually issued, but after being several times postponed it was ultimately abandoned. The king was enough of a statesman to foresee the disastrous influence of a Jewish expulsion upon the economic stability of the country. Torquemada continued his solicitations with every argument that might appeal to the religious fanaticism of the queen or the cupidity of the king. As the Moors were pushed back, both sovereigns began to waver. The vision of a homogeneous Christian Spain was

[1] *Ibid.*, 174.

inviting; more so was the prospect of confiscating the valued possessions of the Jewish population.

In 1491, before Granada fell, an embassy was sent to Pope Innocent VIII requesting his blessing for the proposed banishment. The Pope, though an abandoned, immoral creature, refused to sanction a project so inhuman. Torquemada's influence, however, was now so great that he prevailed upon the king to proceed without the papal permission. On March 31, 1492 the edict went forth from the Alhambra ordering all Jews, on pain of death, to leave the country within four months. They could dispose of their property as well as they were able and could take with them goods and chattels, but neither gold nor silver nor precious stones. No good Christian, on penalty of the confiscation of his possessions, could give shelter or assistance to the banished people after the expiration of their time in the country.

The Jews were stunned by the frightful edict. For fifteen hundred years their forbears had lived in the Peninsula; they had contributed liberally to its wealth and culture. Now suddenly they were turned adrift—compelled to dispose of homes, of real estate, of debts, of all possessions, within a limited period, in a falling market; forbidden to take other than bills of exchange with them. Even the expulsions from France and England had been more humane.

One of the chroniclers tells the story that the more influential Jews made a desperate appeal to Ferdinand to avert the decree. Abrabanel offered the king a huge sum of money in lieu of the banishment and would have won his point but for the intervention of Torquemada. The inquisitor, violating all the rules of courtly etiquette, interrupted the conference by rushing into the room, holding a crucifix aloft, and crying out: " Behold the Saviour, whom the wicked Judas sold for thirty pieces of silver. If you approve that deed, sell him for a greater sum. I resign my power, nothing shall be imputed to me, but you will answer to God! " Whether it was Torquemada's dramatic warning or the influence of other ecclesiastics, Ferdinand and Isabella were not moved by any other attempts to stay the edict which ordered the most frightful exodus in Jewish history.

Many communities purchased immunity by accepting baptism. The greater number made ready to go, accepting their misfortunes as tests to prove their loyalty to God. They sold their homes and possessions for bagatelles, a mansion for an ass, a vineyard for some yards of cloth. The accumulations of generations of brilliant management and thrift melted into nothing. Communal property was taken by the states. The exiles pleaded that decent care be taken of the cemeteries, so that at least the dead might rest in peace. Even this plea was denied; the tombstones were appropriated for building-purposes or adapted to domestic uses. As the date of the departure came near, the wealthy shared what they had with the poor, each trying to dissipate the heartsickness of his neighbour. In many communities the rabbis ordered that music be played before the exodus to bid a last defiance to the persecutors.

On the second of August, the ninth day of Ab, already a sorrowful anniversary, at least a hundred and fifty thousand Jews left the country. Some historians place the total as high as eight hundred thousand. Certainly the strongest characters went, elements which formed the backbone of Spanish commercial and industrial life. For a while the country showed no disastrous effects of the depopulation. Aided by fortunate discoveries in the New World, material prosperity and artistic and intellectual vigour continued and hid the importance of the groups who had been expelled. But when a century of warfare with England had exhausted the country, and the golden goose in Peru and Mexico ceased to lay golden eggs, the loss of the Jews and the Moors, the sinews of the middle class, told severely. Spain slowly decayed, economically and intellectually; a pernicious anæmia set in which attacked her national enterprise, and Spain sank into the ranks of the third- and fourth-rate powers.

5 · THE FATE OF THE EXILES

The edict of 1492 scattered the proudest and most prosperous Jewish community in Europe to the four winds. The expulsion, however, was but half the tragedy. Where were the exiles, uprooted and beggared, to go? England and France had already driven their Jews out — most of the German and Italian states felt overgorged with the Jews who already lived in the country. For all it concerned the charitable princes of Europe, the seas might swallow up the unfortunate people, or the earth open up to receive them.

About twelve thousand Jews who lived in northern Spain turned to Navarre for shelter. Here the rulers, who had steadily resisted the introduction of the Inquisition, seemed to be free from the virus of intolerance. The Jews hoped at least for a breathing-space during which they could seek out more permanent places of refuge. But the arm of the vigilant Ferdinand was long, and his insistence won over the King of Navarre. The choice between expulsion and baptism was again placed before the exiles. Unable to endure the strain the majority adopted Christianity; even the famous community of Tudela yielded to the intolerable pressure.

Some thousands who did not wish to wait till the last day of grace in Spain made their way to the African seaport towns. The account of their ruin and decimation is a tale for the masters of the horrible. Many were killed, as soon as they landed, by the infuriated inhabitants, who feared the effects of overcrowding. When the sultan was prevailed upon to allow the remnants to land, they were not permitted to enter towns. They lived in the open fields, and when their resources gave out, they fed on the grass like beasts. Many starved to death; others died of disease and exposure. Still others were captured by avaricious sea-captains and sold into slavery. Only a few of the sturdiest and luckiest survived and, miraculously, became one of the important Jewish communities of northern Africa.

Many of the exiles boarded ships to find refuge in Italian ports. They were charged exorbitant rates, and often they were robbed of all their possessions and set adrift. Or they were sold as slaves and suffered a thousand deaths until ransomed by compassionate fellow Jews in more fortunate lands. The Genoese sea-captains were a particularly bloody and piratical lot. Some of them, hearing that the exiles had swallowed precious jewels which they were forbidden to carry away, ripped them open and searched in their entrails for the treasure! One bedraggled group arrived in Naples and received shelter from the friendly Ferdinand I. But a plague broke out among them and they were compelled to bury their beloved dead at night, secretly, as if they were criminals, to hide the seriousness of the plague from the inhabitants. Another miserable group were landed in Genoa, but they were not permitted to remain for more than three days. While they waited for ships to carry them farther into nowhere, missionaries went among them, tempting them with food and drink. Most of the poor martyrs, driven nearly insane by their sufferings, yielded. Some arrived in Rome only to find that their fellow Jews, in terror for their own safety, had petitioned the Pope not to allow them to enter.

More than a hundred thousand Jews made their way into Portugal, but here too they found no welcome either from the king or from their own people. Thirty very wealthy families were permitted to settle in Oporto and six hundred other families, who paid a hundred crusados and agreed to a poll-tax of four crusados, were given refuge. The rest were granted a temporary shelter of eight months if they paid eight crusados a head for the privilege. Even then a cruel fate pursued them. A pestilence broke out among them which carried off great numbers and then smote the Portuguese as well, rousing the bitterest hatred against the cursed folk that had spread the contagion.

Vessels were gradually provided for these unfortunates and they were herded into them by the hundreds. Like so many others who had trusted to the mercy of the sea-captains, they were robbed and beaten and often left to die in forgotten places. Thousands who remained after the expiration of the eight months were sold as slaves, and their children were seized, baptized, and sent off as Christians to the newly-discovered island of Saint Thomas.

King Manuel, who succeeded John in 1495, was more humane, and for a moment the Jews hoped that their miseries were over. He freed those who had remained beyond the time limit and had been forced into slavery, and refused the presents which the Jews gratefully offered. But even now the bigotry of the Spanish sovereigns had not diminished, and when a match was arranged between Manuel and the daughter of Ferdinand and Isabella, one of the conditions was the expulsion of the Jews and the Moors from Portugal. In December of 1496, therefore, a new edict was issued giving the Jews and the Moors one year in which to leave. Before then, however, all young people under twenty-five were seized and forcibly baptized. Many desperate parents killed their children and themselves rather than submit. Bishop Coutinho writes: "I have seen many dragged to the font by the hair, and the fathers clad in mourning, with veiled heads and cries of agony, accompanying their children to the altar, to protest against the inhuman baptism. I have seen still more horrible, indiscribable violence done them."

As the day for the expulsion drew near, Manuel, fearful of the economic consequences of his edict, placed so many hindrances in the way of departure that great numbers of Jews were still in the country after the final date of grace. Manuel at once announced that they were his slaves and used every inhuman means to bring about their conversion, even dragging them by force to the churches. One rabbi who refused to set an example by submission was buried to his neck and so kept for seven days, until he died of his agonies.

Many thousands of Jews thus became Christians, continuing, however, to practise Jewish rites in secret, and watching every opportunity to flee the country and return to Judaism. Others remained to suffer at the hands of the ever vigilant Inquisition, whose severity was not abated for another century. Until the present day their descendants, many of them as *marranos,* live in Portugal, recalling the heroism of their steadfast ancestors.

One moment of retribution was permitted for all of the miseries which the Portuguese Jews had endured. Eighty years after the expulsion Manuel's great-grandson, Sebastian, led an army into Africa and was disastrously defeated. Thousands of his men, the scions of the noblest houses, were killed; other thousands were captured and sold into slavery. The descendants of the miserable Jews who had fled from Portugal were now in a position to buy as slaves the descendants of those who had driven them out!

Meantime a whole people was beggared and ruined. For years after the expulsion wretched families were found in every corner of the world still seeking a place of refuge, still trying to bring together the broken fragments of their lives. There is no way of reckoning the toll of the whole terrible episode — the toll in lives lost, homes and families disrupted, fortunes melted, spirits bent. And yet there were none to raise their voices in protest. Spain was not damned by the public opinion of Europe. Some astute princes considered that it was stupid and unstatesmanlike to drive out the thriftiest and most energetic elements of the population; but there was no cry of horror at the brutality and inhumanity of the Spanish policy. Rather, praise. In 1496 Pope Alexander VI bestowed upon Ferdinand and Isabella the title of "Catholic" sovereigns, enumerating among their services the expulsion of the Jews. Even the cultured and liberal Pico della Mirandola praised the Spanish rulers. What a bleak and inhuman thing the divine teachings of Jesus had become in the hands of his fifteenth-century apostles!

6. THE ROMANCE OF THE ABRABANELS

No story of Jewish life in Spain and Portugal is complete which does not include the romance of the Abrabanel family, one of the most interesting and unusual in all history. Their talents were remarkably preserved, passing unimpaired from one generation to another for nearly two centuries. Their fortunes were bound up with the fate of the Jews, rising and falling as the circumstances changed for their people. Half a dozen times a member of the house brought it to the heights only to see it dashed to the ground when the Jewish situation changed for the worse. Yet, despite all vicissitudes, the family maintained its courage and faith; misfortune merely stimulated it to redoubled efforts.

The Abrabanels were an ancient family. They were fond of tracing their ancestry back to the royal stock of David, following the family line through centuries of scholarly and public-spirited men. The modern family was founded in the fourteenth century by Judah of Seville, who served as royal keeper of the wardrobe. His son, Samuel, became one of the wealthiest men in Castile and was employed by King Henry II in several important undertakings. These were happy years when the persecutions of France and England were not yet known in Spain, and Jews could soar to any heights on the wings of their talents.

The terrible year of 1391 wrecked the fortunes of the house, and in the epidemic of forced conversions even the proud Abrabanel submitted to the cross. Samuel became Juan de Seville. Later he returned to the faith of his ancestors, but he was obliged to migrate to Portugal to do so.

In Portugal, Samuel's son, Judah, now sought to retrieve the fallen fortunes of his house. There were endless opportunities for the resourceful. This was the era of Prince Henry the Navigator, whose magnificent enterprises made the country conscious of a unique geographical destiny. Portuguese ships went sailing, exploring, experimenting everywhere, and soon there were rich rewards as the unknown world opened out under Portuguese daring. Judah rose on the tide of this new prosperity, and ultimately he became the treasurer to King John's brother. He financed many of the exploring trips and some of the wars against the Moors. There is a record of a return of half a million reis blancos to the treasurer from his patron in 1437.

It was in this tranquil period that Judah's son, Isaac, destined to become the most famous of all the Abrabanels, was born in Lisbon. Isaac was very carefully educated under the best teachers, and early showed bright promise. His mind was clear and penetrating, and at twenty he was already writing on abstruse philosophical subjects. His father's position and his own undoubted capacity made the way easy for him in the royal court and within a few years he began

to serve the king, Alphonso V, as treasurer. Isaac did not permit his high position to blind him to the fate of his people. He spared neither his resources nor
his energies to bring assistance to the distressed. When nearly a hundred Jews
were made slaves in Morocco, he personally solicited contributions to purchase
their freedom.

Fortune, however, did not permit him long possession of his high position.
A new king " who knew not Joseph " came to the throne, and Abrabanel found
that he was no longer in royal favour. He was soon implicated in a conspiracy,
led by the Duke of Braganza, to upset the government. The king acted quickly.
Braganza was seized before his plan matured, his fellow conspirators were
stabbed in their beds, and a messenger was sent to Isaac summoning him immediately to court. He did not wait. Putting together whatever of his possessions
could be moved, he flew towards the Spanish border. He barely had time to
elude the clattering cavalry that followed closely on his heels, determined to cut
him down and end his traitorous life. So ended the Portuguese period.

Isaac was now a very humble person in Toledo. Far from the cares of State,
he spent his days writing commentaries on various Biblical books, drawing
analogies from the adventurous days of Joshua, the judges, and Samuel. Evidently, however, he let no opportunity slip by to improve his fortunes. Within
a year he was associated with a friend in collecting the royal taxes, supplying
provisions for the army, and performing other responsible duties. Soon after,
the Portuguese exile had become treasurer to the mighty Spanish sovereigns,
Ferdinand and Isabella!

Life in Spain for minority groups was no longer enviable. The Moors were
being pushed back steadily into the ocean, the *marranos* were being roasted
in every public square, the Jews were facing every hardship which human
ingenuity could devise. It was an eloquent tribute to the capacity of Abrabanel
that through all this calamitous period he was able to maintain his position
at court and use it to alleviate the condition of his people.

When Torquemada finally induced his sovereigns to expel the Jews from
Spain, in 1492, Abrabanel was not included in the edict. He was a member of
the royal household and was much too valuable a public servant to lose. Abrabanel was not flattered by the immunity. It was he who engineered the last
desperate attempt to dissuade the king, collecting thirty thousand ducats from
the wealthiest Spanish Jews and offering them as a bribe for the recall of the
edict. When the attempt failed, he determined to throw in his lot with his
people. For a second time a brilliant career was clouded by political currents.

Abrabanel joined the group which embarked for Naples, and his prestige
secured shelter for a limited number. He gained the complete confidence of the
king, Ferdinand I, and within the year the twice exiled treasurer was in control
of the royal finances of a third state. It seemed that here at last was a refuge
which would be permanent. But the fate of Abrabanel was like the fate of the

classical Sisyphus, doomed for ever to roll his huge stone up the hill only to see it crash to the bottom again when apparently the goal had been reached. In 1494 the ill-balanced and worthless King of France invaded Naples, scattered its forces, and drove out the king. Abrabanel followed his patron to Sicily after witnessing the plundering of his beautiful Neapolitan home, the confiscation of possessions accumulated for a third time, and the destruction of his choicest treasure, a library of rare and ancient volumes. He remained in Sicily until the death of Ferdinand and then made his way to Venice. His indomitable will was not yet conquered by adversity. Within a year he had entered the inner councils of the Venetian government and served in several important diplomatic posts. In Venice he finally died, worn out in body, but as defiant and buoyant in spirit as when he served his first patrons in Portugal.

Abrabanel was blessed with a number of children, some of whom surpassed him by their talents. Judah León, or Leo Hebræus, became private physician to the Spanish captain-general Gonsâlvo de Córdoba, who served as Viceroy of Naples after the French were expelled. He retained this post until the Inquisition compelled the dismissal of his patron in 1507. Leo migrated to Venice, where he wrote his beautiful *Dialogues of Love,* counted by critics as among the most polished in the literature of the Medicean period. He is now recognized as one of the most distinguished philosophers of the Renaissance.

There was a younger son Samuel, who also remained in Naples after his father's departure. He was accounted *tremegisto,* thrice blessed, in scholarship, in wealth, and in glorious ancestry. He was employed as financier by the Spanish viceroy and amassed an enormous fortune of more than half a million ducats. His wife, the amiable Benvenida, enjoyed the friendship of the Duchess of Tuscany. But the ill fate which pursued all the Abrabanels did not pass Samuel by. The Emperor Charles V came into possession of Naples when he ascended the throne of Spain, and he introduced all of the degrading restrictions upon Jews which already existed in his other dominions. Samuel preferred exile to disgrace and migrated to Ferrara, where he died soon after.

With Samuel ended the outstanding members of the Abrabanel house. But the descendants continued a tradition of scholarship and public service until the last of the family in the male line, the head of the rabbinate at Lissa, Prussia, passed away in 1863. No family in Jewish history had so consistently lived up to the highest standards of the teachers whom they followed. They were worthy to symbolize the best in the Jewish life of Spain.

CHAPTER SEVENTEEN

HAVENS OF REFUGE

I. UNDER THE CRESCENT

As the doors of Christian Europe closed on the Jews, new doors were providentially opened in Turkey and Poland to receive them. Eastern Europe now became the leading centre of Jewish life.

The powerful Ottomans, conquerors of Turkey, were boils and locusts and all the other plagues to the powers of Europe. Since the fourteenth century, when Osman created his famous dynasty, the new lords of the East had been sweeping forward irresistibly. By 1389 they had conquered practically all of the Balkans and had pushed their frontiers to the Danube. In 1453, Constantinople, once the proud capital of the Eastern empire, fell, and the gorgeous cathedral of St. Sophia became a Moslem mosque. All through the sixteenth century the Christian monarchs were compelled to reckon with the might of the new power in the Mediterranean.

Jews had found a refuge in the Ottoman dominions for many decades before the expulsion from Spain. During the fifteenth-century persecutions in Germany, thousands had fled eastward and had been well received in the Turkish provinces. Life was secure and the morrow could be greeted without terror. There were no degrading badges and no oppressive residential or trade restrictions. The Code of Omar imposed a special costume upon the Jews, but the law was not enforced. The Jews were liable only to a negligible poll-tax, which all non-Moslems paid.

The hospitality of the Turkish rulers was a godsend to the victims of Spanish and Portuguese bigotry. Thousands who were fortunate enough to survive the perils and privations of the long journey came pouring into the Turkish dominions. The rulers were happy to engage their energies and talents. The Jewish merchants and trained artisans brought new life to commerce and industry, and the skilled physicians were unable to meet the many demands upon them. It may be that the exiles helped also to introduce the newly-invented fire-arms to Turkey. Little wonder that the Sultan, Bejazet II, cried out: "You call Ferdinand a wise king, he who has made his country poor and enriched ours!"

Soon Constantinople boasted the largest Jewish settlement in Europe, numbering more than thirty thousand souls. Salonica, a close rival, enthusiastically termed by a grateful poet "the mother city in Israel," became the centre of an active cultural life. Everywhere in Turkey proper, in Asia Minor, and later in Egypt, great Jewish communities developed and prospered. The exiles, who were a more enterprising and more broadly educated group than the original Jewish inhabitants, easily moulded Jewish life in Spanish and Portuguese patterns. Even Palestine, long neglected and sunk in sloth and ignorance, increased its Jewish population to more than five hundred families; the dry bones stirred again in Safed, Tiberius, Jerusalem, and the larger cities. Here every variety of cultural activity thrived, rationalism and mysticism, Talmudic dialectic and free-lance speculation. What was produced was not always inspiring, nor even useful, but at least there was freedom for creative activity. The Jews were at home!

In 1551 one Nicolo Nicolai, chamberlain to the King of France, who accompanied the French ambassador to Constantinople, wrote with astonishment of the ubiquitousness of the Jews in the Turkish dominions. " There are so many Jews throughout Turkey, and in Greece especially, that it is a great marvel and downright incredible. They increase daily through the commerce, money-changing, and peddling which they carry on almost everywhere on land and on water; so that it may be said truly that the greater part of the commerce of the whole Orient is in their hands. In Constantinople they have the largest bazaars and stores, with the best and the most expensive wares of all kinds. In addition, one meets among them many skilled artists and mechanicians, especially among the *marranos,* who some years ago were driven out of Spain and Portugal. These, with great harm and injury to Christendom, have taught the Turks to make implements of war. The said Jews have also established a printing-press, which is a wonderful thing to the Turks. They print books in Latin, Greek, Italian, Syrian, and Hebrew; but in Turkish and Arabic they are not allowed to print. Besides, they know most languages; so that they are employed as interpreters." [1]

The tolerant regime of the sultans made it possible for one of the exiles to become an influential figure in Turkish politics. Joseph Nasi, whose sensational career shed lustre upon his people, came of a distinguished Portuguese *marrano* family. The Inquisition had compelled their withdrawal from Portugal in the sixteenth century, and several of the more enterprising members settled in Antwerp. Here Joseph founded a banking-house and became one of the wealthiest men in the country. Despite his success, however, he was unhappy while he wore the mask of Catholicism and he determined to take advantage of Turkish tolerance to begin life anew. He migrated to Constantinople, presented letters of introduction from French statesmen and at once gained the favour of the sultan, Suleiman II. His knowledge of European affairs and his financial prestige made him invaluable as an adviser and he was given several high positions at the court. His influence may be measured from

1 Cited in the *Jewish Encyclopedia,* XII, 281.

the circumstance that the sultan called upon France to return some confiscated property belonging to the Nasi family, and when the request was refused, he seized, in reprisal, a third of all cargoes brought to Turkish ports by French ships!

Joseph was a close friend of the young prince, Selim, who soon afterwards ascended the throne and heaped further honours upon the Jewish statesman. The former exile was given a group of islands in the Mediterranean and created the Duke of Naxos. He ruled his little province from a palace in Constantinople, and Christian powers seeking concessions from the sultan often found it advisable to negotiate through him. The Holy Roman Emperor, in whose dominion Jews were scum of the earth, the Prince of Orange, the King of Poland, all sent ambassadors to sue for his favour.

On the death of Selim, in 1574, Joseph lost his political power, but he retained his wealth and offices and spent the last five years of his life in honourable retirement in his Constantinople palace. He attempted to rehabilitate a strong Jewish community in Palestine, encouraging settlers to live in Tiberius, which had been granted to him by the sultan. None of his work was destined to last, but his munificent generosity to his people earned him their undying gratitude. His career was inspiring, too, as a symbol. It was a source of comfort to a dispersed and unfortunate race to recall that one of their own earned and enjoyed the favour of the politically elect. It was a forerunner of a new era when Jews would again be permitted to use their talents in the service of kings and princes and parliaments.

2. THE POLISH REFUGE

Just as Turkey served as a refuge for Spanish and Portuguese Jews, Poland became the promised land of the harried Germans. Jews had been drawn to the Vistula, the Dnieper, and the shores of the Black Sea from the beginning of the Christian era. In the eighth century a whole Tartar kingdom, the Khazars, in South Russia, had been converted to Judaism, and maintained an independent and successful existence for more than two centuries, until it fell, in 969, before Sviatoslav, the Duke of Kiev. In the eleventh century there was a wealthy community of Jews in Gnesen, at that time the religious centre of Poland.

Nevertheless, it was not until the crusades destroyed the stability of German Jewish life that Poland became an important Jewish centre. The Polish kings heartily welcomed the refugees, anxious to utilize their capital for the development of the country, and their revenues to render themselves independent of the obstreperous nobles. All through the twelfth century Jews prospered as merchants, traders, and tax-farmers. Many of them were in charge of the mints, and the Polish coins sometimes bore the name of the princes in Hebrew characters! After the Tartar invasions of the middle of the thirteenth century foreigners were doubly welcomed, and the Jews, who migrated in thousands, became the only commercial class in a country of landlords and peasants.

Boleslav the Pious in 1264 issued a favourable charter which promised the Jews complete freedom and excellent opportunities for honourable livelihoods in Great Poland. Nearly all of his successors renewed these promises. As the news of Polish tolerance reached the stricken communities of Germany, flayed by Rindfleisch and outraged after the Black Death, a steady stream of refugees flowed eastward. Indeed, it seemed as if the whole balance of Jewish life was to be shifted.

The hopes of the wanderers were not disappointed, for under Casimir the Great (1333–70) every happiness was theirs. Casimir was one of the most enlightened sovereigns of the Middle Ages, intent upon raising the standards of life among all classes of his people. He subordinated war to politics, crushed the lawlessness of the nobility, created a famous code of law, built cities, promoted commerce, developed the trade of his country, and earned the epitaph: "He found a Poland of wood and left behind him a Poland of stone." He welcomed the Jews as an essential factor in his reconstruction policy and extended Boleslav's charters to apply in all the Polish dominions. His generosity to Jews and peasants and his severity to all who disturbed their peace gave him the title "King of the serfs and the Jews."

In the fifteenth century the Polish rulers were not so uniformly favourable. Moreover, two strong orders fought bitterly against the extension of "godless privileges" to the Jews. German merchants, long established in the land, rightly feared the effects of Jewish competition and seized every opportunity to discredit the new-comers. Much more formidable was the opposition of the clergy, who already in the days of Boleslav had opposed his charter, protesting that the Jews would endanger "the tender plant of Christianity." Every year they found new reasons for the restriction of Jewish enterprise. When their insistence won over some weak or pious king, the old charters were annulled and Jewish existence in Poland was endangered. Capistrano, who nearly ruined every Jewish community in Germany in the middle of the fifteenth century, wrought immense havoc in Poland. Occasionally there were riots and local persecutions, and some municipalities introduced special restrictions. In Posen a ghetto was created and the number of Jewish houses was limited to forty-nine; this regulation obliged the Jews to raise their dwellings to many stories. Warsaw for long permitted no new Jewish families to settle in its territory. In 1407 there were disturbances in Cracow, during which a number of Jewish lives were sacrificed and nearly the whole community was forcibly baptized.

Yet, by comparison, Poland remained a refuge, and for two centuries continued to beckon to the Jews of the west, especially during the expulsion epidemic. It is computed that between 1501 and 1648 the Jewish population of Poland increased from fifty thousand to half a million. The settlements were strong and well established, not limited to money-lending and petty peddling. Jews were permitted, during the regimes of most kings, to engage in all productive enterprises; many followed rural vocations as far as the feudal system of the country permitted. During the liberal regime of Sigismund I (1506–48) every minority group was cordially treated. Sigismund was a pious Catholic, but passionate devotion to his faith did not blur his vision. Jews were chosen for public service, and a number were conspicuous among the favourites who surrounded the king in his court.

The Jewish community in Poland was now large enough to form a distinct order, like the clergy or the nobility. It was in keeping with the political ideology of the day to permit the creation of a state within a state, for in the absence of an efficient bureaucracy such an arrangement facilitated the collection of taxes. Hence in 1551 the famous charter of Sigismund Augustus, justly termed the "Magna Charta of Jewish self-government," was issued. By its provisions the Jews were given virtual autonomy, their own courts, their own schools, and their own governing agencies. Each city and town with a Jewish population had its *kahal,* or assembly of elders, elected during the Passover, for one year. The *kahal* served as the general administrative body, with authority even over the rabbis. It was responsible for the collection of taxes and for the management of all Jewish communal institutions. Already in the sixteenth century, regional meetings of the outstanding rabbis and the leaders of the *kahal* became common. These were originally called to settle important litigation between communities or to adjudicate appellate cases. Gradually they assumed administrative functions as well and supervised the local *kahal.* At the end of the century a new organization had developed out of these meetings, the Council of the Four Lands, a supreme council which controlled the Jewish activities of Great and Little Poland and the provinces of Lemberg and Volynhia.

It is clear that in the sixteenth century Poland was no mere refuge for bedraggled and broken exiles; it had become the new centre of a vigorous Jewish life, well able to develop a rich cultural activity. Its " firmly-knit organization of communal self-government could not but foster among the Jews of Poland a spirit of discipline and obedience to the law." But it also " provided the stateless nation with a substitute for national and political self-expression, keeping public spirit and civic virtue alive in it, and upholding and unfolding its genuine culture." [1]

3. THE ITALIAN STATES

The disunity of mediæval Italy made it possible for several thousand Jewish exiles to settle in the more tolerant provinces which did not share the bigotry of Spain. Already for several centuries there had been small but thriving Jewish communities scattered through the peninsula. A number of Jewish names

[1] Dubnow: *History of the Jews in Russia and Poland.* I, 113.

appeared among the philosophers and thinkers who were the glory of mediæval Italy. To Jewish scholars, writes a modern critic, " is largely due the building up of the School of Salerno, which we find flourishing in the tenth century. . . . Still more important is the rise of the School of Montpellier; this was due almost entirely to Jewish physicians, and it developed medical studies to a yet higher point, doing much to create a medical profession worthy of the name throughout southern Europe." [1] Jews also contributed to the thirteenth-century Renaissance, which made Italy the centre of European culture. They helped the earliest humanists to study original Hebrew sources by teaching them the language and interpreting the documents with them. Their own critical researches were useful additions to the scholarship of the renaissance. Jews lived on excellent terms with Christians. Immanuel of Rome, who introduced Hebrew secular poetry into Italy, was probably a friend of the immortal Dante, and the brilliant Hebrew grammarian Elijah Levita lived for thirteen years in the splendid palace of the Cardinal di Viterbo. Elijah Delmedigo, whose beautiful literary Latin style and thorough knowledge of philosophy established his reputation as an original thinker, was appointed, at the age of twenty-three, professor of philosophy in Padua and taught successively in Florence, Venice, Perugia, and Bassano. He became the teacher of Pico della Mirandola, one of the most brilliant lights of the Florentine Renaissance, who learned his Hebrew and his philosophy from his gifted Jewish teacher.

The tolerant Italian provinces now became the loadstone for thousands of the Spanish exiles. Naples, under the enlightened king Ferdinand I, welcomed the little group led by the former Spanish financier Isaac Abrabanel. Even the plague which broke out among the Jews and spread to the Neapolitan population did not shake the king's determination to give the unfortunates a home. Ferrara, under the dukes of Este, was another refuge, and scores of families who escaped the rapacity of the villainous ship-captains took advantage of its unexpected hospitality. Curiously enough, the Papal States, which already had a large Jewish settlement, were not averse to receiving new immigrants. The Renaissance popes were a worldly group, and, though they had no hesitation in issuing bulls which assailed the Jews in other lands, they were too clever to overlook their economic importance in Rome. The cost of the pomp and pageantry which characterized life at the Vatican was staggering, and every lucrative source of income was welcomed. The wealth which flowed from Jewish hands was as eagerly sought as wealth from less tainted sources.

Unfortunately, most of the Italian settlements proved temporary. Naples fell before French and Spanish invaders, and the inevitable Inquisition was introduced. *Marranos* were hunted down with other incorrigible heretics, and the Jews again found it necessary to take up the wanderers' staff. Venice fell into the hands of less liberal doges. Several times the Jews were altogether expelled, to be recalled when the mood of bigotry passed. The haughty oligarchy,

[1] White: *Warfare of Science with Theology,* II, 33, 34.

mistress of the Adriatic, introduced the ghetto in 1516, and the most important Jewish merchants, whose capital helped to send the Venetian fleets into all the seas, lived in the poorest and vilest parts of the city.

The Papal States also lost their tradition of tolerance when, towards the middle of the century, the succession of humanist popes and cardinals ended. In an attempt to silence the criticism of the Protestants that the Church was worldly, a Catholic counter-reformation was inaugurated, which brought into the Vatican devout and ascetic ecclesiastics who frowned upon follies and banished the Muses and Graces. There were no longer cardinals who avoided the Church Fathers because they corrupted one's Latin style, or Mediceans who were determined "to enjoy the papacy." As part of the restoration of the Church's pristine vigour came the old legislation against the Jews. Their enterprise was crippled, they were confined to a filthy ghetto along the banks of the stinking, noxious Tiber, they were again burdened with the humiliating Jew badge, and annually they were compelled to listen to special conversion sermons in their own synagogues. These conditions remained in force until Napoleon conquered Italy.

The revival of the narrow, persecuting spirit weakened every Jewish community and reduced its numbers. By the close of the sixteenth century no city in Italy held more than two thousand Jews. Yet, despite all restrictions, the few Italian provinces which admitted Jews were welcome asylums. Those which remained tolerant were blessed with loyal Jewish communities who never stinted to show their gratitude. Those which imposed onerous restrictions were at least stopping-places for thousands who looked to Turkey or Poland as permanent havens of refuge.

4 · GERMANY AND THE REFORMATION

At the opening of the sixteenth century it appeared as if there would be a change in the status of the German Jews, who for centuries had been as dust under the feet of kings, clergy, and masses. The Protestant Reformation shook the country out of its mediæval lethargy and broke the hold of the papacy on spirit and intellect. The reformers leaned heavily on Jewish scholarship to guide them in understanding the Bible in the original Hebrew. Indeed, the first skirmish in the long struggle which ultimately rent the unity of the Church centred about the value of Hebrew literature. Unfortunately, the new developments did not liberalize the German spirit. The Protestants proved as narrow and intolerant as the Catholics had been. Years of religious strife intensified religious hatreds, and the Jews were crushed between the contending factions.

At the beginning of the century a determined effort was made to convert the Jews of Germany. It was the opinion of Johann Pfefferkorn, a Jewish apostate, whose early training as a butcher was his sole claim to scholarship, that the centre of Jewish resistance was the Talmud and its commentaries. If these volumes, filled with libels on Christianity, could be destroyed, he said, Jewish solidarity would be weakened and ultimately dissolved. Pfefferkorn was supported by the Dominicans of Cologne, and, in 1509, he obtained permission from the Emperor Maximilian to confiscate all literature of an antichristian nature. Fortunately Germany possessed a distinguished humanist, Johann Reuchlin, who had studied under Jewish teachers and had a more enlightened appreciation of Jewish literature. When summoned by the emperor to give his opinion on the suppression of the suspected books, he paid a glowing tribute to Jewish scholarship and deplored the sacrifice of its creations simply because they had no connexion with the Christian faith. He went so far as to suggest that, for ten years, the emperor should endow two chairs in Hebrew at every German university!

Impressed by Reuchlin's plea, the emperor recalled his decree, and the Dominicans rightly threw the blame for the miscarriage of their plans upon Reuchlin. A fierce battle of books was now begun which continued for nearly ten years. The humanists of Europe as well as of Germany sided with Reuchlin. The obscurantists attacked his scholarship and his honesty. The issue passed beyond the merit of the Talmud and Hebrew literature. Public opinion was stirred on the whole question of freedom of thought and the Church forces received blows from which they did not soon recover. The famous *Epistolæ obscurorum virorum* was evoked by the controversy; the volume poured such ridicule upon the monks and their allies that they became a laughing-stock. Soon after, Luther, who had consistently sided with Reuchlin, began his tremendous assaults on the whole fabric of the Catholic Church.

At the beginning of his career this vigorous Protestant reformer was almost a liberal crusader, with a breadth of vision which was rare in the sixteenth century. He denounced the clergy for their brutal and senseless fulminations against the Jews and reminded them of the obligations which Christianity imposed upon them. " The Jews are the best blood on earth," he wrote; " through them alone the Holy Ghost wished to give all books of Holy Scripture to the world; they are the children, and we are the guests and the strangers; indeed, like the Canaanitish woman, we should be satisfied to be the dogs that eat the crumbs which fall from their master's table." [1] In a fervent pamphlet entitled *Jesus was Born a Jew,* which was republished seven times in one year, he sent a thrill of hope through Jewish hearts by saying: " If we would help them, so must we exercise, not the law of the Pope, but that of Christian love — show them a friendly spirit, permit them to live and to work, so that they have cause and means to be with us and amongst us. . . . And if some remain obstinate, what of it? Not every one of us is a good Christian."

Luther's gentleness, however, seems to have been dictated by a desire to

1 Cited in the *Jewish Encyclopedia,* VIII, 213.

convert the Jews, who proved to be no more amenable to persuasion than they had been to force. Meantime, Luther was beset on every side by virulent enemies, and as he grew older and his difficulties increased, he became harsher and less patient. It seemed impossible that the same man was speaking when, in 1543, appeared the stinging pamphlet *Concerning the Jews and their Lies*. Here the monk who had defied all the power of organized Christendom in his search for truth, joined with the worst bigots in accusing the Jews of poisoning wells, murdering Christian children, and remaining impossibly stubborn in the face of Christian revelation. He urged the princes to destroy the Jewish synagogues and to confiscate their wealth and devote it to maintain those who accepted Christianity. One of his last sermons denounced Jewish physicians for "understanding the art" of poisoning their patients, and concluded with the ominous admonition: "I say to you lastly, as a countryman, if the Jews refuse to be converted, we ought not to suffer them or bear with them any longer."

Inevitably the Protestant communities took to heart the later utterances of Luther rather than his early and more charitable ones. The tyranny which the reformer had so often denounced became part of the inheritance which he bequeathed to his devoted followers.

Throughout the sixteenth century the few German communities which still permitted Jews to breathe their air vied with one another in devising methods to degrade them. Typical were the regulations which the council of Frankfurt am Main enacted in a revolting document called the *Judenstattikeit* ("permissive residence of Jews"). Four thousand souls were confined to a narrow ghetto and reduced to the status of criminals. Jews could not leave the ghetto except on important business, and two could not walk together, especially past the town hall. They were obliged to lower their voices so as not to offend Christian ears by their odious speech. They could not receive visitors, or even patients in their hospitals, without reporting the fact to the magistracy. On their clothes they were to wear special badges, and on their homes they were obliged to place identifying shields with such symbols as an ass, or a dragon, or garlic. For all of which rights they were to pay heavier taxes than the Christian inhabitants.

Sixteenth-century Germany tolerated the Jews. They could breathe, they could work, they could sleep, they could be buried. And by comparison with other lands in the West the country was accounted a haven.

5. THE DUTCH JERUSALEM AND ENGLAND

Late in the sixteenth century a new refuge was unexpectedly opened in the gallant little Dutch republic. Jews had long been attracted to the thriving cities of Flanders and the Low Countries and after each outburst of fanaticism during the Middle Ages had filtered in. *Marranos,* too, sought protection in the north from the vengeance of the Inquisition. Unfortunately the Netherlands passed into the hands of the Habsburgs and were bequeathed to the gloomy Philip II of Spain when the empire was divided, in 1556. Soon the Inquisition was established and the free air of the north was polluted by the smoke of the *auto-da-fé*. The Emperor Charles V and his son Philip several times ordered the Jews to leave and the inquisitorial torture-racks and the stake virtually cleared the country of the panic-stricken *marranos*.

The Dutch, however, chafed under Spanish control, and the restlessness which was apparent under Charles came to a head under the less tactful Philip. Financial extortion, administrative inefficiency, and intolerance of Protestants combined to unite the northern provinces in a long and desperate struggle for freedom, one of the most inspiring in all history. For long the issue was in doubt, and several times the Dutch bravely flooded their fields, by cutting the dikes, to drive the enemy from their hearths. Gradually the patience and resistance of the mighty Spanish empire was worn down, and when Elizabeth's seamen swept the Spanish Armada from the seas, in 1588, the last menace to Dutch independence was removed.

Holland showed no enthusiasm in welcoming Jews, but it was eagerly sought out, especially by refugees from Spain and Portugal. In 1593 a little group of *marranos* landed in Amsterdam and worshipped secretly in a private home. Four years later, at Yom Kippur service, they were attacked by suspicious citizens who mistook them for Catholics. When the worshippers explained that they were secret Jews, the council granted them permission to remain, and in 1598 a synagogue was publicly dedicated with almost extravagant joy.

Every pinch of the Spanish Inquisition brought new Sephardic families to Holland. The rabbi of Amsterdam received more than two hundred and fifty *marranos* back into Judaism within a few years. By the early seventeenth century the capital of the little republic became known as the Dutch Jerusalem. It numbered more than five hundred Jewish families, most of them wealthy, enterprising, and highly cultured. Opportunities which had been denied in Spain were eagerly grasped in Holland. The Jews became interested in the carrying trade, and their capital helped to build up the Dutch East and West India Companies, which, as if in retribution, were the chief instruments in the destruction of Spanish and Portuguese commercial supremacy. Rembrandt's many portraits of Jewish worthies are a significant tribute to the comfortable and influential positions attained by the erstwhile exiles.

The success of the Jews in Holland prompted other monarchs to encourage Jewish settlement. In 1622 Christian IV of Denmark invited a number of Jewish families to settle in his own cities, promising them every privilege. The Duke of Savoy held out similar hopes for those who came to Nice, and the Duke of Modena urged settlers to take advantage of a thoroughly unrestricted life in

Reggio. But perhaps the most important consequence of Dutch liberalism was its influence on England, where negotiations were now opened to end the four-hundred-year-old banishment of Jews.

The appeal for readmission was made by Manasseh ben Israel, one of the Jewish leaders of Amsterdam. Manasseh's universal reputation as a scholar and teacher was perhaps undeserved, for none of his works showed much originality or profundity. Yet he was a fervent Jewish patriot, and his name carried prestige everywhere in Europe. In 1650 he petitioned Oliver Cromwell, now virtually dictator of England, to allow the Jews to return. He based his appeal on a curious combination of sound economic fact and mystic speculation. A typical child of his century, he pointed out that the Jews must first be dispersed "from one end of the earth to the other before the redemption could be realized." More to the point, he suggested that the Jews were useful citizens wherever they settled and could prove invaluable in building up the prosperity of the country. Manasseh was assisted by the *marrano* Antonio Carvajal, the first "endenizened" Jew in England, who had entered the country during the reign of Charles and had rendered considerable service to the Commonwealth by his extensive operations in the West Indies.

Cromwell received the petition with genuine friendship. Like Charles before him, he required no persuasion to convince him of the commercial usefulness of the Jews. Besides, he was influenced by the millennial ideas of the time and hoped by friendliness to bring about the conversion of the Jews. For some years, however, the matter hung fire. There were strained relations between England and the Dutch state which several times blazed into open war. Moreover, the merchants of London and the clergy vigorously objected to a new Jewish immigration. At length, in 1657, Cromwell rode roughshod over all opposition and consented to the settlement of the Jews, with the condition that they were not to conduct public worship or engage in religious propaganda. The readmission of the Jews to England was not official, therefore, and for long their legal status remained in doubt. Yet a "back door" had been opened and a little Jewish community was gradually formed in the country. It was destined to take the lead in the battle for the political and social emancipation of the Jew.

CHAPTER EIGHTEEN

DEGENERATION

THERE is a comfortable theory, commonly advanced, that persecution strengthens the vitality of a people and adds to its stamina. The forces of repression, the argument runs, call forth hidden powers of resistance; they whet the mind and give it sharpness and keenness. "The purest ore," says Colten, "is produced from the hottest furnace, and the brightest thunderbolt is elicited from the darkest storm." This theory, quite plausible, finds no application in mediæval Jewish history. We have already noted how little of quality had been produced among Jews since the fearful period of the crusades. There was the same devotion to the ideal of learning, the same respect for scholars, the same energy; but breadth of view was impossible in physical and mental isolation. Cut off from contact with European civilization, the Jews were compelled to draw into their own shells and to feed on their own heritage. Mulling over the same material decade after decade, they produced little that deserved to survive. "Even Phidias," Macaulay suggested, "could have done nothing with an old tree and a fish-bone, or Homer with the language of new Holland."

Occasionally there were happy exceptions. Jewish translators and commentators served as the bridge between Arabic and Christian culture. Jewish teachers opened the treasures of the Bible to Christian humanists. These contributions, however, stand out conspicuously by their very rareness. Most of the scholars and teachers, embittered by sorrow and denied all creative opportunity, spent their choicest years poring over the pages of the Talmud, splitting hairs and spinning laws.

As the centuries passed and the hope for a better day faded and died out, the situation became graver. Jews lost their resiliency of mind, and their power of judgment. Too often the Bible became a vehicle of superstition. Rendered desperate by the burdens of life, many Jews juggled its letters and its sentences, hoping to discover some magic incantation which would give them control of events or, at least, power over their enemies. Others flung themselves into complete dependence on a strict religious code, seeking to forget their miseries by sucking dry the very marrow of every precept. Still others hearkened to every charlatan who promised them a way out. In every generation there were dupes who succumbed to the wiles of rascals and fanatics who claimed to be Messiahs, sent by God to usher in a new world, where Jewish suffering would cease and mankind would live in peace. Intellectual and spiritual degradation nearly everywhere, producing the perversions of the Cabala and the *Shulhan*

Aruk, a blind faith in false Messiahs, and a narrow, uncompromising loyalty to rites and dogmas which drove some of the noblest and ablest spirits out of Judaism.

I. THE CABALA

A mystical strain had never been absent in Jewish philosophical or religious speculation. Jews, like other peoples, were deeply concerned with the eternal mysteries, with God and the creation of life, with the soul, its divinity, its destination, its redemption. From the dawn of their history their mystics yearned to bridge the gap which separated man from an understanding of God. Those who were philosophers exhausted their ingenuity in inventing phrases to express their nearness to Him, to define Him without limiting Him. Those whose mysticism disclosed itself through religion strained after experiences which would lift them outside of themselves and bring them into communion or identification with God. The Cabalists, or Jewish mystics, often helped to stir Judaism into renewed life, especially when over-emphasis upon creed and dogma had dried up the estuaries of religious inspiration.

One of the most important Cabalist volumes developed by the speculation of the Middle Ages was *The Book of Creation,* the oldest philosophical work in the Hebrew language. A modern authority suggests that " it had a greater influence on the development of the Jewish mind than almost any book after the completion of the Talmud." It was variously attributed to Abraham, to Akiba, to a number of Talmudic sages. It is likely that some parts of it date back to the early Christian period; certainly it was compiled earlier than the ninth century, when Saadiah wrote a commentary upon it. The little volume was concerned primarily with the problems of cosmology and sought to explain the creation by means which afterwards became orthodox in Cabalist circles. Logic, inadequate to pierce the mystery, was abandoned. Instead words and numbers were employed to penetrate to the heart of reality. The letters of the alphabet and the ten numbers, the *sephiroth,* were the thirty-two paths of wisdom; by some divine arrangement they had brought about the creation and all that followed. They were mysteriously related to the things which they were meant to represent.

Given these premises, Cabalist imagination ran riot. It became possible to lose oneself completely in the subtleties of such symbolism. In every generation enthusiasts turned to the volume. In the twelfth century Azriel ben Menahem, a Spanish mystic, built almost a Cabalist system upon it. God, Azriel declared, could be described only in negative terms. Positive qualities or attributes of intention or desire limited Him. How then was creation possible? Obviously, God could not create the world without subtracting from Himself. Azriel fell back upon the idea that the universe was latent in the essence of God, whom he termed " *En Sof* (the illimitable)," and that creation was simply the transformation of potential into realized existence. He then developed the idea of emanations, the basis of future Cabalist speculation, by which God maintained His relation with the finite world. The ten numbers, the *sephiroth,* came from God's presence, one out of another, like sparks from a flame, and these were the intermediates between the material and the infinite.

This kind of speculation had a peculiar fascination in the Middle Ages and captured the imagination of every type of thinker, learned and unlearned. But it worked havoc with fragile vessels. Weak-minded and mediocre men were more injured than helped as they rushed in where angels feared to tread. They misunderstood the true purposes of Cabalist speculation; they were confused by symbolistic utterances. They began to dabble with names and numbers and opened the way to the crassest superstitions. Unfortunately, in a period of distress, when Jews were rendered desperate by the hopelessness of their status, when the logical world was a nightmare, the methods of the pseudo-Cabalists were seized upon as a possible way out. The most gifted individuals lost their equilibrium and led whole communities into demoralizing extravagances.

The dangers of mystical speculation were well illustrated in Abraham Abulafia, an interesting intellectual vagabond of the thirteenth century. His lively mind revelled in the propositions of the Cabalistic literature, and, though he attacked the propositions of *The Book of Creation,* the *Bahir,* and its other successors, he was enchanted by the infinite mystery of word combinations and numerical computations. At the age of eighteen he was wandering eastward in search of the river Sambation, by the banks of which the lost ten tribes of Israel were reputed to dwell, awaiting the coming of the Messiah. When he returned, his attempts to prophesy and to explain heaven-sent visions brought upon him the wrath of the authorities and he was expelled from Spain. Off to Rome in 1281, he hit upon the idea of converting the Pope, Nicholas III, to Judaism! He soon found himself in a papal dungeon and was released only when he had manufactured the most ingenious of excuses. His restless spirit then carried him to Sicily, where he announced himself as the long-expected Messiah and drew a number of credulous followers to him. Harassed by the ridicule and animosity of the saner inhabitants, he fled the island and continued his wanderings until death overtook him. He left behind him a vast collection of mystical writings, which were much used by later Cabalists. Truly a character for harlequinade!

The most influential of all the Cabalist literature was the *Zohar* (*Brightness*), issued in the thirteenth century by Moses de Leon, who claimed that it was the record of revelations vouchsafed to the famous sage Simeon ben Johai, who lived in the second century. There is considerable controversy as to the origin of the celebrated volume. Some authorities accept it as an actual creation of the second century, compiled and edited by Moses. Others regard it as a pure forgery by Moses, attributed to Simeon in order to gain a hearing for it. Franck, one of the leading modern critics, believes that its essence came from teachers perhaps as far back as the second century; it was amended, revised, and altered as it passed through the generations, and it was finally brought together by Moses, who honestly believed it to be the literal revelation of Simeon. Whoever was the actual author, he profoundly influenced modern Jewish life, for the *Zohar* became the Bible of the Cabalists, and Simeon, its traditional inspirer, was counted above the greatest prophets. Divine honours were paid to him and it was suggested that Simeon was meant in the Biblical verse: " All men are to appear before the Lord! "

The original purpose of the *Zohar* was a worthy one. It sought to leap the gulf which separated man from the infinite, to define God without limiting Him. It followed Azriel's premises rather closely and emphasized the doctrine of emanation by which God had linked Himself with the finite world. The Pentateuch was, of course, the basis of faith, for all Cabalist speculation was rooted in the Holy Writ. So far there was no harm done. But the *Zohar* went far beneath the literal reading of the text. Indeed, there was ridicule for the " simple " who found in the Bible only what was clearly stated therein. " Every word of the law holds an exalted meaning and a sublime mystery. . . . The simple-minded take heed of nothing but the vestments or the recitals of the law; they know nothing else, and do not see what is hidden under this garment. The well-informed think not of the vestment, but of the body that the vestment covers." [1] The most astonishing methods, some old, others new, were devised to unearth these hidden meanings. Certain verses were placed over other verses and when read vertically, formed new words by the light of which the text was reinterpreted. Or words were joined up and then redivided in new ways. Sometimes the initials and final letters of words were taken to bring new meanings. Or words were reduced to their numerical values and then explained in terms of other words of like numerical composition.

The ablest men in every community spent lives in this type of word jugglery. Many of them swooned into superstitions and began to employ the symbols as charms by which to control events. The very subtlety of these dialectitians betrayed them into futility.

> As skilful divers to the bottom fall
> Swifter than those who cannot swim at all;
> So, in this way of writing without thinking,
> Thou hast a strange alacrity in sinking.

It was this degenerate quibbling which brought the whole study of the Cabala into disfavour with rationalists who denounced the *Zohar* and kindred literature as the " dreams of a diseased mind — *ægri somnia vana*." [2]

---

[1] Franck: *The Kabbalah*, pp. 140–1.   [2] Ibid., p. xxx.

Part of the Cabalist literature naturally won the admiration of the keenest Jewish and Christian thinkers. Pico della Mirandola and other leading humanists of Renaissance days were almost effusive in their praise; Reuchlin explained to an irate emperor that it was worthy of the soberest study. Unfortunately it was the worst side which took hold of men's minds and spread through Europe. During the persecutions of the fifteenth and sixteenth centuries the pseudo-Cabalist gibberish of numbers and letters was frantically explored to disclose the date of the Messiah's advent and to confound Israel's tormentors.

Every community was affected — Bible, Talmud, Rashi, faded into insignificance before the dancing symbols. They entered the Holy Land itself, where a new Jewish population had only just been settled. There they captured the imagination of a young Talmudist, Isaac Luria, who was soon to become the most influential Cabalist apostle of the century. Luria procured one of the first printed copies of the *Zohar,* and his whole world at once rotated about it. He began to live the life of a hermit, returning to his home and family only on the sabbath. In 1569 he established himself in Safed, where his ascetic way of life brought on trances and visions, in which he imagined himself to be the forerunner of the Messiah. Together with a small community of faithful disciples he made regular pilgrimages to the tomb of Simeon ben Johai; there he prayed and studied in the familiar Cabalist way, hoping to be rewarded with a glimpse into the infinite. Luria had no important popular following, but when he died of the plague, in 1572, one of his disciples, Haym Vital, an eccentric young Italian immigrant, spread his doctrines and related stories of wondrous miracles that had been wrought by them. The invention of printing helped further to popularize Luria's work, and the Cabalist teaching, speculative and practical, penetrated into every village in Europe.

In addition to a Talmudic Judaism there was now a Cabalistic Judaism, which threatened to gain ascendancy in Jewish life. Few could escape its appeal in an era of dreadful persecution. "Kabala," writes Silver, "was no longer the handmaid of Rabbinic Judaism, modest and deferential. It became imperious and aggressive. . . . And it fast degenerated into a miracle-mongering, wierdly superstitious affair, in which demonology, necromancy, spiritism and all forms of magic played the chief rôles." [1] At the very time that Europe was emancipating itself intellectually, saturating itself in a new Renaissance spirit, the harried Jewish masses were credulously sinking more and more deeply into the bogs of a hocus-pocus.

2. CARO AND THE *SHULHAN ARUK*

While the perversions of the pseudo-Cabalists turned men's thoughts to word and letter somersaults, another work was created which inadvertently helped

[1] Silver: *Messianic Speculations in Israel,* pp. 110–11.

further to circumscribe Jewish life. The great code of Joseph Caro was completed in 1555 and published in four parts in 1567; it eclipsed every previous compilation and became the most important religious influence in modern Jewish history.

Caro was born in Spain or Portugal just before the edict of expulsion sent his people flying to all parts of the globe. After considerable wandering he was brought to Turkey by his parents. Here his astonishing mastery of Talmudic literature gave him an immense reputation. At thirty he began to work over Jacob Asher's *Four Rows,* which had brought together Talmudic laws for practical use. For twenty years he explored the sources for every law and added to them the commentaries of the last centuries. It required twelve years more to revise his work, *The House of Joseph.* His prodigious feat of compilation marked Caro as the outstanding Talmudic scholar of the time. His reputation stood higher than that of any rabbi since the golden days of Maimonides.

Despite his sternly disciplined mind and his genius for symmetry Caro could not escape the mystical tendencies which surrounded him. He was completely carried away by the Messianic fervour of his day and lent credence to the pretensions of Solomon Molko, who was venerated by thousands of Jews in every land as the precursor of the millennium. When the young visionary was burnt at the stake, Caro too wished to be "consumed on the altar as a holy burnt offering"! Visions came frequently to him and he believed that his genius was merely the spirit of the Mishnah, which had chosen him as its interpreter because he had devoted himself to its service.

After Caro had settled in Palestine, he determined to make his commentary available for popular use. He felt that nothing could so well preserve Jewish unity in the chaos of dispersion as a compact code of the law. He toiled for years to prepare the popular abstract, the *Shulhan Aruk,* a "*Prepared Table,*" where the young and unlearned could feed without difficulty.

The abbreviated code was finally published in 1567 and it enjoyed immediate success. Its appearance coincided with the popularization of printing and it was therefore given an unprecedented circulation within a few years of its completion. It became only less important than the Talmud and served as the centre of study and the guide of practice for centuries following Caro's death. It served, as Caro hoped it would, as a bond of union for scattered and disunited Israel. Its meticulous regulation of activity re-emphasized the old Jewish principle that religion and life were closely associated. Yet it wrought more harm than good. "It put Judaism in a strait jacket." The healthy growth of religious thought was checked. Freedom was inhibited. Every act in life was ticketed and marked, this permitted, this forbidden. Once the code was accepted as authoritative, it became almost impossible to effect changes in Jewish religious practice. The industrious compiler of the *Prepared Table,* innocent of any intention to crystallize the law finally, helped in the general demoralization of Judaism.

3. REUBENI AND MOLKO

The astonishing popularity of the pseudo-Messiahs in the sixteenth and seventeenth centuries was another symptom of disease. The sanest of peoples was led, largely because of its sorrows, to trust in the promises of a succession of rascals and self-deluded fanatics who convulsed Jewish life for two centuries. The Cabala with its Messianic predictions stimulated faith in the claims of the impostors, but Jewish unhappiness was the real cause for the blind and extravagant devotion of whole communities.

One of the strangest careers of the sixteenth century was that of David Reubeni, who came out of the East, ostensibly to win European assistance for the reconquest of the Holy Land. He claimed to speak for the descendants of the lost tribe of Reuben, who, he said, dwelt thousands strong in the wilderness of Khaibar in the interior of Arabia. He was a swarthy, emaciated dwarf, who spoke a Hebrew dialect which Jews themselves could scarcely understand; it appeared that he would be turned back with a flea in the ear. When he came to Rome in 1524, however, and rode into the Vatican court on a white charger, he created a sensation. So little was known of the geography of the world that his claims and plans were soberly discussed. The Pope, Clement VII, was just then in serious political difficulties. The Turks were sweeping up through Europe and had already taken Belgrade and the key island of Malta; the Protestant heresy was undermining the stability of the Catholic Church. Clement welcomed every development which seemed likely to divert the Christian monarchs to unified endeavours. The diminutive Hebrew's promise of warriors from the interior of Asia was tempting — and the Pope's astrologers saw favourable signs in the heavens. Why not a new crusade?

Reubeni was well received by Clement, who forwarded his credentials from merchants in the East to the King of Portugal, who was in the best position to pass upon their importance. Meanwhile the Jews of Rome, astonished by the reception accorded to a Jewish emissary of a lost tribe, gave themselves over to the wildest hopes. Was he the forerunner of the Messiah? Was he the Messiah himself? Reubeni was astute enough to make no claims, but men and women dogged his shadow, beseeching his blessing as he rode in state through the streets of Rome.

Soon Reubeni's credentials came back with the notation that they were indeed authentic. The Pope suggested that he proceed to Portugal, where he could most easily secure the troops which he required. The swarthy adventurer was thereupon transported to Portugal in a ship which carried a Jewish flag at the mast. He was welcomed by King John III, who had several conferences with him on the matter of weapons and men for assisting the Israelite tribes in Arabia! While the negotiations proceeded, John ceased his prosecutions of the *marranos*. The unexpected dispensation seemed another proof that Reubeni's mission was divinely inspired. In several communities some poor fanatics fell into trances, saw visions, babbled prophecies, and otherwise disturbed the public peace. A number of minor uprisings were crushed with loss of life before the dementia passed.

Reubeni's appearance stirred the latent mysticism of a young *marrano* of excellent family, Diego Pires, who was serving as royal secretary in a high court of justice. He had immersed himself in the Cabala and was thoroughly convinced that the Messianic era was at hand. He sought out Reubeni, but the wily charlatan refused to interview him. Diego attributed the rebuff to the circumstance that he was a *marrano,* living in falsehood and sin. He returned to Judaism, adopted the name of Solomon Molko, submitted to circumcision, saw visions in which he was commanded to preach the coming of the Messiah, and secretly left Portugal. He travelled as far as Palestine, where his personal attractiveness and his Cabalist learning created a remarkable stir. The greybeards listened in awe as the scion of a noble Portuguese family expounded metaphysical mysteries and poured out his confident prophecies of doom. A series of desolating events seemed to prove the truth of all he said. There were floods and fires and plagues; in 1527 Rome, the Eternal City, was sacked by the soldiers of Charles V and almost ruined.

Molko, who probably looked upon himself as a Messianic messenger, now determined to come to Italy and to speak fearlessly to its abandoned inhabitants. The millennium was nigh and yet so few understood the need for penance and contrition! He preached to vast audiences of wondering Jews and in 1529 arrived outside of Rome. In conformity with the Messianic tradition, he remained in rags for a month, among the poor and the leprous, and then, starved and worn by his self-inflicted privations, he entered the city of wickedness. He, too, mysteriously won the favour of the Pope, who kept him from falling into the hands of the Inquisition.

Meantime Reubeni had outstayed his welcome in Portugal, and before the suspicions of the king were turned against him, he left the country. At Venice, Reubeni and Molko met face to face. The meeting must have been dramatic, a fit subject for the romantic historian. What did each now think of the other? What could a clever rascal and a poor deluded fanatic say to each other?

There were floods in Rome again next year and a terrifying comet. In January 1531 an earthquake shook Portugal and devastated Lisbon. Molko's prophecies were being fulfilled. He returned to Rome, where he had innumerable adventures, escaping the clutches of the Inquisition almost miraculously. At last in 1532 both adventurers again met and together went to interview the emperor at Ratisbon, hoping to convince him that a crusade against the Turks was still practical. The emperor threw both men into chains and conducted them to Italy, where Molko was turned over to the Inquisition. He refused to recant, glorying in the thought of dying for his convictions. Not to be martyred was martyrdom. The Inquisition made short shrift of him, and he was burnt at the stake as a relapsed Christian. Reubeni was carried off to a Spanish prison and probably died there in obscurity.

The importance of these two spectacular careers lay in the pathetic hopes which they aroused among the Jewish masses. The living world was full of sorrow; there seemed to be no hope for a better day except through the miracles of God's own messengers. Whole communities were carried away as much by the cunning of Reubeni as by the melancholy sincerity of Molko. Men believed in them because their burdens made them wish to believe.

4 · BOGDAN CHMIELNICKI

By the middle of the seventeenth century even Poland had ceased to be a haven of refuge. The clergy, an austere and intolerant caste, had insinuated themselves into the very heart of political life, and the Jesuits had won complete control of education. The German tradesmen, long a thorn in the side of the Jews, were more powerful and more unscrupulous than ever. Jews continued to serve the nobles as tax-collectors, tax-farmers, financiers, and particularly stewards and overseers of their estates. But these positions, while adding to their power, increased popular animosity. The peasants, who were being exploited by the nobles, hated the tools of tyranny more than tyranny itself.

The bitterness between classes and creeds was nowhere worse than on the banks of the Dnieper where lived the Zaporozhian Cossacks. These rude frontiersmen, who served as a bulwark against the Tartars and Turks, enjoyed virtual autonomy under an ataman of their own selection. They despised the Poles, who, as Catholics, scorned their Greek Orthodox faith and, as landlords, oppressed them. But their loathing was intensified a hundredfold against the Jews, who lived in large numbers in the Ukraine and were so often the instruments of the nobles' tyranny.

In 1648 came the inevitable uprising of the Cossacks. It was led by the Cossack chieftain Bogdan Chmielnicki, one of the outstanding figures of the seventeenth century. Bogdan was brave, resourceful, a natural genius in warfare, but a creature of impulses, a terrifying savage. Not only did he enter the revolt as the champion of his people's rights; he was an offended chieftain seeking vengeance for personal injuries which he had sustained at the hands of Poles and Jews. The Polish squire on whose estate he lived had stolen his hayricks and flogged his infant son to death. Some Jews had apparently spied upon him and involved him in difficulties with the Polish lords. He thirsted for vengeance against all members of the cursed races. Fate threw victims to him. He was able to win victories over the flower of the Polish military forces. As he triumphed, the serfs everywhere rose against their masters. The fury of the revolt was without precedent. Houses and castles were torn stone from stone. Whole villages were uprooted. The Polish gentry were hunted down, burnt, flayed alive, sawed asunder. Catholic priests were hanged to trees together with hogs and Jews.

The Jews died in their tens of thousands after suffering cruelties which have rarely been equalled in all history. Their infants were slit like fishes, their women were ripped open, live cats were let into their bowels, and they were then sewn up again. "Often they did not attain to burial, dogs and swine feeding on their dead bodies."[1] In Tulcin two thousand Jews and six hundred Poles sought to keep off the Cossacks. When resistance became futile, the Jews were betrayed by the Poles and ruthlessly massacred. The Cossacks then cynically slaughtered the traitors as well. The story of Tulcin was repeated everywhere; rape, murder, pillage, in every village, in every town. When Bogdan entered Kiev in triumph in 1649, he at once ordered a general massacre of the great community of Jews who lived there. Fortunate were those who fell into Tartar hands, for they were sold in the markets of Constantinople and were later ransomed by compassionate co-religionists.

In the fall of 1649 the new King of Poland, John Casimir, patched up a truce with Bogdan by which the Cossack leader was recognized as a semi-independent prince. It was part of the convention that Jews were no longer to live in the Cossack districts. For a moment there was a respite for the terrified and broken people. Only for a moment. The civil wars soon flared up again, and the Cossacks began a new series of depredations. Suddenly in 1654 hordes of southern and northern Scythians poured into the country, and next year the Swedes also began their invasions. The new wars "resembled nothing so much as a hideous scramble of ravening beasts and obscene fowls for the dismembered limbs of a headless carcase, for such did Poland seem to all the world before the war was half over."[2] Not until 1658, when Poland had agreed to the most humiliating concessions, did peace come at last.

It is impossible to estimate accurately the toll of these awful years, perhaps the worst in Jewish history since the destruction of national life. High estimates say five hundred thousand Jews perished; conservative estimates place the dead at not less than one hundred thousand. Seven hundred Jewish communities were destroyed. Everywhere there was ruin and desolation, and scarcely a family had been spared. For years the Western world was filled with derelicts, as in the dreary days of the Spanish expulsion. The darkness seemed never to lift and Jews turned more and more to the comfort of the Talmud, to the promises of the Cabala, and above all to the pseudo-Messiahs who continued to bring emollient messages from Heaven.

[1] Cited in Dubnow: *History of the Jews in Russia and Poland*, I, 150.
[2] David Hannay in *Encyclopaedia Brittanica*, XXI, 915.

5. SHABBATHAI AND HIS SUCCESSORS

The most influential and popular of the modern pseudo-Messiahs was Shabbathai Zebi, born in 1626, in Smyrna, of a family of Spanish immigrants. He came to a world ruined by the Thirty Years' War and desolated by natural calamities. Jews and Christians both were crazed with superstition. "Among the Princes of the age we find every kind of fixed delusion—from the visions of Christian of Denmark to the ravings of John Frederick of Weimar. Nor should the inveterate endurance and rank growth of countless petty superstitions be overlooked, which seemed to place life and death under the control of dealers in astrological certificates and magical charms."[1] Shabbathai, a child of the chaos and the delusions of the period, was very early led away by the Cabala and the mysticism of Luria. No penance was too severe for him. He mortified his flesh, fasted, bathed in the Mediterranean in the coldest days, and, though twice married, refused to live with his wife and was immediately divorced. His asceticism aroused widespread comment; it was whispered that he performed the most astonishing miracles. He gathered a group of enthusiastic disciples about him who prayed and sang with him and studied the hidden meanings of the Cabala. The world buzzed with Messianic predictions and expectations; after the Chmielnicki massacres the very stones cried out for a saviour. Shabbathai became convinced that he was the destined Messiah, and in 1648, a miracle year by Cabalist calculations, he proclaimed himself by pronouncing the Ineffable Name.

The leading Jews of Smyrna were horrified by his presumption, and in 1651, after his claims had nearly disrupted the community, he was driven out. He travelled through the East, preaching and praying, everywhere inspiring followers who were anxious to believe. In Salonika he took the Torah to him as bride in a mystical ceremony which shocked the rabbis and awed the Cabalists. In Cairo he won over the wealthiest families. He converted the leaders of the Jerusalem community when he secured financial assistance to satisfy the exactions of the wolfish pasha.

Fate now brought the strange Messiah a worthy spouse whose colourful and spectacular career matched his own. The beautiful and vivacious Sarah came from Poland. She was a mere infant of six when her parents fell as victims before the fury of Chmielnicki. Fortunately the little orphan found a refuge among some sisters in a convent, who cared for her until she reached womanhood. Restless, craving excitement, she fled one day and began several years of adventurous vagabondage, which carried her through most of the European countries. In Amsterdam she was deeply swayed by the Shabbathaian hysteria and proclaimed herself as destined for the Smyrna Messiah. When he heard of her pretensions, he called her to Cairo and at once fell in love with her.

[1] Ward in *Cambridge Modern History*, IV, 6.

What did it matter that her life had not been above reproach? Had not the prophet Hosea taken Gomer to his heart, and was there not an ancient tradition that the Messiah would have an unchaste woman as bride? The marriage attracted international attention and henceforth the two adventurers played out their thrilling roles with the eyes of the world upon them.

The furor caused by Shabbathai and his claims was astonishing even in the mystical seventeenth century. The miracles described by his disciples were everywhere believed. In Smyrna, to which he returned in triumph, the community greeted him with shouts of " Long live the Messiah! " Twelve hundred children of ten and twelve were hastily married off so that the unborn souls could be united in their bodies and could thus share in the redemption soon to come. Residents of Dutch and English houses in the East reported the achievements which were attributed to the Messiah; the news travelled through Europe and became a topic of interest in the exchanges. Even in the West the Jews were deeply stirred. Not only the credulous and the ignorant, but the best minds in every community believed. Glückel von Hameln tells how her father-in-law left his home, after sending on to Hamburg two barrels of food and clothes, in preparation for embarking for the Holy Land. The Amsterdam presses poured out new prayer-books containing special prayers for Shabbathai. In England it was reported that a ship had been seen near Scotland with silken sails and ropes, with sailors speaking Hebrew, and with a flag bearing the inscription of twelve Tribes or families of Israel. Pepys noted in his diary that there were Jews in London who offered a hundred pounds to ten that within two years Shabbathai would be owned by the princes of the East as the King of Jerusalem — " And certainly this year of 1666 will be a year of great action; but what the consequences of it will be, God knows."

Shabbathai was now called by the Sultan to Constantinople. The young knight-errant was not at all nonplussed. He calmly divided up the world among twenty-six faithful disciples, creating them kings and princes and investing them with weird Cabalist titles. Then he set sail with a magnificent retinue. There were storms all the way, but, according to the vivid accounts of his disciples, he bested the elements in every crisis. Nevertheless, he arrived virtually shipwrecked and was at once arrested. He was buffeted about by the guards, but he played the suffering servant very successfully and won the favour even of the Moslems.

The Sultan was in a quandary. He could not execute Shabbathai without creating him a martyr. He could not leave him at liberty without adding to his prestige. He therefore dispatched him to a fortress in Abydos and ordered that he be kept in nominal confinement. Shabbathai made the most of his opportunities, and his life became a continuous fête. Thousands of visitors flocked to see him, usually bringing valuable gifts, and he was enabled to live in regal splendour. His guards, who received enormous sums from the visitors, joined in honouring him. And all Europe prayed for his success. On every sabbath-day hundreds of congregations intoned with fervour: "Bless our lord and king, the holy and righteous Shabbathai Zebi, the Messiah of the God of Jacob."

For three months the curious pageant went forward without interruption. Then another competing Messiah, who had interviewed Shabbathai, denounced him as a conspirator against the Moslem state. The Sultan now offered Shabbathai the choice of Islam or death. The farce ended quickly. Shabbathai at once chose Islam, adopted the name of Mehamed Effendi, and became the royal door-keeper! A large number of followers passed over into Islam with him. Later he was disgraced for continuing his Cabalistic agitations and was banished to Dulcigno in Albania, where he died in obscurity.

The Jews of Europe were overwhelmed with shame and horror when the news of Shabbathai's apostasy became public. The rabbi of Smyrna, who had publicly hailed the Messiah, almost died of his humiliation. To be so tragically duped by any man after so many honours had been lavished upon him! In every community Christians ridiculed the Jews for following an impostor like Shabbathai, having rejected a saint like Jesus.

But some credulous souls refused to be shaken. Shabbathai, they insisted, had not been converted. He had been transported to heaven, and a phantom had taken his place. Or he had accepted Islam in order to undermine the Moslem faith and thus prepare the world for the coming of the Messiah. Long after Shabbathai's apostasy and death little groups of believers continued to cherish his memory and to follow disciples who too often exploited their gullibility.

A certain Cardoso, who proclaimed himself as a successor, for years excited the communities of the East by his prophecies and his nonsensical Cabalist writings. One of Shabbathai's widows passed off her brother as Shabbathai's son; the young charlatan was venerated by a host of followers as he advocated licence and indulgence in order to hasten the coming of the end of the world. They outraged public opinion in Salonika until the Sultan put an end to their rites. Frightened lest they fall before the Sultan's wrath, four hundred families went over to Islam. They lived together, married only amongst themselves, and perpetuated the sect to the present day. They are known as the Donmah; they number nearly four thousand in Salonika and practice a curious combination of Moslem and Jewish rites.

The last and perhaps most vicious of the Shabbathaian impostors was a Podolian Jew, Jacob Frank (d. 1791). He had travelled considerably in his youth and had come into contact with Shabbathaian communities in Turkey. He reiterated the doctrine that the Messiahs were all incarnations of each other; that David, Elijah, Jesus, Mohammed, and Shabbathai were essentially one person, taking on different forms. He announced himself as the last of the succession and worked out a mystic theory by which he became the second person in the Trinity! No claim was too extravagant for the credulous, and a little Frankist sect was born which began to indulge in every kind of licentiousness.

The rabbis of Poland found it necessary to excommunicate the sect, and to protect the Jewish communities from other impostors they made it unlawful for any student under thirty to occupy himself with the Cabala. The proscribed sect, pretending that it was being persecuted for its attacks upon Talmudic Judaism, appealed to the bishop for protection. The degradation of Jewish life was so complete that not a single rabbinical leader could successfully defend Judaism against the charges of the Frankists, and in 1757 thousands of copies of the Talmud were publicly burnt. Other disputations were held with similar results.

Meantime, in 1759, Frank accepted baptism in the Catholic Church and carried over with him several thousand followers. Later the Catholic authorities learned that the charlatan continued to voice his claims as the Messiah, and Frank was arrested and imprisoned for thirteen years. After his release he called himself Baron von Frank and practised his impostures in western Europe for twenty years longer. His daughter Eva carried on the tradition until 1817.

6. ACOSTA AND SPINOZA

Persecution rarely makes a harried sect more liberal. In strengthening resistance it usually develops a very narrow loyalty. Those whose faith is being assailed draw within their shells to guard every iota of their heritage. Exactly these consequences followed from the hardships of Jewish life in the sixteenth and seventeenth centuries. Talmudic Judaism, despised and scorned by the enemies of Israel, became a precious heritage to be guarded with life itself. Criticism of its tenets by Jews was sternly denounced as treason by the communal leaders. Their intolerance and impatience of any liberalism, products of historic circumstances, were responsible for two of the most poignant personal tragedies of the seventeenth century.

Uriel Acosta (1590–1640) was descended from a *marrano* family of Oporto. His father had yielded to the logic of the executioner and the argument of blazing fires and escaped cremating through Christianity. Uriel was brought up as a noble, studied the law, and prepared to seek a career in the Church. In 1615 he became chief treasurer of an abbey. But he was sorely troubled by religious doubts and found no solace in the unbending doctrines of the Catholic Church. One day he read the Old Testament, and his restless spirit found an echo in the vigorous social and religious protests of the prophets. He determined to renounce the rich perquisites of his career, to fling aside honours and ambitions, and to return to the faith of his ancestors. He fled with his mother and brothers to Amsterdam, which had once swept back the enemies of religious liberty, and there the little family were received into the Jewish faith.

He was soon disillusioned, however. He could not find in the Judaism of seventeenth-century Amsterdam what he had found in the prophets. The synagogue was a formal affair, and religious life seemed to be as clogged with creed and petty detail as the Catholic faith which he had abandoned. Acosta felt that he had sacrificed enough for conscience' sake to have the right to protest. He denounced the oppressive ordinances, criticized their intolerant guardians, and cavilled at their authority. His protests culminated in a long pamphlet, *Proposals against Tradition.* He was at once excommunicated for his daring, cut off from all human intercourse, isolated even from his own family. For fifteen years, from 1618 to 1633, he gnawed out his heart in a living death, berating the narrow stupidity of the community and cursing the day that he had entered the covenant. As the years passed, his bitterness grew venomous. He drifted beyond the bounds of any religion, threw off all moderation and restraint, and fiercely attacked the foundations of all faith. The civil authorities were called in to chastise his sacrilegious hand and reckless pen. He was fined and imprisoned and his writings were publicly burnt. Fifteen years he held out, uncowed, and then, unable to bear the awful loneliness which excommunication brought, he yielded, declaring cynically that he would try to be an ape among apes.

But he was carefully watched and his departures from ritual regularity were reported to the elders. It was said that he refused to keep the dietary laws, that he scoffed at Jewish sanctities, that he dissuaded possible converts from accepting the appalling yoke of Judaism. Again he was excommunicated, this time much more severely. For seven long years, well into middle age, he lived as a social leper. His sorrows were his society; his wrongs were his nourishment. It could not go on for always, this blank, dull misery and despair. Acosta could no longer stand the strain. Again he yielded and petitioned for reinstatement. The penance ordered for him is a sad commentary on the degeneration of Jewish life. He was compelled to acknowledge his transgressions publicly, to submit to scourging, to lie on the threshold of the synagogue and allow the community to walk over his prostrate body. The humiliation was too much for the proud spirit of a Spanish hidalgo. He went home, wrote a short sketch of his life, bitterly denouncing the Jewish community, and then shot himself. His baffled, wasted life came largely from a restless nature that could not be at home in any formal faith. He lacked judgment, even temper, patience; he hurried into war and then crawled into peace. But assuredly the tragedy would not have been possible if the demoralization of Jewish life had not driven its leaders into a fearful and thoroughly un-Jewish intolerance.

The fate of Baruch Spinoza, whom Renan has called the greatest Jew of modern times, was not so tragic, but it also left a deep scar in Jewish life. The brilliant thinker was born in Amsterdam in 1632 of parents who had fled from the persecutions of Portugal only a few years before. He received the usual Jewish education, but showed himself keenly interested in every type of learning, and at fifteen he was badgering his teachers with painfully embarrassing questions about faith and doctrine. He dipped into the works of Ibn Ezra, Hasdai Crescas, Maimonides, and the other Jewish philosophers of the golden age. He was profoundly influenced by the mellow wisdom of the ablest of his teachers, Van den Ende, a heretic destined to die on a scaffold for his opinions. He became devoted to the natural sciences and to the methods of Descartes's revolutionary thinking. He loved the writings of the philosopher Bruno and was thrilled by his magnificent defiance of the Church. All of these elements in his education helped to enthrone reason as his guide, and very early he began to attack beliefs which seemed founded on superstition and muddled thinking.

Gradually he discarded Talmudic Judaism. He could not go on pretending nominal conformity, however. When he disagreed, he was obliged to say so. He ceased synagogue attendance and began to influence other young people to follow his way of life. The Jewish community was highly alarmed. His beliefs in the imperfectibility of the Bible, his radical notions about God, his denial of immortality, struck at Christian as well as at Jewish doctrines. They therefore endangered the security of the Jewish community in Amsterdam. The Jews were merely tolerated, and if they permitted such blasphemies to go unpunished, they might all be driven out. Besides, Jews who had borne privations and exile for their faith could not bear with patience powerful attacks upon all that they held dear.

The elders pleaded with Spinoza to be discreet, ultimately promising him a pension if he would only keep his opinions to himself. Spinoza naturally refused and the elders were compelled to excommunicate him. Even his own kin turned against him, and, like Acosta, he found himself bitterly alone. When, soon after, a fanatic attempted to take his life, the daring heretic, at the age of twenty-three, cut himself for ever adrift from his people. He did not accept another faith, but it is probable that he never again came into contact with Jews.

Spinoza seemed quite happy in his exile. He earned enough to satisfy his humble wants by teaching privately and later by grinding lenses, as if to symbolize his mission to help men to see the truth more clearly. He had his books, peace, and independence. What more could a philosopher ask? Alone, unfettered, he wrote the epoch-making works which induced Hegel later to say that before one could be a philosopher, one had to be a Spinozist.

He guarded his independence carefully. He constantly refused offers of pensions and the gifts of admirers. In 1673 he refused a post in the University in Heidelberg where he was promised "the most perfect freedom in philosophizing, which His Highness feels assured you would not abuse by calling into question the established religion of the State."

Physically he was always frail, having inherited from his mother a tendency to consumption. His condition was doubtless aggravated by the nature of his work. Early in 1677 he became seriously ill, and died soon after, little more than forty-four years of age. He was buried in a church in Spuy in a grave which can no longer be identified.

Spinoza's philosophy, which placed him among the world's greatest speculative thinkers, need not here be discussed. But it is clear that he could have pursued his work within the fold of Judaism if historic conditions had not conspired to drive him out. His magnificent concept of God, which bordered on pantheism and which earned him the title of "the God-intoxicated man," was not too revolutionary for Judaism. His reiterated emphasis upon freedom of thought in religion and philosophy was later accepted by the makers of Reform Judaism. Unfortunately the time was not ripe for daring speculation. His religious message was as deeply misunderstood as his lovable nature. He was looked upon as a danger and an evil influence by Jew and Christian alike. For a century after his death European philosophers alluded to him only casually and Hume denounced his "hideous hypothesis." "People talked of him," Lessing said, "as if he were a dead dog."

It remained for later generations to right the wrong done to his memory. In 1882 a monument was unveiled at The Hague, contributed to by admirers from all over the world. Renan said then, in moving words: "This man from his granite pedestal will point out to all men the way of blessedness which he found; and ages hence the cultivated traveller passing by this spot will say in his heart: 'The truest vision ever had of God came, perhaps, here.'"

The tragedy of the three centuries which followed the Spanish expulsion lay not alone in the physical suffering endured by the Jews. The spiritual and mental degradation was a far worse tragedy. A whole people was made to grope in the dark, mumbling over Cabalist letters and numbers, believing blindly in rascals and fanatics who called themselves Messiah, regulating their lives meticulously with the narrowest laws of conduct, fearing to think freely, fiercely persecuting the more daring spirits who sought to broaden the bases of their faith.

Persecution had been successful beyond the fondest expectations of the Jew-baiters. They could look with complacency upon the eighteenth-century Jew — bent, broken, superstitious and ignorant. They could laugh at his pathetic claim, still fervently intoned, that he was the guardian of the prophetic faith.

CHAPTER NINETEEN

THE JEW IN THE MEDIÆVAL WORLD

I. THE JEWISH DISPERSION

AT the threshold of modern history, in the middle of the eighteenth century, the Jews were scattered in every corner of the globe, but probably they did not total more than three millions and formed only a small proportion of the general population. Insanitary conditions, plagues, and epidemics everywhere wore down mediæval populations. Among the Jews there were also rigorous economic restrictions which limited the means of livelihood and helped further to keep the Jewish population static. Hostile observers often lamented the alarming growth in the Jewish numbers and strength, but they were misled by the circumstance that Jews were usually concentrated in limited districts and were restricted to particular occupations.

Of the three millions the vast majority dwelt in eastern Europe, whither they had been gravitating since the crusades wrecked Jewish life in the western countries. Poland sheltered more than a million and a half until the end of the eighteenth century. When the independence of the country was suddenly snuffed out in the infamous partitions, the Polish Jews passed under the jurisdiction of the despoiling powers, Russia, Prussia, and Austria. In the Roumanian provinces Jews had been settled since the early Christian centuries and had grown in numbers all through the Middle Ages. They were all expelled in the sixteenth century by the despotic Aaron, himself of Hebrew descent, but early in the seventeenth century many of them returned and new strains were added through a heavy Polish immigration. So long as the tolerant Turk remained in control, the Jews led relatively happy and comfortable lives.

In the other Balkan states also under Turkish jurisdiction, much smaller communities thrived, following special occupations. About a hundred thousand lived in Asiatic Turkey, especially in Constantinople, which in the sixteenth century claimed thirty thousand Jews and fifty-four synagogues. In Egypt the new influx of Spanish refugees far outnumbered the original inhabitants, and their Sephardic way of life was superimposed upon the Egyptian communities.

In central Europe the Jews were concentrated mostly in the Austrian dominions. German Austria had always housed a large number, and some of the most glorious traditions as well as the bloodiest memories were associated with the vivacious capital, Vienna. The Polish partitions swept the province of

Galicia into the empire, and Maria Theresa, whose sentimental tears at Poland's fate did not prevent her from taking her share, became the mistress of one of the largest Jewish centres in Europe. Bohemia and Moravia, which champed at the Austrian bit, also included thriving Jewish centres, despite the frequent expulsions of the sixteenth century which followed the Hussite disturbances and the unfortunate blood libel of Trent in 1475. In the German provinces the Jewish population was confined to the larger cities, Berlin, Hamburg, Frankfurt am Main, and others. Here they were wedged between the upper millstone of the Catholics and the lower millstone of their Protestant enemies, innocent victims in the rancorous religious squabbles which still distracted the country.

There were much smaller communities in England, France, Italy, and Holland. In England, indeed, it was only since Cromwell's day that the Jews were readmitted to the country by a back door, and in France and Italy life was too precarious to attract any but the most daring and the most cunning. In the Dutch provinces the Jews had grown, in 1780, to thirty thousand, of whom twenty-two thousand lived in Amsterdam. They took a leading part in the diamond and precious stones industry and were influential as importers and exporters.

In America the Jewish population was still negligible. A few hundred Jews and *marranos* had settled in the newly-opened Spanish colonies, but the long arm of the Inquisition reached even into the New World, and those who were not apprehended fled to more congenial soil. In the English colonies in North America there were less than two thousand Jews, mainly refugees from the repressions of Europe. They were established mostly in New York, Pennsylvania, Massachusetts, and Rhode Island, receiving, in the latter colony, the most liberal treatment accorded by any State in the world.

In addition there were small but historically interesting Jewish settlements scattered through Africa and inner Asia. In Morocco the Spanish exiles who escaped the perils of their flight began life anew, and by the eighteenth century their descendants had become the leading citizens of the country, with a well-organized and autonomous Jewish life. The black Falashas of Abyssinia were another ancient community, historically allied to the Jews, living by a pure Mosaism. They were proud of their supposed descent from Menelek, the son of the Queen of Sheba by King Solomon. The Jewish dispersion extended even to the Great Wall of China. There Jewish communities had dwelt since the early Middle Ages, and they were cited by Marco Polo in 1286 as a powerful element in the political and commercial life of China. Until recently there survived a remarkably interesting sect, Chinese in appearance and habits, but adhering to a faith which faintly resembled Mosaic Judaism.

2. THE GHETTO AND ITS CONSEQUENCES

The main currents in the political, social, and intellectual life of mediæval Europe touched the Jews only slightly. They were a class apart, denied any of the rights of citizenship, excluded from nearly all social relationships, and, consequently, little affected by the cultural influences which slowly transformed the European world. Even the Church used its vast authority to keep Christians and Jews apart. Too free commingling, it was feared, would undermine the Christian faith. The papal bulls thundered anathemas upon those who permitted Jews to sit in places of trust. Municipal councils insisted upon the degrading badge. "Although the Jews are tolerated by the church," the Ravenna council of 1317 declared, "yet they ought not to be tolerated to the detriment or severe injury of the faithful; because it frequently happens that they return to Christians contumely for favors, contempt for familiarity. Therefore, the provincial council held at Ravenna some time since . . . thinking that many scandals have arisen from their too free commingling with Christians, decreed that they should wear a wheel of yellow cloth on their outer garments, and their women a like wheel on their heads, so that they may be distinguished from Christians." [1]

There were always exceptionally placed individuals who maintained cordial relations with Christians. The supposed friendship between the Hebrew poet Immanuel of Rome and the immortal Dante was a source of pride to the Jews of Italy and has been much romanticized by later generations. There were famous Christians who were deeply influenced by Jewish writings and enjoyed perusing them. Albertus Magnus drank from the well of Maimonides's wisdom and Pico della Mirandola immersed himself in the Cabala. Yet these instances of cordiality and sympathetic understanding were rare exceptions, the more conspicuous by their rareness. Albertus, with all his reverence for Maimonides, endorsed the burning of the Talmud, and Pico could see no evil in the expulsion of the Jews from Spain.

The institution most closely associated with Jewish isolation in the Middle Ages was the ghetto, a restricted district within a city, outside of which Jews were not permitted to live.[2] Even before the days of the compulsory ghetto, Jews naturally centred together. There were undoubtedly advantages. They were more at ease among their own people and could more readily carry through religious and social functions. They felt more secure, too, in a ghetto, where

---

[1] Cited in Philipson: *Old European Jewries,* pp. 40–1.

[2] The origin of the term is obscure. Some scholars believe that it is derived from the word *gietto,* or gun-foundry, the earliest ghetto in Venice having been established in close proximity to a cannon-foundry. Others believe that it is a degeneration of Judaca, the name of the district assigned to Jews. Still others maintain that it is an expansion of the Talmudic word " get," meaning " a separation."

they avoided the insults and the dangers which would be inevitable if they were scattered in a hostile community. In Majorca, in the fourteenth century, the Jewish community begged for the continuance of the ghetto as a protection against the growing intolerance of the Balearic Islands.

Already in the early Middle Ages a number of cities had established compulsory segregation. Salerno had its ghetto in the eleventh century and Bari even earlier. In Toledo the Cortes ordained in 1480 that " all Jews and Moors of every city, town, and place in these our kingdoms . . . shall have their distinct Jewries and Moories by themselves, and not reside intermixed with Christians nor have enclosures together with them." But the sixteenth century was the ghetto age. City by city and province by province the institution was established until there was scarcely a spot in Europe where Jews were not herded together. The ghettos were usually marked out in the filthiest and most unwholesome parts of the towns, and, though their population grew, their areas were not increased. Incredible overcrowding, with its attendant illnesses and plagues and its frequent devastating fires, made Jewish existence a torment. " Congestion," says Zangwill, " was the characteristic even of the ghetto graveyard, as is still to be seen at Prague, where the tragic huddle of countless gravestones in every stage of decrepitude and defacement and at every angle of declension, almost suggests a struggle for death, for a place not in the sun but in the earth." [1]

The ghetto of Rome was the physical symbol of all that was foul in papal bigotry. It was recreated by the zealous, pious, narrow-minded Paul IV, who came to the Vatican in the reaction from the liberalism of the Renaissance popes. All the Roman Jews were herded into a restricted area near the stinking, disease-breeding Tiber, whose annual overflow brought untold hardship and sometimes loss of life. " When I visited it [the ghetto] the first time," writes a nineteenth-century traveller, " the Tiber had just overflowed its banks, and the yellow flood flowed through the Fiumara, the lowest street of the Ghetto, the foundations of the houses of which stand partly in the water; the river also coursed along the Octavia . . . and covered the lower portions of the lowest houses. What a melancholy sight to see the wretched Jewish quarter thus sunk in the waves of the Tiber! Yearly must Israel in Rome experience the deluge, and the Ghetto survives the flood, like Noah's ark, with human creatures and animals. The danger increases when the Tiber, swelled by rains, is driven back from the sea by west winds; then all who live in the lower stories of the houses must seek refuge in the upper apartments." [2] Every year, too, the Jews were compelled to plead anew for permission to continue to live in the Gehenna, paying a liberal tax for the privilege.

Another typical ghetto was established in Frankfurt am Main. It consisted

---

[1] Zangwill: *The Voice of Jerusalem*, p. 27.
[2] Cited in Philipson: *Old European Jewries*, p. 125.

of a narrow Jews' street, only twelve feet wide, into which were thrust four thousand persons, distributed through a hundred and ninety houses. A few brothels were thrown in to add repute to the district. When the terrible fire of 1711, the worst in mediæval Germany, completely destroyed the ghetto, it was necessary to overcome enormous difficulties before the homeless Jews were permitted to build it up again. Then there were further restrictions.

The ghetto in Prague, the most famous and least squalid of them all, originated in the early Middle Ages. Here a whole section of the city was set apart for the Jews, who enjoyed an autonomous life. They had their own town hall, a large number of picturesque synagogues, and four guild halls. Many Jews became fairly prosperous, especially in the tolerant early seventeenth century. Even here, however, the Jews were at the mercy of every ruler's caprice, and the frequent expulsions and readmissions made life and property most unstable.

No mediæval institution moulded the Jew more than the ghetto. It contributed to his physical degeneration and, by divorcing him from nature, deprived him of every opportunity for æsthetic development. The children of the ghetto, who could scarcely see the sun from their narrow, dingy streets, knew nothing of flowers and birds, of nature's happy secrets. They could never say with Landor:

> I strove with none, for none was worth my strife:
> Nature I loved, and, next to Nature, Art;
> I warmed both hands before the fire of life;
> It sinks, and I am ready to depart.

The ghetto, in encysting the Jew, also deepened the prejudice against him. The ordinary Christian could know little of the mysterious life beyond the ghetto walls and he usually lent credence to the twaddle which was spread by the ignorant or the malicious. Even the sunny Goethe, the literary colossus of the eighteenth century, a philosopher who took all humanity for his theme, thought of Jews as vile, unclean beings, deservedly hidden in the fusty places of the earth.

It was inevitable that the hardships and the isolation of ghetto life should weaken Jewish loyalty to the rulers. Patriotism in the Middle Ages was, even among the elect of the earth, merely a personal loyalty. It would have been unnatural for the Jews to give their love to the monsters who bled them with every opportunity. Thrown in with their own, understanding only their own, many of the Jews did not even speak the language of the country in which they lived. By the fifteenth century they were using everywhere in eastern Europe a degenerate German, interspersed with Hebrew and other languages, the Yiddish jargon which has survived to the present. In the Sephardic communities the language became the Ladino, a corrupted Spanish-Hebrew dialect.

Perhaps the sorriest effect of ghetto life was the loss of Jewish self-respect.

The Jew had always cherished his honour. A just pride in his faith had, especially in Spain, bred a desire to appear well and to speak with dignity. The ghetto broke down the ancient tradition. It produced the bedraggled, unkempt type, hunted in appearance and obsequious in demeanour, the type by which the world judged the Jew and his Judaism. Europe made the Jew into a caricature and then scorned him for playing the part.

Yet it is easy to exaggerate the evil effects of the ghetto. The institution had its brighter side too, and life was not devoured entirely by "the worm that never dies." Thrown close together, always in view of each other, the Jews built up an esprit de corps which was stronger than death. The home, with high moral standards, became an impregnable rock against which time and adversity beat in vain until the subtler influences of the nineteenth century began to wear it down. A strong Jewish consciousness was developed, a folk-life with folk-ways, remarkably virile for a people divorced from a land of their own and denied opportunities in any other. And, as will be explained later, there was joy and conviviality within the ghetto walls which compensated for many of the miseries which the Jews were obliged to endure.

The most interesting feature of mediæval Jewish life was its autonomous nature. Jews were regarded as a distinct class, like the clergy and the nobility. This was not anomalous, for in feudal society every person belonged first to a class and second to the State. Jews, with no place in the social order, were virtually aliens, and as such were the wards of the king. In Germany they actually became *servi cameræ,* chattel of the king, and were dealt with, invariably, through special legislation. It was natural, therefore, that they should have their own communal organization, their own educational system, their own law-courts and code of law, even separate prisons, or, at least, specially reserved rooms in the general prisons.

To the government the arrangement was a distinct convenience, for it materially facilitated the collection of Jewish taxes. There were all too many of these, poll-taxes and communal taxes, special taxes and protection taxes. In Spain there was a hearth tax and a tax for the king's dinner; in France, a coronation tax whenever a new ruler ascended the throne; in England, a heavy tax upon the renewal of charters. There were taxes to build and taxes to demolish, taxes for safe-conduct and taxes for participation in fairs, taxes for acquiring ground in which to bury the dead, and taxes for the burial. There seemed to be taxes for all things in the heavens and on the earth and in the waters of the sea. In England the Jewish revenue before the expulsion totalled one twelfth of the national income! In other countries the proportion was often higher. All of these dues and tolls passed through the hands of the Jewish communal agencies that were responsible for them.

The larger communities usually had their local governing bodies. These were at first rather democratically organized, but gradually they passed into the hands of those who paid the most taxes. They were charged with the care of communal institutions, and they governed the social and religious life of the people. They answered the challenge of the apostate who vilified the Jews, and they eased the poverty of the Jewish transient. In Germany they collected the golden *Opferpfenning* introduced by Ludwig the Bavarian; in Italy they collected the pound of pepper and two pounds of cinnamon which every Jew paid as tribute upon the accession of a new pope.

Often the representatives of a number of communities met in synods to discuss affairs affecting the common weal. During the lifetime of Jacob Tam, a public-spirited scholar of the eleventh century, the synods of France were unusually vigorous. We have already discussed the effectiveness of the synod of the Four Provinces in eighteenth-century Poland.

Every community, too, usually had its *Bet Din,* a court presided over by the rabbi or the spiritual leader, where judgments were rendered according to the Talmudic law. The *Bet Din* retained complete jurisdiction in all cases where Jews were involved, and often it was permitted to apply corporal punishment. Its most dreaded weapon was the power of excommunication, a power which made it almost impossible for Jews to defy public opinion. The excommunicant was cut off from all intercourse with society and even the milder form, the *niddiu,* usually brought him to heel. Uriel Acosta, the seventeenth-century heretic, was driven to his death by the horrors which excommunication brought upon him.

3. ECONOMIC LIFE

Turning to the economic life of the mediæval Jew, the survey leads through endless restrictions and disabilities. All too many Jews were obliged to descend to the unworthiest and most undignified tasks to keep body and soul together. To begin with, mediæval trade and commerce were almost exclusively in the hands of the guilds. These bodies, chartered by the king or by town governments, combining social and religious functions with business, controlled production and distribution. None but members of a craft-guild could manufacture and none but guild merchants could sell. Jews were rigidly excluded from the guilds; there are not half a dozen cases in all mediæval history of Jewish membership in these powerful corporations. The feudal organization of society made it difficult for Jews to own land; law or custom excluded them from the professions.[1] In the Bohemian provinces and Silesia there were astonishing disabilities which destroyed all enterprise and almost disrupted family life. The *" Familienten Gesetz "* which, in practice, prevented more than the eldest in

---

[1] In the early Middle Ages Jewish physicians were prominent despite the persistent opposition of the clergy. But when the universities began to train their students in a scientific spirit the Jewish and Arabic monopoly disappeared.

each Jewish family from marrying, usually compelled the other children to emigrate. The outrageous law was not repealed until the revolutionary movements of 1848!

There were exceptions, of course, to all of these restrictions. Many Jews managed to become prominent in international trade, acquiring fortunes as importers and exporters. Jews controlled the Levantine trade which brought the luxuries of the Far East into Europe. In Sicily they were the producers and distributors of silk; they continued to export their products to France and Italy until their profitable enterprises were destroyed by unscrupulous rivals. They were among the pioneers in the tobacco industry. When printing was invented, they mastered the new craft and established famous presses in Hebrew and in other languages. There were also Jewish artisans and skilled metal and pottery workers in every country. The diary of Benjamin of Tudela, the twelfth-century Jewish Marco Polo, describes the occupational versatility of the Jews whom he met everywhere on his travels.

There were always the romantic court Jews too, special favourites of the princes, who won exemption from the usual Jewish disabilities. They flourished during the seventeenth and eighteenth centuries, primarily in Austria and Germany. They were permitted to own their homes, to carry on every variety of enterprise; and they were exempted from Jewish taxes and from the necessity of wearing the Jewish badge. Jacob Bassevi, one of the financiers of the Thirty Years' War, was the first Jew to be raised to the nobility, receiving the title " von Treuenberg." Samson Wertheimer, who rose high in the court of the Habsburgs, served as their banker during the long Rhenish, French, Turkish, and Spanish wars. The quixotic Joseph Süss Oppenheimer, court Jew in Württemberg, led a brilliant and adventurous career until he was suddenly disgraced and executed at the age of forty.[1]

These singularly fortunate exceptions did not affect the general economic status of the Jews. Denied entrance into the guilds, barred from the professions, excluded from the soil and from large-scale enterprise, most Jews were reduced to petty commerce in limited commodities and to buying and selling second-hand goods. They were the pedlars, who lived from hand to mouth and rarely went to bed without the taunts of a hostile multitude in their ears. They were the small tailors, whom patrons scrupled little to cheat; in eighteenth-century Rome three quarters of the Jewish population sweated out a miserable existence by the needle, near the filthy Tiber. In Poland the soberest of peoples became dealers in liquor and, quite naturally therefore, innkeepers. The more thoughtful European travellers may have wondered at the paradox as they received shelter from Jewish innkeepers in a land where the Jews themselves lived in insecurity.

By a queer twist of fate many Jews also became money-lenders, existing

[1] Feuchtwanger's *Power* is a fascinating historical novel dealing with the Jew Süss and his times.

precariously on the interest of their loans. Money-lending had, of course, always been common. In Greek and Roman days the practice had been carried to lengths of extortion which wrought disastrous social effects. Aristotle vigorously denounced the acceptance of interest as immoral, and his opinion profoundly influenced the Church Fathers, who drew no distinction between loans at moderate, legitimate rates, and extravagant exactions. This prohibition of interest charges by the Church threw money-lending into the hands of the Jews. They interpreted literally the Deuteronomic command which forbade taking interest from a brother. But why not from a stranger? Since few other means of livelihood were available, the Jews served in disproportionate numbers as bankers to the ever impecunious people among whom they lived.

Often they were usurious in their dealings, and their harshness undoubtedly contributed in good measure to the hatred of the masses for them. But it is fair to point out that usury was not limited to the Jews, nor were they the most ungenerous in their terms. The following passage from Thomas Wilson's famous *Discourse upon Usury* has been often quoted: " And for this cause they [the Jews] were hated in England, and so banyshed worthelye, with whom I woulde wyshe all these Englishemen were sent, that lende their money or other goods whatsoever for gayne, for I take them to be no better than Jewes. Nay, shall I saye: they are worse than Jewes, for go whither you will throughout Christendom, and deale with them, and you shall have under tenne in the hundred, yea sometimes for five at their handes, whereas englishe usurers exceed all goddes mercye, and will take they care not howe muche, without respecte had to the partye that borroweth, what losse, daunger, or hinderaunce soever the borrower sustayneth. And howe can these men be of God, that are so farr from charitie, that care not howe they get goods so they may have them." [1]

Indeed, it was not the Jews who profited most from the practice of money-lending. The kings and nobles were the chief beneficiaries and, in the long run, the real usurers. For a generous consideration they permitted the Jews to continue their traffic until the popular protest became formidable. Then they suddenly mulcted their erstwhile protégés of their wealth and expelled them or punished them heavily, thereby enriching their treasuries and earning an easy popularity. As Abrahams well puts it, the Jews all through the Middle Ages served as " unwilling sponges," sucking in the wealth of the land and then being squeezed dry again by their unscrupulous rulers.

In consequence of the intolerable economic pressure, the majority of Jews lived on the bare margin of subsistence. Fortunate was the family which could look forward to a fat fowl roasting in the pot even for the sabbath dinner. Fortunate, too, were the youngsters whose garments were not out at the elbow or whose shoes were not down at the heel. In eastern Europe the grim spectre

[1] Cited in Abrahams: *Jewish Life in the Middle Ages,* p. 243.

of poverty haunted nearly every home. An alarming proportion of the population lived on charity or received doles, at least for the holidays. The *shnorrer,* the perpetual mendicant, was a common character. The Jewish poor differed from the oppressed peasants, whose faces were also ground in the dust, only because they usually remained sober despite their sorrows.

Yet the legend persisted of the universal wealth and the conquering power of the Jews. " Rich as a Jew " passed into the common speech. Perhaps the legend was due to the survival of the Jews despite the burdens which seemed impossible to bear. Perhaps it was due to the rise of individual Jews to outstanding power. Perhaps the type of enterprise carried on by some Jews, who dealt always in gold, created the impression that all Jews had mastered its secrets. At any rate the legend persisted. It is surprising that the dunder-pated oafs who swore by the legend did not expect, when a Jew was burnt at the stake, to find precious gold in the charred remains.

4. SOCIETY AND RELIGION

Social life was closely intertwined with religious life. Worship was only one of the many functions of the synagogue. Men gathered in its dingy little rooms for communal meetings or for an hour or two of study. They came to announce happy tidings and sad ones, and all the community shared in the dispensations which Fate brought. They listened to the reading of the Takanoth, or ordinances, of *kahal* or synod, and they stood in awe during an excommunication service as the black candles were solemnly extinguished and the *shophar* sounded its fearful notes. Often the results of lawsuits were made public or lists of stolen articles were read, to place the community on guard against buying them. The synagogue took in the orphan and the stranger and assigned them to the community, combining functions which the Church delegated to special orders.

The synagogue thus was house of worship and town hall, school and forum. It was the tangible symbol of the old Jewish concept that religion was an integral part of life. Perhaps it was inevitable that a people without country and without civic life should give to the synagogue all the loyalty which found no other outlet.[1]

The mediæval Jew, however, was most clearly revealed in his home. In almost a literal sense his obscure little dwelling was his castle. Here he shut out the hostile world; he set aside the Jew badge and straightened up, a human being again. On the sabbath he was lord in his own right. Attired in holiday *sarabal,* surrounded by a devoted family, quiet, peaceful, he could forget for a moment the ugly realities just under his window. " When the lamp is lit, sorrows flit."

In the background was the Jewish housewife, usually unschooled, yet pos-

[1] The flavour of the mediæval synagogue is remarkably well preserved in *The Dybbuk* of S. Ansky.

sessed of much native wit, especially in a business way. She had a thorough knowledge of religious customs and it was her task to transmit them to the children. Few other opportunities remained, for oriental influence materially circumscribed family life. Men and women were usually separated and at banquets were served separately. Even in the synagogue the women usually sat in a little balcony or in reserved seats partitioned off by a curtain. Kissing and embracing were prohibited by custom, and in the eighteenth century the prohibition extended even to betrothed couples. To the present day eastern European families are reserved in openly displaying affection, a reserve which extends even to parents and children.

Life, it is clear, was a serious business, and a man's responsibilities began very early. A lad in his early teens had lost his animal spirits and was well settled, a full-fledged member of the community. Marriage came early; indeed, it was considered sinful for a man to be unmarried beyond his eighteenth year, and a girl of the same age was rapidly becoming an old maid.

Marriages were usually arranged by the parents, and their will was followed without question. Often they employed the services of a *shadchan,* or marriage broker, a picturesque figure who has persisted into modern times. He knew all the available young people of his own and near-by communities and was ever ready to explain and elaborate upon their charms. He served as go-between and received fees for successfully consummating an alliance.

Until the fifteenth century the Jews were perhaps the most literate of peoples, despite all the disabilities which they endured. Nearly every male child could read and write and the proportion of truly educated was commendable. Boys began their study of the Bible almost as soon as they could speak and then went forward, without a qualm, into the intricacies of the Talmud. All types studied, even business men and labourers, for study was a mode of worship. Every fairly cultured home had its library of Hebrew books; certainly a Bible and a "Shas," a set of the Talmud.

There was immense respect for the learned, and ignorance was regarded with contempt. The rabbi, who until modern times combined a secular occupation with his ministry, was the outstanding citizen and wielded considerable authority. Wealthy Jews supported study, and it was a high distinction for them to marry a daughter to a promising young rabbi. Poorer scholars, who wished to devote their lives to cultural pursuits, were usually assigned to the householders for meals during the years of study. Many of them married early and lived with their wife's family. This practice was not materially different from the system of endowed livings in the western European communities, which relieved young churchmen of financial embarrassments as they devoted themselves to cultural activities.

In summary, the darkness of Jewish life in the Middle Ages was not unrelieved. Political and economic restrictions were often not enforced, and sometimes several years passed without a storm to disturb the humble Jew's peace and contentment. The sabbath and the holidays, the engagements and marriages, the fair-days and the visits of the stork, all brought their joys and refreshed life within the ghetto walls.

Yet, with all of its brightness, Jewish existence remained too precarious to be comfortable, and the years of travail cast their shadows over the years of quiet. Limited intellectually, ground down economically, despised socially, disinherited politically, the Jews were also decried and persecuted for race and religion. It was not astonishing that, with no hope for participation in the life of the country, Jews swaddled themselves in their own traditions and placed their reliance in a personal Messiah who would some day come to restore them to the ancient homeland in Palestine.

PART THREE

CHAPTER TWENTY

THE END OF THE JEWISH MIDDLE AGES

FRIAR: Nathan! Nathan! You are a Christian! By God, you are a Christian!
There never was a better Christian!
NATHAN: We are of one mind! For that which makes me, in your eyes, a
Christian, makes you, in my eyes, a Jew!

Nathan the Wise

THE eighteenth century in European history was an age of rationalism, of intense intellectual activity, producing a new and prodigious Renaissance. It stood sponsor to the genius of Voltaire and Rousseau, of Newton and Adam Smith, of Goethe and Pope. Mediævalism was still strongly entrenched, but the hosts of the emancipated were battering at its foundations under the standard of the leader whose watchword was " Crush the infamous thing."

In Jewish life, however, the early eighteenth century was the nadir of a long history. Jews were everywhere sunk in superstition; learning had decayed and leadership had so far degenerated that it was impossible to find a worthy champion in the libels which were concocted against Jewish literature. It was the age of Eybeschutz and his curious controversy over the miraculous powers of amulets; of Messianic impostors who, despite their incredible claims and almost patent rascality, attracted large followings. It seemed that Judaism had become a mass of meaningless formulas, totally divorced from life, unworthy of the respect and loyalty of sincere and sensible men.

Yet the spark of life had not been completely extinguished. It smouldered in the very heart of the dry-rot. And at last, when it appeared as if it would go out altogether, three magnificent characters appeared to give it strength and to guide Judaism out of the cave of death. Israel of Moldavia, labouring in the recesses of the Carpathian Mountains, created a warm, emotional faith which brought new life to thousands of neglected souls in eastern Europe. Elijah, the venerable sage of Vilna, revitalized Talmudic studies, destroying the old intolerable hair-splitting which had reduced it to gibberish. Moses Mendelssohn, one of the most lovable figures of the eighteenth century, restored self-respect to the Jews and ushered them into the intellectual and æsthetic life of the European world. The trio, each appealing to a different element, at length closed the dreary Jewish Middle Ages, which had lasted for several hundred years.

263

I. BAAL SHEM TOB

Israel of Moldavia, reverently known as the Baal Shem Tob (the "Master of the Good Name"), was in the truest sense a religious revivalist, akin in spirit to the saintly John Wesley, who thrilled the English multitudes of the eighteenth century. The sect which he founded, known as the Hasidim, depended as much upon his own radiant personality as upon his teachings. Indeed, the Baal Shem himself "is still the real center for the Hasidim; his teachings have almost sunk in oblivion."[1] The legends woven about his name, extolling his kindliness, glorying in his miraculous achievements, and even bespeaking for him an intimate relationship with God, are the product of a devotion little short of idolatry.

Israel was born of humble parentage about 1700, somewhere in or near the province of Bukovina. He probably did not receive the usual scholastic training, and he was never at home in the intricacies of Talmudic dialect. Whenever possible, he escaped to the hills, where he spent his hours in carefree companionship with nature. The elders frowned upon his apparent idleness, for he had no worldly ambitions and was content to make his way by performing odd jobs. After an unfortunate early marriage he took a second wife and settled in the heart of the Carpathians, his entire wealth consisting of a horse, which his brother-in-law had given him. He supported himself by digging lime in the ravines, which his wife transported for sale in near-by market towns. Here, in the midst of some of nature's most magnificent scenery, he was happy and content. He spent his days in praying and teaching, and, having learned the healing secrets of plants and herbs, he ministered with great effect to the peasants of the region.

When he returned to civilized life and settled in Miedzyboz, he continued his simple, unaffected existence. Perhaps now he gathered about him a group of disciples to whom he expounded his teachings. His following, while not large, was significant enough to call down the dislike of the Talmudic authorities, although their actual hostility was not aroused until after his death, in 1760.

Israel's philosophy opened no new vistas in Jewish thought, for it simply suggested ways of life which had been often taught before. But the re-emphasis was sorely needed in his day. When he taught, Judaism rotated about Talmudic prescriptions. Learning was much respected, but it was a cold, unappealing learning, a learning that had little relation to reality, that emphasized mental subtlety beyond reason. Every academy specialized in *pilpul*, hair-splitting. There was profound contempt for the artisan, the labourer, and the peasant who had no Talmudic ingenuity. These were regarded as *Am Aratzim*, the crude, uncultured masses who served no useful purpose in life. Israel revolted against

[1] L. Ginzberg in the *Jewish Encyclopedia* (s. v. "Ba'al Shem-Tob").

the whole tradition. The law, he felt, was more than pedantry, more than a series of syllogisms. The rabbis were judging with narrowness and blindness. In their search for the meanings of dots and dashes they were neglecting life itself and the beauty and comfort of the divine presence.

Israel substituted a warm mysticism for the arid scholasticism which he attacked. His basic concept was the omnipresence of God, in all the universe, in mind and in matter, in every relationship, in evil as in good. This type of pantheism a hundred philosophers had already expounded, but it had not affected the lives of the masses. Israel drew corollaries from it which made a metaphysical system into a practical way of life. Unfortunately it is difficult to ascertain the exact expression of Israel's teachings. He left no writings, and all that we know is gathered from the sayings of his followers, who, too often, did not discriminate between Israel's words and their own commentaries. Yet the leading principles which grew into Hasidism are quite clear. God's omnipresence, the Baal Shem preached, vitalized human judgments on the worth of men. God is as close to the sinner as to the saint, to the ignorant as to the wise. He is not to be approached through learning, but through a strong, sincere faith as expressed in genuine prayer. "All that I have achieved," the Baal Shem is said to have remarked, "I have achieved, not through study, but through prayer." Again, the nature of God called for cheerfulness, for optimism. Evil is only a relationship, it lies in man's view of things rather than in the things themselves. Consequently no man is sunk too low to raise himself through faith in his own betterment. Plaguing oneself with fasts, mortifying the flesh, wallowing in sorrow, all these are unworthy ways of glorifying the name of God. They serve Him best who live fearlessly and cheerfully and accept the inevitable with resignation.

It is easy to understand the immense vogue of the Baal Shem's teachings among a people whose lives held out no promise and who were despised by the aristocracy of the learned. The rabbinical pedant might belittle the value of a mystical devotion to God, but to thousands of humble souls it opened a new heaven and a new earth. These turned to the Carpathian saint as to a Messiah, and when his teachings were disseminated by loyal disciples, all of southern Russia became Hasidic.

It is one of the melancholy facts of history that nearly every faith suffers most from its own followers; too often they misunderstand and distort a great teacher's words and ruin the good which he creates. Israel's ideals did not long survive his death. The fervent devotion for which he appealed degenerated into hysterical prayer and vulgar spiritual antics. His subordination of learning to faith was taken to imply contempt for learning. The ignorant masses prided themselves upon their ignorance. It became a dogma in Hasidic circles that "where there is much learning, there is little piety."

But especially obnoxious and degrading was the veneration of the Hasidic rabbi, the *Zaddik*. The Baal Shem had taught, it was said, that pious men who could, through faith and prayer, lose their sense of individuality and achieve communion with God, were endowed with the gifts of the prophets and were entitled to the respect paid to the prophets. Their worth was so high that they could serve as a connecting link between God and His own creations. Several of the Baal Shem's disciples were soon regarded as possessing such virtues. These *Zaddikim* were venerated as holy beings, capable of interceding for the down-trodden and the afflicted, endowed with almost miraculous powers. Sickly men came to them for healing, barren women for the blessings which would give them their hearts' desire. A veritable worship of the *Zaddik* began, which debased the spiritual life of the Hasidic communities. Many of the *Zaddikim* were sincerely pious men who proved able shepherds of their flock. But when the institution became hereditary and the spiritual gifts of saintly fathers were not vouchsafed to their children, the office of the *Zaddik* was degraded and ruined. And there were rascals who lived on the credulity of the masses and exploited them for their own material well-being.

With all the errors into which it fell, however, Hasidism was a force for good. It compelled the rabbis to take stock and helped to destroy the tyranny of the Talmud. It made prayer more meaningful and enriched the liturgy of the synagogue. Its emphasis upon cheerfulness and optimism dispelled the clouds which so often obscured the sun and the promise of a better tomorrow. Circumstances were never too black for the Hasidim — congenial spirits, lovers of a good story and a good drink.[1] Through every restriction and every persecution they continued blithely to serve their God and hope for the best. In the literary revival of the nineteenth century it was natural that scenes from Hasidic life furnished the inspiration for many a novelist and poet.

2. ELIJAH, THE VILNA GAON

Meantime in the heart of Lithuania, which had become a prominent Jewish centre in the seventeenth and eighteenth centuries, another attempt was made to raise the tone of eastern Jewish life. It came from Elijah, popularly known as the Gaon of Vilna, who was born in the thriving capital of Lithuania in 1720. He was a prodigy in an age of prodigies, tradition ascribing to him the feat of mastering Bible and Talmud before he was nine! Like Lessing, he was "a steed that required double fodder." Contrary to the practice of his generation, he was vastly interested in Hebrew grammar. He loved to browse in the sciences also and was thoroughly at home in the leading Jewish philosophical works. He wrote a brief work on astronomy and was the inspiration for a Hebrew translation of Euclid. Though he refused to serve as the official rabbi of his community, the Jewish leaders through all the eastern European world appealed to him in their disputes. His scholarship, his perspicuity and liveliness of mind, were

---

[1] It must be added that some of the Hasidim remained ascetics.

everywhere respected and it was considered a signal honour to be permitted to speak with him.

Elijah was an indefatigable student and a voluminous author. There was scarcely a field in Hebrew literature which he did not enrich with commentaries, notes, and elucidation. He even wrote a treatise on the *Zohar*. One purpose ran through all of his work. He wished to bring Jewish scholarship back to the simple textual meaning of Bible and Talmud, to end the rule of *pilpul* against which the Baal Shem had also vigorously protested. All of his lectures and his writings, which he modestly refused to publish during his own lifetime, hammered the lesson that casuistry was not learning.

While Elijah trained a select group of distinguished students in the little synagogue of Vilna, Hasidism spread through the country and made inroads even in the anti-mystical stronghold of Lithuania. The whole motif of the Baal Shem's teachings was incomprehensible to such a mind as Elijah's. He was roused to action against the Hasidim, especially when stories come to him of the more degenerate form of their teachings. Ordinarily he was a peaceful man, unwilling to participate in any public affairs, but this dispute, the only one into which he ever entered, took all of his energies. Attack and recrimination became so fierce that, in 1781, the erstwhile gentle Elijah excommunicated the Hasidim and forbade intermarriage with them.

It was as much a desire to combat Hasidism as to stimulate a more useful study of Hebrew literature that induced the Gaon to plan a great Talmudic academy. Unfortunately he died before his ambition could be fulfilled and the task was delegated to a favourite pupil, who opened the famous institution in Volozhin in 1803. In order to attract the ablest men to the new academy it was decided to admit only those who had distinguished themselves in Talmudic study. The mediæval method of assigning students for daily meals to various homes was also abolished, and those who came were either self-supporting or else were maintained by the institution.

In the new academy the spirit of Elijah's reforms found a congenial home. The most distinguished young people came from all over Europe, eager to be trained in the tradition of the famous Gaon. The old scholasticism was not completely broken down, but its worst evils disappeared, and the obscurantism of the previous centuries was somewhat dissipated. Students who left the halls of the academy carried back to the communities of Europe, in which they became rabbis, a new respect for the law and custom of the Talmud, based on rational study.

3 · MOSES MENDELSSOHN

" How free from bias is his spirit, how open his heart to every virtue, how attuned to all beauty! " This encomium on Moses Mendelssohn was not overdrawn, for he was indeed one of the most winning characters in all Jewish history. He was born in Dessau, Germany, in 1729, the son of a humble scribe. The father denied himself necessaries in order to give the young lad a good Hebrew training, and Moses did not waste his dearly purchased opportunities. Before he had passed his Bar Mitzvah days, he was working, with intense delight, in material far beyond his years. His diligent application to the philosophy of Maimonides brought on an illness which left him weak and delicate and deformed. "I have my hump," he used to say with a wan smile, "from the great Moses."

At fourteen Mendelssohn begged his way into Berlin, from which Jews were rigidly excluded, except in the rarest instances. Here he carried on a fearful battle against illness and poverty, all the while, however, meeting useful teachers and assimilating important works. The Berlin of Frederick the Great's day teemed with intellectual effort, and young Mendelssohn's mind responded with ease to every stimulating influence. He learned to use the German language with a facility which made him a leading figure in German literature.

It was a momentous day for him when, in 1754, he met Gotthold Lessing, the brilliant German critic and dramatist, one of the most liberal spirits of the eighteenth century. Lessing was immensely impressed, and, in a letter to the friend who had brought them together, he wrote: "His integrity and philosophical mind make me anticipate in him a second Spinoza, lacking only his errors to be his equal." The two became fast friends, and the élite of fastidious Prussia looked in wonder at the spectacle of the leading man of letters boasting of an intimacy with an ugly little hump-backed Jew.

Lessing had already begun to preach his gospel of tolerance in a youthful drama entitled The Jews, published in 1749. He had there pointed out the excellent qualities of the Jews and had pilloried Protestant bigotry which ignorantly degraded a noble people. The little drama was theory spun out of Lessing's breadth of heart. In Mendelssohn the young critic met the type which he had idealized, a brilliant intellect, a lovable nature, an expansive spirit. Nathan the Wise, the masterpiece of Lessing's maturest genius, was undoubtedly created around the personality of his gifted Hebrew friend. Lessing took the keenest delight in assisting Mendelssohn on his road to fame, and his patronage was of invaluable assistance. Mendelssohn's first work, in which he criticized the national neglect of native philosophers, was published through Lessing's influence.

Thenceforth Mendelssohn's rise was rapid. His essay, published in 1755, on the philosophy of the beautiful, became the basis of æsthetic criticism in Germany. His reviews in philosophy and literature were always as well written and as courageous as they were profound. He dared to criticize even the verse of the Emperor Frederick and almost alienated the royal poet, whose " dirty linen " Voltaire had been obliged to wash. Mendelssohn became a national figure when the remarkable lucidity and clearness of his prose enabled him to win the first prize in a contest on a metaphysical subject, sponsored by the Berlin

Academy. The achievement was the more spectacular because the future king of German philosophers, Immanuel Kant, was also a contestant. A few months later Mendelssohn was given the privileges of a *Schutzjude,* which released him from all onerous Jewish burdens.[1]

In 1767 Mendelssohn, taking Plato's famous dialogue the *Phædo* as a model, wrote *Phädon,* a discussion of immortality, in which the current cynicism and materialism were attacked. It was written with amazing charm and clearness, far from the German tradition of ponderousness in learned works. Translated into nearly all languages and reprinted innumerable times, it became the most widely read book in Europe. It won for Mendelssohn the name of the " German Plato " and the esteem of the leaders of German thought.

Mendelssohn had always associated himself with the life of his people even when his society was sought by the leaders of German thought. But he had little opportunity to become a leader until an attempt was made by a well-wisher to convert him to Christianity. The ensuing controversy made him a zealous champion and he was soon launched upon the formidable task of raising his people from a degraded and misunderstood position.

In 1783 he translated the Pentateuch into beautiful German prose and added a clear, concise commentary, disburdened of all dialectic and theological bias. Its influence was enormous. Rarely has a volume created so profound an intellectual revolution. The Jews, whose long confinement within physical and mental ghettos had corrupted their speech, learned German from the translation. Like children with a new toy, they used the instrument to dabble in every field, and their minds, long cut off from the channels of Western thought, were now flooded with new ideas and new points of view. Gradually the whole motive of Jewish education was changed. The Bible was no longer taught merely to inculcate religious principles. Its literary and æsthetic qualities were also emphasized, and Hebrew grammar, long neglected, was at last scientifically investigated. By one masterful stroke Mendelssohn thus opened a new world to his people. They became interested in Germany and in German thought. They began to long for citizenship, for participation in the life of the nation. They became Germans and Europeans.

It was to be expected that opposition to Mendelssohn's work should arise from the more conservative elements among the Jews. They believed that it was a degradation to take the Holy Writ out of the sacred tongue and they feared the effects of contact with European life. When the news was broadcast that the Berlin sage was working over a Biblical translation, there were protests, and when it was issued, some of the leading rabbis threatened to

---

[1] The story has it that he received the honour at the request of the Marquis d'Argens, who said to Frederick: " A bad Catholic philosopher begs a bad Protestant philosopher to grant the privilege to a bad Jewish philosopher. There is too much philosophy in all this for justice not to be on the side of the request."

excommunicate those who read it. Mendelssohn was not unprepared. "As soon as I yielded to Dubno to have my translation printed," he said, "I placed my soul in my hands, raised my eyes to the mountains, and gave my back to the smiters."

Yet until the full effects of Mendelssohn's teachings were seen, the opposition did not become violent. The rabbis respected Mendelssohn too much and it was significant that though they issued an interdict against reading his work, they made no attack upon him.

Mendelssohn now became a vigorous advocate of Jewish emancipation, fighting to relieve his people of their onerous restrictions. The battle was long and victory did not come until Mendelssohn had been in his grave for many decades. But his contribution was a fundamental one, the first scientific presentation of the case for Jewish emancipation. In the same year in which his translation appeared, he published the epoch-making little volume *Jerusalem,* in which he pleaded for freedom of conscience for all peoples. He pointed out that no religion could boast of a monopoly of truth, that the test of religion lay in its effect on conduct, and that all religions were true which affected their believers for good. Therefore, he argued, half a century ahead of his time, "let everyone who does not disturb public happiness, who is obedient to the civil government, who acts righteously towards his fellow man, be allowed to speak as he thinks, to pray to God after his own fashion, or after the fashion of his fathers, and to seek eternal salvation where he thinks he may find it." *Jerusalem* had no immediate influence, but the day was to come when its principles, as Kant wrote to Mendelssohn, would affect not only the Jews, but other nations too.

The gallant little philosopher, however, was not to live to see that happy day. He died in 1786, just before the mighty French Revolution came to shake the world out of its lethargy and to tear down the last relics of an outworn feudalism. It was symbolic that he met his death from a cold that he contracted while going to deliver to his publishers a manuscript in which he sought to vindicate the memory of his beloved friend Lessing.

Mendelssohn's influence initiated a renaissance in Russia as well as in Germany. The paths of the renaissance, however, led into very different fields. Whereas in Germany the disciples of the great teacher employed the German language to open the wonders of German culture, in Russia the use of the native tongue was profitless; there were no worth-while Russian intellectual treasures. Consequently the young Russian Jews turned to Hebrew and gave their best talents to its development. It was natural for the German humanists to be led into the modern Reform movement and for the Russian humanists to follow the path of Jewish nationalism.

The death of Mendelssohn did not diminish the enthusiasm for his teachings. Students flocked in their thousands to apply his gospel to their own lives.

Every city in Germany which had Jewish communities spoke of nothing and thought of nothing but the cultural affiliations which German and secular studies opened. Soon there were Biblical translations in the vernacular in Italy, in Poland, in France, and in other countries. The presses of Europe poured out the famous European classics in Hebrew translation, and young Jews everywhere could not devour them fast enough.

One of Mendelssohn's leading disciples, Hartwig Wessely, a brilliant German humanist, began to apply his master's theories to Jewish education. Already in 1782 he addressed a Hebrew letter to the congregations of Austria, where Joseph II had just inaugurated an era of tolerance, in which he insisted that a true knowledge of Judaism was impossible without the background of a general culture. Biblical and Talmudic training were indispensable, but education could not end there. The natural sciences, philosophy, history, the wisdom of the world, were fully as important. His appeal evoked considerable opposition, but it was heeded in several Italian communities, in Austria, and in Germany, where secular schools were established with the curriculum which he recommended. A group of Hebrew enthusiasts in Königsberg founded the journal *Ha-Meassef* (the Gatherer), which published articles on religious and secular subjects in Hebrew and which became the organ of the leaders of the new thought.

Unfortunately, many of those who climbed out of the traditional rut were completely carried away by their newly-found freedom. The Prussia of Frederick's day had many temptations for the unwary. The Church had found it difficult to wrestle with the cynicism called the "Berlin religion," and the synagogue now faced the same problem. French dilettantism, as popular in Germany as in France, often worked havoc with minds not accustomed to free-thought. Thousands of young men threw over every restraint and became utter pagans. Others, enamoured by the apparent superiority of Christian beliefs, accepted baptism. Still others, finding their newly-awakened ambitions checked by their Jewish loyalties, dropped them and as Christians knocked at the gates which they hoped to enter.

The tendency towards disintegration was hastened in the famous salons of Austria and Germany. The salon was an important institution in the latter eighteenth century. It brought together socially the leading political and literary figures, who discussed, with wit and charm and without restraint, the politics, drama, and literature of the day. Several Jewish salons became enormously popular and helped to raise the tone of German intellectual life. Mendelssohn's drawing-room was a favourite gathering-place. After his death the cultured élite came of an afternoon to the home of his dear friend Dr. Marcus Herz, whose clever wife, Henrietta Herz, became the most popular hostess of the day. It was said that when the revolutionary statesman Mirabeau came to Prussia, in 1786, on a secret mission, he spent more time in the Herz home than at court. For several years the salon of the beautiful and cultured Rachel Levin, the wife of Varnhagen, critic and biographer, was counted the most cultured centre in Europe. It became the rendezvous for men like Jean Paul Richter, Schlegel, Schelling, von Gentz, and other philosophers and *littérateurs*.

Christians and Jews, meeting on equal terms in such an environment, learned to understand each other better. But in nearly every case loyalty to Judaism disappeared. Henrietta Herz was soon involved in Christian amours; Rachel, though never disinterested in the welfare of her people, accepted baptism. Mendelssohn's own daughters cut themselves adrift from the faith which their father had laboured to revitalize and followed their husbands and lovers into Christianity.

The older, more conservative folk, frightened by the defections of so many brilliant Jews, naturally decried the new influences which had come to disrupt Jewish life. They insisted that a liberal education was a curse, that it were better to live completely in the Talmudic world than to be led astray by every will-o'-the-wisp philosophy. They fought bitterly against the educational innovations, condemning the good and the bad alike. But they could more easily stop a rain-storm. The old regime was ended; Jewish life could never again be confined by the traditional literature. This was made clearer when the French Revolution came, a few years later, to tear down the ghetto walls and to add political and economic equality to the new-found intellectual freedom.

In the transition period many rudderless souls were carried out, lost to Judaism for ever. But others, hardier and more stable, found in their new contacts a firmer and deeper basis for their faith.

Chapter Twenty-one

THE FALL OF THE MEDIÆVAL CITADEL

1. VOICES FRIENDLY AND OTHERWISE

The few decades preceding the French Revolution were noteworthy for their spirit of self-examination. Thoughtful observers became keenly alive to the absurdities and stupidities which had survived out of the past, the evils of serfdom, of guild restrictions, of privileged classes, of lawless laws and orderless orders. With biting wit and incomparable literary skill they began to attack the old regime, ever reiterating their conviction that genuine progress was not possible unless men were set free from outworn institutions and hateful prejudices.

It was now possible to speak up more boldly for the long-victimized Jews, to insist upon the dissolution of the political and economic restrictions which had stamped a whole people as pariahs. Lessing's courageous advocacy of the Jewish claims has already been noted. His drama *Nathan the Wise,* "the song of songs of tolerance," was immensely influential. Banned at first by self-righteous Christians, attacked as absurd and impossible, it became highly popular and was never read or performed without dissipating ugly clouds of prejudice. It gave cultured Germany a view of a despised race which put arrogant Christians to shame. Perhaps not least among its benefactions was the new self-respect which it awakened in Jews themselves.

Another influential champion of Jewish rights was Christian William von Dohm, a Prussian councillor of State and the supervisor of the royal archives. Following an outbreak of Jew-baiting in Alsace, he prepared a historical vindication in two volumes, the celebrated *Upon the Civil Amelioration of the Condition of the Jews,* published in 1791, in which he made a direct plea to the Crown to end the age-old restrictions. In an enlightened day, he wrote, it was disgraceful to maintain that religious convictions were an obstacle to the proper performance of civic duties. If Jews possessed the obnoxious characteristics which were imputed to them by detractors, they were not inherent in the people, but were forced upon them by their degraded position. It was obviously brutal and unfair to restrict the Jews to petty peddling and money-lending and then to condemn them for following unworthy means of earning a livelihood. Von Dohm proposed for them equal political rights with other subjects, complete freedom in economic and professional life, and, above all, unrestricted educational opportunities.

The ablest of the eighteenth-century political philosophers, Montesquieu, also denounced the hypocrisy of a Europe which prided itself on its Christianity. His power for satire had been sharpened in the guerrilla wars against the general social and political abuses of his day. Christians, he said in his epochal *Spirit of the Laws,* complained of Chinese barbarism, but were themselves guilty of practices towards Jews, harsher and infinitely more cruel. "If any of our descendants should ever venture to say that the nations of Europe were cultured, your example will be adduced to prove that they were barbarians."

The *littérateurs* and philosophers who were influenced by the general humanitarianism of the Age were reinforced by a number of statesmen. Most important, perhaps, was Joseph II, Emperor of Austria, the most tolerant and benignant, though not the ablest, of the enlightened despots of the eighteenth century. It is one of the paradoxes of history that so genial a sovereign sprang from the loins of the narrow, unreasoning, Jew-hater Maria Theresa. Joseph changed the whole motif of government as soon as he ascended the throne, and capped his reforms with an Edict of Toleration, issued in 1782, which breathed a strange spirit of friendship to Jews and alien peoples. Of course his purpose was primarily to break down the separateness of the many groups in his crazy-quilt empire. And his edicts bristled with qualifications. They did not end occupational and residential restrictions and they did not put Jews on the same plane with Catholics. But they ended the degradations which made the Jews feel ashamed and unclean. The obnoxious body-tax and the distinctive Jewish dress were both abolished. Jews were permitted to take part in large-scale enterprises, to build large factories, to worship as they pleased, to send their children to schools and universities. Joseph's policy was very quickly reversed when he passed to his grave, but it was a significant act of friendship, the first in centuries which Jews had enjoyed from any great European state.

Another interesting champion of Jewish rights was Mirabeau, the most impressive orator and the most powerful statesman in France on the eve of the Revolution. A hard liver, a hard fighter, a hard worker, as influential with the Crown as with the complaining Estates, he would have changed the history of the Revolution if he had been spared beyond its opening years. He was a firm friend of several important Jews and was especially fond of Mendelssohn, the fine texture of whose intellect fascinated him. He was a frequent visitor in the Jewish salons, and his friendship with the clever Henrietta Herz brought him into contact with the most distinguished Jews of the day. Several times during the meeting of the Revolutionary National Assembly he advocated complete political equality for the Jews, and, though he did not live to see his hopes fulfilled, his booming eloquence helped in the long, uphill struggle.[1]

---

[1] Yet we know from his correspondence that he wished for Jewish emancipation partly because this radical action might incite the masses to rise against the Jacobins.

Nevertheless, it required more than a few voices in a wide wilderness to destroy a system almost as old as the serpent in Eden. The ignorance of the masses, the prejudice of the most cultured, the religious scruples of the pious, the deeply-rooted notion that a state must be Christian, were walls which seemed to recoil little against the most determined batterings of the hosts of enlightenment.

Who can blame the benighted masses for their animosity? With their mother's milk came the belief that Jews were outcasts, moral lepers, eternally damned for a dreadful crime nearly two thousand years old. It was well-nigh impossible to cast out the belief, for they themselves lived in darkness, oppressed by a few social superiors, enslaved by a fanatical priesthood, embittered by the relentless struggle for a livelihood. Education was closed to them, and they grew up the children of superstition, the tool of every blackguard who exploited their passions.

The power of popular prejudice was demonstrated in mid-century in England, one of the more enlightened countries. Here several thousand Jews, who had been admitted by a back door, as it were, had been living for nearly a century without political or civil rights. Little effort had been made to remedy their status and they were themselves content to follow Walpole's dictum to "let sleeping dogs lie." When the Jews who lived in the American colonies were naturalized, however, it seemed stupid to deny the same rights to the Jews of the mother country. Accordingly, in 1753 the new Prime Minister, Pelham, introduced a naturalization measure, which passed both Houses of Parliament and received the signature of King George II. As soon as the implication of the Act became clear, there was furious opposition in the country. Merchants who feared competition, and churchmen who feared the wrath of God, united to fire the masses, who feared everything. One well-meaning defender of the Jewish cause was overwhelmed with abuse, and his effigy was burnt by a mob in Bristol. The blind fury compelled Pelham, in 1754, to withdraw the measure "because it had provoked displeasure, and the minds of many loyal subjects had been disquieted thereby"!

Another dreary manifestation of mob hysteria came in Alsace, where four fifths of the French Jews lived. Since economic restrictions compelled the Jews to seek the most unpopular means of livelihood, they were cordially hated. Before the Revolution a blackmailing lawyer, Hell, rode them hard and made them feel the full significance of his name. Though he was himself ultimately jailed and exiled, he almost succeeded in obtaining the expulsion of the Jews and he remained for many years a popular idol.

In Prussia every anti-Jewish pamphlet which was issued obtained a wide circulation. A representative gutter sheet proposed not only to enclose the Jews in ghettos and to compel them to wear the hateful Jew badge, "but, in order to limit their increase, the second male child of each Jew should be castrated."

The ignorant masses were given no lead in tolerance by those who counted themselves the salt of the earth. Even the most emancipated thinkers, the philosophers, the leaders of the new rationalism, were subject to instincts which proved more powerful than their intellectual convictions. There was no more enlightened ruler in the eighteenth century than the versatile Frederick the Great of Prussia, who prided himself on his popular title, the "Philosopher King." Assuredly he had no religious convictions, and his cynicism was notorious. Yet he despised Jews, and his *General Privilege,* written in 1750, was filled with the mediæval spirit of intolerance. He granted protection to certain groups of families, but, in the attempt to limit the number of Jews in his dominions, he decided that only the eldest sons could succeed to their fathers' rights. The edict virtually compelled the younger children to emigrate and destroyed the stability of family life. When its severity was modified, the Jews paid dearly for the king's indulgence.

An even more astonishing instance of prejudice was furnished by the brilliant iconoclast Voltaire. His was a colossal mind, a mind which never ceased, throughout a long life, to make war on existing abuses and superstitions. He defended the weak and the downtrodden; in the famous Calas case he made Europe ring with the iniquities of the bigots who hounded the unfortunate family to death. Yet this enemy of injustice used his biting pen and tongue to attack the Jews as a greedy and selfish race, whose only ideals were more money and more children. It may be that some disagreeable personal experiences with Jews influenced his attitude. A London Jewish banker on whom he had drawn a draft went bankrupt, and Voltaire lost twenty thousand francs. Later he made an unsuccessful attempt to outdupe a Prussian Jew and he was mercilessly satirized by his ever watchful enemies; even King Frederick twitted him for his cupidity. The most rational beings are apt to transfer an animosity against individuals to a whole people, and Voltaire very likely succumbed to the weakness. Or it may be that, like many clever men, he could not resist the temptation to be sharp; and where was there a better-stocked armoury for a master of caricature than in the habits and customs of a strange and little-known people? Yet, if the intellectual arbiter of Europe could select the Jews for his gibes simply because they were convenient scapegoats, it is easy to understand why they were selected by those whose motives were grounded in malice.

The sage and rational Goethe, pre-eminent among German poets, shared the popular prejudice and looked upon Jews, whom he had rarely seen, except through the gates of the ghetto, as inferior and degraded beings. The brilliant Fichte opposed Jewish political emancipation strenuously. Jews, he argued, were incapable of performing civic duties, for they had no civic patriotism. "The only way I see by which civil rights can be conceded to them is to cut off all their heads in one night and to set new ones on their shoulders, which should contain not a single Jewish idea. The only means of protecting our-

selves against them is to conquer their promised land and send them thither." [1]
Herder reacted instinctively in like manner and could never meet even Mendelssohn without feeling some repugnance.

The ostracism of the Jews, at least politically, was not based entirely upon
fear and prejudice. The theory of a Christian state was an integral part of the
political philosophy of the day. Some of the most liberal statesmen insisted that
Christianity was the foundation upon which the State was built, and that none
but Christians should participate in it. As late as 1834 the Archbishop of Canterbury declared, seriously, in the House of Lords, opposing a bill to permit Jews
to sit in Parliament, " that the blessings of the Divine Providence had been
bestowed upon this country as a Christian country, and he should be apprehensive lest these blessings should be withdrawn when the country ceased to
retain that character." All men had a right to their lives and to their property,
the argument ran, but not to power or political privileges. It was no injustice,
therefore, to disfranchise the non-Christians and the heretics who would not
subscribe to the oath, the prerequisite for voting or holding office, which included the profession of Christianity.

It did not help the Jewish cause that the Jews were themselves broken up
into mutually hostile groups. Spanish Jews looked down upon German Jews,
German Jews upon Polish Jews, and Polish Jews upon Lithuanian Jews. Snobbishness entered into every social relation and necessitated the creation of separate synagogues. In one instance the intra-group antipathies nearly precipitated
a terrible disaster. In Bordeaux lived a large community of Spanish and Portuguese Jews, who had built up an honourable reputation. In 1760 about a hundred
and fifty immigrants came to the city from Germany and Poland, and their
settlement was bitterly opposed by the older Jewish inhabitants, who went so
far as to petition Louis XV to expel the new arrivals as vagrants. One leader
wrote a pamphlet in which he pointed out the inferiority of the German Jews
to the Spanish. Only the confusion in pre-Revolutionary France prevented
the shameful fratricidal tragedy from taking place.

Such was the situation in 1780. The Jews remained disinherited politically,
restricted economically, and despised socially. A few of the more enlightened
spirits protested against the existing iniquities, but their voices could scarcely be
heard. The mass ignorance, the selfishness of classes who feared the Jews, the
emotional repugnance even of the educated, the notion of a Christian state,
were tremendous obstacles, through which mere phrases about equality and
brotherhood could not cut. It required a great convulsion, a readjustment of
social and economic values, to create a new system. Towards the end of the
eighteenth century the convulsion came which destroyed the *ancien régime*
and laid the foundations for a new world.

[1] It is fair to add, however, that later, as rector of the University of Berlin, he went out of his
way to assist a Jewish student who had been victimized by intolerance.

2. THE FRENCH REVOLUTION

Hardly had the brilliant historian Gibbon ventured to congratulate the world that the age of great political and social catastrophes was past when the French Revolution burst upon Europe. The deliberations and achievements of the National Assembly and its successors profoundly affected every other land. " When France sneezes, all Europe catches cold." Despite the guillotine and the Reign of Terror, the crude worship of Reason, and the brutality of mobs who shouted the *Marseillaise* as they paraded with the heads of aristocrats on their pikes, despite sordidness and excesses, the Revolution was a gigantic force for good, abolishing innumerable absurd and vexatious institutions. It destroyed the political monopoly of the aristocracy and the economic strength of the Church. It made possible the political supremacy of the middle class, which had already grown powerful as a result of vast changes in industry.

For the Jews the Revolution was perhaps the most important influence in modern history. It fulfilled an almost impossible dream by bringing them political emancipation. For the first time in a thousand years they became citizens of the states in which they lived. Even more important, it completely changed their economic status and opened new worlds of opportunity to them. After all, paper rights meant little without economic strength. Such strength the Jews were able to obtain in the new liberal states controlled by the middle class.

At first, though, the Revolution seemed to bring nothing but sorrow. Louis XVI, shorn of his despotic power, could not keep order, nor could his " transient, embarrassed phantoms." There was considerable rioting against the privileged classes, and, since no riot is ever complete which does not involve the Jews, they suffered severe material losses. On the very night when the Bastille fell and Frenchmen rejoiced in the collapse of the old regime, riots began in Alsace which compelled thousands of terror-stricken Jewish families to flee to Switzerland, where they received a very cool and reluctant welcome. The delegates who represented Alsace in the Estates General clamoured for further legislation to restrict the Jewish locusts who, they were sure, ate up the country.

These incidents were perhaps inevitable in a time of stress. Fortunately, other developments were taking place which held better promise for the France which was emerging from the Revolutionary furnace. On the night of August 4, decrees were passed abolishing the survivals of an outworn feudalism; the scions of the oldest houses, caught up in the enthusiasm of the moment, vied with each other in surrendering their privileges. On August 23 the momentous debates began to determine the rights of the individual citizen. The Catholic clergy alone protested against granting equality to all sects and creeds, and at last even its resistance was overcome. After three days the Declaration of the

Rights of Man, one of history's noblest documents, was adopted amid general enthusiasm. Theoretically all men became equal before the law, regardless of birth, status, or belief.

Abstractions, however thrilling, require practical application before they become important. In the case of the Jews this took time. When concrete demands were made to enfranchise the Jews and to remove all annoying economic barriers, the motions were regularly tabled. Mirabeau, the liberal Abbé Grégoire, Robespierre, and other Revolutionary patriots, all joined in supporting the Jewish cause, but for long the stubborn opposition of the Alsatian delegates and the clericals prevented a favourable decision. One deputy warned the assembly that a decree which granted the Jews full citizenship would mean their destruction in Alsace.

The inevitable could not be continuously postponed, however. Late in January 1790 the Portuguese and Avignonese Jews of southern France were declared full citizens. At the end of 1791 similar privileges were granted to all the Jews in France. At last a great European country had abolished all restrictions; the Jews had liberty, equality, and, at least in theory, fraternity. They were no longer aliens.

The fervent loyalty of the Jewish population to the principles of the Revolution was the clearest answer to those who had opposed Jewish rights. The emancipated people outdid themselves in their devotion to what had at last truly become for them "la patrie." Those who could enlisted in the Guard, others poured out their treasures, and all prayed for the success of the Revolution against enemies at home and abroad. The very candelabra of synagogues were sold to contribute to the war fund.

Indeed, material and moral support of every kind was urgently needed. At one time it appeared as if all that had been wrought by the Revolution would be swallowed up in the internal anarchy which suddenly convulsed the nation. It was brought on largely by the fear of foreign invasion. Danton met the challenge by throwing down " as gage of battle " the head of the poor king. Late in 1793 came the Reign of Terror, bloody months during which systems, parties, and individuals bitterly fought each other for survival and supremacy. Every excess was made possible in the general loosening of discipline. Hébert carried through his mad proposal to abolish Christianity and establish a regime of Reason, and a handsome Parisian actress became the centre of the new worship. Scores of churches became temples of Reason and the old religious forms were everywhere derided and persecuted. "The star of liberty was paling before Mercury, Mars and Venus." But, on the whole, Judaism emerged from the saturnalia without harm. Some synagogues were burnt, some Jews were killed in local riots. It was difficult to preserve the holidays and the sabbath when the new calendar was enforced and the observance of traditional customs was made a misdemeanour. But after a year the terror ended and

France came out into the open. The worst crisis of the Revolution had been weathered.

Meantime a general European war had been precipitated by the Revolution. Austria, Prussia, and England, alarmed by the excesses of the republicans and horrified by the execution of the king, sought to turn back the clock and restore the old regime. But the tricolour swept all before it, and, in 1795, the allied forces were driven out of Holland, and the Dutch provinces were organized into the Batavian Republic. What Louis XIV, with all his military institutions, could not accomplish, the Revolution had achieved with pure spirit. "With bread and iron we can get to China," the ragged and unpaid troops of the Republic cried!

Holland had long been a haven of refuge, and Jews had thrived and multiplied there. When the victorious French troops arrived, there were about fifty thousand in the new republic, more than twenty thousand centred in Amsterdam. They enjoyed no political rights and were hampered by restrictions, but in comparison with their co-religionists in other countries they were in a fortunate position. The spirit of the Revolution was infectious, however, and the Jews felt that they had the right to make demands. Political disfranchisement and economic disabilities were considered degrading in the new age. Petitions were accordingly sent up to the recently created assembly, appealing for the naturalization of the Dutch Jewish community. The way was difficult. The Dutch were a hard folk to convince. They shared the prejudices of most other peoples, and they feared the influence which the Jews might exert if their talents and energies were in no wise restricted. France ran no risk in setting fifty thousand Jews free among a population that ran into many millions. But in Holland fifty thousand Jews in a population of two million could give a Jewish tone to the whole country! To add to the difficulty, many of the conservative Jewish leaders were themselves not convinced that emancipation was beneficial. They feared that it would mean the destruction of the Jewish faith. They had seen what havoc had been wrought in several German communities when the young Jewish intellectuals had become absorbed in the "alien" cultures that invited them. Those who fought for Jewish emancipation, therefore, battled on two fronts, against the prejudices of the Dutch and against the fears of the more conservative Jews.

In 1796 the issue came to a climax. The clericals and the other champions of the old order combined to resist all attempts at innovation. The liberals were losing ground and it appeared as if the Jewish cause was lost. French intervention, however, saved the situation; it was made clear to the assembly that emancipation must come. On September 2, 1796 a second great equalization measure was passed and the Jews in Holland became as free as the Jews in France.

3. NAPOLEON BONAPARTE

After 1796 the story of Europe was nearly synonymous with the story of Napoleon Bonaparte, soldier, statesman, despot, adventurer, the most spectacular personality in modern history. Napoleon undoubtedly brought great evils upon the world, draining the man-power of his own country and plunging the rest of Europe into years of strife and bloodshed. Presented with the most amazing opportunities ever vouchsafed to an individual, he kicked them aside to follow the path of selfish glory, until, in the magnificent words of Victor Hugo, " God became bored with him " and brought him to a deserved ignominy at Saint Helena. Yet it would be grossly unfair to deny that he was a factor for immense good as well. Even when pursuing his crassest personal ambitions and wasting enormous numbers of lives, he scattered blessings by destroying mediæval restrictions and outworn institutions.

It is difficult to estimate his personal attitude to Jews. Often he was quite friendly and there are many legends of his benefactions in France and Germany. More often he was distinctly hostile, and a number of his edicts smacked of the spirit of the meanest Jew-baiters. Yet, at least indirectly, his actions had undeniably useful consequences for Jewish life. Wherever his victorious legions came, the walls of the ghetto fell and the Jews walked forth free and unafraid. To this day German Jews look upon him as the father of their emancipation.

He won his first glorious victories in Italy, against the flower of the Austrian forces. He struck with bewildering speed, with deadly accuracy, and within a few months the fairest cities of the peninsula lay at his feet. The Italians greeted him as a saviour, for he had, at least temporarily, destroyed the hold of the hated Austrian. The Jews rained blessings upon him, for he destroyed the barbarities that made their lives miserable. The ghettos fell in Venice, in Livorna, even in Rome, where, in 1775, the benighted Pope Pius VI had again reduced the Jewish community to virtual serfdom.

After his Italian success Napoleon dreamed of a French empire in the East, with Egypt and the Holy Land as a nucleus. Perhaps he would be able to cut the artery that connected England and India and reconquer the lost provinces for France. The jealous Directorate was only too happy to be rid of a popular hero and gave him all the rope he needed with which to hang himself. He transported an army to the East and won several impressive victories, but the project was too vast, even for a Napoleon. Nelson destroyed his fleet and the British navy dogged his heels wherever he attempted to force the issue. For months the little general struggled valiantly against inevitable disaster. He seized upon every straw to bolster up his wobbling structure. There is a persistent newspaper tradition — not authenticated, however — that after capturing Gaza and Jaffa, in 1799, he appealed to the Jews of Asia and Africa to rally to the French standard, promising them a homeland in Palestine when he had completely conquered it. If the appeal had been made, it would have been a spectacular moment in Jewish history. A new world-conqueror was offering the ancient homeland to the Jews as a French protectorate. The Jews were not dazzled, however. They continued to support their sovereign with loyalty, and those who lived in Jerusalem worked feverishly to throw up earthworks to repel Napoleon's invasion.

Late in 1799 Napoleon deserted his army and slipped back to France, where his personal magnetism enabled him to cover his defeats and to make himself master of the country. He soon atoned for the disasters in the East. A rejuvenated French army scattered to the four winds every foe that dared to contest his supremacy. He conquered half of Europe in half a dozen battles. Then he sheathed his sword for a moment to consolidate the fruits of the Revolution in France.

The Jews were now equal before the law, but the outcry against them continued. The Alsatians remained their bitterest critics, for a period of depression had set in and the peasants were at the mercy of their debtors, many of whom were Jews. They besieged Napoleon with tales of Jewish usury, of brutal, inhuman exploitation. Others who bore the Jews no goodwill hinted that the Jews were avoiding conscription. The gifted writers Chateaubriand and Bonald added their dignified philosophic objections to Jewish equality.

At the outset Napoleon was very angry. In his council, early in 1806, he spoke like a Capistrano, repeating the rubbish ten thousand times chewed over by every enemy of the Jews. Jews were not like decent Catholics or Protestants; they were unassimilable; they formed a state within a state; they had no loyalty. Alsace and Strassburg, the keys of France, must not be left in their hands; they were a nation of spies. They ought to be punished or scattered.

Fortunately he was mollified by friendlier members in the council and contented himself by suspending for one year all debts due to Jews in the eastern departments. Then he determined to call together an assembly of Jewish notables from all the provinces under French control for the purpose of getting a promise of civil patriotism, and of putting an end to the " unfair " practices of the Jews. He would revive, he said, " the civic morality of the Jews, lost during the long centuries of a degraded existence."

It was a frightened and thoroughly subservient gathering that met in Paris, in 1806, at his request — a hundred and twelve of the leading Jews of France, Italy, and Germany. Twelve questions were presented to them publicly, dealing with patriotism, social morality, intermarriage, and other national and religious problems. The assembly completely reassured Napoleon, answering all charges with as much ability as dignity. The leaders pledged their loyalty to France and to Napoleon and asserted their determination to enter fully into the life of the country, although they would never sacrifice their loyalty to Jewish traditions.

Now the brilliant imagination of Napoleon seized upon the idea of making the body permanent, modelling it on the ancient Sanhedrin of Temple days. Perhaps such a dramatic move would rally the Jews of the enemy countries to his support. At any rate it would be useful to have a representative Jewish body always at hand through which the Jews of France could be reached for every imperial purpose. The project was enthusiastically received by the French Jews, who were carried away by the romantic thought that the ancient glory of Jewish life was being resurrected.

The first Sanhedrin met in Paris in 1807 and re-emphasized the pledges of loyalty which had been given by the previous assembly. It was not destined to become a permanent body, however. It had no real work to perform and even the emperor, now completely absorbed in a new Prussian war, forgot his early grandiloquent designs. The Sanhedrin therefore died of inanition.

That Napoleon was not motivated by any special love of Jews in these organizing projects was clear from the special legislation which followed the dissolution of the Sanhedrin. Consistories were created in every department which had more than two thousand Jews. These imperial bodies were material aids in regulating religious life, but their primary purpose was to facilitate conscription. Further, by the "infamous decrees," restrictions were placed for ten years on Jewish loans to peasants and new trading-enterprises were forbidden without express permission. In the majority of the departments the Jews obtained exemption from the operation of these measures, but not until thousands of families had been ruined by them. The consistorial organization of Jewish life remained in force until State and Church were separated, in 1905.

So far Napoleon had brought nearly as much evil to the Jews as he had alleviated. During the remainder of his career he proved to be a magnificent Jewish benefactor.

After the collapse of the Third Coalition he carved out of the western German provinces the kingdom of Westphalia and placed his tolerant and well-meaning brother Jerome on the throne. By the royal edict of the new king, issued in 1808, the Westphalian Jews were made full citizens of the new State. Their special taxes were abolished and they were admitted to all means of livelihood. They were then organized into a consistory, on the French model, which was to regulate their congregational activity and to serve as intermediary between them and the government.

From the ruins of the Holy Roman Empire Napoleon created another important unit of government, the Confederation of the Rhine, of which Frankfurt was the centre. Here lived five hundred Jewish families, in mediæval degradation. The Frankfurt ghetto had already been bombarded and partially destroyed during the earlier Napoleonic campaigns in Germany. Now, in 1811, when the duchy of Frankfurt was created, serfdom came to a sudden end and the Jews were made full citizens. The archduke and the populace were violently opposed to the edict, but Napoleon's guns thundered too effectively not to be promptly obeyed. The archduke submitted and was compensated for the loss of his special taxes by a payment of four hundred and forty thousand gulden from the Jewish community.

In most of the other German communities edicts of equality, with some reservations, were also decreed. In Baden all Jews except money-lenders and petty traders were granted citizenship; in Hamburg, Lübeck, Bremen, and other Hanse cities, the restrictions of centuries were abolished as soon as the French troops entered. In the Prussian communities, where Napoleon's influence was much more superficial, the battle for emancipation took longer. The king and his advisers could not overcome their personal animosities. After the humiliation of Jena, however, in 1806, the State was reconstituted by liberal administrators, and many mediæval abuses were swept out in the general cleaning. In 1812, on the eve of the War of Liberation, equality was granted to the Jews, with the qualification that they were not eligible for State offices.

A few German states, however, resisted to the bitter end all efforts to destroy the existing system. Catholic Bavaria, where thirty thousand Jews lived, remained adamant, and when citizenship was extended to the Jews, it was full of restrictions. Saxony, because of its mediæval attitude, became known as the Protestant Spain of the Jews, and even the degrading poll-tax was not abolished until the allied armies compelled its repeal, in 1813.

Meantime the Napoleonic forces spread their conquests to every corner of Europe, and the ancient ghettos continued to fall. Even Spain was affected when Napoleon annexed the Peninsula and placed his brother Joseph upon the throne. The Inquisition was at once destroyed, and, though there were no Jews to be freed, the *marranos* probably breathed easier. In 1820, when complete freedom was decreed, a number of *marrano* families in the Portuguese cities of Lisbon and Oporto openly proclaimed their long-hidden Jewish faith.

The French Revolution and its heir, Napoleon, inaugurated a new era in Jewish history. Despite later reactions, which temporarily rescinded the earlier liberal legislation, the Jews became a definite part of the European world. Henceforth it became the leading motive in Jewish history to readjust Jewish life to the new situation.

Chapter Twenty-two

THE TRIUMPH OF LIBERALISM

I. THE REACTION

THEN came a momentous day in the summer of 1815 when the English and Prussian forces broke through the faltering French lines at Waterloo and shattered the power of the Little Corporal. The drain of the Peninsula campaign, the tremendous pressure of the English blockade, the disastrous expedition to Russia, in which "General Winter and General Hunger" destroyed more than half a million Frenchmen, the rise of a vigorous nationalism in the countries conquered by Napoleon, all combined to bring him from his high estate to the sunset of Saint Helena.

With his fall a great European reaction set in and statesmen drunk on "legitimacy" tried frantically to turn back the clock to 1789. "We are now," said Stein, "in the days of small things and mediocre men." Liberalism, democracy, reform, the gods of the former generation, became anathema. Metternich, the new dictator of Europe, and its vigilant policeman, denounced all change as revolution, "a hydra with open jaws to swallow the social order." Europe needed, he said, quiet and peace, not liberty.

In such an atmosphere it was impossible for a free Jewish life to thrive. The rights which had been painfully won were part of the revolutionary settlement and were trampled down in the general reaction. In most places equality had been grudgingly conceded at the point of the sword, and with the removal of Napoleon it became almost a patriotic task to restore the old conditions. Nor was this all. A new wave of hate swept the Continent. The ordeal of the long war had aroused an intolerant nationalism which brought suspicion upon every alien group. The blows which the Church had received inflamed the clericals and they joined with the nationalists in attacking those who had upset the old order. The Jews, who served as convenient scapegoats, were blamed for unemployment, social derangement, economic distress, the inevitable concomitants of a long war.

The Jewish leaders expected grave reverses when it was planned to undo the Napoleonic settlement. To forestall the changes delegates were chosen in every country to present the case for Jewish rights at the peace conference in Vienna. In Germany several communities united to finance the efforts of a number of Jewish and Christian advocates. Private pressure was also brought to bear upon the statesmen at Vienna, especially by the powerful Rothschild family. In consequence of months of propaganda, no official restrictions were enacted. Indeed, by the principles of the Holy Alliance the rulers solemnly averred that they would be fathers to all their subjects and would rule by the precepts of justice, Christian mercy, and peace.

Yet the pious platitudes of the Congress did not limit the individual states. When a constitution was drawn up for the new German Confederation, a resolution was suggested that "the rights already conceded in the several federated states will be continued." The proposal was strenuously opposed inasmuch as several states had been forced by the French to grant privileges, and the resolution would compel their continuance. A Bremen deputy finally discovered a way out of the difficulty. The word "in" was changed to "by," and all was right. For by the revised clause the rights granted willingly by the states would be continued, but those which were forced upon the states by external pressure would be permitted to lapse.

The old Jewish restrictions now reappeared nearly everywhere in Germany. Almost as soon as French control had disappeared in Frankfurt, the ghetto was re-established and the Jews were again forced to live under the irksome regulations which had embittered their lives for centuries. Lübeck and Bremen at once expelled most of their Jews and deprived the others of civil and political rights.

The cry for repression did not proceed solely from the ignorant classes. Goethe, the choicest spirit of the new Germany, was a leader in the movement of 1823 to reimpose humiliating disabilities upon the Jews of Saxe-Weimar. Professor Ruhs, from the newly-organized University of Berlin, advocated the restoration of the mediæval badge, "that the German who could not recognize his Hebrew enemy by face, gait, or speech might do so by the doubtful badge of honour." A rabid Teutomania developed idealizing a Christian Germany and warring upon "the godless" and "the soulless."

There was no constitutional way of fighting the obscurantism. All liberal movements were sternly forbidden. The Prussian king decreed that all constitutional projects must be left to his "paternal solicitude." With every lawful avenue of protest closed, the liberals inevitably turned to revolution. Many Jews were prominent among these enemies of reaction, and an orgy of Jew-baiting began, encouraged by the authorities. In Würzburg the cry was raised: "Hep, hep" ("*Hierosolyma est perdita* — Jerusalem is destroyed"), and Jews were beaten and robbed. It spread through Franconia, through all Germany, echoes reaching as far as Copenhagen. Four years after the Holy Alliance had pledged itself to Christian conduct, Germany was visited by every mediæval outrage, — and killing, pillaging, burning. In Heidelberg the criminal raper of a Jewish maiden was freed by an infuriated mob. As late as 1840 there was a ritual murder case in a Prussian community!

In the polyglot Austrian empire the situation was nearly as tragic. Here the reaction had begun almost as soon as the enlightened Joseph II had been laid in his grave. After Waterloo, repression was elevated into a system of government, and Metternich, who was personally not unfriendly to Jews, closed his eyes while all the miserable disabilities of Maria Theresa's day were restored. Some very wealthy and influential Jews escaped the general ignominy. But the masses suffered in darkness; they were forced back into ghettos and confined to narrow filthy " Jew streets." In the Tyrol and in the mountain villages of Bohemia Jews were excluded and in the great cities of Moravia they could only remain overnight.

In Italy the brief period of freedom established by Napoleon came to an end all too soon. Pope Pius VII dedicated himself to remove every vestige of French "infidelity," the Inquisition was restored, and a strict censorship was re-established. Miracle-working, eye-winking madonnas again gave audiences. It was even proposed to destroy a bridge over the Po because Napoleon had built it. The Jews were thrust out of their new homes into the ghetto along the Tiber, and the old restrictions were again restored, with the Argus-eyed inquisitors to enforce them. Every wretched device was used by the papacy to gain converts; it was not considered unseemly to introduce even the conversion sermon to which Jews were regularly compelled to listen. In 1848 there was a breath of hope when Pius IX, a liberal and broad-minded statesman, received the papal tiara. But his moment of liberalism soon passed too and he became as much a tyrant as his predecessors had been.

In Spain the restoration of Ferdinand, with " the heart of a tiger and the head of a mule," naturally carried with it the restoration of the Inquisition; as late as 1826 a Quaker and a *marrano* suffered martyrdom together for their beliefs. Even when the Inquisition was abolished, the clericals remained supreme until the close of the century and by their intolerance continued the spiritual imprisonment of their country.

Thus the world which was remade by the Treaty of Vienna promised only new sorrows for the Jews. Europe needed time, it was clear, to regain its sanity after the long travail of war and hate. Meantime the reaction helped to renew Jewish solidarity. Thousands of Jews in every Western country, intoxicated by the freedom which followed the Revolution, had rushed to take advantage of their new opportunities. Many of them severed all connexions with their people and sought to identify themselves completely with the European world, but the persecutions which followed the fall of Napoleon did not discriminate between the assimilated and the unassimilated. The cry of " Hep, hep" was hurled at both. Those who had left the fold now looked wistfully back. With all its sorrows, the old life seemed to promise more peace, more stability. The weary and the disillusioned who had sought to escape began to turn again to their people.

2. THE BATTLE AGAINST REACTION

All of the repression after Waterloo, the thirty years' war on liberalism, did not crush the revolutionary spirit. It merely drove it underground. Movements for national freedom, combined with movements for constitutional liberty, agitated every country. In Italy the fervid eloquence of Mazzini made a new religion of nationalism, and Young Italy, which he organized and which embodied his ideals, set the heart of the nation on fire. The Burschenschaften attempted to waken the slumbering spirits of patriotic Germans, and brave young souls strove to end the reproach that Germany, like Italy, was a mere geographical expression. In Hungary, Kossuth became the apostle of the aspirations of his people and led the struggle for freedom against the Austrian "charnel-house." Every country had its revolutionary heroes, and, while they could only express themselves through secret societies or through abortive rebellions, their influence grew steadily. Time was surely on their side.

In the revolutionary movements the Jews played no unimportant role. Circumstances made them liberal; the black reaction in every country drove them into the ranks of those who opposed the existing regime. By training and temperament, too, most of the Jewish leaders opposed the suppression of constitutional and national liberties. A people with their history could as soon believe in the miracles of saints as in autocracy. They were therefore prominent in every movement which led to the revolutions of 1830 and 1848. Sometimes they were associated with the middle-class struggle for democratic reform, sometimes with the working-class struggle for radical social reform, or again with the nationalists in their attempts to win independence or autonomy. In any case they met on common ground in their animosity to the bigotry and narrowness of reactionaries in every camp.

Of course there were prominent Jews among the conservatives as well, but their conservatism had no kinship with the current reaction. Disraeli, a converted Jew, who rose from the humblest ranks to "the top of the greased pole," the English prime-ministership, after the most sensational career in Victorian history, served for years as the Tory leader. But his Toryism was truly enlightened. He laboured to remove disabilities, he devoted pen and tongue to better working-conditions, he educated his party to make social legislation their distinctive program. Near the end of his premiership, speaking of the long battle against the slums and disease, he could say jocularly: "*Sanitas, sanitatum, omnia sanitas.*" He left his party as truly liberal as the Liberal party.

One of the most interesting of the great liberals of the nineteenth century was Heinrich Heine, "the wicked favourite of the Graces and Muses." He is known primarily for his beautiful poetry, for lyrics which have become immortal, and for a sparkling prose style which helped to break down the lumbering literary methods of many of his contemporaries. Yet his political contribution was by no means meagre. His keen and brilliant wit cut into every type of political despotism and intellectual repression. He asked, with justice, before he died, that a sword be placed upon his grave, "for I was a soldier in the war for liberalism." Matthew Arnold's famous epigram bears repeating:

> The spirit of the world
> Beholding the absurdity of men, —
> Their vaunts, their feats, — let a sardonic smile,
> For one short moment, wander o'er his lips.
> *That smile was Heine!*

The famous poet was born in Düsseldorf, Germany, in 1797, of comfortable middle-class Jewish parents. He grew to manhood in the midst of the revolutionary enthusiasm of a generation which evoked extravagant adulation from Wordsworth:

> Bliss was it in that dawn to be alive,
> But to be young was very Heaven!

Though he received very little Jewish training (his education had been irregularly conducted by French free-thinkers and Jesuits!), he loved the ancient Jewish traditions and denounced the rationalists who worked with their "chiropody" upon the body of Judaism, cutting away its very life. "They wish to pour the ocean into a neat little hand-basin." Some of his most exquisite writings, especially the *Confessions,* are an eloquent testimonial to the genuineness of his Jewish loyalty. For some years he struggled to satisfy his ambitions for a career without deserting Judaism. But when this was impossible, when it became plain that "Judaism was not a religion, but a misfortune," he succumbed, declaring that he was "merely baptized, not converted." "If the law had permitted the stealing of spoons," he said, "I should not have been baptized." The step, he soon learned, helped him very little. "I am hated alike by Jew and Christian," he wrote in 1826. "I regret very deeply that I had myself baptized. I do not see that I have been the better for it since. On the contrary I have known nothing but misfortune and mischances."

All his life the "German Aristophanes" stormed and fretted against existing institutions. His tongue knew no restraint. One moment he was intensely reverent, writing in a spirit which overflowed with delicate sentiment, the next he approached the blasphemous in his acid denunciations of religion and religious hypocrites. "God will forgive me, however; it is His business!" The profundity of his ironic analyses was almost hidden beneath his easy, fluent, flippant style. "An Englishman," he wrote, "loves liberty like his lawfully wedded wife. She is a possession; he may not treat her with much tenderness, but he knows how to defend her. A Frenchman loves liberty like his sweetheart, and he will do a thousand follies for her sake. A German loves liberty like his old grandmother.

And yet, after all, no one can tell how things will turn out. The grumpy Englishman, in an ill temper with his wife, is capable of dragging her by a rope to Smithfield. The inconstant Frenchman may become unfaithful to his adored and be off flirting round the Palais Royal with another. But the German will never quite desert his old grandmother; he will always keep for her a nook near the chimney-corner where she can tell fairy-tales to the listening children."

Heine's wicked tongue and impertinent daring raised up innumerable enemies, who never ceased to plague him. Prussia has boycotted his writings to the present day, for he looked upon the towering giant of the North as the evil genius of Germany. "I do not trust these Prussians, these long, pietistic heroes of the spick and span uniform, with their wide stomachs, big mouths, and corporal's clubs dipped into holy water preparatory to striking." Most of his life he remained an exile, living on the meagre proceeds of his writings and on pensions from his uncle and the French government. He was subject to physical ills, brought on by his nervous dissipations, and he died in his prime after eight dreadful but courageous years of suffering on a "mattress grave." No one influenced the new liberal Germany in literature and politics more than he. He was, as he yearned to be, a soldier in the war of liberation, undisciplined, as likely to fire into his own ranks as into his enemy's, but brave and loyal to the core.

Another powerful influence in laying bare the shame of post-Waterloo Europe was Karl Ludwig Börne, whose career in many ways resembled Heine's. He came of a well-to-do middle-class family and was prepared for a professional career. He was early drawn into a remarkable intellectual group in Berlin; under their influence he abandoned his professional ambitions and determined to devote himself to literature. He was gifted with a keen, virile, incisive style, which he employed in the cause of freedom for more than twenty years. His work earned him an important place in the history of German journalism.

Though he had left the Jewish faith soon after he passed his thirtieth year, he, like Heine, never tired of assaulting the bigotry of his generation. "German minds," he wrote, " dwell on Alpine heights; but German hearts pant in damp marshes." "What you call human rights, which, it must be conceded, you grant Jews, are only animal rights. The rights of seeking food, of devouring it, of sleeping, of multiplying, are enjoyed also by the beasts of the field — until they are slain, and to the Jews you grant no more."

Soon after his conversion, in 1818, Börne became editor of *Die Wage,* in which he presented his advanced views on contemporary art, literature, and politics. His writings created a sensation and he was compelled to conduct a continuous guerrilla warfare with the ever vigilant censor. The revolution in France in 1830 fired him to his most enduring work. He wrote his famous *Letters from Paris,* in which he struck at every social and intellectual abuse and pleaded for a new Germany, freed from kings and lords and other tyrants and united in amicable relationship with the reborn France. The *Letters* roused a storm, and he was denounced as more French than German, but those who rushed into the arena with him found themselves pinned by his deadly shafts. The statue on his grave, done by the sculptor David, tells the true story of his place in the Liberation movement. Beside the head of Börne is a relief which represents France and Germany extending hands to each other, under the blessing of the goddess Freedom.

Gabriel Riesser was another liberal who ate the rotten political system in his bread. He differed from both Heine and Börne in remaining loyal to Judaism, though he was never very much interested in its formal doctrines. His own dreary struggle to make headway as a jurist and as a professor roused him to the seriousness of the Jewish disabilities. When success came to him at last, he toiled to emancipate his people and won some notable local victories in Hesse and other German provinces. It was due to his influence that Jewish rights became part of the liberal platform of Young Germany.

Riesser saw clearly that the forces which opposed the modest claims of his people were the same forces which opposed liberalism in broader fields. The enemies of one were the common enemies of all. He became one of the most active leaders in the Young German party. The vice-presidency of the first German national assembly, which was bestowed upon him in the "mad year" 1848, was a deserved tribute to his selfless service in the battle to destroy the old despotic forms in which he had been reared.

3. THE TRIUMPH OF LIBERALISM

In 1848 Europe was literally drenched with revolutions. The liberal laws, so long boiling and bubbling beneath the earth, suddenly burst through the craters and surged out in all directions. The white-haired Metternich, who symbolized the old order, was compelled to flee in disguise to England. Nearly every state in Europe was reorganized and it appeared as if the long battle for constitutional freedom was ended at last. Reaction died hard, however. It required two decades more before the revolutionary settlement became permanent. By 1870 nearly every state was regulated by a liberal constitution and men's lives and destinies were no longer at the mercy of a despot's caprice.

In France the Jews had already in the thirties attained full political manhood. Most of the old Bourbon restrictions were swept out by the Revolution of 1830, which brought to the throne the genial and well-meaning idol of the bourgeoisie, Louis Philippe. A resolution was soon introduced and passed through the Chamber which placed Judaism on an equal footing with the two Christian creeds. In 1830 it was further enacted that rabbis and rabbinical institutions were to be maintained by the government, and the arrangement was continued until State and Church were separated, in 1905.

The German states followed much more slowly. Despite the strivings of Young Germany, liberalism could not seem to get a strong foothold. Even the national heroes who had helped to destroy Napoleon's power were persecuted. In Prussia, Frederick William IV set his face like flint against all talk of constitutions. "No sheet of written paper shall ever thrust itself, like a second Providence, between God in heaven and this land." Then suddenly, in 1848, the foundations of every state were violently shaken by the revolutions which swept the country, and constitutions were hastily granted by the terrified kings and princelings. The Jews were included in the privileges which were distributed. They were elected to parliaments and joined in the deliberations which sought a solution to the new constitutional problems. Next year came a sharp reaction, and most of the democratic innovations which had been granted under coercion were quickly annulled. But it was impossible to return to the Middle Ages and to rescind the principle of religious freedom. Though Germany remained disunited and under autocratic governments until 1870, no distinctions were drawn between races and creeds.

The middle of the century also inaugurated an era of immense material prosperity, and with no restrictions to hamper initiative several hundred thousand Jews faced the future with new hope. During the regency of William, afterwards the first emperor of the new German state, Jews were identified with every important enterprise and they became a powerful element in the bourgeoisie. Though there were occasional outbursts against them, their position could no longer be challenged. The time had passed for ever when a whole people could be sent flying from the country because of a wave of popular hatred.

In Austria there was a temporary liberal regime when the revolution of 1848 drove Metternich out of the country. Religious freedom was proclaimed, the ghettos were abolished, special Jewish taxes disappeared, and in the first Parliament the grey-bearded rabbi Meisels of Galicia, with *caftan* and *streimel,* deliberated side by side with prominent Christian deputies. But the next year brought a woeful reaction. Autocracy quickly recovered its strength and sternly repressed every vestige of liberalism. In Germany, despite the reaction, the Jews had been left in possession of their privileges; but in Austria there were no such dispensations. In a land ruled by firing squads and martial law, drill-sergeants and spies, and unforgiving clericals, one was fortunate to preserve life and property. Only when Austrian military power was crippled in the Italian wars, and the prestige of the clericals had been irreparably shattered, did the government yield to the spirit of the day. A new constitution, the *Ausgleich,* was proclaimed in 1867, and it became the Magna Charta for minority races. The Jews could now live everywhere in the land; they were made eligible for all positions, and eventually they were admitted even into the hereditary nobility.

Hungary, which had always been a rebellious member of the Austrian confederation, seized the opportunity in 1848, when the governing State was beset by internal and external troubles, to strike for freedom. The Magyars struck quickly and their early successes terrified the Austrian emperor. The Hungarian Jews readily joined in the rebellion. About twenty thousand served loyally in the Hungarian armies, and a Jewish battalion fought with distinction against the Croatians, in the critical days of 1848-9. Kossuth, the Hungarian national leader, strongly favoured Jewish equality, and in the first Hungarian national assembly, in July 1849, complete civil and political rights were granted to them, "wiping out the enormous debt owed to the heroic descendants of the illustrious Maccabeans." But, as in Austria, their Cinderella dreams soon turned to rags. Nicholas I of Russia helped his kinsman Francis Joseph to suppress the Hungarian uprising, and, with its collapse, the Jews were reduced to the status of their Austrian brethren. They remained bondsmen for another two decades, until the *Ausgleich* gave autonomy to Hungary. Then, at last, the Jews were released from all restrictions. Official equality was proclaimed when, in 1895-6, Judaism was recognized as one of the legal religions of the country.

In the Italian peninsula freedom came to the Jews, as to the Italians themselves, by piecemeal. For half a century after Waterloo the unhappy country lay in the grip of reaction — the north in the hands of Austria, "the fire department of Italy"; the south in the hands of the vile Bourbon despots; and the central states in the hands of the papacy. The Italian patriots never lost hope, however, and unity and democracy were achieved, province by province, through the astute statesmanship of Count Cavour and the buccaneering courage of Garibaldi. Wherever these epic heroes triumphed, the darkness lifted for the Jews. Freedom came first in northern Italy when Austria was expelled, in 1859. It came in Naples and Sicily when Garibaldi and his gallant red-shirts drove out the hated king. Rome held out for another decade, and Pope Pius IX gave Europe an example of bigotry which paralleled the days of Innocent III. In 1858, in the infamous Mortara case, he prevented the restoration to Jewish parents of a child who had been secretly baptized by a Christian servant. He continued the ghettos and the conversion sermons and a score of other harsh restrictions until 1871, when the Papal States were wrested from the Church. Then, at last, the country was united under a liberal, democratic king. The Jews began at once to play an important part in Italian political and intellectual life. Within a generation Ernesto Nathan, a Jew, was elected mayor of the Eternal City, and Luigi Luzzatti rose to one of the highest positions in the State when he took charge of the Treasury portfolio.

The Jews of England had not suffered from intolerable restrictions on trade or residence. Their situation was perhaps the most favourable in all Europe.

But along with Dissenters and Catholics they were deprived of many civil rights. They were denied admission to the bar, high rank in the Army and Navy, the right to hold important municipal offices and to sit in Parliament, and admission to a degree at Oxford or Cambridge. Most of the civil disabilities were removed before Queen Victoria came to the throne, in 1837. But admission to the House of Commons, the symbol of complete political emancipation, was for twenty-five years longer made impossible by the oath "on the true faith of a Christian" which Parliament required of all members. Prejudice, indifference to the claims of a small and uninfluential minority, and the fiction of a Christian state, were the chief obstacles. Year by year emancipation bills were passed in the House of Commons, where Macaulay, Russell, Disraeli, and other leaders of both parties spoke eloquently for the Jewish claims. Macaulay poured ridicule on the stupid futility of the existing system which gave the Jew all the substance of power, but denied him the shadow — "the maces, and gold chains, and skins of parchment with pieces of wax dangling from their edges." The Jew could make members of Parliament, he said, or East Indian directors, through his control of boroughs, but he could not pass the bar of the House, or sit down on the mysterious cushions of green leather and cry out: "Hear, hear!" Despite the eloquence of the leading debaters in the Commons, the House of Lords held out obstinately until 1858. It finally became a nuisance to the Tory party to have the unsettled issue disturbing the relations of the two Houses. So principle eventually gave way to persistence and the Lords yielded to expediency what they would not yield to argument. Lionel Rothschild became the first Jewish member to sit in the Commons, more than a decade after he had been first elected. Later Lionel's son was admitted even into the exclusive ranks of the peerage, and the Prince of Wales, the later King Edward VII, attended a Rothschild wedding in a Jewish synagogue. In 1871 Jews and Dissenters were admitted to the degree in Oxford and Cambridge, and the last relics of exclusion disappeared. The veneered and fastidious society of the mid-Victorian period would have been amazed to witness twentieth-century developments, when Lord Reading, formerly Sir Rufus Isaacs, became the ruler of the Indian empire with its teeming millions, and Sir Herbert Samuel arbitrated the disputes of races and religions as the High Commissioner of His Majesty in the Holy Land.

4 · THE INDUSTRIAL AND FINANCIAL REVOLUTIONS

Meantime there were even more basic upheavals in the economic and social order which profoundly altered the lives of all men. An astonishing number of inventions harnessed the forces of nature and substituted machines for the nimblest of hands. Industry moved out of homes into factories, population more than doubled, cities grew into busy metropolises, new comforts and luxuries came within the reach of the common man. Above all, production increased a hundredfold and the whole world became the manufacturers' market.

The Industrial Revolution gave added significance to capital, which was indispensable to support and expand a myriad of projected undertakings. A new class came into existence, the capitalists, eager to invest their savings in factories and mines, in workshops, railroads, and steamships, in every enterprise which promised a secure profit and a quick turnover. Thousands of these captains of industry amassed riches as a consequence of their daring and they became the nucleus of a new nobility. "Chimney aristocrats," they were at first contemptuously called, but they wielded enormous economic power and gradually they supplanted the ancient landed aristocracy.

In all of these changes the long-repressed Jews found remarkable opportunities to test their talents. For the new society was little concerned with hoary feudal restrictions. An enterprise which required capital did not probe into the religion or the social background of those who could supply it. A hard-pressed foreman who was short of workers did not stop to examine the racial antecedents of those who had willing hands and who could be of immediate service. In a period of expanding capitalism inherited prejudices were not permitted to interfere with profits, and they were conveniently pushed into the background. Economic changes were therefore more crucial in winning political equality for Jews than all the glittering generalities about the rights of man and the sanctity of human personality.

Some Jewish families, notably the Rothschilds, became powerful enough to influence European history. Indeed, their political strength sometimes brought the criticism that the Jews formed cliques to control international finance. The charge was not true. The Jews were not disproportionately represented among the capitalists and the bankers, nor was there co-operation among them. Heine's famous jest that the Foulds and the Rothschilds were the rabbis of finance, opposed to each other as strenuously as the House of Shammai and the House of Hillel, was a commentary on the rivalries which divided all Jewish concerns.

Yet there were enough well-established Jewish families in each country ultimately to affect the political position of the Jews. Usually when they had achieved financial strength, they turned to relieve the disabilities of their people, and their powerful advocacy won precious concessions. The Montefiores, the Goldsmids, and the Salomons in England, the Pereires in France, the Bischoffsheims in Germany, the Rothschilds everywhere in Europe, were typical products of the industrial and financial revolutions whose intercession in the battle for Jewish emancipation was often decisive. Lord Macaulay put it bluntly in the House of Commons when he pleaded for the right of Jews to sit in Parliament: " How was it possible to deny a Rothschild a seat on the grounds of his race when his signature on the back of a piece of paper was worth more than the royal word of three kings! " By the third quarter of the nineteenth century Jewish political equality had been won in nearly every western European country.

Less spectacular but even more important than the success of the Rothschilds was the changed status of the great Jewish middle class. Thousands of enterprising Jews in every country took advantage of the dissolution of the feudal system to shake off the more or less degraded means of livelihood which had long limited them. They were among the pioneers in the tremendously accelerated international trade which followed the expansion of production. They helped to build the bustling city life of the new commercial and industrial world. All the restrictions which reactionary governments placed upon their enterprise could not now retard their progress.

Just as the Industrial Revolution created capitalist entrepreneurs, it also brought into being a huge proletarian population, concentrated in the larger cities, who soon developed a keen class consciousness. They realized that they could not rely for the defence of their rights upon the sense of justice or fair play of their employers. If they were to obtain concessions in wages and working conditions they would have to fight for them. Hence they began to organize into unions and guilds to protect themselves against possible exploitation.

There were large numbers of Jews in this labouring group who shared the hazards and the insecurities of their fellow workers. Many came to feel that their economic interests were more binding than their religious loyalties. Often they were extremely critical of traditional Jewish observances. The more radical among them went so far as to dismiss church and synagogue as bourgeois superstitions or as instruments deliberately created by their economic masters to keep labour in leash. But even those who did not break with the religion of their fathers were deeply affected by the new ways of living. As the old domestic economy was displaced by the factory system, it was found increasingly difficult to maintain the Sabbath and the Jewish holidays in the traditional way. Competition and the exigencies of the new commerce made inroads upon rigorous orthodox practices. Gradually, in western Europe, the dietary laws and other time-hallowed customs began to drop away and the traditional Jewish home lost its vitality.

Out of the inevitable conflict of labour and capital a fiercely militant proletarian philosophy emerged, Socialism, which sharply attacked the existing order and sought to substitute for it a system of production for use rather than for profit. The father of this philosophy, which was destined completely to change modern history, was a dour, plodding, scientific-minded German, Karl Marx, who came from a well-to-do Jewish family. Marx's uncompromising criticism of capitalist sanctities was responsible for his exile from his native land. Most of his life he spent in penury in the libraries of France and England. From his painstaking research he created his ponderous magnum opus, *Das Kapital*, which was destined to become the Bible of the Socialist Utopia.

Marx was mainly a closet philosopher. His genius lay in the devastating logic with which he deduced his principles from revolutionary axioms. Men of action were required to turn his dialectic into social realities. Among these was the brilliant Ferdinand Lassalle, who forged the theories of the British Museum book-worm into the powerful Social Democratic parties of continental Europe. Lassalle was the son of a wealthy Jewish merchant of Breslau. He lived only thirty-nine years; he was killed in a duel over a quixotic love-affair at the very climax of his career. But in his narrow span of life he created a potent working-class movement in Germany which later mightily influenced the destiny of all the Western nations. Bismarck began to wonder, as he noted the reformer's great strength, whether the future of Germany would be under the ægis of the Hohenzollerns or the Lassalles!

The fact that Marx and Lassalle sprang from the Jewish group was neither forgotten nor forgiven by anti-Semitic detractors, who inevitably linked all forms of radicalism with the Jews. Yet Marx's family had been early converted to Christianity and young Karl was reared in the adopted faith of his parents. Some of his bitterest diatribes were reserved for Jews and Judaism. At the beginning of his career Lassalle was, indeed, determined to help free the Jewish people from the degrading status to which obscurantist governments condemned them. His youthful diary records a loyalty which ran into chauvinism. But later he too dissociated himself completely from Jewish life. The redemption of his own people became infinitely less important than the redemption of the workers of the world.

In truth, there was nothing specifically " Jewish " about Socialism or Capitalism or any economic philosophy, just as there was nothing specifically " Jewish " about the mathematics of Einstein or the physics of Michelson. Many Jews who were sympathetic to Socialism took pride in the achievements of Marx and Lassalle just as many Jews who were completely unsympathetic found no occasion to wax enthusiastic over their achievements. But demagogues were not usually inhibited by facts, and the Jewish origins of Marx, Lassalle, and other creators of Socialism were to play a crucial part in the anti-Semitic movements of modern history.

Labour and capital continued their battle for position and advantage all through the nineteenth and part of the twentieth century. In countries like Russia, Italy, Germany, and the Balkans the struggle was uncompromising, and extremists in both camps won the major victories. But in Britain, France, Switzerland, Holland, Belgium, and the Scandinavian countries the struggle did not jeopardize the steadily growing strength of political democracy, whose acids dissolved many of the restrictions of the old feudal system. Citizenship became a right and not a privilege. Freedom of speech, freedom of press, right of assembly, all became cherished bulwarks, warmly defended by the vast majorities of the population.

In such an environment the Jews, like all minority groups, found it possible to complete their Europeanization. The old order which had segregated them without the pale of civilized life now seemed far, far away. Here was a new world which called for the talents of the individual man who, regardless of faith or creed or race, could develop his potentialities and take whatever places he could win by competition. Jews could now set forth with courage, with heads held high, to build their homes in peace and security. They did not dream that the new order was only a respite, a strange interlude for a brief century; that it depended upon the vicissitudes of the new economic system. In the twentieth century there was to be another violent social revolution which would smash most of the rights which had been so painfully won. But for the moment there was only buoyant optimism. Democracy was the dominant philosophy of the day. Buttressed by the strength of the Industrial Revolution, its permanence seemed as assured as the sun and the stars in the firmament.

CHAPTER TWENTY-THREE

FACTORS IN AMERICAN JEWISH HISTORY

How came they here? What burst of Christian hate,
What persecution merciless and blind,
Drove o'er the sea — the desert desolate —
These Ishmaels and Hagars of mankind?
            Longfellow: *In A Jewish Cemetery at Newport*

THE history of the Jews in America is the history of three distinct tides of immigration. Soon after the New World was opened to European adventurers, the Sephardic group came, some directly from Inquisition-ridden Spain and Portugal, others by way of doughty little Holland, and still others by way of the South American settlements. This first group was not very large, however, and for more than three hundred years the Jewish element in America remained negligible. With the dawn of the nineteenth century a steady German immigration began, swelling perceptibly after the reaction of the post-Waterloo era and the failure of the liberal revolutions of 1848. Finally came the Polish-Russian-Roumanian group, a thin stream in the sixties, and then a veritable flood after the May laws in Russia in the eighties. The Slavic immigrants, who numbered more than two and a half million by the outbreak of the World War, completely submerged the other groups and deeply influenced American Jewish life.

All of this immigration came without let or hindrance to American shores. Until the cataclysm of 1914 the United States welcomed the immigrant and drew no distinctions between sect or creed or country of origin. It interpreted freedom liberally, without reference to race theories or a cephalic index. All peoples found in America as ideal a land as could be imagined, endowed by nature with every richness and generously offering this bounty to those who came for it. It has been often observed that Europe passed so peacefully through the dislocations of the long industrial revolution because the discontented could always migrate to America.

To the Jews, particularly in the nineteenth century, America became the Promised Land. Unhampered by disabilities, they developed with the country and grew strong with its strength. They became passionate defenders of its institutions and served it loyally in every crisis. Their contribution to the complex product known as American civilization pointed a significant moral to those who were blind to the relationship between freedom and loyalty.

I. THE FOUNDATIONS OF AMERICAN DEMOCRACY

America was discovered in the very year in which the Jews were expelled from Spain; three hundred thousand Jews sorrowfully left their ancestral homes on August 2, and on August 3 Columbus began his memorable trip westward. It was almost as if one haven was providentially opened as another was closed. Several Jews were associated, directly and indirectly, with the voyages of discovery. The researches of Jewish geographers and astronomers, notably Abraham Zacuto, rendered Columbus immense service and on one occasion saved his crew. The expenses of the expedition were met not, as the romantic story has it, by the pawning of Queen Isabella's crown jewels, but by treasures derived from confiscated Jewish property and by the loans of *marrano* financiers. Luis de Santángel, one of the royal treasurers, furnished seventeen thousand florins to equip the expedition. Several men of Jewish origin were among the crew of Columbus, and it is said that the first to land on American soil was Luis de Torres, the *marrano* interpreter.

In the first century after the discoveries numbers of Jews and *marranos* came, with glowing hopes, to the New World. Like other pioneers, many of them were lured on by fame and adventure and by the dreams of wondrous El Dorados. But the majority turned westward because of the persecutions which gave them no respite in Europe. The flight from persecution has ever since been the dominating motive in Jewish immigration.

The earliest Jewish settlements were made in the Spanish and Portuguese dominions of South America, Mexico, and the West Indies. Only *marranos* could come, however; professing Jews were strictly forbidden on Spanish soil, and, after 1508, on Portuguese soil. The *marranos* were compelled to keep their Judaism hidden, for the Inquisition had ten thousand eyes and, towards the end of the sixteenth century, was already burning heretics and relapsed Christians. The number of victims rose steadily, and in 1639 sixty-three *marranos* were condemned and ten were burnt at the stake in one ecclesiastical orgy, whose preparation involved enormous expense and fifty days of uninterrupted labour! Among those burnt were Manuel Perez, reputed to be the wealthiest man in Peru, at whose death an immense fortune passed into the coffers of the State.

The effectiveness of the Inquisition in Brazil came to an end when the Dutch seized the country in 1631. The tolerant policy of the conquerors attracted an important community of *marranos* to the leading city, Recife or Pernambuco. Many of the new-comers took the opportunity to throw off their mask and to declare their Jewish faith openly. The community grew to several thousand, with a congregation and a vigorous Jewish life. Its fame spread to the Old World, and Manasseh ben Israel dedicated the second part of his *Conciliador* to the Jewish leaders of the fortunate city. The Jews watched carefully over the independence of the State and were frantic as the Portuguese planned to reconquer it. Its capture would snuff out their security, perhaps their lives and fortunes. Their fears were fully justified, for upon renewal of warfare the Portuguese were finally victorious, in 1654. The Jewish population scattered at once throughout the territories of the New World.

Yet, despite all restrictions and a troubled history, a number of the Jews became wealthy and controlled many of the large sugar plantations in South America and the West Indies. Indeed, it is probable that sugar-cane was first transplanted from the island of Madeira to Brazil by Portuguese Jews. After 1654 the Jews transferred their activity to the Barbados, Jamaica, Martinique, and Santo Domingo, largely increasing the sugar production in these islands.[1]

The history of the Jews in the United States begins with their settlement in New Amsterdam, later New York. A group of twenty-three refugees from Pernambuco arrived in 1654, in the *St. Catarina,* so impoverished that their personal effects were sold to pay for their passage. Peter Stuyvesant, the brusque old governor of the colony, was at first unwilling to give the poor derelicts permission to land. Later he was ordered to do so by the Dutch East India Company, several of whose important stockholders were Jews. Stuyvesant, however, continued to put obstacles in the way of the despised settlers, and for long they enjoyed no more than the right to shelter. But one aggressive young Jew, Asser Levy, fought Stuyvesant's edicts to a finish, and his appeals to Holland were usually upheld. Levy won the right to serve as a soldier, to trade, to own real estate, and even to share in the privileges of the community as a burgher. Within ten years of his arrival in the colony Levy had become one of its most influential and popular citizens. Levy's rights, however, were not shared by his people. When the English captured the territory, in 1664, they made few changes in the status of the Jews. Up to 1727 no Jew could be naturalized, and in 1737 the New York Assembly decided that Jews could not vote for assemblymen.

In the New England colonies Jews lived in inconsequential numbers, enjoying economic freedom, though not sharing in political life. Even the Pilgrims, themselves hunted and persecuted, set up sharp barriers between Christian and Jew, and their intolerance made the establishment of Jewish communities well-nigh impossible. Yet most of their laws were based squarely upon the Old Testament and were often taken verbatim from its codes.[2]

When Roger Williams was forced to leave Massachusetts because of his religious convictions, he established a colony in Rhode Island upon the principle of tolerance for all groups. Even here some distinction was drawn between Jews and Christians, and the General Assembly ordained in 1684, referring to the Jewish settlement: "They may expect as good protection here as any stranger,

---

[1] Jacobs: *Jewish Contributions to Civilization,* p. 223.

[2] " One can form some opinion of the measure of Old Testament influence when one considers that in the code of colony laws adopted in New Haven in 1656 there are 107 references to the Old Testament to 29 to the New, and of the latter 5 are of an ecclesiastical character." *Jewish Encyclopedia,* XII, 364.

being not of our nation, residing among us in His Majesty's colony, ought to have, being obedient to His Majesty's laws." Yet Rhode Island was the most tolerant community in the world, and Jews came in numbers to Newport and Providence, its chief cities. Their leading spirit was Aaron Lopez, one of the most prominent merchants of the period, who carried on an extensive West Indian trade. Ezra Stiles, later president of Yale College, said of him: "For honor and extent of commerce he was probably surpassed by no merchant of America." The famous Newport settlement did not flourish undisturbed, however. In the Revolutionary War the Jewish traders sided with the colonists, and when the city was captured by the British, the Jews lost their ships and their cargoes.

There is virtually no early Jewish history in the southern colonies, for only a few individuals drifted into the territory before the Revolution. Georgia is the only exception. Soon after the colony was founded by Oglethorpe, in 1733, forty Jewish immigrants arrived; they were heartily welcomed by the liberal-minded governor, though he knew that the trustees of the colony were not anxious to have Jewish settlers. One of the oldest Jewish congregations in America grew up in Savannah.

Up to the Revolution there were scarcely twenty-five hundred Jews in the whole country, and American Jewish history was largely the history of prominent individuals. The immigrants were usually of Sephardic stock, who came by way of England, happy to find golden opportunities in the New World. They were strangers in most communities and were obliged to submit to some limited political disabilities. But life and labour were free and secure; no one feared the morrow. In contrast with the situation in Europe, America was a paradise.

Most of the original settlers were wealthy merchants, with important trade connexions in England. Yet, when the troubles began which led to the Revolution, there were few loyalists among the Jews. They joined with the other colonists in opposing British imperial methods, and a number of Jewish names appear on the non-importation resolutions of 1765 and 1769. Ministers who justified the rebellion drew much of their inspiration from Old Testament texts. The historian Lecky suggests that "Hebraic mortar cemented the foundations of American democracy." About one hundred Jews served in the Continental armies, and, since they were drawn from a cultured and wealthy group, there was a disproportionate number of officers among them, some of very high rank.

One of the most interesting personalities of this period was Haym Salomon, a Jewish merchant who, after the first partition of Poland, migrated to the United States and settled in New York. When the American Revolution began, he was arrested as a spy by the British and was confined for two years. He escaped in 1778 and settled in Philadelphia, where he established a banking-house and became one of the country's leading financiers. Robert Morris, who superintended the colonial finances, relied almost solely upon Salomon to keep up the credit of the struggling young republic. The Polish exile also served as chief financial agent of the French, and he carried through the negotiations for war subsidies from France and Holland.

Salomon took a keen interest in the careers of the leading colonial statesmen. When James Madison was hard pressed for funds, Salomon insisted upon relieving his embarrassments. "I have for some time past been a pensioner on the favor of Haym Salomon, a Jew broker," writes the future President. ". . . The kindness of our little friend in Front street, near the coffee house, is a fund which will preserve me from extremities, but I never resort to it without great mortification, as he obstinately rejects all recompense. The price of money is so usurious that he thinks it ought to be extracted from none but those who aim at profitable speculations. To a necessitous delegate he gratuitously spares a supply out of his private stock." James Wilson, too, was able to continue in public service because of Salomon's assistance, "administered with equal generosity and delicacy." It is unfortunate that to this day there has been neither repayment of Salomon's loans to the United States nor recognition by Congress of his patriotism, although House committees have several times recommended favourable action.

Soon after the successful culmination of the Revolution most of the colonies changed their charters or constitutions to place all groups upon a plane of equality. In a few instances, however, it required considerable pressure before the liberal principle triumphed.

In Virginia, only professing Christians could hold public office, and all the inhabitants of the dominion were required to contribute to the upkeep of the churches. Madison and Jefferson began a determined fight to liberalize the constitution. They were opposed by the fiery oratory of Patrick Henry, who won his point in the House of Burgesses in 1784. The two future Presidents did not surrender, however, and carried their fight into the colony itself, pleading from every hustings for equality. Their persistence was rewarded next year by the passage of the Religious Freedom Act, which carried through all of their wishes.

In North Carolina, where the bogy was the Roman Catholic, the state constitution enfranchised only the Protestants. The restriction was not enforced, however; Catholics served in the highest offices, and, in 1781, a Catholic was elected to the governorship. In 1808 an attempt was made to unseat a Jew who had been elected to the General Assembly, but the attempt failed. Yet the law remained upon the statute-books until 1868.

In most of the colonies the question of Jewish equality was largely academic, for there were too few Jews to make the issue important. In Maryland, however, there was a strong Jewish community, centred in Baltimore. The constitution disqualified those who would not subscribe to the Christian faith from serving in any public office. A long struggle was necessary before the oath was changed, in 1828. Maryland was the last colony to retain restrictions.

Meantime a constitution had been drawn up for the United States, and one of the first principles adopted by the new-born republic was the guarantee of full political rights for all groups. The federal Constitution provided that "no religious test shall ever be required as a qualification to any public office or public trust under the United States." This was strengthened by the first amendment, which declared that "Congress shall make no law respecting an establishment of religion, or prohibiting the free exercise thereof." Only North Carolina, fearful of Catholic influence, protested against the abolition of religious tests for federal offices. These unequivocal enactments were epoch-making, for they established, at the very beginning of the nation's history, that there were to be none of the weary battles against ecclesiastical privilege which sullied the history of other countries.

2. THE ERA OF GERMAN IMMIGRATION

The Jewish population increased steadily after 1815, when the reaction in European countries sent thousands flying to more congenial climes. The immigrants came mostly from Germany where "Hep, Hep" was now substituted for soothing platitudes about equality. Virtually every German principality joined in harrying the frightened Jewish settlements. In Bavaria the difficulties became so serious that whole communities were obliged to migrate. The tragedy of Spain was being repeated as a whole people looked eagerly to the day when they could begin life again in a new world. The first money earned by the immigrants in the United States usually went for passage money to bring in relatives and friends who had been left behind.

The peak of emigration came in the few years following 1848. The revolutionary movements of the period found many Jews enlisted among the rebels. Their lives were intertwined with reform not only because they hated tyranny but also because of the obscurantism of the established governments in relation to the Jews. But the liberal struggle ended in the crushing disaster of 1849 and thousands of Jews joined in the exodus of liberals who fled to the United States from the wrath of the reactionaries. By 1880, when the tide began to slow down, the Jewish group had grown to 250,000, of whom the majority were refugees from the German and Austrian dominions.

Most of the new arrivals remained in the already well-established Jewish centres in the East. But the more adventurous pushed out with other pioneers into the thinly settled districts in the South, the Middle West, and across the desert and mountains to the coast. They came to Cincinnati, Chicago, and St. Louis, to Mobile and New Orleans, to little trading posts in Iowa and Minnesota, and there was a *minyan* for Yom Kippur services in San Francisco during the gold-rush year, 1849. Usually the Jewish travellers began as merchants in small towns and grew in wealth and prestige with the growth of the territory. Some of the most prominent Jewish families of the South and the Middle West have their origin in some enterprising pedlar of the covered-wagon era.

DISTRIBUTION OF JEWS
IN THE
UNITED STATES, 1940
with Chief Centers of
Jewish Population

Based on statistics of American Jewish Year Book

The German settlers were therefore a vigorous element. They were rather ill informed about Jewish life and learning and not very well advanced in general culture. But they were able, intelligent, and willing to learn in a land of unique opportunity. Their children were given every advantage and many of them rose to distinguished leadership in Jewish and American life. Franz Lieber writes in 1869: "The application of Germans for all possible appointments is at present enormous, the Jews among them being naturally in the majority. The German Jews in America gain in influence daily, being rich, intelligent, and educated, or at least seeking education. They read better books than the rest of the Germans, the booksellers tell me."[1]

The outstanding Jewish personality of the period was Judah Touro, a merchant of New Orleans, who set a tradition of philanthropy which redounded to the credit of all his people. Touro came to Louisiana just before it passed from France to the United States. He served under Andrew Jackson in the defence of New Orleans and was critically wounded; he was left for dead and was saved only through the bravery of a young friend. Having achieved immense success in all of his mercantile undertakings, Touro turned to dispense his vast wealth for worth-while causes. He achieved a national reputation when he contributed a substantial sum for the Bunker Hill monument and enabled the committee to carry through its project successfully. He saved the Congregational church from being sold under the auctioneer's hammer; he preserved historic landmarks; he never neglected the poor and the homeless. Upon his death he distributed half a million to the most varied types of charitable enterprise, not limiting his bequests to any race or creed. Today large-scale philanthropy is not uncommon; in Touro's day it was the sign of unusual breadth of heart and nobility of soul.

Another interesting career which fell in this period cannot be neglected, though it affected Jewish life very little. Mordecai Manuel Noah came of an old Portuguese family which had long been settled in America; he was brought up in Philadelphia, then the capital of the country. As a young man he became interested in journalism and play-writing and achieved a popular success in both fields. He was rather a swashbuckler and was involved in several duels, in one of which he killed his opponent. In 1813 he was appointed consul to Tunis, and was captured by the English on the way to his post. After his release he carried through the difficult undertaking of ransoming Americans who had been kidnapped by Barbary pirates. He exceeded the subventions allowed by the government, however, and was recalled.

So far Noah's career was merely adventurous. He now turned to solve the Jewish problem by attempting to organize a Jewish state in the heart of the United States! With the aid of friends he acquired a plot of territory near Buffalo and invited the harried and the persecuted of all lands to settle in the new Ararat, the city of refuge for the Jews. On September 2, 1825 the founda-

[1] Cited in Lebeson: *Jewish Pioneers in America*, p. 289.

tion stone for the state was laid with extravagant ceremony, participated in by federal and state officials, clergymen of all denominations, and Indians, whom Noah identified with the lost ten tribes of Israel. He himself was most impressive, in crimson silk robes trimmed with ermine. No settlers, however, flocked to Ararat, and the colony was soon abandoned. Noah turned back to his plays and his books and later to the law and capped his extraordinary career by becoming an associate justice of the New York Court of Sessions.

Meantime the new republic, with sharp internal quarrels over states' rights and slavery, was tending rapidly towards disintegration. In 1861 the divergence between North and South passed into disunion and secession, and then into the bloody Civil War, which almost destroyed the nation.

There was, of course, no specifically Jewish attitude in the disputes which led up to the war. Those who lived in the South usually defended states' rights and the institution of slavery. David Yulee (Levy) rose to a senatorship from Florida and served with distinction in the Confederate Congress. Judah P. Benjamin, of Louisiana, "the sphinx of Confederate history," whose legal talents were so highly respected that he was offered a place in the Supreme Court of the United States by President Pierce, became one of the leading men in the Confederate government, serving successively as Attorney-General, Secretary of War, and finally Secretary of State.

On the other hand, those who lived in the North defended Lincoln's policies and vehemently denounced slavery. Perhaps ten thousand Jews served in the armies of both sides, the majority of course, with the federal forces.

3. THE NEW RUSSIAN IMMIGRATION

Between the Civil War and the new Russian immigration of the eighties the growing Jewish communities developed an unprecedented number of philanthropic and educational institutions which became a permanent feature of American Jewish life. Organizations to aid needy immigrants, to assist the poor, to encourage agricultural settlements, and to stimulate education, fraternal societies, Americanization groups, and societies to train immigrants in trades, all grew up within a generation. The development was providential, for America was thus partly prepared to receive the tremendous new wave of immigration which poured into the country and taxed the resources of the best American leadership.

Already in 1845, when conscription was extended to Poland, the tide had begun. It continued after the failure of the Polish rebellion of 1863. It rose higher when the emancipation of the Russian serfs created an economic crisis in Russia which compelled thousands of young Jews to emigrate to better their economic condition. The new arrivals settled in the larger Eastern cities, and the

Jewish population of New York City rose, in 1872, to seventy thousand, served by twenty-nine synagogues.

Early in the eighties the May laws and the violent *pogrom* epidemic in Russia sent tens of thousands of Jews flying towards the United States. Whole communities migrated *en masse,* and more than twenty thousand Jews entered the United States annually. In the nineties the Russians inaugurated the policy of wholesale Jewish expulsions, and the great majority again turned to the ever hospitable shores of America. Between 1881 and 1900 it is estimated that about six hundred thousand Russian and Roumanian Jews entered the United States, swelling the total Jewish population to more than a million. Then followed more fearful *pogroms,* the Russian Revolution, and the massacres by the Black Hundreds, precipitating the migration of nearly a million more Jews to the United States. Within a generation America became one of the most important Jewish settlements in history.

The two hundred thousand Jews of Sephardic and German origin were now completely inundated by nearly two million immigrants from the eastern European countries. The earlier settlers had come dribbling into the country in small groups and had become easily assimilated. The new-comers migrated, not by families, but by communities and by provinces, with a well-developed group consciousness, desiring to live together, forming huge ghettos in the metropolises of the East.

The constant stream of immigration that poured into the country year by year alarmed many American leaders, who feared that the original stock would be submerged and that the high standard of living characteristic of the American worker would be forced down in competition with cheap foreign labour. In 1897 Congress approved a measure which required immigrants to pass a slight literacy test before they could enter the United States, but President Cleveland vetoed it and it failed to become law. After the opening of the century further attempts were made to restrict the numbers of immigrants, and from 1906 to 1913 new and more drastic bills were introduced in Congress, which called for a literacy test and certificates of character from the home country. This latter provision would almost automatically cut off Jewish immigration from Russia and Roumania, for it was well-nigh impossible for Jews to procure such certificates from their bigoted governments. The "certificate" provision was finally eliminated, but the literacy test passed both houses of Congress. President Taft vetoed it in 1913, just before retiring from office, and when it passed in the new Congress, President Wilson again refused his signature.

Unrestricted by legislation, Jews came in their tens of thousands past the shadow of the Statue of Liberty. The immigrants were mostly manual workers, in contrast with the older settlers, who earned a livelihood as middlemen. They joined the vast army of industrial labourers, toiling long and hard for every dollar, as tailors, garment workers, carpenters, tinners, and in a score of other humble occupations. Life was a continuous struggle. The immigrants lived concentrated within a few industrial areas in congested tenement dwellings; the hours of sweated labour were long, the wages were miserable. Yet the hardships of their lives did not depress them. There was freedom in the Promised Land, endless opportunities to rise, to move into a more congenial environment, to educate children in the American tradition. Many immigrants were able, in phenomenally short periods, to save enough to become employers, to build little factories, to taste the sweets of moderate wealth.

The more alert and ambitious revolutionized several industries by their initiative. The clothing industry, for example, very largely in Jewish hands, underwent a fundamental transformation and became one of the key manufacturing-enterprises in the country. " The Boston System," which introduced a minute division of labour and enormously accelerated production, was the result of Jewish enterprise. In 1880 only sixty millions was invested in clothing; by 1910 the capitalization had been increased fifteen hundred per cent. Modern economists declare that the vast increase was due more to the intelligence of the Russian Jews than to the tariff bills.

This was the era of the trade-union, and the Jewish proletariat took a prominent part in asserting the claims of labour. The Amalgamated Clothing Workers of America, one of the most powerful organizations in the country, grew, through the skilful management and aggressive leadership of Sidney Hillman, to a membership of 180,000, nearly all Jewish. It helped to wipe out sweatshops and vastly improved labour conditions. The International Ladies' Garment Workers' Union, also predominantly Jewish, attained a membership of 140,000. " They established machinery of conciliation from the shop to the industry, which in spite of many tempests and serious crises, will probably live on indefinitely. Perhaps the greatest achievement to their credit is that they have jointly with the employers, through a Joint Board of Sanitary Control, wrought a revolution in the hygienic conditions in the shops."[1]

The Jewish trade-unionist was a new type. Radical in politics, radical in economic outlook, he was also a radical in religion. The exigencies of the industrial organization usually compelled him to dispense with the sabbath and holiday observance and made inroads in the traditions of the old faith. Many of the workers shed no tears, however, for they looked upon both church and synagogue as tools in the hands of capital and they exulted in their emancipation from all traditional dogmatic observances. Religious leaders soon discovered that the Jewish workingman was one of their most serious problems.

4. RELIGIOUS AND CULTURAL DEVELOPMENTS

Meantime a sturdy religious life was being developed in the United States. Most of the immigrants were brought up in the tradition of rabbinic Judaism,

[1] Perlman: *A History of Trade Unionism in the United States*, p. 220.

but the new conditions in America often made changes necessary. As early as 1824 a group of Jews in Charlestown revised the service and the ritual, and in 1841 the first Reform temple was dedicated. Its prayer-book was modelled upon the famous revision of the Hamburg congregation. The movement for reform gained headway after 1848, the impetus coming from the German liberals, who poured into the country when their revolution was crushed. Reform congregations were established in New York, Baltimore, Philadelphia, Cincinnati, and other centres of Jewish population.

The father of American Reform Judaism was Isaac Mayer Wise, who came to the United States from Bohemia in 1846. After an early charge in Albany he settled in Cincinnati, where he served as rabbi of Bene Yeshurun congregation for forty-five years—a ministry which profoundly influenced the development of religious life in America. Wise was a firm believer in adaptation, and, despite the opposition of conservative elements, he introduced a great number of reforms in ritual and service. A characteristic effort was his revised prayer-book, the *Minhag America* (American Rite), which was used by Reform congregations until nearly the end of the century. Despite his Reform enthusiasm, however, Wise would not sacrifice old traditions to pure theory; and while he fought the conservatives to accomplish reform, he fought the radicals to maintain traditions which had been glorified by the devotion of the ages.

Wise's genius did not lie in original theology. He was primarily an organizer. Early in his American career he began an agitation for a union of Reform congregations and his efforts were crowned with success in 1873, when the Union of American Hebrew Congregations was organized. He felt the need also for a seminary to train native-born ministers. He was appalled by the incompetency of the men who posed as spiritual leaders. After a campaign of twenty-five years the Hebrew Union College was opened in 1875, and eight years later its first ordained rabbis came from its halls. Wise's appeal for an authoritative synod of rabbis to govern religious life in America resulted, in 1889, in the creation of the Central Conference of American Rabbis. With all his activity, Jewish, civic, and national, Wise found the time and the energy to write voluminously and to edit the *Israelite,* a weekly journal in which he formulated the philosophy of American Reform Judaism.

Meantime the conservative groups were not idle. Already in the early part of the nineteenth century the task of preserving the traditional faith in the changing life of America was undertaken by Isaac Leeser, who came from Germany in 1824 and five years later began a memorable ministry in Philadelphia. He was more of a pedagogue than a preacher and was always busy with grammars and catechisms; his translation of the Bible into English remained a standard work until about a decade ago. His journal, the *Occident,* which he edited for twenty-five years, became the organ for those who believed in the vitality of conservative Judaism.

The new immigration from Russia, Poland, and Roumania was composed, almost exclusively, of orthodox Jews, who were anxious to link themselves with religious institutions as soon as they arrived. By 1910 the number of synagogues had increased to several thousand, more than eight hundred in New York alone, and there were schools and cultural organizations in proportion. Most of the rabbis were imported from Russia and Poland. It soon became clear that there was a need for spiritual leaders who had been bred and educated in the United States. To meet this need the Jewish Theological Seminary, which had been organized in 1886, was reorganized in 1902 and, under the guidance of the brilliant and lovable scholar Solomon Schechter, played an increasingly important role in American Jewish life. The Isaac Elchanan Yeshibah was organized in 1912 to train rabbis for congregations whose orthodoxy had not yet been modified into conservatism.

One of the most important developments since the Russian immigration has been the creation of a thriving Yiddish and Hebrew press. Before the War there were half a dozen dailies in New York alone, some with a circulation running into the tens of thousands; and there were a number of weeklies and monthlies. Pamphlets and books were issued in such profusion that New York became the largest Yiddish book-market in the world. Much of the literary material which came into the immigrant's home was of a remarkably high standard and helped to raise the general level of Jewish intelligence. Often the foreign press kept the Jew from learning the English language, but more often it facilitated the process. For having learned the facts of the New World, its social life, its politics, its ideals, he was eager to know more. In the night-schools for immigrants the Jews were represented in greater proportion than most other immigrant groups. " Surely nothing can be more inspiring," writes the publicist Abraham Cahan, " to the public-spirited citizen, nothing worthier of the interest of the student of immigration, than the sight of a gray-haired tailor, a patriarch in appearance, coming, after a hard day's work at a sweat shop, to spell ' cat, mat, rat,' and to grapple with the difficulties of ' th ' and 'w.' "[1]

It had all been a unique development. The tiny group of derelicts who came in the *St. Catarina* in 1654 to the shores of New Amsterdam had grown, before the World War, to three millions, of whom all but a quarter-million had entered the country since 1880. Within two generations America had become the most important Jewish settlement in history. The immigrants came from everywhere, Sephardic refugees from Spanish and Portuguese inquisitions, German and Austrian refugees from the despotism of central Europe, and, above all, Polish, Russian, and Roumanian refugees from the barbarous bigotry of eastern European tyrants. Here in the New World the refugees from every corner of the Old mingled, pooled their cultural and religious ideals, and modified them by the new American tradition, to produce a new Judaism and a new Jew, upon whom rests the chief responsibility for the future of the race.

[1] Bernheimer: *The Russian Jew in the United States*, p. 32.

CHAPTER TWENTY-FOUR

THE RUSSIAN JEWISH NIGHTMARE

UNTIL the outbreak of the World War nearly half of the Jews of the world lived in the vast Russian empire. Their history as the subjects of the Romanovs is a record of constant misery. No people has so many tearful associations, so little reason to cherish rulers and country-side as worthy of devotion and sacrifice. Even in the twentieth century, when nearly all of western Europe had shaken off the primitive brutalities that had long disgraced it, Russia still clung to her Tartar traditions. She climaxed her outrageous legal disabilities and savage economic restrictions with *pogroms* and massacres which horrified the civilized world. In the very year in which the Tsar Nicholas II called for a world peace conference, bloody riots were being planned and perpetrated in the unhappy Jewish pale.

The benighted policy of Russia was partly due to the colossal ignorance of the masses, to the bigotry of the Church, and to the stupid incompetence of the rulers. It was assuredly complicated by the fact that the five million Jews of the empire refused to fall in line with the Russification policy of the pan-slavists. They demanded the right to live their own lives in their own way. The clash was, consequently, inevitable, but the ruthlessness with which the tsars conducted their warfare on the helpless little people made the name of Russia a synonym for barbarism and inhumanity.

I. THE PARTITIONS OF POLAND

In the middle of the eighteenth century the Jewish population in eastern Europe totalled more than a million and a half, of whom the greatest number were concentrated in Poland. They were primarily the descendants of the refugees who had fled from the malevolence of Christian Europe during the Dark Ages. For centuries they thrived under hospitable rulers, and Poland remained the Promised Land. Towards the middle of the seventeenth century foreign merchants and grasping nobles combined with the ubiquitous Jesuits to harass the Jewish population. Year by year as the Polish state degenerated into administrative anarchy, the burdens of Jewish life became heavier. In 1733 the Polish Church synod declared that the Jews should be tolerated so that "they might remind us of the tortures of the Saviour and, by their abject and miserable condition, might serve as an example of the chastisement of God inflicted upon the infidels."

In Russia the Jews were confined to the outlying districts. There were large and compact groups in Lithuania, in the north-west and south-east Russian provinces, and in the provinces north of the Black Sea, especially in the Crimea. Jews were strictly forbidden to enter central Russia, and severe penalties were imposed upon those who were found in the country without special permission. Peter the Great, while welcoming foreigners, denounced the Jews as rogues and cheats. His successors continued his prohibitions and expelled the Jews who managed, despite restrictions, to smuggle themselves into the interior. Elizabeth placed her animosity to Moslems and Jews upon religious grounds; in the edict by which she expelled the latter from Little Russia she stated that " no other fruit may be expected from the haters of the name of Christ the Saviour than extreme injury to our faithful subjects."

But it was fated that the great Russian bear, hating the Jews and desiring to be free of them, should gobble up Poland and become the leading Jewish state.

The partition of Poland was one of the great crimes of history, but it was well-nigh inevitable. The country was surrounded by three greedy powers, Austria, Prussia, and Russia, who took full advantage of her economic weakness and her internal chaos. After numerous attempts to control the country indirectly, they conspired to divide it up among themselves. In 1772 the infamous bargain was carried through, and in 1792 and 1795 the final partitions took place, and the political life of Poland was snuffed out. The Poles fought desperately under Kosciuszko to retain their freedom, but it was too late. The nation wakened when its vitality was gone and as Kosciuszko fell, the historic State was effaced from the map of Europe. In the last struggle the Jews forgot their grievances and fought shoulder to shoulder with their former persecutors. One young patriot, Berek Joselevitz, received permission from Kosciuszko to organize a Jewish legion of light cavalry. Five hundred Jews responded to his call, and nearly every one of them died fighting in the defence of the doomed Polish capital.

Catherine II, " the Semiramis of the North," who took over most of Poland and with it nearly a million Jews, was one of the ablest sovereigns in Europe. She had a keen mind and an imperious will and was a shrewd judge of character. She was fond of posing as an enlightened despot and was constantly mouthing liberal sentiments. She welcomed the French philosopher Diderot to her court as tutor to her son and carried on a dilettante correspondence with the titanic Voltaire. But at heart she was little moved by the needs of her people and she once wrote quite frankly to the governor of Moscow: " My dear prince, if I institute schools, it is not for us — it is for Europe, where we must keep our position in public opinion. The day when our peasants shall wish to become enlightened, both you and I will lose our places."

Little wonder that despite her liberal protestations Catherine's Jewish policy was cruel and coercive. Her " Placard," issued in 1792, guaranteed the Jews their lives and religious freedom, but continued the restrictions which had been in force under the Polish regime. She recognized the *kahal* as the Jewish governing body and granted it the authority to try specifically Jewish cases. But she was shrewd enough to utilize it primarily as a fiscal instrument to collect special and general Jewish taxes. In a manifesto which she issued encouraging foreigners to settle in Russia, she used the phrase " *kromye zydov* (except Jews)," which was constantly repeated in subsequent Russian legislation.

Towards the close of her reign came the French Revolution, which frightened out of her even a sentimental liberalism. She closed the door completely on all manner of reform and applied the knout to all who defied her wishes. Her awakened severity naturally reflected itself in her attitude to the Jews. A series of ukases restricted the long-established Jewish right to sell liquor, to keep taverns, and to participate in a number of other commercial enterprises. She began the pernicious system of denying to the Jews everything which was not specifically permitted by the law.

The climax of the reaction came in 1791 when the pale of settlement was created. For this Catherine was perhaps not entirely to blame. Narrow, jaundiced officials in the Senate and in the Jewish districts pressed her to take the step, and she yielded. Her ukase, by forbidding Jews to join merchant and artisan guilds in certain provinces, practically confined them to a limited district. But even in the pale itself Jews were excluded from the military ports and from certain towns and crown-lands. It was hoped through the new law to protect Russians from Jewish competition and to keep the greater part of the country clear of Jews. Every effort was made to squeeze the Jews out of the country-side. Once the Poles had driven the Jews out of the cities into the villages; now the process was reversed and the Jews were again driven back into the cities.

Until the opening of the nineteenth century, statesmen under Catherine's phantom successors busied themselves with "investigations" of the Jewish problem. They were much concerned with the outcries of peasants, who complained that Jews were enslaving them, and of nobles, who used the Jews as convenient scapegoats to evade complaints against their own harshness. In 1800 the poet Derzhavin published an *Opinion,* in which he analysed the Jewish problem, and through which he hoped that "the stubborn and cunning tribe might be set to rights." He came to the conclusion that the Jews were a menace to Russian progress — first, because they were middlemen, economic parasites; and, second, because, trained, as they were, exclusively on the Bible and the Talmud, they were a clannish, unassimilable people. The Jewish problem could be solved satisfactorily to the Russian state only when the Jews placed themselves in a position to be readily absorbed. He proposed that measures should be taken to restrict Jews from continuing in " unproductive" occupations, and that the old Talmudic educational system should be uprooted. The autonomy of the *kahal* should surely be destroyed, for it tended to create a state within a state. The *Opinion* was an important influence on subsequent generations of statesmen, who often dipped into its wisdom for inspiration in restrictive legislation.

Thus at the opening of the nineteenth century, when everywhere in Europe the ghettos were being battered to bits by the blows of Napoleon, new experiments in disabilities were being created for the millions of Jews who lived under the tsarist despotism.

2. KICKS AND KINDNESS UNDER ALEXANDER I

The accession of Alexander I, in 1801, filled the Jews and all Russian liberals with hope, for he was a well-meaning, tolerant dreamer, anxious to govern his country and to regulate its international relations by Christian principles. He listened earnestly to counsel on the Jewish question and was much influenced by the liberalism of his leading minister, Speranski, whom Napoleon once termed " the only clear mind in Russia." But the commission which Alexander appointed to report on the Jewish situation was largely averse to such liberalism. Its scheme of reform was a curious mixture of amelioration and repression. On the one hand, every privilege was promised to Jews who became agriculturists. They could live in two districts outside of the pale, Astrakan and the Caucasus; they could buy unoccupied lands or live on crown-lands. All schools, the highest as well as the elementary, were thrown open to Jews and they were permitted to have their own as well, if the language of instruction was Russian, Polish, or German. On the other hand, severe attacks were made again upon " unproductive " Jewish enterprises. Jews were no longer to keep taverns on the countryside; they could not lease lands, and they were uprooted from a number of frontier villages where they had lived for generations.

The tsar himself, " favored with all the gifts of Heaven except common sense," was motivated by no malice towards the Jews. He honestly believed that the limitation of Jewish industry would break down the " parasitism " and the separateness of a strange and stubborn people. Hence the paradox of a well intentioned sovereign who contributed liberally towards the erection of a Jewish hospital and, at the same time, issued orders for the expulsion of Jews from ancient villages.

During the critical days of 1812, when the Grand Army of France invaded the country, the Jews turned a deaf ear to the blandishments of the wily Napoleon and loyally supported the government. Their patriotic attitude amazed even the future autocrat Nicholas, then an arrogant young prince. Alexander was touched by their devotion and for a brief moment was inclined to mitigate his severity. He suspended the edicts which had turned a few hundred Jewish families to the soil, but had ruined thousands of others, and he permitted the Jews to take surnames as a special mark of royal favour.

He soon abandoned his liberalism, however. After Waterloo all Europe turned reactionary, and Alexander, alarmed by a military mutiny in his capital and by the seditious activity of secret societies, turned his face against his youthful dreams. The Jews were early victims of his changed policy. When a curious movement began in the twenties in which thousands of southern Russians turned to practices which resembled Judaism, Alexander uprooted the neophytes and exiled them to Siberia and the Caucasus and forbade the Jews to live in the infected districts. He also attempted, by every artifice, to make converts and bitterly resented his lack of success. Towards the close of his reign he was frankly persecuting. Old laws were now rigidly enforced. The expulsion policy which had been interrupted was now renewed. In the dead of winter in 1824, twenty thousand Jewish families of Moghilev and Vitebsk were ruthlessly expelled and left to die on the roads or to struggle along in the already badly congested Jewish pale.

Before Alexander died, in 1825, the Jewish situation had become deplorable. The vast Jewish population was now confined to the governments of the pale. How they subsisted is a mystery. One thinks of the famous Irish village where the women lived by taking in each other's washing. There were still a small number of wealthier Jews who carried on commerce in furs and skins with foreign lands and moved about freely, attending great international fairs. But these were the exceptions. The masses of the people lived in poverty, hemmed into a narrow district, learning to subsist under an ever increasing load of repression.

3. NICHOLAS I: RUSSIAN HAMAN

Alexander was succeeded by his brother, Nicholas, a military autocrat who believed in ruling his country as if it were a barracks. Strong as an ox, loving the breath of the battlefield, he became the reactionary gendarme of Europe, dedicating himself to the principles of autocracy, nationalism, and orthodoxy. He loved Russia sincerely and resolved to protect it from the influence of all Western liberal ideas. The censorship which he established was so stringent that even musical compositions could not enter, lest the notes be used as a revolutionary code. He once replied to a petitioner who craved mercy: " We all expect mercy from God; but from me, the ruler of the lands, my subjects must look only for justice." Such a type could not be sympathetic to any minority group, and he despised the Jews above all. To him they were leeches and parasites and an unassimilable element in Russian society. With his accession there began a relentless thirty years' war against them.

In 1827, soon after his accession, all able-bodied Russians above the age of eighteen were made liable to serve in the army for twenty-five years. He hoped by universal military training not only to create the finest army in Europe, but also to break down the solidarity of the alien groups. Hence his military policy was devised to bear heavier upon these minorities. Conscription affected seven in a thousand of the Russian population, but ten in a thousand among Jews. Moreover, the period of military service was increased by six years for the Jewish population, through the provision which compelled them to attend cantons, or preparatory camps, from the age of twelve. Every effort was made to wean the young reservists from Judaism. They were transported long distances from their native towns, away from every Jewish influence. They were flogged and prevented from sleeping; they were served salt foods and denied water. It was impossible for more than the most stalwart to survive. There were enormous numbers of forced baptisms, which took the most virile elements out of Jewish life. It is estimated that by 1839 more than forty thousand had been converted in Moscow and Piltushey alone.

The law of conscription was made more cruel and more demoralizing through the provision which placed the responsibility for recruiting upon the *kahal*. When the quota was short, the leaders in the *kahal* were obliged to supply the deficiency by fair means or foul. Bands of hunters prowled about the centres of Jewish population, kidnapping young men without passports, *poimaniki,* whom they could use as substitutes to fill the quota! These *lovchiki* (catchers) were the terror of Jewish life; Jews preying on Jews to fill the maws of the Russian Moloch. The system went on for thirty years, sacrificing the youth and destroying the morale of Jewish life.

In the conviction that Jewish separatism was nurtured by Jewish religious literature, Nicholas now turned to attack the root cause. He listened eagerly to his Minister of Education and other councillors, who pointed out how separatism was nurtured by the Talmud and the old-fashioned Jewish teachers. By the ukase of 1844 he established special secular schools, in the attempt to counteract the overweening influence of the teachers and the stubborn nationalism of the Talmud.

In itself the idea attracted many Jewish liberals who looked for intellectual progress through the development of a broad secular education. They were also anxious to free the Jews from the belief that the Talmud was the all in all of Jewish life. The German Jewish liberal Max Lilienthal, and several other Jews who had been liberally trained, supported the program of the Minister of Education and assisted in the organization of the new schools. But they soon realized that Nicholas's true motive was not the enlightenment of the Jews, but their conversion or assimilation. They quickly abandoned their co-operation; Lilienthal migrated to America in 1845. All of Nicholas's efforts to destroy the traditional system of Jewish education failed.

Meantime, outraged by his lack of success, the resourceful tsar continued to impose new disabilities upon the unfortunate people. The pale of settlement was further narrowed through a series of edicts which nearly ruined Jewish life. More than a hundred and fifty thousand Jews were affected by the expulsions, which became scandalous enough in 1843 to evoke the protests of all civilized Europe. The English philanthropist Sir Moses Montefiore came to plead with the tsar for leniency, but though he was well received, his mission brought no change in the attitude of the government.

Nicholas was already busily attacking Jewish "parasitism." He proposed to clear Russia of Jews who lived as hand-to-mouth middlemen. His laws of 1851 were levelled against all Jews who were not engaged in "productive" occupations. The Crimean War made it necessary to suspend the edicts, but the fear of exile and oppression continued to hang over the Jews and to unsettle their spiritual and economic life.

Even the Russian novelists and poets of the period, the pride and glory of the country, joined in the crusade of Nicholas against the hated Jews. Pushkin pictured the Jew as the poisoner of *Skupoi Rytsar;* Gogol, as the sneaking, cowardly, obsequious pedlar of *Taras Bulba;* Lermontov, as the professional spy of *Sashka.* Even the tolerant Turgeniev developed, in his *Zhid,* a horrible Jewish spy who bartered away his own daughter. The versatile genius of these artists was an incalculable influence on the intellectuals of Russia, who were further convinced that the Jews were merely shrewd, grasping money-grubbers who lived on the miseries of the peasantry.

The experiments of Nicholas were not tried in Poland, where the Jews were most numerous. But even here their lot was not enviable. The Poles, though themselves oppressed by the Russians, did not hesitate to persecute the Jews. The districts in which they could live, and the occupations which they could follow, remained severely limited. A literary anti-Semitism also fuelled prejudice, and occasionally there were riots. During the revolution of 1830, when Poland again tried desperately to throw off the Russian yoke, leading Jewish patriots begged for an opportunity to serve. The Polish nobles contemptuously turned from them, remarking that they could not mix their blood with that of the Poles. They were permitted, however, to serve in inferior capacities and managed to die in great numbers in the fruitless attempt to win Polish independence. After the revolt was crushed, the old disabilities were continued as before.

4. ALEXANDER II AND THE RIFT

Nicholas I died in 1855 in the midst of the Crimean War, whose disastrous mismanagement revealed the rottenness of the autocratic regime. The accession of his son, Alexander II, was hailed as the beginning of a new era. The young prince had been well educated, and, while not a liberal, surrounded himself with enlightened statesmen, whose counsels he usually followed. He inaugurated his reign with a series of epoch-making reforms, political and judicial, which met the highest expectations of the liberals. He cut down the powers and privileges of the clergy. And he capped his early reform enthusiasm by liberating forty million serfs. Russia was almost cut loose from its ancient moorings.

The Jews gained immensely in the general liberal high tide. Alexander's reforms in their status were, perhaps, only homœopathic and were largely dictated by a desire to assimilate them to the Russian population. But they at least dissipated the horrors of Nicholas's system. The deadly policy of juvenile conscription came to an end at once, after being in force thirty years. The age limit of conscription was now set alike for Jew and Christian. The schools and universities of the country were again opened to the Jews. The great Russian cities were also opened to certain favoured classes, merchants of the first guild, skilled artisans and mechanics, and university graduates, whose talents, intelligence, and wealth were considered useful in developing the resources of the country.

The benefits which flowed from Alexander's early liberalism must not be exaggerated. The vast majority of the Jews were still not permitted to move from the overcrowded provinces of the pale. The concessions to the privileged were often not honestly carried out, and merchants and artisans were subject to serious annoyances from corrupt officials. The emancipation of the serfs created a bitter economic crisis in the country, during which thousands of Russians were compelled to leave and seek new homes in America. Yet living-conditions had at last become tolerable; hearth and home were no longer threatened. Many Jews took advantage of the new educational opportunities and flocked to the schools and colleges. They entered the professions, and Jewish names began to appear among those of prominent lawyers and, in some instances, judges. Jewish physicians and surgeons found useful careers even in the army. Jewish financiers invested in Russian national enterprises, exploiting mines, building railroads, helping in the development of the country and in their own economic advance.

Above all, a vigorous intellectual life was developed in the unexpectedly favourable environment, and for the first time there were Jewish periodicals published in the Russian language. European culture was also brought into old-fashioned Jewish homes by means of Hebrew and Yiddish periodicals and books. It seemed as if Russia was to come at last into the concert of civilized European peoples.

Unfortunately a curse seemed to hang over the Russian tsars. However liberal they began, they invariably turned reactionary. Alexander, like many of his forbears, was of a volatile nature, and when his reform enthusiasm had spent itself, he forsook his dream of a liberal empire. He had been sadly disillusioned when all of his paternalistic efforts brought no peace. Liberalism, instead of diminishing dissension, had encouraged it, and the rise of revolutionary nihilism, which struck down officials and attempted the life of the tsar himself, convinced him that repression alone could succeed in Russia. He severely censored the press and harried suspects out of the country.

Alexander's abandonment of liberalism naturally vitally affected the Jews of the empire. The tsar now frankly regretted his former generosity, for all of his concessions had not broken down Jewish solidarity. Many Jews, too, were identified with the liberal movements which terrorized the tsarist government. From the Russian interior came protests by the nobles against the roguery of the Jews in their relations with the peasantry. From every source came the whole tribe of familiar accusations. Committees now began their ominous investigations, and the usual restrictions followed. In 1871 a number of *yeshibahs* were closed. Conscription of Jews was no longer accompanied by the right to military advancement. At the Congress of Berlin, in 1878, Gorchakov, the Russian minister, was the only important statesman who opposed the grant of legal equality to eastern European Jews. Accusations of ritual murder began to crop up, forerunners of the horrors of the next reign, which began in 1881, when Alexander II was blown to bits by revolutionary fanatics. Russian history now became, in Herzen's words, a long list of martyrs and a register of convicts.

5. ALEXANDER III AND ORGANIZED *POGROMS*

The new tsar, Alexander III, resembled his grandfather Nicholas in his soldierly training and bearing and in his narrow Russian prejudices. But he was infinitely less able and earned the title "the crowned peasant" which critics gave him. The brutal assassination of his father reinforced his natural hatred of liberalism, and his first proclamation was a challenge in which he vowed the continuance of the autocracy "which we are called upon, by the voice of God, to strengthen and preserve for the good of the people."

Alexander surrounded himself with pan-slavist advisers, who wished to cut Russia off from the pestilential ideas of western Europe. They were convinced that Russia had a destiny of her own, more glorious than the industrial, rationalist, godless civilization of the West. "*Para Domoi,*" cried Aksakov to Russia, in thrilling accents; "it is time to go home, time to stop aping Western habits and ideals of life. Let Russia turn again to the glorious days which preceded Peter's disastrous reforms." Unfortunately the return to a "Russian" civilization meant too often the return to the indiscipline and the primitive barbarity of Ivan the Terrible.

The most influential personality in the new government was Pobedonostsev, the former tutor of the tsar, who now became procurator of the Holy Synod.

Pobedonostsev was a man of broad education, but book-learning had not liberalized his spirit. He was a convinced reactionary who despised parliamentary institutions, tolerance, or free discussion. To him the ideal government was an autocracy under the protecting care of the Orthodox Church. He began a war on all minority groups who would not accept his program, and his fanaticism earned him the unenviable title of the "Second Torquemada."

The new regime was worthily inaugurated with a series of anti-Jewish riots, which raged through the year and spread to all parts of Russia, affecting the thriving metropolises as well as the obscure, ignorant villages where Jews still lived. The riots, or *pogroms,* were undoubtedly centrally organized and the government did little to check them. In the Kiev government, where Jews were most thickly settled, General Drenteln would not "endanger the lives of his soldiers for the sake of a few Jews." Ignatiev, the Minister of the Interior, insisted that the *pogroms* were the natural consequence of the unfair economic practices of the Jews. Instead of taking measures to put an end to the outrages, he appointed commissions to investigate Jewish exploitation; the Jews were placed on trial for arousing *pogroms* against themselves!

At the beginning of 1882 the government finally checked the excesses, but in effect it took the monopoly of persecution into its own hands. "Temporary Rules" were issued in May which remained in force until the outbreak of the war in 1914. The pale district was materially narrowed and it was decreed "that the Jews be forbidden to settle anew outside of towns and boroughs, exceptions being made only in the case of existing agricultural colonies." As the law was interpreted, the Jews were prevented from moving at all, and they became interned in the villages in which they lived when the regulation was issued. Furthermore, Jews were forbidden to own mortgages and leases, and since the prohibition was interpreted retroactively, the claims which Jews already had were cancelled without compensation.

The special classes of Jews who had settled throughout the empire during the tolerant decade of Alexander II's reign were severely examined, and those who could not prove their right to remain were expelled within twenty-four hours. Security of residence disappeared and whole communities were placed at the mercy of the police, who were paid immense bribes in return for lenience in the execution of the brutal laws. The corruption of officials and the subordination of law to the bureaucracy ultimately served as a boomerang, reacting disastrously on Russian civil and political administration. The May Laws aroused the indignation of the civilized world, but all protests were unheeded.

There followed, in 1887, new educational restrictions which limited the number of Jews in universities to ten per cent within the pale, and to five per cent outside of the pale, except in St. Petersburg and Moscow, where the limitation was placed at three per cent. The restrictions brought untold sorrow to thousands of students who were left stranded in the midst of their educational program. The drastic operation of the law is clear from the fact that during the nineties there were eighteen hundred Jewish students in Russian universities and at least twenty-five hundred abroad. Barriers were also placed in the way of a legal career. Jews had been prominent in the law, but in 1889 it was decreed that no Jew could be called to the bar without the permission of the Minister of Justice. Few Jews were consequently called until 1904.

Pogroms, civil disabilities, legal and economic restrictions, increased military obligations, all gave a tremendous impetus to Jewish emigration. At first the Russian officials attempted to check the great flight which began after the May Laws, and the emigrants were plagued wherever they turned. The world shuddered at the horrors through which the Jews passed. They huddled in their thousands on the western frontiers, without funds, without any definite destination, hounded by the officials and by *pogroms.* Yet, despite all difficulties, tens of thousands left during the eighties, and in the last three years of the decade more than a hundred thousand escaped from the Russian hell. Most of them turned to the United States, where they completely submerged the older stocks and profoundly influenced Jewish life.

By the end of the century the Russian administration changed its attitude towards emigration and began openly to encourage it. It seemed to be the easiest solution to an apparently insoluble problem. The Russian leaders looked forward to a time when at least the larger cities would be *judenrein* (cleansed of Jews). Then came an astonishing offer from Baron Moritz de Hirsch, one of Europe's wealthiest Jews. He sought the co-operation of the Russian government in the attempt gradually to remove the majority of the Russian Jews to the Argentine republic. He was prepared, through the London Colonization Society, which he organized in 1891, to spend hundreds of millions on his scheme. He hoped to transport and establish, with economic stability, about twenty-five thousand Jews annually. Russia accepted with alacrity, and the most remarkable phenomenon in all history was witnessed — a civilized government co-operating in a scheme to remove a whole population! The project was, of course, too gigantic to be successful. In ten years only ten thousand Jews had emigrated to the Argentine. Despite Baron de Hirsch and the lure of the United States — which drew more than a hundred thousand Jews in 1891 alone — millions were still left to suffer as the Russian nationalists experimented with plans to annihilate them.

6. NICHOLAS II: THE PUPPET

Nicholas II, the last Autocrat of All the Russias who ascended the throne, inaugurated the two worst decades in the bloody history of the Jews in Russia. Nicholas was a weak-willed, superstitious puppet whose court was a refuge for fanatical pilgrims and reactionary advisers. His reply to the liberal addresses on his accession was significant: "Let everybody know that I shall guard the principle of autocracy as firmly and uncompromisingly as it was guarded by my never-to-be-forgotten deceased father." He rebuked a group of representatives who petitioned for a constitution by denouncing their projects as "senseless dreams."

The Jews soon learned that the change of rulers meant that they were to be scourged with scorpions rather than with whips. Persecution began immediately. In the large cities there were raids to ferret out Jews who could not prove their right to remain. The premium offered for each Jew was equal to the premium for two burglars. In 1897 the Grand Duke Sergius practically uprooted the whole Moscow Jewish community. *Pogroms* came every year as regularly as the return of the winter snows. By the end of the century Jewish economic and social life had been completely demoralized. The census of 1897 revealed an astonishing amount of pauperism among a race always too proud to beg. On the average, nineteen per cent required Passover aid. In Odessa the proportion ran to 33.5; in Vilna it reached 37.7 per cent.

The opening of the new century brought a new wave of revolutionary activity in Russia. The liberals were undismayed in the face of every terror; the gallows, imprisonment, exile to Siberia, took heavy tolls, but new recruits filled the ranks as quickly as they were decimated. Many Jews were prominently involved in the complicated conspiracies, and the government, in despair, labelled the whole liberal movement as a vast Jewish conspiracy and called upon loyal Russians to save the State from the machinations of aliens. When the ultra-reactionary von Plehve became Minister of the Interior in 1902, the government deliberately incited the masses against the Jews. *Pogrom* horrors, on a larger scale than ever, again horrified the world. During the Easter holidays of 1903 a well-organized massacre occurred in the Bessarabian province of Kishinev, in which about fifty Jews were killed, six hundred were wounded, and more than fifteen hundred shops and homes were plundered or destroyed. The massacres continued for several days before orders came from the government to dispatch troops to the district.

> The old grey spider spinning in the garret.
> She knows a lot of stories — bid her tell them!
> A story of a belly stuffed with feathers,
> Of nostrils and of nails, of heads and hammers,
> Of men who, after death, were hung head downward,
> Like geese, along the rafter.
> A story of a suckling child asleep.
> A dead and cloven breast between its lips,
> And of another child they tore in two,

Thus cutting short its last and loudest scream,
For " Ma— " was heard, but " Mama " never finished.
And many, many more such fearful stories
That beat about thy head and pierce thy brain,
And stab the soul within thee, does she know.
And, stifling down the sob within thy throat,
Thou rushest headlong down the stairs and out —
To see again the world of ev'ry day,
The usual sun, outpouring unashamed
A wealth of beams at every guilty threshold,
And lavish of its store on worse than swine.[1]

In the trials which followed the outrages, it was plain, from the evidence, that the government had connived at the *pogroms* as a means of diverting attention from liberal agitation. The leading rioters were dismissed with light sentences, and many Jews were convicted for using arms. The liberals of Russia and all the civilized world thundered their protests, but Pharaoh's heart had turned to stone.

The liberals were not to be denied, however. The Russian disasters during the Japanese war brought the revolutionary movement to a climax. " Jap the Giant-killer " proved beyond all doubt the inefficiency of the Russian autocracy. Strikes, riots, the assassination of prominent officials, at last frightened the autocracy into concessions. The tsar promised to convene a Duma, to promulgate a constitution, and to grant rights to the discontented minorities.

But, in the very act of calling the Duma, the leaders planned a horrible means of vitiating the reforms. Bands of ruffians, the Black Hundreds, were organized, to perpetrate new *pogroms* on the Jews, who, it was urged, were responsible for all of the Russian misfortunes. During the summer and autumn of 1905 Jewish blood was spilled in more than fifty localities. October 18 to 25 was the blackest week in Russian Jewish history, a St. Bartholomew's massacre on a larger scale. In Odessa alone, hundreds of Jews were cut to pieces, thousands were wounded, and more than forty thousand homes and shops were destroyed. In the first Duma, which met next year, Dr. Schmarya Levin and other prominent Jewish leaders protested against the outrages and demanded that the perpetrator be brought to justice. But the assembly could offer only academic sympathy. Its own existence hung on a thread. Indeed, within a few months the government, which had been gradually recovering its equilibrium and its courage, felt strong enough to dismiss the assembly altogether and to call for a new election.

The government tried every means to secure the return of a friendly Duma, but the new body proved more obstreperous than the first. After a

[1] Bialik: *The City of Slaughter*. Translated from the Hebrew by Helena Frank.

little more than three months of continuous quarrelling the tsar again sent the delegates packing; he was obliged to take the step, he said, because too many of the members were implicated in revolutionary conspiracy. The government now tinkered with the electoral franchise and, in November 1907, when the third Duma was convened, it was found to be a thoroughly chastened body. Stolypin, the Prime Minister, was a pliable tool of the court group, and his policy was frankly reactionary. " First, pacification," he said; " then reform." In 1907 alone his " necktie " hanged eighteen hundred liberals implicated in the revolutionary movements, and there were hundreds of Jewish victims. Persecution and legal restriction were revived at the very time that the tsar was appealing to the world for international peace and brotherhood. In 1911 a ritual murder case was permitted to disgrace Russian justice when Mendel Beilis was accused of the murder of a Christian child to satisfy the Passover ritual. The case dragged on for years and diplomatic pressure alone compelled the eventual release of the martyred victim.

The outbreak of the European conflict in 1914 compelled the suspension of all repressive legislation. In a fervent appeal for the loyalty of his subjects Nicholas promised equality to all races and creeds who would rally to the support of Mother Russia in her fiery ordeal. Unfortunately the belated promises meant nothing. Russia was rotten to the core, and under the impact of a gigantic war its whole structure collapsed. The unhappy millions who lived within the empire were to suffer miseries whose recital would tax the masters of the horrible.

For nearly a century and a half the Jews of Russia had lived in darkness under the most brutal despotism in modern history. It is fair to add that the Russian statesmen were baffled by a serious problem. The Jews formed a vast mass, three million strong, rapidly increasing in numbers, unassimilated, apparently unassimilable, hard as steel, stubborn as death, sticking like a huge bone in the gullet of the nationalists. But though one may appreciate the toughness of the problem, it is difficult to understand the stupidity and the brutality of the means used to solve it. Europe was justly amazed that a country with as distinguished an intelligentsia as developed in Russia could deliberately adopt a policy of butchery and pursue it relentlessly. It was not strange that the Jews were usually identified with liberal and radical movements, aiming to overthrow the disgusting despotism which compelled them to eat the bread of affliction.

CHAPTER TWENTY-FIVE

CULTURAL AND RELIGIOUS CHANGES

1. THE NEW SCIENCE

THE battle for freedom which convulsed the nineteenth century was not confined to the political field. In the field of thought, too, there were daring liberals who insisted upon exploring every nook and cranny of their world, to the discomfort of truculent theologians and timid philosophers. The researches of these pioneers completely revolutionized the natural and physical sciences and offered new explanations for the world of matter and nature. Problems which were considered long solved were again opened to be probed without preconceptions.

Until the nineteenth century it was generally believed that the earth was not more than five or six thousand years old; indeed, according to Archbishop Ussher's calculations, it had been created in the spring of 4004 B.C. The Biblical account of the origin of life was taken literally, and, though there were critics in every generation to voice their doubts, they were few, and usually their attacks were not convincing. The new century brought with it a scientific spirit which spared neither creed nor doctrine. In 1833 Sir Charles Lyell published his *Principles of Geology,* in which he demonstrated that the earth had been formed, not by a series of catastrophic changes, but by the steady and constant operation of causes which were still at work. Some years later he again jolted an orthodox generation by suggesting that the earth, judged by fossil remains, was at least tens of thousands of years old. He was socially ostracized for having helped, however indirectly, to discredit the Pentateuchal accounts of the Creation and the Deluge.

Meantime the gentle Charles Darwin had been patiently working out a theory of the origin of species which was destined to give much greater offence to the theologians. His theory of evolution, published in 1859 and amplified in 1871, declared that all existing beings have been gradually developed from previous species, that unchanging laws have governed this gradual development, laws which have always been, and still are in operation. Man consequently was not a sudden creation. He evolved as other beings evolved, from an inferior species, and he arrived at his superior position by virtue of a magnificent power of adjustment and adaptability. Darwin's theory was of course not new. It had been suggested in vague fashion by Lamarck, Goethe, Kant, and others, and it may be traced back twenty-four hundred years to the brilliant Greek philosopher Heraclitus. But Darwin developed his thesis on scientific premises and did not publish it until it had simmered in his mind for fifteen years. It was enthusiastically received by the leading scientists of Europe. Huxley popularized it in England, Ernest Haeckel proclaimed it in Germany, and Spencer built his whole philosophy upon it.

The theory made necessary a complete readjustment of older generalizations. Theology was in difficulty immediately and the theologians found themselves sharply on the defensive. If Darwin was right, if man had gradually developed through the ages from lower species, what of the Biblical story of the origin of life? What of the other dogmas which were involved in the Biblical account of Eden, especially the dogma of human corruptibility? What of the miracles in the Bible, the sudden interruptions of nature's orderly processes? Could they be reconciled with the story of evolution?

The conflict which was precipitated by the publication of Darwin's thesis agitated England and Europe for decades. Disraeli could dismiss the whole matter glibly with the epigram that the whole battle was whether man is an ape or an angel and " he was on the side of the angels." But it was no laughing matter to men whose entire religious life had been built up about a document which they regarded as verbally inspired, who felt that, when a jot or tittle of the Sacred Word was demolished, the foundations of religion collapsed. In 1860 a little volume, *Essays and Reviews,* which attacked the citadel of Biblical orthodoxy, divided English public opinion. Two ecclesiastical contributors, who had criticized the traditional view of Biblical inspiration and the doctrine of rewards and punishments, were deprived of their livings. They were, however, sustained in a secular court and Lord Westbury jocularly lamented that the judgment had " dismissed hell with costs, and deprived earnest churchmen of all hope for everlasting damnation." Other cases followed and Christian Europe was convulsed as argument and recrimination came fierce and fast.

The Jewish world felt the impact of the new thought as severely as the Christian world. The great masses, to be sure, knew little of the implications of the quarrel, but those who understood found that their thinking was profoundly influenced. A sharp conflict arose between those who believed in revelation and those who accepted an evolutionary view of religion. These latter, influenced by Darwinism, took the thesis that all religions, and Judaism too, had grown just as man had, higher forms from lower forms in conformity with natural law. Judaism did not come suddenly from the traditional Sinai; it was the product of ages of painful building. It came out of primitive animism, totemism, nature worship, polytheism, monolatry, each the product of environment and historic conditions. Only under the magnificent tutorship of the prophets did it blossom into a sublime ethical monotheism.

The popularization of this evolutionary view of religion gave an immense impetus to scientific Biblical criticism. Since Israel's religious genius had been continuously unfolding, and since the Bible was the most important record of the development, it was necessary to study the Bible from a new viewpoint. There had, of course, been critical views of the Scriptures for many centuries. Ibn Ezra, Spinoza, and numbers of Christian thinkers had hinted at the composite origin of the Pentateuch and of the historical and prophetic books of the Bible. Throughout the eighteenth and early nineteenth century the higher criticism laboured steadily to separate the independent documents from which later chroniclers had compiled the traditions of Israel. But after Darwin's day the evolutionary school went forward more surely to rearrange the Biblical accounts, linking them up with new information from other sources. They were able to discover what fragments probably were the product of more primitive thinking and what portions sprang from the maturer genius of Israel. They analysed the influence on the early Hebrew sages of contact with other peoples and other environments. By the end of the century the radical Biblical critics had completely reconstructed the history of Israel and its religion.

It is easy to imagine the turmoil in Jewish life as Darwin's views and their implications were defended and attacked. Many Jews, fascinated by the new thought, and finding it impossible to reconcile the temple of creed with the temple of science, threw over Bible, dogma, and all religious affiliation and followed Huxley into agnosticism, aggressively spelling God with a small g.

Others readjusted their religious ideas, insisting that evolution, far from harming true religion, strengthened it. There was surely no fundamental conflict. Religious faith was still a necessity, for science solved none of the mysteries of life and death, the secrets of creation, the wonders of religious inspiration. As for the Bible, one could discard its limited scientific concepts and still look upon the old, old writ as a magnificent ethical and spiritual repository.

Then there were conservatives who accepted the new science in part. They used Maimonides's method of rationalizing. After all, they suggested, evolution was not incompatible with a view of the Bible as a verbally inspired document. The miracles and stories which did not square with science were allegories. The view that religion had developed gradually was met with the defensible thesis that remarkably gifted religious personalities were the most important factor in the developing-process. There was nothing in evolution to deny that Moses, by divine intuition, could create a religious system which was far in advance of all that subsequent ages painfully realized.

Finally, there were thorough-going traditionalists who firmly refused to accept any of the new teachings. They rested on the position that man's mind was much too limited to question the word of the divine law and they read out of Judaism all who followed the new will-o'-the-wisp heresies.

The conflicts in the various groups had their effects in the development of Reform Judaism, the Haskalah, and a new militant orthodoxy. Their influence is not yet ended; they are still transmuting Jewish life. But the changes have already been sufficiently significant to make clear that no intellectual revolution in modern history has been so important as Darwinism and its attendant philosophies.

2. LEOPOLD ZUNZ: HUMANIST

The outstanding figure in the history of modern Jewish thought is Leopold Zunz, whose astounding genius gathered the best in the new scientific spirit and turned it to illumine the soul of his own people. Zunz was more than a historian, more even than the creator of the "*jüdische Wissenschaft,*" the Jewish Humanism. He reopened the rich stores of Jewish experience and used them to create a pride in Jewish achievement. This was virtually to re-create the Jew. For, apart from a superficial knowledge of Biblical history, the Jews had lost all knowledge of their past. The great Middle Age was a Sahara with a few oases, and even these were only vaguely known. The Talmud, in which thousands of Jewish scholars spent their lives, was only a vast compendium, and few knew who the sages were that had treated it, when they had lived, or the conditions under which they had worked. Before Zunz wrote, Jewish literature and Jews received similar treatment; both aroused the most violent passions, and both were either greatly undervalued or overestimated.

No people can remain vigorous without a glowing pride in its past. The finest Jewish intellects turned wistfully to other fields, and Christian thinkers made haste to point out that the Jewish contribution had ended with the Bible. "Abused," writes Oko, "by her collateral relatives, the Christian theologians, and left by her nearest kin to vegetate in a corner, the Cinderella among the literatures found in Leopold Zunz both the good fairy that intervened in her behalf and the noble prince who fell in love with her." [1]

Zunz's career was not adventurous. Born in 1794 in Detmold, Germany, of poor parents, he received the usual education in Hebrew grammar, the Bible, and the Talmud. But he soon branched out into other studies, and after earning a few marks as a student teacher he entered the University of Berlin. Here he passed under the influence of Wolf, de Wette, and other brilliant critical scholars who were revolutionizing the study of literature and theology. From them Zunz received an excellent grounding in the scientific method. He was already contributing to periodicals and received an appointment as one of the editors of a local political daily, an appointment which he soon resigned, however, because of his uncompromising liberal views.

All the while poverty stalked his doorstep. For, though he passed from one position to another in the attempt to keep the bread-box filled, he would never sacrifice his independence. He served as preacher in the new Temple in Berlin in 1820, and again in Prague in 1835, but neither congregation could under-

[1] S. Baruch (pseud.): "Leopold Zunz — Humanist," *Menorah Journal,* IX, 4 (February 1923).

stand his idealism, and his resignations were not lamented. Lecturing brought him no release from cares, for the proceeds were "in worthy parallel to the income of a chicken-slaughterer." For a few years he acted as principal of a Jewish teachers' training college in Berlin, but the institution was closed in 1850. Fortunately he was voted a small pension by the congregation, and this was sufficient for his needs. His wife, "the Zunzin," was an extraordinary housekeeper and was able to manage fishes and loaves with a pittance.

Despite his poverty and his devotion to books Zunz was no recluse. He was keenly interested in the politics of his day. During the mad year 1848 he spoke often at political rallies for the liberal cause; and whenever the Jews were threatened by bigots or tyrants, his pen became a halberd on their behalf.

Throughout a long life, which extended over ninety-two years, Zunz laboured to re-create the Jewish past. Only knowledge, he insisted, could destroy the mental ghetto in which Jews still lived. "In order to know which of the old is still valid, which of the outlived is to be rejected, which of the new is to be adopted, we must betake ourselves to the study of the people, both in its political and its moral sense." Already in 1818 he had penned a little brochure on rabbinical literature, a program of study for scholars and students, a program not fully realized to this day. He followed this first systematic survey of post-Biblical literature with a series of special studies in recondite fields, all immensely useful, however. The biography of Rashi, which dissipated a host of trashy legends that had grown up about the mediæval commentator, was a model of historical research.

Zunz's next work, on the history of the Jewish sermon, was the direct result of the intolerance of German nationalism, which followed Waterloo. The Prussian government forbade preaching in German in the synagogues, on the pretext that preaching was an exclusively Christian institution. Zunz at once began on a reply, published in 1832, which proved irrefutably that preaching was associated with Jewish life long before Christianity was born. But his volume was more than a defence. In developing his theme Zunz covered all of the Midrashic literature. Here he was ploughing through a vast, confused wilderness, and the order and system which he introduced, the skill with which he reconstructed ancient works from fragments, the historical information which he extracted, the structure of post-Biblical literature which he reared, made it clear that a master of Jewish science had appeared. The volume, bearing the unassuming title *Gottesdienstliche Vorträge der Juden* (*History of the Jewish Sermon*), became the most important Jewish work published in the nineteenth century.

After another series of highly original studies in the mediæval field Zunz began on his most extensive and most difficult work, the history of the Jewish liturgy. He discovered that the prayer-book was not primarily theological; it was a record of Jewish martyrdom for more than a thousand years. Stamped upon the prayers and the chants and the penitential laments were the unforgettable experiences of a people which knew no peer for suffering. The rationalists could jeer at the old-fashioned liturgy, and point out its shortcomings and naïvetés, but a Jewish humanist would understand. No æsthetic spirit was there, no appreciation of poetic rhythm, but a people that could not lift its head for pain, even to God Almighty, was in no position to hear or feel the music of their world. " The *Payyetanim* do not reveal new beauties in sky and in field and in flower. They describe not the felicities of Solomon; they recount the afflictions of Job. These troubadours were either chained to their thresholds in the ghetto, or, worse still, driven from land to land. Weary wanderers, they longed for shelter and rest rather than for the beauties of hill and dale, field and forest. Homeless slaves, they did not sing ballads in praise of kings and princes; they wailed *Kinot* or elegies lamenting the martyrdom of the *Kedoshim,* the saints of the synagog. Hounded, they uttered cries of pain and anguish, often disregarding form and order, grammar and style. And so, if the investigation of the *Piyyutim* did not yield an abundant vintage of ' sweet food of sweetly uttered knowledge,' it uncovered a rich vein of Jewish history." [1]

Zunz toiled for nearly fifty years on this masterpiece, which was published in three parts. He searched the world for manuscripts, ransacking every library, every synagogue, every museum where a new prayer or a new explanation of it could be found. It is said that Macaulay would walk miles to inspect a battlefield or a cathedral for a paragraph in his history. Zunz went hundreds of miles for a sentence. His astonishing diligence was rewarded by the fact that though there has been much new material unearthed since his day, his conclusions have scarcely required amending. He created a superb standard of Jewish scholarship and raised a host of disciples who blessed his name as they walked in his paths.

3. THE DEVELOPMENT OF REFORM JUDAISM

We have already discussed the far-reaching influence of Moses Mendelssohn and the renaissance for which he was largely responsible. Thousands of keen minds were lifted out of the narrow environment which had stultified Jewish life for centuries and were brought into contact with the stimulating currents of the European world. Then, providentially, came the French Revolution, which let down political barriers and granted the Jews, at least temporarily, the opportunity to achieve the economic independence which is the prerequisite of a stable cultural development.

Yet, after all, it was not an emancipated world. Christians and Jews were bound by ancient prejudices and theological preconceptions. There was little scientific Biblical criticism. The Bible was still regarded as a verbally inspired

---

[1] S. Baruch (pseud.): " Leopold Zunz — Humanist," *Menorah Journal,* IX, 217–18 (February 1923).

document, every letter of which was unchallenged truth, sanctified by ages of devotion. Mendelssohn, with all his progressive views, still belonged to the old world.

The first few decades of the nineteenth century brought important changes in the structure and content of Judaism. The changes followed two tendencies, the first opportunist and empirical, the second philosophical and doctrinaire. Many of the Jews who entered the European world wished to reshape Jewish practices to fit easily into European life. Too many of the traditional customs and ceremonies were obsolete; too many prevented intimate intercourse with the cultured men of other faiths. There was urgent need, therefore, to cut away those elements in the old faith which were no longer essential.

The second impetus to change was more fundamental. It came from groups of vigorous thinkers, deeply influenced by contemporary scientific developments, who sought to re-examine the very foundations of their religious faith. Timidity or sentiment, they declared, must no more interfere with the development of religious thought than with the progress of scientific thought. They probed to the roots, analysing the meaning and purpose of religion and revelation, of the law and its fulfilment, of the mission of Israel and its relation to the non-Jewish world. They completely reconstructed Judaism until it seemed to be almost a new religion.

At first the desire for simple adaptation was the more prominent. The changes which were made in services and practices followed no definite philosophy of reform. Thus, after much agitation, a congregation was organized in 1796 in Amsterdam, the Adath Jeshurun, which abolished from the services some of the more involved liturgical poems and introduced a sermon in the vernacular. Nearly ten years later Israel Jacobson, the president of the Westphalian consistory, which was established by Napoleon, introduced several further changes in his temple at Seesen. Realizing that the services had become unæsthetic and the prayers unintelligible, he sought to revitalize both by introducing German prayers, German songs, and German sermons. After several cautious preliminaries another modern temple was opened in Hamburg, in 1818, with all of the innovations which Jacobson had already established. Organ and choir were installed, several changes in the liturgy were made, and it was agreed that only such ceremonies would be permitted as could be easily followed and understood by those who had been German born and bred. Similar innovations were introduced in Berlin, in Leipzig, and in other large German communities. Soon the movement spread to Austria, Hungary, France, and Denmark, and to other lands.

There were as yet no radical departures from traditional Jewish practice; the authority of the *Shulhan Aruk* remained unchallenged. But one principle was already implied — namely, that the hold of the past could not remain absolute, that ceremonies and practices had no sanctity in themselves. They were symbols, the result of environment and historic conditions, and could be changed to keep pace with the spirit of the age. Because this principle was clearly involved, even minor innovations aroused immense opposition. The conservatives insisted that the slightest departures would lead to greater ones, that they struck at the body of Judaism, and that they were conducive of great harm, particularly in a time of religious laxness.

In 1819 a number of earnest young men organized a society for the scientific study of Judaism. The leading spirit was Leopold Zunz, and it attracted the keenest-minded young Jews of Germany, among them Heine, Jacobson, Gans (a disciple of Hegel), and Moses Moser, whom Heine called "a living appendix to Nathan the Wise." The society intended, "through culture and education, to bring the Jews into harmonious relations with the age and the nations in which they live." Zunz hoped that thorough study and research would rid Judaism of its outworn elements and place it upon a rational and defensible basis. It would remove the barriers that existed between Jew and non-Jew, by finding a common cultural and ethical ground. Zunz edited the journal of the society with conspicuous ability, but the program appealed only to a few intellectuals and it made little headway. Gans accepted baptism, the other leaders drifted away, and the society died. It served an eminently useful purpose, however, in stimulating discussion of the principles of Judaism and their effectiveness in modern life.

The foremost leader of modern Reform Judaism was Abraham Geiger, a brilliant German scholar and critic, admirably educated in Hebrew and secular learning, hating all manner of intellectual compromise. He believed, like many of his generation, that Judaism was not fixed and immutable, but was a continuously developing religion. Revelation had not been vouchsafed to man once and for all many thousands of years ago, but was the gift of the sages and seers of every generation. Traditions were, of course, valuable, but they were not to petrify the healthy life of religion; as they became antiquated, they were to be discarded. Geiger distinguished between the spirit of tradition and the separate traditions. He held that the spirit of tradition is continuous, while separate traditions must pass when they have outlived their significance.

In the light of these concepts Geiger stressed the ethical side of religion rather than the ritualist. He was little interested in phylacteries or dietary laws or Passover dishes, but he was vitally interested in social justice. He maintained that all references to a restored national life and to a personal Messiah should be dropped from the creed. For he refused to link up the destiny of Israel with Palestine, or to consider the Diaspora as necessarily an abnormal and unfortunate status. It was Israel's mission to be an example to all nations, to strive for a society in which the prophetic ideals would dominate the life of men.

For the moment Geiger's ideas, though vigorous and stimulating, were merely academic. But when the reformer was elected rabbi of Breslau as a colleague of S. A. Tiktin, who represented the older, conservative point of view, a tremendous controversy began. Tiktin and his followers tried every means to prevent Geiger from ascending the pulpit and even called in the assistance of the Prussian government. Geiger's friends were persistent, and after two years the young heretic was able to preach his first sermon. His words were a clarion to the hosts of reform: " Judaism is not a finished tale; there is much in its present form that must be changed or abolished; it can assume a better and higher position in the world only if it will rejuvenate itself; all should unite in this work." When Tiktin died, three years later, and Geiger was elected chief rabbi in his place, the conservative opposition withdrew to form a new congregation.

The conflict had become more than a local matter. Rabbis in Germany and Austria gave their opinions on the disputed points, and soon their own congregations were divided and there were secessions everywhere. In Hamburg the issue which precipitated the schism was the revision of the prayer-book. In Frankfurt a long dispute began over the importance of circumcision. In England the Reform wing petitioned for a choir, the revision of the prayers, and sermons in English. When the petition was denied, a new congregation was organized, which, however, could gain no recognition from the conservative Jewish Board of Deputies. The schism caused considerable inconvenience, for the Reform minister, not being officially certified by the board, could perform no religious ceremonies. It required a special act of Parliament, in 1856, to secure official recognition of the reform congregation.

The immediate cause of dissension varied in each community. Yet the fundamental issues were similar. Was Judaism a developing religion which could be adapted in each generation, or was it a revealed faith whose development was circumscribed by definite and immutable premises?

After the revolutionary year of 1848 the Reform agitation died down. On the whole, a reaction set in and reform made little further headway. The leadership of the movement passed to the United States, where the authority of the *Shulhan Aruk* was repudiated and the most radical readjustments were made. Yet even in Europe, though reform lost its early vigour, it included among its champions some of the most influential leaders in Jewish life. After 1860 the impetus given to scientific thought by the work of Darwin and his disciples strengthened the Reform position and clarified its aims.

The comparison that has often been made between Geiger and Luther and between Reform and the Reformation is quite superficial and requires much qualifying. Geiger went much further than Luther. He broke from the dead hand of the past, he interpreted religious ceremonies and dogmas as symbols, not as sacraments, and he placed his faith squarely in the currents of progressive thought.

For I had found
That outward forms, the loftiest, still receive
Their finer influence from the Life within.

Too often, unfortunately, Reform Jews were little concerned with the true significance of their faith. They flocked to Reform because it made life more comfortable or because it enabled them to climb higher upon the social ladder. But where the true spirit of Geiger's ideals was caught, there was a happy revitalization of Judaism.

4. THE HASKALAH

The Haskalah (Enlightenment) is the general term applied to the remarkable cultural renaissance which developed in eastern Europe in the nineteenth century. It began with a revived interest in Hebrew and Hebrew learning. It passed into a broad humanism which aimed to break through Jewish exclusiveness by bringing the cultural richness of the European world into Jewish life. The Maskil, the product of the Haskalah, was usually an emancipated individualist, his critical faculties admirably sharpened, who took literally the Haskalah watchword: "Let there be light." He assimilated European literature and philosophy, he familiarized himself with grammatical Hebrew, and he emphasized the value of the poetical and critical parts of Hebrew literature. He broke sharply from the old theory that Jewish education was a religious exercise or a spiritual discipline rather than a means of developing the intellectual and æsthetic potentialities of men.

The Haskalah first grounded itself in Galicia, where the magnificent work of Mendelssohn deeply influenced Krochmal and Rapaport, the two outstanding humanists of eastern Europe. Nachman Krochmal, a frail, shy, scholarly type, caught up in the liberating enthusiasm which was inspired by the Berlin sage, set to work to investigate critically the vast stores of Jewish history and rabbinical literature. He hoped, through scientific study, to dissipate misconceptions, to demonstrate to his own people and to the Gentile world that Jewish lore was not a mummified body of legalisms. The results of his life's work he set forth in his epochal *Guide for the Perplexed of Modern Times,* posthumously published, "the most original piece of philosophic writing in modern Hebrew," in which he pointed out the peculiar spiritual genius of Israel, and the place into which it fitted in the universal scheme.

Krochmal had considerable influence upon a younger colleague, Solomon Rapoport, who also applied an alert and searching mind to a critical study of the Jewish past. Rapoport wrote several luminous biographies of mediæval notables, Saadiah, Hai Gaon, and others who had become mere names, but whose literary and philosophical contributions were well worth resuscitating. Rapoport's studies influenced the work of Zunz, Jost, and the whole modern school of scientific investigators of Jewish cultural history. Stimulated by the two great humanists, Galicia produced an important school of Hebrew writers, Erte, Letteris, and a host of others.

The chief stronghold of the Haskalah, however, lay in Lithuania and in Russia itself. The earliest Maskilim, like most of the Russian intelligentsia, were almost entirely dependent on German stimulus. There was nothing in Russia to inspire them; the great giant still slept; the day of the flowering of Russian genius had not yet come. Young Jews consequently turned to Mendelssohn's German translation of the Pentateuch and the Psalms. They mastered the language and wandered joyously into the green German pastures, their cup running over. The wisdom of the German thinkers was theirs, Goethe, Schelling, Hegel, Fichte, and, above all, Kant. So great was the adulation for the philosopher of Königsberg that one ingenious student linked up the letters of his name with the Hebrew initials of the Psalmist's verse: " My heart panteth after thee."

The deep interest in German learning led directly to a renaissance of Hebrew, for it sent the humanists to the springs of Hebrew culture. The poetry and the prose which was produced in the first flush of enthusiasm was often not of very high calibre, but the young writers were just beginning to find themselves and were blazing the trail for the maturer and more disciplined artists of the next generation.

But it was not easy to be a Maskil. The conservatives were fearful that irresponsible wanderings into other fields would weaken the solidarity of Jewish life. They noted with alarm the laxness in religious observance which characterized many of the Maskilim, and when several passed into apostasy, they became panic-stricken. They opposed the "prostitution" of the holy tongue for secular purposes; they condemned the popular German works and threatened to read out of Judaism all who followed the Dessauer philosopher or imitated the "Deitcher." Many families were rent by the dissensions which developed between old and young. The Maskilim were obliged to turn their talents more to satirizing the violence of the traditionalists and the Hasidim than to creative endeavours.

The attempt during the regime of Nicholas I to wean Jews from the Talmud and to promote secular education seemed to give an impetus to the Haskalah. The German liberal Lilienthal co-operated zealously with Uvarov, the Russian Minister of Education, in establishing secular schools, and many of the Maskilim were employed as teachers. But Nicholas's motive was not Jewish enlightenment, but Jewish assimilation. The oppressions which accompanied his educational reforms, and the onerous candle tax which supported his schools, united liberals and conservatives in opposition and brought discredit to the Maskilim who had been associated with the tsar's policies.

One earnest attempt was made in all the sound and fury of conflict to bring the orthodox to reason. Isaac Bär Levinsohn laboured, during a long life, despite physical ailments and the traducings of the fanatics, to reconcile the Haskalah spirit with traditional Judaism. In old age, almost blind, " with neither brother, wife, child, nor even a sound body," he still persevered in his thankless task. At one time the condemnation of his work became so bitter that he was compelled to leave his native town.

Levinsohn was himself a profound rabbinical scholar and a good student of the classics, philosophy, and the Oriental languages. In 1828 he published his *Learning in Israel,* dedicated to Science, a vigorous appeal to link up Talmudic studies with the best in secular learning. He pointed out that the great Jewish teachers, authorities in their own fields, needed supplementing. " Art and science," he wrote, " are steadily progressing. To perfect ourselves in them we must resort to non-Jewish sources." The little volume won the admiration of the tsar, who presented the author with a thousand roubles as a mark of his esteem. But the orthodox looked on sullenly. Only those who wished to be convinced were convinced.

Having, to his own satisfaction at least, justified the activity of the Maskilim, Levinsohn now sought to explain the richness of traditional Judaism to the Christian world, " to expose to Christian eyes the world of Jewish spiritual life, founded on the principles of the highest morality, a world then unknown to Russian Christians." In *The House of Judah,* published in 1838, he developed his philosophy of Judaism and pointed out its excellent qualities. This work, however, was more of an influence upon his younger contemporaries who were being drawn from their Jewish loyalty than upon the Russian Christians.

Levinsohn lived till 1860, long enough to see the fruits of the first generation of Maskilim, to whom he had been an endless source of inspiration. He fully deserved the title bestowed upon him, " the Russian Mendelssohn."

The most important impetus to the Haskalah was given by the early liberalism of Alexander II. Taking fullest advantage of his reform edicts, thousands of young Jews flocked to the schools and universities and eagerly sharpened their intelligence on the whetstones of European culture. In 1860 a splendid journal, *Ha-melitz* (the *Interpreter*), was founded, and it became the organ of the new intelligentsia. Three years later came the organization of the Society for the Promotion of Culture among the Jews in Russia. Its object was " to spread the knowledge of the Russian language among the Jews, to publish and assist others in publishing, in Russian as well as in Hebrew, useful works and journals — and, further, to assist the young in devoting themselves to the pursuit of science and knowledge." It was a healthy sign that the most influential Jews in the country supported the new society. Soon there were several Jewish publishing houses which not only printed original Hebrew works but also made available in Hebrew and Yiddish the classics of European literature. A class of Jewish literary men developed who lived entirely by the pen. Despite poor pay and the precarious Grub-street existence which, like their compeers in other lands, they were obliged to lead, their artistry lit up the darkness of Russian life and helped to make it tolerable.

It is possible to name only a few of the representative Maskilim who thus made the late nineteenth century memorable in the history of Jewish literature. There was Abraham Mapu, the pioneer Hebrew novelist, whose *Painted Vulture* was the first realistic novel in Hebrew and whose *Love of Zion* sold in hundreds of thousands of copies. Many were the young readers who were compelled to conceal their copies from the eyes of irate parents. There was Mendele Mocher Seforim (Solomon Abramowitch), the Jewish Cervantes, whose chief power lay in his story-telling. He probed the life of the masses and detailed it with gentle humour. There was Judah Leib Gordon, the leading Hebrew poet of the day, who surveyed Jewish history from Biblical times to the present in magnificent poetry and whose fluent, mellifluous prose, bitingly satirical of fanatical obscurantism, made him as feared by his opponents as he was loved by his admirers. There was Shalom Aleichem (Rabinowitch), the prince of Jewish humorists, who found no subject too humble to adorn with his subtle art. And finally there was Judah Leb Peretz, the interpreter of Hasidic life, with all of its beauty and pathos.

It was natural that the Haskalah should arouse an intense nationalism among the Jews, just as it was aroused by the cultural revival among contemporary peoples, the Balkan nationalities, the Italians, the Hungarians, the Irish. When Alexander II turned from his youthful liberalism, and legal emancipation became an empty formula in Russia, the masses turned in weariness to other dreams. Those who found the doors of Russian life closed upon them fed hungrily upon the new nationalistic literature, which gave the disillusioned a hope and the discontented a program. The Haskalah, in this sense, was a forerunner of Zionism.

The foremost of Maskilim, Perez Smolenskin, a fervent apostle of Jewish nationalism, began to turn the cultural renaissance in the direction of his ideal. In his journal the *Dawn* he sought to inculcate among his youthful readers a love for the Hebrew language, and he never tired of pointing out that the acquisition of broad culture meant nothing unless it made the Jew more conscious of his Jewishness. "You wish to be like the other peoples," he cried out to the assimilators. "So do I. Be, I pray you, be like them. Search and find knowledge, avoid and forsake superstition; above all, be not ashamed of the rock whence you were hewn. Yes, be like the other peoples, proud of your literature, jealous of your self-respect, hopeful, even as all persecuted peoples are hopeful, of the speedy arrival of the day when we too shall reinhabit the land which once was and still is our own."

In *The Eternal People*, published in 1873, Smolenskin developed the thesis that the Jews are a nation and required Palestine for the normal development of their genius. It was highly significant that in his theme he dissociated, for the first time in Jewish history, the ideal of a Messianic restoration from a religious program. Smolenskin believed that the Messianic era would be realized when the Jews achieved political and moral emancipation in a land of their own.

Of the last generation of Maskilim by far the greatest is Nahman Haym Bialik, the final and most complete representative of the new Hebrew renaissance. His more enthusiastic admirers count him the profoundest poet in all Jewish history, ranking with the best in Biblical literature. He was born in 1873 in the province of Volhynia and spent a youth of sorrow, ground down by poverty and a fanatical orthodoxy. Neither succeeded in repressing his lyrical gifts, however, which were the more miraculous as coming from one who had been artificially trained in the Hebrew language. He mirrored the life of his day, its intellectual anæmia, its disproportion, its tortured longings. The massacre of Kishinev stirred him to prophetic fury and his *City of Slaughter* was not only a slashing indictment of the barbarities of Russian civilization, but also a flaming indictment of his people, " heirs to Hasmonæan glory," but now rendered craven in the face of persecutors. " One has the feeling," writes Maurice Samuel, the ablest of Bialik's translators, " that somehow a greater drama than Hamlet will never be written, that there will never be a greater religious utterance than that of the prophets. So one feels that the struggles of a people in bondage, wakening vaguely toward a new life, loving building the new but not yet assimilated to it, the past and yet breaking with much of it, will never be more perfectly expressed than in Bialik." [1]

> There are abandoned corners of our Exile,
> Remote, forgotten cities of Dispersion,
> Where still in secret burns our ancient light,
> Where God has saved a remnant from disaster.
> There, brands that glimmer in a ruin of ashes,
> Pent and unhappy souls maintain the vigil —
> Spirits grown old beyond the count of time,
> Grown old beyond the reckoning of days.
> And when thou goest forth alone, at nightfall,
> Wandering in one of these, the sacred cities,
> When heaven above is quick with breaking stars,
> And earth beneath with whispering spirit-winds —
> Thine ear will catch the murmur of a voice,
> Thine eye will catch the twinkle of a light
> Set in a window, and a human form —
> A shadow, like the shadow of death — beyond,

[1] *Selected Poems of Bialik*, Introduction, p. 14.

A shadow trembling, swaying back and forth,
A voice, an agony, that lifts and falls,
And comes toward thee upon the waves of silence.
Mark well the swaying shadow and the voice:
It is a Masmid in his prison-house,
A prisoner, self-guarded, self-condemned,
Self sacrificed to study of the Law. . . .

All, all of you do I remember yet,
In all my wanderings you go with me —
Your likeness graven in my heart for ever.
And I remember, too, how strong, how sturdy
The seed must be that withers in those fields.
How rich would be the blessing if one beam
Of living sunlight could break through to you.
How great the harvest to be reaped in joy.
If once the wind of life should pass through you,
And blow clear through to the Yeshivah doors.
All, all of you do I remember yet —
The hungry childhood and the bitter manhood,
And my heart weeps for my unhappy people . . .
How burned, how blasted must our portion be,
If seed like this is withered in its soil. . . .[1]

[1] From "The Masmid," translated from the Hebrew by Maurice Samuel.

CHAPTER TWENTY-SIX

THE REVIVAL OF ANTI-SEMITISM

I. CAUSES AND CHARACTERISTICS

By the end of the nineteenth century the intellect had won mighty conquests. Scientific progress was revolutionizing life and living. Every type of humanitarianism was enthusiastically encouraged. A brilliant French bacteriologist predicted that disease would soon be conquered; the tsar of an enslaved empire entered the lists for world peace. It appeared as if the savage in man was fast being stilled. Yet human history is shot with paradoxes. The era which filled liberals with hope for a new world-order witnessed the slavery of competitive armaments, and the preparation for wars on a terrifyingly large scale. As all Europe "breathed a harsher air," a most rabid kind of anti-Semitism appeared, taking possession of every country and endangering all that the Jews had laboriously won.

The political conditions in Europe after 1870 were largely responsible for the animosities which suddenly flared up again. A number of new nations had just been born, proud of their heritage and jealous of their independence. Germany came together, welded by Bismarck's blood-and-iron policy, and the victorious empire was baptized in a fierce war with France. Italy proved that it was more than a geographical expression and flung Austria out of the peninsula. The dry bones of the Balkan states stirred themselves and shook off the Turkish yoke. Other peoples who were not successful in winning national freedom vowed never to rest content until their oppressors had been overthrown. Half a dozen militant nationalities in the Austrian empire gave the emperor no respite, and it was necessary several times to drown Poland's revolutions in blood. So Europe flamed with national hatreds and fears and jealousies and the cult of the one-hundred-per-cent patriot became supreme. Nations which had just emerged fought desperately against every minority group which threatened its homogeneity. Nations threatened by internal revolts ruthlessly harried those who would not conform.

In such a Europe the Jews were unable to find peace. Everywhere they were looked upon as an alien group, a particularly stubborn, unassimilable group. They spoke and wrote the idiom of the country perfectly, they filled prominent places in the political, economic, and intellectual life, they gave their blood for its ideals. Yet the fierce nationalists could not trust them. They were different and they remained different. In theory it was admitted that variety in culture and tradition enriched the national life. In practice those who did not readily fit into this national pattern were instinctively hated.

The triumph of the bourgeoisie was another circumstance which fuelled the anti-Semitic tendencies in modern Europe. The industrial middle class, after a continuous struggle which lasted for more than a century, succeeded, by 1870, in entrenching itself in the places of the mighty. The Jews were an important element in this bourgeoisie, a disproportionately prominent element. They were the leading financiers; they controlled the press and exercised a prodigious influence in political life. " Jewish capitalism," " a Jewish press," were terms flung about indiscriminately to prove that the Jews unduly dominated the life of the country. On the other hand, the Jews seemed to stand out too clearly, too prominently, among the radical proletariat who preached various brands of socialism. It was just as easy, then, to prove that radicalism was a Jewish monopoly, that discontented, reckless Jews were in a league to undermine the foundations of capitalistic society.

Then there were the grievances of the clerical groups, who were rapidly losing their favoured positions in the modern State. Until nearly the middle of the century their monopoly of education, their right to innumerable tolls and taxes, their close association with the political and social life of the nation, had been scarcely questioned. With the modern development of rationalism and the growing tendency towards secularization a sharp reaction took place. Liberals in every land strove to emancipate education from Church control, to end the partnership of State and Church, to secularize the State. By 1870, though not entirely successful, they had won notable victories. Jewish liberals naturally associated themselves with the anti-clerical cause. Nurtured in the noble traditions of the rationalist philosophers, they attacked denominational education and the ideal of a state officially dominated by sect or creed. The Church groups never forgave Jewish participation in the struggle. They pilloried anti-clerical liberalism as a Jewish conspiracy and added their thunder to the denunciation of Jews and Judaism.

These political, economic, and religious factors, all operating together, gave rise to modern anti-Semitism, which influenced not only Jewish life, but the life of every European country. Political parties were organized, active in every election, whose most important aim was to combat Jewish control in the State. In vain the liberals sought to dissipate fears, to point out fallacies. Argument was useless, for anti-Semitism was a disease, not a syllogism.

2. ANTI-SEMITISM IN GERMANY

Anti-Semitism burst upon Germany soon after the Franco-Prussian War, and it gained in strength until it became a powerful political and social force. The German victory over France brought the enormous indemnity of one billion dollars into the country within two or three years. As money became cheap and sought lucrative outlets, Germany entered into an orgy of wild speculation. Every kind of enterprise was sponsored and eagerly supported until the bubble burst in 1873 and ruined a great number of individuals and firms. In the searching investigations which followed, it was revealed that many Jews were involved in the scandals. The cry was at once taken up by the enemies of the bourgeoisie that Germany was in the grip of Jewish corruptionists. Wilhelm Marr's pamphlet *Der Sieg des Judenthums über das Germanthum* (*The Victory of Judaism over Germanism*), which discussed the overweening influence of Jews in the commercial life of Germany, became an anti-Semitic textbook. Glogau's *Die Börsen und Grundergeschwindel in Berlin* (*The Bourses and the Company Swindlers in Berlin*), dealing in detail with the Jewish participation in the scandals of 1873, added to the furore. " The agitation gradually swelled, its growth being helped by the sensitiveness and *cacoëthes scribendi* of the Jews themselves, who contributed two pamphlets and a much larger proportion of newspaper articles for every one supplied by their opponents." [1] Until 1879, however, the outcry remained literary, and those who refused to lose their heads hoped that it would die out when passions were cooled.

Now Bismarck himself helped to turn the agitation to more serious channels. Personally he was perhaps not unfriendly to the Jews, though he is said to have remarked that he was born with an anti-Jewish bias. But he was overwhelmed by a triple fight, against the Catholics, the National Liberals, and the Socialists, and as he felt himself losing ground, he found that he could cover his failures by making scapegoats of the Jews.

The Catholics, by their firm loyalty to the Vatican and to the doctrine of papal infallibility, were becoming a menace, in Bismarck's view, to the development of the empire. In 1871 two acts were passed, one making it a penal offence for priests to attack the government from their pulpits, and the other expelling the Jesuits from the country. These were followed by the May Laws, which compelled candidates for the priesthood to attend government schools and to pass government examinations. By these acts Bismarck hoped to release education from Church control. The Church fought back, and for six years the " *Kulturkampf*," as the struggle was grandiloquently called, subordinated every other issue in Germany. The " Diocletian persecution " strengthened the Church, and in the end Bismarck surrendered and repealed most of the anti-Catholic legislation. But on his way " to Canossa " he skilfully threw the blame for much of what had happened upon the Jewish leaders who had been in the forefront of the battle. Even before the surrender Catholic animosity against the Jews had been aroused, and Pope Pius IX celebrated Christmas of 1872 by issuing a diatribe denouncing the Jews as enemies of Christ and a pernicious influ-

---

[1] Wolf in *Encyclopædia Britannica*, II, 136 (s. v. " Anti-Semitism ").

ence in civilized society. The papal pronouncement, widely advertised, excited all the centres of Catholic strength, especially in Germany.

Meantime the National Liberals, who had loyally supported Bismarck while the German state was being fashioned, were growing restive and insisted upon democratic changes in the constitution. When Bismarck flatly refused, two German Jewish liberals, Lasker and Bamberger, led a secession of the party into opposition. Bismarck, to continue in office, was compelled to seek a new majority among the Conservatives and Catholic Centrists. He shrewdly attempted to discredit the opposition as a Jewishly dominated group and his hints that Jewish influence should be destroyed brought an anti-Semitic political party into existence.

The whole situation was complicated by the Iron Chancellor's battle against the Socialists. He bitterly opposed the party, less for its economic doctrines than for its pacifism and internationalism, which sapped the foundations of the military State which he had created. At his request the Reichstag passed a series of "exceptional laws" which struck at Socialist propaganda. But the more Bismarck fought, the stronger the enemy became. In each new election the Socialists polled an increasing number of votes. Bismarck realized that he was beaten and repealed the restrictions which had driven the discontented underground. At the same time he determined to "kill Socialism with kindness," and he took over many of its more attractive social reforms, such as workmen's compensation, health and old-age insurance, and a "few more drops of social oil." Having proved his friendship for the fundamental needs of the German proletariat, he joined with the court chaplain, Adolf Stöcker, the founder of the Christian Socialist party, in drawing a distinction between decent Socialism, which was moderate and Christian, and Jewish socialism, whch was subversive.

When the anti-Semites began to organize into a political party after 1879, Bismarck did nothing to check them. Nor did the leading nationalist historian, von Treitschke, who rather encouraged it and lent prestige to it with his serenely developed philosophical anti-Semitism. "Even in the circles of highest culture," he said, "among men who would reject any idea of religious intolerance with horror, one single cry is heard, 'The Jews are our misfortune.'" The anti-Semites, recruited from extreme nationalists, junkers, clericals, and opportunists, grew in strength, and Germany rang with their venomous denunciations. Petitions were introduced to exclude the Jews from the schools and universities and from holding any public offices; pamphlets and books attacking every phase of Jewish life were broadcast through the country. Hardly a day passed without a duel between Jews and their detractors.

Soon cultured Germany, the centre of learning, the ideal of Hegel's dreams, was in the grip of mediæval Jew-baiting. A wave of physical violence swept enlightened cities as well as ignorant hamlets. Associations of women were formed to boycott Jewish merchants. In 1880 a priest remarked in the Bavarian

Diet: "If you wish to assist the starving population in the Spessart, make one brief law: 'Every Jewish pedlar is to be shot or hanged.'" Late in the eighties Herrmann Ahlwardt, a clever scoundrel and charlatan, electrified the country by his violent and unqualified fulminations against the Jews, and, though he was ultimately imprisoned for libel, he became a national hero. When the American Congress passed a resolution of sympathy on the death, in New York, of the famous German liberal Lasker, Bismarck curtly refused to transmit it to the Reichstag. A ritual murder case occurred in Xanten, Prussia, in 1891.

The climax came in 1892 when the Centrist group became strong enough to strike up an alliance with the Conservative party, which went on record with a new plank in its platform: "We combat the oppressive and disintegrating Jewish influence on our national life; we demand for our Christian people a Christian magistracy and Christian teachers for Christian pupils; we repudiate the excesses of anti-Semitism." Later a revolt of the more extreme Conservatives made it necessary to expunge the last phrase!

Ultimately the agitation collapsed, especially when several of the leaders were found guilty of forgery and swindling and when the Conservatives realized their mistake in linking the fortunes of the party to the stupidities of an Ahlwardt. But the movement left deep scars. Jews were no longer so sure of their stability. The glowing hopes which they had built upon political emancipation collapsed as they realized the impossibility of ever becoming identified completely with the German people. A blighting pessimism settled upon them, and the most progressive elements abandoned the country to seek new life in the Promised Land, America. The exodus was not stayed until the outbreak of the World War.

3 · AUSTRIA-HUNGARY AND ROUMANIA

In Austria the clericals and the aristocrats had never been reconciled to the loss of authority which the *Ausgleich* of 1867 had entailed. Their chagrin was not diminished by the knowledge that the new constitution, which destroyed their prestige, gave legal equality to the Jews and the other despised races of the empire. They hastened to join in the clamour of the nationalists who despised the Polish Jews of Galicia, herded together in the great cities, speaking their own language, adhering to their own queer customs, and resisting every attempt to nationalize them.

The financial crisis of 1873, which ruined thousands of German speculators, had reverberations in Vienna too. There were sharp attacks on the liberal bourgeoisie and the Jews, who were disproportionately large among them. The Christian Socialists joined in these attacks, denouncing the Jewish control of land. Individualism in landed property, they held, was legitimate only when the landlords were "the families of the nation" and not "cosmopolitan financiers."

As in Germany, the literary anti-Semitism became a political force by the turn of events. In 1879 the Liberals seceded from the Taafe ministry, which threw itself upon the support of the Czechs, Slavs, and clericals, and to keep this support the ministry made concessions to the reactionaries. There followed a series of laws which debarred Jews from teaching-positions in country districts and established commercial and educational restrictions. In Vienna the anti-Semites became strong enough in 1895 to capture the municipal council and to elect Karl Lueger, a notorious Jew-baiter, as burgomaster. For some time the emperor refused to sanction the election, but Lueger was twice returned by growing majorities, and ultimately the emperor yielded. Until the outbreak of the war Vienna was ruled almost continuously by the anti-Semites, and the example of the capital was followed in other districts of Lower Austria. Meantime there were outrages throughout the country, culminating in the disastrous riots in Prague in 1897. In Polna, Bohemia, in 1889, a young Jew, Hilsner, was convicted of ritual murder and languished in prison until he was freed after the revolution of 1918.

In Hungary anti-Semitic propaganda had also been carried on by the clericals since the promulgation of the *Ausgleich* of 1867. The movement made little headway, however, for liberalism was strongly entrenched, and the Jews, by their loyalty and patriotism, had earned an honourable position in the State. Even the influx of Jewish refugees from the persecutions of Russia did not arouse the nation. It was not until the revival of the dreadful blood accusations in the eighties that the ignorant and the superstitious were swept into an orgy of hate that threatened the Jewish life of the country.

For some years Dr. Rohling, professor of Hebrew in the University of Prague, had been lending his name to the anti-Semitic attacks of the clericals. In 1881 he declared that the murder of Christians for ritual purposes was part of the secret Jewish doctrine. Though his arguments were easily exposed by eminent scholars, the refutations, as usual, were much less influential among the masses than the accusations. In April 1882 a Christian girl disappeared from the Hungarian village of Tisza Eszlar and the anti-Semites at once seized upon the event for their own purposes. They supervised the investigation and brought about the arrest of fifteen Jews. The best legal talent that they could muster came to the trial to damn the accused. The case was one of the most dramatic and sensational of the century and proved the debacle of the Hungarian anti-Semites. They were so completely discredited that they did not raise their heads again.

The Jews of Austria and Hungary were taught the emptiness of mere legal equality. They had tried hard to be optimists. They had identified themselves with liberal and radical parties to fight against the bigots and the rascals who misrepresented the finer traditions of the nation, hoping always that history would not repeat itself. Yet in every political and economic crisis a whole nation lost its equilibrium, and the most elementary rights of the Jews, rights taken for granted by every self-respecting person, became woefully insecure. So the pious Jew of Cracow and the sensitive critic of Vienna and the keen-eyed student of Prague were all brought together again to face the common problem of spanning an apparently endless gulf where glowed the unreasonable hates and passions of unemancipated men.

Anti-Semitism needed no external stimulus in bigoted little Roumania. The country was among the most backward in Europe. Nearly ninety per cent of its population of five and a half million were ignorant peasants. During the eighteenth century a large Jewish population filtered in, constantly augmented by refugees from Austria, Poland, and Russia. The Jews formed the only middle class, practically the only intelligent class, and the commerce of the country usually passed into their hands. They were bitterly hated by the Roumanian peasantry, but so long as the Turks were in control of the territory, the Jews suffered no hardships.

Early in the nineteenth century, however, the sultan's grip began to relax and gradually Roumania freed itself. Along with autonomy came a revived Roumanian nationalism, fierce, cruel, and intolerant of every alien minority. Long before Hegel glorified a homogeneous nationalism, the Roumanians were unconsciously applying it. The Jews were the first to feel the change of masters. Every prince who ruled the State had new whims to make them uncomfortable. Jewish residence and occupations were limited and the whole code of discrimination which the Russians had developed was applied in Roumania — with this difference: in Russia oppression came from a benighted autocracy; in Roumania it came from the elected representatives of a constitutional state.

It was only a short step from discrimination to violence. Jews were blamed for plagues and for national misfortunes. Blood libels cropped up with sickening frequency. In 1867 persecution on a large scale began, countenanced by the premier, Bratianu, who revived obsolete laws and expelled the Jews from the villages. The European world protested and the American counsel, Peixotto, tried strenuously to bring the government to reason. But the promises given were not kept and Roumania continued to rival Russia in its bigotry.

After the Russo-Turkish war the statesmen at Berlin agreed to recognize Roumania as a sovereign state. Disraeli insisted that independence be conditional upon the grant of religious and civil liberty to all the inhabitants of the land. He won over the cynical Bismarck and the other delegates, although Gorchakov of Russia consented most unwillingly. The famous Article xliv, guaranteeing full political and civil equality to all minorities, was incorporated into the treaty. Roumania found pretexts, however, for evading the conditions of the clause, and until 1902 only about eighty Jews were admitted to citizenship. Restrictions and persecutions continued. Jews were denied entrance to professions, to posts in the public service, to free academic opportunities. Until 1914 the Jews of Roumania remained legal helots, and the tragedy of their situation was increased tenfold by the horrors of the World War.

The persecutions of the government naturally drove the Jews into the liberal and radical parties. They also stimulated a continuous exodus from the country, and in 1902 the number of emigrants, an element which Roumania could ill afford to lose, ran into the thousands.

4 · FRANCE AND THE DREYFUS CASE

Even France, which had been a centre of liberalism for several decades, was deeply affected by the new anti-Semitism. The establishment of the third French Republic in 1870 meant a serious diminution of clerical influence in the State; in fact, the new government was definitely anti-clerical in its policies. The discomfited group joined with the Royalists, who were also desperately inimical to the bourgeoisie, in denouncing the whole liberal movement as a Jewish conspiracy. Because France had attracted a large number of German Jewish financial adventurers, they maintained that the Jews were in a league with Germany to destroy France, repeating the arguments of the German anti-Semites that the Jews were in a league with France to destroy Germany.

A series of sensational events now crystallized the opposition of the anti-Semites and lent it vitality. In 1877 Paul Bontoux, a former employee of the Rothschilds, attempting to break down the so-called Jewish and Protestant financial monopoly in France, organized the Union Générale. It was subscribed to by Catholics and blessed by the Pope, and for nearly five years its operations were so successful that its shares rose from 125 francs to 3200. But its prosperity was built on the bubble of wild speculation, and when it burst, the Union collapsed, with liabilities amounting to more than two hundred million francs. The cry was at once raised by those who had been ruined that the company had been strangled by the machinations of Jewish financiers.[1]

Meantime a determined fight against royalists and clericals was being waged by Gambetta, the eloquent leader of the liberals. His unalloyed republicanism was linked with sound statesmanship, and his policies went forward steadily to victory. When he dissolved two hundred and sixty-one monasteries and destroyed Jesuit influence in the State, the clericals were beside themselves. Their rage against the Jews was not diminished by the knowledge that Jewish liberals were among their most stalwart opponents and that Gambetta himself had Jewish blood in his veins.

A formidable anti-Semitic representation was returned to the Chamber of

[1] Much of the ruinous competition had come from Lebaudy, a Catholic sugar-merchant.

Deputies in 1885. Next year came the most exhaustive and exhausting of modern works on anti-Semitism, Drumont's *La France juive (Jewish France)*, in which the author brought together all the propaganda that he could unearth or manufacture. Unfortunately, soon after its publication the Panama Canal Company, in which several Jews were involved, crashed, ruining thousands of gullible stock-holders. Drumont's accusations seemed to be grounded in fact, and his work went through hundreds of editions. In 1892 his journal, *La Libre Parole (Free Speech)*, began to appear, with a regular lesson on Jewish corruption. It devoted itself to ferreting out scandals and gained an immense popularity when it exposed the swindles of the Panama Company.

The culmination of the long period of anti-Semitic agitation came in 1894 when a Jewish captain, Alfred Dreyfus, was accused of selling military secrets to the German government. He was court-martialled and summarily condemned to solitary confinement for life on Devil's Island, off Guiana. His punishment was dramatically advertised when he was publicly degraded in the court of the military school in Paris. Dreyfus protested his innocence to the end, crying out in the face of the adjutant who tore off his insignia and broke his sword: "You are degrading an innocent man! Long live France!" In 1896 young Lieutenant-Colonel Picquart, head of the Intelligence Department, became convinced that a terrible injustice had been done. He carefully inspected the *bordereau*, the list of military secrets which it was alleged Dreyfus had attempted to sell to the Germans, and found that it was filled with grammatical and technical inaccuracies. Picquart brought the matter to the attention of his superiors, but he was warned to let matters be and was transferred to a foreign station. The gallant young officer at once began a fight to save Dreyfus from the terrible injustice which was ruining his life.

Picquart's evidence was convincing to the liberals of France, and Émile Zola, Anatole France, Georges Clemenceau, and other brilliant intellectuals put their resources at the command of those who insisted upon a retrial for Dreyfus. Zola stormed like a new Voltaire. Despite all threats to him he denounced the martyrdom of an innocent man, at length opening himself to imprisonment for libel by his famous letter to the President of France: "*J'accuse.*" "For a moment," said Anatole France, "he was the conscience of man." Still the army officers refused to yield and maintained their stand in the face of the most conclusive evidence of foul play. Picquart was dismissed from the service; Zola was prosecuted for libel, financially ruined, and compelled to flee France; and other prominent liberals were assailed with every weapon of a desperate opposition. The liberals soon realized that the issue had become more than justice to an individual, more even than the power of anti-Semitism. It had become a test of strength between clericalism and militarism on the one hand, and anti-clericalism and civil supremacy on the other. The very stability of the republic was involved.

For years the agitation dragged on, until the country was divided into

Dreyfusards and anti-Dreyfusards, and all Europe rang with the issues of the conflict. Ultimately the real culprits, Esterhazy and Henry, who were guilty of forgery and duplicity, confessed; Henry cut his throat and Esterhazy fled to England. Even then the military would not restore the good name of the convicted Jewish captain. By five votes to two: " Dreyfus is declared guilty of treason — *under extenuating circumstances"!* His final vindication did not come until 1906. It was significant that the year before, Church and State were separated in France and a death-blow was give to " the alliance of the sword and the holy-water sprinkler."

The victory of Dreyfus cleared the good name of the Jews and ruined official anti-Semitism. Yet the whole affair had disastrous consequences. Years of inflammatory anti-Semitic propaganda inevitably increased racial animosities. No progress was possible in a land where one's very existence was a political question.

5. SOME CONSEQUENCES

In the countries where anti-Semitism rooted itself — Russia, Germany, Austria, Roumania, France — it left a deep impression. It moulded the policies of political parties; it stirred the savage animosities of the masses and blinded them to other issues. It had more constructive consequences too, however, for it stimulated Jewish unity just when the ancient solidarity was being threatened. Thousands of young Jews who had thrown themselves passionately into the life of their country, renouncing their own people, were now flung back. Many turned to Zionism and to a vigorous Jewish nationalism. Others identified themselves more fully with the life of their people, eager to learn their history, to understand how Israel came to be. Anti-Semitism, writes Mr. Lucien Wolf, " so far from injuring the Jews . . . has really given Jewish racial separatism a new lease of life. Its extravagant accusations, as in the Tisza Eszlar and Dreyfus cases, have resulted in the vindication of the Jewish character. . . . The bond of a common race, vitalized by a new pride in Hebrew history and spurred on to resistance by the insults of the anti-Semites, has given a new spirit and a new source of strength to Judaism at a moment when the approximation of ethical systems and the revolt against dogma were sapping its essentially religious foundations. In the whole history of Judaism, perhaps, there have been no more numerous or remarkable instances of reversions to the faith than in the period in question." [1]

For the first time since the days of emancipation Jews everywhere felt that they were one people. " Common sorrow unites man more closely than common joy," says Renan. The feeling of unity overflowed geographical boundaries. Those who lived in more liberal lands created agencies to assist those who

[1] *Encyclopædia Britannica*, II, 145.

were not so fortunately situated. Already after the Mortara affair in Italy, in 1858, and the Damascus blood libel two years later, the Alliance Israélite Universelle was organized in Paris through the efforts of a French Jewish lawyer, Adolphe Cremieux. Contributions came in from all over the world to be distributed to the needy in the dismal lands of persecution.

England and Austria soon followed the lead of France. The Anglo-Jewish Association was established in London in 1871 and the Israelitische Allianz in Vienna. Besides the usual philanthropic activities, the organizations strove to secure Jewish rights in Roumania, and in 1878 they exerted considerable influence upon the statesmen at the Congress of Berlin.

After the great Russian *pogroms* in 1906 the American Jewish Committee was formed, with representatives from every American district. The committee spoke for American Jews and several times aroused American sympathy for the oppressed Jewish peoples of the world.

Perhaps the most important agency for the alleviation of Jewish distress was the Jewish Colonization Association, established by Baron de Hirsch in London. The fabulous sum of fifty million pounds was set apart to transport Jews from Russia to the Argentine and other lands. The scheme was not successful in solving the Russian Jewish problem, but farm colonies were established in South America, the United States, Palestine, and other lands, and an immense amount of good was accomplished. In the Argentine 212,000 colonists were settled, and though their economic status was never entirely secure, they were rescued from the pit of Acheron and granted new opportunities to live normal lives.

All of these agencies were godsends in the bitter days of the revived anti-Semitism. But they were of course established for the purpose of rendering temporary relief. They bound up wounds, they healed sores. But they did not attack the root disease. Other means had to be devised for a fundamental solution, if there was a solution.

CHAPTER TWENTY-SEVEN

ZIONISM

THE revival of anti-Semitism, which brought the Jew moral expulsion from Europe, gave new meaning and purpose to an ancient hope. Small groups of Jews, roused by their afflictions, took up the dominant idea of the age, nationalism, and applied it to their own people. The Jews, too, were a nation, they maintained, older than any of the others, with a more glorious heritage and with a magnificent destiny. If only Jews would will it to be so, they would again flourish in the ancient homeland, Palestine. The Maccabees would rise again. Those who were harried and storm-tossed would find it a refuge; those who wished to live a normal Jewish life in a healthy Jewish environment would find it a home. " The world will be freed by our liberty," cried Herzl, " enriched by our wealth, and magnified by our greatness." This reawakened spirit of nationalism, firing the most vigorous elements in Jewish life, gave birth to modern Zionism, one of the miracles of modern history.

I. FORERUNNERS

The idea of a restored Jewish life in Palestine was not new. Ever since the destruction of the political state by the Roman legions the Jewish masses had hoped, some vaguely, some fervently, some merely piously, for the fulfilment of ancient prophecies.

> And I will turn the captivity of my people Israel,
> And they shall build the waste cities and inhabit them;
> And they shall plant vineyards and drink the wine thereof;
> They shall also make gardens, and eat the fruit of them.
> And I will plant them upon their land,
> And they shall no more be plucked up
> Out of their land which I have given them,
> Saith the Lord thy God.

Zionides, lamenting the loss of the ancient glory and praying for its speedy restoration, were the commonest form of Jewish lyrical hymns, and many of the most beautiful passed into the liturgy. The Passover festival was not complete without the hearty conclusion: "Next year in Jerusalem"; and every year, as the last blast of the *shophar* was sounded on the high holy-days, the same hope was echoed.

This age-old attachment to Palestine was responsible for the support which Jews gave to the false Messiahs of the sixteenth and seventeenth centuries, who promised the dawn of a better life in Palestine. It also explains the coldness with which Jews received offers of a Jewish state in Uganda and the Argentine, in the Dutch West Indies and French Guiana, and in other forsaken spots of the earth which European statesmen were anxious to have peopled.

But, though a sentimental attachment to Palestine was an integral part of Jewish life, no attempts were made to give it reality. The pious hoped for a miraculous restoration and insisted that it was blasphemous to force the hand of God by action. Had He not promised an end of captivity in His own good time? Others, who saw no practical way to fulfil their aspirations, gave their backs to their persecutors, and their souls to their books.

When the French Revolution destroyed the ghettos and later introduced legal equality for all peoples in Europe, even the sentimental attachment began to dissolve. The Jews gloried in their identification with the life of the Western world. They turned their faces from the East; they insisted that they were not a separate national group; only their religious beliefs marked them off from their neighbours.

Only a few lone notes sounded dissent. The most aggressive challenge came from Moses Hess, a picturesque German Jewish Socialist, who, already in 1840, during the Damascus troubles, had written: "We shall always remain strangers among the nations; these, it is true, will grant us rights from feelings of humanity and justice; but they will never respect us so long as we place our great memories in the second rank, but in the first the principle '*Ubi beni, ibi patria.*'" In his *Rome and Jerusalem,* one of the classics of Zionist literature, published in 1862, Hess pointed out the historical bases for Jewish nationalism, and its indestructibility. He went so far as to suggest that if nationalism was incompatible with Jewish emancipation in each country, the latter should be sacrificed. Hess made little impression on German Jews, but he stirred the historian Graetz to remark, in 1864, that the new nationalist spirit just awakening in Jewish life was bound to rejuvenate it.

Almost at the same time Rabbi Hirsch Kalischer startled the orthodox Russian Jews, in the very heyday of Alexander II's liberalism, by declaring that they must not wait for God to perform miracles, but must begin practical work to help themselves. He advocated colonization work in Palestine and was instrumental in establishing the first colonization society in Frankfurt in 1861.

A number of Christians, too, manifested deep concern in a restored Jewish homeland in Palestine. Henri Dunant, a Genevese philanthropist whose remarkably vivid account of military sufferings at Solferino had inspired the Geneva Conference, tried repeatedly, from 1863 to 1876, to interest Jews and Jewish organizations in Palestine. He personally organized colonization societies to carry through his projects. But though his motives were appreciated by Jewish leaders, he received no support.

Even more impressive was the note sounded by George Eliot, who in *Daniel Deronda* placed in the mouth of her hero sentiments so vibrant with Jewish national feeling that the author must herself have been carried away. " Looking forward to a land and polity, our dispersed people in all the ends of the earth may share the dignity of a national life which has a voice among the peoples of the East and the West—which will plant the wisdom and skill of our race so that it may be, as of old, a medium of transmission and understanding. . . . Then our race shall have an organized centre, a heart and a brain to watch and guide and execute; the outraged Jew shall have a defence in the court of nations, as the outraged Englishman or American. And the world will gain as Israel gains. For there will be a community in the van of the East which carries the culture and the sympathies of every great nation in its bosom; and there will be a land set for a halting-place of enmities, a neutral ground for the East as Belgium is for the West. Difficulties? I know there are difficulties. But let the spirit of sublime achievement move in the great among our people and the work will begin. . . . Let the central fire be kindled again, and the light will reach afar. The degraded and scorned of our race will learn to think of their sacred land, not as a place for sacred beggary, to await death in loathsome idleness, but as a republic where the Jewish spirit manifests itself in a new order founded on the old, purified, enriched by the experience our greatest sons have gathered from the life of the ages. . . . The vision is there. It will be fulfilled."

The revival of anti-Semitism in modern Europe made these isolated voices more meaningful. Russia seethed with hate after 1881 and even the more enlightened communities in Germany, Austria, and France turned against their Jewish populations. The vast majority of Jews continued to hope that the phenomenon, born of unnatural conditions, would soon spend itself. But there were now important groups in every country, particularly in eastern Europe, who turned to Palestine for comfort. The Haskalah, producing hosts of brilliant thinkers and artists, pulsated with a new-born faith in the power of Jewish nationalism, and nearly every Maskil threw his whole soul into the attempt to stimulate the humble masses.

In the forefront of aggressive nationalists stood Leo Pinsker, a Russian physician who soon proved that he was skilful in diagnosing spiritual ailments too. He had been reared on the glowing cosmopolitan hopes of the mid-century, but the renewal of persecution, abetted by the governments themselves, destroyed his hopes. He was an eyewitness to the inhumanities of the May laws of 1881, and before their horror had passed into the cold pages of history, he struck off his epochal brochure, *Auto-Emancipation,* published in 1882. His thesis was not original, but its timeliness gave it a great vogue. He believed that Jews were nourishing illusions when they hoped for identification with the life of the countries in which they lived. Nor could they be treated even as self-respecting aliens, for they had no national homeland. Governments regarded them as rudderless groups or individuals, ghosts in every land. He pleaded for self-emancipation through the creation of a national homeland, preferably in Palestine, but, if that was not feasible, in any other desirable land.

Stimulated by the persecutions and by the eloquence of the Maskilim, a society was organized in Odessa, known as the Lovers of Zion. By 1890 it had many branches in Russia and had spread to other countries. Its original purpose was to finance and encourage the settlement of small bands of immigrants in Palestine. Such a group was the Bilu, made up of earnest young enthusiasts, mostly professional men, who left Russia and Roumania to begin life anew in the Holy land. Their efforts resulted in the founding of Rishon Le Zion in Judæa, Zichron Jacob in Samaria, and Rosh Pinah in Galilee.

The path was not strewn with roses. The pioneers had a desperate struggle for bare existence, and their lovely dreams dissolved before the dread realities of Palestinian life. They had only limited support and there was constant difficulty with the Turkish government. The land, neglected for centuries, resisted the first attempts at cultivation, and malaria, cholera, and trachoma took a fearful toll. Baron Edmund de Rothschild lent generous assistance to help save the struggling colonies, but his early philanthropic efforts broke the self-reliance of many of the colonists. The pioneer efforts of the nationalist dreamers seemed then to end in a few miserable settlements which struggled for breath in the suffocating night that surrounded Jewish life.

More serious, however, was the apathy of the Jews of the world. Even when the early settlements began to show signs of permanent vitality, they embodied the aspirations of only a tiny minority of Jews. The nationalists then learned what Mazzini, the prophet of modern Italy, had learned a few decades earlier — that the dreams of a few gallant spirits cannot build a nation. A whole people must be aroused, a national will must be created. The warmth of Jewish nationalism would have to penetrate to every fragment of Israel.

Then, providentially, came Herzl.

2. THEODORE HERZL

Theodore Herzl, the founder of modern political Zionism, was the most important, as undoubtedly he was the most interesting, Jewish personality of the nineteenth century. He was endowed with all of the qualities which the leader must have — above all, the leader of a cause which seemed quixotic even in his quixotic era. Physically he was cast in the heroic mould, with a prophetic face, an aristocratic poise, and a manner which enthralled his followers and impressed his intellectual opponents. " A majestic Oriental figure . . . you would say one of the Assyrian Kings, whose sculptured heads adorn our Museums, the very profile of Tiglath-Pileser. . . . In a Congress of impassioned rhetoricians he remains serene, moderate. . . . And yet beneath all this statesmanlike prose, touched with the special dryness of the jurist, lurk the romance of the poet . . . the fantasy of the Hungarian, the dramatic self-consciousness of the literary artist, the heart of the Jew." [1] Tactful, witty, radiating amiability, he was as much at home in the Yildiz Kiosk where ruled the cunning sultan of a " declining robber-empire," as in a Vienna café, where he sipped wine between paragraphs of a spicy review of the latest play. These qualities were vitally needed, for Herzl had nothing else with which to create a Jewish state out of a poetic dream. He had not even a Jewish background.

He was born in Budapest in 1860, when Jewish hopes were highest for a complete identification with Magyar life. His education was thoroughly German, with scarcely a Jewish note to make him conscious of any other heritage. Though he was prepared for the bar, he passed into journalism and became a correspondent and later literary editor of the *Neue Freie Presse* in Vienna. He wrote plays, sketches, criticisms, stories, with the light and whimsical fluency of the easy-going *fin de siècle* Viennese *littérateur*. If he ever thought of Jews, it was as of another people. If the echo of their oppression reached him, he was sure their night would pass, as soon as they shook off the ghetto and became adjusted to the new world. " The Jews will adapt themselves. They are like seals which, through an historical accident, were driven into the ocean. There they took on the appearance and properties of fish, which of course they are not. If they return to dry land and are allowed to remain there a few generations, they'll do away with their finny feet." [2] Once he even thought that a mass conversion to Christianity might solve the problem. Yet this sophisticated creator of witticisms, as alien to his people as to the simple peasant who spent half her life on her knees before the Virgin Mary, was destined to inspire the most passionate hope in the Jews since the Temple went up in flames!

It is not clear what brought Herzl to his own people and compelled him, almost despite himself, to give himself body and soul to their regeneration. He was in Paris during the furious anti-Semitic campaign which was a concomitant of the Dreyfus case, and the affair may have touched a sensitive chord in him and accomplished his conversion. At any rate he began to analyse the Jewish question, and, as was usual with him, the whole problem was envisaged in a flash and a plan for its solution became clear.

Herzl was completely unaware of the work of Hess, Pinsker, and other nationalist leaders. His idea of a Jewish homeland in Palestine came with all the violence of a revelation; and his imagination glowed as he planned a vast international Jewish society, with a capitalization of millions, to rebuild the Holy

[1] Zangwill: *Dreamers of the Ghetto*, pp. 433, 434, 436.
[2] Cited in Lowenthal: " Herzl's Diaries." *Menorah Journal*, X, 220 (June–July 1924).

Land, to draw off surplus Jewish populations in all countries, to minimize anti-Semitism, to regenerate the Jews—on and on, in an endless torrent of ideas and dreams—the more fantastical because they came from the usually restrained and level-headed. He at once interviewed Baron de Hirch, and though the famous philanthropist pooh-poohed his "fantasy," it became an unquenchable flame. "I believe for me life has ceased and cosmos begun."

In his diaries Herzl tells how completely his plans, embodied in *The Jewish State,* now dominated his life. He wrote "lying down, in the street, at dinner, at night, when it hounded away sleep." When he finished, after three weeks of heat and labour, he read the draft to a friend and was advised that he was out of his senses. Herzl did some sums in arithmetic to convince himself that his friend was wrong. He wrote to Bismarck asking him, as an expert statesman, whether the plan was really a solution or merely a clever fantasy. Bismarck did not reply. Nor did Alphonse Rothschild, whom Herzl also attempted to draw out. Herzl refused to despair. Optimism was his forte. "What will come of it is too early to say. However, I have experience enough to tell me that even as a dream it is remarkable. . . . If no action comes out of this romancing, a Romance at least will come out of this activity." Besides, "who wants to be right in thirty years must be thought crazy the first two weeks." [1]

The publication of *The Jewish State,* in 1896, precipitated an immense amount of discussion. On the whole, its reception was unfavourable. It was rent, Herzl wrote, "with the viciousness with which the theatre hyenas tear down a *première.*" He must have wondered how there could be such unanimity of scepticism and downright opposition among a scattered and divided people. But there were friendly voices too. In Vienna the Kadimah society encouraged him. Dr. Max Nordau, who had won fame as a philosopher and critic, became interested, and Israel Zangwill, the most eminent Jewish man of letters, was also profoundly impressed. Herzl interviewed leading Jewish financiers and addressed various Jewish organizations. He could not win the bigwigs, but he fired the humbler masses nearly everywhere. He was so far encouraged that early in 1897 he called for a Jewish congress, which met in Basel, Switzerland, attended by Zionist representatives from all over the world. In itself the congress was a romantic gesture. It was the first time in more than eighteen hundred years that a Jewish body, representing communities from nearly everywhere in the Diaspora, gathered to discuss the problem of the Jewish future. Here was drawn up the famous Basel program: "The object of Zionism is to establish for the Jewish people a publicly and legally assured home in Palestine." The historic movement was launched.

It is easy to understand the violent opposition which was aroused by the birth of the Zionist movement. Western European Jews insisted that Jewish nationalism was a delusion and a myth, that it could only endanger whatever position

[1] Cited in Lowenthal: "Herzl's Diaries," *Menorah Journal,* X, 216, 229 (June–July 1924).

the Jews in Europe had already painfully won. The enemies of Israel were saying that the Jews were strangers in every land; the Zionists were creating tangible proof that the anti-Semites were right. Such damnable propaganda was a menace to Jewish security! The opposition was so fierce in Munich, where the first Zionist congress was to be held, that Herzl transferred the meeting to Basel.

Reform Jews, who had already eliminated all references to Zion from the prayer-book, insisted that Judaism had outgrown Palestine, that it was the mission of modern Israel to be a light unto the Gentiles, to spread justice and right by precept and example through all the world. Zionism was not progress, but retrogression. "The newest thing in the Jewish movement," wrote Herzl wrathfully, "is the protest rabbi. Max Nordau branded this type in a sentence that will persist. 'They are people who sit in a safe vessel and who use the oars to beat in the heads of those drownlings who try to hang on the sides of the vessel.'" [1]

Orthodox Jews still rested on the traditional Messianic ideas and refused to force the hand of Providence. Besides, Herzl and the leaders of Zionism were advocating a purely secular state in Palestine; they were themselves not observant religious Jews; in their hands Judaism could not be safe.

Many who wished Herzl well saw only too clearly the impracticability of his project. Herzl's vision was magnificent, but it was not based on statesmanship. It aimed to make a nation of a people scattered for nearly two thousand years, to settle them in a forsaken land controlled by the irresponsible Turk, and to accomplish these impossibilities despite the opposition of all the influential elements in Jewish life. "Zionism," said a cynic, "is a splendid idea, and practicable for any other people but the Jews."

Meantime, unperturbed by opposition, Herzl proceeded as if the whole nation were unanimous in support of his ideas. Several instruments were at once fashioned to make the program of Zionism practical. A Jewish Colonial Trust was organized in London, as an English joint-stock company, for credit and banking, supported by tens of thousands of small Jewish stockholders. The Jewish National Fund, maintained by voluntary contributions, was established in 1901, to purchase land in Palestine as the property of the entire Jewish people. A small yearly tax, the *shekel,* was placed upon all Zionists, to help defray administration expenses. The funds were inadequate for so vast an undertaking, yet the work went forward steadily. Within a few years there were several new colonies, agricultural enterprises, schools, and a few thousand new settlers, under their vines and their fig-trees, on the soil of the ancient homeland.

Yet it was all slow and precarious, "an egg dance with the eggs invisible." In the long run, Herzl felt, little was to be gained by "smuggling" a few Jewish families into Palestine. Even the little practicable work was not secure so

---

[1] De Haas: *Theodor Herzl*, I, 157.

long as the Jewish settlements were at the mercy of the rapacious Turkish officials. Indeed, bribery alone stayed the execution of anti-Jewish laws. In 1900 all
that the Zionists had built in Palestine was endangered by the threat of the
sultan, Abdul-Hamid, to enforce the law prohibiting Jews from owning land
or remaining in the country for more than three months.

Hence Herzl devoted most of his energies, in the few years that were still
left to him, to diplomatic negotiations. He had no social standing, no powerful
organization behind him, no influential friends in the European chancelleries.
The great Jewish financiers fled at his approach as from a plague. He had nothing to offer in return for the grant of an autonomous Jewish life in Palestine. Yet
he negotiated with the sultan and the kaiser, with the leading officials in Russia,
and the British secretaries of State, even with the Pope. He fenced admirably,
now by cajolery, now by flattery, now by an appeal to Christian sympathy, now
by skilful bluffing. In the end he had gained only some vague promises, little
that was tangible; but at least he had raised Zionism to the status of a factor
in diplomacy. And there was always the possibility of a fortunate turn, an
unexpected twist, in the European diplomatic situation which could bring
success.

The negotiations with the sultan involved five years of patient waiting for an
audience, running the gauntlet of blackmailers and spies, bribery and chicanery.
"The north wind was blowing through the fir-trees." In 1896 Herzl, for a price,
got as far as the chief lieutenants of the sultan, only to be stopped by the impene-
trable wall of red tape, rascality, and corruption. Just a round of coffee-drinking,
clouds of cigarette smoke, promises, and more promises. At last, in May 1901,
the long-wished-for interview with Abdul-Hamid materialized. Herzl offered to
play Androcles to the Turkish lion, to place the huge Turkish debt into hands
friendlier than those which now pressed heavily upon the sultan. In return His
Majesty was to grant a charter to the Jews at a price equal to the capitalization
of the present revenues from Palestine, about ten million dollars. The sultan
nodded and smiled, and smiled and nodded, and was able later to get better
terms from his bankers by threatening them with Herzl's offer. Herzl was kept
guessing for three years by "Ali Baba and his forty thieves" and had nothing for his pains and expense except membership in the Order of the Medjidie
(first class) and a scarf-pin set with brilliants. It is only fair to add, however,
that even if the sultan had accepted Herzl's plans, there would not have been
sufficient financial support from the Jews themselves for Herzl to proceed with
his side of the bargain.

After the sultan, Herzl tried the kaiser, whose influence in the Porte was so
dominant that Guedalla's jest fairly summarized the situation: "*Deutschland
über Allah.*" Again there were the intermediaries and months of diplomacy
to pave the way for an interview. Herzl prepared himself thoroughly, even
attending the opera to study the kaiser and his mannerisms. The long-awaited

meeting finally took place in the fall of 1898 during the kaiser's visit to Constantinople, the first visit of a Christian potentate to the Turkish capital. The conversation lasted more than an hour in the presence of the unfriendly Chancellor Bülow, who interrupted to mention Jewish radicals and Socialists and Jewish ingratitude in Germany. Herzl worked desperately on the weaknesses of the kaiser — his youth, his ambition, his innate theatricality. What a heroic gesture to help restore a Jewish state under German protection! What an excellent opportunity to stop the embarrassing anti-Semitism of Germany by drawing off many of its Jews! And was there not an ancient prophecy that the millennium could not come until the Jews were again in the Holy Land? The kaiser promised to take up the matter with the sultan. But despite a later friendly meeting in Jerusalem, nothing developed, and in December Herzl wrote in his diary: "No news from Berlin. That means snow — and Bülow." Months later, gossip reported that Bülow had thus expressed himself: "Dr. Herzl made an excellent impression upon me, but I did not believe in his cause. His people have no money. The rich Jews would not aid, and nothing can be done with the lousy Polish Jews." [1]

Herzl now turned to the Russian bear, the ancient implacable enemy. Perhaps Russia would recognize the enormous advantage of losing tens of thousands of her troublesome Jews and would intercede with the sultan. It was worth attempting. For four years Herzl negotiated for an interview. It was not until after the horrors of the Kishinev *pogroms* in 1903, when all the civilized world recoiled from the Russian brutalities, that he was ushered into the presence of Plehve, the Minister of the Interior and one of the instigators of the *pogroms*. Plehve had a surprising knowledge of the Jewish situation in Russia, and the conversation was bitterly frank. The minister expressed himself as willing to forward any movement which diminished the number of Jews in the country, but he was vehemently opposed to the nationalist aspirations of the Jews within Russia itself, propaganda which made them all the more unassimilable. Herzl felt the intense Jew-hatred of Plehve in every sentence. "I stood before a panther, a strong, sinuous unrelenting beast, whose every move was a guarded offense. . . . The arch anti-Semite, cool, frank, a butcher." [2] Plehve practically agreed to permit Zionist propaganda to continue in Russia and to use his good offices with Turkey. With a fair promise of success at last, Herzl's hopes were dashed by the assassination of the Russian consul in Constantinople, which ruptured the good relations between the two countries.

In the last year of his life the ever optimistic Herzl had his first interview with Goluchowski, the Austrian Foreign Minister. The Jewish problem concerned Austria vitally; Galicia was almost a Jewish province. Goluchowski enthusiastically supported Herzl's plans and thought that the Great Powers should sponsor them, even to the extent of financial support. "Excellency,"

---

[1] De Haas: *Theodor Herzl*, I, 271.   [2] Ibid., II, 145.

Herzl suggested, " will you head such an effort? " " This is not the moment. We are not finished in Macedonia." Sympathy, paper promises, and again " but."

Without great expectations, but merely to exhaust the armoury of possibilities, Herzl interviewed the Pope, " a good, heavily built village priest, whose Christianity has remained alive in the Vatican." Would he not intercede with Turkey, or at least declare officially that the Vatican would not oppose Zionism if the holy places were extraterritorialized? The Pope sternly refused to lend any sanction to Herzl's program. The Jews denied the divinity of Christ. The Church could not declare itself for them without stultifying its principles. He would do nothing in opposition, however, and if the Jews did come to Palestine, " we will have priests and churches ready to baptize all of you."

Just before the interview with the Pope, Herzl saw the King of Italy and was graciously received. Victor Emmanuel liked the genuine Jews. " There are Jews who come here who obviously are nervous when they hear the word ' Jew.' When I really talk with Jews, I like those who are willing to be what they are." He went on to declare himself whole-heartedly for the Zionist aspirations. " The country will and must be yours. It is only a question of time." Victor Emmanuel was a constitutional monarch, however, and spoke only for himself. Herzl could get no more than the assurance that the Italian ambassador in Constantinople would use his personal influence to support every diplomatic endeavour in favour of Zionism.

Only in England was Herzl more successful. He was dealing at last with a sympathetic government and he was now ready to consider temporary shelters other than Palestine. In July 1902 he had been called in as an " expert " by the royal commission which was considering the advisability of restricting immigration. His appearance before the group gave him an excellent opportunity to suggest outlets for the Jewish refugees from persecuting countries. In the fall he interviewed Joseph Chamberlain, the British colonial secretary, the most prominent minister in the Cabinet, a man " without literary or artistic resources, a business man with a cloudlessly clear head." Herzl suggested that El Arish and the Sinai peninsula, which were under Anglo-Egyptian control, would make an admirable place for Jewish settlement. Chamberlain was not very certain where these places were and suggested that there would be difficulties if the Jews settled in Egypt. " No," replied Herzl, " we will not go to Egypt. We have been there." Herzl then made clear that El Arish and Sinai could serve as a gathering-centre for Jews near Palestine, which might later be joined. Chamberlain was extremely friendly and offered his support if the Egyptian officials approved. But the matter was allowed to die primarily because of Egyptian opposition.

Soon, however, came a much more important offer. While touring the British possessions in Africa, Chamberlain conceived the idea that the attractive lands in Uganda, in British East Africa, could serve as a Jewish homeland. " It is hot on the coast, but as you travel inland, the climate improves and is splendid even for Europeans. You can raise sugar and cotton there." Chamberlain's suggestion was followed by an official offer from the Foreign Minister. The scheme would comprise " the grant of a considerable area of land, the appointment of a Jewish official as the chief of the local administration, and permission to the colony to have a free hand in regard to municipal legislation as to the management of religious and purely domestic matters, such local autonomy being conditional upon the right of His Majesty's Government to exercise general control."

Herzl came to the Sixth Zionist congress in 1903 in a serious dilemma. He had just finished his fruitless negotiations with Plehve; the Jewish situation in Russia was deplorable. Some temporary shelter would be a godsend. Yet he knew only too well the Zionist soul and its instinctive shrinking from any project which set Zion aside, even temporarily. He was very cautious in his presidential address and said clearly: " East Africa is not Zion and can never become it." Nordau earnestly supported the British offer and termed Uganda a " *Nachtasyl,*" a refuge for the night.

The scenes which followed the presentation of the British offer were highly dramatic. The project threatened to disrupt the congress and divide the Zionist Organization. The opposition was led by the Russian delegates themselves, representing the millions whom it was intended to relieve. Herzl succeeded in having a commission appointed to investigate the territory and to report to the next congress upon its usefulness. While the commission carried on its work, both sides organized. The fervent Zionists pledged themselves never to consider any land but Zion, the territorialists insisted that it would be criminal to neglect opportunities to relieve the pressure of anti-Semitism. The opposition was so bitter and the dissension so great that the matter was allowed to drop quietly. Meantime, in his forty-fourth year, Herzl suddenly died, worn out by his exertions and perhaps, too, by the quarrels which had been precipitated by the Uganda project.

Measured by concrete achievements, Herzl had accomplished little. No important diplomatic victory had been won and even the Jews remained disinterested. At his death there were a few new colonies in Palestine and a struggling Zionist organization with a membership of some tens of thousands. Meagre material indeed with which to divert the course of history.

Yet Herzl was a genuine state-builder and one of the most influential personalities in Jewish history. He turned sentimental and philanthropic hopes into nobler and more worth-while channels. He stimulated a new Jewish renaissance, which expressed itself in a love for the Hebrew language and Hebrew literature. He awakened a nationalist sentiment which was not to remain limited to small groups of Jews, but was to expand and warm the heart of all Israel. And his faith in Israel's destiny as a reborn nation was to receive vindication barely thirteen years after his death when the power which he trusted most conquered Palestine and set it apart as a Jewish homeland.

3. FROM HERZL TO THE WAR

So long as Herzl lived, the emphasis in the Zionist program was laid upon diplomacy. It was considered almost useless to pour money and energy into petty colonization in Palestine when even security had not been obtained. Much of the funds which had been gathered were held in trust until such time as the success of the diplomatic program would warrant their investment. This diplomatic policy was sharply challenged during Herzl's own lifetime, especially by the Russian Zionists. Every moment was precious, the opposition insisted. One could be kept for ever waiting at the portals of the chancelleries and get nowhere. With the development of a practical program there would be action, accomplishment. There would be a miniature life in Palestine, and the world would be shown that Zionism was not a closet philosophy or a poet's dream.

After Herzl's death the conflict between the "politicals" and the "practicals" became clearer, with sentiment gradually shifting towards the views of the latter. A growing number of Zionists counselled a peaceful but active penetration of Palestine, utilizing whatever funds were available for planting colonies and colonists. From 1904 to 1911 the "practicals" gained ground and at length were strong enough to govern the executive.

While the political and practical Zionists debated methods of achieving their common goal, another point of view was leavening the Zionist movement. It came from Ahad Ha'am (Asher Ginzberg), one of the most brilliant thinkers of the Haskalah group, who declared that Palestine could make no appeal as just another political state. He envisaged Palestine as a cultural centre, a home for Judaism rather than for Jews. To fulfil this ideal the Zionists needed to stress schools and education above farms and buildings, to nurture the Hebrew tongue and a Hebrew literature and to think less of shares and bonds and the purchase of land. Palestine had only to contain a tiny fragment of the Jewish people, living a healthy, vigorous Jewish life, serving to inspire the Jews of the Diaspora. These would be the "saving remnant."

Cultural Zionists often went to extremes in their enthusiasm for a Hebrew renaissance. They sometimes failed to remember that men must live before they can become creative artists, that though financial transactions are vulgar as ends they are essential as means to an end. But Ahad Ha'am's philosophy was a useful reminder to the state-builders that Zionists could not live by bread alone, and that the spiritual needs of Jewish life were of vital importance. The emphasis on Palestine as a centre of culture appealed also to many who were alienated by the political program of Zionism. Many Reform rabbis found no incompatibility between such ideals and their own program of Reform Judaism.

Meantime the practical program of the Zionists went forward steadily during the decade after Herzl's death. Before the war the Jewish population had risen to nearly a hundred thousand. There were a score and more of new colonies, many of them struggling, to be sure, and always on the bare margin of subsistence, yet persevering, with a contented, buoyant population, happy amidst every hardship. What if there were sand in the bread? The sand was of Palestine.

The new life, it was clear, was producing a new race of Jews. The average colonist was a sturdy, healthy soul, well able to stand a full day's toil in the fields, to ride hard, and to shoot well, and with no fear in his heart for any man. "They are the pioneers, the workers. And what they see is not shrine or sarcophagus, but stone to be quarried, fields to be digged, water and power to be brought into the wastes of this desolate land, new cities on hill tops fronting the same old stars. They see a new Jerusalem, too. Not a city of mystic forms or golden stairs. A city of houses and parks and theatres and seats of learning. The plans for that new city are laid and that city is being built. There are new houses and new quarters; there are schools and hospitals; there is the beauty of trees where for centuries no shade fell." [1] What a change from the bent and broken hulks who stood by the Wailing Wall of Jerusalem and prayed, who came to the Holy Land that their bones might find a resting-place in its holy sod!

Yet all this new, vigorous life, filled with such glorious promise for the future, hung always on the flimsiest thread. Danger was never absent after 1908, when the Young Turk revolution drove out Abdul-Hamid the Damned and established a constitutional government. The Young Turks were passionate nationalists and set about to Ottomanize the races in their scattered dominions by establishing a central administration and a uniform system of education. They looked with disfavour upon Zionism and the vigorous nationalist population which it was creating in Palestine. The Zionists soon learned that they had more to fear from the liberalism of the Young Turks than from the tyranny of the old sultan. When the War burst upon the world, it seemed a certainty that the frail little structure of Zionism would be shattered and cast to the winds.

[1] Lewisohn: *Israel*, p. 136.

CHAPTER TWENTY-EIGHT

FROM SARAJEVO TO SAN REMO

1914-20

THE pistol-shots at Sarajevo and the World War which they precipitated completely changed the Jewish situation in Europe. Five years of bitter warfare destroyed millions of lives and wrecked millions of others. No people, with perhaps the exception of the Armenians, suffered more. The Jews had only their proportionate number in the armies of the combatants, but their civilians went through worse miseries than were endured by the soldiers in the trenches. The most sanguinary fighting took place along the frontiers of Russia, Austria, and Germany, in the "three Polands," where more than three and a half million Jews were concentrated. In normal times their legal and social disabilities were distressing enough. Now there were added the carnage of war, *pogroms,* looting, and expulsions.

Physical wear and tear was only part of the price exacted by Armageddon. The untold hardships which all peoples experienced reawakened passions and hatreds which engulfed Europe in a new anti-Semitism. The collapse of Russia, and the Bolshevik triumph, revolutionized the social, economic, and religious status of half the Jews in the world.

One constructive feature emerged from all the welter and chaos. The British conquered Palestine, and the Zionist dream became a reality. Nothing short of the violent diplomatic convulsions of the War could have brought such a miracle to pass.

1. THE WORLD WAR

For more than four years millions of soldiers advanced and retreated through bitterly contested territory along an eastern front which extended for hundreds of miles. Russia took the offensive in August 1914,sending forth two huge armies, one into eastern Prussia from the salient of Russian Poland, and the other into Austrian Galicia. The Russians were beaten back in Prussia, by the remarkable strategy of General Hindenburg, in one of the colossal engagements of the war, the battle of Tannenberg. But the Galician campaign was more successful. The Russians took the great fortresses of Jaroslaw and Przemyśl and by March of 1915 were masters of nearly the whole province.

To relieve the immense pressure on Austria, Hindenburg launched a new drive in the north. All through the summer months of 1915 the German guns pounded at the Russian key fortresses, and at the end of the year nearly all of Poland had been conquered. Russia lost more than a million and a half men in the offensive and vast quantities of military equipment and stores. Simultaneously came the tremendous drive of Mackensen which drove the Russians out of Galicia. Next year the Russians, under Brusilov, returned in a desperate offensive which extended over a two-hundred-and-fifty-mile front along the Polish and Galician borders. Brusilov pushed back the Teutonic lines from twenty to fifty miles, but he could not penetrate the Hindenburg defences. And then in 1917, thoroughly exhausted, with a rotten government, inadequate means of transport and supplies, and a shattered morale, the Russians were pushed back almost at will and soon rushed headlong into revolution and chaos.

Meantime, in 1916, Roumania, encouraged by Brusilov's early success, threw in her lot with the Allies and quickly conquered the Hungarian province of Transylvania. Roumania, however, was not prepared for large-scale warfare and, after her first easy victories, was quickly overwhelmed. Within three weeks the economically valuable parts of the country, with its grain and oil supplies, fell before the combined assaults of Germany, Austria, and Bulgaria.

Through all of this violent fighting on the eastern front millions of Jews were caught between millstones of the invading and retreating armies. During the engagements in Russia and Poland they were harried by the advancing Russians; when the Russians retreated before the fury of Hindenburg's counter-offensive, hundreds of thousands of Jews were expelled at two or three days' notice and were brought to the interior provinces of Russia, lest they give up important military secrets. The deportations were conducted with an inhumanity unique even for brutalized soldiers. Whole communities were crowded like cattle into sealed box-cars, which were opened at infrequent intervals; it was a miracle that only half of the exiles perished. Other communities were driven afoot for hundreds of miles, the weakest succumbing by the road-side, only the strongest surviving to struggle for existence in strange, unfriendly worlds in the interior. The German advance was so rapid, however, that the Jews could not all be evacuated in time. Their homes were now subjected to the withering artillery of the German invaders and, after the conquest, to the brutalities of the war-drunk victors. As an appropriate accompaniment to the deportations and invasions, hundreds of Jews were executed as spies by both sides.

As the Russians marched into the densely populated province of Galicia, the Jews fled in terror, receiving orders for evacuation first from the retreating Austrians and then from the advancing Russians. The process was continued when the positions of the armies were reversed. The Roumanian debacle involved another half-million Jews, and the eastern world, none too friendly to Jews even in times of peace and quiet, was crowded with broken, desolated, penniless refugees. It is impossible to measure the extent of the ruin wrought in the congested districts through which the armies marched and counter-marched.

In western Europe Jewish life was affected no more adversely than the life of the other elements in the population. But the foreign Jews who lived in these countries soon found that they were not to escape altogether from the horrors which were being endured by their people in the eastern war-sector. During the *pogrom* years thousands of Jews had migrated and had settled in the western countries and in Palestine without becoming naturalized. When the war came they were expelled as enemy aliens, or deported as war slackers. The great colony of Galician Jews was compelled to leave Belgium; the Russian and Roumanian Jews in Palestine were harried out of the land by the Turkish officials. In England it was intended at first to ship the Russian Jews back to the land of their origin, but later the alternative was given to them of joining the British army and thereby winning naturalization.

The unparalleled Jewish tragedy, which rendered a whole people homeless and placed millions on the threshold of starvation, strained to the limit every Jewish agency which was in a position to render assistance. The German Jews formed the Eastern Committee to succour the Jews of the devastated provinces in Poland, and the Austrian Jews laboured selflessly to make the lot of the Galicians easier. The Jews in the few neutral countries in Europe also organized to bring relief.

But the mightiest efforts came from American Jews, who were ideally situated to serve as godfather to the afflicted. The wealthy gave princely sums, and the poorest contributed their mites. The Joint Distribution Committee raised millions, and, though the most colossal sums could relieve only minute areas, the saving in life and family integrity was incalculable. Committees were stationed in the chief Russian Jewish centres to mitigate the horrors of the summer of 1915, when the Jews were scattered to the winds. The committees helped to secure transportation, to supply food and lodgings at way stations, and to find employment for some of the wanderers. Other relief groups ministered to the needs of the refugees in Galicia, Roumania, Transylvania, and far-off Palestine. The service was continued even after the United States entered the War. Through the good offices of the State Department and of the neutral countries, money and food still came into enemy lands, for relief purposes.

Meantime military events were altering the fortunes of the belligerents. A series of amazing German successes in 1917 made it appear that the Allies would soon be compelled to sue for peace. Italy was crushed at Caporetto. German submarines sank nearly a million tons of British shipping monthly. German air raids demoralized the civilian populations of England and France. In November Russia, which had already passed under Bolshevik control, withdrew from the war and released the pressure on the German east front. Finally, in the spring of 1918, Hindenburg began a new offensive, which carried the German troops to the very gates of Paris.

Yet the British and the French held on grimly, desperately, and the tide turned at last. Already in early 1917 the British had begun the drive in the Near East which ultimately crumpled Turkey. The army in Mesopotamia recovered Kut-el-Amara on February 24, entered Bagdad about two weeks later, and soon practically took control of all Mesopotamia. Another army, under General Allenby, began a memorable march from Egypt into Palestine and, on December 9, captured Jerusalem. Next year the whole Turkish army was routed, and Palestine, for the first time in more than seven centuries, was again in the control of a Christian power.

The collapse of Turkey was the signal for the end. Bulgaria had already capitulated in September 1918. Now the whole Austrian empire disintegrated and the government surrendered early in November. An attempt was made to muster the German fleet for a last rally, but the sailors mutinied. On November 10 the kaiser fled to Holland, and next day the armistice was signed which ended the greatest war in history.

2. THE TRIUMPH OF POLITICAL ZIONISM

From the beginning of the World War it was apparent that an Allied victory would mean the partition of the Ottoman empire. Suggestions for a partition were made in the Franco-British treaty, the Sazonov agreement, and the Anglo-Italian convention of 1914; in the London pact and the Anglo-Hejaz treaty of 1915; and in the Saxonby-Paleologue convention between France and Russia in 1916. In May of 1916 official steps were taken to arrange for the disposition of "the sick man of Europe." By the secret Sykes-Picot agreement it was decided to create a series of Arab states in the Near East, France to control Syria and the Mosul, England to control northern Arabia and central Mesopotamia, and Palestine to be internationalized.

All through 1916, however, the war went steadily against the Allies and it became necessary to redistribute the spoils in the East to bring in Arab support. Already the remarkable young Oxford don, Colonel T. E. Lawrence, had gained the confidence and friendship of the powerful Sherif Husain of Arabia, and a new treaty was now worked out which won the Arabs to the Allied side. It was agreed that, as soon as the Turk had been expelled, three Arab kingdoms would be created under the control of the three sons of the Sherif. Syria and Palestine would pass to the Emir Feisal, Mesopotamia to the Prince Zeid, and the Hejaz to the youngest son, the Prince Abdullah. England and France, of course, were to guard their economic interests in their own spheres of influence.

This agreement, too, was soon superseded. Indeed, the Allied plans changed with bewildering frequency. Every military event compelled revisions. Pledges were nothing but moves in the diplomatic game. Each country engaged in complicated manœuvres and backdoor intrigues in the attempt to guarantee and advance its own political and economic interests. And then, in the midst of all the conferences and negotiations, Britain officially endorsed the Zionist program, and the Zionist dream suddenly and dramatically became a reality.

It is not yet possible to determine fully the British motives for this astonishing move. Those who looked at issues with an eye to English imperial interests suggested that a Jewish state in Palestine would make a strong rivet in the long chain which bound the Suez and India to Britain. Some observers believed that the declaration would win the support of powerful Jewish financial interests in the United States and Europe; others that it would be bait to the Jews of Russia, who might be influential in keeping Russia in the war; still others that it would add another to the discontented and aspiring minority groups among the Central Powers.

Yet there was assuredly more than political opportunism behind the British declaration. The material motives were sustained by the liberalism of several statesmen who applied to the Jews the doctrine of self-determination, and by the traditional British policy of friendliness to Zionist aspirations. For some years before the declaration Zionist leaders had been actively engaged in creating a favourable attitude among the Allied governments towards the Zionist program. Early in 1915 Herbert Samuel, one of the leading liberals of England, had presented a memorandum to the British cabinet calling for a Jewish commonwealth under British protection, a memorandum which evoked an interesting comment from Prime Minister Asquith. "It reads," he writes in his war diary, "almost like a new edition of 'Tancred' brought up to date. I confess I am not attracted by this proposed addition to our responsibilities, but it is a curious illustration of Dizzy's [Disraeli's] favourite maxim that 'race is everything' to find this almost lyrical outburst proceeding from the well-ordered and methodical brain of H. S. . . . Curiously enough, the only other partisan of this proposal is Lloyd George, who I need not say does not care a damn for the Jews or their past or their future, but thinks it will be an outrage to let the Holy Places pass into the possession or under the protectorate of 'agnostic atheistic France.'"[1]

Nahum Sokolow, one of Herzl's closest confidants, had been travelling from one chancellery to another—Rome and the Vatican, London and Paris —pressing the Zionist claims. In the United States, Louis D. Brandeis, risen to an associateship in the Supreme Court, was doubtless an important influence in eliciting from President Wilson a commendation of the Zionist aims. And above all there was Haym Weizmann.

Weizmann, who was born in Poland in 1874, had early migrated to England,

[1] Asquith: *Memories and Reflections, 1852–1927* (1928), II, 71, 78 (under date of January 28, and March 13, 1915).

where he distinguished himself as a brilliant chemist and was attached to the University of Manchester. He was an amiable and winning personality, with infinite shrewdness and a keen sense of diplomatic values. He gained the friendship of some of the leading English statesmen and influenced them to view the Zionist program favourably. He won the gratitude of the British government by placing at its disposal a formula which made T.N.T. practical for war purposes.

For nine months during 1917, negotiations went forward between Weizmann and Sokolow and the British government. There were communications with France and Italy and with the President of the United States. The statement defining the British policy was cast and recast to cover every contingency. At length, on November 2, 1917, the historic Balfour Declaration was issued by the Foreign Minister in a letter to Lord Rothschild. "His Majesty's Government," it read, "view with favour the establishment in Palestine of a national home for the Jewish people, and will use their best endeavours to facilitate the achievement of this object, it being clearly understood that nothing shall be done which may prejudice the civil and religious rights of existing non-Jewish communities in Palestine or the rights and political status enjoyed by Jews in any other country."

Soon after the declaration was made public, the Allied governments added their official commendation. Even far-off China and tiny Siam hastened to salute the Zionist program and promised their support to its fulfilment. The Central Powers were not to be outdone. The Turkish Grand Vizier, Talaat Pasha, called attention to the traditional friendliness of Turkey to the Jews. Germany went a step further and took for granted that Turkey intended "to promote flourishing settlements within the limits of the capacity of the country [Palestine], local self-government corresponding with the country's laws, and free development of their [Jewish] civilization." All of which Germany fully approved. Fifteen years before, Herzl would have been rejoiced by a friendly gesture from a single European country. Now all the Great Powers were vying with each other in soliciting Zionist support!

Meantime the conquest of Palestine went forward rapidly. In December General Allenby took Jerusalem and made ready to push his conquest to the northern limits of Syria. In March the Zionist Commission arrived in Palestine, welcomed by the British government as a liaison organization between the military officials and the Jewish community. It was to give advice "on all matters relating to Jews or the Jewish people." It was highly significant that almost its first official act, before the implications of the Balfour Declaration had been made clear, before even strife had ceased, was to lay the corner-stone for the Hebrew University on Mount Scopus. The gesture evoked a warm tribute from President Wilson, who wrote: "I think that all Americans will be deeply moved by the report that even in this time of stress the Weizmann

Commission has been able to lay the foundation of the Hebrew University at Jerusalem with the promise that it bears of spiritual rebirth."

3. THE PEACE CONFERENCE

After months of planning and preparing, the most important peace conference in history assembled in Paris to reshape the world, in which twenty-seven nations had been at war for more than four years. The brilliant French capital was host to the rulers and premiers of large nations and small, diplomatic delegations, political and economic commissions, emissaries from groups which aspired to independence and from those which coveted new territory, ambassadors and generals, fakirs and grafters, famous journalists and literary lights, princes and men who wished to be princes, all gathered together to observe or to create, to plead causes or to fight them. " The Paris of the Conference," says Dillon, " ceased to be the capital of France. It became a vast cosmopolitan caravanserai teeming with unwonted aspects of life and turmoil, filled with curious samples of the races, tribes, and tongues of four continents who came to watch and wait for the mysterious to-morrow."

Amidst the multitude of delegations, with their hundreds of conflicting requests, were also those representing Jewish communities and organizations. They came from nearly every country, most of them democratically created by popular election, others, like the Alliance Israélite Universelle, representing committees which had a long tradition of philanthropic Jewish service to recommend them. Unfortunately the various bodies were in sharp disagreement over the program which they wished to urge upon the Peace Conference and over the methods which were to be adopted in pressing the Jewish claims. The representatives from eastern European countries were passionately intent upon obtaining minority rights for their afflicted people, a need which the western representatives could hardly understand. Nearly all the delegations were pledged to support the Zionist program and to insist upon the incorporation of the Balfour Declaration in the peace treaties. But this was vigorously opposed by delegations from Britain and France.

The United States had sent two delegations, one representing the American Jewish Committee, the other representing the newly-organized American Jewish Congress. Fortunately the American representatives were highly respected by all the delegations and were able, after much delicate negotiation, to bring the conflicting groups to a compromise. Louis Marshall, a member of both American delegations, arranged an agreement, upon a *modus vivendi,* to the effect that the delegations were to co-operate in all non-controversial matters and to engage in no open conflict upon the matters in dispute. This accomplished, Marshall conducted the negotiations which resulted in the formulation of the various minority treaties.

These treaties guaranteed full and complete civil and political rights to all religious, racial, and linguistic minorities residing in the countries with which the treaties were made. The right of citizenship, it was declared, was not dependent upon naturalization or upon any other formality, but was to spring into existence upon the execution of the treaties. It was further established that, in places where the minorities were of appreciable numbers, a share of the public money was to be allocated for the educational or charitable institutions of such minorities. Since the treaties were to apply to all minority groups, the word "Jew" did not appear in them, except in the guarantee that Jews could observe their own sabbath without let or hindrance.

The attempt to incorporate the Balfour Declaration into the peace treaties was a much more difficult matter. It required immense pressure to persuade the delegations from England and France to refrain from openly fighting the Zionist program. At length a memorial was submitted to the Peace Conference, which asked that Britain become the mandatory for Palestine and allow the Jewish settlements to develop in accordance with the Balfour Declaration. The memorial was reinforced by a tentative economic program, the principles of which had been adopted at the Pittsburgh Zionist Convention in 1918, which aimed to develop Palestine into "an autonomous commonwealth dedicated to the advancement of social justice."

Now the battle was begun in earnest. The Balfour Declaration was, after all, but one of a number of promises made under the pressure of military needs, and each contradicted the other. The Arab delegation, under the Emir Feisal, insisted upon the fulfilment of the British promise for an Arab Palestine and Syria. The French clung stubbornly to the terms of the Sykes-Picot agreement. Effendi landlords of Palestine, whose hold over the ignorant Arab peasantry would be broken under an enlightened regime, stormed against any arrangement which included a Jewish State. Missionary interests, Catholic and Protestant, worked behind the scenes to forward their own claims. Above all, the British military administration in control of Palestine strenuously opposed the plan which would make the country, with an Arab population nearly ten times as large as the Jewish, a Jewish homeland. From a purely military and policing point of view, the safest and sanest policy was to create one large Arab State, under British control.

So long as the Peace Conference remained in session, the fate of a Jewish Palestine hung on a hair. The Jewish leaders knew only too well how quickly the Balfour Declaration would be scrapped if British imperial interests demanded a revision of policy. By April 1919 new political factors had appeared which practically killed all hopes of Zionist success. There was grave unrest in India and in the Near East, aggravated by the news of the approaching disruption of the Turkish empire. At any moment an all-Arab-Moslem uprising was likely. Meantime an official commission, dispatched by the Peace Conference to investigate the Near Eastern situation, had reported unfavourably upon a Jewish Palestine. If the Turkish treaty had been signed in 1919, it is likely that Britain would have been obliged to yield to the military advisers. But it was impossible to conclude the Turkish treaties before the conference adjourned, and it was agreed to postpone final action upon them until a later date. The postponement gave the Zionists a breathing-space. The Balfour Declaration had not been sanctioned, but at least all hope had not been crushed for more favourable developments at another time.

In the year or more which elapsed before the Treaty of Sèvres with Turkey was signed, the Zionist work in Palestine went forward as if all had been assured. And behind the scenes the Jewish delegations continued their propaganda. They were vastly encouraged by the reaffirmation of the Balfour Declaration by Lord Curzon, the new British Foreign Minister, by the assurance of Colonel Lawrence, Feisal's most important adviser, that Zionism was " the only practical means of setting the new Semitic Near East in order in our own days," and by the activity of Major Ormsby-Gore, the liaison officer between the military government in Palestine and the Zionist commission, who continually urged upon Parliament the need for supporting the Balfour Declaration.

Powerful assistance was never more necessary, for the enemies of the Declaration were winning significant victories also. The military government in Palestine was filling important posts with anti-Zionists and quietly sabotaging every concession which the Zionists had won. The Arab leaders were active in every European capital, working upon statesmen, press, and public. Then, in March 1920, an attempt was made at a *coup d'état,* which, the Arabs hoped, the European diplomats, sadly divided among themselves, would be obliged to acknowledge. A Syrian congress suddenly proclaimed Feisal king of Syria and Palestine and his younger brother, Abdullah, king of Mesopotamia. They were both actually crowned as Europe looked on bewildered.

In Palestine the coup brought matters to a climax. The Arab population, long in ferment, began to organize demonstrations and there were rumours of approaching bloodshed. The military administration, warned by the Zionist commission, forbade the use of arms and threatened dire punishment for violations of the order. The demonstrations continued, and during Passover of 1920 there were disastrous riots in Jerusalem, lasting over three days, in which a number of Jews were killed.

Fate plays strange tricks. The coup, which threatened to undo the Zionist cause, made the Balfour Declaration a reality. The whole world protested against the Arab demonstrations and their tragic climax. In England the leading newspapers insisted that the government make good its promises to the Jews. Petitions poured in upon Parliament and upon the Supreme Allied Council sitting at San Remo. President Wilson and leading members of his Cabinet sent cables reiterating their friendliness to the Zionist aspirations. The storm carried away the Allied diplomats. Feisal was called in and told that an independent Syria and Palestine was out of the question. Then, on April 25, 1920, the Balfour Declaration was incorporated in the Turkish treaty and Britain was made the mandatory for Palestine. A month later Sir Herbert Samuel, who already in 1915 had argued in the Cabinet for a Jewish commonwealth, was appointed the first High Commissioner for Palestine.

CHAPTER TWENTY-NINE

EUROPE BETWEEN THE WARS

THE close of the war was greeted with hysterical joy by all the world, even by those who had suffered disastrous military defeat. The beating of the wings of the Angel of Death had ceased at last. Men could turn again to their fields and their factories and not think of them in terms of wheat for the armies and shells to blast the enemy. They could plan again for homes, for the schooling of their children, for travel, for the pleasant amenities of life. They could speak with confidence of tomorrow, even of the day after tomorrow.

No people were more thankful than the Jews, who had endured most. For them peace meant not only the end of the horrible carnage, of blockade and starvation, of cities laid waste and homes destroyed. It meant also the end of pogroms and expulsions, of torture and looting, of sadism and bestiality. It meant, if God had pity again, a new world order with security for the smaller peoples, the stepchildren of Europe.

But the glowing hopes of those who had suffered were soon turned to bitterness. Past experience had demonstrated that after every great war the forces of black reaction swallowed up the social system. For it was not possible to drench the world with blood, to blast away every ancient sanction, and then to turn back the waves of hate by the mere fiat of peacemakers. History repeated itself. Through the two decades that followed the peace treaty, Europe teetered dizzily on the brink of destruction. Each year brought its civil disturbances, its war crises, and its mounting horror of debt and poverty and unemployment. And then, in 1939, despite all the vaunted intelligence of the twentieth century, despite all the fervent prayers for peace, Europe plunged into more fearful warfare than ever before, with every indication that this time it would finally destroy itself.

The focal centre of disturbance was Germany, which rose from its defeat in the World War to exact a bloody revenge from its conquerors. During the first years of the peace the people were too exhausted by the sacrifices of the four long years' conflict to do more than nurse their wounds in sullen hate. They watched almost contemptuously as their new leaders, who had supplanted the Hohenzollern bureaucracy, sparred with the Allied statesmen to gain concessions that would restore some of the normal channels of trade. Then, when their democratic representatives failed, they turned to other men, frankly anti-Christian, anti-rational, anti-spiritual. They turned to one of the great fanatics of history, Adolf Hitler, whose shadow was to darken the whole country, then every part of Europe, finally all the world.

Hitler succeeded in making himself master of the German people because he was the perfect symbol of their own frustrations. He had been thwarted in every youthful undertaking. He had suffered from shrapnel wounds and gas. His pride had been outraged. He had personally tasted the bitterness of military defeat. Now destiny gave him the reins of power in a land where all the millions like him were glad to gear their lives for the purposes of revenge. Hitler ruled without squeamishness. He smashed all opposition and turned the country into a vast military training camp. For seven years all the resources and the energies of his people were corralled to prepare for a gigantic military gamble. Hitler was clever enough to take advantage of the dissensions which distracted the rest of Europe; of the fears of the ruling classes in England and France that his fall might plunge Germany into Communism. For seven years he kept building a new war machine, the most efficient and most powerful in the history of the Western world. Then he threw off all restraints and began a march to power which was not approached even by Cæsar and Napoleon.

One of the avowed aims of Hitler was to destroy the Jews of the world. Indeed, his early success was due in no small measure to his emphasis upon anti-Semitism. In the long history of the Jews they had been often attacked by men who despised them; but none remotely approached Hitler in personal malevolence or in the opportunity to implement this malevolence. When Hitler took control of Germany, it meant the complete annihilation of the ancient Jewish community there. When he went on to power in Austria, Czechoslovakia, Poland, Holland and Belgium, nearly every Jewish family in these historic lands was quickly and savagely liquidated. By 1942, the high point in Hitler's drive to world conquest, it appeared that his ambition was about to be fulfilled, for Europe approached the Nazi *judenrein* goal. The victorious Brown Shirts sang:

> Crush the skulls of the Jewish pack
> And then the future, it is ours and won;
> Proud waves the flag in the wind
> When swords with Jewish blood will run.

I. GERMANY AND THE NAZI WAR MACHINE

It is not difficult to understand the collapse of civilized values in defeated Germany. The years of warfare took a terrific toll; more than two million men, the cream of German youth, went to early graves. Many more millions were wounded, billions in property were destroyed. The economic and military provisions of the Treaty of Versailles added to the burden of the unhappy population, for they sheared away precious resources which were essential for recovery.

To denounce Germany specifically in the treaty as the criminal instigator of the war did not help to restore morale.

What did it matter then if the new republican Germany functioned under one of the world's most enlightened constitutions? It was a republic only in name, and its constitution was a paper façade which hid from view the evils which were gnawing at the vitals of the country. The old Junker guard still retained its crushing economic power. The industrialists who had profited from post-war inflation were determined to hold on to their ill-gotten gains and to sabotage all attempts at reform. The military clique, though discredited by defeat, were not deprived of their posts and they plotted in secret against the republic. The German people were offered political liberty, freedom of the press, the right of assembly, proportional representation. But they could not eat freedom, and the embittered younger generation found that glittering generalizations about the glories of democracy were a sorry substitute for jobs and homes and an honourable place in the social order.

A violent anti-Semitism spread through the country. Liberals, Social Democrats, honourable Christians, denounced the movement as uncivilized and unworthy of a cultured people, the people of Lessing and Goethe and Beethoven. But the Junkers and the clericals, the militarists and the disgruntled nationalists found it easy to divert attention from social distress by pillorying every Jew as a profiteer. The Jews had caused the war, they had engineered the disastrous peace, they had brought on the inflation, they had pre-empted the positions which belonged to deserving Germans. . . . The propaganda mills deluged the country with hate, and a sick people had little resistance to fight back against it. It was a portent of the horrors to come when Albert Einstein, the most original of modern scientists and one of the greatest geniuses of all time, was hooted by nationalist hooligans in the university lecture halls of Berlin.

Then, out of the fears and the distress and the national humiliation of the German people developed a powerful new party, the Nazis, organized for the purpose of smashing the republic, rebuilding the military strength of Germany, defying the Allies, and driving the Jews out of the country. The creator and spearhead of the party was the ruthless, half-crazed golem Adolf Hitler, whose career was to change the history of Western civilization.

Hitler was born and reared in old Austria, but he was early influenced by the pan-German pamphleteers of his youth and he dreamed of a powerful European bloc of slave states which would serve the master German people. He had none of the personality attributes which would normally be associated with the born leader. Unimpressive in appearance, ignorant of civilized values, highly neurotic, he was not taken seriously until he gained control of Germany. When he made an early attempt, in 1922, to seize the state by force, he was quickly captured. But the republican leaders discounted his menace so completely that, instead of shooting him as a traitor, they let him off with a short prison term. He used the period of incarceration to write his program in an autobiographical farrago, *Mein Kampf,* which, despite its turgid prose, called clearly for war to the end upon "the criminal democracy which corrupted the country's life." His appeal to hate and vengeance struck a responsive chord in the bankrupt mood of his people. The legitimate doctors had failed to bring healing and hope. Perhaps this violent brown-shirted Messiah would be more successful. What was there to lose?

Against this spirit the more disciplined and reasonable statesmen of Germany found it almost impossible to fight. Chief among them was Walther Rathenau who envisaged a Europe where all the great powers could collaborate to restore the economic health of the Continent. Rathenau came from a well-known Jewish family. His father had built up the A.E.G., the most valuable electrotechnical enterprise in the world. At the outbreak of the war Walther took charge of the Department of War Materials, and his genius made possible the four years of German resistance. One critic declared that his was the greatest single service rendered by any civilian during the war. As Minister of Reconstruction in 1921, Rathenau negotiated the treaty with France, which was a first step in improved relations between the former combatants. He also negotiated an advantageous economic agreement with Russia, which opened vast potentialities for Russo-German co-operation. As Foreign Minister Rathenau held the highest office ever attained by a Jew in Germany.

But his type of pacific statesmanship was fast becoming alien in a Germany where hate was counted a national virtue. Rabid nationalists denounced Rathenau's concessions to France. The Junkers exploded with wrath over the agreement with Russia. The Nazis and their anti-Semitic fellow-travellers grew purple with rage as they thought of a Jew so prominent in the councils of government. In June 1922 half a dozen pistol-shots from Nazi guns killed Rathenau. It was the opening salvo in the destruction of democratic Germany.

During the next decade, as economic conditions grew steadily worse, the Nazi party increased its popular strength until in 1932 it drew more than thirteen million votes, winning the largest number of seats in the Reichstag. It was no longer possible to keep Hitler out of the government. In January 1933 he was named Chancellor in the hope that responsibility would tame him and chasten his intransigence. "No soup is ever served as hot as it is cooked," the liberals said assuringly. But Hitler was not to be tamed. He quickly destroyed all opposing political parties and compelled a rubber-stamp Reichstag to assign dictatorial power to him. He then launched a revolution in the social life of Germany that smashed most of the political, cultural, scientific, and artistic canons that were the glory of the past.

Hitler did not wait long to fulfil his election promises with reference to the Jews. Six hundred thousand lived in the country, among the oldest and most valuable part of the population. They were dismissed from all public posts, in

the courts, the administration, the educational institutions, the railroads, and all
the nationalized utilities. The bar associations and the hospitals purged all of
their Jewish members. Those who were ousted included some of the world's
outstanding personalities, among them five Nobel prize winners. Pressure was
applied to Jewish business and commerce, and since there was neither ethics nor
national gratitude in the technique of despoliation, the economic fabric of Jewish life soon collapsed. In 1935 came the infamous Nuremberg laws which deprived all Jews of citizenship and set them apart as a special slave caste.

In 1938 a young Jewish exile in Paris, driven frantic by the sufferings of his
parents, who had been deported to Poland by Nazi orders, assassinated a subordinate official of the German Embassy. The hysterical act precipitated a nation-
wide pogrom in Germany, which was planned and engineered by the Nazi propaganda ministry. During several days and nights of unrestrained violence every
synagogue in the country was burnt down, thousands of Jews were killed
and wounded, and millions in property were destroyed. The impoverished
Jewish community was then ordered to pay the incredible fine of four billion
marks (four hundred million dollars), a fine assessed upon every Jew who still
owned more than two thousand dollars. When the second World War began
in 1939, the *coup de grâce* was administered. Every able-bodied Jew left in the
country was drafted for manual labour as part of the military program of the
Nazis.

Hitler had vowed before he came to power that he would exterminate the
Jews of Germany. He was unable to keep most of his economic and political
promises, but he succeeded beyond the wildest fears in completely annihi-
lating one of the most cultured and valuable Jewish settlements of the Western
world.

The first World War disrupted the proud Austrian empire which was partitioned among half a dozen succession states. Only a small rump, with a population of six and one-half million, remained of a once powerful imperial confederation that had played a dominant part in European history for more than
a thousand years. It would have been best, perhaps, if this segment, German in
population, had been added to republican Germany. But the French government
stubbornly opposed any *Anschluss;* even a customs union was sternly vetoed.
The French were unwilling to strengthen a defeated enemy by adding several
thousand square miles to her territory. They could not see that a liberal, democratic Germany, economically sound, absorbing Austria, was a factor for peace.
The decision of the Allies made of Austria one of the perennial problems of
post-war Europe. For two decades its history was a succession of economic
crises, hunger riots, attempts at revolution, and frequent national bankruptcy.
When the flimsy economic structure of the country collapsed in 1929, there
were repercussions in every part of the world.

These disasters played into the hands of Hitler and his followers. They established Nazi branches in Austria that worked from within to gain control of the state. When the opportune moment came to strike, the Trojan-horse technique made it easy to take over the country bloodlessly. In 1938 Hitler boldly defied the Allies, marched into Austria, dissolved its corporate existence, and declared it to be an integral part of the greater Reich.

A quarter of a million Austrian Jews were at once brought under the jurisdiction of the Swastika. In one devastating "spring cleaning" they were swept out of their place in the social order and were relegated to a new caste of untouchables. Even the world-famous Sigmund Freud, father of modern psychoanalysis, was not spared, and, as he went into exile, his contribution to modern science was contemptuously referred to as "Jewish pornography." Within two years emigration emptied the country of those Jews who could obtain precious visas, the young, the vigorous, the ambitious. Those who were left were the old, the infirm, the hopeless, who now waited wearily for death to release them from the Nazi prison.

Perhaps the happiest and most contented Jewish community of central and eastern Europe was centred in blessed Czechoslovakia. Here lived more than 350,000 Jews, a sturdy middle-class group, highly respected, well educated, justly proud of a cultural and religious tradition which went back to the early Middle Ages. The thriving cities of Prague and Karlsbad, Brünn, Pilsen, and Brataslava had been built by Jewish and Czech genius, and they were islands of democratic strength in the bleak Fascist and semi-Fascist desert of the east and south.

Czechoslovakia had long been part of the Austrian empire. It became an independent state through one of the few statesmanlike provisions of the peace treaties. Its freedom and prosperity were carefully guarded by its noblest sons, the architects of the country's independence, Masaryk and Beneš. For nearly two decades they resisted all threats to its integrity, earning the plaudits of the world by their enlightened economic policies and by their treatment of minority groups.

Then in 1933 Hitler became the next-door neighbour of the little country, and its independent life could no longer be taken for granted. A series of internal crises was artificially stimulated by Nazi agents, who were sheltered by the democratic principles of free speech and the right of assembly. In the fall of 1938 Hitler dispatched an ultimatum, ordering the surrender of the strategic defences of the country. Britain and France had sworn to protect the integrity of Czechoslovakia, but the promise was repudiated by the appeasement twins, Chamberlain and Daladier, whose quavering diplomacy was later to bring their own nations to disaster. Beneš was obliged to capitulate. By the Munich Pact, the Czech defences were abandoned to Hitler in the hope of slaking his appetite and, in Chamberlain's words, "winning peace in our time." Six months after Munich, Hitler cynically tore up the pact, annexed the whole country, and converted it into another Nazi outpost.

Among the first victims, as usual, were the hundreds of thousands of Jews. As soon as the Nazi lorries rolled into the land, the attacks upon them began. The same pathetic routine, already so familiar, was followed — expulsion from positions, destruction of all civil rights, homes raided, property expropriated, physical brutality, executions, degradation. With the usual German thoroughness every piece of property, all valuables, even wedding rings and ornaments, were taken from the Jews. Those who were fortunate enough to leave the country went forth into exile as bereft of possessions as of spirit and hope.

Germany, Austria, now Czechoslovakia. A new German empire was being built, but the foundation stones rested on millions of broken lives and the cement was mixed with human blood.

2. THE RISE AND FALL OF POLAND

Poland was a prime favourite of the Allied statesmen at the peace conference. They went to unusual lengths to satisfy the most extravagant claims of the Polish representatives. Some were motivated by the sentiment of historical justice; a long-suffering people, enduring alien rule for more than a century and a half, was at last to break its fetters. Some thought of strategic factors: a powerful Poland would be a useful guard upon Germany's eastern frontier. Poland emerged from the peace conference the fifth largest state in Europe. Nineteen million Poles were given control of eleven millions of non-Polish minorities, including more than three million Jews. The minority groups were protected by a series of treaty provisions which guaranteed their civil and political equality as well as their cultural autonomy.

But the actions of the Poles, whom Zangwill once called "beggars on horseback," were a disgrace to the high pretensions of the new state. Freedom came to Poland after centuries of oppression, but as soon as her own national life was secured, she became more imperialistic and intolerant than her oppressors had been. The boundaries established by the peace conference were too narrow for her. There were wars with Russia, Czechoslovakia, Lithuania, and Estonia in the attempt to gain more territory. Like a pauper suddenly raised to wealth, Poland became unbearably drunk with pride.

Her Jewish policy was of a piece. The promises made at the peace conference to respect the rights of minorities were scrapped. The nation which had pleaded for more than a century that a minority must not be submerged now carried through a policy of ruthless Polonization.

The pans and the szlachta, the powerful nobles who controlled most of the Polish economy, continued to exploit the millions of peasants and workers. Social restlessness became dangerous and the parasites turned to anti-Semitism as a ready-made lightning-rod to divert revolution. Year by year, restrictions were introduced to cut away the economic opportunities of the Jews until nearly half of them were reduced to virtual beggary. Many of them were kept alive by the remittances of relatives in other countries or by the charitable disbursements of Jewish relief agencies. Registration in universities and the higher institutions of learning was severely restricted. There were special ghetto benches assigned in the classrooms for the few Jews who were able to make their way through the legal loop-holes. Pogroms were frequent and were condoned by the government leaders. With all the paper guarantees of Versailles, the Jews of Poland were no better off than in the worst Tsarist days. Then, at least, the persecutions were not paraded in the name of " national honour."

Fate ultimately brought retribution upon the heads of the Polish rulers. Hitler's ambitions clashed with the continued independent existence of the newly created state. The second World War was begun with the attack by Hitler upon Poland. In an incredible blitzkrieg, a lightning war of less than two months, the twenty-year old state was again wiped off the map of Europe. Polish territory was partitioned between Germany and Soviet Russia in conformity with a prearranged plan made by the Red and Brown *Plunderbund*. A million Jews passed under the jurisdiction of Stalin; two and one-half million, in the great industrial area of Poland, fell into the clutches of Hitler and the Nazis.

During the next six months, as the greatest looting expedition in modern history was under way, neither foreign correspondents nor relief officials were permitted to enter the country. The Nazis took everything in sight — wheat, oil, steel, rolling stock, the linen from the hospitals, the door-knobs on the house fronts, the copper wiring on the trolley lines, everything of value that could be carried off. The war destroyed several hundred thousand Jews; in the period of 'reorganization' that followed virtually all who still survived were annihilated by disease, starvation, execution, or suicide.

Poland had long been one of the chief reservoirs of Jewish life. Its cultural and religious tradition had continued despite the tyranny of its conquerors. But Polish Jewry was now not merely passing under another tyranny. It was in the talons of a maniac with a lust for destruction, uninhibited by pity or chivalry. As the months of occupation passed, hope diminished that there would be anything left except debris and the sorry hulks of broken, blasted, starving Jews.

3. DARKNESS IN THE BALKANS

Roumania emerged from the World War as the largest of the Balkan States, its territory doubled, its population increased from seven to eighteen millions. Like Poland, there was little humility or generosity in its post-war policies. Its chief scapegoats were the Jews, who made a compact minority of more than a million. Anti-Semitism was almost a government policy. Party leaders fought bitterly over domestic or foreign issues, but there was little difference in outlook where the Jews were concerned. Jew-baiting received the blessing of the heads of universities and the church patriarchs, as well as of the diplomats who represented the playboy King Carol in foreign capitals.

Roumania was quick to adapt the lessons that it learned from Poland and other clever neighbours in their political disposition of the Jews. But it set up an original pattern for others to follow in dealing legally and "humanely" with the Jewish economic position. Shrewd bureaucrats insisted upon rigid examination of all Jewish citizenship rights and they were able to entangle the proceedings in labyrinths of red tape. In the confusion they succeeded in depriving whole communities of their naturalization. By 1939 nearly 320,000 Jews were declared stateless. This was a kind of cold pogrom. For those who were not citizens could not engage in gainful employment nor could they conduct profitable enterprises. In this way, without bloodshed, without scandal, half the Jews of Roumania were swept out of the economic structure to make room for "good" nationals of unimpeachable background.

It was inevitable that hundreds of thousands of Jewish families should begin the desperate hunt for emigration outlets. But not many could leave, since nearly every country in the world now had air-tight immigration restrictions. The terror of the trapped Jewish inhabitants increased as Hitler moved ever closer to the Roumanian orbit. No one could be sure that the country would escape his clutches, for he coveted the rich oil reserves which were its most precious possession. In 1940 a million Roumanian Jews lived fearsomely under the shadow of a rumbling volcano.

Hungary's post-war history was dominated by its tragic memories of the soul-searing experiences of 1918–19. It suffered disastrous military reverses and was cut to pieces by the Allied treaty-makers. The country was overrun by enemy troops, Serbs, Czechs, and Roumanians, and there was a brief interregnum of Bolshevik control. This Red government was headed by an opportunist scoundrel, Béla Kun, of Jewish origin, whose Cabinet also included a number of Jewish officials. All the Jews of the country, mainly middle-class, and passionately devoted to their Fatherland, were ultimately to pay, and to pay dearly, for this accidental circumstance. It was never forgotten that the brief but bloody Red dictatorship had been engineered by an alien firebrand who had Jewish blood in his veins.

Béla Kun's regime collapsed in 1919. The new Regent, Admiral Horthy, at once proclaimed martial law, sternly repressed all free institutions, and converted Hungary into one of the most reactionary states in Europe. Anti-Semitism now had free reign. For nearly twenty years the war on Jewish rights continued, actively abetted by government officials. It took the form of economic boycott, political and social discrimination, interspersed with riots and physical brutality. In 1938, special laws were enacted which radically reduced the proportion of Jews in every economic enterprise. More than two-thirds of the Jewish population were automatically deprived of their means of livelihood. Even this legislation, however, did not satisfy the powerful Nazi party in Hungary. They were determined to destroy completely the 700,000 Jews of the country. When Hungary became part of the Fascist axis in 1939, it was plain that soon the Nazi program would be entirely fulfilled.

4 · SOVIET RUSSIA

In March 1917, after three disastrous years of war, which brought millions of casualties, the old Russia collapsed. The Tsar abdicated and a liberal provisional government, headed by Alexander Kerensky, took control of the country. For a brief moment it seemed that the blessings of democracy were to be extended to the oppressed Russian masses and that the persecuted minorities were to share fully in the promises of the new day. The subject provinces, Poland, Finland, Lithuania, Latvia, and Estonia, were granted a generous degree of autonomy, and all the anti-Jewish legislation which had embittered six million lives was automatically swept away.

There was no opportunity, however, to test the generous intentions of the new government. Kerensky, under great pressure from the Allies, agreed to continue with the war effort. But the people were sick to death of bloodshed, and in the months which followed the March revolution Russia, demoralized by economic distress and military disaster, drifted rapidly into anarchy. In November the vigilant, aggressive Bolshevik minority seized the reins of government and established a proletarian dictatorship. One of its first acts was to sign a separate peace treaty with Germany.

Theoretically the new revolution made no change in the Jewish situation. In the very first week of the Bolshevik coup the government announced the abolition of all restrictions and privileges. Yet the new revolution was destined to disrupt the lives of the Russian Jews more completely than any other event in their varied history.

To begin with, a deadly civil war broke out between the Bolsheviks and those who wished to maintain the old economic order. The opposition parties, sensing greater danger to their way of life from the Reds than from invaders, willingly accepted assistance from foreign armies. The irreconcilables, patriotic and selfish, liberal and reactionary, assailed every frontier, and the Russian people sank further in the sanguinary abyss.

The Jews, as usual, were caught between the warring hosts. The conflict raged most fiercely in the cities of the south and west, where the Jews were concentrated. Three million souls lived in the stricken Ukraine, and every invading army plundered them, the Poles because they were Bolsheviks, the Bolsheviks because they were not, the Germans because they were Ukrainians, Petlura's guerrilla bands because they were Jews, Denikin's robber forces because they were worth plundering. Nearly two thousand pogroms were perpetrated, in which, by conservative estimates, more than a hundred thousand Jews were destroyed, and, by other estimates, nearly a quarter of a million. The year 1920 brought back all the horrors of Chmielnicki's day, three centuries before.

For five years, until well into 1922, the Soviet government fought desperately against its enemies. One by one the foreign interventionists withdrew and gradually the remarkably organized Red armies re-established order. The Bolshevik leaders were then able to turn with clearer minds to the vast problems of internal reconstruction.

Already a fundamental economic revolution had taken place. It was decreed that all the resources of the nation were to be controlled by the state. The institution of private property disappeared as competition was outlawed. The substitution of state planning for private enterprise eliminated the middleman and smashed the bourgeoisie.

Millions of Russians were reduced to poverty by the confiscation of fortunes and enterprises and by the destruction of their means of livelihood. But the Jews were affected more than all other groups; Tsarist restrictions had cut them off from most callings except those of middlemen. The Soviet attack upon their economic position was not launched because they were Jews; but they paid heavily for the accident of history which had given them disproportionate representation in the now tabooed economic categories.

Gradually, after immense suffering, a complete realignment of Jewish life took place. Many thousands of the younger generation moved into government positions. The corrupt Tsarist bureaucracy had to be completely scrapped. There was unusual opportunity in the reorganized state service.

In 1927 the Soviet officials announced the first of a series of Five-Year Plans by which they hoped to carry through the industrialization of Russia. The giant had slept too long. If he hoped to survive he must meet the challenges of the mechanized twentieth century. The Soviet blueprints which aimed "to overtake and surpass the advanced countries of the West" called for labour, for willing hands to forge the shafts of steel for the new Russia. Hundreds of thousands of young Jews joined in the rush to fit into the new plans. They went into mines and timber regions, into oil fields and the metal trades. The best trained and the most gifted were placed in charge of technical enterprises in the giant cities which began to rear themselves in every part of the country. The rank and file moved into the foundries, onto the girders, into the very bowels of the earth, forming a vast new proletariat of nearly half a million Jews.

Simultaneously the Soviet leaders inaugurated a back-to-the-land movement through which they hoped to absorb another large segment of declassed Jews.

Special consideration must be given to Jewish families, President Kalinin announced, for they had been denied legitimate creative outlets under Tsarist tyranny. Fertile areas were opened for colonization in White Russia, the Ukraine, Northern Crimea, and in the Far Eastern province of Biro-Bidjan. The program was placed under the direction of a special board, the *Komzet,* which supervised the land distribution, arranged for loans of seed and implements, and served as liaison between the workers and the government.

Within ten years more than 250,000 Jews had been settled on the soil. The transition, of course, was not an easy one. Most of the colonists came from an urban environment and they were totally untrained and unprepared for their new mode of life. They had to learn how to clear the land, drain the swamps, build roads, and erect homes. But they gladly accepted these pioneering challenges, for they were now, at last, associated with enterprises which were blessed by the state.

The creation of a Jewish proletariat and a Jewish farmer class involved far-reaching changes in Jewish life, in family relationships, in the social structure, in population distribution. But there were to be others, even more fundamental. A determined effort was made by the Soviet officials to root out the curse of anti-Semitism, which was condemned as counter-revolutionary activity. In 1917 Lenin wrote in a margin of a decree condemning anti-Semitism: "Pogromchiks and those who carry on pogrom agitation are to be considered outside the law." It was announced that those who were found guilty of inciting hatred of one group against another would be punished by death or long imprisonment. There were educational campaigns to teach the people to be on guard against the prejudices which could serve only the enemies of "the classless society."

After the first terrifying years of readjustment, most of the two and one-half million Jews who lived under the jurisdiction of the Hammer and the Sickle became an integral part of the Soviet social order. They lived on a plane with every other group, for there was no discrimination against them as Jews.

Yet the story was not all honey and clover. Like the millions of other inhabitants in the state, the Jews shared the many repressions which are inevitable in a totalitarian tyranny. Human beings were robots, cogs in a vast economic machine, to be manipulated by the whim of the cocksure despots who arrogated all authority to themselves and ruthlessly shot or exiled those who dared to disagree. Jews in other lands who were unduly enthusiastic about the Communist "solution" were often brought up sharply by the reports of purges and liquidations. A Russian court of justice evidently had only one wall. . . . It was a heavy price to pay for what was called economic security.

Nor could Jews live as Jews, following the faith of their fathers if they had the wish to do so. For the Bolsheviks waged relentless warfare upon all organized religion. "The destruction of religion," Karl Marx had written, "the phantom happiness of the people, is a necessary condition for their real happiness." Priests, ministers, rabbis, and mullahs were all anathema, parasites who preyed upon the gullibility of the people. Religion was opium; it was devised to hoodwink the workers by holding out to them the promise of an other-worldly paradise in order to divert them from the task of building a paradise on earth. Religious services were not prohibited, but a special edict forbade the teaching of religion to children under the age of eighteen. In the public schools all the devices of a brilliant propaganda system were applied to bring home the lesson that religious faith was the superstition of the ignorant.

For those who had no concern about Jewish group survival, the Soviet war on Jewish religious practices was shrugged off as inconsequential. But for those who believed ardently in the right of the Jewish people to maintain its corporate existence, this enforced assimilation, by edict and propaganda, was mourned as a major tragedy. For it was plain that it would ultimately be much more effective in undermining the fabric of Jewish life than all the brutal persecutions of the Nazis.

5. THE DEMOCRATIC WEST

The gloom that settled over Jewish life in most European countries, darkening the homes of many millions, was, for a while, not extended to the centres of the democratic tradition. France, Belgium, Holland, Switzerland, and England, remained, as in the past, strong bulwarks of liberty and humaneness. Their peoples, enjoying a comparatively high standard of living, were fervent supporters of democratic institutions. They were proud of their parliaments, their bills of rights, their reputation as asylums for the weary and the heavy-laden.

Among them lived more than a million Jews, most of them old settlers. In Holland they traced their community tradition back to the days of the Spanish Inquisition; in France, far beyond, to the beginnings of national growth. There was no permanent guarantee of security in the tumultuous post-war decades, but it was a great comfort for the Jews to realize that their fate was inextricably bound up with the fate of the democratic dogma. So long as their beloved homelands remained free and independent, it was not likely that Jewish rights would be assailed. These could be jeopardized only if internal revolution or external aggression extinguished the free life of all the people. And who, in his right mind, would treat such a danger as near or real?

Hence the Jews of the Western democracies lived with an easy optimism that was the envy of their coreligionists in other parts of Europe. They shared the burdens of taxation and unemployment and the sacrifices of military preparedness which no nation, not even the victors, could escape after Versailles. But no responsible agency threatened their right to fullest opportunity. The law was a precious sanction, and they placed as much trust in it as in the ways of the stars.

No task seemed impossible, no post of honour seemed too remote. A number of Jews won the highest distinctions within the gift of the state. In Britain they served creditably in Parliament, in the courts of justice, and in the most famous institutions of learning. Lord Samuel was chosen as the leader of the Liberal Party; Lord Reading became the Viceroy of India, arbitrating the destiny of millions of Hindus and Moslems. In France, Léon Blum, scion of an ancient and distinguished Jewish family, was twice Prime Minister in periods of difficult social crisis. Belgium sent Paul Hymans as its representative to the League of Nations and rejoiced in his elevation to its presidency.

Where Jews were so providentially situated, they were naturally called upon to extend assistance to those who were less fortunate. They did not shirk their responsibility as their brothers' keepers. Relief drives were generously supported; indeed the per capita contributions from Britain were much larger than those which came from the richer communities of the United States. Appeals for help to build the Jewish homeland in Palestine elicited an enthusiastic response. London, Paris, Geneva, Amsterdam, Antwerp, and other citadels of Jewish life became indispensable clearance points for refugee service. Most heartening of all, as Hitler's terror mounted, was the sympathy and goodwill of Christian leaders. Churchmen, educators, journalists, scientists, all publicly denounced Nazi barbarism and joined in the attempt to assist its victims. The millions that were raised by Christian friends were no more important than the spirit of goodwill that bolstered the morale of the sorely tried Jewish communities condemned by fate to live in the very heart of disaster.

To be sure, no country could escape the ubiquitous operations of the Fascist termites. Mosley in England, Mussert in Holland, Degrelle in Belgium, Gustloff in Switzerland, were the spearheads for Nazi penetration in these countries. They demonstrated extraordinary resourcefulness in spreading their propaganda, utilizing the technique of anti-Semitism to bring confusion into democratic ranks. But the meagre popular support they received in free electoral campaigns clearly indicated that they were a tiny, contemptible minority, regarded by all decent, responsible people as national garbage.

In 1939 the irresistible hammer blows of Hitler's legions destroyed all dreams of security and placed in jeopardy the ethical sanctions of the Western world. France was soon fighting desperately for survival against the most powerful war machine in history. It was quickly overwhelmed, and the worst elements in the population were given authority in a broken, dispirited vassal state. Belgium and Holland strove frantically but unsuccessfully to remain neutral. Hitler had never respected promises or treaties, and he tore through both countries with such speed that the legend of Nazi invincibility became as effective a weapon as guns and planes. The Jewish communities were singled out for special treatment. Only when Hitler had been defeated and the authentic story of what happened inside conquered Europe had been pieced together, did the world learn the awful significance of this special treatment. Britain itself—powerful, traditionally inviolate Britain—narrowly escaped invasion. The air assaults that rocked the island by day and by night, reducing huge parts of the industrial centres to rubble, brought democratic hopes to the lowest point in generations. Until the tide turned, in 1942, it appeared that nothing could any longer save what the free, rational, critical spirit of the Western world had patiently built since the days of the Enlightenment.

6. SUMMARY

The summary of Jewish history in Europe during the two post-war decades is uniformly tragic. In Germany, Austria, and Czechoslovakia more than a million Jews, who had built the most promising settlements in modern history, were annihilated. In Poland twenty years of economic attrition, climaxed by the barbarity of the Nazi and Soviet blitzkrieg, devastated another three and a half million Jews. In Roumania and Hungary nearly two million more were caught in an economic trap, and, living in the shadow of Nazi conquest, faced total extinction. In the Baltic states, in the Arab world along the Mediterranean, and in Italy, the Jewish communities knew that disaster was a matter of an inexorable Nazi time-table. In Russia there was some hope for bare physical survival, but the two and a half million Jews of that country were being rapidly assimilated in the vast Communist melting-pot.

In two decades ten million Jews were brought into the Valley of the Shadow of Death. No similar period in all the centuries that followed the bloody crusades of 1096 had been so disastrous, so void of security or comfort. Even when the paranoiac ambitions of Hitler had been thwarted, there was no hope for continued creative living in eastern, central, or southern Europe. The historian who writes realistically cannot end the chapter, even though it includes the downfall of the Nazis, in the exultant spirit of Hallel, the traditional prayer of hope and gratitude. His summary must be written in the solemn spirit of the Kaddish, the prayer for the dead.

CHAPTER THIRTY

THE WESTERN HEMISPHERE IN THE TWENTIETH CENTURY

I. LATIN AMERICA

THE rich Latin American continent had always been a strange, exotic world to the European and the American. Knowledge of its people and its economy filtered through sporadic trade contacts, which brought out coffee, rubber, wool, and frozen meats for Western use. It played only a small role in international affairs and emerged in the news only through an occasional political upheaval, usually dismissed as just another typical South American explosion, "bald men fighting over a comb." After World War I, however, the situation changed completely. The highly industrialized European countries, their own economies shrivelled and crippled, began to hunt for trade and raw materials in the few comparatively undeveloped areas that were left. Latin America became the answer to the statesman's prayers. Long identified with romantic trivialities, the continent was now studied by finance experts in terms of manganese and copper, wheat and hides, exports and imports, and trade balances. And incidentally, but not too incidentally, naval and air bases.

Britain and the United States, who long enjoyed an uncontested trade hegemony, were rudely jolted into the realization that the salesmen of other nations were now determined to exploit the vast resources of the continent. And their rivals, chiefly Italy and Germany, followed none of the leisurely, gentlemanly techniques of pre-war days. They moved in with the usual Fascist ruthlessness, with cunning propaganda, bewilderingly unorthodox economic legerdemain, "barter" and "boycott," with power politics actively abetted by local Fascist cells. Latin America became high stakes in the game of economic and political control, a game that completely unsettled the mañana tempo of a slow-paced continent.

Nearly half a million Jews lived peacefully in this area. Their numbers were negligible in relation to the vastness of the continent. But they enjoyed unusual security in the Argentine, Brazil, Mexico, and in many subordinate states where small but influential communities had been established under friendly auspices. Many were families whose proud tradition went back three or four centuries to the beginnings of European penetration. Others were more recent arrivals from lands that evoked only painful memories. All were grateful that fate had set them down in more pleasant pastures, and they watched fearfully lest the fortunes of war and diplomacy bring back the woes from which they had fled. For they knew that if totalitarian states succeeded in transplanting their corrupting ideologies, they would soon be helots.

The Argentine possessed the largest and most influential Jewish settlement in Latin America. The foundations of this community had been laid at the end of the nineteenth century by Baron Maurice de Hirsch, Europe's fabulous railroad king. Hirsch invested millions of dollars in a dream of transplanting large Jewish groups from the congestion and misery of eastern Europe to the spacious farm lands of the Argentine pampas. Here, he was convinced, there could be an escape from the economic vulnerability of the Pale of Settlement. Jews would be able to return to the soil and transform the image of the peddler, the *Luftmensch,* the marginal middleman, into the image of the dynamic Jewish farmer.

Hirsch's grandiose hopes for a major alleviation of the Jewish problem in Russia were not fulfilled. By the outbreak of World War I, less than 35,000 souls were settled in three hundred farming units. Nevertheless, Hirsch's colonization attempt produced consequences far beyond the few surviving agricultural settlements. His widely publicized plan brought the Argentine into every Russian-Jewish household. Like the United States, his name became a talisman, carrying the promise of a clean break with the frustrations of the past. Between 1904 and 1915, the years of severest pressure in Czarist Russia, 83,000 Jews migrated to the Argentine. When the outbreak of World War II shattered further hope for emigration, 350,000 Jews already lived in the country. Buenos Aires, the magnificent capital, was listed among the world's most influential Jewish communities. In a sense, too, even the farming dreams were partially realized. By mid-twentieth century more than 40,000 Jews were living happily on the tracts that Baron de Hirsch had purchased. Their success would have brought joy to the Baron's heart, had he lived to see these Jewish agriculturists win coveted prizes for produce or breeding at the great provincial and national fairs.

But the vast majority of the Jews of Buenos Aires and the other cities of the republic belonged to the lower middle classes. They made their contribution to the national economy by developing a number of small industries—knitted wear, furniture, mirrors, luggage, office supplies, and allied articles. Except for a few leading merchants, they were virtually unrepresented in the key enterprises— shipping, transportation, and refrigeration. But if they were insignificant in economic influence, they were an unusual leavening force in the cultural life of the Argentine, especially in journalism, *belles-lettres,* the theatre, and the arts. They were well represented in the school system and they helped to mould educational policy.

Before the twentieth century there were less than three thousand Jews in Brazil. The United States, Canada, and the Argentine offered more attractive opportunities, and Brazil was scarcely mentioned in the turbulent decades of exodus that followed the Russian May laws. Then the Johnson Bill of 1924 closed the doors of the United States and diverted tens of thousands of immigrants to Brazil, among other places, and before World War II the Jewish population had increased to 110,000. They settled in the urban centres, Rio de Janeiro, Pernambuco, Bahia, Porto Alegre and Curtiba, working primarily as minor merchants, artisans, and professional men. A small number became manufacturers and foreign traders. The Jewish population was a tiny speck in a total Brazilian nation of forty million. It was completely absorbed in the task of winning economic security; few of the new arrivals learned Portuguese well enough to participate fully in the cultural life of the country. It would take another generation before the recently augmented Jewish community could strike roots and make its influence felt, as it had in the neighbouring Argentine.

The many smaller Latin American countries and the West Indies islands came into contemporary Jewish history primarily through the frantic search for immigration outlets. The most forgotten corners of the earth were sought out for the victims of Hitlerism. Yet some of the new settlements proved to be ideal havens, and none more so than Uruguay, the Switzerland of Latin America. Its wealth of resources and its superb climate offered excellent opportunities for the talented and the courageous. Since 1917 a small but steady stream of immigration was drawn to the country, and by 1945 the Jewish population had grown to 27,000, centred primarily in the lovely resort capital, Montevideo.

Jews were associated with Mexican history from the dramatic days of early European conquest. But the number was never large, and before 1914 there were less than a thousand Jews in all the land. The early post-war governments, anxious to build up the national economy, especially industry and commerce, encouraged large-scale immigration. In June 1922 President Obregon welcomed eastern European Jews as colonists in the sparsely populated territory along the American border. Late in the summer of 1924 General Calles, President-elect of Mexico, declared that if there were sufficient financial support from American Jews, he would urge the settlement of extensive tracts of arable land. He also favored a system of co-operative guilds to provide employment for many thousands of Jews in the garment and allied industries. It turned out that each of the proposed plans required substantial investment, and the major Jewish colonization and relief agencies felt that this was unpractical in the light of the dubious benefits. Consequently there was no large scale immigration. But the patent friendliness of the Mexican government drew smaller family groups, and before World War II the Jewish population had increased to 20,000.

Most of those who came were really transients. They intended to stop briefly in what they regarded as a half-way station en route to the United States or Canada. Yet only a small proportion carried through this original resolve. The country had charm, the government was hospitable, the opportunities for normal living were limitless. Many Jews took to peddling, penetrating into the remotest Indian villages. They found friendly natives and an unharried tempo of living, which appealed mightily after the tensions of Europe. When the natives were little attracted by hose, neckties, and other wearing apparel, hardly necessary in the primitive outland, the resourceful pioneers turned to hardware or to sacred objects. Many a crucifix was sold between the morning *Shachris* and the afternoon *Minchah* by former Talmudic students from Lithuania.

The majority of the newcomers settled in Mexico City, where they were soon engaged in minor commerce. Those who were trained abroad as artisans became tailors, shoemakers, or jewellers. The more enterprising began to manufacture their own goods in order to avoid the heavy expense of importation from American sources. Mexican light industry stemmed directly from this newly stimulated native market for men's and ladies' wear, shoes, hats, and other manufactured articles.

It was all a providential development, and it was hoped that the Latin American countries, virtually at the beginning of their economic expansion, might mature into another United States. The total population of the Argentine was only thirteen millions; Brazil, larger than the United States in geographical area, had only forty millions. The racial mixtures of the continent, the ease of assimilation, the complete absence of ethnic arrogance, limited group hostility to the blatherings of a few irresponsible agitators on the lunatic fringe. Why was it not possible for these youthful lands to receive hundreds of thousands of Jewish settlers, so that the continent could become the fulcrum for a new Jewish civilization in the Western world? Once, when the lights went out in Babylon and the East, the Jewish centre of gravity shifted to Spain and North Africa, and a rich civilization was built there. The lights were again dimmed, indeed extinguished, in Europe. Why should not the new centre of gravity now be shifted to a rehabilitated Palestine and to the Western hemisphere, where the Latin countries would complement in absorptive capacity and in creative Jewish living the example of the United States?

It was a beautiful dream. But it turned out to be pathetic wishful thinking. The Nazi plague reached out across the oceans and worked its poison into the interstices of every community, the simple villages as well as the most sophisticated metropolises.

The Jews of the Argentine were the first to feel the consequences. The advent of Hitler in 1933 brought ruin to many Jewish firms whose well-being depended upon business connections with Germany. The Nazi propaganda machine began to pound away at the large German population of the Argentine, which numbered nearly a million and a half, to boycott Jewish enterprises, and to serve as the spearhead for anti-Semitic attacks. This was the usual fifth-column technique to weaken the solidarity of a country and to bring confusion into its foreign policy. Germans who were loyal to their lifelong friendships were denounced as traitors to *Volk* and *Boden*. They were threatened with boycott, with loss of passport privileges, and with reprisals against relatives and friends in the old homeland. There was a large infiltration of German professors and exchange students, all carefully prepared by the Nazis, and huge sums were spent by German business houses to advertise the "beneficent" achievements of the Hitler regime. In 1937 the novel *Oro* by the Nazi author Hugo Wast reached best-seller status. It was a violent attack upon the Jews which treated the *Protocols* as genuine and called for a Jewish purge *à la* Hitler.

The democratic forces in the Argentine fought vigorously to protect the country from Fascist engulfment. But it was a losing fight. The restlessness of millions of poverty-stricken bondsmen frightened the top industrialists, clericals, and bankers, and made them natural allies of reaction. The adroitness of Nazi penetration and the unbridled ambitions of the army clique further contributed to the rout of the constitutional forces. In June 1943 came the Coup of the Colonels, which brought to power a tough military dictatorship, with Juan Perón exercising the control from behind the scenes. The government became increasingly anti-American, anti-democratic, and anti-Semitic. The other Latin American countries had joined the Pan-American front in war on Germany, Italy, and Japan. The Argentine remained neutral, and its neutrality was definitely slanted towards the Fascist powers. At the last moment, when Hitler was already doomed, the Argentine joined the Allies, but it was a cynical declaration of war intended only to gain a seat in the international conferences that considered the peace.

In 1946 Perón emerged from behind the façade of puppets who had officially represented the government, and stood personally for election as President. His program included all the demagogic nostrums that the Fascists of Europe had used to ride to power. He promised bread and circuses on a scale that even the most intransigent workers had never dared to expect. The United States considered Perón such a potential menace that the State Department issued a Blue Book on the eve of the election which catalogued his long record of Fascist complicity and co-operation. This unwittingly played directly into Perón's hands. He appealed to the latent anti-American sentiment of the populace, and went into frenzies of indignation over Yankee "interference" in internal affairs. He was overwhelmingly elected.

As President, Perón did not officially sanction anti-Semitic measures. But he was so tainted by his Fascist associations that the Jews of the country prepared for the worst. The incidents began to multiply. The usual anti-Jewish slogans were painted in the streets. Synagogues and cemeteries and schools were desecrated and damaged, and there were arson attempts on the homes of prominent Jews. The Jewish community leaders of the Argentine protested repeatedly; after each protest Perón blandly expressed official regret, but the outrages continued and grew more serious. There could be no wide public protest, for Perón had muzzled the democratic press, retired the liberal members of the Supreme Court, and dismissed professors and school-teachers who had opposed his regime.

The Argentine announced that it desired large-scale immigration to build up

the country and develop its magnificent potentialities. But the immigration program was placed in the hands of Dr. Santiago Peralta, a well-known Fascist and
anti-Semite whose writings had vilified the Jews. His danger did not lie so much
in prohibitive restrictions on Jewish immigration which he sponsored. It lay in
the fact that the new immigration was sought from Spain and Italy and Poland,
and every effort was made to bring in those who would be most compatible in a
Fascist state. Such immigration would provide steady reinforcements for those
elements who looked to the Argentine to become the leader of a new Fascist bloc
in the Western world. A deep despair blanketed the spirit of the Jewish communities. Those who had recently escaped from Europe's nightmare felt that
history was repeating itself, and that, though the war had been won, the Fascists
were using the Argentine as a new reservoir from which to build back to strength
and power.

Yet, as the Czech statesman Eduard Beneš once remarked, dictatorships are
all-powerful until a few minutes before they are overthrown. On a fall day in
1955 the pent-up resentment against the Perón regime suddenly erupted in revolution. Under the popular leadership of Air Force General Pedro Aramburu, the
dictatorship was swept out. Perón fled, together with his brassy and ambitious
wife, Evita, and the entire grafting cabal that surrounded them. Aramburu
moved vigorously to purge all the Peronista elements in the armed forces, the
labour unions, and the universities. The Peronistas, in their turn, fought back
desperately, attempting a general strike in late 1955 and a military uprising in
1956. But, except for the fanatical support of the *descamisados,* the impoverished
proletarians of the cities, both attempts at counter-revolution failed. Astutely
guided now by Aramburu, the Argentine government was determined to bring
the country into the mainstream of modern Western life.

By now the Jewish community had grown to more than 400,000 souls, far indeed from the isolated, fledgling settlement of only a generation earlier. Although
some of the business tycoons had been guilty of collaborating with Perón, the
more responsible Jewish leaders repudiated these self-proclaimed spokesmen and
reorganized their communal life to conform to the prevailing climate of cultural
autonomy. Social and religious practices in the Argentine, with the country's
overwhelming Catholic dominance, dictated separatism. Hence the steady expansion of Jewish elementary and high school education was accomplished by
and large through the medium of the parochial schools, attended by thousands of
Jewish children. By now, too, a thriving Jewish press had emerged. Moreover,
since Buenos Aires had now become the fourth largest Jewish city in the world
(after New York, Los Angeles, and Tel Aviv), it was hoped that the Argentine
capital could take its place as a major centre of Jewish influence.

To be sure, the dangers were not over. The Peronistas had bequeathed serious
economic problems and a raging inflation and these could not be quickly overcome. All the efforts of the new regime, as well as of the agencies created by the

American Government and the Organization of American States, could not contain an almost endemic restlessness. Indeed, in the 1961 election an alarming Peronista resurgence took place; it polled the largest number of votes of any competing political party. Accordingly, the military felt obliged to step in to prevent Perón's return. By now democratic stability depended on a race between the reforms recommended by the American Alliance for Progress, with its hundreds of millions of dollars in economic and social aid, and the intransigence of the unemployed and the discontented who threatened all established institutions.

The nascent anti-Semitic elements in the Argentine sensed their opportunity. Gang depredation and vandalism again became common, usually concentrating on the desecration of synagogues and cemeteries. In 1961 and 1962 a native Fascist group, the Tacuara, was continuously in the forefront of demonstration and attack. Earlier it had drawn its recruits from high school students, but it was now strongly reinforced by ranking military men and a few bigoted priests. Nests of Nazi expatriates who had found refuge in the Argentine also seized the opportunity to emerge from their festering anonymity. After the kidnapping of Adolf Eichmann by Israeli agents, they took advantage of popular resentment to move openly into terrorist activities, for they imagined that they could once again re-enact the days of the Nazi blood brawls. The Jews were not unprepared. They had created strong self-defence groups, organized on the Haganah model. Retaliating quickly, they met the Nazi hooligans full force, sending scores of them to hospitals.

Fortunately, the 1963 national elections eased the tensions. The Peronistas were roundly beaten. A committed democratic leader, Arturo Illía, received an overwhelming mandate. His victory was interpreted to mean that the Argentinians were now eager to end the oscillations that converted every election into a survival crisis. The flight of capital was arrested, and Jewish emigration preparations tapered off. With somewhat greater confidence now, Argentine Jewry anticipated that the master plan for social and economic reforms proclaimed by the new government would at last bring the country to the fulfillment of its democratic hopes.

As a result of economic and political upheaval, following the world crisis of 1929, Brazil, too, had become an uneasy and dangerous shelter. The country's major export had been coffee. As the world market dried up, vast quantities of this commodity remained as surplus to be burned or dumped into the sea to avoid further price collapse. Growing unemployment and the ugly temper of the impoverished population frightened Brazil's reactionary elements; these in turn encouraged the activity of Fascist groups. It happened that a million and a half Italians and nearly as many Germans composed a disproportionately large minority of Brazil's population. Fascist cells proliferated among them, working closely with the propaganda bureaus of Italy and Germany.

In 1934, however, when Getúlio Vargas came to power, the subversive movements were temporarily driven underground. Serving twice as president, from 1934 to 1945, and again from 1951 to 1954, Vargas dominated the public life of his country for more than twenty years. Vargas was an ardent Brazilian nationalist, and he had little patience with the Nazi cells. He made it patently clear that he would not tolerate foreign-sponsored agitation nor the disruption of his country's unity through the importation of foreign loyalties. Yet he was no committed democrat himself. He was as autocratic a type as the turbulent politics of South America had produced—tough, steel-willed, ruthless; he maintained his grip on the presidency by a frank alliance with the army.

The Jews of Brazil were justifiably apprehensive as a result; they knew that they could expect no permanent security so long as they lived by the whim of a dictator. For the present the authoritarian government was anti-Nazi. But all dictatorships were opportunistic, and the turn of the diplomatic or economic wheel could easily bring catastrophe. Apart from his determination to stamp out an alien Fascism, Vargas gave the Jewish community, indeed, all minority groups, cause for intense concern when they planned for cultural autonomy. He opposed Zionist activity, the publication of Yiddish newspapers, the expansion of Jewish parochial schools. None of this was based on anti-Semitic sentiment. Vargas himself cherished a number of personal Jewish associations. But he sought complete homogeneity for his country, and he believed that his goal would be achieved more rapidly if he discouraged cultural separatism.

Then, in 1954, Vargas's own generals suddenly turned on him, forcing his resignation, and driving him to suicide. Perhaps he had anticipated the almost complete repudiation of his political philosophy which was to follow. For succeeding presidents demonstrated little sympathy with the Vargas brand of militant nationalism. João Café Filho, for example, who followed him, was especially friendly to the concept of cultural pluralism, and took pleasure in dedicating Jewish institutions and participating in special Jewish communal functions. President Kubitschek in 1960 rejected the application for naturalization of a Latvian Nazi mass-killer who had settled in Brazil after the fall of Hitler. President Quadros insisted on the careful editing of the official school dictionary to eliminate defintions that were derogatory to Jews. He lent his prestige to the campaign for a public school which was to be named for Anne Frank. When Nasser came to power in Egypt and demoralized the Jewish life of that country, Brazil offered sanctuary to more than five thousand Egyptian Jewish refugees.

By 1964 the Jewish population in Brazil had grown to 200,000. This still represented a miniscule proportion in a land of 54,000,000, although the principal Jewish concentration remained in Rio de Janeiro and São Paulo, where the commercial and cultural role the Jews played was quite significant. They blessed their good fortune that Brazil had now become a promising homeland rather than merely a providential refuge. Yet, since the foundations of constitutional government were still not anchored in mass loyalty, the Jews could not become complacent. It was disquieting that one's personal and family fate, indeed that life itself, had to be related to the fluctuations of domestic politics.

In Mexico, after World War II, the usual storm clouds gathered wherever Fascist elements sought a foothold. Several Fascist parties developed measurable strength. They were encouraged by a number of leading Catholics who had never been reconciled to the reforms of the radical Mexican governments. Powerful industrialists, too, kept up their drumfire of opposition to labour policies. All three groups were very ready to exploit anti-Semitic unrest, and the Jews understandably felt an intense concern as they witnessed the subsidized rallies of the Sinarquist Party, or noted the multiplication of anti-Semitic articles and publications sponsored by the Fascist Yellow Shirts.

Yet the chances for Fascist success in an increasingly proletarian nation remained slim. The workers were well organized and made it clear that they would not easily yield to a Fascist *coup*. It was evident, too, that the United States, despite Mexico's expropriation of American oil companies, would not permit the establishment of a Fascist staging base in its backyard. Nor were the dangers of a Communist take-over any more likely. To be sure, Mexico retained cordial relations with the Soviet Union. When Cuba succumbed to Castro and Communism, Mexico refused to suspend diplomatic or trade relations with that country, and the Communist parties in Mexico carried on an extensive propaganda campaign. Nevertheless, the public response remained apathetic, even hostile.

Mexican Jewry, for its part, enjoyed comparative peace of mind. The community grew steadily and by 1964 its population, augmented by families in flight from Europe and North Africa, approached 30,000. Mexico City, the capital, remained the focus of Jewish cultural life, and its activities, as in most Latin American countries, were rooted solidly in the traditions of the Old World. Indeed, the spoken language of the older generation, a substantial minority even in the 1960's, remained Yiddish. As for the children, 85 per cent of them were enrolled in Jewish parochial schools. The economic base remained primarily commercial and industrial, with perhaps ten per cent of the adult population concentrated in the professions. It was, on the whole, a reasonably healthy community whose optimism was linked to the committed democratic orientation of the strongly entrenched labour forces of the country.

2. CANADA

Canada shared with the United States the responsibility for carrying the democratic hopes of the Western hemisphere. Nature had endowed her with abundant physical resources for the role. Canada is a magnificent granary and a lumber reservoir, and she has long supplied the world with wheat and precious raw materials. To avoid the dangers of building the national economy exclusively upon exports, her statesmen gave every encouragement to industrial and commercial entrepreneurs. This meant a liberal immigration policy. For the potentialities of Canada called for population in the millions—workers to till the fields, pioneers to open the wildernesses, consumers to absorb the products. Yet, before the twentieth century most European immigrants preferred the United States. Canada grew slowly, peopled mainly by her original French and by the English, Scotch, and Irish. Before World War II the population still stood at only eleven million in a land that could easily absorb five or six times that number.

Because most of the Jewish immigration to the Western world went to the United States, there were in 1900 less than fifteen thousand Jews in all of Canada. But later when the American doors were closed, large groups were channelled into Canada, and the Jewish population rose to 175,000, mainly concentrated in the larger cities: Montreal, Toronto, and Winnipeg. These were unclouded days when there was little talk of Nordic supremacy and of "unassimilable" aliens. Canada was glad to welcome those who came. In 1924, touched by the desperate plight of the Ukrainian refugees trapped in Roumania, Canada made provision to bring in five thousand of them at the rate of one hundred each week. Jewish immigration bodies co-operated to disperse the immigrants, so that they would not all be concentrated in one area.

The doors of Canada remained open until the world depression of 1929 struck the country full force. Unemployment became serious, and in some provinces there were dangerous riots that reached the proportions of revolt. All parties agreed that immigration must now be curtailed, and the law of 1932 limited entrance to agricultural labourers, domestics, and close relatives of Canadians.

The Jewish community was small, and, in the light of economic realities, was apparently to remain small. It was mainly a commercial group, the older generation concentrating in the clothing and furnishing businesses and in various types of textiles, and the younger generation veering to professional life. There were also a number of interesting agricultural settlements that had been created early in the century through the sponsorship of the Jewish Colonization Association (ICA). These included ten flourishing colonies west of Winnipeg, where a thousand hardy souls lived on the 27,000 acres that were under cultivation. Another thousand were scattered in areas adjacent to the colonies, where they combined agriculture with commerce. In Quebec and Ontario there were still other Jewish farming communities, which supplemented income through the establishment of summer resorts. In all, the Jewish agricultural population totalled about 5,500.

Merchants, small manufacturers, artisans, a sprinkling of farmers, and a younger generation drifting towards the professions—this was the basic structure of the Jewish community. There was none of the fabulous successes of families in South Africa and the United States. Jews were not represented among the railroad, wheat, shipping, insurance, and lumber kings of Canada. But there was no ambition in this direction. The average man was comfortable, secure, and he rejoiced in the liberalism of the country that gave him his bread with dignity and respect.

Canadian Jewry's single most vexing problem related to education. This issue was limited primarily to Montreal, where more than 100,000 of the 275,000 Jews of Canada were concentrated. In Canada the school system was almost entirely denominationally oriented. There were English Protestant schools and there were French Catholic schools, and each network was subsidized by its own group through special real-estate taxes. The Jews were obliged to choose between the two systems, and almost invariably they opted for the Protestant schools. However, as their population grew in Montreal, as additional thousands of their children were affected, the Jews increasingly resented the segregated classrooms that were reserved for them, the penalties imposed for absence during Jewish holidays, and the exclusion of Jews as teachers or as representatives on the school boards.

Not until 1931, after many court battles had been fought, did the Protestant community finally offer a few nominal concessions to end the de facto segregation. Even then, however, only a few token positions were opened for Jewish teachers. The compromise worked with so little satisfaction that an ever-increasing number of Jewish children were enrolled in a third set of Jewish parochial schools, subsidized by the Jews themselves. The danger of this trend was that it deepened the already profound social cleavage in Canadian life. Its one advantage was to intensify Jewish ethnic cohesiveness, which by now was notably stronger among Canadian Jewry than among the more acculturated Jewish communities across the American frontier.

Except, then, for quarrels over the structure of the educational system, Jewish life in Canada was not particularly uncomfortable. To be sure, occasional problems of anti-Semitism had to be faced. They usually erupted in the predominantly French province of Quebec, the stronghold of a parochial and rather bigoted Catholic Church faction. In the 1930's the provincial government fell into semi-Fascist hands; for the first time, as a result, Jew-hatred was encouraged by government officials, and for a while assumed disquieting proportions. The Church, through its control of the major organs of education, preached the virtue of the Fascist "corporative" technique for the settlement of labour difficulties. The French Catholic press ardently supported Mussolini in Ethiopia, Franco in Spain, and de la Rocque in France. Then, in 1935, Adrien Arcand, a French Canadian firebrand who made no secret of his admiration for Hitler, became the Minister of Labour. Urging his followers to boycott the Jews, Arcand denounced the "business control" that ostensibly rested in the hands of "those who are not of us." He was warmly supported in his pronouncements and in his campaign by the Premier of the province.

These attacks were usually more spectacular than effective. They aroused no response whatever in the English community. When World War II committed the Canadian government to the side of the Allies, support for the Nazis and Fascists became a matter of treason. Arcand attempted to stage a comeback after 1945, through his Fascist Front. But by then he was completely identified with Nazi collaboration during the war, and his political career reached a dead end.

Throughout this period of unrest, the more responsible Canadian leadership continually assured the Jewish community that it had nothing to fear, even in Quebec. An occasional anti-Semitic demonstration could not be equated with the totalitarian disasters of Europe. Hate-mongers surely were incapable of infecting the democratic spirit of a nation like Canada. The Jews believed this whole-heartedly. Nevertheless, they refused to let down the guard. Supporting defense agencies with more than nominal philanthropic loyalty, they focussed attention on every instance of bigotry, however minor or obscure. For they had learned from the European experience that they could not afford to treat too cavalierly any form of overt or covert hostility, even if it found no immediate hospitality in the responsible institutions of the country.

3. THE UNITED STATES

Ever since 1881, when the benighted governments of eastern Europe virtually declared war on their Jewish populations, the United States had been a Promised Land for all the areas of hopelessness. There was a steady exodus of younger sons, followed by the importation of whole families, climaxed by the transplantation of entire communities. By the end of World War I, America counted more than four million Jews. Then came the Johnson Act, passed by Congress in 1924, which virtually closed the doors of the country except to a minor stream of specially selected groups. The Johnson Act, undramatic to the point of dullness, adopted without fanfare, proved to be one of the three or four most significant and far-reaching events in modern Jewish history. For, in effect, it dammed up in Europe all the discouraged and the hopeless victims of successive repression and misfortune. The United States had always been the safety valve. No matter how mean and poverty-stricken life had been in the towns and villages of the Old World, there was always the blessed expectation of a letter from a relative in America, a letter with financial help or with a steamship ticket enclosed. This hope had now been destroyed, and its demise profoundly affected, not only the Jews, but all the expanding populations of the world.

For the Jews who were already in the United States, the new immigration law was a warning and a challenge. The American Jewish community could no longer expect the reinforcements that had always been fed into their cultural and religious institutions. They could no longer rely upon the great European centres to provide inspiration for scholarship and art and religious growth.

ICELAND

DISTRIBUTION OF JEWS IN EUROPE AND NORTHWEST ASIA AS HITLER CAME TO POWER, 1933

with Chief Centers of
Jewish Population

Based on statistics of American Jewish Year Book

ATLANTIC

OCEAN

NORTH SEA

NORWAY **0.06**

SWEDEN **0.**

0.

2.4 DANZIG

IRISH
FREE STATE **0.17**

GREAT
BRITAIN **0.6**

DENMARK

2.2

Amsterdam
London NETH.

Antwerp
Brussels BELG. **0.5**

Paris

Berlin

GERMANY **0.9**

0.5
LUX.

SAAR
5.1

Prague
CZECHOSLO **2.**

Vienna

5.3 AUSTRIA

HUNG. **6.0**

FRANCE **0.5**

SWITZ. **0.54**

PORTUGAL **0.01**

SPAIN **0.02**

CORSICA

Rome

ITALY **0.13**

YUGOSL

0.

ALBAN **0.0**

5.1
Gibraltar

Tangiers **23.1**

SP. MOROCCO **1.4**

Oran

Algiers

SARDINIA

MEDITERRANE

SICILY

Tunis

FR. MOROCCO **2.8**

ALGERIA **1.5**

TUNISIA **3.1**

LEGEND
Above 10%
8 to 10%
3 to 8%
1 to 3%
½ to 1%
Below ½%

0   100   200   300   400   500 MILES

NLAND
0.05

Leningrad

NIA
41

5.18

TVIA
A

7.15

SOVIET   RUSSIA

Moscow   0.36

WHITE
RUSSIA
16.1

nā

ND
aw

Kiev   Kharkov

ow

UKRAINE
6.6

Czernowitz

Kishinev   Odessa

CRIMEA

CASPIAN SEA

MANIA
5.5

Bucharest

0.6

BLACK SEA

GEORGIA
0.9

AZERBAIJAN
1.1

0.7

ULGARIA   9.5

fia   Istanbul

T.

0.5

T   U   R   K   E   Y

PERSIA
0.4

onika

E

SEA

SYRIA
1.6

3.1

IRAQ   Bagdad

Herlin

The casualties of assimilation had usually been equalized through the blood plasma that came from abroad. There was to be no more blood plasma. American Jews were on their own, and leadership had to be nurtured and prepared in native ranks. In the years that followed 1924, Jewish institutions and ideologies were slowly but surely modified and transformed as the family associations and the loyalties of Europe faded and dissolved.

After mid-century the transformation reached decisive proportions. By 1964 five and a half million Jews lived in the United States, and more than eighty per cent of these were native born. Immigration had narrowed to an insignificant trickle. In 1960, for example, less than 6,600 Jews entered the country, and when the number momentarily increased in 1962, it occurred only as a result of the special crisis in Cuba, precipitated when Castro came to power there, destroying virtually the entire middle class of Havana's Jewish settlement and compelling these people to flee.

Yet American responsibility for the continued physical and cultural survival of European Jewry did not taper off. Rather it increased. American Jews loyally responded to the substantial demands made upon them. Although the opportunity to evacuate refugees was drastically limited by American immigration laws, several hundred thousand Jews, many of them leaders in the scientific, artistic, and economic life of Europe, were brought to American shores in the fifteen years that followed the rise of Hitler. In turn, this all-encompassing concern with philanthropy transformed Jewish community organization. The need to provide relief, to establish a Commonwealth in Palestine, to rehabilitate the refugees who came to America, all were met by united appeals, demands upon every "responsible" Jew to contribute as a compelling moral duty. The great national campaigns became an established part of community living.

Thus, between 1948 and 1964 the United Jewish Appeal provided nearly three quarters of a billion dollars for Jewish communal needs both in America and abroad. Similarly, Hadassah, the Women's Zionist Organization of America, contributed more than 125 million dollars to the medical care of immigrants in Israel; most of these funds were pieced together out of small offerings from Hadassah's committed membership in each community. The Israel Bond organization netted more than 600 million dollars for long-term loans. There were, in addition, regular campaigns month in and month out, for the programs sponsored by the educational institutions of Israel, for ORT, an international body that was devoted to the vocational rehabilitation of young Jews in the distressed areas of the world, and for many other causes. These funds, it should be noted, were rarely at the expense of support for general civic campaigns.

In the cultural life of the pre-war Jewish community the dominant pattern seemed to be the passion for adaptation, for quick assimilation to the ways of America. The sociologist and the novelist found a perennially fascinating theme in the reactions of Jewish immigrants to their new environment. An

impressive literature was created to describe the tortuous road from Ellis Island
to Hester Street, and thence, through a labyrinth of heartache and happiness,
to the goal of Americanization—educated children, economic security, a genteel
neighbourhood, perhaps even membership in a fashionable club. Some of the
newcomers remained loyal to the core of their Old World practices, but they
made constant, sometimes startling, compromises to adapt them to the norm
of fashion. Others were so anxious to conform that they threw every tradition
overboard, even before the effects of the acquired civilization had begun to
mellow their own lives. They imagined that genuine Americanism demanded
the devitalization of every uniqueness, not alone in dress and speech and manners, but in culture and folkways, in fundamental convictions.

It was startling to note the extremes to which great multitudes went in this
passion to conform. They had just arrived from Pinsk and Kishinev, from
Breslau and Bucharest; they could not yet manage the *W* and the *Th;* but they
stubbornly resisted the synagogue or the school or the charity federation on the
grounds of Americanism. These were the vast unaffiliated who made up a substantial part of the new immigration, and they were identified with their people only when they experienced the pinch of discrimination. They were *"pogrom"* Jews who felt no obligation to Jewish institutions or to the communities
from which they had themselves been rescued, until they were frightened by
the continued threat of Hitler and his imitators.

Jewish educators realized early that group survival in the United States depended upon the school fully as much as upon the synagogue. Loyalty to a
minority culture could not be long sustained without knowledge of its meaning. The orthodox immigrant groups simply transplanted the Old World *cheder,*
the daily Hebrew school that was later modernized into the *Talmud Torah.*
Only a small portion of the orthodox-reared children attended these schools,
however, since they met after the regular public-school sessions and demanded
the sacrifice of the precious afternoon play periods. The Sunday schools of the
conservative and the reform groups were better attended, but their effectiveness
was also limited, since they met for only an hour or two, once or twice a week.
Besides, few of the youngsters continued after confirmation day and the inevitable gift of a fountain pen. Most children did not enjoy even these restricted
benefits. The total enrolment in the religious schools, it was estimated, came to
about eight per cent of the Jewish population. This was from three to fourteen
times less than the proportion registered by every other creed in the United
States. Approximately 350,000 Jewish children attended the public schools in
New York City. Of these, 260,000 never saw a Hebrew alphabet or had any
instruction in a religious school. And New York was the centre of Jewish life.[1]

After World War II, a major transformation occurred. The elimination of
the great centres of Jewish life in Europe, the establishment of Israel, gave over-

[1] Engelman, in *American Journal of Sociology,* Vol. XLI, p. 50.

whelming impetus to the appeals for adequate programs of Jewish education. The pioneer bureaus of Jewish education were now reinforced with scores of others under expert professional leadership. Though maximalist programs were still rare in a country where the established public school system was the indispensable norm, Jewish education was at least no longer relegated to a perfunctory ritual in deference to parents or family, to be terminated as soon as the filial amenities had been observed. For the first time, highly respected Jewish educational systems were functioning in such urban centres as New York, Los Angeles, Chicago, Philadelphia, Boston, Cleveland, Detroit, Minneapolis, St. Louis, Miami, and in many smaller communities.

Meanwhile the development of elaborate express highways accelerated a revolutionary movement toward suburbanization in American life. Millions of families were fleeing from the cities. The breadwinners commuted each weekday to their work in the metropolitan area. Entire new Jewish communities mushroomed in these suburbs, stimulating almost immediately the growth of a well-integrated organizational life, combining synagogues, schools, welfare federations, and membership chapters in various Jewish national and international agencies. The younger generation gravitated quite spontaneously to the essentials of Jewish life in city and in suburb. In the old days, in the passion to demonstrate their complete Americanization, their parents or grandparents might have been sensitive about Jewish commitment. The native-born "second" generation shed its insecure defensiveness, and its participation in Jewish activity no longer raised painful cultural conflicts.

The maturing process was further demonstrated in the vast amplification of existing Jewish institutions. The rabbinical seminaries, drawing increasing numbers of native-born young people for the tasks of the ministry, established a firmer hold on the totality of the Jewish community, rather than on small enclaves of the religiously oriented, as had been the case two and three decades earlier. The Jewish Publication Society grew into a major cultural influence, and its volumes, dealing with all phases of Jewish life, combined most effectively poular appeal and first-rate scholarship. The B'nai B'rith Hillel Foundations, beginning modestly, almost timorously in 1923, grew to more than 250 units by the 1960's. Dedicated to the stimulation of the cultural and religious loyalties of Jewish student body. Hillel units were also established in the major universities of Canada, in Britain, France, Holland, and in South Africa and Australia. The expansion was climaxed by the establishment of units at the Hebrew University and the Technion in Israel.

Two major educational institutions were part of the developing patterns of this period. In 1955 the Albert Einstein Medical School was added to the responsibilities of Yeshiva University in New York City. It quickly attracted some of the country's most distinguished physicians and scientists, and the high level of its student body added to its reputation as one of the best medical schools in

America. In 1948 Brandeis University was established in the Boston suburb of Waltham, in the heart of New England. It was an institution founded within the framework of the American educational tradition. All other religious denominations had created nonsectarian universities, from the days of Harvard, Yale, Princeton, Fordham, Columbia, Swarthmore, down to the beginnings of the twentieth century. Hence the first nonsectarian contribution of the Jewish people to American higher education was heartily welcomed. Within a decade and a half Brandeis had completed its initial physical master plan with a fifty-million-dollar building program; it had recruited one of the most respected liberal arts faculties in the country for its undergraduate and graduate studies and its research; and it had enrolled a student body of such high quality that Phi Beta Kappa accreditation came to the university in its thirteenth year, the shortest period of time for such accreditation of any university since the eighteenth century.

Happily it was not necessary for the Jews of America to be obsessed with the problem of rights, of personal or group security. The United States was one of the few countries in the modern world that established the principle of complete equality from the very beginning of its life as a nation. Social discrimination existed, but this was almost inevitable, except in Utopia. Indeed there were social cleavages among the Jews themselvs. Pompous families who had lived for several generations in America manifested the same *hauteur* in relation to recent immigrants that blue-blooded Yankee dowagers expressed when they spoke of "those foreign Jews." Such social snobbishness encouraged the climate of restriction and prejudice in more vital areas and called for constant resistance. But it did not interfere seriously with opportunities to live, to study, to work, to exercise all the privileges of citizenship. This freedom, in contrast to Europe's festering hatreds, was not due to the superior intelligence of the American people or to their deeper devotion to Christian principles. America was a rich country; it had endless resources; its standards of living were comparatively high. There was, in consequence, infinitely less strain upon Americans than upon the exploited, hate-stimulated groups of eastern and central Europe.

The unfailing relationship between tolerance and abundance, and between intolerance and depression, was clearly demonstrated, even in bountifully endowed America. For the only periods when anti-Semites achieved any following, or for that matter, any notice, were those in which the country went through the cycle of depression, unemployment, or the tensions of post-war shortages. Only then did the propaganda of a small minority of racketeers, chauvinists, and cranks penetrate into wide enough areas to warrant counteraction. Father Charles Coughlin, a rabble-rousing Catholic priest, disgraced his cloth and his Church by preaching hate in the name of religion. There were scores of imitators in many parts of the country who scented profit or power from similar activity. The Nazis undoubtedly spent millions through their native representatives to stimulate anti-Semitism and in this way to confuse and demoralize the American people.

The responsible leadership of the country—in politics, the Church, education, the press, the radio—quickly dissociated themselves from such utterances and proudly asserted that they represented nothing but the off-scourings of national life. These assurances were comforting to the Jews as they lived through the barrage of calumny of the radio priest and of the Nazi fellow-travellers. Yet after the astonishing success of the campaigns in Europe, it was no longer sensible for the Jews to dismiss lightly the vapourings of crackpots or humbugs, or to rely exclusively upon Christian goodwill. The major Jewish organizations, B'nai B'rith, the American Jewish Congress, the American Jewish Committee, strengthened their defence arms. Their strategy was to focus the spotlight of publicity upon their enemies and to expose their lies. They published authoritative studies to clarify the convictions of those who moulded public opinion. They kept open diplomatic and political contacts so as to facilitate redress in the courts or in the legislative chambers when the assaults of the unprincipled required action.

In recent years, there were occasional, rather minor instances of anti-Semitic activity that grew primarily out of international developments or out of Jewish participation in controversial social action. The Arabs perfected propaganda techniques in the years that followed the establishment of the State of Israel. They appealed to the American democratic dogma and asked how the infiltration of Jews into an ancient Arab homeland could be justified. They circulated accounts of unbridled Israeli imperialism, and of Israel's shabby treatment of Arab refugees.

They quoted Arnold Toynbee, the British historian who had not forgiven the Jews for refusing to become "fossils" after their rejection of Christianity. Toynbee had equated the Israeli treatment of Arab refugees with the Nazi treatment of Jews and he was, therefore, a reliable Arab reference. In keeping with the American tradition, the Arabs were given every opportunity to present their case, and they made an impact on many sincere, well-motivated liberals. University centres, social clubs, the halls of Congress where speeches were read into the record and then franked in the millions, all became part of a continuing forum.

On still another front, the Jews were drawn into the struggle to maintain the scrupulous separation of Church and State. In 1963 the Supreme Court issued a number of historic decisions prohibiting Bible reading and the recitation of the Lord's Prayer in public schools. The decisions were violently attacked by many Christian groups as "driving God out of the schoolroom." Virtually all Jewish organizations associated themselves with the liberals who supported the Supreme Court decision, insisting that religious indoctrination belonged exclusively in the home and in the church. Inevitably there were right-wing groups that seized upon the stand of the "godless" and "atheistic" Jews as the excuse for mounting their anti-Semitic attacks.

Meantime, in the early 1960's, the campaign for Negro civil rights came to a riotous climax. The major Negro organizations, after decades of resentful and festering moderation, decided that the time had come to turn defiantly militant. The Supreme Court had decreed in 1954 that desegregation was to be introduced with all "deliberate speed." The deliberate aspect had become the established tempo; the speed had been conveniently forgotten. An aroused Negro leadership rejected the Fabian tactics of the past and called for boycotts, strikes, and massive demonstrations. Liberal sympathy for the Negro demands was overwhelming, and predictably, the most respected Jewish spokesmen announced their solidarity with the Negro cause. The moment the Jews exposed themselves, the racists and segregationists found their opportunity to stigmatize the demonstrations as Communist and Jewish propaganda.

None of these troublesome developments appeared to represent a dangerous trend. The defence groups remained vigilant; they performed a not ineffective service in keeping the record straight. In the long run, however, it was recognized that the basic defence for all minority groups lay in the preservation of the democratic system. If a functioning democracy should survive, all groups would be safe. If the democratic system should fail through assault from abroad or economic catastrophe at home, then all values would be in jeopardy—Christianity, the liberal tradition, the national standard of living. The task of resisting foreign and domestic enemies was a common one, hardly less crucial for Christians than for Jews, for the rich and highly placed than for the marginal men who were in the front line of vulnerability.

CHAPTER THIRTY-ONE

THE EPIC OF PALESTINE

THE story of modern Palestine is a welcome oasis after the odyssey of horror in post-war Europe. For the years between the San Remo Conference of 1920, which gave the sanction of international law to a Jewish Homeland in Palestine, and the outbreak of World War II, were a period of remarkable constructive achievement. In the face of diplomatic difficulties, armed Arab opposition, administrative sabotage by British colonial officials, and the physical inadequacies of the country itself, Palestine was converted by Jewish genius and enterprise into a modern, healthful, highly civilized commonwealth. The Permanent Mandates Commission of the League of Nations, assuredly not given to lyrical appraisal, characterized the Jewish achievement as "the greatest colonizing enterprise of modern times."

I. PHYSICAL GROWTH AND MATERIAL PROGRESS

In 1917, when General Allenby conquered Palestine, there were barely 35,000 Jews left to acknowledge their new allegiance. They were mainly old men and women, infirm, ill-clad recluses, subsisting on *Haluka,* international charity, waiting only for the redemption of death to give them the privilege of interment in hallowed soil. The elimination of Turkish control and the guarantees of San Remo began a period of reconstruction that transformed the spirit of the land even as it brought in a new race of men. The Jewish population mounted every few years. In the first official census of 1922 it rose to 82,700; in 1928 it nearly doubled and reached 151,000. By 1931 it had climbed to 175,000, and Palestine was no longer regarded merely as an exotic symbol.

Then came Hitler, and his malevolence pressed out tens of thousands of Germans and Austrians and other central Europeans in a phenomenal exodus. Many of those who were uprooted, even though they had never been Zionists (some had been anti-Zionists), looked to Palestine for the opportunity to re-fashion their broken lives. The ordinary restrictive labour quotas did not apply to them, for usually they entered in the unlimited capitalist category. The Nazi shakedown system had not yet been perfected, and hence the Jews were not penniless when they escaped. With capital, goods, and furnishings, they often also brought superb technical and business experience. They were a new type, very different from the ardent nationalists of earlier migrations. They offered

few problems in absorption. For instead of requiring employment, they created
it by developing enterprises, building homes, establishing European trade contacts.

But the steadily increasing immigration brought endless friction with the
Arabs and with the British mandatory power. Arab nationalists stormed against
any new immigration at all; the British colonial officials tried to whittle it down
to negligible numbers that would not affect population proportions in the
country. Yet, despite the most cunningly devised restrictions, the refugees continued to come. They came by land and by sea, "legally" and "illegally," suffering every hardship, squirming out of mazes of red tape—but getting in. By
1939, when a new British White Paper sought to freeze Jewish immigration,
the population stood at half a million, and every Jewish soul was determined to
defy restrictions so that other waiting tens of thousands could join them.

The increase in Jewish population was not at the expense of Arab rights or
living standards. The Arab population in 1918 was 664,000. By 1939 it had risen
to well over a million. At the same time Arab population remained static in all
the surrounding Arab states, and there was no comparison between the gratifying health and economic standards of Arabs in Palestine and their racial brothers
in adjacent Arab territory. A British investigating Commission said in 1937
(the Peel Report): "The general beneficent effect of Jewish immigration on
Arab welfare is illustrated by the fact that the increase in Arab population is
most marked in urban areas affected by Jewish development."

But, of course, the population proportion changed radically as a result of
Jewish immigration. In 1922 the Jews comprised about 12½ per cent of the
population; in 1929 the proportion was beyond 30 per cent, and it was this
changed relationship that excited the Arabs and perturbed the British colonial
officials.

The passion for normal living which impelled most of the Jewish immigrants to come to Palestine became a driving power for building a fecund
civilization. In a generation the face of the ancient land was transformed. Soon
there were impressive cities, as progressive as any in the world. Tel-Aviv had
been founded in 1909 on the dunes of the Mediterranean just beyond the limits
of primitive, stagnant three-thousand-year-old Jaffa. Its population had grown
to 15,000 in 1920. Two decades later it was a busy, thriving all-Jewish city of
200,000, as up to date and alive as Chicago, with well-appointed hotels, advanced
schools, smart shops, trim boulevards, the most diverse amusements, modernis-
tic homes, a brilliant literary and artistic life. Jerusalem had been the shrine of
three world religions, but until 1920 it was left primarily to the pilgrims, the
tourists, and the beggars. By 1940 the Jewish population of 65,000 outnumbered
all other groups. To the Old City, the symbol of the romantic past, were added
many new sections, beautiful garden suburbs, soon to become the heart of the
æsthetic and scientific achievements of renascent Palestine. Equally spectacular

was the development of Haifa, the country's chief port, the oil terminus from Iraq, and the aerial hub of the Near East. In 1922 the Jewish community numbered 6,230; in 1940 it was a booming city whose 60,000 Jews comprised more than two-thirds of the population.

The striking growth of the cities was matched by the development of the rural settlements, gratifying because the men who came to them had only yesterday been declassed white-collar flotsam and jetsam. Because of their determination, thriving colonies studded the countryside from the borders of Syria in the north to the edge of the great desert in the south. Most of them were small units, where fifty or sixty families grouped to enjoy the thrill of life close to the good earth. But there were also many large units that were almost urban in their social advantages. Petach Tikveh, with its population of 20,000, its busy streets, schools, and recreation centres, could easily pass for a fair-sized town. Rehoboth was the seat of the Daniel Sieff Research Institute, where the Zionist leader, Dr. Chaim Weizmann, conducted his most important chemical experiments. Rishon Le-Zion was famous as much for its prosperous citrus culture as for its world-renowned wine-cellars.

The agricultural conquest of Palestine did not come easily. It demanded unflagging cultivation of a niggardly, grudging soil. For the country had been neglected for centuries by Turkish maladministration. It was parched, disease-ridden, a menace to the pioneer who dared to challenge its reputed sterility. The new Jewish settlers were not frightened or discouraged. They hewed to their tasks. They applied modern science to the sick soil and lovingly nursed it back to health. They brought in water by modern boring methods. The luxuriant groves, rich with oranges, lemons, and grapefruit, the almond plantations, the wheat fields, were all redeemed from areas that had been abandoned as barren, and in their redintegration they testified to the courage and consecration of the Jewish pioneers. The Peel Report paid tribute to this miracle of redemption. "The Arab charge," it said, "that the Jews have obtained too large a proportion of good land cannot be maintained. Much of the land now carrying orange groves was sand dunes or swamp and uncultivated when it was purchased."

Out of the physical enrichment of Palestine came a new economic order that strove to avoid the errors and the injustices of monopoly capitalism. The Jewish settlers envisaged Palestine as a co-operative commonwealth where there would be minimum opportunity for the evils of exploitation. Hospitality was extended to the private entrepreneur and others whose resources and initiative were desperately needed in a new country. But Jewish labour was determined to prevent the control of the country from passing into the hands of private capitalists.

Consequently, few places in the world have created so many voluntary collectivist units. Palestine is dotted with little agricultural communes where the workers share the fruits of their labour as if in one united family. *Histadruth,* the General Labour Federation, includes in its membership more than one-half of the adult population of the country, virtually all who work with hand or brain, skilled and unskilled, white-collar and proletarian, men and women. It controls trade-union activities, health insurance, workers' banks, the transportation system, schools, theatres, producers' and consumers' co-operatives, and hundreds of other enterprises. Palestine has become a laboratory where it is hoped to create new economic relationships on the basis of prophetic principles.

Paralleling the agricultural progress of Palestine was a thoroughgoing industrial revolution. Brilliant engineering harnessed the Jordan to supply electrical energy for the rapidly expanding needs of the country. The Dead Sea was tapped for its mineral resources, especially potash and bromide. Before the Mandate it was necessary to import nearly every manufactured product. Now Palestine planned to supply its own materials for building, furnishings, clothing, and all the arts of life. The country was knit together through a modern bus system. Harbour facilities were also expanded to meet growing shipping and passenger needs. A maritime training school was established, and fine clear-eyed young people soon emerged to join their ancestors in the tradition of Jews "who go down to the sea in ships."

The resuscitation of the country inevitably affected health standards. Though Palestine was semi-tropical in its geographical position and had been neglected for centuries, the new settlers were not daunted. They gave their best energies to swamps and marshes, and ingenious drainage projects opened new areas for colonization. Hadassah, a splendid American organization of Jewish women, built and maintained a chain of hospitals, training schools, and nurseries that helped to place Palestine among the most advanced countries in Europe in sanitation and health standards.

There was endless hope for the future, if only Jewish scientific resourcefulness and energy were given full play. Walter Lowdermilk, Assistant Chief to the Soil Conservation Service of the American Department of Agriculture, no starry-eyed mystic, saw unlimited power opportunities in Palestine. He had studied the great reclamation projects of the world, the Yellow River in China, the Zuider Zee in Holland, the Tennessee Valley Authority and Boulder Dam in the United States. He envisaged a Jordan Valley Authority through which the entire land could be brought to blessed productivity and strength, with room for five million Jews without displacing a single Arab. For in the Jordan Valley, in Lowdermilk's sober estimate, there were all the potentialities "for one of the greatest and most far reaching reclamation projects in the world." [1]

[1] Lowdermilk: *Land of Promise.*

2. CULTURAL RENAISSANCE

The chief glory of the new Palestine did not come from its material progress. This progress assuredly opened it out as a refuge, a sanctuary that rehabilitated the lives of hundreds of thousands who were drawn out of the recesses of Hell. But Palestine was also the matrix of a renewed cultural inspiration, destined to raise the dignity of the Jews everywhere.

It was an achievement that did not come easily. The resurrected land did not even have a common language. A decisive battle had to be fought and won to establish Hebrew, with its roots in the ancient Bible, as the mother tongue of the Jewish population.

Hebrew had never really passed into the limbo of forgotten languages. After the destruction of the national state by the Romans in A.D. 70 it remained the language of prayer and of scholarly communication. Wherever Jews were dispersed they naturally assimilated the language of the country. But since their religion was bound up with the hope of an ultimate return to Zion, the Hebrew language was always the vehicle for their prayers. There were also periods of literary revival, in Moslem Spain, in mediæval Poland, in the Enlightenment of the eighteenth century, and in nineteenth-century Russia.

But, on the whole, Hebrew remained a language for the scholarly elite. It was not spoken by the common folk, nor was it understood by most of those who used it in their prayers. It belonged with Greek and Latin as a key to ancient literature, but no more than Greek or Latin was it a tool for contemporary living.

The transformation of Hebrew into a folk tongue grew out of the compelling needs of the newer settlers. They were far different in spirit and determination from the weary dependents and recluses whose last wish it was to die and to be buried in the Holy Land. These newcomers also reverenced the glories of the past, but they came to live, to work, to create. With their arrival there was renewed impetus to make Hebrew the language of the national Homeland. At first there seemed little prospect for success. The older inhabitants spoke the Yiddish jargon of eastern Europe, or Ladino, a Spanish-Jewish *patois* favoured by the Sephardic or Oriental Jews. The devout argued that it was blasphemous to vulgarize the sacred words of Scripture by applying them to routine purposes. Nor were such misgivings limited to the devout. Ardent Zionists, quite secular in outlook, confessed to a feeling of incongruity as they heard traffic disputes or read soap advertisements in the language of Isaiah. Hebrew, to become the language of home and school and street, required fanatic missionary effort and a completely reorganized educational system. The vision and the zeal to accomplish the miracle were supplied by one of Palestine's most eccentric heroes, Eliezer Ben Yehuda, the creator of modern Hebrew.

Ben Yehuda, born in Russia in 1858, migrated to Palestine in 1881, determined to devote himself to the enthronement of Hebrew as the mother tongue of the Jewish people. Ill and frail, one lung already eaten away by tuberculosis, he set out with a young wife. On board ship, under the stars, both took a vow that no words would ever again pass their lips except in Hebrew, a vow that proved to be one of the turning points in the history of Palestine. For more than thirty years Ben Yehuda fought with divine obstinacy to accomplish his mission. His toughest opponents were the practical people who insisted that their children be taught some European language, German, or English, or French, some "useful" language, so that they would not be disqualified when they sought to earn a living. Ben Yehuda went on with his research and propaganda against a background of continuous abuse. Poverty-stricken, desperately ill, ridiculed, he toiled steadily to complete a Hebrew dictionary. He tracked every word down to its roots, creating new words to meet modern needs. After fifty years he produced a monumental work that is the basis of the present Hebrew language. He placed his chief reliance upon the children, and knew that the victory was assured when Hebrew, championed by the nationalist teachers, became the language of the schools. From there the youngsters took it into their homes and their play. When they swore at each other affectionately in Hebrew, the long struggle was over.

As it turned out, it would have been impossible to unify the people of Palestine and give them a sense of common nationhood without the Hebrew language. For Jewish immigration flowed into the country from every part of Europe, primarily from Poland, Russia, Roumania, and Germany. Each immigration tide brought its own language, and Palestine sounded like a Tower of Babel. The synthesizing factor was Hebrew, and its role in deepening the Jewish nationalist spirit cannot be overestimated.

The battle for Hebrew was fought on one front; the determination to maintain a model school system was pressed irresistibly on another. Even as the settlers came to grips with the most elementary problems that beset a pioneer land, they would not permit any compromise in their educational goals. There were never enough funds for land and tools and shelter and defence, yet a good portion of these slim resources were always set apart for the educational fabric. Hundreds of excellent schools were built, and even the smallest village was not left out. The system reached from the kindergarten through the elementary and secondary schools, supplemented by teachers' training and vocational colleges. Teaching was a highly respected profession, and the calibre of instruction could not be surpassed anywhere in the world.

At the apex of the educational hierarchy was the Hebrew University, the pride of the new Palestine. It was still only in its beginning, developed primarily on the scientific side. But it was already the most advanced educational institution in the Near East. It had a brilliant faculty, drawn from the great universities of Europe that were emptied of Jewish genius by the stupidity of Hitler and his Aryan ignoramuses. It was significant that where the Hebrew University stood on Mount Scopus, it overlooked not only the Dead Sea, symbol of decay and desolation, but the historic city of Jerusalem, teeming with new life, and the ancient hills of Judæa, blooming with the vineyards and the harvest fields of renewed fertility.

Jewish Palestine is still too young, and its population has been too completely preoccupied with political, economic and military problems, to have produced any considerable native literary and artistic genius. The talents of nearly all of the influential figures in its intellectual life really matured in eastern and central Europe early in the century. But in most instances the source of their inspiration was the Zionist ideal, and, once settled in the land, their creativity came to fullest maturity.

The outstanding poet in modern Jewish history was Chaim Nachman Bialik, master of all the poetic modes of the Hebrew language, whose profundity and wealth of diction aroused as much amazement as pride. In Russia, where he was born, he was a prime factor in the Hebrew renaissance. He was a proud, self-respecting artist, and his *Songs of Wrath,* written after the *pogroms* in Kishinev, mercilessly castigated the Jews for tamely submitting to slaughter, for foolishly accepting, almost without resistance, a sterile martyrdom.

Bialik migrated to Palestine after World War I and turned from poetry to prose exposition. He began also to edit and publish the classics, gearing his work primarily for children, upon whom he counted to break the last links with the Diaspora spirit. He was the creator of the *Oneg Shabbat,* the Sabbath-afternoon cultural salon, which became a national institution and quickly spread to all parts of the Jewish world. His last poem was a call to renewed dedication to the Homeland, inscribed to the third generation of Palestinean pioneers, *Al Shilleshim.* When Bialik died in 1934 it was universally acknowledged that not since Biblical days had Israel produced such authentic literary genius.

Almost as influential was the work of Saul Tchernichovsky, whose poetry was related to the love of nature and the passion for beauty. He translated the Homeric epics, the Greek tragedies, the works of Shelley and Burns, of Molière and Goethe. Because he moved with such satisfaction in the naturalist traditions of European culture, and, even more, because he often lashed out against dogma and ceremony and institutional rigidity, he was sometimes listed as belonging to the "pagans." To be sure, he was not at home in Talmudic Judaism and he reserved his most effective barbs for rabbinic disciplines. His powerful poem, *Before the Statue of Apollo,* storms against the "bloodless ones":

> I kneel to live, to beauty and to strength,
> I kneel to all the passionate desires
> Which they, the-dead-in-life, the bloodless ones,

The sick, have stifled in the living God,
The God of wonders of the wilderness,
The God of gods, who took Canaan with storm
Before they bound Him in phylacteries.

Yet even such sentiments were not alien to the Jewish tradition. They came from the mood of the prophets, who, while unfair in their generalizations about all priests and all cults, crystallized the pioneer revolt against institutional restraint. The sainted chief rabbi of Palestine, Abraham Kook, a model of piety, understood this surge of restlessness and was sagely tolerant. During the strenuous, uncertain days of the building of the Temple, he said, even the Holy of Holies, later to be reserved exclusively for the High Priest on the Day of Atonement, was calmly entered, without any sense of sin or desecration, by the workers who made the building possible!

Bialik and Tchernichovsky were only two among scores of writers and artists who found new release as the land hummed with pioneering effort. The tradition of these giants divided and subdivided into every form of prose and poetry. Novelists, essayists, musicians, artists, poets, strove for the distillation of their experience in their chosen format. Yet a listing of educational institutions, newspaper and magazine articles, dramatic and musical creations, could not convey the spirit of the neo-Hebraic renaissance. One had to sit in the cafés and listen to the conversation, ride in the buses, participate in a workers' meeting in one of the co-operative communes, overhear an argument on the Tel-Aviv beach, attend an *Oneg Shabbat*. For here culture was not limited to a thin veneer of educated aristocracy. It was shared—shared more fully by all classes than in almost any other country in the world. There was a direct link between this strange, resurgent generation and the tumultuous but vastly creative days of the Bible.

3. PROBLEMS OF ARAB RESISTANCE

The remarkable record of achievement written in field and industry and school in two short decades presaged a flourishing and enduring civilization, if only effort were unimpeded. But there was the rub. Effort was constantly impeded by Arab resistance. Climate and marshes could be subdued, indifference and sloth could be overcome, self-interest and individual incentive could be harnessed to social needs; but the Arab problem grew rather than diminished with the passing years. The Jews never tired of pointing out how much headway had been made— the development of the soil, the growth of the villages, the improvement in health conditions, the modernization of the country, changes that raised the standards of living for the Arabs as for the Jews. The Arabs remained sullen and unimpressed. They were constantly fomented to resentment and riot by a small clique of Arab landowners who were violently opposed to Jewish immigration. For centuries these parasitic *effendis* had with impunity exploited their peasant vassals, the share-croppers, the poor *fellahin*. Now they were alarmed because the Jewish pioneers, with high living standards, protected by wholesome labour safeguards, set a dangerous example for the wretched *fellahin* who could easily move from dissatisfaction to revolt. In one area was the Jewish colony, green, tidy, productive, the labourers well paid, educated, secure, singing at their work. Adjacent to it was the miserable, squalid, dirty Arab village, ignorance the rule, discouragement the climate. Romantic outsiders could sentimentalize over the picturesqueness of Arab life and lament that Jewish immigration was eliminating the flavour and colour of the story-book stereotype. But there was little of the picturesque in villages full of tuberculosis and amoebic dysentery, where food was scarce and shelter primitive, where cow-dung was applied to wounds and camel's urine to diseases of the eye, where children slept almost completely covered by flies. The Arabs worked as hard as the Jews did, but they were paid practically nothing and were left with nothing. How long would it be before the dispossessed and the disinherited, stirred by the example of Jewish standards, cried out for a decent way of life? It was in the interest of feudal self-defence to forestall such demands by persuading the *fellahin* that the Jews were trespassers who had come to rob the Arabs of their land, to steal their jobs, to subjugate them, to pollute their holy places.

This does not mean that there was no legitimate nationalist feeling among the Arabs. The post-war younger generation, stimulated by the independence movements of surrounding Arab countries, fed by the ebullient nationalism that swept every part of Europe and Asia, became fervent patriots. They loved Palestine, and were prepared to endure any sacrifice to tie it in with Arab tradition. But such nationalism was not in the least incompatible with equally valid Jewish aspirations. During the Peace Conference that followed World War I, when territorial settlements were still in flux, several highly placed Arab leaders, including their official representative, Emir Feisal, looked to mutually advantageous co-operation in Palestine. After signing a treaty of friendship in 1919, Feisal wrote: "We Arabs look with the deepest sympathy on the Zionist movement. . . . We will wish the Jews a most hearty welcome home." The extreme nationalists, however, were adamant against any co-operation. They kept impressing upon their youth that Jewish penetration would reduce the Arabs to peonage and destroy their culture and religion. The commitments of the great powers belied such fears; they emphasized that no Arab rights were, or could be, in jeopardy. Such assurances were written into the Balfour Declaration. They were confirmed at San Remo. They were reiterated by every commission and in every White Paper. But none of these assurances influenced the young nationalists when their chauvinism was envenomed by the agitators. "*The* underlying cause," said a Jewish spokesman as he discussed the grievances of the extremists, "is that we *exist*."

The whole problem was aggravated because the British civil administration in Palestine was not anxious to co-operate with the plan for a Jewish Homeland. From an administrative point of view it was much easier to create one Arab state and to govern it in the hard-boiled tradition of the crown colony. Ruling over the Jews, an educated European people, acutely sensitive about their rights as human beings, prepared, at the drop of the hat, to demonstrate these rights, brought exasperating problems. Later, successive British governments in England, despite their promises while in opposition, grew less and less enthusiastic about building a Jewish Homeland, for every attempted British solution of the Palestine problem which offered the slightest concessions to the Jews brought violent protests from the Arab states that surrounded Palestine. And the British colonial office never relinquished the idea of a power life-line that would include the Arab states.

Arab-Jewish embroilment was further complicated by Mediterranean power politics. After 1934 Britain tried desperately to thwart Mussolini's design to build a new Italian empire at the expense of smaller peoples and of the British imperial holdings. Mussolini used every artifice to stir up trouble for the British, and a most effective way was to sow dissension among all Moslem subjects. Italian propaganda blared from the radio station of Bari, and considerable sums of Italian money flowed into Palestine for literature, guns, and guerilla pay. Soon Nazi propaganda was added to the witches' cauldron. Special emissaries were trained in Berlin for fifth-column service among the Arabs. They carried through their missions with all the cunning and thoroughness that had already corrupted most of Europe.

All of these factors then—the *effendi* fears that their racket would be spoiled, the developing nationalism of the younger generation of Arabs, administrative sabotage, British concern over the effect of a Jewish Homeland upon Moslems everywhere else, and the propaganda of the Fascists and the Nazis—all of these factors combined to make the period that followed 1929 years of growing tension, culminating in riot and civil war.

The first serious outbreaks came in 1929 and were precipitated by an appeal to religious fanaticism. The responsibility for the bloodshed rested upon a wily, red-bearded Arab chieftain, the Grand Mufti, whose career in Palestine and, later, in an exile spent with Nazi hosts in Germany, was one long provocation to *pogrom*. The word was spread that the Jews were planning to seize and desecrate the Moslem holy places. Every Arab village was informed, with hysterical appeals for vengeance, that the Mosque of Omar had been dynamited! The British, instead of dealing with the aggressors, treated with maddening neutrality both those who attacked and those who defended, as if the Jews were equally responsible for the bloodshed. The rioting did not bring the mass rebellion that the Grand Mufti hoped would follow. It was put down, as much by sturdy Jewish resistance, as by the British armed forces that finally reached the affected areas.

There followed an uneasy truce for seven years, during which the Grand Mufti's work of provocation went forward ceaselessly. Then, in 1936, as the Axis powers grew stronger and bolder, the Arabs struck again in many parts of Palestine. If ever firmness was called for, it was now, to teach the Arabs, once and for all, that no political decisions would be influenced by wanton assaults on peaceful villages. But the British administration, confused, deep in the strategy of appeasement everywhere else, was not firm. It permitted a minor rebellion to drag on for three years. Then it sponsored still another Royal Commission report with instructions to bring in recommendations. There had already been a series of Royal Commissions, each going back over the same ground. There had been a Shaw Report in 1930, followed by a Hope-Simpson Report the next year. Now, in 1937, there was a Peel Report. After each report the pledges of the Balfour Declaration were whittled down a little more. Immigration quotas, already tragically small, were steadily restricted. Land sales to Jews were surrounded with increasing difficulty. Immigration had been guided by the principle of "absorptive capacity" of the country. After successive Commission reports, immigration was regulated according to political circumstances. This unilateral reinterpretation of responsibility by the mandatory power was roundly denounced by the Mandates Commission of the League of Nations as "a departure from the spirit of the Mandate." But by this time the League was little more than a debating society, and the shadow of Hitler and Mussolini played a much larger role in formulating British policy in Palestine.

None of the British concessions satisfied the Grand Mufti. Why should they? He had seen that every British decision was subject to revision whenever the Arabs fired some shots or tore up some oil pipe-line or attempted to burn down some villages. Despairing of a solution that would bring Arabs and Jews together in all of Palestine, the Peel Report of 1937 now proposed partition of the country into Arab, Jewish, and British states.

For the Jews it was a heart-breaking compromise. The area of the original Mandate, pledged by the nations of the world, had been shorn of Trans-Jordan in Sir Herbert Samuel's administration in order to placate the Arabs. Now even the miniscule area that was left was to be partitioned and mutilated. But Jewish leadership, saddled with the awful responsibility of providing for hundreds of thousands of desperate refugees, who were, indeed, later sent to gas chambers by Hitler, was almost ready to surrender rights to a large section of Palestine in order to obtain sovereignty in what was left. The Zionist Congress of 1937, after a historic debate, gave its Executive Committee the authority to negotiate with Britain for modifications in the compromise plan which would make partition more acceptable.

Still the Arabs refused even to negotiate. They insisted upon the whole country, every last dunam, the exclusively Jewish sections included. And to prevent any further discussion, they broke the truce that had been established during the Commission's study, and precipitated the worst disturbances that had yet confounded the peace of Palestine.

Through all the deadly strife, though scores of Jews were cut down by sniping and in continuous ambush, the Jewish community was bound by its leadership to *Havlagah,* strictest self-restraint. Defence was crucial, of course, and every colony, every village, every city group, was prepared to resist, and did resist, Arab acts of aggression. But reprisals against the innocent were condemned as cowardly, as succumbing to the gangsters' own methods. Yet, as the months dragged on with mounting lists of murdered men, women, and children, with the social and commercial life of the country seriously disrupted, the patience of the Jewish population wore precariously thin.

The Revisionist group, which had always scoffed at reliance upon British good faith and had opposed moderation and forbearance in relationship with the Arabs, repudiated the "luxury" of moral restraint. One of its members fired upon an Arab bus. He was promptly tried, sentenced to death, and executed by a British military court. Despite appeals by Jewish leaders for maintenance of *Havlagah,* group discipline cracked and there were sharp reprisals. Flesh and blood could stand only so much, the Revisionists cried. For years the terror had gone on, snuffing out lives, burning property, uprooting precious trees, the life-line of Jewish Palestine. A great Empire, defied so long by miserable Arab gangsters, stirred to decisive action and stern punishment only when Jews were involved! Bombs began to explode in Arab market places, in Arab homes. These acts of vengeance and defiance in turn called forth further Arab terrorism. Britain was obliged to rush in whole squadrons of planes and ships, until the largest concentration of military forces since World War I was stationed and alerted in the Holy Land.

By the fall of 1938 the international situation had changed radically. Hitler and Mussolini had burst through the status quo and were threatening the security of the British Empire. Successfully gambling on the peace-at-all-costs psychology of the democratic governments, they threatened and bluffed their way to major bloodless victories on the Continent and in the Mediterranean. Now there were ominous hints in the inspired British press to indicate that the government was seriously considering major concessions to the Arabs, in the hope of ending their major disaffection and keeping them in line. The Jews sensed, with sinking hearts, that a Palestine Munich was being planned by the quaking, faltering statesmen in Whitehall. Appeasement had become the pattern of democratic action, or rather inaction. Manchukuo, Ethiopia, Spain, Austria, and Czechoslovakia had been sacrificed for peace, and the price continued to rise. Now apparently Palestine was to be added to the tragic list.

Soon the worst Jewish fears were realized. In November 1938 the controversial partition plan was discarded as unpractical. Then the Colonial Secretary issued a call for a new Round Table. The negotiations dragged on for weeks, and, as the international situation deteriorated, the British leaders pressed for a quick decision. Lord Halifax, British Foreign Minister, said bluntly: "Ethical principles must give way to administrative necessity." In May 1939 the Chamberlain Government issued the famous White Paper, Command 6019, which scrapped the Balfour Declaration. There were to be admitted only another 75,000 Jews in the next five years; land sales were to be drastically limited. The core of the White Paper lay in the assurance that after a ten-year period of transition, Palestine would become an independent state with the population frozen permanently at the ratio of two Arabs to one Jew. Bombs and terror had triumphed over justice and sacred international obligations.

4. CHAMBERLAIN AND APPEASEMENT

The release of the White Paper by the Chamberlain government elicited extraordinary protests from every quarter of the globe. There were strikes in Warsaw and in Buenos Aires, fasts in Johannesburg and New York. In the United States, Congressmen and educators, governors and labour leaders, university presidents and churchmen, cabled their sense of shock. President Roosevelt authorized the American Ambassador to express the grave effects that the British intention would have on American public opinion. In Britain itself, where the government won a very narrow Parliamentary majority for the plan, there were mass meetings attended by tens of thousands, addressed by leading Christian statesmen, churchmen, and publicists who added their voices to the world-wide protest. The most vehement statements came from the Labour Party whose leaders denounced the Tories for a betrayal of sacred promises. They pledged an unceasing battle to rectify the injustice. Herbert Morrison, later Deputy Prime Minister in the Labour Government, said, "If we do this thing today, we shall have done a thing which is dishonourable to our good name, which is discreditable to our capacity to govern, and which is dangerous to British security, to peace, and to the economic interest of the world in general and of our own country." The words were to be remembered as an ironic commentary, only a few years later when the Labour Party came into power and proceeded to out-Tory the Tories.

Through all the stunning defeats that preceded and followed the White Paper, new colonies were staked out in Palestine. The Jewish community looked upon these acts of faith as the most effective response to British appeasement and Arab terror. In the three years since the disturbances began, nearly fifty such settlements were founded. All stood their ground. Men and women fell under knife and bullet and bomb, but no settlement was abandoned, in the north, at the Jordan, on the hills, in the valleys. The White Paper really accelerated the pace of colonization. Volunteers from adjacent areas would gather on the chosen site in the middle of the night to begin their work. By morning the foundations were laid—stockade, watch-tower, barracks, and fences—and another link in the Jewish defence system would be complete.

Then, a few months after the publication of the White Paper, the entire settlement was blown up by Hitler's bombs on Poland. When World War II was launched, Britain found itself engaged in a titanic struggle for survival. Years of Nazi provocation and international mischief-making had finally made it clear even to the appeasement bloc that there could be neither peace nor security in Europe until the Brown plague was eradicated. A united British nation vowed that it would continue the conflict until Hitlerism had been destroyed, root and branch.

The war came just as the Zionist Congress was meeting in Geneva. It had been convened to devise methods of fighting against the implementation of the White Paper. It resolved at once to lend unlimited support to Britain and its Allies. Dr. Chaim Weizmann sent a message to Chamberlain in which he pledged fullest Jewish co-operation. In Palestine the tens of thousands who had registered for resistance to the establishment of an Arab state gave immediate assurances that their lives and resources were at the disposal of the British. Thirty thousand men and three thousand women enlisted in the British fighting forces in Palestine, equivalent in proportion to total populations to an American volunteer force of eight million! *Great Britain and the East,* official organ of the Colonial office, commented: "The leaders of Zionism may be assured that the British people will not forget their attitude in this hour of destiny." Chamberlain, replying to Weizmann, promised that "the public-spirited assurances are welcome and will be kept in mind." The Jewish response was all the more significant because the Arab leaders remained sullenly neutral and the Grand Mufti himself used the war to stir up bitterest opposition to the British. He escaped from Palestine and took refuge in Nazi Germany as Hitler's personal guest, and from there continued to direct Arab opposition to the British war effort. The British leaders promised the Jews that they would never forget. And the Jews implicitly trusted these grateful promises, in the darkest hours of British history.

CHAPTER THIRTY-TWO

WORLD WAR II AND AFTER

I. PLANNED EXTERMINATION

A NEW term, "Genocide," had to be created in the period of World War II to cover the full criminal intent of the Nazi leaders. Genocide is the scientific attempt to exterminate a whole people, and the Nazis left nothing undone to carry through their appointed mission. The result of their thoroughness and ruthlessness dragged the Jewish people through the most tragic experiences of their long history.

For several years during the war period, as stories filtered out of sealed countries, hinting at what was going on, they were discounted as the usual atrocity creations of the propagandists. In August 1942 some Polish women, exchanged for German war prisoners, arrived in Palestine and gave eye-witness accounts of vast slaughter-houses in Poland and occupied Russia which were systematically consuming millions of Jews, rounded up from everywhere in Europe. Still the world did not believe. It could not believe. Even the testimony of escaped victims, with documentary proof and ineradicable marks in their flesh, could not establish that there were human beings outside of insane asylums who would go to such frenzied lengths to consummate a theory of extermination. It was only when the invading armies of the Allies burst into Nazi-held territory and, taking over the concentration camps, saw with their own eyes the monstrous instruments of torture and decimation, that the truth began to take shape. Later the details were worked into the fabric of horror when the Nazi war trials began. The confessions of the top officials, some expressed with sorrow, but most freely offered in arrogance and defiance, went into the record. At last the world began to realize the full implications of Nazi depravity.

The victories of the Nazis put virtually all of Jewish life in Europe under their control. The master plan had long been prepared to kill off every last Jew. It was important, however, to achieve the goal without rousing the suspicions of the victims or of the more decent Christians among whom Jews lived. Hence great concentration camps and ghettos were set apart; the Jews were rounded up from everywhere in Europe and transported to these receiving points. Here, behind huge walls or barbed wire, far from the eyes of the Christian world, the Nazis could devour their defenceless prey without let or hindrance.

The sickening details were later supplied, during the war trials, by some of the captured guards. Only enough precious food or fuel was "wasted" to keep the inmates temporarily alive. They were beaten at the slightest provocation, or with no provocation at all. Since part of the purpose was to degrade the Jews, they were worn down by hunger or by sadistic sports. Leading Nazi medical men admitted at their trials the use of the Jews as guinea pigs in every kind of pseudo-scientific experiment. They were put to torture to test air pressures in planes, to determine the limits of starvation or thirst, to test out poisons. Their skin was taken for grafting operations on wounded German soldiers. The children were drained of their blood to supply the war blood banks. Here a military purpose was served. Apparently the purpose was purely ornamental when human skin was peeled off to make ingeniously tattooed lamp shades.

Meantime, giant gas ovens and crematoria had been built in which bodies could be disposed of in wholesale numbers, mechanically, and without undue inconvenience. The Nazis wanted no revolts on their hands, even hopeless revolts of fists against machine guns. The extermination was to be accomplished cheaply, with no Nazi lives endangered. Hence the most ingenious stratagems were used to send the victims to the gas chambers in the belief that they were headed else-where. Announcements were made that they were being sent for work opportunities in other parts of Europe, or that they were part of the promised contingents of forced labour needed in occupied Russia. Great numbers flocked eagerly to the deportation trains when they were told that they had been chosen for transportation to Palestine. Soon forged letters and post cards flooded back, strategically released by the Nazis, to tell of better conditions in the interior where the earlier contingents had gone. Motion pictures of tolerable living in these new centres were shown, and they lulled the suspicions of the miserable remnants and kept them from revolt.

The deportations themselves were on the lowest animal level. Thousands died in the sealed trains for lack of food, lack of water, lack of air. Those who survived to reach the extermination points were held only brief periods before consignment to the gas chambers. Children were often torn away before their mothers. One survivor said later with icy bitterness: "Even a cat is led away before her kittens are taken." [1] The bodies were pushed out of the gas ovens like so much garbage and then burnt in huge crematoria or buried in long common graves. The liberating hosts later found piles of baby shoes, gold teeth, spectacles, toys, all sorted out meticulously. For the Germans, even horror had to be methodical.

These were stories usually told dully, sullenly, at the war trials, by the guards in charge of the camps and the ovens. Some of them were pathological creatures, congenitally unable to understand the enormity of their crimes. But the evidence made it plain that the German people were also deeply implicated. They may not have condoned the sadism but they could not have been unaware of the mass murders. Perhaps they were helpless to protest in a tightly controlled Fascist police state. But how could they have rationalized that the Jews deserved their fate? By

[1] Syrkin: *Blessed Is the Match*, p. 145.

what psychological perversity could they have carried over their hatred beyond the fall of Hitler? The names of the great horror camps—Treblinka, Buchenwald, Oswiecim, Maidanek, and others—remain not only as enduring symbols of the Jewish tragedy; they remain as irrefutable witnesses of deeply rooted German folk guilt.

2. RESISTANCE

Even Nazi ingenuity could not forever conceal the wholesale pact with Death, and at last the surviving Jews began to understand the horror that was engulfing them. A determination to sell their lives dearly knit together the younger men. Most of the Jews had died without a struggle. They had no alternative. They had been disarmed. They were isolated. They were surrounded by the Nazi military forces and by hostile populations. But those who could, resolved, with full understanding of its hopelessness, that there must be resistance if only to make the cowardly fully armed supermen pay something for every Jewish life.

Their determination was strengthened by emissaries who broke through from the outside to tell them what was happening. Palestine sent parachutists who dropped from the skies into the Balkan lands and then worked their way even into sealed Poland after feats of heroism that would strain the credulity of motion-picture thrillers. They were able to smuggle some Jews out. Some Jews escaped to the woods and joined up with Partisan underground groups to carry on the fight against the Nazis. These were the fortunate exceptions; the great majority were destined to die. But they determined to die as allies in a war of liberation rather than as casualties or victims in a rat-trap massacre.

The Warsaw ghetto resistance was the most heroic, as it was the most dramatic, of all the resistance attempts. Here half a million Jews had been cooped up by October 1940, most of them siphoned out of every country in Europe. For nearly two years they lived in their tomb, with less than animal security, crowded, miserable, fighting epidemic without medication, winter rigour without fuel, but trying desperately to maintain some kind of dignity. They continued their schools, their sports, their pathetic theatricals and amusements. A symphony played, a carefully trained choir sang. There was a children's library to keep open the lifeline with other happier worlds, and even vocational classes to train hands that death was so soon to claim.

In July 1942 the deportations to the extermination camps began, from six to ten thousand souls going daily. For a year those who went, simply disappeared, but the forged letters and cards that came back brought a measure of assurance. In May 1943 only about forty thousand remained in the ghetto. For several months stories had been trickling in which began to open out the whole ghastly truth. Now the resistance was organized, led by a few courageous spirits, men and women, who demonstrated remarkable skill in converting defenceless ghetto remnants into a crack fighting brigade. In the wretched hovels home-made hand grenades and incendiary bombs were prepared. The Partisans on the outside smuggled in other weapons and ammunition through the sewers and through some Aryan-appearing Jews. The Nazis had hoped that there would be no cost for the liquidation, but the surprise of the resistance and its fury took a heavy toll. The ghetto was not subdued for weeks, and then only when tanks and machine guns were brought in. The battles went on street by street, house by house, and ultimately room by room. The men fought on until there was no ammunition left, and they used their last bullets for themselves, so as not to fall into Nazi hands. Only a few escaped through the sewers of the ghetto to join with the Partisan underground.

There was similar last-ditch resistance in some of the other ghettos and extermination centres. In August 1943 an eight-day battle raged in Bialystok before all Jews were killed off. There was similar gallant though hopeless resistance in Tarnow, Vilna, and Czenstochowa. In one of the most infamous death camps, Treblinka, the final victims, on their way to the gas chambers, fell upon the guards and were able to kill many of them. The gas chambers were fired, and some of the Jews escaped into the woods.

Resistance that had more than token dramatic value took the form of underground fighting against the Nazis. But only small groups were able to pass through the fine Nazi sieve. Even after escape there was scarcely a moment of blessed respite for these fortunate few. It was difficult enough for any European people to carry on resistance as guerilla partisans against as thorough and efficient an enemy as the Nazis. For the Jews it was a demand for daily, almost hourly, miracles. They were deeply resented by the civilian population. Poles, Lithuanians, Ukrainians, hated the Nazi oppressors but they had no sympathy for the Jews and would not think twice about betraying them. Even the Partisans of Poland and the Baltic states, fighting for survival, were often implacable enemies, as likely to fall upon them and destroy them as they would the common Nazi enemy. Jewish Partisans had to live in a jungle world of their own.

There were honourable exceptions. In France the Jewish guerilla fighters achieved spectacular results with the Maquis forces; they all fought together as comrades against the Nazis and the Vichy regime. In occupied Russia, in Czechoslovakia, and in Yugoslavia they were either assimilated into the guerilla groups or organized their own fighting units. They worked as dynamiting teams in a "track war," destroying communications and transportation; they served as intelligence teams, carrying crucial military messages. They were ideal emissaries in sure-death missions, for they fought with extraordinary desperation and fanaticism. They had to get through or die; if they fell into Nazi hands they could expect no mercy. They felt, too, that for them this was beyond war. Every blow struck by them was a shared act of vengeance. It was participated in by relatives and dear ones who had gone under namelessly.

While the extermination mills continued to devour their millions of victims, there were several sensational attempts by Nazi officials to "sell" some of these lives in return for gold or military equipment. The Nazi leader, Wislitzeni, a brother-in-law of Heinrich Himmler, agreed to use his good offices to stop the deportation of the Jews of Slovakia and the Balkan states in return for two million dollars. Since about a million Jews were involved, this meant that the rate was set at two dollars per Jewish life. Responsible Jewish groups in Palestine and representatives of American Jewish relief agencies probed cautiously to determine whether there was sufficient good faith to warrant further action. But advance payment would have meant risking precious relief funds on the off chance that a minor Nazi leader actually had enough influence to stop the deportations and thereby to alter a master Nazi extermination plan. A down payment, with the promise to pay in full after the Jews had been redeemed, was flatly turned down by the Nazis, and the negotiations came to an abrupt end.

Two years later, in 1944, another Nazi chieftain, Eichmann, offered to spare surviving Jews and permit them to emigrate if ten thousand trucks were delivered for action on the Eastern front against the Russians. Britain promptly denounced the offer as a not too clever ruse once again to drive a wedge between the Western allies and their Russian comrades in arms. Whether any of the deals would have been honestly carried through or not is a subject for speculation. That negotiations with the Nazi butchers were actually opened and explored is the best index to the plight of the Jews and the desperation of their leadership.[1]

3. THE COST OF HITLERISM

In the spring of 1945 Nazi power finally collapsed under the mighty blows of the Allied armies. Hitler and his mistress committed suicide in a bunker under the Chancellery in Berlin as, overhead, the city was reduced to rubble by ceaseless air pounding. Many of Hitler's closest cronies also shot themselves or took poison. The chief lieutenants who preferred escape were gradually rounded up, and later, after thoroughly prepared public trials, were hanged or given long prison terms. A great weight was lifted from the hearts of the democratic peoples. Only after the crisis had passed was it fully realized how close the Nazis had been to victory and the eclipse of Western civilization.

The liberation troops poured into Germany and into the long-despoiled territories. The oppressed peoples came out into the light again. Their inheritance, abused and drained by the Nazis, was damaged, deeply damaged. But the core remained. The land was there, and the people and the basic resources that nature

[1] The whole fantastic story is brilliantly told by Marie Syrkin in *Blessed Is the Match,* pp. 91–129.

had provided. For the Jews there was little rejoicing and less comfort. Even the
suicide of Hitler and Goebbels and Himmler and the Haman fate of the other
Nazi top men brought only hollow satisfaction. For the cost of the ghastly years
of Hitlerism, in life and property and human dignity, defied description. The
worst stories that had filtered out of the Continent, and which had been dismissed as the exaggerations of a hysterical people, were found to be understate-
ments. Six million Jews had perished; most of those who survived had no land,
no homes, no means of livelihood, not even elementary security.

Virtually all of the Jews of Germany were gone. Before Hitler came to
power, there were 600,000 in the country, and old and deeply rooted community.
More than half migrated in the first years of the Nazi scourge. Then the war
closed in, and when the curtain was lifted in 1945, there were, outside of Displaced Persons' camps, less than 15,000 left. A few thousand more gradually
returned from concentration camps or came out of hiding or emerged from
Christian homes where they had been mercifully sheltered. Most of the rest
had perished in the gas chambers. Austria suffered as disastrously. The pre-
Hitler community had numbered a quarter of a million. When the war broke
out this had been cut to 43,000. The end of the war left six thousand broken
and hopeless derelicts.

The most awesome decimation came in Poland. Of the three million Jews,
half mercifully escaped extermination when the eastern parts of the country
were absorbed into Russia. After Hitler's downfall, even with the repatriation
of thousands who returned from concentration camps or from hidden refuge,
there were only 250,000 left. Then the Poles, only yesterday released from their
own bondage, turned in hatred on the Jews and a wave of *pogroms* precipitated
a new exodus. By 1946 the most populous centre of Jewish life, with a tradition
of culture and service that went back to the Middle Ages, was left with 105,000
harried souls, all praying for deliverance.

The record in western Europe was almost as melancholy, for the Nazi deportations left no land untouched. The Jews of Belgium were cut down from
90,000 to less than 25,000. Holland had a pre-war population of 145,000, and was
left with 28,000. Of these, most were married to non-Jews or had partial Christian parentage; there had to be special circumstances for any Jew to survive
the Nazi purge. The Netherlands Red Cross reported on the fate of 117,000
Jews who were uprooted. One concentration camp at Westerbork had received
34,000 Jews, the end result of the 1943 deportations on nineteen trains. Three
men and sixteen women survived to tell the tale. The last eight hundred organized a revolt against their guard. They took an unexpected toll from their
tormentors, but not a single Jew remained alive. The record of Westerbork,
except for names and places, can be used for any other land where the Nazis
cast their shadow. Perhaps the best way, then, to summarize the fantastic impact
of Hitler's black years upon the Jewish life of Europe is merely to refer to the

appended statistical table. The simple figures speak so eloquently that embellishment is an anticlimax.

4. DISPLACED PERSONS' CAMPS

When the war ended in the summer of 1945, the liberating Allied armies found about thirty thousand Jews still alive in the concentration camps. They were a broken, dispirited lot, worn down physically by the hardships they had undergone, and further depressed because of the fate that had befallen all of their dear ones. They had no strength to return to their native lands, nor was there the slightest desire to live again in areas that carried only tragic memories. The military authorities did not press them to return, and they set up camps to receive them and to care for them until some more permanent haven could be found for them. This was the origin of the Displaced Persons' camps, initiated to provide temporary shelter and status for the victims of Hitlerism, with no expectation that leaden-footed years would pass without any solution to the problem of their rehabilitation.

The camp population was soon oppressively increased. Tens of thousands of Polish Jews, appalled by the anti-Semitism of the civilian groups whose sufferings they had shared under Nazi domination, began a flight from Poland into the American-occupied zones of Germany and Austria. The movement was turned into a mass migration after the *pogrom* in Kielce in early July 1946, when forty-two Jews were murdered in a community lynching party. Balkan Jews, too, from Hungary and Roumania, convinced that it would be less difficult to reach Palestine through the German camps, also joined in the flight. The American military authorities, first General Dwight Eisenhower and afterwards General McNarney, opened the borders and the camps to the refugees, and the army was ordered to care for them. The greatest numbers moved into the American zone. The British strenuously resisted the pressure. Few of those who fled were attracted to either the French or the Russian zones. By April 1947 the American military authorities had closed the borders and had stopped further registration in the camps. But already more than 150,000 Jews were in the American zone in Germany, and about 27,000 in the Austrian zone. They comprised about one fourth of the population of the camps, the others being mainly Christian Poles and Balts who could not or would not fit into their homelands.

Every effort was made to extend sympathetic assistance to these victims of Nazism. The essentials of food, shelter, and clothing came from American military resources. The major relief agencies, UNNRRA and the Joint Distribution Committee, added supplementary support to make existence more tolerable. Social, cultural, and religious activities were encouraged, and a Central Committee drawn from the camp inhabitants themselves served as a self-

ESTIMATED JEWISH POPULATION OF EUROPE*

Country	1939	1947	
Albania	200	—	
Austria	—	—	300
Displaced Persons in U. S., British, French and Russian zones..	—	35,000	—
Others	—	7,000	—
Total	60,000	—	42,000
Belgium	100,000	—	34,500
Bulgaria	50,000	—	46,500
Czechoslovakia	360,000[1]	—	60,000
Denmark	7,000	—	5,500
England	340,000	—	345,000
Estonia (U. S. S. R.)	5,000	—	500
Finland	2,000	—	1,800
France	320,000[2]	—	205,000
Germany	—	—	—
Displaced Persons in U. S., British and French zones	—	170,600	—
Others	—	18,000	188,600
Total	240,000	—	—
Greece	75,000	—	8,000
Holland	150,000	—	33,000
Hungary	403,000[3]	—	180,000
Irish Free State	4,000	—	4,500
Italy	—	—	—
Nationals	—	30,000	—
Displaced Persons and Refugees..	—	26,000	56,000
Total	51,000	—	—
Latvia (U. S. S. R.)	95,000	—	12,000
Lithuania (U. S. S. R.)	155,000	—	20,000
Luxembourg	3,500	—	500
Norway	3,000	—	1,000
Poland	3,250,000	—	105,000[4]
Portugal	3,500	—	4,000
Rumania	850,000[5]	—	430,000
Soviet Union	3,020,000	—	2,000,000[6]
Spain	4,500	—	3,500
Sweden	7,500	—	15,500
Switzerland	25,000	—	25,500
Turkey	80,000	—	80,000[7]
Yugoslavia	75,000	—	11,900
TOTAL	9,739,200	—	3,920,100

*Table from *American Jewish Year Book. 1947–48.*

[1] Figure in 1939 column refers to the Jewish population within pre-Munich boundaries. Figur⸻

governing liaison with the military authorities. Health improved rapidly, and, in truth, there was no real want, even in the toughest weather.

But what these uprooted people wanted more than physical comfort was the opportunity for normal family and community living in a background of permanence and security. They wanted the restoration of dignity, an end of the humiliating identification as letters in the alphabet—DP's. They hoped that after a few months they could migrate to Palestine, or perhaps to the United States, where hands would work again, where creative effort would renew self-respect. But the weeks lengthened into months, and the months into years, and promises were buried under official paper, and hopes were snarled up in diplomatic red tape. The mood of the people changed. Exaltation turned to anxiety, then to cynicism, and then to bitterness. Relations with the German people among whom the camps were placed became tense. The Germans deeply resented the presence of the Jews as their own position deteriorated in terms of housing, food, and fuel shortages. The Jews deeply resented the Germans who, with all their low standard of living, still had private homes and personally owned lands and farms. There were insulting words, then blows, then even riots. New contingents of American soldiers came over for occupation duty, younger, less experienced, with little understanding of what the Nazis had done to the world. They were influenced by German women, and a thinly veiled but steadily spreading anti-Semitism among them further embittered the displaced Jews. The pressure to get out, to migrate, to reach Palestine, became the one overwhelming passion. By 1947 a kind of mass desperation had engulfed the camps, and the men in charge knew that there must soon be an explosion somewhere unless some doors were opened.

5. FORCING THE DOORS OF PALESTINE

The White Paper of 1939, the bastard child of Chamberlain's appeasement program, had kept legal immigration to Palestine at a farcically minimum level.

---

for 1946 includes about 11,000 refugees from Ruthenia and Poland.

[2] Figures refer to European France.

[3] These figures refer to Hungary within 1938 frontiers. After 1938, the Jewish population in Hungary increased to 745,000 due to the annexation of Czechoslovak and Rumanian territory and some influx of Jews from Poland and other Nazi areas.

[4] About 140,000 Jews were repatriated from the U. S. S. R. in the first part of 1946. After the Kielce pogrom, however, large numbers fled westward.

[5] The figure for 1939 refers to Greater Rumania which included Bessarabia, Bucovina and Transylvania. The figure for 1946 refers to the present boundaries, thus excluding Bessarabia and Northern Bucovina. The 1946 figure includes repatriates from Soviet territory; this repatriation is still continuing.

[6] Including Asiatic provinces.

[7] Including Asiatic Turkey.

Nevertheless, all through the war period the Jews of Palestine toiled loyally and fought gallantly under British direction, confident that victory would bring recompense through the abrogation of the White Paper and the other creatures of the appeasement era. When the Labour Government came to power, pledged to the limit to establish Palestine as a Jewish commonwealth and to open immigration without restriction, it seemed that the long, long travail was at last to be ended.

The Labour Government not only refused to modify the White Paper, but proceeded to enforce it with unprecedented severity and cruelty. An Anglo-American Committee of Inquiry had been appointed through the joint action of the British and the American governments. It, too, recommended unanimously that, pending the ultimate solution of the Palestine problem, one hundred thousand Jewish refugees, drawn mainly from the DP camps, be admitted to Palestine within the year. The Labour Government flatly repudiated its own Committee and refused to yield any interim concessions. This policy was applied just when the pressure from the camps had become overwhelming, when the years of suffering and hopelessness should have been an irresistible compulsion on the Christian conscience.

There is no simple explanation for the bewildering change in the policy of the Labour Party, from staunchest support to lukewarmness to unyielding hostility. Of course, promises made by an opposition without responsibility do not always square with the actions of such an opposition when it becomes a government with responsibility. A still more decisive influence stemmed from the permanent Foreign Office and Colonial Office staffs. Governments rose and fell, the fortunes of political parties swelled and ebbed, but these officials remained at their posts. They were almost uniformly pro-Arab. They firmly believed that highest British interests were linked to the friendship of the Arab states. They overwhelmed the freshly appointed Cabinet members with data designed to prove that a Zionist orientation by the new Government would have disastrous effects throughout the Middle East at exactly the time when Britain and Russia were struggling for vital position in that explosive area. The Labour leaders, even those most sympathetic to the Zionist cause, were apparently impressed by this briefing, and began to play for time. They were unwilling to commit themselves to any action or to repudiate any policy that would alienate the Arab states and the Moslem world.

Not to be discounted, furthermore, was the personal equation interjected by the new Foreign Minister, Ernest Bevin. Bevin rose to political eminence from the trade-union ranks. For years he had been secretary of the Transport and General Workers' Union, and he had been constantly involved in quarrels with the Communist left wing of this all-powerful group. They were a thorn in his side. Some of the Communist leaders were Jews. Bevin, a man of narrow, provincial training, apparently never emancipated himself from these early associations where Jews and Communists and unpleasant people all fused into one *mélange* and emerged as one stereotype. In the light of the pressure from the permanent civil service, the Labour Government would probably have scuttled Jewish hopes anyway. But the harshness with which this policy was applied, the attacks upon the motives of the Jews of the United States who were appealing for those whose voices had been muted, the uncomplimentary references to the Jews of the DP camps at the very time when they were plunged into profoundest despair by the turn of events, all pointed to the influence of Ernest Bevin. It was part of the unhappy fate of the Jewish people that, in the decisive hour when a historic hope was on the threshold of fulfilment, the head and front of British policy was not a Lloyd George or a Balfour or even a Churchill, but a harsh and obdurate Ernest Bevin.

The Jews refused to accept the Labour Government decisions supinely. If the doors of Palestine were not to be opened by the Jewish contributions to the total war effort or by the honourable fulfilment of sacred British pledges, then they would have to be pried open by underground action or blasted open by defiance. These considerations reinstated on a larger scale than ever the *Ha'apalah*, the "illegal" immigration whose dramatic story was to crowd the headlines for the next two years.

This tenuous but crucial immigration life-line was planned to its minutest detail. The base was in Palestine where Haganah, the Jewish militia, took over the secret organizing tasks. There were agents in every part of Europe and in the United States who purchased or leased the ships, selected the fortunate immigrants, shepherded them across frontiers, and then tried to run them past the rigid British blockade. Failure was much more common than success. The odds were always heavily stacked against the desperate caravans. In Europe there were diplomatic and military obstacles wherever there were frontiers, and the frontiers were endless. In the Mediterranean and at the approaches of Palestine, modern devices for detection were virtually surprise-proof. Only a few of the illegal ships could hope to get through. The others were apprehended, and the British then transferred the disappointed but undaunted cargo to specially built concentration camps on the island of Cyprus. Even Cyprus, with its primitive facilities and its heart-breaking monotony, became a sought-out goal, for Britain usually permitted those on the island to head the list of legal immigrants in each month's new quota.

The ships hardly deserved their name. They were usually leaking little tubs whose captain and crew exacted heavy recompense for the extraordinary risks that had to be run. They were always loaded to three and four times their proper capacity. They stole out at night or in fog from Constantza or Athens or Bari, or from other obscurer ports. If they were not intercepted en route, they transferred their human cargo to little fishing boats close to unpatrolled Palestine shores. Those who finally landed, after all these hazards, were then whisked by truck to the villages to be quickly swallowed into the general population so that their whereabouts could not be ferreted out.

How narrow was the margin for success was well known in the ghettos of Europe and in the DP camps. Yet the competition to get on the favored lists and to try for Palestine increased rather than diminished. Thousands who could not be immediately chosen formed into determined little bands and walked across Europe to strange ports whose advantages had been puffed up by the flimsiest rumours. There they negotiated for any available ship or boat, however small or unseaworthy. And from there, with fantastic but understandable fool-hardiness, they sailed. Men and women who had so often heard the beating of the wings of the Angel of Death could not be deterred because their schemes were reckless. If they were linked to the thousandth off chance of getting into Palestine, it was enough.

Up till this point there was still rigid group discipline in relation to the Mandatory power. Haganah sanctioned no terror. It did join in blockade-running and in diversionary stratagems to help open the way to freedom for the boatloads who flung themselves on Palestine's shores. Yet no matter how severe was the provocation, Haganah would not authorize reprisals against the British.

But there were smaller dissident groups, Irgunists and Sternists, who became intractable and refused to accept any such discipline. Their dear ones had nearly all been destroyed. A few remnants here and there now approached Palestine, a last brother, a lone surviving son. Were those fortunately already on the land to stand by as these precious remnants were sent back to new sorrows? What good was moderation now? What had it brought in rewarding concessions? The British had yielded only to the Arabs, and usually when Arab bombs went off to spell out the warning in blood and debris, that force was the only recognized arbiter. These dissident bands, emotionally exhausted by disillusionment, harried by the desperation of those who came up to the gates of Palestine only to be transported to new concentration camps, derided the ethical inhibitions of Haganah and repudiated their authority. The strange turn of events in Palestine paralleled with amazing fidelity the pattern of recent Irish history. Sein Feiners and Republicans were often at odds over the limits of guerilla resistance and reprisals in the battles for Irish independence which ultimately wore down the British.

Terror dominated the headlines of 1946 and 1947. There was continuous bombing of oil pipe-lines, railway stations, and trains, and there were assaults upon the police and military personnel. The King David Hotel, headquarters for the British, was blown up with sickening loss of life, British, Arabs, and Jews. These acts of violence were widely condemned by authorized Jewish leadership. But these leaders linked the British in responsibility for the outrages. They maintained that they were not the acts of gangsters and murderers, terms used by the British. Rather they were the acts of men crazed by the pain and disappointment that were the products of British opportunism.

Terror brought swift reprisals by the British. Several captured Irgunists were court-martialled and executed. Their comrades responded by kidnapping some British soldiers and hanging them as hostages, "an eye for an eye, a life for a life." The British imposed martial law on nearly half the settlements in Palestine, bringing trade and commerce to a standstill and paralyzing the economic life of the country. "Let's hit where it will hurt the Jews most, at their pocketbooks," the commanding British general blurted out, and the venom in the statement indicated how far British-Jewish relationships had deteriorated. But even martial law did not halt the rising tide of terrorism. Each episode provoked the opposing forces into more violent retaliation. The tempo of executions increased. Jewish Agency leaders were imprisoned as accomplices of terror. Whole communities were subjected to mass searches to dig out weapons or to round up the extremists in hiding. The curfews blacked out normal living.

In 1947 came a climactic act of stupid callousness which turned many Jewish moderates into extremists. Several thousand refugees who attempted to get into Palestine were herded back on their ship, appropriately enough named the *Exodus,* and the crowded boat was sent on to Germany. When the Jews refused to disembark for German concentration camps, they were beaten by the British in the presence of Nazi civilians, who stood by exultantly as their fondest hopes came true within two years after Hitler's suicide. Briton and Jew were now openly engaged in what Winston Churchill, who heartily condemned the reckless hostility of the Bevin policy, termed "the Labour Government's war with the Jews in Palestine."

6. THE END OF THE BRITISH MANDATE

Neither martial law nor executions nor deportations ended the terror; they intensified it. Early in 1947, drained by military complications in many parts of the globe, the Labour Government decided that Palestine had become too great a liability, and announced that it planned to surrender the Mandate. Bevin, in making the sensational statement, threw the responsibility for failure on the other nations. The real difficulty, he said, was that no country, including the United States, was willing to admit Jews. "There has been a failure of international moral consciousness." Bevin felt that such shirking of moral responsibility made it intolerably hard for Britain. The United Nations would now have to take over the problem and work towards a settlement of its own.

A special session of the United Nations Assembly was convened in the spring of 1947. After stormy debates a new international Commission was authorized to make an exhaustive study of the whole problem and to present its recommendations for final United Nations' action. The Commission was made up of representatives of smaller states not themselves directly involved in the long dispute.

There was little optimism among the Jews that after so many futile Commission reports this new one would bring any relief. The Arabs had denounced the action that placed the discussion on the United Nations agenda; they had attempted to block the right of the Jews to be heard; they had threatened to boycott the hearings of the Commission. Bevin had made the ominous statement that Britain would not necessarily be bound by the recommendations of the Commission or by the decisions of the United Nations. How could there be room for optimism when the Commission embarked on its mission in such a charged and threatening climate? But there was no alternative, and Jews took comfort in the slender hope that, if the recommendations were favourable, a decision by the representatives of all the nations might have a deeper compulsion than the discarded reports of the past. In the DP camps the Jews prepared for additional months of sterile waiting while another Commission stirred the embers for new evidence.

Once again there were exhaustive hearings and on-the-spot inquiries. As in the past, the investigators could not divorce the question of a Jewish Commonwealth from the fate of the dispossessed Jews of Europe. Nor could they by-pass the historic claims of the Jewish people, especially when they were placed against the overgenerous territorial grants that the Arabs had received after World War I. Yet they too could find no solution within the framework of a united Palestine. Cantonization, federalization, bi-nationalism, all the suggested plans and expedients threatened to raise more problems than they solved. The Commission therefore came back to radical surgery, the partition of the country into Arab and Jewish states, with complete independence for each, adding the pious hope that the two units would co-operate to preserve the delicate economic balance of the area.

The territory recommended for the Jewish state was tiny, divided into widely separated segments, vulnerable to attack, hardly a viable entity. But it included the undeveloped Negeb in the south, which could perhaps be brought to fertility by Jewish scientific resourcefulness. Partition would mean independence, with freedom to open the doors of Palestine for unrestricted immigration. It would mean sovereignty, an end to the humiliation of perpetual minority status. Above all, it would mean the right to speak with dignity in the council chambers of the world. Hence the Jews acclaimed the recommendations and prayed that they would not end again in the sterility of empty words. But the British government, which had hoped for a pro-Arab decision, stood by sullenly. Bevin's first reaction indicated that though the Mandate would be surrendered as promised, there would be no British co-operation in implementing partition. The Arabs violently denounced the recommendations and girded for the battle in the Assembly of the United Nations to prevent them from being adopted.

The Arab states, with seven votes in the Assembly, entered the decisive debates with considerable initial advantage. This was further strengthened by their bargaining power in the international markets. For they had precious oil reserves to release or to withhold; they had strategic bases that loomed large in the clash of power politics in the Middle East. The Arabs used their bargaining power to the full, and did not hesitate to threaten reprisals if partition was voted. The Jews had only one slender asset to match all of this diplomatic strength. They were a political force in the United States. There was no Jewish voting bloc in American politics, but here was an extraordinary issue that involved the destiny of the whole Jewish people. Their indignation or their gratitude could swing elections in crucial states. This hardly needed underscoring for the party leaders, who were always sensitive to the mass reactions of the major immigration strains. Such political considerations had influenced diplomatic action in the 1920's when the Irish voters had pressed for the recognition of Irish independence. Such factors had counted heavily with the State Department in modifying American hostility to Franco's Spain when the pressure of the Catholics had been exerted. Politics had all too often impaled Jewish hopes. Here was one time when it worked advantageously, and the Jewish leaders employed it as a counterfoil to Arab oil and Arab bases in their struggle to win a Jewish Homeland.

The American representatives, under prodding from President Truman, took a firm stand for partition and worked zealously to line up the other delegations. Astonishingly enough, the partition proposals also received staunch support from Soviet Russia. Indeed, when the Russian and American delegations voted together, it was the first time that these implacable East-West antagonists were in co-operation on a major issue. It had been prophesied that the millennium would be preceded by miracles and wondrous doings. As Russian and American representatives joined to support the partition plan, some bewildered Jews half expected to hear Gabriel's horn.

Affirmative action required a two-thirds vote in the Assembly, and it was nip and tuck until the last moment of debate. Several representatives changed sides a number of times. One delegate expected to vote one way, and then when his government at home fell over internal issues, he voted with the opposite camp. Late Saturday afternoon, November 29, as the dusk came to close the Sabbath, the momentous decision was made. With only three votes to spare, the United Nations authorized the establishment of independent Arab and Jewish states in a partitioned Palestine.

The world response to the decision was overwhelming. Liberal Christians rejoiced that an age-old problem was approaching solution, and that the weary remnants of a people were about to find salvation. Jews in the DP camps, by now almost impervious to the call of hope, began to speak again in the accents of free men. God's ways were everlastingly unpredictable. Only yesterday a whole people was within thrusting distance of the gas chambers. But the last thousands who had also been marked for extermination were now, it was hoped, to be the spearhead for a new life in a resurgent Homeland. In the midst of the ruins of Italy's Fascism, at the base of the Arch of Titus, which was erected two thousand years before to commemorate the extinction of a stiff-necked people, five thousand Jews gathered, the survivors of other crematoria, to express their gratitude at the miracle of resurrection. In Egypt, undaunted by Arab threats, Jews rejoiced in the shadow of the Cairo museum where reposed the famous parchment stele of Mnepthah, one of the earliest of the Pharaohs. He had written thirty centuries before: "Israel is no more," using the term "Israel" for the first time in recorded history, introducing Israel with the salutation of an epitaph. But in 1947 the Jews of Egypt were still there to hail a United Nations decision that seemed to offer new opportunities to attest their indestructibility.

The Partition Resolution of November 29 was followed by a revolutionary change in the British strategy. Within a few weeks the Colonial Office declared that it was the intention of the government to relinquish the mandate over Palestine as of May 15, 1948. The Foreign Minister, his prestige at stake, doubtless hoped that the ensuing civil war between Jews and Arabs would end in the overwhelming defeat of the Jews. A newly constituted Arab Palestine would then lean heavily upon British support, and the Bevin policy would be sustained without all the travail that had followed from the Balfour Declaration. It was risky reasoning and, as events proved, it was to be as disastrous for Britain as virtually everything else had been which Bevin had attempted in Palestine.

At first, however, Bevin's strategy seemed to bring dividends. For it was accompanied by a calculated unwillingness to co-operate in any orderly liquidation. Without waiting until May 15 to begin sloughing off responsibility, the British forces moved out piecemeal, area by area, making no provision to transfer authority. The United Nations Security Council offered to send a commission to Palestine to help bridge the interregnum between British withdrawal and the establishment of the partition states. But the British delegate announced that Britain would flatly refuse to transfer any authority to the commission until the mandate was surrendered, nor would Britain allow the commission to recruit militia or form provisional governments in any area while British troops remained. This was almost open sabotage of the United Nations plan for a solution through partition. The American delegate made this plain, though his diplomatic language had to be limited to the restrained comment that the policy of the British was not "entirely helpful."

Arab guerrillas and mercenaries struck almost as soon as the partition resolution had been passed, attacking in many parts of the country, especially in outlying little settlements of Galilee and the Negeb. Communications became less and less reliable and many areas were soon completely isolated. There were increasing riots, and the disturbances were aggravated as the law courts ceased to function. The British military, while exercising moderate police supervision, took no strenuous measures to restore order. The Arabs were defying an international mandate; the seven Arab states were openly marshalling their armies to fight against partition. But the British continued to sell arms to the Arab states on the ground that contracts completed earlier had to be fulfilled. On the other hand, when the Jews demanded that they be given the right to defend themselves, the British refused to recognize the Haganah as a militia and disarmed Haganah members at every turn. The bitterness of the Jewish population became so intense that the most irresponsible elements, which had for so long been held in check by public opinion, gained increasing respectability.

It was a pathetic end to thirty years of mandatory administration by the British. To be sure, their colonial officials had not at any time been genuine allies of the Jews. They had cribbed and cabined and confined the development of the country as a Jewish homeland. But, taken in historical perspective, Britain had offered thousands of uprooted Jews their first opportunity, however qualified, for a new freedom. It had set standards of modern administration in a part of the world which had been misgoverned for centuries. Anglo-Saxon law and order had been its most estimable export. The extraordinarily devious policy of deliberately courting chaos, a policy summed up succinctly by Winston Churchill as "Bevin's sulky boycott," was a contemptible and tragic valedictory.

7. RECENT DEVELOPMENTS IN BRITAIN AND FRANCE

Fortunately the modern story of Jewish life in Britain was not to end with Bevin nor with the acrimony that accompanied the surrender of the Palestine mandate. The hostility of the Labour Government had not been rooted in malice, but rather in *Realpolitik,* the evident need to retain the support of the Arab world. The English people themselves demonstrated their fundamental goodwill during the Nazi horror, when refugees from Germany, Austria, and Czechoslovakia were made welcome. There were nearly 200,000 of these newcomers. Most of them came without resources. Yet, with the sacrificial co-operation of the Jewish community, the refugees were given every opportunity to reconstitute their shattered lives. The British policy of humaneness, at a time when so many other doors were closed, was continued after the war at the very time that refugee ships were turned back from Palestine's shores.

Then, in 1956, in the face of a common danger, *Realpolitik* converted this earlier hostility into a virtually outright alliance. For within two years after coming to power in Egypt, President Gamal Abdul Nasser openly repudiated his nation's dependence upon Britain. Supported by the Soviet Union in his bid to challenge the traditional Near Eastern balance of power, Nasser defiantly na-

tionalized the Suez Canal, the historic British lifeline to India. Whitehall's re
sponse was almost reflexive. Britain promptly joined with France and Israel in a
three-pronged attack on Egypt aimed at eliminating Nasser and his regime. The
Western Allies, as it happened, failed in their attempt. Yet the Israeli forces
startled the world by the speed and efficiency with which they accomplished their
more limited objectives. Many an Israeli soldier must have wondered at the
caprice of fate as he recalled that, only a few years before, British soldiers were
in a tacit pact with the Arabs to prevent the establishment of the State of Israel.
It was but another corroboration of Palmerston's dicum that Britain had no permanent friendships, only permanent interests.

Meanwhile the Jewish community in Britain, reinforced substantially by
refugees from the former centres of Jewish life in Europe, was gradually, and
all but totally, transformed. The well-established Brahmins who had dominated
the principal Jewish communal organizations were now being challenged for
leadership by second and third generation families of East European origin.
There had been a steady attrition of social lines, especially when the children of
both groups married into each other's families. The effects of the new leadership
became apparent when the conservative policies of the past were scuttled as no
longer relevant. Thus in 1960 the Anglo-Jewish Association, once a pillar of
aristocratic conservatism, passed a series of forthright resolutions severely condemning the apartheid policies of South Africa. The querulous arguments of the
older families, that the Jewish "newcomers" had no right to jeopardize the security of their co-religionists in South Africa, were firmly brushed aside. This
was a new age, the "newcomers" insisted, and Jewish institutions could no longer
be effective if they shrank from the responsibility of social action where right
and justice were involved.

One small measure of disquiet, especially for those who had escaped from
Hitler's surrealist world, appeared in the anti-Semitic activities of the British
Fascist party, led by Sir Oswald Mosley. During the war, and in the period
immediately following, the Fascists had not dared come out into the open. Too
many British families had lost their sons to German bullets and armament. In
the social and economic dislocation of the post-war period, compounded by the
progressive and humiliating dismantling of the British Empire, England's native
Fascists again took heart. They began to circulate their incendiary leaflets; they
fulminated from the soap boxes of Hyde Park; they organized provocative demonstrations in order to precipitate rioting. The British tradition of freedom of
speech and assembly provided them with considerable leeway. The extremists
were able to preach their doctrines with impunity, but only until they attempted
to invade Jewish neighbourhoods with insulting placards and slogans. The Jewish
war veterans did not rely upon the police to do their work for them. They were
well organized and more than eager to pay off old scores. When enough of the
mauled Fascists ended up in hospitals, the hooligan invasions came to an abrupt

end. It was evident that the anti-Semitism of post-war Britain was more nuisance than danger.

One sentimental note should be added to underscore the close of an era. Because of ancient religious prohibitions, the universities of Oxford and Cambridge were forbidden to grant degrees to Jewish graduates. In 1870, in the rarified days of Gladstone and Disraeli, the restrictions were lifted. The final symbolic step was taken in 1959 when the provision was eliminated which required the Regius Professor of Hebrew to be a canon of Christ Church.

When Hitler's troops marched down the Champs Élysées in the summer of 1940, it appeared as if one of the oldest settlements in Jewish history was destined for liquidation. And, indeed, the rule of the Nazis from 1940 to 1944 was almost as disastrous for the Jews there as it was in other areas of occupied Europe. With the acquiescence of the Vichy puppet government, tens of thousands of French Jews were rounded up, shipped off to concentration camps, and ultimately murdered. The process of extermination was no less grisly here than in Poland or Germany proper. Fortunately, it was somewhat less thorough. When the Liberation came, some 200,000 Jews of their original community of 325,000 still survived. Moreover, enough vitality and faith were left to rekindle the hope that the distinguished Franco-Jewish cultural tradition, a tradition dating back to Gershom and Rashi in the eleventh century, would somehow be sustained. It was in fact a happy augury that the venerable Léon Blum, the widely esteemed Popular Front premier of 1936, and a prisoner of the Nazis through the war years, was called back to leadership as a mentor in the tasks of reconstruction.

Further proof, too, that Nazi ideology had not struck root on French soil was forthcoming when Pierre Mendès-France, the descendant of a distinguished Sephardic family, was elected premier in 1954. Brilliant, resourceful, courageous, trained as an economist with a distinguished record in the French Resistance, Mendès had one of the clearest and most original political minds in Europe. He utilized all these qualities in full measure now as he confronted the terrifying problems spawned by the impending collapse of the French colonial empire. In the post-war years, France had been losing thousands of its sons in futile wars to preserve its holdings in Asia and North Africa. Mendès scored the flabby grandiloquence of his predecessors in office, and insisted upon dealing realistically with the erosion of French military power. Indeed, within a few months after accepting the premiership, he managed to negotiate a practical, honorable settlement both in Indo-China and in Tunisia. If his proposals had also been accepted for Algeria, it is not unlikely that the long years of exhausting warfare that followed might have been avoided. Winston Churchill voiced the prevailing consensus in Western capitals when he hailed Mendès as the ablest statesman produced by France since the days of Clemenceau.

Anti-Semitism had by no means vanished in France. Yet it was significant

that when Jew-hatred reappeared in more than isolated personal incidents it was
not a heritage of Nazism. Rather the reaction drew both from the classical anti-
Dreyfusard vocabulary of the past half century and the crises that plagued
France's economy in the early 1950's. Jews were natural scapegoats. In 1954 and
1955, as the nation's mounting inflation endangered savings and wages, a petit-
bourgeois demagogue, Pierre Poujade, launched a bid for political support by
appealing to his countrymen's traditional hatred of the tax collector. Shrewdly
identifying the Jews with the nation's ills, Poujade demanded the elimination
of "the Rosenkranzes and the Rosenkopfs" and the Jewish "brain trusts" who
were "corrupting" French economic life. At the peak of his influence he won
fifty-two seats in the Chamber of Deputies. But within a year, as the inflation
was brought under control and the economic crisis eased, Poujade was repudiated
and took his place in history along with Edmond Drumont, Jacques Doriot, and
the other forgotten marginal men of the lunatic fringe.

In truth, the diplomatic climate in which France functioned did not encourage
anti-Semitism. For even as the nation struggled to retain its North African
holdings, Egypt had become a prime staging area for the training and indoctrination of Algerian rebels. Israel and France, each menaced by the accelerating
xenophobia in the Moslem world, found themselves in a natural alliance. Israel's
search for defensive weapons was thereupon rewarded by the French government. A steady stream of planes and tanks, often the newest models, flowed
from France to Israel. As was noted, the two countries co-operated closely in the
1956 military assault upon Egypt.

In the internal life of French Jewry, however, the problems of sustaining and
strengthening a creative group identity proved to be uncommonly serious. Assimilation had made major inroads in Jewish community life. The rate of intermarriage was high, indeed the highest in Europe. Moreover, there appeared to
be a curiously widespread conversionary movement to Roman Catholicism, a
trend centred mainly among those who had suffered most from the Nazis! By
a strange irony, reinforcements arrived from the fugitive Jews of newly independent Morocco and Algeria. These were a backward, semi-literate population,
who for years had depended upon the Alliance Israélite Universelle for philanthropic and cultural support. Now, for all the financial burdens the newcomers
imposed on their kinsmen, they brought with them at least an unquestioning,
"integral" Jewish loyalty which provided a stimulus and an example for the
more acculturated European Jews who had lived in France for generations.

Nor was it possible to underestimate the impact of the State of Israel upon the
Jewish intellectuals of France. Many of these were leaders in French literary
and artistic life. Visiting Israel not infrequently, borrowing from the unself-
conscious pride of Israel's citizens, the nativized French-Jewish intelligentsia
turned with reawakened interest to Jewish themes for their self-expression. Only
the passage of time will determine whether this newly aroused folk-identity

represents the wave of the future in the largest Jewish community on the continent of Europe.

8. CONTEMPORARY RUSSIA: STALIN AND KHRUSHCHEV

For nearly two decades after the death of Lenin in 1924, Russian history was dominated by the iron personality of Josef Stalin. His dictatorship was as thorough and ruthless as any in history. Stalin and his colleagues on the Politbureau justified Soviet totalitarianism as a cruel but necessary transition until the ingrained corruptions of bourgeois civilization had been permanently eliminated.

All the Soviet Union's multitude of nationalities suffered from the subordination of law to caprice, the sacrifice of consumer goods for military strength, with its consequent sub-marginal standard of living. For the Jews, however, the Stalin period brought with it a subtle, but measurable return of pre-revolutionary discrimination. The rosy promises of the early Bolshevik days, that anti-Semitism would be treated as a counter-revolutionary movement and severely punished, were not only forgotten but were contemptuously repudiated. Neither Stalin nor his close advisers made any secret of their personal anti-Semitic bias. Jews were hounded out of key party positions, denied equal opportunity in educational institutions, and increasingly exposed to ridicule or public scorn.

The pressure of Stalinist tyranny was felt in yet another way. All minority groups within the Soviet empire had been encouraged to develop and sustain their ethnic individuality, thus fulfilling the Leninist concept of "socialism in content but nationalism in form." But the principle of hospitality to folk distinctiveness was not extended to the Jews, one of the largest of Russia's national minorities. The government's official explanation of its policy was that the Jews were unassimilable, that they were congenitally loyal to Palestine—or, later, Israel—and that they could not be trusted to place devotion to Moscow above other ties. In a dictatorship where the cardinal sin was the likelihood of deviation or diversion, a suspect group, homogeneous, intellectually vibrant, internationally minded, would naturally be a prime target. Similarly, too, the Jews fulfilled a a classical role: as scapegoat for the more than occasional failures within the Soviet regime.

The war on the Jews therefore assumed two forms. Every attempt was made to destroy their ethnocentrism, to sever their historic connexions with their folk history and with their kinsmen in other nations. The Jews were listed as a separate cultural group, yet not permitted to develop their culture freely. On the other hand, paradoxically, instead of providing opportunity for those who chose assimilation, who were eager to fit into the total Russian pattern, the government systematically closed these avenues. The official policy was apparently to deracinate the Jews in every way possible, to abolish their distinctiveness, but simultaneously to prevent their absorption into the mainstream of Soviet life.

During the early years of World War II, this anti-Semitic policy was not quite as overt. Jews who won decorations for exceptional service received their awards; but they were hailed as Russians and not as Jews. The galling prohibitions in worship and education were relaxed somewhat. In the last year of the war, however, and afterward, when the Nazi danger passed, Soviet anti-Semitism acquired official status. Indeed, until the death of Stalin, in 1953, the Jews lived through "the Black Years," an experience that recalled the grimmest period of Nicholas II. The drive was resumed to purge Jewish civil servants who had moved back into the government hierarchy. Employment opportunities were again severely restricted. Jewish schools were closed down. When synagogues fell into disrepair, their renovation was prohibited. The public explanation for the anti-Semitic program rarely varied: the Jews were Zionist-oriented; their leaders were in the pay of the American Central Intelligence Agency; they yearned for the old bourgeois culture; they could not fit into Soviet objectives.

The purge extended rapidly to the Soviet Union's satellites. When the Communist leadership of Czechoslovakia was labeled as traitorous, a disproportionate number of those who were hanged were Jews. Jews were evicted from all party positions in Poland and Roumania. The climax of this intensified Judeophobia took place in 1953 when Pravda announced that a group of physicians had been arrested for the "murder," several years earlier, of the two ranking Soviet leaders who were closest to Stalin. Six of the doctors were Jews. When placed on trial, they "confessed" their guilt, dutifully admitting their participation in a "conspiracy" with the Zionists and the CIA. These admissions were widely publicized, and set the stage for an anti-Jewish campaign unprecedented, in the Soviet Union, for its virulence. The caricatures that appeared in the Soviet press were duplicates of those Streicher had used in Nazi Germany. Many Jewish families sought desperately, though unsuccessfully, to flee the country. But the very attempt was cited as further proof of Jewish unreliability.

Then, in December of 1953, Stalin died. Slowly, but perceptibly, the miasma of fear and terror that had befogged the country for so long began to lift. For a year or more, all moves in the direction of reform were timorous, as if the new leadership was not quite sure that Stalin's ghost had been laid. Then suddenly the breakthrough came. After a scramble for power, Nikita Khrushchev, a wily Ukrainian party veteran, emerged as undisputed leader of the Communist Central Committee. At the Twentieth Congress in 1956 he launched into a detailed and passionate denunciation of the Stalinist crimes and promised an end to "the cult of personal leadership." A thaw set in. Tensions began to ease. Khrushchev promised greater emphasis upon consumer goods, a higher standard of living for the Soviet people, indeed a standard that would steadily improve until it would surpass the vaunted achievements of the Western capitalist world.

Above all Khrushchev promised to end police state terrorism. Western statesmen and journalists who visited the Soviet Union in ensuing years reported that he kept his promise. The law apparently was moving into a more dominant role in Soviet society, and was gradually supplanting the mechanism of terror. In 1960 the dreaded MVO, the secret police apparatus, was dissolved. It was significant that the anti-Party leaders who had challenged Khrushchev's rise to power, notably Malenkov, Molotov, Bulganin, and Zhukov, were not executed, but rather were given minor assignments, and, in this way, were contained. In 1961 Khrushchev felt strong enough to dictate the removal of Stalin's body from its place of honor next to the tomb of Lenin; it was reburied beside the graves of lesser functionaries near the Kremlin wall.

Unhappily, the thaw did not bring with it a fundamental change in the status of the Jews. As Soviet citizens they may have shared in the general relaxation of terror tactics and procedures. Nevertheless, the Moscow regime remained unalterably determined to emasculate Jewish identity. Overt religious persecution had stopped; but the proscription of religious teaching continued. Khrushchev was less blatant in his methods than Stalin; but, in his relations to Jews, he was hardly more sympathetic. Again and again observers left interviews with the premier sensing his undoubted personal animus.

As in other spheres, however, the Soviet regime discovered that its Jewish policy could no longer be formulated entirely independently of public opinion. In 1961, for example, a national celebration was planned in honor of Ilya Ehrenburg, a widely renowned Soviet journalist who had somehow survived all changes in government policy. Ehrenburg, after a lifetime of opportunism, now spoke feelingly of his Jewish identity. "Yes," he said, "I am a Russian writer, but so long as there is even one anti-Semite, I will continue when asked about my nationality to answer with pride and vigour, a Jew." What was significant in this statement was less Ehrenburg's sentiment than its candour; he could speak feelingly in public and still be heartily respected by his fellow craftsmen and by government officials. Another episode in the autumn of 1961 also raised hopes that a more tolerant climate was emerging. Evgeny Evtushenko, Russia's most popular young poet, published a poem in the *Literary Gazette,* the organ of the Soviet Writers Union, which paid tribute to the Jews of Babi Yar. A huge ravine near Kiev, Babi Yar served as a mass grave for the thousands of Jews who had been slaughtered in the single largest Nazi extermination action of World War II. Evtushenko indicted anti-Semitism in history and, by implication, in Russian life itself. He mourned the fact that the sacrifice of the Jews at Babi Yar had been forgotten; indeed, he wrote as one who carried the guilt with shame. Many of the literary set attacked Evtushenko for his sentiments. But the fact remained that he had written with complete forthrightness, challenging the Party Line, and his poem had been published and was hailed by his younger contemporaries.

In 1964 the Jewish population of Russia numbered between two and a half and three million people. Although Soviet nationality laws no longer required ethnic groups to show proof of their identification, two and a quarter million

Jews preferred to state their national identity in the registration of 1959. In view of the advantages of "passing," this was a remarkable folk-commitment. It hardly signified a religious commitment, however. Forty years of government and Party hostility left their impact. Less than one hundred synagogues now remained in the whole of the Soviet Union, and these were frequented mainly by old people, wistfully fingering their tattered prayer books. The cemeteries were falling into neglect, and were gradually being converted into public parks. Each time the government launched a new attack on religion, and these were frequent, it singled out the Jewish faith. Judaism's reliance on Bible, Talmud, and Jewish education, was a special target.

Thus it was that one of the largest Jewish settlements in history found itself in a tragic, an all-but-hopeless impasse. The government brought every pressure to bear to destroy the Jews' individuality, their *esprit de corps*. At the same time, the Communists recognized that if the Jews were to be assimilated their influence on national life would become even greater, and this was feared with pathological intensity. When Jews sought to live as Jews, they were punished. When they sought to merge into the totality of Russian life, they were turned back. When they sought to emigrate, they were denounced as disloyal. For the Jews, at least, there is little evidence yet that the era of Khrushchev has signified more than a kind of false dawn.

In the realm of foreign policy, too, the Jews were destined to serve the Soviet premier as a favourite *bête noire*. Admittedly, Russia's belligerent and hectoring attitude toward Israel could not be attributed to anti-Semitism. Here naked *Realpolitik* was the key, as the recurrent shifts in Soviet diplomacy made abundantly clear. In 1948, when the Jews of Palestine were involved in a bitter civil war against the British mandate, the Soviets lent their support to the Zionist cause. Later the Russians voted for Partition in the United Nations, and promptly recognized Israel's independence. Of course, Moscow's purpose in backing the Jews was transparent; an independent Jewish State appeared to offer a more likely base for Soviet expansion in the Near East than either a British mandate or a feudal Arab sheikhdom. Unfortunately for the Soviets, the Republic of Israel proved to be ardently democratic, and firmly committed to Western ideals, if not always to Western policies. Indignant at this "betrayal," the Soviet government swiftly and radically altered its Near Eastern policy. The Party Line now depicted Israel as a tool of Wall Street, an agent for imperialism, a cog in the apparatus of capitalist exploitation. Economic ideology exerted little influence on this diplomatic position. In its new love affair with the Arabs, Moscow preferred to ignore the feudal structure of Moslem society, the poverty and hopelessness of the Arab *fellahin,* the fundamental irreconcilability between Islam and Marxism. Conversely, the Soviets reserved special poisoned bouquets for Ben-Gurion, for Histadrut, Israel's labour federation, and for Mapai, the powerful Labour party of Israel.

During the early 1960's the Soviet government denounced Israel's developing commercial and cultural relations with Africa as a conspiracy designed to hoodwink the emerging nations of that continent. After the French exploded an atomic bomb in the Sahara, Khrushchev linked the French and the Israelis as partners in a "vicious imperialism." In 1956 when Nasser defied the British and the West by seizing the Suez Canal, Moscow warmly hailed the Egyptian president as an emancipator. In the Suez campaign of the same year, when England, France, and Israel struck virtually simultaneously to end the Nasserist threat to the Near Eastern balance of power, Russia threatened to loose its rockets unless the invaders withdrew. Soviet arms aid to the Arabs, particularly the Egyptians, reached nearly a billion dollars by 1964, and economic aid in this period extended even beyond that. For Khrushchev, however, the enormous expenditure seemed to represent a worthwhile investment; he viewed the Arab bloc as his likeliest weapon of penetration into the Near and Middle East.

CHAPTER THIRTY-THREE

THE NEW STATE OF ISRAEL

I. THE WAR FOR INDEPENDENCE

THE period between the first Arab attacks and the final withdrawal of the British offered the largest challenge to Jewish fortitude and tenacity. The basic strategy was a delaying action, an action to hold the territory that had been assigned by partition, to protect the laboriously created Jewish settlements that were marooned in the proposed Arab zones, and to keep open all lines of communication, especially the lines to Jerusalem. There was considerable loss of life and there were dark periods when thoughts turned from the glorious tradition of Maccabean victory to the tragic defeats of Bethar and Masada. But after the first calamitous setbacks the Jews were able to hold their own. Indeed, on May 13, by a series of brilliant stratagems, they captured the all-Arab city of Jaffa and watched unbelievingly as the huge population fled in terror. Confidence returned with a rush as the days of British occupation ran out and freed both sides to test their fullest strength.

At midnight of May 14 the High Commissioner and his staff and the last soldiers of the British colonial power left Haifa, officially terminating the thirty-year mandate. Even as the British colours were hauled down, the provisional government, in a deeply moving scene, proclaimed the independent State of Israel and vowed to defend it to the end with life and honour. Arab armies attacked at once, on all sides, in full-scale war, confident that sheer numbers and vastly superior armament would quickly overwhelm the tiny island of Israeli resistance. The issue was joined at last, and it was to be determined not in Whitehall nor in Washington, nor in the Vatican, nor at Lake Success, but on the field of battle.

There were few responsible statesmen among the nations of the world who doubted that the Arab victory would be quick and decisive. For the odds seemed to be overwhelming. All the Arab states were involved—Transjordan, Syria, Lebanon, Egypt, Yemen, Iraq, and Saudi Arabia. There were additional volunteers who came from the Sudan and from the North African states. The Arabs drew from a population of about 30,000,000; the total Israeli population was approximately 650,000. These did not live in a compact territory, but were dispersed among hundreds of thousands of Palestine Arabs. For months the Arab states had been permitted to accumulate modern warcraft, including tanks and planes. Behind them was the powerful influence of Britain. Indeed, Transjordan's crack Legion was financed and officered by the British.

But the Israelis had a different kind of strength. Theirs was a small but firmly disciplined army, the nucleus of which had been trained while fighting with the British and the Allies as comrades in arms in World War II against a common enemy. They had young, vigorous, brilliant commanders. They were reinforced by volunteers who came from the United States and the Western democracies, and these were especially helpful in the tiny Israeli air force and in coping with the bewildering problems of organization and supply. But more than armament and tight military discipline was the desperate last-ditch spirit with which the Israelis fought. The Arabs who invaded the land never fully understood how much this counted. Their own men were almost listless by comparison, for they seemed to have little personal stake in the outcome of the war. When Dr. Weizmann was asked why the Egyptians did not stand up well, he replied: "The men were too lean, and the officers were too fat." But the Israelis knew in their hearts that the land they defended represented the last stop. If it were lost, there could be no other alternative, either for them or for the millions who were still encysted in the transit camps and the waiting points of Europe, Africa, and Asia.

The war was fought in a series of short intense efforts, punctuated by truces enforced by the great powers through the United Nations. The first stage lasted about four weeks, from May 15 to June 11, and the main assaults came from the Arab forces of Egypt, Transjordan, Syria, and Lebanon.

The Egyptians crossed the frontier at several points and quickly occupied all the territory that had been assigned by the Partition Commission. But they failed to capture Tel Aviv, their main objective. Tiny settlements all along the way offered frenzied resistance, slowing the advance and exacting heavy casualties from the invaders. Even as in the last days of the British mandate, it was Israeli strategy to fight a holding action, waiting for much-needed armaments, for reinforcements of manpower, and for better organization and consolidation. The Negeb was lost, and with it such centres as Bethlehem and Beersheba. But so long as the capital held out, despite ever mounting daily air assaults, there was faith that the Arabs would be turned back.

The attacks of Transjordan also led to stalemate. In the months following partition there had been many skirmishes during which the Arabs had aimed at the capture of Jerusalem. They had quickly secured the Old City. Now, when full-scale war began, they struck out against the New City, which was one of the chief sources of Israeli strength. After bitter fighting, the north approaches fell. The loss was heartbreaking, for it meant that the Hebrew University and the Hadassah Hospital passed into Arab hands. The ring kept tightening and there was constant danger that all communication with the rest of Palestine would be cut. Heavy shelling went on day and night and food and water grew scarce. But the courage of the New City defenders never wavered and convoys somehow kept getting through. Operation Burma Road carved out a new precariously defended highway, and though no day passed without a bloody toll of men and equipment, the route remained open. Even when the Legion was joined by forces of Egypt, Iraq, and Syria, the crucial Israeli defences could not be breached.

Meantime the Syrians, occasionally reinforced by the Legion, struck in Galilee. The Israelis were strongly entrenched in a solid belt across the south, but they were committed to many scattered settlements in the north and the east, and here they were quite vulnerable. The Syrians were led by General Kaukji, who was a formidable military figure with a reputation for ruthlessness which he had won in the disturbances of the 1930's. At first there was an almost clean sweep by the Arabs. But after the initial stunning defeats the Israelis rallied. They saved the Rutenberg works on the Yarmak River. They captured the Arab fortress and the city of Acre, which boasted the remembrance of the long resistance against Napoleon. When the Israelis moved to the offensive and took the approaches to Mount Gilboa, a thrill of hope passed through the beleaguered little state. On June 11 the United Nations, through Count Folke Bernadotte of Sweden, forced a truce. Israel was sure now that the combined might of the Arab states would no longer suffice to crush out the reinforced national will.

When the results of the first phase of the war were recapitulated, it was evident that Israeli confidence was not the artificial buoyancy of desperation. The severest test had been successfully met. In the south, Egypt had taken the Negeb, assigned to Israel by the Partition Commission; but the Israelis had held firmly everywhere else and had added the city of Jaffa. The Legion was in firm control of the Old City of Jerusalem and had taken over Mount Scopus with its revered Jewish buildings and treasures. But the New City had not fallen, and a route had been carved out which linked it to Israeli-held territory and nullified all efforts at siege. Although the Arabs held a solid section of Galilee, the western areas that had been assigned to the Arabs had now fallen into Israeli hands. The most decisive change was in the status of the Arab population. In the area originally assigned to Israel there had been more than 400,000 Arabs. All but 60,000 had fled precipitously during the preliminary skirmishes and the month of all-out war. A Jewish state, with almost as many Arabs in it as Jews, had been part of every plan and had been resignedly accepted by the Israeli leaders. The battlefield was apparently resolving issues that all the delicately balanced diplomatic settlements had until now only complicated.

The four weeks' truce was an uneasy period of scarcely concealed impatience on both sides. The Arabs resented the truce, believing that their best opportunity for success lay in pressing their initial advantage before the Israelis could weld their regular and guerrilla units into a more efficient military force. The

Israelis waited only for the reinforcements, which had not come more quickly because there were endless embargoes and international restrictions to bypass.

The Arabs struck again, on July 9, to usher in the second phase of the war. The renewed fighting lasted less than ten days and resulted, despite serious casualties, in a devastating Israeli victory. This time, after rolling with the first Arab punches, the Israeli forces took the offensive. Their main objective was to remove all threat to the New City of Jerusalem and to protect its corridor to the rest of Israel. On July 11 Operation Dani brought the capture of Lydda; the next day the equally important strategic centre of Ramleh fell. Thousands of Arabs who lived in the area fled. The Israeli attack carried so much power that Latrun and Ramallah were endangered. Their fall would have led to the capture of all of central Palestine, including Jerusalem and Hebron. A second truce, firmly imposed by the United Nations, intervened. Meantime, in the north the renewed fighting also brought startling Israeli victories. Operation Dekel was launched primarily against the Syrians. Tiberius was cleared and the all-Christian city of Nazareth fell to the Israeli forces. General Kaukji barely escaped capture, and his armies were saved from annihilation only by the second truce.

The United Nations truce chief was a Swedish nobleman, Count Bernadotte, head of the Swedish Red Cross, a seasoned diplomat who had served as intermediary between the Allies and Nazi Germany in the closing days of World War II. Under the best circumstances his role as impartial arbitrator could not have been a happy one, for the issues were ulcerated and both sides were violently contumacious. The Arabs assailed Bernadotte for beginning with the assumption that the Israelis had certain fundamental rights in Palestine. The Israelis accused him of being too much under British influence and speaking too often in Bevin's accents. Bernadotte moved patiently between the torrents of abuse, exploring his tortuous way on the realistic principle that there could be no peace unless each contender made concessions. He pressed for a settlement that recognized the results of the fighting. The Negeb and all of Jerusalem ought now to go to the Arabs, with international supervision of the Holy Places. Western Galilee, which the Israeli forces had won in the resumption of the war, ought now to be assigned to Israel. From every point of view, he reasoned—geographic, economic, and military—this made more sense than the partition arrangements did.

The Israeli government flatly rejected the bid. They could not yield on Jerusalem, for this would be as catastrophic morally as it would be politically. They could not sign away their hopes in the Negeb, for this was the one great undeveloped reservoir upon which depended the economic expansion of the little state and the possibility of absorbing large masses of immigrants. The Arabs were just as adamant; they denounced any settlement that recognized Israel as a sovereign state, however delimited its territory. In their refusal to negotiate they revealed serious cleavages in their own ranks. Transjordan was assailed by the other Arab states. The latter had no intention of permitting Abdullah to enlarge the state of Jordan by absorbing Arab Palestine. Nor, even more emphatically, would they stand by supinely and allow Jerusalem, with all its hallowed Moslem memories and traditions, to go to Abdullah. Abdullah's reply scarcely hid his contempt for his allies. In a proclamation on August 6 to the Arab Legion he said: "Your army has preserved the holiness of Jerusalem. We and the others went into this fight jointly. Here we are. Where are the others? We have fought and progressed, but we have not seen the progress made by others." Count Bernadotte had not brought Arabs and Israelis any closer; he had inadvertently succeeded in driving a wedge between the Arabs themselves!

On September 17 the world was shocked by the news that Count Bernadotte, while visiting the New City of Jerusalem, had been assassinated. The crime was apparently committed by a group of Sternists, irresponsible terrorists who imagined that they were helping the cause of freedom by eliminating the Count. The Israeli leaders denounced the "insanity" of the gunmen who by their act had shown again that they were "traitors to the people and enemies of its liberty." Members of the Sternist gang were rounded up and jailed and the guerrilla groups were outlawed. Irgun announced that it would immediately disband and accept the discipline of the Haganah. But the guilty parties were never discovered and it took many months for the infant state to live down the embarrassment and the obloquy of the assassination. Dr. Ralph Bunche, a brilliant and resourceful American Negro, who had been assisting Count Bernadotte, became the Acting Mediator. He declared that the best memorial to his fallen chief would be the successful culmination of the truce negotiations.

Before Dr. Bunche could really square away, however, there was a third round in the war, the decisive round, and it brought the Arabs to the gloomy realization that the Israelis had become too strong and too well entrenched to be attacked with impunity. The Egyptians learned this in two disastrous campaigns. They attacked in mid-October and were beaten back to their own frontiers, the Israeli forces taking over a good portion of the Negeb. They tried again late in December, and this time they were routed so thoroughly that not only was the rest of the Negeb taken over, but Israeli troops actually crossed into Egypt. They could have marched straight on to Cairo, but the Security Council sternly ordered a halt. Other Israeli columns pushed down to the southern end of the Red Sea and threatened to move into Transjordan. This precipitated a dramatic international incident, for the British had defence treaties with Transjordan and threatened to go to war with Israel if there were any violation of Abdullah's territory.

By now Egypt was ready for an armistice. The stunning military defeats had bred an ominous restlessness among the people, and the efficiency and the integrity of the military and the governing cliques were being openly questioned. This was to lead ultimately to a sweeping revolution in which King, councillors, and their hangers-on were driven out. On February 24, 1949, after weeks of patient negotiation, Dr. Bunche brought the Egyptian and Israeli representatives together and the armistice was signed which, for all practical purposes, ended the war.

Dr. Bunche now applied his unusual talents to provide a face-saving formula for Abdullah and Transjordan. The wily old Emir was now not too obdurate. Much of what he wanted he already had, and the unity of the Arab League had never been a principle worth defending too strenuously. He had been proclaimed by his Parliament as King of both Transjordan and Arab Palestine. The Old City of Jerusalem was tightly in his control. The furious protests of the other Arab states against his unilateral decisions left him completely unperturbed. Dr. Bunche made steady headway with him, and when Iraq commissioned Transjordan to act on its behalf as well, it was possible by April to sign an armistice with both states.

Meantime the ever sanguine General Kaukji, leading reorganized forces from Syria and Lebanon, tried still again to overwhelm Israel. His appetite was whetted by a few preliminary victories. But on October 28 the Israelis turned to the offensive in what they called Operation Hiram. This time all of Galilee was overrun and the Israelis crossed the Lebanon frontier and took over a number of Lebanon villages. Kaukji was completely routed, and retired in disgrace. Syrian resentment was so deep over the humiliating showing of its forces that a revolution ousted the old regime and brought in a new dictator. The time was now opportune for the resumption of truce negotiations, and Dr. Bunche pressed hard to bring Syria and Lebanon to reason. The negotiations dragged on for many months, but on July 20 Syria and Lebanon joined all the other Arab states in signing the armistice. By mid-August the United Nations, recognizing that the war in effect was over, recalled Dr. Bunche and terminated the office of the Mediator. Dr. Bunche had every reason for satisfaction and thoroughly deserved the Nobel Peace Prize which was awarded to him for his extraordinary services.

The Israeli triumph created a new power in the Near East. The kaleidoscope of shreds and patches which had been pieced together in the earlier United Nations discussions had been scrapped completely. There was now a strong State of Israel, its territory small but homogeneous, its viability no longer jeopardized by bizarre political boundaries or grotesque economic compromises. The dilemma of an unmanageable Arab population in the Jewish areas had been virtually resolved by the action of the Arabs themselves, who had fled into the surrounding Arab lands. There were still enormous problems to be faced, but they would now be met, not in the spirit of panic, but in the spirit of confidence and dignity.

2. SYMBOLS OF SOVEREIGNTY

In the waning hours of the British mandate the independent State of Israel was proclaimed. After an eloquent preamble that summarized the historic struggle to establish a free new life in Israel, the Declaration of Independence went on to pledge unrestricted immigration from all the lands of the world; full social and political equality, without distinction of religion, race, or sex for all citizens; freedom of religion, conscience, education, and culture. It pledged co-operation with the United Nations in bringing peace to Palestine and appealed for admission to the United Nations. It offered a neighbourly hand to all Arab states and their peoples.

Within a few hours after the Declaration of Independence, President Truman announced *de facto* recognition of the new state. It was appropriate for the oldest republic to be the first to welcome the newest democracy into the family of free nations. While this was not full *de jure* recognition, it was a decisive act of friendship at a moment when the outlook for survival seemed bleak indeed. Russia, which had spearheaded the resolution for partition, was not to be outdone. Three days after Truman's announcement, the Kremlin extended *de jure* recognition and, because it was the first to make this gesture, the Soviet Minister to Tel Aviv became the dean of the diplomatic corps in Israel. The United States then imperturbably raised its mission to an Embassy and at once the American Ambassador took precedence over the Soviet Minister! This kind of diplomatic nose-thumbing was part of the developing cold war between the East and the West. What mattered much more was the prompt recognition of Israel by the nations of the world. Within a few months after the Declaration of Independence, all but the Moslem states had followed the example of the United States and Russia. To a tiny beleaguered state, fighting off enemies on every frontier, such recognition meant infinitely more than diplomatic amenities. It meant morale and it was almost as valuable in sustaining resistance as any shipments of arms.

In November, on the first anniversary of the partition resolution, Israel applied for membership in the United Nations. It was sponsored by the American and the Russian delegates. The initial application encountered stormy weather and was laid over mainly through British opposition. Sir Alexander Cadogan, still following the line of the sulky boycott, objected that Israel had not yet demonstrated sovereign capacity, and that its application was premature. The British government apparently required sterner guarantees from Israel than from many of the shaky states whose admission it had sponsored or supported. The diplomatic battle was renewed in later sessions of the Security Council and the General Assembly. Then on May 11, 1949, when the war had been won, regular elections had been held, and a firm democratic government had been established, Israel was voted in, to become the fifty-ninth member. It called for no artistry to find drama in the historic moment when the blue and white flag of Zion went up on the flagpole in front of the United Nations meeting-place, nor again when Moshe Sharett, the Israeli Foreign Minister, was escorted to his seat in the Assembly of the United Nations.

Equally stirring was the symbolism involved in the return to Israel of the body of Dr. Theodore Herzl, the father of modern Zionism. On August 14, 1949 Herzl's coffin was taken from the cemetery in Vienna and flown on an Israeli plane to Lydda. There it was received by the Prime Minister and the entire Cabinet, who accompanied it to Tel Aviv. The bier rested in the esplanade in front of the building used by the Parliament, and multitudes from every part of Israel passed by to salute the man whose dream had now so miraculously come true. It was then slowly driven to Jerusalem, following the route that Herzl had taken when he went to meet Kaiser Wilhelm in a historic interview fifty years before. The permanent grave was on one of the highest hills of Jerusalem, where it had been dug out of solid rock. Into the grave with the remains of the founder of Zionism went little bags of earth from each community, brought with reverence by a chosen delegate. The solemn ceremony ended when the guards presented arms and the ancient Kaddish was recited.

The first government of the newly created state was little more than a provisional council, drawn from representative elements and clothed by the emergency with the authority to make the initial far-reaching decisions. But from the very beginning, right in the heart of siege and assault, it was planned to establish permanent democratic institutions and to govern through them. A census was taken in November 1948. It listed 728,000 inhabitants, of whom 471,000 were men and women above the age of eighteen, and therefore eligible to vote. The first elections were held on January 25, 1949, and 440,000 cast votes, an extraordinarily large proportion of those who were eligible. The voters included many thousands of Arabs who had chosen to cast their lot with the Israeli state. And since women had equal rights with men, thousands of Moslem women voted for the first time in history.

Israel was inevitably influenced by Continental practice, and there were many political parties, divided by economic and religious issues and by deep divergencies in foreign policy. In the first election only four groups polled more than ten per cent of the electorate. The Mapai, the moderate Socialists, Ben Gurion's own party, polled about thirty-four per cent of the total and represented the largest single bloc. The Mapam, also Socialist but closer to the Soviet foreign policy than to the orientation of the Western democracies, polled fourteen per cent. The religious groups, with theocratic aspirations for the new state, polled twelve per cent. The Herut, comprised of remnants of the Irgun and the Sternists and others who were violently nationalistic, polled about eleven per cent. The great surprise of the election was the negligible vote drawn by the General Zionists, who primarily represented the middle class and the moderate economic approach of free enterprise. These polled only nine per cent.

The first Parliament, the Knesset, met in Jerusalem on February 14. The choice of Jerusalem as the newly proclaimed capital, apart from sentimental reasons, was meant as a clear warning to those who still hoped that it could be placed under international control. Dr. Chaim Weizmann came forward to convene the first Jewish Parliament in two thousand years. Infirm, tired, in pain, he could scarcely see through the blinding cataracts of his ailing eyes; but he rose to the climactic moment of his life as he linked the fate of Israel with the fate of the democratic principle in the Western world. "Today is a great day in our lives," he told the distinguished audience, which included diplomatic representatives from all the world. "Let us not be thought too arrogant if we say that it is also a great day in the history of the world. In this hour a message of hope and good cheer issues from this place, from this sacred city, to all oppressed people and to all who are struggling for freedom and equality." By now the venerable old man had little more to contribute; it was a time for youth and vigour. But the Knesset would not forget the past and what Weizmann had meant in the days of the locust. They elected him the first President of Israel, and to the sound of the shofer he took the oath of office.

The first Prime Minister was, of course, David Ben Gurion, whose preparation for the historic task went back to the days when Palestine was a wilderness. He was born in Poland in 1886 and, after abortive revolutionary activity there, came to Palestine in 1906, undeterred by the fact that his assignments fell in what were then the death valleys of Galilee. His early interest in the political aspects of Zionism embroiled him with the Turkish government, which arrested him, sentenced him to death, and only at the last moment commuted the sentence to deportation. He was in the United States at the outbreak of the First World War and returned at once to join the Jewish Legion, which fought with distinction in the liberation of Palestine. After the war he rose to leadership in the Palestine labour movement and created Histadruth. Through all the unhappy years of the British mandate Ben Gurion built the strength of labour, guided the economic life of the Jewish settlements, and laid the foundations for Haganah and the Army of Liberation. During the long months of war he served as civilian commander-in-chief and, more than any other man, was the fulcrum and the rallying-point for victory. Now the white-maned hero was called to the tasks of peace as the first Prime Minister.

It was foreordained that the nucleus of the new government would be Ben Gurion's own Mapai party. Almost from the beginning the economy of the country had been a democratic collectivism. The means of production and the channels of distribution were largely controlled by the labour groups, primarily through the great labour confederation, Histadruth. As Ben Gurion sought to build a coalition, he knew that he must avoid any partnership with Mapam. Apart from his own loyalty to the democratic principles of the West, he would otherwise sacrifice any expectation of help from the United States. Nor could he have any traffic with Herut, for these firebrands represented extremist positions in politics and diplomacy which were abhorrent to the great majority of the people. There was some hope that he might seek an alliance with the General Zionists and in this way encourage private investment when it was so desperately needed; but Ben Gurion was unwilling, at this stage, to qualify any of the objectives of the labour groups, even if modification meant the immediate bracing and buttressing of the economy.

The Prime Minister turned therefore to the religious groups and invited them to join the coalition he was building. The resultant partnership was loaded with grief. The demands of the religious bloc in the field of education and in regulating the social life of the country were a far cry from the secularist program of socialism and from the religious libertarianism of Mapai and the majority of the people. But Ben Gurion apparently preferred the occasional embarrassments that stemmed from the alliance with the religious bloc more than the concessions in economic objective and practice which must follow from any relationship with the General Zionists.

For nearly four years, though plagued by internal disputes and by frequent parliamentary crises, the Prime Minister kept to his resolve. Late in 1950, when the problems of holding the coalition together became too oppressive, Ben Gurion resigned and called for new elections. The mandate was no clearer, but Ben Gurion still refused any relationship with the General Zionists, though their proportion of the votes nearly doubled to sixteen per cent. It was not until late in 1952, when inflation, unemployment, and declining foreign trade seriously threatened the economy, and when the General Zionists won impressive new strength in the third election, that Ben Gurion yielded. When he promised to modify economic controls and to encourage the investment of private capital, the General Zionists joined the new government. The combined strength of Mapai and the General Zionists in the Knesset was solid enough to ensure a stability that the country had not enjoyed since the beginning of its national life.

3. THE INGATHERING OF THE EXILES

A pledge had been made in the Declaration of Independence that immigration would be welcomed from every part of the world. Under the British it had been held to a minimum, and it averaged about eighteen thousand a year. In the last months of the mandate the number was considerably stepped up. Once the British were gone and it was no longer necessary to link immigration with smuggling and underground activity, the flood really began. In little more than a year, a quarter of a million newcomers entered Israel. The next year the tempo was again accelerated, and then again. Soon the average touched eighteen thousand a month and reached a peak of more than a thousand a day! By June

1951, in three years of independence, a total of 638,000 Jewish immigrants had been brought in, virtually doubling the original population. There was no precedent for such an extraordinary voluntary absorption.

The consequences, in terms of radically decreased standards of living, frightened the more conservative elements in the original population. They clamored for some practical restrictions on the tempo of increase. But in the first years none of the problems of absorption seemed so serious as the need to rescue the remnants of the Nazi fury, and the need to bring in manpower to defend the land and to pre-empt its open spaces. So they came, in their tens of thousands, the miraculous remnants of the millions who had been done to death. For all too many it was already too late to hope for a new life. They were too old, too broken, too distraught, to be of any use in a country that required youth and strength and hope. The doors of the most powerful democracies remained closed, but Israel continued to set an example of humaneness in a world where pity and sensitiveness were fast becoming alien and unwelcome virtues.

The Nazi concentration camps had been succeeded by huge centres for displaced persons, and Israel felt that its prime obligation was to empty these as fast as transportation could be provided. In these camps were nationals of central Europe, the last survivors of the Western lands that the Nazis had overrun and looted—Germans, Austrians, Czechs. There were also many tens of thousands of east Europeans who had been uprooted or had been captured by the Nazis in the years of their military heyday—Poles, Roumanians, Hungarians, and Russians. Many chose to return to their former homes, but the great majority eagerly welcomed the opportunity to begin afresh in Israel. The displacement camps therefore provided a large proportion of immigration in the first years of independence. Before 1951 there were no heavy restrictions on the emigration of Jews who wished to go to Israel from the Iron Curtain countries; hence there were large contingents each month from Roumania and Poland. They had been living under Communist influence for many years, and there was always the danger that the indoctrination of these years would create problems of adaptation in Israel. But the same liberal policy that prevailed in the case of the physically hampered and impaired was set in the case of divergent ideologies. All Jews were welcome if they wished to come, and there was complete confidence that the miracle of free living in Israel would be an effective counterbalance to any imported bias.

Virtually every boatload of immigrants required extended processing. One group, however, far from adding to Israel's problems, was of crucial immediate help. This was the group of about twelve thousand internees from the island of Cyprus. In the last years of the mandate the British had followed the practice of deporting to Cyprus many of the refugees who attempted to get into Palestine illegally. There had been brutal skirmishes as the refugees resisted deportation, and a number of British transports had been blown up so that the shipments to

Cyprus would be blocked or delayed. Even after the mandate had been relinquished, the men of military age were not released, but remained closely
guarded, by specific order of Bevin. In the last days of the war, however, Britain
peevishly yielded. Twelve thousand strong, highly spirited men, who had been
selected from all the lands of Europe and had been carefully prepared during
their internment for their new life in Israel, came in as most welcome reinforcements.

Migrations from the Arab lands of the Near East and North Africa were
severely limited by hostile government restrictions. There was no love for the
native Jews, and their departure was devoutly sought by the discredited Arab
effendis. But the Nazis had taught despotic governments how to use their
scapegoats as hostages and how to profit from them, whether they stayed or
left. Thus every migration plan, whether managed individually or by accredited
Jewish international agencies, became a nightmare combination of negotiation
and blackmail. But despite all obstacles and restrictions, tens of thousands of
Jews in the Arab lands managed to get out. Most dramatic was the complete
transplantation of the historic Jewish community of Yemen. Here nearly fifty
thousand Jews lived, in incredible misery and degradation. Their roots in the
land went back to Biblical days, but they had scarcely ever risen above the
status of pariahs. Permission was obtained for them to leave for Israel if they
forfeited their possessions and paid a silver tax of three dollars per person. By
the thousands they were transferred to the British port of Aden, whence, in
Operation Magic Carpet, they were flown, in C-54 Skymasters, 150 to the plane,
to Israel!

Other thousands came from Morocco and Tunisia and Algiers. They came
from the slums and the bazaars of Egypt and Syria. Operation Ali Baba flew
out a thousand Jews a day from Iraq. They bribed and smuggled and connived
and even fought their way out. They came in ever increasing numbers, which
began to approach sixty per cent of all immigration. Those who counted on a
European base for the population structure of Israel began to worry over the
ultimate fate of the nation when so many Oriental Jews became an integral
part of its fabric.

The problems were more than ethnic—much more. They were cultural and
social and religious. When the Yemenites were transported by the extraordinary
air lift they came not only from Aden to Lydda. They flew from the Middle
Ages into the twentieth century. They had to learn everything from the alphabet to elementary sanitation. Shlomo Barer, who made an exhaustive study of
the Yemenites, reports that the men had to be taught how to wear a pair of
pants, that there were women who avoided the maternity ward until *after*
childbirth, that it required special vigilance to prevent the marriage of twelve-
year-olds. Other groups were not quite so bewildered by the novelties of the
twentieth century, but their dress, their ethical standards, their state of culture,

their way of life, called for patient adaptation. Many were ill with trachoma, malaria, colitis, malnutrition, tuberculosis, all the ailments of the primitive civilizations from which they emerged.

The immediate need was housing. Where were these incredibly heterogeneous masses to be accommodated, even temporarily? The old British military camps were pressed into service; then the homes that the Arabs had abandoned; then even their most primitive huts and caves. Special transit camps were established, but these were quickly filled, too. At one period there were more than one hundred thousand new immigrants in temporary lodgings, harried by crowding, by weather, by the lack of useful activity, never knowing the blessed luxury of privacy. The government sent them on as fast as more permanent quarters could be found or as quickly as they could be absorbed into the economy. But there was not sufficient employment even for a fraction of those who came, and these were men and women who could not be put off with comforting phrases about patience. They had already suffered the agonies of endless waiting in the concentration camps or the displaced-persons centers, and they had had their bellyful of group living. "My golden dream fulfilled would be a small table," said one wretched camper to a visiting housing authority. "For eight years we have eaten with thousands of others at long tables. My children have never known what a home is!" There were protests and demonstrations and piteous appeals not to spread out too long the period of readjustment. No one envied the government officials who, beset by so many other problems, had to bridge these early years of unrestricted immigration in a land that had to import every scrap of lumber and steel and plumbing.

There was a compensating corollary however in the new generation of children. No one surveying the realities of Israel could fail to be impressed by the wholesome, buoyant, healthy stock that abounded even in the shacks and the tents of the transit camps. The birth-rate among the immigrants was high, and in 1950 fully one fourth of the population of Israel was under fourteen. These youngsters had few memories of concentration camps and the humiliations of life in the world of their parents. If they had memories they soon lost them in the uninhibited creativity of these fresh new experiences. Jewish life in Europe was doomed when the Nazis destroyed virtually all of the young people; Israel was a land where children thrived. Though their laughter and their freedom from fear could not be counted as assets in trade and population statistics, those who were building the land knew that here lay the promise of the future.

4. EXPANSION OF THE ECONOMY

By the end of 1951 two forces began to merge which automatically ameliorated the problems of immigration. There were virtually no facilities left to receive a heavy daily load. Simultaneously there were increasing police restric-

tions in the Iron Curtain lands, which began to constrain the sources of emigration. For example, in Poland, which had supplied a good proportion of the new
population, the severest penalties were now attached to any attempts to leave.
After 1951 there were purges in the Soviet Union and in the satellite lands, and
the lists of applicants who had only yesterday registered in good faith were
turned over to the authorities for police action against "deserters." In the fourth
year of independence emigration dropped to 23,370, as compared with 173,901
in 1951. But the total population by the end of 1952 stood at 1,500,000, of whom
all but 200,000 were Jews.

The best hope for the absorption of these immigrants as well as for the
welfare of the over-all economy lay in opening out the undeveloped land. The
Negeb received primary attention. A whole series of pumping stations were begun to provide irrigation, which it was hoped would transform the desert into
life-bearing soil. The early settlements there were steadily reinforced, and every
advance in cultivation was accompanied by a rush of new population. In March
1951 the drainage of the Huleh marshes was begun, a most ambitious and far-
reaching project through which it was expected to reclaim about 12,500 acres of
soil that had been uncultivated for centuries. There were other similar projects
wherever there seemed to be the slightest hope of fertility and habitation. In the
three years following independence there was more colonization and settlement
than in the fifty previous years.

The industrial and commercial progress of the country in the years since
independence was more restrained. The block came from the fear of private
investors that the socialist economy of Israel made large-scale ventures too risky.
Nevertheless, there was impressive expansion. Every week licences were granted
for the opening of new factories, and there was soon a steady flow of shoes,
watches, tires, glass, ceramics, paper, artificial teeth, plastics, furniture, and a
hundred and one other articles, whose local manufacture helped to stem the
flight of hard currency even as it provided increasing employment. A number of
important American firms were persuaded to make modest initial investments.
The Ford Motor Company and Kaiser-Frazer set up automobile assembly
plants. Philco refrigerators now had a Palestine branch. The General Shoe Company of Nashville opened a Zipper factory. Quaker Oats established a plant in
Rehovet. The little merchant marine grew to thirty-four ships, with a tonnage
of 120,000, and there was more than ordinary pride in the scheduling of regular
service between Lydda and New York through the Israel-owned El Al Airlines.
Trade agreements were concluded with Holland, France, Yugoslavia, Finland,
Turkey, and many other European states. One agreement had more than passing significance and boded well for the future: in May 1949 Britain accepted the
facts of life and signed a trade accord with Israel, restored full commercial
relations, and released all of the funds that had been blocked during the period
of hostility.

But outweighing all of these developments was the bounty that came from the United States; more than half a billion dollars from the United Jewish Appeal and the sale of Israeli bonds, and another three hundred millions in the form of grants from the Export-Import Bank and the Point Four and Mutual Security programs. Such a transfusion into the veins of the faltering Israeli economy brought renewed vitality.

Of more dubious value was the completion of negotiations with Western Germany for a grant to cover some of the costs of resettling the victims of the Nazi holocaust. Ever since the defeat of Hitler and the establishment of a democratically based West German state (the eastern portion of Germany fell into Soviet hands), there had been pressure to compel some form of indemnification. The issues were highly complicated and required the most delicate kind of diplomacy. On the most elementary level, legislation was called for to reimburse those who had been looted, or their known heirs. Here there was a measure of progress, accelerated undoubtedly by the desire of the West German government to vindicate the confidence of its recently acquired democratic allies.

But what of the losses sustained by the numberless families that had been completely destroyed, leaving no legal heirs? And what of the thousands who had survived, but whose property had been caught up in so many legal skeins and mazes that it could no longer be retrieved? The Israeli government and representatives of the major international Jewish organizations co-operated to demand a collective indemnity to subsidize a portion of the heavy costs of rehabilitating the survivors in Israel and in other lands. It was made clear that, as far as the Jews were concerned, no monetary payment would wipe out the monstrous guilt of the Nazi regime. But the material indemnity would at least make the tasks of rehabilitation a little easier. The claim was set at one and a half billion dollars.

At first it was difficult to get the West German government even to consider discussion and negotiation. The subject was not a popular one among defeated and embittered people who were divided on most subjects but were remarkably united on the presumption that they were in no way responsible for the excesses of the wicked and unrepresentative Nazis. Chancellor Adenauer, however, soon realized that a return to the family of nations and inclusion in the Atlantic Alliance depended in large measure on tangible evidences of good faith. On September 27, 1951 he accepted the principle of negotiation in a statement to Parliament wherein he admitted that there was an obligation on the part of the German people to make "moral and material amends" for the "unspeakable crimes perpetrated in the name of the German people. . . . The Federal government is prepared, joining with representatives of Jewry and the State of Israel, which has admitted many homeless Jewish refugees, to bring about a solution of the material reparation problem in order to facilitate the way to a spiritual purging of unheard-of suffering." The Bonn Parliament, by a standing vote, endorsed the offer.

In Israel the reaction was by no means unanimously favourable. All too many victimized families could not bring themselves to sanction negotiations with a people that had shown no real contrition, despite the pious and unctuous phrases of politically minded leaders. How could Israel be rebuilt through the use of blood money? The argument was quixotic, but who could blame men and women for indulging their emotions at the expense of their practical interests after so much grief and terror? The Herut party and the Communists took full advantage of the poignant confusion to harass the government by touching off demonstrations and riots. The Knesset, after exhaustive debates, took the attitude that no moral whitewash was involved or intended. But there was no reason to permit the German people to emerge scot-free when an indemnity, taken from their standard of living, could solve some of the formidable problems of rehabilitation. The Knesset therefore voted full authority to their representatives to seek an official German settlement.

The negotiations were long and full of vexation. They were several times broken off by the Israeli representatives, who accused the Germans of bad faith. At the most critical junctures there was prodding of the Germans by American intermediaries, and this prodding resulted in fruitful concessions, which saved the negotiations. In September 1952, agreements were reached whereby West Germany agreed, through treaty with Israel, to pay out 715 millions in commodities and services over a period of twelve to fourteen years. An additional 107 millions was to be paid over to Israel for ultimate transmission to a Conference on Jewish Material Claims against Germany, organized to indemnify victims of the Nazis outside of Israel.

Despite a number of misgivings, the treaty was meticulously fulfilled. Indeed, payments arrived ahead of schedule. Whether the agreement had been entered into out of a sincere feeling of repentance or because of diplomatic and political pressures, the results ultimately justified the accord. The German government had been forced publicly to confess its responsibility for the Nazi atrocities. And the hundreds of millions of dollars worth of ships, tractors, heavy machinery, and vehicles that were carefully chosen by Israeli experts, all designed and manufactured with traditional German efficiency, brought renewed strength to Israel in a period when the little country's economy desperately required infusion.

5. THE UNFINISHED BUSINESS OF STATE-BUILDING

In the long run, the problems of immigration, employment, inflation, austerity, industrial and commercial development, were all somehow manageable, for they were subject to domestic legislation and control. But the dark shadow that loomed over all Israeli life and activity was the implacable hostility of the Arabs, their refusal to accept the existence of the Jewish State, to recognize that the Palestine war had been decisive, and that Israel was a fact. The Arab nations were hardly less bitter against the West, particularly the United States, for having supported the original partition plan in the United Nations. They bided their time, maintaining an economic blockade against the Jews, reorganizing their armies in the expectation that within a few years they would try again to drive the Israelis into the sea. In the early 1950's, however, the time apparently was not yet ripe. Unity was still far off in the Arab world, despite the impressive façade of the Arab League. No single Arab country was strong enough to take the military initiative against the Jews.

The possibility of a "second round" against Israel was augmented by the rivalry of the Cold War. Russia nurtured its traditional determination to move into the Near and Middle East. If Western-oriented Israel was unwilling to serve as a cat's paw for Soviet expansion, perhaps, from Moscow's point of view, more could be accomplished by offering inducements and encouragement to the Arabs. The joinder of Arab and Soviet policy took place in the wake of a major political revolution in Egypt. Hundreds of young Egyptian officers, veterans of the Palestine war, were convinced that the rotten feudal structure of their nation was responsible for the humiliating defeat at the hands of the Jews. In July 1952, this group made its move. Led by Colonel Mohammed Naguib, the military sent King Farouk into exile, and in the following year proclaimed an Egyptian Republic. In 1954, Naguib himself was replaced by a brother officer, Colonel Gamal Abdel Nasser, also a veteran of the Palestine war.

Nasser was a dynamic and imaginative man, and his ambitions for his country seemed legitimate. There was much to do in solving the problems of disease, poverty, illiteracy, and the feudal exploitation that cursed Egyptian life. At the outset, therefore, foreign policy did not appear to be a matter of burning concern for the new government. Nasser was content to negotiate a rather mild agreement with Britain by which the occupying garrison would be withdrawn within two years, though with the right of re-entry in case of emergency. In return, Egypt agreed to respect the 1888 Suez Convention, which guaranteed free and unfettered traffic through the Suez Canal. For the most part, Nasser focussed his attention in this period on his ambitious plan for the Aswan Dam, an enormous enterprise that might take twenty years to complete, and that would require an investment of a billion and a third dollars. Such an engineering miracle would bring into cultivation two million acres and revolutionize the economy of the parched country. Nasser was hailed in these first years as an Arab Kemal Mustapha, who would modernize Egypt even as the Turkish genius had Westernized his country.

None of his initial successes gave Nasser peace of mind, however. The Suez Canal remained under Western control. Israel was just across the frontier, a proud, independent, self-reliant nation; its very existence mocked him, for no

man could assume undisputed leadership in the Arab world without first se-
questering the Canal, and then driving the Jews into the sea. For this purpose,
however, weapons were needed in quantities heretofore unknown in the Near
East. And then, incredibly, Nasser acquired his arsenal—from the Soviet Bloc.
In the summer of 1955 Nasser completed an agreement which was destined
radically to shift the balance of power in the Eastern Mediterranean. By its terms,
he promised the Soviets ten million bales of cotton, in return for which Moscow
assured Nasser of millions of dollars worth of tanks, jet airplanes, and other late-
model weapons of modern warfare. Only a year later, Nasser exploited his shining
new arsenal by nationalizing the Suez Canal, in purposeful defiance of his earlier
treaty with the British.

At the same time Nasser's preparations for an attack on Israel grew increasingly bolder. Bands of *fedayin*—terror raiders—crossed the frontier, killing Jews
and burning their property. The raids became ever more frequent, and the reprisal casualties the Israelis inflicted on the Arabs simply encouraged the latter
to redouble their efforts. Arms were now pouring into Egypt, together with
Soviet technicians and instructors. Nor was Nasser idle in exerting his influence
among the other Arab nations. There were riots in Jordan, stimulated by pro-
Nasser forces; soon thereafter General John Glubb, British commander of
Jordan's army, was dismissed from his post and exiled. Indeed, the election in
Jordan a few weeks later demonstrated that the country had turned violently
anti-British, anti-Western, and pro-Nasser. The Jordanian chief of staff announced that "the time has come for the Arabs to choose the appropriate time
to launch the assault for Israel's destruction." Syria, too, was on the move after
careful Nasser cultivation, especially among the armed forces. Israel's closest
neighbours were now mobilizing. The Jewish State faced the most serious crisis
since the early days of its independence.

Yet the Ben-Gurion government was not entirely without allies abroad. France
was deeply concerned over Nasser's activities. Cairo had not only nationalized
French holdings in the Suez Canal; it had also become the centre for Algerian
rebel disaffection. Accordingly, Premier Guy Mollet made available to the Jews
a limited quantity of modern planes, tanks, and other mechanized equipment.
Some modest help also came from England. Incensed by Nasser's expropriation
of the Canal, British Prime Minister Anthony Eden came to Paris for consulta-
tions in October 1956, and was apparently joined by several Israeli representatives.
The details of these negotiations have never been made public, but evidently
agreement for joint action against Egypt was reached. Hence, on October 29,
Israel launched its attack. Within a few hours its troops had penetrated deep into
Sinai and were on their way to the Canal Zone. Other Israeli contingents moved
into the northern Gaza strip. Still others quickly captured the fortified islands
that controlled the Gulf of Aqaba at the tip of the Red Sea, and the outlet to
the Indian Ocean. The Jews seized huge stores of arms, together with thousands
of Egyptian prisoners. Of these, 5,600 were later exchanged for four Israelis who

had been captured. Ironically, in the face of this devastating Israeli assault, not a single Arab state felt constrained to come to Egypt's assistance.

The day after the invasion's opening, October 30, France and England sent official ultimata both to Israel and to Egypt, indicating that the Western powers intended to protect their rights by occupying Port Said, Ismailia, and the Canal Zone. Whereupon British and French bombers launched an attack on Egyptian airfields. A few days later paratroopers dropped on Port Said, quickly occupying the town. Nasser by now was within a few miles of disaster, and another few days probably would have completed his ruin.

By now, however, the diplomatic world was in an uproar. Egypt asked for an immediate meeting of the Security Council, where Israel, Britain, and France were condemned almost unanimously. Henry Cabot Lodge, the American representative, spoke with bitterness about Israel and the Allies and their aggression. President Eisenhower delivered a stern warning that "there can be no law if we work to invoke one code of international conduct for those we oppose, and another for our friends." From Russia Khrushchev added his bit, insisting on a ceasefire and an immediate withdrawal of the invaders, lest Soviet "volunteers" be released to participate in the struggle. There was a well-founded rumour that the Russian premier had threatened to loose rockets on London and Paris.

The timing of the Western allies had been incredibly bad. Earlier, during the summer, world-wide indignation had been aroused by Nasser's action in nationalizing the Suez Canal, without redress or compensation. But, by the autumn, service in the Canal had been restored and Egyptian pilots were directing traffic quite efficiently. The military operation, too, had been bungled. Israel, to be sure, moved with astonishing precision, quickly accomplishing its goals. But England and France, ostensibly world powers, permitted a week to pass before completing a minor military operation against a smaller, almost defenceless foe. The concentration of pressures, especially from the United States, compelled retreat. So complete was the disaster for the Western allies that Anthony Eden's government fell; while the badly defeated Nasser, now fully restored, emerged with his prestige all but untarnished.

Israel, on the other hand, had gained the most important of its objectives. For the time being at least, the Jews had completely blunted Egyptian military might. The Sinai campaign ended the dreaded *fedayin* raids, secured control of the Aqaba enclave, thus opening out Israeli commerce to the Red Sea, the Indian Ocean, and the Far East. Above all, the short war had once again demonstrated Israel's determination to survive. The Ben-Gurion government well understood that it had violated technical assurances to the United Nations by its preventive war. But hardly a nation had stirred to offer the Jews protection during the formidable Egyptian military build-up, or had chosen to take notice of the ever mounting threats of the surrounding Arab states. As one Israeli official noted: "Israel had a choice a fortnight ago either to be wiped off the map, and then be eulogized and mourned by her friends, or to counter-attack, to survive, and then to explain to her friends why she tried to survive." The crisis was not over. There would assuredly be other campaigns. For Egypt and her Arab allies were no less determined to destroy the alien enclave in their midst. But Israeli initiative and courage had once again indicated that no attack or threat would be treated with impunity.

6. THE WOUNDS OF THE PAST: KASTNER AND EICHMANN

Meanwhile the terrible wounds of the past were still unhealed. The survivors who had miraculously managed to reach Israel carried with them the searing remembrances not only of their deliverance but also of the destruction of their loved ones. During the inferno of the Hitler epoch, Jewish communal leaders had often been forced by the Nazis to decide who of their fellow Jews would live and who would die. The survivors of that leadership now were judged bitterly by those who had lost their kinsmen in the heartbreaking lottery. How deeply the wounds were felt became clear in the famous Kastner case that convulsed Israel for many months, and in 1955 toppled a government.

Rudolf Kastner was a former leader of the Hungarian Jews who had settled in Israel after the Nazi defeat. One of his countrymen, Malkiel Gruenwald, accused him of collaborating with the Germans, assisting in the murder of thousands of his people, saving known Nazi criminals, and sharing in the loot that had been squeezed out by the tormentors. Gruenwald presented evidence that of the 1,685 souls who had been released, 388 came from Kastner's native town of Kluj and these included many members of Kastner's own family. It was alleged that in rescuing this pathetic remnant he had lulled the rest into fatal complacence and prevented many more from escaping in time.

The Gruenwald assault was soon submerged in the rancour of party politics, for the Ben-Gurion government was assailed for keeping in power the same men who had co-operated during the war with "scoundrels" such as Kastner. The government, in turn, brought a criminal libel suit against Gruenwald; to everyone's astonishment, however, the presiding judge, Benjamin Halevi, found some of Gruenwald's allegations valid and expressed his view that Kastner "had sold his soul to Satan." In June 1955, motions of no confidence were presented in the Knesset by the Herut party, speaking for all the intransigeants who despised the Labour government for its moderation. The General Zionists, until then partners in the ramshackle government coalition, used this occasion to abstain from a vote. Whereupon the government felt obliged to resign. By now the entire country was convulsed by the ugly denunciations that besmirched friend and foe.

While the case dragged on through the courts, Kastner was ambushed near his home in March 1957, shot down, and died a week later. Three terrorists were arrested; their defence counsel, predictably, was a rightist leader who had himself been implicated in the murder of the Swedish mediator, Count Folke Bernadotte, in the days when the fate of Palestine was in the balance. The terrorists were found guilty and given long prison terms.

Then, in 1958, the supreme court reversed the judgement of the lower court, upheld the government's libel action, and imposed a suspended one-year sentence on Gruenwald. Kastner was posthumously exonerated of the charges of wilful collaboration with the Nazis. The court noted with compassion that no one could pass judgement upon individual actions committed under the terrifying duress of the war years. The entire case, the recriminations, the political vendettas, the unrestrained partisanship, the murder, all revealed that one of the most lamentable consequences of the Nazi horror was the scars it inflicted on the psyche of the Jewish community itself.

Soon the Kastner case was overshadowed by a new and far more sensational development. It was an episode which re-created even more effectively for a short-memoried world all the bestiality of the Nazi period. One of the principal Nazi butchers, Adolf Eichmann, who had been responsible for implementing Hitler's master plan for exterminating the Jewish people, had mysteriously disappeared following Germany's defeat. Rumours persisted that he was living in disguise in Spain, in Egypt, in the hidden fastnesses of Germany, in the Argentine, even in Israel. A team of Israelis, survivors of German death camps, had dedicated themselves to the task of hunting down escaped Nazi criminals. Eichmann remained at the top of their list. For years they worked with fanatic relentlessness, patiently exploring every clue to Eichmann's whereabouts. In 1960 they completed their search. In May of that year the world was electrified to learn that Eichmann had been trapped in Buenos Aires, had been kidnapped and placed on an Israeli passenger airplane, and had been transported to Israel. Prime Minister Ben-Gurion himself made the announcement that the arch-criminal was in Israeli hands, and that he would be tried for the liquidation of the Jews of Germany, Austria, Czechoslovakia, Poland, and Hungary.

The Argentine government immediately protested the violation of its sovereignty. Israel expressed its deepest regret, and asked that the Argentine people take into account the extraordinary circumstances of Eichmann's abduction. Indeed the volunteers who had apprehended Eichmann were themselves survivors of massacres that had immolated their entire families. Ben-Gurion followed with a personal message to the president of the Argentine, expressing faith that "only a very few persons in the world would fail to understand the profound motivation and supreme moral justification for this act." The Argentine government still felt obliged to defend its national honour, and it temporarily recalled its ambassador, lodging a formal complaint in the United Nations. There were further apologies, both in the United Nations and in Buenos Aires, and after four months, normal diplomatic relations between the two countries were re-established.

But the dispute did not end with the diplomatic charade. For more than a year the Eichmann case was vigorously debated in every part of the Western world. The various protests against Israel's action, and the trial itself, were later incorporated in the presentation of the defence. Israel had disqualified itself to try Eichmann because of the illegality of the kidnapping, the argument went; it had no right to speak in the name of the total world Jewish community. Moreover, how could Israel pass judgement on the crime of genocide if such a crime did not exist when Eichmann carried out his mission? Properly he could be tried only in an international tribunal, or perhaps in a German court, for it was in Germany that Eichmann had lived and worked.

Israel was not deterred by the avalanche of argument. It proceeded with the trial, ensuring only that every legal protection was afforded Eichmann. Its government contended that Israel's jurisdiction in this case was precisely the same as that claimed by other nations when they try cases of piracy or slave-trading. The method of bringing an alleged criminal to trial had no bearing on a country's right to try him. Israel, the argument declared, had as much right to speak for the world Jewish community as it had to receive reparations from the West German government in symbolic atonement for Nazi crimes. What other tribunal could try Eichmann? Germany wanted no part of him. It was impossible to convene a new Nuremberg tribunal; and if it were possible, could there be a meaningful trial in the climate of the Cold War? But above all, why all these legalisms in a situation that had no precedent in all recorded history for the sheer magnitude of annihilation? In truth, Israel insisted upon the trial not because this wretched creature's life meant anything, or because any punishment, however drastic, could atone for his role in slaughtering millions of human beings. The trial was essential to put the story of the holocaust on the record. That record had to be made available for a generation of Israeli young people; to revive the memory and conscience of the Christian world; to remind the Western democracies that what began as a narrow anti-Semitism ended with the destruction of all liberal and democratic and Christian values.

Eichmann's trial lasted four months, from April until August 1961. It was conducted in Jerusalem, presided over by three judges—all of them German Jewish refugees who had themselves escaped Nazi Germany before the war. Five hundred journalists from every part of the world attended the trial; every word, every action, was fully reported, from the given testimony of the long parade of witnesses to the behaviour of the defendant in the glass-enclosed, bullet-proof prisoner's dock. Eichmann was given efficient and resourceful counsel, headed by a Cologne attorney, whose fee was partially covered by the Israeli government.

The basis of Eichmann's defence was not a denial of the mass murders, but rather insistence that he had merely been a petty functionary in the rigidly organized Nazi apparatus; he had "loyally" fulfilled the orders that he received from above. The prosecution refuted this claim, reminding the court that a similar defence had been attempted by the Nazi war criminals at the Nuremberg trials of 1945. Eichmann was identified as the new type of mass killer, "the man who exercises his bloody craft behind a desk." Incredible details poured into the record, personal tragedies, the death of entire communities, the destruction of huge national settlements. How, it was asked, could human beings survive so much heartbreak and terror? The answer came from the testimony of a Dr. Wells. When asked how he had generated the stamina to survive the nightmare of torture he replied: "One of us had to fight through to tell the world. . . . We shielded each other so the strongest could live to speak for the dead." And the trial offered such a historic opportunity to speak for the dead.

Eichmann was being tried in the dock. Others were on trial, too. For the devastating truth was implicit in the evidence of nearly every witness: the vast unconcern of the Christian world, of the Polish and Hungarian and Roumanian peoples; of the Allied governments, of the Vatican. And the unconcern was not limited to the war period when each people brooded over its own tragedies. A Protestant minister from West Germany described how he and a comrade had saved many Jewish families in Germany—and then pleaded anonymity for that comrade; if it became known that the man had saved Jews he would *today* be overwhelmed with abuse from his German neighbours!

Even as the tale of horror unfolded, the Israeli younger generation expressed bewilderment. How, wondered these young people, could thousands of European Jews have permitted themselves to be slaughtered like sheep without any attempt to fight back? To be sure, witnesses had pointed out that it was impossible to fight armed enemies with fists, that in all instances the Nazis held precious hostages, that the machinery of death had been fashioned with fiendish ingenuity. But the replies seemed inadequate to the young Israelis, men and women who had won their own independence with the rarest courage. The trial deepened their commitment to their nation, which they considered their protection forever against such humiliating helplessness and dependence.

After the long months of testimony ended, the panel of judges required many weeks to complete their verdict. But when it was issued, it was unanimous. Eichmann was pronounced guilty and sentenced to death by hanging. "In fulfilling [his mission]," the verdict read, "the accused acted in accordance with general directives from his superiors, but there still remained to him wide powers of discretion, which extended also to the planning of operations on his own initiative. He was not a puppet in the hands of others. His place was amongst those who pulled the strings." The moment sentence was pronounced still another international debate began on the issue of the death sentence. Curiously, strongest pressure for commutation came from Jewish leaders in the United States. Capital punishment in itself was abhorrent to them; yet they pleaded for mercy to demonstrate to the Christian world that the rationale of the trial was not the passion for vengeance. This appeal, in turn, evoked the profoundest astonishment from Israel's refugee population. They asked how such a doctrinaire protest could be voided by those who had raised little outcry when the Nuremberg tribunal condemned the Nazi leaders, but who now found voice only when an Israeli court condemned a monster like Eichmann. He was hanged on a morning as dark as his own soul, and his ashes were scattered over the Mediterranean waters—lest they defile Jewish soil.

7. STRENGTH AND CONFIDENCE THROUGH AYN BRAIRA

Despite the enormity of its problems, the doughty little republic gained strength with each passing year. Its population mounted steadily, both through a burgeoning birth-rate and through immigration. Each major crisis in other lands brought thousands of refugees to Israel. The growth of national liberation movements in the Moslem world was a principal source of concern. Thus, when Tunisia won its independence in 1954, a vague feeling of uneasiness circulated among the eighty thousand Jews of that country. To be sure, most of them had lived in Tunisia for centuries. At first, too, they were given assurances of security and equality by Habib Bourguiba, the national liberator. Initially, Bourguiba was considered a modern, enlightened leader, and was counted upon as an ally of the Western powers. In 1959, however, a violent dispute with France over the naval base at Bizerte drove Bourguiba to hostility, and raised doubts about his reliability as a partner in the Cold War. For the Jews, the change spelled disaster. Bourguiba was soon receiving Cairo-inspired agents who spoke of rapprochement with the Arab League. The diplomatic *volte face* inevitably stimulated emigration to Israel; tens of thousands of Tunisian Jewish families joined the exodus.

Similarly, when Morocco obtained its independence from France, more than a quarter million Jewish inhabitants were obliged to make a sober reappraisal of their status. Ulcerated Berber nationalism evoked the usual proposals of economic autarchy; soon the ominous cry was raised of "Morocco for the Moroccans." There were overtures, too, for closer relations between Egypt and Morocco, in the common "Arab" interest. Although they had lived in the country for centuries, the Jews were the first and inevitable victims of the aroused xenophobia. Thousands of them migrated to France. But even greater numbers prepared for a new life in Israel. Indeed, after 1956, the determination to emigrate was so marked that more than seventy thousand Moroccan Jews were registered with the Israeli authorities. The Moroccan government realized that such a vast uprooting, consisting mainly of artisans, businessmen, and professional leaders, would seriously affect the economy of the country. Efforts were made to stem the flight. After 1960, however, despite the threat of severe penalties and long prison terms for those who gave aid to illegal emigration, thousands managed to evade the regulations and escaped.

In the disintegration of the French colonial empire, the experience of Algeria proved to be the most traumatic of all. No satisfactory compromise seemed possible between the Berbers and the European colonists; guerilla warfare between the two communities grew steadily worse. In the last days of the Fourth Republic, Pierre Mendès-France had suggested a formula agreeable to the rebels, but it was rejected as far too extreme by the European settlers. As the situation in Algeria deteriorated, however, Charles de Gaulle, who had come to power in 1958, was obliged to go much further. In 1961, he granted Algeria its complete independence. Even as de Gaulle's critics had feared, within a year of its liberation the Algerian Republic not only repudiated its ties with the West, but aligned itself increasingly with Nasser's Egypt, and the so-called neutralist camp.

The Jewish community was caught in a fearsome crossfire. It numbered more than 120,000 of whom the great majority were indigenous settlers tracing their ancestry back not only long beyond French rule, but to the pre-Moslem Carthaginian era. In 1930, when the French first occupied Algeria, every opportunity had been granted the Jews to develop close ties with the Europeans. Accordingly, the ablest, most intelligent and most ambitious had responded eagerly to this offer. In 1870, moreover, as a direct result of this loyalty, the French government passed the "Cremieux Law" (after the French Jewish leader who proposed it), granting Algerian Jewry French citizenship. From then on the Jews became an integral part of French economic and cultural life.

Yet when the nationalist crisis in Algeria came to a head after World War II, the Jews resisted being labelled as belonging *en bloc* to one camp or the other. Some actively supported the French and wished to remain associated with the French community; others joined in the revolutionary movement, working and fighting at the side of the Moslem nationalists. Earlier Mendès-France had stated the dilemma, and also offered a formula for action to those who wished to make a choice: "When a definitive settlement for Algeria is reached," he declared, "when a new state is established, all the people who live there should have the right to practice their own self-determination. Those who wish to be French should under all circumstances have the right to be French. Those who want to become Algerian citizens and play their part in the new Algerian state should have the right to do so."

The formula was simple, but its application was swallowed in the intense hatreds that were spawned by the civil war. Jews were assailed by the French terrorists who resented their identification with the rebels; they were repudiated by the rebels because of their identification with the French. The tragedy was dramatized by the fate of the William Lévy family, one of whose sons was ambushed and killed by the Berber terrorists, while another son was assassinated a few years later by the French colonial underground. It was inevitable therefore that emigration should be viewed as a solution to the intolerable impasse. Thousands of Jews fled to France to begin new lives there. Other thousands sought refuge in Israel. By 1961 the emigration approached a thousand monthly, despite every effort on the part of the authorities to block the loss of the important professional and business elements.

Even Europe remained a not altogether exhausted reservoir of immigration to Israel. When the 1956 uprising in Hungary was brutally suppressed by Soviet tanks, thousands of Jews were among the hordes who fled the Communist police-state. A momentary relaxation in the tight exit restrictions of Roumania and Poland opened in the same year, and this encouraged additional thousands of Jews to seek refuge in Israel. The apartheid crisis in South Africa, and the withdrawal of that country from the British Commonwealth, were largely responsible for the departure to Israel of three thousand Jews—who brought with them superb technical and professional skills. The Nasserist reaction which followed the Suez campaign in Egypt sent another 13,000 Jewish refugees fleeing for sanctuary to the Israeli haven.

But it was not tragedy alone that brought immigrants to Israel. A small but growing stream arrived from Britain, Canada, and the United States; most of these were younger people who were intrigued by the challenge of creativity in a new frontier world. And so the Israeli population grew from 650,000 in 1948 to 1,629,000 in 1953 to 2,031,000 in 1958 to 2,300,000 in 1963. All but 280,000 of these Israeli citizens were Jews, and seventy per cent of these were under thirty years of age. In the majority of cases, they were superb raw material for the Zionist renaissance.

The nation's economy, too, was steadily growing. By 1964 the expansion of the gross national product compared favorably in rate of growth with that of those countries of Western Europe that had been revitalized by the Marshall Plan. Additional thousands of dunam of land came under cultivation, enriched by the research of Israel's leading scientists, by the counsel of expert advisory teams from the United States, and, above all, by the Israeli government's imaginative and extensive irrigation projects. New industries for products such as cut diamonds, textiles, plastics, tires, automobiles, even airplanes, changed the skyline not only in the major cities but in the Negev area which was further opened out by investment and mounting immigration.

Equally gratifying was the expansion of the merchant marine and the air service. Israeli ships and planes operated between the major cities of Europe, Africa, Asia, and the United States. In the last decade tourism, one of the principal "industries," has brought much-needed hard currency into the country, afterwards sending home inspired interpreters to detail their admiration for what they had seen and been shown. The measure of the little nation's international reputation was evidenced by the establishment of cordial relations with a number of African and Asian states. Israel's assistance to the emerging countries, her co-operation in solving technical and educational problems, was gratefully received, for the Jews, representatives of a tiny nation, elicited no fear or suspicion of imperialism, a sensitive point for peoples only now shaking off past exploitation.

Israeli scientists, educators, and technicians were heartily welcomed as they converted blueprints for industrial plants, irrigation projects, public-health programs, and school systems into realities. Israel co-operated with Ghana in organizing the Black Star Line, with joint stock control in a merchant marine. Friendly trade and cultural relations brought Israelis to Guinea and Ethiopia and far-off Burma. Thousands of foreign students registered in Israel's universities and technical institutes. The Asian and African states who were indebted to Israel in this fashion provided vital diplomatic support in resisting Arab political and economic pressures.

Yet with all the pride and exaltation of success, a persistent danger continued to haunt every aspect of national life: Israel remained a tiny enclave of two and a third million people, almost completely surrounded by seven Arab states, with a combined population of forty million, that were fanatically committed to the destruction of the Jewish nation. Whether it came from the West or from Israel itself, every overture for peace was turned aside. The Israeli government still found it necessary to assign a vastly disproportionate share of its budget for defence. In a frenetic period, when hundreds of thousands of penniless immigrants had to be absorbed and acculturated, the burden of military preparedness was all but insupportable. Soviet Russia, shrewdly reinforcing the Arab menace, vastly compounded this burden and tension. Israel found some momentary reassurance in its ability to create a modest source of nuclear power from one of its own reactors. But this achievement was quickly counterbalanced when technical aid was rushed to Egypt from Russia and its satellites, including rocket missiles that brought all of Israel within firing range of the enemy.

These perils notwithstanding, the Jewish nation remained extraordinarily optimistic. Perhaps some of this spirit was a form of fatalism. After all, if disaster should engulf this last bastion, there was no place else for the people of Israel to go. *Ayn braira,* no alternative, was the challenge, and this challenge bred a strong determined resistance. There was no longer the Messianic exaltation that had pervaded the climate when the state was proclaimed. There was instead a kind of grimness, a tough-minded realization that there were no easy solutions in the frothy sentimentalities of the verbalizers and the mystics. Juicy phrases, even when adorned with Biblical references, could not change the meaning of an import balance that was eight times the amount of exports. Yet faith had by no means been banished. It was a faith that transcended the immediacies of logic and fact. It was faith in a unique destiny, faith that a war for survival could not be lost, that a nation grounded in so much sacrifice could not founder. When Iraq repudiated its Western alliance and the Bagdad Pact, and still another Arab nation joined the military alliance against Israel, the Jewish reaction was almost arrogant: "Now we have the Arabs completely surrounded!" In such a mood, Chaim Weizmann had declared his deep conviction "that God has always chosen small countries through which to convey His message to humanity." The confident folksaying was repeated, not as a boastful cliché, but as a fact of national life: "In Israel, the inevitable rarely happens, but the impossible often does."

SELECTED BIBLIOGRAPHY

The Bibliography which follows is limited to references in English which are usually accessible in the library of a fair-sized community. Wherever possible the most recent authoritative studies have been given preference. Since the volume is divided into three parts — Biblical, Mediæval, and Modern — the references have followed this topical arrangement.

GENERAL REFERENCES

BARON, SALO: *A Social and Religious History of the Jews.* 3 vols. Philadelphia. Jewish Publication Society. 1937.

FINKELSTEIN, LOUIS (ed.): *The Jews: Their History, Culture, and Religion.* 2 vols. 2nd ed. New York. Harper & Brothers. 1955.

GRAETZ, H.: *A History of the Jews.* 6 vols. 2nd ed. New York. Hebrew Publishing Company. 1926.

GRAYZEL, SOLOMON: *A History of the Jews.* Philadelphia. Jewish Publication Society. 1947.

Jewish Encyclopedia: 12 vols. New York. Funk & Wagnalls. 1906.

KASTEIN, JOSEF: *History and Destiny of the Jews.* New York. Viking Press. 1933.

MARGOLIS, M. L. and MARX, A.: *A History of the Jewish People.* Meridian Books ed. 1958. Philadelphia. Jewish Publication Society. 1927.

ROTH, CECIL: *The Jewish Contributions to Civilization.* New York. Harper & Brothers. 1940.

SCHWARTZ, LEO W. (ed.): *Great Ages and Ideas of the Jewish People.* New York. Random House. 1956.

Universal Jewish Encyclopedia. 10 vols. New York. Universal Jewish Encyclopedia, Inc. 1939–43.

WAXMAN, MEYER: *A History of Jewish Literature.* 3 vols. New York. Bloch Publishing Company. 1930–6.

I

THE BIBLICAL WORLD

BARON, SALO: *A Social and Religious History of the Jews.* Vols. 1 and 2. Rev. and enl. New York. Columbia University Press. 1958.

BARTON, GEORGE A.: *Archæology and the Bible.* 7th ed. Philadelphia. American Sunday School Union. 1937.

BENTWICH, NORMAN: *Hellenism.* Philadelphia. Jewish Publication Society. 1919.

———: *Josephus*. Philadelphia. Jewish Publication Society. 1914.

BERTHOLET, ALFRED: *A History of Hebrew Civilization*. New York. Brentano's. 1926.

BEVAN, E. R. and SINGER, CHARLES: *The Legacy of Israel*. Oxford. Clarendon Press. 1927.

BEWER, JULIUS A.: *The Literature of the Old Testament in Its Historical Development*. Rev. ed. New York. Columbia University Press. 1933.

BLUNT, ALFRED W. F.: *Israel before Christ*. London. Oxford University Press. 1932.

BOKSER, B. Z.: *Pharisaic Judaism in Transition*. New York. Bloch Publishing Company. 1935.

BOX, G. H.: *Judaism in the Greek Period*. London. Oxford University Press. 1932.

BREASTED, JAMES H.: *The Conquest of Civilization*. New York. Harper & Brothers. 1938.

BURNEY, C. F.: *Israel's Settlement in Canaan*. 2nd ed. London. Oxford University Press. 1919.

BUTTENWIESER, MOSES: *The Prophets of Israel*. New York. The Macmillan Company. 1914.

CASE, S. J.: *Jesus*. Chicago. University of Chicago Press. 1927.

CHEYNE, THOMAS, and BLACK, JOHN: *Encyclopædia Biblica*. New York. The Macmillan Company. 1914.

COHEN, MORTIMER J.: *Pathways through the Bible*. Philadelphia. Jewish Publication Society. 1947.

ENELOW, H. G.: *A Jewish View of Jesus*. 2nd ed. New York. The Macmillan Company. 1930.

FINEGAN, JACK: *Light from the Ancient Past*. Princeton. Princeton University Press. 1946.

FINKELSTEIN, LOUIS: *Akiba: Scholar, Saint and Martyr*. New York. Covici, Friede. 1936.

———: *The Pharisees*. 2 vols. 3rd rev. ed. Philadelphia. Jewish Publication Society. 1962.

FOAKES-JACKSON, F. J.: *The Rise of Gentile Christianity*. New York. George H. Doran Company. 1907.

GARSTANG, J.: *The Heritage of Solomon*. London. Williams and Norgate. 1934.

GASTER, M.: *The Samaritans*. London. Oxford University Press. 1925.

GLUECK, NELSON: *The River Jordan*. Philadelphia. Jewish Publication Society. 1946.

———: *Rivers in the Desert. A History of the Negev*. Philadelphia. Jewish Publication Society. 1959.

GOODSPEED, E. J.: *The Story of the Apocrypha*. Chicago. University of Chicago Press. 1939.

GUIGNEBERT, CHARLES: *The Jewish World in the Time of Jesus*. New York. E. P. Dutton and Company. 1939.

HASTINGS, JAMES: *Dictionary of the Bible*. New York. Charles Scribner's Sons. 1909.

HESCHEL, ABRAHAM: *The Prophets*. Philadelphia. Jewish Publication Society. 1962.

KAUFMANN, YEHEZKAL: *The Religion of Israel*. Chicago. The University of Chicago Press. 1960.

KENYON, KATHLEEN MARY: *Archæology in the Holy Land*. Praeger. New York. 1960.

KITTEL, R.: *The Religion of the People of Israel*. New York. The Macmillan Company. 1925.

KLAUSNER, JOSEPH: *From Jesus to Paul*. New York. The Macmillan Company. 1943.

———: *Jesus of Nazareth*. New York. The Macmillan Company. 1925.

LAUTERBACH, J. Z.: *The Pharisees and Their Teachings*. New York. Bloch Publishing Company. 1930.

LODS, ADOLPHE: *Israel*. New York. Alfred A. Knopf. 1932.

MARGOLIS, MAX L.: *The Hebrew Scriptures in the Making*. Philadelphia. Jewish Publication Society. 1922.

MENKIN, JACOB S.: *Herod*. Rev. ed. Yoseloff. New York. 1959.

MOORE, G. F.: *Judaism in the First Centuries of the Christian Era*. Cambridge. Harvard University Press. 1927.

NOTH, MARTIN: *The History of Israel*. Trans. by Stanley Goodman. New York. Harper & Brothers. 1958.

PEET, THOMAS ERIC: *Egypt and the Old Testament*. Boston. Small, Maynard and Company. 1923.

RABBEY, BEATRICE: *A Short History of the Hebrews*. London. Oxford University Press. 1937.

RADIN, MAX: *The Jews among the Greeks and the Romans*. Philadelphia. Jewish Publication Society. 1915.

———: *The Life of the People in Biblical Times*. Philadelphia. Jewish Publication Society. 1929.

SKINNER, J.: *Prophecy and Religion*. New York. The Macmillan Company. 1922.

SMITH, GEORGE ADAM: *The Historical Geography of the Holy Land*. 25th ed. New York. Harper & Brothers. 1932.

———: *Jeremiah*. Garden City, New York. George H. Doran Company. 1923.

YADIN, YIGAEL: *The Message of the Scrolls*. Simon and Schuster. New York. 1957.

II

THE MEDIÆVAL WORLD

ABRAHAMS, ISRAEL: *Jewish Life in the Middle Ages*. 2nd ed. London. Goldston. 1932.

Agus, I. A.: *Rabbi Meir of Rothenburg.* 2 vols. Philadelphia. Dropsie College. 1947.

Altmann, A.: *Saadya Gaon.* Oxford. East and West Library. 1946.

Baron, Salo: *A Social and Religious History of the Jews.* Vols. III–VIII. Rev. and enl. New York. Columbia University Press. 1960.

Blumenfield, Samuel H.: *Master of Troyes: A Study of Rashi.* New York. Behrman Book House. 1946.

Danby, H.: *The Mishnah.* Trans., with introduction. London. Oxford University Press. 1933.

Dubnow, S. M.: *A History of the Jews in Russia and Poland.* Vol. I. Philadelphia. Jewish Publication Society. 1916–18.

Finkelstein, Louis: *Jewish Self-Government in the Middle Ages.* New York. Jewish Theological Seminary of America. 1924.

————: *Rab Saadia Gaon: Studies in His Honor.* New York. Jewish Theological Seminary of America. 1944.

Fleg, Edmond: *A Jewish Anthology.* New York. Harcourt, Brace & Company. 1925.

Halper, B.: *Post-Biblical Hebrew Literature.* 2 vols. Philadelphia. Jewish Publication Society. 1921.

Husik, Isaac: *A History of Mediæval Jewish Philosophy.* 2nd ed. Philadelphia. Jewish Publication Society. 1930.

Katsh, Abraham: *Judaism in Islam.* New York. New York University Press. 1954.

Lea, A. C.: *A History of the Inquisition in Spain.* 4 vols. New York. The Macmillan Company. 1906–7.

Liber, Maurice: *Rashi.* Philadelphia. Jewish Publication Society. 1906.

Malter, Henry: *Life and Works of Saadia Gaon.* Philadelphia. Jewish Publication Society. 1921.

Mann, Jacob: *The Jews in Egypt and Palestine under the Fatimid Caliphs.* 2 vols. London. Oxford University Press. 1920–2.

Millgram, A. E.: *An Anthology of Mediæval Hebrew Literature.* Philadelphia. Associated Talmud Torahs. 1935.

Neuman, Abraham: *The Jews in Spain.* 2 vols. Philadelphia. Jewish Publication Society. 1942.

Oesterley, W. C. C. and Box, G. H.: *A Short Survey of the Literature of Rabbinical and Mediæval Judaism.* New York. The Macmillan Company. 1920.

Philipson, David: *Old European Jewries.* Philadelphia. Jewish Publication Society. 1894.

Roth, Cecil: *A History of the Marranos.* 2nd rev. ed. Philadelphia. Jewish Publication Society. 1959.

————: *A History of the Jews in Italy.* Philadelphia. Jewish Publication Society. 1946.

————: *The Jews in the Renaissance*. Philadelphia. Jewish Publication Society. 1959.

————: *Life of Menassah ben Israel*. Philadelphia. Jewish Publication Society. 1934.

————: *Venice*. Philadelphia. Jewish Publication Society. 1930.

SCHOLEM, GERSHOM G.: *Major Trends in Jewish Mysticism*. New York. Schocken Books. 1946.

SCHWARTZ, LEO W.: *Memoirs of My People through a Thousand Years*. Philadelphia. Jewish Publication Society. 1945.

SEGAL, FRAU GLÜCKEL: *The Memoirs of Glückel von Hamelin*. Trans., with introduction and notes, by Marvin Lowenthal. New York. Harper & Brothers. 1932.

SILVER, ABBA HILLEL: *Messianic Speculations in Israel*. New York. The Macmillan Company. 1927.

STOKES, H. P.: *A Short History of the Jews in England*. New York. The Macmillan Company. 1921.

TORREY, C. C.: *The Jewish Foundation of Islam*. New York. Bloch Publishing Company. 1933.

VISHNITZER, M.: *The Memoirs of Ber of Bolechow*. London. Oxford University Press. 1922.

YELLIN, DAVID, and ABRAHAMS, ISRAEL: *Maimonides*. Philadelphia. Jewish Publication Society. 1908.

ZEITLIN, SOLOMON: *Maimonides*. New York. Bloch Publishing Company. 1935.

III

THE MODERN WORLD

AGAR, HERBERT: *The Saving Remnant*. New York. Viking Press. 1960.

ANTONIUS, GEORGE: *The Arab Awakening*. London. H. Hamilton. 1955.

ARENDT, HANNAH: *The Origins of Totalitarianism*. New York. Harcourt, Brace & Company. 1951.

BEIN, ALEXANDER: *Theodore Herzl*. Philadelphia. Jewish Publication Society. 1940.

BENTWICH, NORMAN: *Israel Resurgent*. New York. Praeger. 1960.

BEN-ZVI, ITZHAK: *The Exiled and the Redeemed*. Philadelphia. Jewish Publication Society. 1961.

BERNSTEIN, MARVER H.: *The Politics of Israel. The First Decade of Statehood*. Princeton. Princeton University Press. 1957.

BILBY, KENNETH W.: *New Star in the Near East*. New York. Doubleday & Company. 1950.

BUBER, MARTIN: *Tales of the Hasidim: The Early Masters.* New York. Schocken Books. 1947.

COHEN, ISRAEL: *Jewish Life in Modern Times.* Rev. ed. New York. Dodd, Mead & Company. 1938.

——: *History of the Jews in Vilna.* Philadelphia. Jewish Publication Society. 1943.

——: *The Zionist Movement.* London. Frederick Miller. 1945.

CROSSMAN, RICHARD H. S.: *Palestine Mission.* New York. Harper & Brothers. 1947.

CRUM, BARTLEY: *Behind the Silken Curtain.* New York. Simon and Schuster. 1947.

DUBNOW, S. M.: *History of the Jews in Russia and Poland.* Vols. II and III. Philadelphia. Jewish Publication Society. 1916.

EISENSTEIN, IRA and KOHN, EUGENE: *Mordecai M. Kaplan: An Evaluation.* New York. Jewish Reconstructionist Foundation. 1952.

ELBOGEN, ISMAR: *A Century of Jewish Life.* Philadelphia. Jewish Publication Society. 1944.

EYTAN, WALTER: *The First Ten Years. A Diplomatic History of Israel.* New York. Simon and Schuster. 1958.

FLENDER, HAROLD: *Rescue in Denmark.* New York. Simon and Schuster. 1963.

FRIEDMAN, LEE M.: *Jewish Pioneers and Patriots.* Philadelphia. Jewish Publication Society. 1942.

GINZBERG, LOUIS: *Students, Scholars and Saints.* Philadelphia. Jewish Publication Society. 1928.

GLATZER, N. N.: *Leopold and Adelheid Zunz.* London. East and West Library. 1960.

GOLDBERG, ISRAEL (Rufus Learsi, pseud.): *The Epic Story of Zionism.* Cleveland. The World Publishing Company. 1951.

——: *The Jews in America.* New York. The World Publishing Company. 1954.

GOODMAN, ABRAM V.: *American Overture: Jewish Rights in Colonial Times.* Philadelphia. Jewish Publication Society. 1947.

GOODMAN, PAUL: *Moses Montefiore.* Philadelphia. Jewish Publication Society. 1925.

HALASZ, NICHOLAS: *Captain Dreyfus.* New York. Simon and Schuster. 1955.

HALPERN, BEN: *The Idea of A Jewish State.* Cambridge. Harvard University Press. 1961.

HERTZBERG, ARTHUR: *The Zionist Idea.* Meridian Books ed. Philadelphia. Jewish Publication Society. 1960.

HITLER, ADOLF: *My Battle (Mein Kampf).* Boston. Houghton Mifflin Company. 1938.

HOURANI, A. H.: *Minorities in the Arab World.* New York. Oxford University Press. 1947.

HUREWITZ, J. C.: *The Struggle for Palestine*. New York. W. W. Norton & Company. 1950.

INFIELD, HENRIK F.: *Cooperative Living in Palestine*. London. Kegan Paul. 1946.

JACOB, HEINRICH E.: *The World of Emma Lazarus*. New York. Schocken Books. 1949.

JANOWSKY, OSCAR I.: *The Jews and Minority Rights*. New York. Columbia University Press. 1933.

JOSEPH, DOV: *Faithful City: The Siege of Jerusalem*. New York. Simon and Schuster. 1960.

KIMCHE, JON and DAVID: *A Clash of Destinies. The Arab-Jewish War*. New York. Praeger. 1960.

KORN, BERTRAM W.: *American Jewry in the Civil War*. Philadelphia. Jewish Publication Society. 1951.

LEBESON, ANITA L.: *Pilgrim People*. New York. Harper & Brothers. 1950.

LEFTWICH, JOSEPH: *Israel Zangwill*. New York. Yoseloff. 1957.

LEVIN, ALEXANDRA LEE: *The Szolds of Lombard Street*. Philadelphia. Jewish Publication Society. 1960.

LIPTZIN, SOLOMON: *Germany's Stepchildren*. Philadelphia. Jewish Publication Society. 1944.

LOWENTHAL, MAVIN: *The Jews of Germany*. New York. Longmans, Green & Company. 1936.

———: *A World Passed By*. New York. Harper & Brothers. 1933.

MANUEL, FRANK: *The Realities of American Palestine Relations*. Washington. Public Affairs Press. 1949.

MARCUS, JACOB: *Memoirs of American Jews*. 3 vols. Philadelphia. Jewish Publication Society. 1956.

MUENZNER, GERHARD: *Jewish Labour Economy in Palestine*. London. Victor Gollancz. 1945.

PINSON, KOPPEL: *Essays on Anti-Semitism*. 2nd ed. New York. Conference on Jewish Relations. 1946.

RAISIN, MAX: *History of the Jews in Modern Times*. New York. Hebrew Publishing Company. 1926.

REITLINGER, GERALD: *The Final Solution*. London. Vallentine, Mitchell. 1953.

REVUSKY, ABRAHAM: *Jews in Palestine*. New York. Vanguard Press. 1935.

SACHAR, ABRAM LEON: *Sufferance Is the Badge*. New York. Alfred A. Knopf. 1939.

SACHAR, HOWARD M.: *The Course of Modern Jewish History*. New York. The World Publishing Company. 1958.

———: *Aliyah: The Peoples of Israel*. New York. The World Publishing Company. 1961.

———: *From the Ends of the Earth: The Peoples of Israel*. New York. The World Publishing Company. 1964.

SACHER, HARRY: *Israel: The Establishment of a State.* London. Weidenfeld & Nicholson. 1952.

SAMUEL, MAURICE: *Harvest in the Desert.* New York. Alfred A. Knopf. 1944.

———: *Prince of the Ghetto: Isaac Loeb Peretz.* New York. Alfred A. Knopf. 1948.

———: *The World of Sholom Aleichem.* New York. Alfred A. Knopf. 1943.

SCHECHTER, SOLOMON: *Studies in Judaism.* Third series. Philadelphia. Jewish Publication Society. 1924.

SCHWARZ, SOLOMON: *The Jews in the Soviet Union.* Syracuse. Syracuse University Press. 1951.

SIMON, LEON: *Ahad Ha-am.* Philadelphia. Jewish Publication Society. 1960.

SPIEGEL, SHOLOM: *Hebrew Reborn.* Meridian Book ed. The World Publishing Company. 1962.

ST. JOHN, ROBERT: *Tongue of the Prophets: Eliezer ben Yehuda.* New York. Doubleday & Company. 1952.

STEINBERG, MILTON: *Making of the Modern Jew.* Indianapolis. Bobbs-Merrill Company. 1934.

———: *A Partisan Guide to the Jewish Problem.* Indianapolis. Bobbs-Merrill Company. 1945.

SYRKIN, MARIE: *Blessed Is the Match.* New York. Alfred A. Knopf. 1947.

———: *Nachman Syrkin.* New York. Sharon Books. 1961.

WEIZMANN, CHAIM: *Trial and Error.* New York. Harper & Brothers. 1949.

WISCHNITZER, MARK: *To Dwell in Safety: Jewish Migrations since 1800.* Philadelphia. Jewish Publication Society. 1948.

———: *Visas To Freedom. The History of Hias.* New York. The World Publishing Company. 1956.

WISE, STEPHEN S.: *Challenging Years. An Autobiography.* New York. G. P. Putnam's Sons. 1949.

INDEX

i

INDEX

INDEX

INDEX

INDEX

INDEX

INDEX

INDEX

INDEX

INDEX

INDEX

Philip II, of Spain, 230
Philistines, invasion of Palestine by, 9; expansion of, along Mediterranean, 30; wars of, with Hebrews, 30 ff.; harry Jews during Exile, 78
Philo-Judæus, 110 ff., 165
Phœnicians, 47
Picquart, Lieutenant-Colonel, 346
Pileum cornutum, 194
Pilgrims, 364
Pilpul, 264, 265, 267
Piltushey, 314
Pinsker, Dr. Leo, 351–2
Pires, Diego, *see* Molko, Solomon
Pius VI, Pope, 281
Pius VII, Pope, 287
Pius IX, Pope, 287, 293, 340–1
Placard (Catherine II), 3, 311
Plato, 109, 110
Plehve, 320, 357
Pliny, 153
Pobedonostsev, 125, 317–18
Poland, Jewish life in sixteenth centuy in, 223 ff.; martyrdom in seventeenth century in, 240 ff.; Jewish life in eighteenth century in, 249, 254 ff.; partitions of, 309 ff.; decline of Jewish life in, 309 ff.; Jewish life in nineteenth century in, 315; postwar tragedy, 378 ff.; effects of Nazi conquest, 424; Communist anti-Semitism in, 440; emigration to Israel from, 469
Polish Church synod (1733), 309
Polygamy, 20, 94, 185
Pompey, 107, 112
Pontius Pilate, 116–17, 131–2
Portugal, 216–17; 238–9, 284
Poujade, Pierre, 438
Prague, Jewish massacres in, during crusades, 189; riot of 1389 in, 201–2; ghetto of, 252, 253
Printing, Jewish contributions to, 222, 256
Procurators, 116
Prophets, characteristics of, 61 ff.; Amos, 64 ff.; Hosea, 68; Isaiah, 70; Micah, 70; persecuted by Manasseh, 71; Jeremiah, 75–6; Deutero-Isaiah, 82; Haggai, 83 ff.; Zechariah, 83 ff.; Malachi, 86; and Book of Jonah, influence of, on Jesus, 127
Proposals against Tradition (Acosta), 246
Proselytization, under Simon, 105; by Jews in Egypt, 111; in Arabia, 155

Provence, 193–4, 196
Proverbs, Book of, 37
Prussia, 275, 284, 286
Psalms, 105
Ptolemy, 99
Ptolemy II, 109
Pumbedita, Academy of, founded, 161; decline and fall of, 167, 170
Pushkin, 315

Q documents, earliest sources for Jesus, 126
Quadros, Janio da Silva, 394

Rab, 150
Raba, 151
Rabina II, 151
Rabinowitch, *see* Shalom Aleichem, 335
Rachel, 96
Rameses II, 9, 15
Rapoport, Solomon, 332–3
Rashi, 185–6, 327
Rathenau, Walther, 375
Ravenna, Council of (1317), 251
Raymond VI, Count of Toulouse, 194
Reform Judaism, influence of science upon, 325; history of, 328 ff.; development of, in United States, 308 ff.
Reformation, Protestant, influence of Rashi upon, 186; Jewish influence upon, 227; Reuchlin-Pfefferkorn controversy and, 228
Rehoboam, 43, 45
Renan, Ernest, on Paul of Tarsus, 136; judgment of, on Spinoza, 246, 248; on common sorrow, 347–8
Resh Galuta (Exilarch), 149
Responsa, 172
Reuben, tribe of, 93
Reubeni, David, 238 ff.
Reuchlin, Johann, 228, 236
Richard I, king of England, 179, 194
Riesser, Gabriel, 291
Rights of Man, 278
Rindfleisch, 198, 203
Rio de Janeiro, 394
Rishon Le Zion, 401
Ritual murder, 203, 322
Robespierre, 279
Rohling, Dr., 343
Rome, Empire of, treaty between Simon and, 105; conquest of Jerusalem by, 107 ff.; conquest of Judah by, 119 ff.; persecutions

INDEX

INDEX

INDEX

PRINTER'S NOTE

This book is set in Granjon, a type named in compliment to ROBERT GRANJON, *type-cutter and printer — Antwerp, Lyons, Rome, Paris — active from 1523 to 1590. The boldest and most original designer of his time, he was one of the first to practise the trade of type-founder apart from that of printer. This type face was designed by* GEORGE W. JONES, *who based his drawings upon a type used by* CLAUDE GARAMOND (*1510–61*) *in his beautiful French books, and more closely resembles Garamond's own than do any of the various modern types that bear his name.*